# Tolley's Internal Aud

Andrew Chambers
Management Audit Ltd

LexisNexis®
Tolley

## Members of the LexisNexis Group worldwide

| | |
|---|---|
| United Kingdom | LexisNexis Butterworths, a Division of Reed Elsevier (UK) Ltd, Halsbury House, 35 Chancery Lane, London, WC2A 1EL, and RSH, 1–3 Baxter's Place, Leith Walk Edinburgh EH1 3AF |
| Argentina | LexisNexis Argentina, BUENOS AIRES |
| Australia | LexisNexis Butterworths, CHATSWOOD, New South Wales |
| Austria | LexisNexis Verlag ARD Orac GmbH & Co KG, VIENNA |
| Canada | LexisNexis Butterworths, MARKHAM, Ontario |
| Chile | LexisNexis Chile Ltda, SANTIAGO DE CHILE |
| Czech Republic | Nakladatelství Orac sro, PRAGUE |
| France | Editions du Juris-Classeur SA, PARIS |
| Germany | LexisNexis Deutschland GmbH, FRANKFURT and MUNSTER |
| Hong Kong | LexisNexis Butterworths, HONG KONG |
| Hungary | HVG-Orac, BUDAPEST |
| India | LexisNexis Butterworths, NEW DELHI |
| Italy | Giuffrè Editore, MILAN |
| Malaysia | Malayan Law Journal Sdn Bhd, KUALA LUMPUR |
| New Zealand | LexisNexis Butterworths, WELLINGTON |
| Poland | Wydawnictwo Prawnicze LexisNexis, WARSAW |
| Singapore | LexisNexis Butterworths, SINGAPORE |
| South Africa | LexisNexis Butterworths, Durban |
| Switzerland | Stämpfli Verlag AG, BERNE |
| USA | LexisNexis, DAYTON, Ohio |

ISBN 0 406 95209 4

Typeset by Kerrypress Ltd, Luton, Beds
Printed and bound in Great Britain by CPI Bath Press, Bath

Visit LexisNexis Butterworths at www.lexisnexis.co.uk

# Preface

'The distinguishing mark of a "profession" is its acceptance of broad responsibilities to the public and its protection of the general welfare.'[1]

Integration, even at a national level, eludes certain cognate professional groups. Internal auditing is a remarkable profession in that it is globally organised.

Paradoxically, to some extent its global reach is a consequence of fewer laws and regulations prescribing the qualities and qualifications for internal auditors across the world, and proscribing others from engaging in the work of the profession: the monopoly rights enshrined within law which protect many professions are much less pronounced for internal auditing. A consequence of this is that the occupational group of internal auditors has had to stand on its own feet, largely unprotected by statute, and so on. It is all the stronger for having to do so.

To some extent the globalisation of internal auditing is due to the vision of The Institute of Internal Auditors' founding fathers, back in the 1940s, and the dedication of the members of the profession which continues. Undoubtedly, it is also a consequence of the transnational character of so much of internal auditing in multinational companies and international agencies.

A common, global *Definition*, *Code of Ethics* and *Standards* bind all the disparate parts of the internal auditing profession worldwide. Subject to proper draft exposure, they have been carefully crafted to capture the essence and essentials of internal auditing wherever it is practised. Great care is taken to ensure that, in their translation into many languages, they retain their authenticity. Then there are the *Practice Advisories* of The Institute of Internal Auditors, which offer non-mandatory guidance on applying the mandatory *Standards*. For most internal auditors, the *Practice Advisories* will, most of the time, be the best way to approach their work. The content of the *Practice Advisories* also often can point to the correct answers to questions within the professional examinations of The Institute of Internal Auditors. All of these, taken together, are the basis of this Handbook – just as they should be the basis of internal auditing wherever it is undertaken.

The 'Best Practice' sections within this Handbook are firmly rooted in the *Standards* and *Practice Advisories* while also referencing into other relevant authoritative pronouncements. The interpretation of these is the author's alone, but I have tried to faithfully reflect the intentions of those who developed them. Readers will find that the exact sources of quotations from The Institute's pronouncements are given as endnotes to each chapter. I am very grateful for permission from The Institute to quote extensively from their mandatory and discretionary guidance – and indeed to reproduce their *Code of Ethics* and *Standards* at Appendices 1 and 2.

Readers will notice that the Supplementary Guidance sections of the Handbook have been drafted, on occasion, with a degree of latitude from the discretionary *Practice Advisories* of The Institute, while still intending to promote an authentic approach to internal auditing.

I have taken the approach of organising the contents of this Handbook sequentially to correspond to the structure of The Institute of Internal Auditors' *Standards* – which have been adopted throughout the world, including within the UK, and are the foundations of the international Certified Internal Auditor (CIA) and UK examinations (PIIA and MIIA). For each major area of The Institute's *Standards*, 'Best Practice' has been developed as a dedicated chapter, to be followed by a chapter of 'Supplementary Guidance' and then, in most cases, by 'Case Studies'. I hope this approach will be most useful to users of the Handbook who in this way will readily be able to find guidance within these pages on most if not all matters covered within the *Standards*.

Apart from being a practitioner guide for use anywhere in the world, the Handbook also sets out to be a textbook to assist trainees to pass the professional examinations of The Institute of Internal Auditors (CIA, CCSA², PIIA, MIIA). Of course, trainees must also consult other books and study guides to learn about (for example) management accounting, organisational behaviour – and so on.

We have attempted to develop a Handbook equally appropriate for those whose focus is in the public, private or not-for-profit sectors.

Much of the practical content of this Handbook has been suggested by our experiences of working on internal auditing projects for a wide variety of clients over the past 13 years, and from involvement on boards and audit committees of listed and unlisted companies and of public sector entities.

The first edition of a Handbook of this sort is likely to have a few rough edges. As a source of reference I am mindful more of its omissions than of any inaccuracies – though there are likely to be some of these too. The responsibility for what you find between these covers is mine alone. I would greatly welcome readers' comments and suggestions for rectifying any limitations.

It will not take long for those who use this Handbook to realise how dependent I have been on the contributions of others. Certainly, there is a vast amount of talent working currently on these issues. I am deeply grateful for the contributions of individual specialists and also, of course, for the opportunity to include the authoritative pronouncements which are an essential part of a work of this kind. I am particularly grateful to that excellent internal auditor, Graham Rand, for his influence and work. If I have failed to seek permission to use any quoted material, I offer my sincere apologies – and will be pleased to rectify the position in future editions of this Handbook.

For me it has been an exciting experience to develop this first edition of the new *Tolley's Internal Auditor's Handbook*. My thanks to LexisNexis Butterworths for putting a fascinating opportunity my way, and for their impressive work on the production side of this volume. Katie Twells at Management Audit has been of sterling assistance too – not least by coping with my preoccupation with this project.

I would like to hear from those who use this Handbook, with comments and suggestions.

Andrew Chambers
April 2005

Management Audit Limited
6 Market Street
Sleaford
Lincolnshire
NG34 7SF
*E-mail:* achambers@management-audit.com
*Website:* http://www.management-audit.com
*Telephone:* +44 (0) 1529 413344
*Fax:* +44 (0) 1529 413355

---

[1]    Practice Advisory 2440–3: 'Communicating Sensitive Information Within and Outside of the Chain of Command', §9.

[2]    Certification in Control Self Assessment.

# Contents

## Chapter A1.3 Understanding internal auditing – case studies

## Chapter A2.1 Internal audit independence and objectivity – best practice guidance

## Chapter A2.2 Internal audit independence and objectivity – supplementary guidance

## Chapter A2.3 Internal audit independence and objectivity – case studies

## Chapter A3.1 Proficiency and care in internal auditing – best practice guidance

## Chapter A3.2 Proficiency and care in internal auditing – supplementary guidance

**Chapter A3.3 Proficiency and care in internal auditing – case studies**

**Chapter A4.1 Quality assurance and improvement programme – best practice guidance**

**Chapter A4.2 Quality assurance and improvement programme – supplementary guidance**

# Part B Performing internal audit

## Chapter B4.3 Performing the engagement – case studies

## Chapter B5.1 Communicating results – best practice guidance

*Contents*

*Part A*

# Internal audit attributes

# Understanding internal auditing – best practice guidance

**A1.1.1**    While we also refer to other important pronouncements, our main source of guidance for the parts of this Handbook which describe internal auditing best practice has been the *Professional Practices Framework* of The Institute of Internal Auditors. This *Framework* includes their *Definition* of internal auditing, *Code of Ethics*, *Standards*, and *Practice Advisories*. Of these, only the *Practice Advisories* are non-mandatory: they explain and elaborate upon best practice in most circumstances, and are important for practitioners and students. Readers can see the current complete list of *Practice Advisories* at www.theiia.org.

Those current on 1 January 2005 are shown in APPENDIX 3 of this Handbook, including a useful topical classification at APPENDIX 3.2.

In addressing this subject we have drawn more widely than those *Practice Advisories* classified by The Institute as applicable to this part of our Handbook, which are:

| **Practice Advisories, by Standard Number** | **Release date** |
| --- | --- |
| Practice Advisory 1000–1: Internal Audit Checker | 5 January 2001 |
| Practice Advisory 1000.C1–1: Principles Guiding the Performance of Consulting Activities of Internal Auditors | 15 May 2001 |
| Practice Advisory 1000.C1–2: Additional Considerations for Formal Consulting Engagements | 7 January 2002 |

*Practice Advisories* carry the *Standard* number to which they principally refer. Readers are advised to consult the applicable *Standards* as we do not in every case reproduce them here. They are to be found in APPENDIX 2.

## A1.1.2    The accepted definition of internal auditing

Internal auditors may experience serious ethical dilemmas. Proximity to management may mitigate against independence and open reporting to the board or its audit committee. Very few would agree that internal audit should be party to the fraudulent financial reporting and other corporate governance debacles which have characterised too much of the corporate scene. Yet, is it legitimate for internal audit to turn a blind eye to unacceptable management practices? Is it acceptable when internal audit fails to uncover significant malpractices, let alone fails to report them promptly and clearly to the board or its audit committee? What is the position of the more junior internal auditor who fails to get the support of the head of internal audit over reporting a questionable practice? And how should members and associates of an internal auditing professional body conduct themselves in roles outside of internal auditing? These are just a very few of the many situations where an accepted *Code of Ethics* will be valuable – and particularly needed in today's world. Of course, there is such a *Code of Ethics* and it should be followed by internal auditors as well as supported by others including top management and boards of directors.

### A1.1.3  *Internal audit qualifications and professional body membership*

There are now four international certifications of The Institute of Internal Auditors – CIA (Certified Internal Auditor), CCSA (Certification in Control Self Assessment), CFSA (Certified Financial Services Auditor) and CGAP (Certified Government Auditing Professional). Due to challenges in developing a truly international version of CGAP without a US bias, its roll out globally was delayed until 2004. Candidates for each of these four certifications as well as those who have achieved any of these certifications are obligated to abide by The Institute's *Code of Ethics* and personally commit themselves to do so. In addition, members of The Institute of Internal Auditors have the same obligation – whether or not they hold any of these certifications.

For the international body, due to US anti-trust considerations, the four certifications are distinct from membership – an individual may hold a certification while not being a member, and may be a member without holding a certification.

The UK position is different. The UK is almost unique in promoting its own national qualifications. There are four UK qualifications – CIABR (Certificate in Internal Audit and Business Risk), PIIA (Practitioner of The Institute of Internal Auditors), MIIA (Member of The Institute of Internal Auditors), and QiCA (Qualification in Computer Auditing). The Certificate (CIABR) is not considered to be a full qualification and so candidates need not be members to actually take it or retain it; but candidates for and holders of the last three of these four qualifications, where in each case there is a requirement to maintain student or full membership of The Institute of Internal Auditors (UK), annually, each time they renew their membership, affirm their commitment to the *Code of Ethics* when they complete their membership renewal form. Except for Anglicisations of the text (from US to UK English) and modified wording to reflect the different status of candidates for the UK qualifications (who are members in the UK, as set out above), the UK's *Code of Ethics* is the same as the international one – indeed, that is one of the conditions of affiliation of national institutes to the international body.

Members of the UK national institute may, of course, also be candidates or holders of one or more of the international certifications and, if so, would therefore make more than one commitment to abide by the *Code of Ethics*.

## A1.1.4 The status of The Institute of Internal Auditors' *Code of Ethics*

The Institute of Internal Auditors' *Code of Ethics* includes both 'Principles' and 'Rules of Conduct', both of which are defined in the preamble to the *Code* as 'essential components'. The Rules of Conduct are stated to:

> 'describe behaviour norms expected of internal auditors'.

Practice Advisory 1200–1: Proficiency and Due Professional Care states that:

> 'The Institute of Internal Auditors' Code of Ethics extends beyond the definition of internal auditing to include two essential components:
> - Principles that are relevant to the profession and practice of internal auditing – specifically, integrity, objectivity, confidentiality, and competency; and
> - Rules of Conduct that describe behaviour norms expected of internal auditors. These rules are an aid to interpreting the Principles into practical applications and are intended to guide the ethical conduct of internal auditors.'

Unlike the UK's Combined Code of Corporate Governance, the Principles as well as the other content of The Institute of Internal Auditors' *Code of Ethics* are both mandatory. One of the Rules of Conduct states that 'internal auditors shall perform internal auditing services in accordance with the *Standards for the Professional Practice of Internal Auditing*'. There is a glossary of terms to the *Standards* and while it is not stated unambiguously that the glossary relates to the *Code of Ethics* as well as to the *Standards* themselves, and the word 'shall' is not defined in the Glossary, the latter defines 'should' as meaning:

> 'The use of the word "should" in the Standards represents a mandatory obligation'.

So, both the *Code of Ethics* and the *Standards* are mandatory for internal auditors associated with The Institute of Internal Auditors as members or as candidates/ holders of any of their certifications. The preamble to the international *Code* states that:

> 'For Institute members and recipients of or candidates for IIA professional certifications, breaches of the Code of Ethics will be evaluated and administered according to The Institute's Bylaws and Administrative Guidelines. The fact that a particular conduct is not mentioned in the Rules of Conduct does not prevent it from being unacceptable or discreditable, and therefore, the member, certification holder, or candidate can be liable for disciplinary action.'

Because of the UK's linkage of their qualifications to membership, the UK *Code* wording can be less complex:

> 'For Institute members, breaches of the Code of Ethics will be evaluated and administered according to The Institute's Disciplinary Procedures. The fact that a particular conduct is not mentioned in the Rules of Conduct does not prevent it from being unacceptable or discreditable, and therefore, the member liable to disciplinary action.'

The Institute covers the circumstance where an internal auditor is prevented from complying with the *Standards*. The Introduction to the *Standards* states:

> **'Unavoidable non-compliance with the Standards**
> If internal auditors are prohibited by laws or regulations from complying with certain parts of the Standards, they should comply with all other parts of the Standards and make appropriate disclosures.'

Standard 1340 itself specifies the correct action for an internal auditor to take in cases of non-compliance:

> **'1340 – Disclosure of Noncompliance**
> Although the internal audit activity should achieve full compliance with the Standards and internal auditors with the Code of Ethics, there may be instances in which full compliance is not achieved. When noncompliance impacts the overall scope or operation of the internal audit activity, disclosure should be made to senior management and the board.'

'The board' may be interpreted as being, for instance, the audit committee of the board. The Glossary definition of 'the Board', as it is used in the *Standards*, reads:

> **'Board** – A board is an organization's governing body, such as a board of directors, supervisory board, head of an agency or legislative body, board of governors or trustees of a non profit organization, or any other designated body of the organization, including the audit committee, to whom the chief audit executive may functionally report.'

## A1.1.5   *The Code of Ethics is binding even outside the internal audit role*

In 1998 when the international Institute of Internal Auditors adopted a policy of non-disclosure of their professional examinations questions so as to build a database of multi-choice questions which could be used again and again, especially when online examining is introduced, they instituted a practice of publishing a *Model Exam* for the benefit of Certified Internal Auditor (CIA) candidates and instructors. Both the 1998 *Model Exam* and also the next (2000) update included one interesting sample question[1] within the Part I (Internal Audit Process) model paper. We reproduce it here:

> 'A CIA, working as the director of purchasing, signs a contract to procure a large order from the supplier with the best price, quality, and performance. Shortly after signing the contract, the supplier presents the CIA with a gift of significant monetary value. Which of the following statements regarding the acceptance of the gift is correct?
> a.    Acceptance of the gift would be prohibited only if it were non-customary.
> b.    Acceptance of the gift would violate The IIA's *Code of Ethics* and would be prohibited for a CIA.
> c.    Since the CIA is not acting as an internal auditor, acceptance of the gift would be governed only by the organization's code of conduct.
> d.    Since the contract was signed before the gift was offered, acceptance of the gift would not violate either The IIA's *Code of Ethics* or the organization's code of conduct.'

Many would be likely to opt for 'c'. but The Institute gives 'b'. as the correct answer. Their expanded answer in their *Model Exam* put it like this:

**'Solution: b**
a.  Incorrect. Acceptance of the gift could easily be presumed to have impaired independence and thus would not be acceptable.
b.  Correct. As long as an individual is a Certified Internal Auditor, he or she should be guided by the profession's *Code of Ethics* in addition to the organization's code of conduct. Article V of the *Code of Ethics* would preclude such a gift because it could be presumed to have influenced the individual's decision.
c.  Incorrect. See response 'b'.
d.  Incorrect. See response 'b'. Further, there is not sufficient information given to judge possible violations of the organization's code of conduct. However, the action could easily be perceived as a kickback.'

The same question and answer also appeared again in the current (2004) *Model Exam* with just the reference to 'Article V' of the old *Code of Ethics* being replaced by 'Rule of Conduct 2.2' to refer to the updated *Code of Ethics*. Article V of the pre-2000 *Code of Ethics* read:

'Members and CIAs shall not accept anything of value from an employee, client, customer, supplier, or business associate of their organization which would impair or be presumed to impair their professional judgment.'

Rule of Conduct 2.2, which replaced Article V in the post-2000 *Code*, is shown here:

**'2. Objectivity**
**Internal auditors:**
2.1. Shall not participate in any activity or relationship that may impair or be presumed to impair their unbiased assessment. This participation includes those activities or relationships that may be in conflict with the interests of the organization.

**2.2 Shall not accept anything that may impair or be presumed to impair their professional judgment.**

2.3 Shall disclose all material facts known to them that, if not disclosed, may distort the reporting of activities under review.'

The key point here is that The Institute of Internal Auditors regards their *Code of Ethics* as binding upon those to whom it applies *whether or not the circumstances relate to internal auditing work*:

'As long as an individual is a Certified Internal Auditor [or in other way(s) committed to the Code of Ethics, as set out above], he or she should be guided by the profession's Code of Ethics in addition to the organization's code of conduct.'

The *Code* is to be applied in contexts outside internal auditing by members of The Institute of Internal Auditors and by candidates/holders of their certifications.

But the applicability of the *Code of Ethics* does not stop there. It has two further, important extensions.

## A1.1.6   *Code and Standards applicable to all internal auditors*

First, The Institute of Internal Auditors considers the *Code* appropriate to be observed even by internal auditors in no way associated with The Institute – not just by candidates or holders of their certifications or by Institute members. Within the preamble to the *Code* is this content (the bold is ours):

> 'The Code of Ethics together with The Institute's *Professional Practices Framework* and other relevant Institute pronouncements provide guidance to internal auditors serving others. "Internal auditors" refers to Institute members, recipients of or candidates for IIA professional certifications, **and those who provide internal auditing services within the definition of internal auditing.**'

The reasoning here is that the *Code of Ethics* and the *Professional Practices Framework* have been developed with immense care, following a due process including proper consideration of comments at the consultation stage. An early part of this process was to establish a new, generally accepted definition of internal auditing which had global buy-in and which encapsulated the nature of contemporary internal auditing. The *Code of Ethics* and finally the *Standards* were then developed to be consistent with this agreed upon definition of internal auditing. It follows logically that The Institute of Internal Auditors holds the position that the *Code of Ethics* and the *Standards* are therefore right for anyone who is providing an internal audit service consistent with the definition of internal auditing.

As membership of, and/or qualification through, The Institute of Internal Auditors becomes more widely accepted for internal auditors globally, the opportunity grows for this Institute to influence how internal audit is conducted, even through the use of disciplinary sanctions. This influence is not dependent on the existence of monopoly rights to practise as an internal auditor, nor upon there being a mandatory requirement for entities to have an internal audit. The latter is sometimes so, but to our knowledge the former is rarely if ever so. With frequently no requirement for an entity to have an internal audit and with discretion to define the role of an internal audit as the entity chooses and to appoint as internal auditors whomsoever the entity desires, clearly the opportunity for The Institute of Internal Auditors to enforce their *Code of Ethics* and their *Standards* is less than it is, for instance, with respect to the external auditing profession. But the force of The Institute of Internal Auditors' *Code* and *Standards* extends beyond those associated with The Institute. Both are widely held as representing best practice. There are many who would be willing to appear in court as expert witnesses to attest that internal auditing, if consistent with The Institute of Internal Auditors' definition of internal auditing, should have been conducted in accordance with their *Code* and *Standards*.

## A.1.1.7   *Code and Standards applicable to internal audit functions as well as to individual auditors*

Secondly, The Institute considers their *Code* appropriate not just for individual internal auditors but for units (whether in-house or outsourced) engaged in internal audit work. Within the preamble to the *Code* is this content:

**'Applicability and Enforcement**
This Code of Ethics applies to both individuals and entities that provide internal auditing services.'

This means *inter alia*, in the estimation of The Institute of Internal Auditors, that:

- individual internal auditors should observe the *Code* and *Standards*;
- internal audit management should facilitate the application of the *Code* and *Standards* by their internal audit staff;
- senior management and the audit committee should use the *Code* and *Standards* as a rubric to determine the approach taken to internal auditing within their entities, and to evaluate internal audit performance;
- legislators and regulators should draft consistently with the *Code* and *Standards*;
- other professional bodies, such as the accounting professional bodies, who need to give guidance to their members on internal auditing practice should either endorse The Institute of Internal Auditors' *Code* and *Standards* or develop their own derivatives. Endorsement rather than development will create less confusion.

In practice, these are happening.

## A1.1.8   Evolution of best practice

The new *Code* (June 2000) replaced the 1988 version shortly after the new definition of internal auditing had been agreed. The new *Standards* (October 2001) replaced the original *Standards* which had been modified only very marginally since they had been first published in 1978. The new *Standards* represented very considerable modification and further significant modifications and additions have been made to them since their introduction in 2001, with the first, major, composite revision taking effect on 1 January 2004.

An IIA's Guidance Task Force, chaired by Tony Ridley, had been established to review the old *Standards for the Professional Practice of Internal Auditing*. They decided to start by updating the definition of internal auditing which appeared in the old *Statement of Responsibilities*. By 1990 that definition had come to read:

'Internal auditing is an independent appraisal function established within an organization to examine and evaluate its activities as a service to the organization. The objective of internal auditing is to assist members of the organization in the effective discharge of their responsibilities. To this end, internal auditing furnishes them with analyses, appraisals, recommendations, counsel, and information concerning the activities reviewed. The audit objective includes promoting effective control at reasonable cost. The members of the organization assisted by internal auditing include those in management and the board of directors.'

Interesting insights are revealed into the development of internal auditing over the second half of the twentieth century if we go back to the original definition of internal auditing in the 1947 *Statement of Responsibilities*, which had read:

'Internal auditing is an independent appraisal activity within an organization for the review of the accounting, financial, and other operations as a basis for protective and constructive service to management. It is a type of control which functions by measuring and evaluating the effectiveness of other types of control. It deals primarily with accounting and financial matters but it may also properly deal with matters of an operating nature.'[2]

As early as 1947 The Institute of Internal Auditors had been allowing that internal auditing reviewed operations as well as accounting and financial matters – a claim which was quite pioneering at the time. Between 1947 and 1990 we see a transition from serving management to serving the organisation, including both management and the board of directors.

The *Statement of Responsibilities of Internal Auditing* is no longer being maintained as its content has been covered in other parts of the *Standards Framework*.

The final agreed upon definition of internal auditing is now:

'Internal auditing is an independent, objective assurance and consulting activity designed to add value and improve an organization's operations. It helps an organization accomplish its objectives by bringing a systematic, disciplined approach to evaluate and improve the effectiveness of risk management, control, and governance processes.'[3]

Ridley was quoted as saying:

'We reworked the definition to capture the changes in the profession throughout the past 20 years and to convey that internal auditing is dynamic and will continue to change. ... The major change from the [definition in the] "Statement of Responsibilities" is the recognition that internal auditors have, for the most part, added new value to their clients by adding consulting activities to their charters. ... These consulting activities are focussed on risk, control and governance.'[4]

The inclusion of consulting services, in addition to assurance services, is clearly the most fundamental change within the current definition of internal auditing. The two together capture how many internal audit functions spend their time and has allowed the development of the new internal auditing *Standards* therefore to cover most, instead of just part, of what internal auditors do. Nevertheless, the launch of a consulting dimension to internal auditing has not been entirely uncontroversial – especially in view of the recent corporate governance debacles which have seen the pendulum swing back towards a greater appreciation of the enduring value of the internal audit assurance role.

While some further light is thrown on the developing role of internal auditors if one compares the current definition with the exposure draft version which preceded it in December 1998, nevertheless most of the changes between the exposure draft and final definitions are just designed to make it less wordy. The exposure draft definition is given here, and we have given the final, agreed upon definition above:

'Internal auditing is an independent and objective assurance and consulting activity that is guided by a philosophy of adding value to improve the operations of the organization. It assists an organization by bringing a systematic and disciplined approach to evaluate and improve the effectiveness of the organization's risk management, control and governing processes. Professionalism and a commitment to excellence are facilitated by operating within a framework of professional practice established by The Institute of Internal Auditors.'

## A1.1.9 Purpose, authority and responsibility of internal auditing

'The chief audit executive should periodically assess whether the purpose, authority, and responsibility, as defined in the charter, continue to be adequate to enable the internal audit activity to accomplish its objectives. The result of this periodic assessment should be communicated to senior management and the board.'[5]

The Institute of Internal Auditors' *Standards* commence with a requirement that the purpose, authority and responsibility of should be defined and endorsed at the highest level:

'**Attribute Standards**
**1000 – Purpose, Authority, and Responsibility**
The purpose, authority, and responsibility of the internal audit activity should be formally defined in a charter, consistent with the Standards, and approved by the board.'

Requirements within these *Standards* relating to 'the board' are taken to have been met if the audit committee of the board, and on occasions other parties, stand in for the board. The Glossary of terms to the *Standards* sets out how terms are used within the *Standards* and defines 'the board' as:

'**Board** – A board is an organization's governing body, such as a board of directors, supervisory board, head of an agency or legislative body, board of governors or trustees of a non profit organization, or any other designated body of the organization, including the audit committee, to whom the chief audit executive may functionally report.'[6]

The Institute of Internal Auditors' definition of internal auditing, which appears in the introduction to both their *Code of Ethics* and their *Standards*, contains the best overall expression of internal audit purpose and responsibility:

'Internal auditing is an independent, objective assurance and consulting activity designed to add value and improve an organization's operations. It helps an organization accomplish its objectives by bringing a systematic, disciplined approach to evaluate and improve the effectiveness of risk management, control, and governance processes.'

This definition went out to exposure twice before it was finalised.

So, the internal audit function should be expressly designed to add value and improve an organization's operations. It is held as axiomatic that internal auditor independence and objectivity are prerequisites for this.

In its second sentence, the definition sets out how internal audit achieves its purpose and the three foci of internal audit work.

There is no suggestion in this definition that internal audit specialises exclusively (or even to any extent) in the audit of financial and accounting matters. Indeed the definition's emphasis is upon 'operations' which includes financial and accounting matters but extends much more broadly across key operational areas such as production, distribution, sales, marketing, R&D, HR and so on. Entities achieve their objectives when they have effective operations, not merely when they have effective accounting and financial processes. Neither is there any suggestion in this definition that the internal audit review of operations is merely, or even largely, a matter of assessing the reliability of the *accounting* for these operations. It is the ways in which *all* operational areas of the business, including but not limited to accounting and financial matters, are managed which should be the focus of internal audit attention.

Since the definition of internal auditing was finalized, undoubtedly there has been a relative swing of the pendulum towards more internal auditing of internal financial control, away from a focus on operational auditing. Chief Executive Officers and Chief Financial Officers are tending to rely on their internal audit functions to assist them in their Sarbanes-Oxley Act assessment and certification of the effectiveness of internal control over financial reporting – and this has left internal audit functions with less time for the audit of operations. This is a distortion of emphasis consequent upon the governance debacles of leading US corporates – many of which involved fraudulent financial reporting. To some extent, therefore, it is a justified emphasis for management teams and audit committees to ask of their internal auditors: internal audit plans should be risk based – and fraudulent or mistaken financial reporting has been and undoubtedly continues to be a significant risk that may be inadequately controlled. But this new emphasis has been more a consequence of legislation and regulation than the conviction of the board and management as to where the risks are greatest. To the extent possible, internal audit functions should continue to allocate significant time to the audit of operations. This should be to the extent applicable based on a careful risk assessment of all the activities of the business. If the risks to the entity achieving its objectives are greater in the non-accounting, non-financial operational areas of the business, then the internal audit function should focus relatively more upon these areas.

This has implications for the competencies needed within a modern internal audit function. A responsibility of the head of internal audit is to ensure that the competencies needed, in order for internal audit to discharge its responsibilities, are available.

First, there is the responsibility of the head of internal audit for the resources of the internal audit function:

#### '2030 – Resource Management
The chief audit executive should ensure that internal audit resources are appropriate, sufficient, and effectively deployed to achieve the approved plan.'

Secondly, there is the related responsibility of the head of internal audit for the proficiency of the internal audit function:

**'1210 – Proficiency**
Internal auditors should possess the knowledge, skills, and other competencies needed to perform their individual responsibilities. The internal audit activity collectively should possess or obtain the knowledge, skills, and other competencies needed to perform its responsibilities.

**1210.A1** – The chief audit executive should obtain competent advice and assistance if the internal audit staff lacks the knowledge, skills, or other competencies needed to perform all or part of the engagement.

**1210.C1** – The chief audit executive should decline the consulting engagement or obtain competent advice and assistance if the internal audit staff lacks the knowledge, skills, or other competencies needed to perform all or part of the engagement.'

The new definition of internal auditing, and the subsequent development of substantially revised new *Standards* based upon this definition, were driven mainly by the complaint of many internal auditors that the old *Standards Framework* no longer adequately reflected how internal auditors spent their time, especially as internal auditors had, in the 1990s, been spending an increasing proportion of their time on other services – most or all of which may be termed 'consulting services' – at the relative expense of providing assurance services. Despite the recent swing of pendulum back to assurance services (especially assurance of the reliability of internal control over financial reporting), it is to be hoped that the worldwide Institute of Internal Auditors will resist the temptation to endorse a re-orientation of internal auditing once again – this time more towards the audit of internal control over financial reporting.

## A1.1.10   *The assurance role*

The first composite revision of the new *Standards* was released in December 2003. The Introduction for the first time included a description of 'assurance services', and the Glossary of terms to the *Standards* set out how this phrase is being used within the *Standards*.

From the Introduction to the *Standards*:

'Assurance services involve the internal auditor's objective assessment of evidence to provide an independent opinion or conclusions regarding a process, system or other subject matter. The nature and scope of the assurance engagement are determined by the internal auditor. There are generally three parties involved in assurance services: (1) the person or group directly involved with the process, system or other subject matter – the process owner, (2) the person or group making the assessment – the internal auditor, and (3) the person or group using the assessment – the user.'

From the Glossary:

'**Assurance Services** – An objective examination of evidence for the purpose of providing an independent assessment on risk management, control, or governance processes for the organization. Examples may include financial, performance, compliance, system security, and due diligence engagements.'

## A1.1.11  *The consulting role*

Similarly, the Introduction to the *Standards* released in December 2003 contained for the first time a description of 'consulting services', and the Glossary of terms to the *Standards* set out how this phrase is being used within the *Standards*.

From the Introduction to the *Standards*:

> 'Consulting services are advisory in nature, and are generally performed at the specific request of an engagement client. The nature and scope of the consulting engagement are subject to agreement with the engagement client. Consulting services generally involve two parties: (1) the person or group offering the advice – the internal auditor, and (2) the person or group seeking and receiving the advice – the engagement client. When performing consulting services the internal auditor should maintain objectivity and not assume management responsibility.'

From the Glossary:

> '**Consulting Services** – Advisory and related client service activities, the nature and scope of which are agreed with the client and which are intended to add value and improve an organization's governance, risk management, and control processes without the internal auditor assuming management responsibility. Examples include counsel, advice, facilitation and training.'

So, for instance, involvement by the internal audit activity in the risk management process of the entity, except to provide assurance on it, would be an example of a 'consulting service':

> 'Management and the board are responsible for their organization's risk management and control processes. However, internal auditors acting in a consulting role can assist the organization in identifying, evaluating, and implementing risk management methodologies and controls to address those risks.'[7]

## A1.1.12  *Purpose and responsibilities of internal audit*

'Purpose' and 'responsibilities' of internal audit overlap very considerably as internal audit is responsible for achieving its purpose. Later we discuss certain specific obligations which fall upon internal audit.

The main purpose of internal auditing is to:

> 'evaluate and contribute to the improvement of risk management, control, and governance **processes using a systematic and disciplined approach**.'[8]

'Risk management, control, and governance processes' overlap hugely – especially so as the internal audit focus on governance processes is perceived as largely to do with the *internal* aspects of governance rather than the accountability of the board to the stakeholders and the exercise of external control by shareholders and other stakeholders, which are essential aspects of corporate governance.

The closeness of COSO's 2004 *Enterprise Risk Management* framework[9] to their 1992 *'Internal Control – Integrated Framework'* is evidence of the high degree of overlap between risk management and internal control.

For internal auditors not to have 'risk management' and 'governance' at the heart of their definition and *Standards* might have risked their marginalization as these concepts have been centre stage over the past decade. But, in essence, internal audit continues to be the independent appraisal of the effectiveness of internal control. The *Standards* of The Institute of Internal Auditors bravely but largely unsuccessfully attempt to show clear blue water between 'risk management', 'internal control' and 'governance'. For instance, ethics programmes are referred to as part of governance but they also belong to the 'control environment' component of COSO's internal control framework and to the 'internal environment' component of COSO's enterprise risk management framework. And, The Institute's *Standards* show the objectives of risk management and internal control to be identical. In the following three boxes we show what the *Standards* say, with December 2003 revisions shown in bold:

---

*'2110 – Risk Management*
The internal audit activity should assist the organization by identifying and evaluating significant exposures to risk and contributing to the improvement of risk management and control systems.

**2110.A1** – The internal audit activity should monitor and evaluate the effectiveness of the organization's risk management system.

**2110.A2** – The internal audit activity should evaluate risk exposures relating to the organization's governance, operations, and information systems regarding the
● Reliability and integrity of financial and operational information.
● Effectiveness and efficiency of operations.
● Safeguarding of assets.
● Compliance with laws, regulations, and contracts.'

---

It is clear that the 'risk management' assurance role of internal audit is to audit the *system* of risk management and to ensure that the entity has evaluated the entity's risks of not achieving its objectives. The categorization of objectives is the same as it is for internal control, and the 'evaluation of risk exposures' has since 1992 been embraced by COSO's 'risk assessment' essential component of internal control. This Institute of Internal Auditors categorisation of the objectives of risk management and of internal control varies from COSO's 1992 internal control objectives in showing 'safeguarding of assets' as a separate objective (it was subsumed within 'effectiveness and efficiency of operations' by COSO) and by adding 'contracts' to the compliance control objective. It is certainly important that key covenants entered into within contracts are known to the board who need to take future decisions consonant with these commitments. They might usefully also have added 'policies of the board' as a further area where compliance control needs to be effective.

There is no suggestion here that internal audit is necessarily the specialist risk management function of the business. Where there is a distinct risk management function it is similar to internal audit in that it does not usurp ownership (in this case 'ownership of risk') from management but rather facilitates the ownership of risk by management. Some entities have allocated to internal audit the risk management function, in which case it is closer to their consulting role than to their assurance role. But when this has been done it does pose challenges for the effective internal audit of the risk management process which is an important internal audit engagement to be conducted. Not only is the *audit* of risk management the authentic role, but it is important that there is an *independent audit* of the risk management process – undoubtedly amongst the most important processes of the entity.

---

**'2120 – Control**
The internal audit activity should assist the organization in maintaining effective controls by evaluating their effectiveness and efficiency and by promoting continuous improvement.

**2120.A1** – Based on the results of the risk assessment, the internal audit activity should evaluate the adequacy and effectiveness of controls encompassing the organization's governance, operations, and information systems. This should include:
- Reliability and integrity of financial and operational information.
- Effectiveness and efficiency of operations.
- Safeguarding of assets.
- Compliance with laws, regulations, and contracts.

**2120.A2** – Internal auditors should ascertain the extent to which operating and program goals and objectives have been established and conform to those of the organization.

**2120.A3** – Internal auditors should review operations and programs to ascertain the extent to which results are consistent with established goals and objectives to determine whether operations and programs are being implemented or performed as intended.

**2120.A4** – Adequate criteria are needed to evaluate controls. Internal auditors should ascertain the extent to which management has established adequate criteria to determine whether objectives and goals have been accomplished. If adequate, internal auditors should use such criteria in their evaluation. If inadequate, internal auditors should work with management to develop appropriate evaluation criteria.

**2120.C1** – During consulting engagements, internal auditors should address controls consistent with the engagement's objectives and be alert to the existence of any significant control weaknesses.

**2120.C2** – Internal auditors should incorporate knowledge of controls gained from consulting engagements into the process of identifying and evaluating significant risk exposures of the organization.

---

The requirement that internal auditors evaluate the extent to which operating and programme goals and objectives have been established (Standard 2120.A2) takes the scope of internal control beyond the 1992 COSO framework, aligning it to COSO's 2004 *Enterprise Risk Management* framework in which 'objective setting' is regarded as an essential component of ERM. Again, there is no suggestion within the Standards' coverage of internal control (or elsewhere) that internal *financial* control should be given a special focus by internal auditors.

---

*'2130 – Governance*

The internal audit activity should assess and make appropriate recommendations for improving the governance process in its accomplishment of the following objectives:

- Promoting appropriate ethics and values within the organization.
- Ensuring effective organizational performance management and accountability.
- Effectively communicating risk and control information to appropriate areas of the organization.
- Effectively coordinating the activities of and communicating information among the board, external and internal auditors and management.

**2130.A1** – The internal audit activity should evaluate the design, implementation, and effectiveness of the organization's ethics-related objectives, programs and activities.

**2130.C1** – Consulting engagement objectives should be consistent with the overall values and goals of the organization.'

---

The given governance focus is, as we have said, on the *internal* aspects of governance. While an important part of 'accountability' is the accountability of the board and top management to the shareholders, it is clearly *internal accountability* which is being referred to in Standard 2130. Only in the suggestion that internal audit has a role in coordinating and communicating with the external auditors is there an implication of internal audit's involvement in the *external* aspects of governance, since external auditors are reporting to external parties. In our opinion this is to understate significantly, indeed to the point of overlooking, internal audit's growing role in the *external* part of corporate governance. The list of internal activities to do with the *external* side of corporate governance continues to grow. We show examples at B2.1.7. See also B2.2.90.

## A1.1.13   *Authority of internal audit*

In general terms, internal audit needs the authority to fulfil its purpose and to discharge its responsibilities. All authority (except for absolute authority) is delegated and internal audit's authority should be derived from the board or the board's audit committee. Clearly internal audit also gains practical authority from a supportive top management team. Internal audit's authority should be such that it can always avoid subordinating its authority to that of any others except to that of the audit committee.[10] For instance, it is important that the scope of internal audit work and the content of internal audit reports are determined by the professional judgement of the internal auditor and are not the result of any pressure exerted by management and complied with against the internal auditor's better judgement. The head of internal audit should approve both assurance and consulting engagements undertaken by internal audit. If this is not so, then the most senior point to whom internal audit reports, which should be the audit committee of the board, should know about this.

While internal audit is an audit *for* management, internal audit also needs the authority to be an effective audit *of* management *for the board*. The decision whether or not to include an audit engagement within the future audit plan should be the decision of the head of internal audit – and this applies to consulting as well as to assurance engagements.

> '2010.A1 – The internal audit activity's plan of engagements should be based on a risk assessment, undertaken at least annually. The input of senior management and the board should be considered in this process.'

> '2010.C1 – The chief audit executive should consider accepting proposed consulting engagements based on the engagement's potential to improve management of risks, add value, and improve the organization's operations. Those engagements that have been accepted should be included in the plan.'

While an assurance engagement may rightly take place even if management is opposed to it, consulting engagements are 'agreed upon' by both internal audit and management. Despite this, information about risk and control gleaned during a consulting engagement is not privileged in the sense that internal audit is barred from utilizing this information in connection with its assurance role. Indeed internal audit has a duty to do so, and also has a duty within a consulting engagement to be alert to the existence of risks generally even if they are beyond the scope of the consulting engagement:

> '2110.C1 – During consulting engagements, internal auditors should address risk consistent with the engagement's objectives and be alert to the existence of other significant risks.

> 2110.C2 – Internal auditors should incorporate knowledge of risks gained from consulting engagements into the process of identifying and evaluating significant risk exposures of the organization.

> ...

> 2440.C2 – During consulting engagements, risk management, control, and governance issues may be identified. Whenever these issues are significant to the organization, they should be communicated to senior management and the board.'

Practice Advisory 1000.C1–1[11] states, in the context of consulting engagements:

> 'CAE Responsibilities-... The CAE retains the prerogative of setting the audit techniques and the right of reporting to senior executives and audit committee members when the nature and materiality of results pose significant risks to the organization.'

Many would hold that the authority of internal audit is rightly assisted if it is the audit committee that appoints, reappoints and dismisses the head of internal audit. At the very least the audit committee should be required to approve these decisions in advance. This is part of a growing awareness that the 'total audit' (external and internal audit) should be more independent of management.

An important element of internal audit authority is the determination of the content of the annual plan of audit engagements to be conducted – which should only need the approval of the audit committee. Within each engagement there should be no imposed scope restrictions. This means there should be open access for the internal auditor to information, members of staff and physical resources 'relevant to the performance of engagements'.[12] Scope restrictions should be reported to the audit committee as they bear upon the degree of reliance that the audit committee can place on the results of internal audit work. Reporting to the audit committee should be direct and not via management. The head of internal audit needs the authority to communicate directly to the chair of the audit committee and its members at any time between meetings, and should have the accepted right to ask that particular items be placed on the agenda of the audit committee. Closely associated with this is the need for internal audit to have 'time alone' with the audit committee without any other executives being present.

## A1.1.14  *Reporting responsibility of internal audit*

Other than what we have discussed under 'purpose' and 'authority', we draw attention here to a further responsibility of internal audit. There is the responsibility of the head of internal audit to report on these and other matters to the audit committee as well as to senior management:

> **'2060 – Reporting to the Board and Senior Management**
> The chief audit executive should report periodically to the board and senior management on the internal audit activity's purpose, authority, responsibility, and performance relative to its plan. Reporting should also include significant risk exposures and control issues, corporate governance issues, and other matters needed or requested by the board and senior management.'

There is the ultimate responsibility of internal audit to ensure that the board is informed of unacceptable levels of risk being accepted by management. The relevant *Standard* on this is obscure as to whether internal audit to ensure this even against the wishes of top management, but we consider the overwhelming weight of argument is that, as a last resort, this should be so. The *Standard* reads:

> **'2600 – Resolution of Management's Acceptance of Risks**
> When the chief audit executive believes that senior management has accepted a level of residual risk that may be unacceptable to the organization, the chief audit executive should discuss the matter with senior management. If the decision regarding residual risk is not resolved, the chief audit executive and senior management should report the matter to the board for resolution.'

## A1.1.15  *Other and non-audit responsibilities of internal audit*

It would be tempting to take the line that internal auditing is only *either* the provision of assurance services *or* the provision of consulting services (*or* sometimes both within a single audit engagement); that anything beyond assurance services belongs to consulting services; and that the nature of each should be set out in the internal audit Charter. Furthermore, both the assurance and the consulting services should marry with the respective definitions of both within the Glossary of terms attached to the *Standards*.

Would that things were so simple! Indeed it would be, were it not for the aberrant sentiment expressed in Practice Advisory 1000.C1–1:

> '*Audit Activities Beyond Assurance and Consulting* – There are multiple internal auditing services. Assurance and consulting are not mutually exclusive and do not preclude other auditing services such as investigations and nonauditing roles. Many audit services will have both an assurance and consultative (advising) role.'[13]

This opens the door a crack to the possibility that there are further internal auditing services as well as non-audit services that an internal audit function might provide beyond assurance and consulting services. Whether to classify a type of further service as 'internal audit' or 'non-audit' is not clear – except that assuming management or operational responsibilities are not audit responsibilities.

A simple, effective 'acid test' is to consider whether internal audit has been built into the system in such a way that were internal audit to stop what they are doing, then day-to-day business operations would start to grind to a halt: if so, then internal audit has taken on a non-audit responsibility.

Safeguards over non-audit services are set out as follows:

> 'When the internal audit activity or individual internal auditor is responsible for, or management is considering assigning, an operation that it might audit, the internal auditor's independence and objectivity may be impaired. The internal auditor should consider the following factors in assessing the impact on independence and objectivity:
> - The requirements of The IIA Code of Ethics and Standards for the Professional Practice of Internal Auditing (Standards);
> - Expectations of stakeholders that may include the shareholders, board of directors, audit committee, management, legislative bodies, public entities, regulatory bodies, and public interest groups;
> - Allowances and/or restrictions contained in the internal audit activity charter;
> - Disclosures required by the Standards; and
> - Subsequent audit coverage of the activities or responsibilities accepted by the internal auditor.'[14]

## A1.1.16  *Internal audit responsibility for fraud*

That all internal audit functions have a responsibility to *deter* fraud as a natural consequence of their responsibilities to evaluate the quality of risk management, control and governance processes, is axiomatic. Heads of internal audit also have the responsibility to *report* fraud 'immediately':

> 'Reporting of fraud consists of the various oral or written, interim or final communications to management regarding the status and results of fraud investigations. The chief audit executive has the responsibility to report immediately any incident of significant fraud to senior management and the board. Sufficient investigation should take place to establish reasonable certainty that a fraud has occurred before any fraud reporting is made. A preliminary or final report may be desirable at the conclusion of the detection phase. The report should include the internal auditor's conclusion as to whether sufficient information exists to conduct a full investigation. It should also summarize observations and recommendations that serve as the basis for such decision. A written report may follow any oral briefing made to management and the board to document the findings.'[15]

Responsibility for *investigating* fraud is not always so clear cut. It does not always fall upon internal audit, though it often does:

> '1210.A2 – Internal auditors are not expected to have knowledge equivalent to that of a person whose primary responsibility is detecting and investigating fraud. Also, audit procedures alone, even when carried out with due professional care, do not guarantee that fraud will be detected.'

But:

> 'Investigation of fraud consists of performing extended procedures necessary to determine whether fraud, as suggested by the indicators, has occurred. It includes gathering sufficient information about the specific details of a discovered fraud. Internal auditors, lawyers, investigators, security personnel, and other specialists from inside or outside the organization are the parties that usually conduct or participate in fraud investigations.'[16]

Clearly, the head of internal audit has a responsibility to ensure that the internal audit function has appropriate competence to investigate fraud where this is an internal audit responsibility. We would expect to see that this responsibility, where present, would be set out within the internal audit charter.

## A1.1.17 *Responsibility of internal audit for information technology*

Rather similar latitude is given by The Institute of Internal Auditors to internal auditors' interface with IT as to their interface with fraud:

> '1210.A3 – Internal auditors should have knowledge of key information technology risks and controls and available technology-based audit techniques to perform their assigned work. However, not all internal auditors are expected to have the expertise of an internal auditor whose primary responsibility is information technology auditing.'

## A1.1.18 **Internal audit charters**

The Institute of Internal Auditors' *Standards* make an internal audit 'charter' mandatory; and also mandatory is that the charter should set out the nature of both the assurance *and consulting* services which the internal audit function provides. The Institute offer a sample charter which we reproduce at the end of this section (A1.1.19) with further examples in use within organizations given at A1.2.39 to A1.2.42.

Remember that:

> 'The use of the word "should" in the Standards represents a mandatory obligation.'[17]

> '**1000.A1** – The nature of assurance services provided to the organization should be defined in the audit charter. If assurances are to be provided to parties outside the organization, the nature of these assurances should also be defined in the charter.

> **1000.C1** – The nature of consulting services should be defined in the audit charter.'

One of the three principal managerial obligations of the chief audit executive is to ensure that the internal audit activity discharges its responsibilities as set out within the charter:

> 'The chief audit executive is responsible for properly managing the internal audit activity so that:
> - Audit work fulfills the general purposes and responsibilities described in the charter, approved by senior management, and accepted by the board.
> - Resources of the internal audit activity are efficiently and effectively employed.
> - Audit work conforms to the Standards for the Professional Practice of Internal Auditing.'[18]

The Institute defines the charter of the internal audit activity as:

> ' … a formal written document that defines the activity's purpose, authority, and responsibility. The charter should (a) establish the internal audit activity's position within the organization; (b) authorize access to records, personnel, and physical properties relevant to the performance of engagements; and (c) define the scope of internal audit activities.'[19]

The Institute's Practice Advisory 1000–1 states that the Charter should be reviewed and approved by management and accepted by the board. We consider this a bit dated: nowadays it could even be the other way around – ie reviewed and approved by the audit committee of the board and accepted by management. Practice Advisory 2060–2 makes the chief audit executive responsible for:

> 'Ensuring that the charter, role, and activities of internal audit are clearly understood and responsive to the needs of the audit committee and the board.'[20]

At A2.1.9 – **Handling impairments to independence or objectivity** we discuss the interface of internal audit with the risk management process and we also address that in A2.2.1. Here we should emphasise that the internal audit activity's role in the risk management process should be set out in their Charter and also in the terms of reference of the board's audit committee:

'The chief audit executive should obtain an understanding of management's and the board's expectations of the internal audit activity in the organization's risk management process. This understanding should be codified in the charters of the internal audit activity and audit committee.'[21]

Permissible involvement by the internal audit activity in the risk management process, apart from assurance auditing of it, would belong to the 'consulting services' role of the internal audit activity.[22]

In part because there may be pressure in legal proceedings and in other (internal and external) circumstance for internal auditing records to be made available to parties for whom they were not intended, The Institute advises that this matter should be addressed within the internal auditing charter and elsewhere:

'Virtually all of an organization's records that are not protected by the attorney-client privilege are accessible in criminal proceedings. In noncriminal proceedings the issue of access is less clear.

Explicit practices in the following documents of the internal audit activity may increase the control of access to engagement records.

…

Internal audit charter should address access to and control of organizational records and information regardless of media used to store the records.'[23]

Practice Advisory 1300–1 on 'Quality Assurance and Improvement Program' states, in the context of the overview of a quality assurance and improvement programme:

'The Chief Audit Executive (CAE) is responsible for establishing an internal audit activity whose scope of work includes all the activities in the Standards and in [The Institute of Internal Auditors'] definition of internal auditing. … To ensure that this occurs, Standard 1300 requires that the CAE develop and maintain a quality assurance and improvement program.'[24]

We discuss the quality assurance and improvement programme in CHAPTER A4.1. Here we should stress that the implication of this Practice Advisory statement is that it is not best practice for the Charter of an internal audit function to describe a scope for internal audit which is narrower than that set out in the definition of internal auditing or in the *Standards*. Taking the definition alone, referred to in this Practice Advisory statement, it reads:

'Internal auditing is an independent, objective assurance and consulting activity designed to add value and improve an organization's operations. It helps an organization accomplish its objectives by bringing a systematic, disciplined approach to evaluate and improve the effectiveness of risk management, control, and governance processes.'[25]

Thus, for instance, an internal audit function which focussed exclusively on assurance services and not at all on consulting services would not be consistent with this Practice Advisory statement. Similarly there should be coverage across risk management, internal control and governance processes. However, we should recall that Practice Advisories, although perceived as 'best practice', are optional. Each Practice Advisory states in bold print within its preamble:

'Compliance with Practice Advisories is optional'.

Part of the purpose of the periodic internal assessment of the internal auditing activity is to determine whether the internal audit activity's Charter is being followed in practice:

'[periodic internal assessments] should be designed to assess (a) compliance with the internal audit activity's charter, the International Standards for the Professional Practice of Internal Auditing, and the Code of Ethics, and (b) the efficiency and effectiveness of the activity in meeting the needs of its various stakeholders.'[26]

The charter should also set out the internal audit activity's responsibility for audit follow-up:

'● Responsibility for follow-up should be defined in the internal audit activity's written charter.'[27]

The Institute suggests that the internal audit charter may address the matter of internal audit communication with outside parties:

'The audit activity charter and the audit committee charter may also contain guidance related to reporting information outside the organization.'[28]

## A1.1.19   *Sample Internal Audit Department Charter*[29]

### MISSION AND SCOPE OF WORK

The mission of the internal audit department is to provide independent, objective assurance and consulting services designed to add value and improve the organization's operations. It helps the organization accomplish its objectives by bringing a systematic, disciplined approach to evaluate and improve the effectiveness of risk management, control, and governance processes.

The scope of work of the internal audit department is to determine whether the organization's network of risk management, control, and governance processes, as designed and represented by management, is adequate and functioning in a manner to ensure:

● risks are appropriately identified and managed;
● interaction with the various governance groups occurs as needed;
● significant financial, managerial, and operating information is accurate, reliable, and timely;
● employees' actions are in compliance with policies, standards, procedures, and applicable laws and regulations;
● resources are acquired economically, used efficiently, and adequately protected;
● programs, plans, and objectives are achieved;
● quality and continuous improvement are fostered in the organization's control process;

- significant legislative or regulatory issues impacting the organization are recognized and addressed appropriately.

Opportunities for improving management control, profitability, and the organization's image may be identified during audits. They will be communicated to the appropriate level of management.

## ACCOUNTABILITY

The chief audit executive, in the discharge of his/her duties, shall be accountable to management and the audit committee to:

- Provide annually an assessment on the adequacy and effectiveness of the organization's processes for controlling its activities and managing its risks in the areas set forth under the mission and scope of work.
- Report significant issues related to the processes for controlling the activities of the organization and its affiliates, including potential improvements to those processes, and provide information concerning such issues through resolution.
- Periodically provide information on the status and results of the annual audit plan and the sufficiency of department resources.
- Coordinate with and provide oversight of other control and monitoring functions (risk management, compliance, security, legal, ethics, environmental, external audit).

## INDEPENDENCE

To provide for the independence of the internal auditing department, its personnel report to the chief audit executive, who reports functionally to the audit committee and administratively to the chief executive officer in a manner outlined in the above section on Accountability. It will include as part of its reports to the audit committee a regular report on internal audit personnel.

## RESPONSIBILITY

The chief audit executive and staff of the internal audit department have responsibility to:

- Develop a flexible annual audit plan using an appropriate risk-based methodology, including any risks or control concerns identified by management, and submit that plan to the audit committee for review and approval as well as periodic updates.
- Implement the annual audit plan, as approved, including as appropriate any special tasks or projects requested by management and the audit committee.
- Maintain a professional audit staff with sufficient knowledge, skills, experience, and professional certifications to meet the requirements of this Charter.
- Evaluate and assess significant merging/consolidating functions and new or changing services, processes, operations, and control processes coincident with their development, implementation, and/or expansion.

- Issue periodic reports to the audit committee and management summarizing results of audit activities.
- Keep the audit committee informed of emerging trends and successful practices in internal auditing.
- Provide a list of significant measurement goals and results to the audit committee.
- Assist in the investigation of significant suspected fraudulent activities within the organization and notify management and the audit committee of the results.
- Consider the scope of work of the external auditors and regulators, as appropriate, for the purpose of providing optimal audit coverage to the organization at a reasonable overall cost.

## AUTHORITY

The chief audit executive and staff of the internal audit department are authorized to:

- Have unrestricted access to all functions, records, property, and personnel.
- Have full and free access to the audit committee.
- Allocate resources, set frequencies, select subjects, determine scopes of work, and apply the techniques required to accomplish audit objectives.
- Obtain the necessary assistance of personnel in units of the organization where they perform audits, as well as other specialized services from within or outside the organization.

The chief audit executive and staff of the internal audit department are not authorized to:

- Perform any operational duties for the organization or its affiliates.
- Initiate or approve accounting transactions external to the internal auditing department.
- Direct the activities of any organization employee not employed by the internal auditing department, except to the extent such employees have been appropriately assigned to auditing teams or to otherwise assist the internal auditors.

## STANDARDS OF AUDIT PRACTICE

The internal audit department will meet or exceed the *Standards for the Professional Practice of Internal Auditing* of The Institute of Internal Auditors.

| |
|---|
| ...............................................................<br>Chief Audit Executive |
| ...............................................................<br>Chief Executive Officer |

```
........................................................
                    Audit Committee Chair

                    Dated   ................................................
```

1    Q64 in the 1998 and 2000 Part I *Model Exams.*
2    The Internal Auditor, September 1947, p20.
3    To be found in the preamble to both the current *Code of Ethics* and the current *Standards.*
4    'IIA Exposes New Internal Audit Definition', Internal Auditor, February 1999, Volume LVI, Issue 1.
5    Practice Advisory 1000–1: 'Internal Audit Charter'
6    Definition revised commencing December 2003.
7    Practice Advisory 2100–4 (February 2004): 'The Internal Auditor s Role in Organizations Without a Risk Management Process', para 1.
8    *Standard* 2100 – 'Nature of Work'. Text in bold added in December 2003 revision.
9    Committee of Sponsoring Organizations of the Treadway Commission, which includes The Institute of Internal Auditors; www.coso.org
10   It is arguable whether and how it is legitimate for internal audit to subordinate its judgement on professional matters even to the audit committee.
11   'Principles Guiding the Performance of Consulting Activities of Internal Auditors'.
12   Practice Advisory 1000–1: 'Internal Audit Charter'.
13   Practice Advisory 1000.C1–1: 'Principles Guiding the Performance of Consulting Activities of Internal Auditors'.
14   Practice Advisory 1130.A1.2: 'Internal Audit Responsibility for Other (Non-Audit) Functions'.
15   Practice Advisory 1210.A2.1: 'Identification of Fraud'.
16   Practice Advisory 1210.A2.1: 'Identification of Fraud'.
17   Glossary of terms to the *Standards.*
18   Practice Advisory 2000–1: 'Managing the Internal Audit Activity', para 1.
19   Glossary of terms to the *Standards.*
20   Practice Advisory 2060–2: 'Relationship with the Audit Committee', para 3.
21   Practice Advisory 2100–4 (February 2004): 'The Internal Auditor s Role in Organizations Without a Risk Management Process', para 3; see also para 4.
22   Practice Advisory 2100–4 (February 2004): 'The Internal Auditor s Role in Organizations Without a Risk Management Process', para 5.
23   Practice Advisory 2330.A1–2:'Legal Considerations in Granting Access to Engagement Records', paras 1, 2 and 3.
24   Practice Advisory 1300–1, 'Quality Assurance and Improvement Program', para 1.
25   Taken from the Preamble to both the *Code of Ethics* and the *Standards.* Discussed in depth at the start of this chapter.
26   Practice Advisory 1311–1: 'Internal Assessments', para 4.
27   Practice Advisory 2500.A1–1: 'Follow-up Process', para 3.
28   Practice Advisory 2440–2: 'Communications Outside the Organization', para 1.
29   Reproduced by permission of The Institute of Internal Auditors Inc, and also available on their website (wwww.theiia.org).

# Understanding internal auditing – supplementary guidance

## A1.2.1 Internal auditors as consultants

At the end of this section, we have included a checklist for internal auditors to use to assess whether their internal auditing activity is leading edge with respect to its involvement in consulting projects.

The second release of the new Standards dated 18 October 2001 contained the first roll-out of 20 'consulting' Standards (indicated by the letter 'C' in their number) and also one additional assurance Standard (1000.A1) to match the new neighbouring 'consulting' Standard (1000.C1).

Specific consulting Standards include the letter 'C' within their Standard number. In every case, the new 'consulting' Standards interpret, in a consulting context, higher level Standards which have existed since the initial publication of the new Standards, and indeed are often a reformulation of the old 1978 Standards. Literally, therefore, it would not be true to say that 'consulting' is a late arrival into the Standards. More to the point, internal auditors engaging in consulting work should regard the higher level Standards, and the Standards as a whole (as well as the Code of Ethics) as essential guidance on their approach to consulting work, whether or not lower level 'consulting' Standards have been enunciated. Where these lower consulting Standards exist, they are interpretive of the higher level Standards in the context of consulting engagements. However, 'compliance with Practice Advisories is optional.[1]

By developing Standards on consulting separately from the assurance Standards, some avoidable duplication has sometimes crept in, since the mandatory guidance on both is sometimes identical in meaning if not in wording.

## A1.2.2 *Revised definition of 'consulting' in the context of internal auditing*

The latest Institute of Internal Auditors' revision of the definition of 'consulting services' which appears in the Glossary to their Standards current from 1 January 2004 and sets out how the term is used in the Standards reads:

> Consulting Services – Advisory and related client service activities, the nature and scope of which are agreed with the client and which are intended to add value and

improve an organization's governance, risk management, and control processes without the internal auditor assuming management responsibility. Examples include counsel, advice, facilitation and training.

The amendments are significant in that, compared with the previous definition (see below) it is now being stressed that internal audit consulting services are, as with assurance services, in the fields of governance, risk management and control – that is consistent with the definition of internal auditing. The Institute has also finally found its way to stressing that internal auditors should not assume managerial responsibilities when they act as consultants. Consistent with eschewing a managerial role is the new avoidance of involvement in process design – an example of consulting services which is notable by its absence from the current definition, a tacit acknowledgement that internal auditors avoid operational responsibilities: in essence internal auditors should avoid responsibilities for activities which they may audit.

The previous revision to the original Glossary definition of 'consulting services' was presumably suggested as the Standards setters developed the new 'consulting' Standards. That definition of 'consulting services' in the Glossary to the Standards for the first time referred to consulting engagements as being 'agreed-upon', in nature and scope, between internal audit and the client; a meeting of minds which may not always be achieved with respect to assurance engagements:

> 'Advisory and related client service activities, the nature and scope of which are agreed upon with the client and which are intended to add value and improve an organization's operations. Examples include counsel, advice, facilitation, process design and training.'

### A1.2.3   'Consulting' in the first release of the new Standards

The original definition of 'consulting services' had read:

> 'The range of services, beyond internal audit's assurance services, provided to assist management meeting its objectives. The nature and scope of work are agreed upon with the client. Examples include facilitation, process design, training, and advisory services.'

The first release of the new Standards of The Institute of Internal Auditors, on 17 June 2001, presaged the subsequent appearance of Standards specific to the internal auditor's consulting role, but contained none of these. They were not long in making their appearance.

Until the appearance of these consulting Standards, reference in the new Standards to consulting was in another context, but it was a new reference nevertheless, and relevant to the internal audit activity's approach to consulting work.

> '**Coordination** – The chief audit executive should share information and coordinate activities with other internal and external providers of relevant assurance and consulting services to ensure proper coverage and minimize duplication of efforts.' (2050)

The old Standard had read:

'**External auditors** – The director of internal auditing should coordinate internal and external audit efforts.'

## A1.2.4 Defining the consulting role of internal auditors

With the new definition of internal auditing, which appears in both the new Code of Ethics and also in the preamble to the new Standards themselves, giving apparent equal stress to 'consulting' and 'assurance' activities for internal auditors, the profession clearly needs firm guidance on both:

'Internal auditing is an independent, objective assurance and consulting activity designed to add value and improve an organization's operations. It helps an organization accomplish its objectives by bringing a systematic, disciplined approach to evaluate and improve the effectiveness of risk management, control, and governance processes.'

The new Standards require that:

'The purpose, authority, and responsibility of the internal audit activity should be formally defined in a charter, consistent with the Standards, and approved by the board.' (1000)

Implementation Standards stipulate that this applies to both the assurance (1000.A1) and the consulting missions of the internal auditing activity:

'The nature of consulting services provided to the organization should be defined in the audit charter.' (1000.C1)

## A1.2.5 Practice Advisories on 'consulting'

Of the 62 Practice Advisories released by 11 December 2001, only one (1000.C1–1: 'Principles Guiding the Performance of Consulting Activities of Internal Auditors' (15 May 2001)) is on the subject of the internal auditor's consulting role, though a number of others are indirectly relevant to this, for instance:

- 1000–1: 'Internal Audit Charter' (5 January 2001);
- 1130.A1–2: 'Internal Audit Responsibility for Other (Non-Audit) Functions' (5 January 2001); and
- 2120.A1–2: 'Using Control Self-Assessment for Assessing the Adequacy of Control Processes' (18 June 2001).

We have an indication in Practice Advisory 1000.C1–1 of the Institute's meaning of the phrase 'systematic, disciplined approach' which appears in the new definition of internal auditing. It could mean that the internal audit plan of engagements to be conducted is to be developed so as to cover the entity systematically over time; or it could mean that each engagement is to be conducted systematically. Practice Advisory 1000.C1–1 indicates that it is, at least, certainly the latter and that this 'systematic approach' is expected of consulting engagements as well:

'**Consistency with Internal Audit Definition** – A disciplined, systematic evaluation methodology is incorporated in each internal audit activity. The list of services can generally be incorporated into the broad categories of assurance and consulting. However, the services may also include evolving forms of value-adding services that are consistent with the broad definition of internal auditing.'

## A1.2.6   'Consulting' perceived as a central internal audit role

Of the 20 new 'consulting' Standards in the release of the Standards dated 18 October 2001, five belong to the 'Attribute' set and 15 to the 'Performance' set of Standards. This compares with 26 'Assurance' Standards by 18 October 2001 (eight of which were 'Attribute' Standards and 18 being 'Performance' Standards), most of which had been present since June 2001. If a simple numeric count is any indication, it is apparent that the internal audit 'consulting' role is today rivalling internal audit's traditional 'assurance' role.

Unlike certain other activities in which internal auditors become involved, it is important to stress that 'consulting' in accordance with the Standards ('consistent with the broad definition of internal auditing') is perceived as being, along with assurance activities, one of the two central pillars of authentic, contemporary internal auditing. Practice Advisory 1000.C1–1 appears to accord co-primacy to the assurance and consulting roles:

> 'A primary internal auditing value is to provide assurance to senior management and audit committee directors.'

It seems that the guidance is at pains to avoid describing the assurance role along the lines of being 'the primary role'. This Practice Advisory ends with a paragraph which states that the internal auditor is first and foremost an internal auditor, but this is not to imply that being an internal auditor only applies when the auditor is engaged in assurance work:

> '**Criteria for Resolving Conflicts or Evolving Issues** – An internal auditor is first and foremost an internal auditor. Thus, in the performance of all services the internal auditor is guided by The IIA Code of Ethics and the Attribute and Performance Standards of the Standards for the Professional Practice of Internal Auditing. Any unforeseen conflicts or activities should be resolved consistent with the Code of Ethics and Standards.'

When the internal auditor provides a consulting service consistent with the Standards, he or she is acting as a mainstream internal auditor, not discharging a non-audit role. The Standards identify other activities which internal auditors sometimes become engaged in which are not internal auditing; but this is not the case with 'consulting'. Practice Advisory 1000.C1–1 again:

> '**Audit Activities Beyond Assurance and Consulting** – There are multiple internal auditing services. Assurance and consulting are not mutually exclusive and do not preclude other auditing services such as investigations and non-auditing roles. Many audit services will have both an assurance and consulting (advising) role.'

There is a tautological confusion in the above statement as 'other audit services' are described as including 'non-auditing roles'. It is safest for us to regard internal audit involvement in activities beyond assurance and consulting activities as defined in the Standards as being involvement in non-audit work, and that internal auditors are expected to abide by the Standards in all their work which is regarded as internal auditing work. We do not see anything in the Standards which bars an internal auditor from engaging in non-auditing work, but it must be clear to all parties that such work is not being done under the guise of being internal auditing.

Practice Advisory 1000.C1–1 acknowledges that:

> 'Internal auditors are expected to use professional guidance to determine the extent to which the guidance provided in this advisory should be applied in each given situation. Special consulting engagements, such as participation in a merger or acquisition project, or in emergency engagements, such as disaster recovery activities, may require departure from normal or established procedures for conducting consulting engagements.'

While both 'assurance' and 'consulting' should now be construed as essential roles for contemporary internal auditors to discharge, consulting engagements tend to be *ad hoc* and by invitation whereas assurance engagements are determined, largely, at the discretion of the chief audit executive, so as to provide systematic coverage of the entity having regard to relative risk. It is true that the new Standards exhort that the chief audit executive should consider the scale of the risk before deciding whether to accept a consulting engagement. And Practice Advisory 1000.C1–1 states, with respect to consulting engagements, that the chief audit executive:

> 'retains the prerogative of setting the audit techniques and the right of reporting to senior executives and audit committee members when the nature and materiality of results pose significant risks to the organization.'

### A1.2.7 'Scope limitations' in the context of the internal audit consulting role

An issue here is whether internal auditors who do not undertake consulting engagements are effectively experiencing 'scope limitations'. By their very nature, consulting engagements are unlikely to provide the same sort of risk-based comprehensive coverage of the entity over time as is provided by assurance engagements, since the need for management to ask for this consulting advice will vary from area to area within the business and the initiation of an internal audit consulting assignment request is at the discretion of management rather at the discretion of the chief audit executive, who does however have the discretion to decline consulting requests.

The new definition of 'consulting' in the Glossary to the Standards is a useful starting point. It refers to consulting engagements being 'agreed-upon', in nature and scope, between internal audit and the client – a meeting of minds which may not always be achieved with respect to assurance engagements:

> 'Advisory and related client service activities, the nature and scope of which are agreed upon with the client and which are intended to add value and improve an organization's operations. Examples include counsel, advice, facilitation, process design and training.'

## A1.2.8  Nature of internal audit 'consulting'

A key issue is to understand the hallmarks of a consulting service which fits into the type of consulting that The Institute of Internal Auditors envisages as being authentic internal auditing.

Although not set out in this Glossary definition, the Standards make it clear that consulting services provided by internal audit should be targeted at risk management, control and governance matters. Being 'advisory and related', an internal auditing consulting assignment should not include the execution of operational tasks or executive duties. It may include advice on the design of processes relating to risk management, control and governance. Another hallmark of consulting engagements, which should also be shared with assurance engagements, is that they should be:

> 'intended to add value and improve an organization's operations'.

The definition distinguishes between 'advice' and 'counsel', making the point that internal audit consulting may entail the giving of either or both. Although not defined, to our knowledge, in the Standards or the supporting Practice Advisories, we define 'advice' as being practical proposals for solutions to day-to-day challenges. An examples of advice in the area of risk management would be a suggestion as to how to embed the review of risk within the business; in the area of internal control an example would be a suggested suitable procedure to avoid recurring errors, or in the area of governance an example would be a suggested solution to a practical problem of the board with regard to how it conducts its business. We define 'counsel' as expert opinion within one's professional competence, relating to a matter or matters on which there are independently established criteria (or frameworks, benchmarks, or bodies of knowledge) against which performance can be assessed. Examples of 'counsel' offered by internal auditors might include the substance of, and extent of compliance with, external regulations; appropriate use of statistical sampling; or the requirements and extent of adherence achieved in the areas of risk management, internal control and governance.

The definition of consulting in the context of internal auditing also includes 'facilitation', which we define as enabling others to achieve an agreed outcome well. An example would be facilitation of CRSA. Another example would be facilitation of risk management: Practice Advisory 2100–3: 'Internal Audit's Role in the Risk Management Process', paragraph 6 puts it in non-prescriptive terms like this:

> 'The internal audit activity's role in the risk management process of an organization can change over time and may be found at some point along a continuum that ranges from:
> – No role; to
> – Auditing the risk management process as part of the internal audit plan; to
> – Active, continuous support and involvement in the risk management process such as participation on oversight committees, monitoring activities, and status reporting; to
> – Managing and coordinating the risk management process.'

We think of 'process design', allowed in the definition as a feature of authentic internal audit consulting, as being to do with the determination of a set of procedures to be applied to a business requirement, or the revision of existing procedures. Examples would include participation in the design of new systems, advising on essential components of managing the change process effectively, or involvement in improving governance. Standard 2130 on internal audit involvement in the governance process, states:

> 'The internal audit activity should contribute to the organization's governance process by evaluating and improving the process through which (1) values and goals are established and communicated, (2) the accomplishment of goals is monitored, (3) accountability is ensured, and (4) values are preserved.' (2130)

Finally, the definition's inclusion of 'training' as a form of internal audit consulting is to do with developing competence in others. Appropriate examples might include developing and running case studies on risk, control and/or governance at management development programmes, or training executives and operational staff in CRSA.

### A1.2.9    Internal audit professionalism when acting as consultants

The relevant Standards read:

> '*Internal auditors should apply the care and skill expected of* a reasonably prudent and competent internal auditor. Due professional care does not imply infallibility.' (1220)

and:

> 'The internal auditor should exercise due professional care during a consulting engagement by considering the:
> * Needs and expectations of clients, including the nature, timing, and communication of engagement results.
> * Relative complexity and extent of work needed to achieve the engagement's objectives.
> * Cost of the consulting engagement in relation to potential benefits.' (1220.C1)

### A1.2.10    Relationships and conflicts between the 'assurance' and 'consulting' roles

The definition of internal audit starts with the words:

> 'Internal auditing is an independent, objective assurance and consulting activity …'.

Just as with external auditors, their assurance role can often lead to consulting opportunities. And, as with external auditors, there can be concerns about the maintenance of sufficient independence and objectivity when this is the case. External auditors attempt to make a positive virtue of the sufficiency of 'Chinese walls' between the consultancy and the assurance sides of their business, as a mechanism to assist in preserving audit independence. The position taken by The

Institute of Internal Auditors is the opposite of this; there should be no 'Chinese walls' between information gathered in the course of consultancy work by the internal auditor, and information available to inform assurance work by the internal auditor:

> **'Communication of Fundamental Information** – A primary internal auditing value is to provide assurance to senior management and audit committee directors. Consulting engagements cannot be rendered in a manner that masks information that in the Chief Audit Executive's (CAE) judgment should be presented to senior executives and board members. All consulting is to be understood in that context.'

and:

> 'When the chief audit executive believes that senior management has accepted a level of residual risk that is unacceptable to the organization, the chief audit executive should discuss the matter with senior management. If the decision regarding residual risk is not resolved, the chief audit executive and senior management should report the matter to the board for resolution.' (2600)

Indeed, consulting Standards require that:

> 'Internal auditors should incorporate knowledge of risks gained from consulting engagements into the process of identifying and evaluating risk exposures of the organization.' (2110.C2)

and:

> 'During consulting engagements, risk management, control, and governance issues may be identified. Whenever these issues are significant to the organization, they should be communicated to senior management and the board.' (2440.C2)

Frequently an audit engagement will have elements of consulting as well as assurance:

> **'Interrelationship between Assurance and Consulting** – Internal audit consulting enriches value-adding internal auditing. While consulting is often the direct result of assurance services, it should also be recognized that assurance could also be generated from consulting engagements.'

## A1.2.11   Independence and objectivity in consulting

While the same high level Standards 1100 and 1130 on 'independence' and 'objectivity' are applicable to both assurance and consulting work by internal auditors, the sentiment of associated Implementation Standards is markedly different:

The applicable Attribute Standards on 'independence and objectivity' read:

> **'Independence and objectivity** – The internal audit activity should be independent, and internal auditors should be objective in performing their work.' (1100)

and:

'**Impairments to independence or objectivity** – If independence or objectivity is impaired in fact or appearance, the details of the impairment should be disclosed to appropriate parties. The nature of the disclosure will depend upon the impairment.' (1130)

While the associated Assurance Implementation Standards are prescriptive in a constraining way, the strictures are much less onerous with respect to consulting engagements:

'**Assurance** – 'Internal auditors should refrain from assessing specific operations for which they were previously responsible. Objectivity is presumed to be impaired if an auditor provides assurance services for an activity for which the auditor had responsibility within the previous year.' (1130.A1)

'Assurance engagements for functions over which the chief audit executive has responsibility should be overseen by a party outside the internal audit activity.' (1130.A2)

'**Consulting** – 'Internal auditors may provide consulting services relating to operations for which they had previous responsibilities.' (1130.C1)

'If internal auditors have potential impairments to independence or objectivity relating to proposed consulting services, disclosure should be made to the engagement client prior to accepting the engagement.' (1130.C2)

## A1.2.12   What sort of consultant?

Although the conflicts between being providing assurance and providing consulting services can be managed effectively, there is no doubt that there are fundamental role conflicts which need to be managed. As with a policeman, a provider of assurance needs to have formal authority which is primarily vested in the office which the provider holds, and it is reinforced by the possibility of coercive sanctions. A glance at the charters of most internal auditing functions confirms these attributes of the internal audit role. On the other hand, a consultant usually has informal authority, vested primarily in the personal ability and reputation of the consultant, and it is reinforced not by the threat of coercion but by the consultant's powers of persuasion. It is necessary for internal auditors to carry these two distinct and often conflicting roles in harness, endeavouring to avoid conflict wherever this is practical.

The parent/child analogy has been used to suggest what sort of consulting relationship internal auditors should have with their consulting clients. Sarah Blackburn suggests that the internal auditor should be not merely an extra resource (where the client is, in effect, the parent, and the auditor is the child). She further suggests that neither should the auditor be the expert resource (where these roles are reversed), with the auditor being the parent and the client being the child. Rather, she suggests that it should be an adult to adult relationship where the internal auditor is the facilitator. While it is unlikely to be appropriate for internal audit to accept consulting assignments which fall into the first category of the auditor being 'the child' and the client being 'the parent', The IIA's definitional characterisation of internal audit consultancy as including, *inter alia*, the provision of counsel as well as facilitation indicates that The IIA sees the consultancy role as fitting into either or both of the remaining two categories.

### A1.2.13   Proficiency

The general Attribute Standard on proficiency, applicable to both assurance and consulting internal audit work, reads:

> 'Internal auditors should possess the knowledge, skills, and other competencies needed to perform their individual responsibilities. The internal audit activity collectively should possess or obtain the knowledge, skills, and other competencies needed to perform its responsibilities.' (1210)

The Standard which elaborates on this for internal audit consulting allows the option that the chief audit executive may decline a consulting assignment where proficiency is in question an option which is not available for assurance work where the chief audit executive is expected to obtain the necessary proficient resources.

> 'The chief audit executive should decline the consulting engagement or obtain competent advice and assistance if the internal audit staff lacks the knowledge, skills, or other competencies needed to perform all, or part of the engagement.' (1210.C1)

### A1.2.14   Due professional care

'Due professional care' refers to the conscientiousness with which proficient internal auditors apply themselves. The general Attribute Standard, applicable to both assurance and consulting internal audit work, reads:

> 'Internal auditors should apply the care and skill expected of a reasonably prudent and competent internal auditor. Due professional care does not imply infallibility.' (1220)

The application of this, within the Standards, to consultancy work by internal auditors acknowledges that the needs and expectations of clients, including the nature, timing, and communication of engagement results, may be, indeed should be, considered. The same does not apply within the Standards to assurance engagements where instead the:

> 'extent of work needed to achieve the engagement's objectives [etc]'.

are the considerations which apply. In other words, the internal auditor is more accommodating to client expectations in consultancy work and in this work the client may be more directive than would typically be the case with 'assurance' assignments:

> 'The internal auditor should exercise due professional care during a consulting engagement by considering the:
> - Needs and expectations of clients, including the nature, timing, and communication of engagement results.

- Relative complexity and extent of work needed to achieve the engagement's objectives.
- Cost of the consulting engagement in relation to potential benefits.' (1220.C1)

Even so, requiring the auditor to 'consider' the client's needs and expectations is not to say that the internal auditor should subordinate his or her professional judgement to that of the client. Bearing this in mind, audit assignments which contain elements of assurance as well as consultancy objectives can be handled effectively.

## A1.2.15   Planning

Notwithstanding that consulting engagements may not be initiated by internal audit, as they are an integral part of internal auditing, they (a) should, as with assurance engagements, be determined in part having regard to relative risk and (b) should be included within the overall internal audit activity plan:

> 'The chief audit executive should establish risk-based plans to determine the priorities of the internal audit activity, consistent with the organization's goals.' (2010)

> 'The chief audit executive should consider accepting proposed consulting engagements based on the engagement's potential to improve management of risks, add value, and improve the organization's operations. Those engagements that have been accepted should be included in the plan.' (2010.C1)

Note that the decision to accept a consulting engagement rests with the chief audit executive, and broadly similar acceptance criteria apply as for assurance audits?

## A1.2.16   Risk management, control and governance

The new definition of internal auditing sets out the nature of internal audit work as focusing on risk management, control, and governance processes:

> 'Internal auditing is an independent, objective assurance and consulting activity designed to add value and improve an organization's operations. It helps an organization accomplish its objectives by bringing a systematic, disciplined approach to evaluate and improve the effectiveness of risk management, control, and governance processes.'

For each of these in turn,[2] and also for the various stages in performing an engagement, we set out the general Standard (as this has applicability to consulting work as well as to assurance work) and the related consulting Standards. In the interests of conciseness we do not provide here the parallel assurance Standards, though we do refer to the differences between the consulting and assurance Standards. Note that the approach to conducting a consulting engagement, as set out in the Standards, is closely similar to the approach for an assurance engagement, though with more deference to the needs and expectations of the client. Indeed, 'the client' is not a term used in the context of assurance engagements.

Note that whereas in the context of assurance work it is the professional responsibility of internal auditors to be effective generally in identifying risks and control and governess weaknesses and in contributing to their improvement, in the context of consultancy work the requirement is not identical. In consultancy work it depends initially on the engagement's objectives, although there is a stated supplementary obligation that internal auditors on consultancy assignments should have a wider alertness. It should be pointed out that consultancy assignments which it may be appropriate for internal audit to accept will be those in the areas of risk, control and governance, it should surely not be the case that any internal audit consultancy would not have a significant focus on one or more of these areas: Standard 2210.C1 reads:

'Consulting engagement objectives should address risks, controls, and governance processes to the extent agreed upon with the client.' (2210.C1)

### A1.2.17   *Risk management*

'The internal audit activity should assist the organization by identifying and evaluating significant exposures to risk and contributing to the improvement of risk management and control systems.' (2110)

'During consulting engagements, internal auditors should address risk consistent with the engagement's objectives and should be alert to the existence of other significant risks.' (2110.C1)

'Internal auditors should incorporate knowledge of risks gained from consulting engagements into the process of identifying and evaluating risk exposures of the organization.' (2110.C2)

### A1.2.18   *Control*

'The internal audit activity should assist the organization in maintaining effective controls by evaluating their effectiveness and efficiency and by promoting continuous improvement.' (2120)

'During consulting engagements, internal auditors should address controls consistent with the engagement's objectives and should be alert to the existence of any significant control weaknesses.' (2120.C1)

### A1.2.19   *Governance*

'The internal audit activity should contribute to the organization's governance process by evaluating and improving the process through which (1) values and goals are established and communicated, (2) the accomplishment of goals is monitored, (3) accountability is ensured, and (4) values are preserved.' (2130)

'Consulting engagement objectives should be consistent with the overall values and goals of the organization.' (2130.C1)

### A1.2.20   **Engagement planning**

While avoiding the word 'plan', a similar intention is expressed for consultancy assignments:

'Internal auditors should develop and record a plan for each engagement.' (2200)

'Internal auditors should establish an understanding with consulting engagement clients about objectives, scope, respective responsibilities, and other client expectations. For significant engagements, this understanding should be documented.' (2201.C1)

## A1.2.21   Engagement work programs

As in other respects, the Standards acknowledge a greater degree of variety with respect to work programs of consulting engagements than would be the case with assurance engagements:

'Internal auditors should develop work programs that achieve the engagements objectives. These work programs should be recorded.' (2240)

'Work programs for consulting engagements may vary in form and content depending upon the nature of the engagement.' (2240.C1)

## A1.2.22   Engagement objectives

The objectives of consulting engagements are expressed similarly to those of internal audit engagements generally, except that the needs and expectations of the client are factored in for establishing the objectives of consulting assignments:

'The engagement's objectives should address the risks, controls, and governance processes associated with the activities under review.' (2210)

'Consulting engagement objectives should address risks, controls, and governance processes to the extent agreed upon with the client.' (2210.C1)

## A1.2.23   Engagement scope

'The established scope should be sufficient to satisfy the objectives of the engagement.' (2220)

'In performing consulting engagements, internal auditors should ensure that the scope of the engagement is sufficient to address the agreed-upon objectives. If internal auditors develop reservations about the scope during the engagement, these reservations should be discussed with the client to determine whether to continue with the engagement.' (2220.C1)

## A1.2.24   Performing the engagement – recording information

The Standards on custody and retention of engagement records are not very dissimilar between assurance and consulting engagements, though the phraseology is not identical.

'Internal auditors should record relevant information to support the conclusions and engagement results.' (2330)

'The chief audit executive should develop policies governing the custody and retention of engagement records, as well as their release to internal and external parties. These policies should be consistent with the organization's guidelines and any pertinent regulatory or other requirements.' (2330.C1)

## A1.2.25   Communicating results

More flexibility is allowed by the Standards with respect to communicating results of consulting assignments.

'Internal auditors should communicate the engagement results promptly.' (2400)

'Communication of the progress and results of consulting engagements will vary in form and content depending upon the nature of the engagement and the needs of the client.' (2410.C1)

## A1.2.26   Disseminating results

While the stress in the assurance Standard (2440.A1) is on communicating assurance engagement results 'to individuals who can ensure that the results are given due consideration', which is for the chief audit executive to decide upon, in the case of consulting assignments it is the client who is specified, but with an override allowed when a consulting assignment uncovers matters which need to be referred higher:

'The chief audit executive should disseminate results to the appropriate individuals.' (2440)

'The chief audit executive is responsible for communicating the final results of consulting engagements to clients.' (2440.C1)

'During consulting engagements, risk management, control, and governance issues may be identified. Whenever these issues are significant to the organization, they should be communicated to senior management and the board.' (2440.C2)

## A1.2.27   Monitoring progress

Even the monitoring of how the results of a consulting assignment are used is made a requirement for an internal auditor who has conducted a consulting engagement, but only to the extent agreed upon with the client. Would that management consultants generally had standards which enjoined them not to walk away without any follow-up! Here we have an example of how the internal audit approach to consulting, drawing upon a tried and tested auditing approach, is able to add value to the consulting process.

'The chief audit executive should establish and maintain a system to monitor the disposition of results communicated to management.' (2500)

'The internal audit activity should monitor the disposition of results of consulting engagements to the extent agreed upon with the client.' (2500.C1)

## A1.2.28   Management's acceptance of risks

There are neither assurance nor consulting Implementation Standards to interpret this general Standard. The general Standard itself therefore applies, without elaboration, for internal audit consulting work:

'When the chief audit executive believes that senior management has accepted a level of residual risk that is unacceptable to the organization, the chief audit executive should discuss the matter with senior management. If the decision regarding residual risk is not resolved, the chief audit executive and senior management should report the matter to the board for resolution.' (2600)

## A1.2.29 Further guidance on internal auditors as consultants

This supplementary section attempts to assimilate a second Practice Advisory on consulting, released on 7 January 2002 (1000.C1.2: Additional Considerations for Formal Consulting Engagements). It had originally been intended that this would have been the first of the two Practice Advisories to date on consulting services, but difficulties in agreeing its wording led to its release being delayed.

This section presents further thoughts based on a study of the new Practice Advisory.

The launch of the consulting Standards has been made at an inauspicious time. Concerned parties, post-Enron, are stressing the importance of assurance services. At a time when the combination of auditing and consulting services by external auditors is being questioned, it is not the ideal time to promote dual assurance and consulting roles for internal auditors.

Although the old Standards allowed that auditors provide advice ('recommendations', 'agreed action') which leads to improvements, many considered that much of what today's internal auditors do was not caught by the old Standards. It was considered inappropriate that the professional pronouncements of The Institute of Internal Auditors should cover only the assurance role of internal auditors, thereby treating everything else as being beyond internal auditing. So the attempt has been made to capture perhaps most of the non-assurance work that internal auditors do, within the category of 'consulting services'. An obvious question is therefore 'when is advice part of an assurance service and when is it part of a consulting service?'. A second obvious question is 'when is a non-assurance service provided by internal auditors an internal audit consulting service and when is it a non-audit service?'.

The further we delve into these pronouncements on internal audit consulting services, the more questions we have to answer. From the new Standards and Practice Advisories released to date, it is extremely difficult to obtain a clear understanding of the intended nature and limits of the internal audit consulting role and its interface with the assurance internal auditing role. We consider this is due to a lack of clarity and consistency in these pronouncements – caused in part no doubt by a lack of agreement within the profession. What is not clearly understood and agreed upon cannot be clearly expressed. It is to be expected that greater clarity will emerge in time, and that this will need to be associated with significant redrafting of these pronouncements. While it is true that compliance with the Practice Advisories is optional, their content is not intended to be inconsistent with the Standards themselves – the latter being mandatory. Candidates for the Certified Internal Auditor qualification are examined on the basis that adherence to the Practice Advisories is the approach to be taken in order to observe the Standards.

For the moment, readers will not find it easy to understand what The Institute of Internal Auditors is requiring and counselling with respect to the consulting role of internal auditors.

Leaving to one side the scope for disagreement between internal auditors as to what *should be* their consulting role, if any, we consider these to be some of the ambiguities in the Standards Framework with respect to consulting services by internal auditors:

- it is not clear that in practice it would be possible to conduct an assurance engagement which did not also have elements of consulting as defined, or *vice versa*;
- it is not clearly stated whether or not assurance services are the core internal auditing service, with consulting being a discretionary optional service;
- it is not clear whether a consulting engagement is always to be 'by invitation' and with an 'agreed upon' remit;
- it is not entirely clear whether *any* 'other activity' undertaken by internal auditors should be regarded as being the provision of a consulting service, nor how to differentiate those that *are* consulting from those that *are not*; especially what are the essential characteristics of an audit engagement which fits into the 'consulting' classification, as distinct from activities (other than assurance engagements) which do not;
- leaving aside 'assurance services', it is not entirely clear, though it appears to us to be probable, that the test of whether a service by an internal audit function is a 'consulting service' as distinct from a 'non-audit activity', is merely whether or not the type of consulting service is defined in the charter of the internal auditing activity.

As lower level, especially 'Implementation', Standards are released it is understandable that some revisions will be required to Standards that have appeared before. Hence, in addition to the already revised definition of 'Consulting Services' in the Glossary to the Standards issued on 15 January 2003, The IIA released the first 'omnibus' of proposed revisions to the new Standards.

'Consulting' in accordance with the Standards ('consistent with the broad definition of internal auditing') is expressed in the new Standards in effect as being, along with assurance activities, one of the two central pillars of authentic, contemporary internal auditing. However, it is not clear what are the criteria to be used to determine whether a non-assurance service falls intrinsically into what may be regarded as a consulting service which may be provided by internal audit within the meaning of the Standards and the Practice Advisories, or falls outside the Standards and therefore outside the remit of internal audit. The description of internal audit consulting services is drawn very widely indeed – especially in Practice Advisory 1000.C1.2. The only unambiguous test we can discern is that if the type of consulting service falls outside what is allowed for in the internal audit activity's charter, then it is outside the scope of internal auditing for that particular internal audit function. This comes close to defining internal audit as being what internal auditors do.

Notwithstanding the almost equal emphasis upon 'assurance' and on 'consulting' internal audit services in the new Standards, we take it that the assurance role is a *sine qua non* and should almost always, if not always, comprise the majority of the internal auditing plan. The new Standards framework feels towards this perspective when it implies that the internal audit charter may even specify no involvement in consulting services – unthinkable for assurance services.

The sentiment in the new Standards is that when the internal auditor provides a consulting service consistent with the Standards, he or she is acting as a mainstream internal auditor, not discharging a non-audit role. The Standards refer to other activities, which internal auditors sometimes become engaged in, which may not be termed 'internal auditing' – but this is not intended to apply to 'consulting'. Practice Advisory 1000.C1–2 states that:

> 'The internal audit activity's risk-based plan of engagements may incorporate and rely on consulting engagements, to the extent deemed appropriate, to provide necessary audit coverage to the organisation.'[3]

This may be interpreted to imply that internal audit consulting services contribute to the assurance objective of internal auditing.

Although formal consulting engagements are usually, or always, 'agreed-upon' between internal audit and the client, Practice Advisory 1000.C1–2 (which, note, is titled 'Additional considerations for Formal Consulting Engagements', rather than informal ones) states:

> 'Internal auditors may conduct consulting services as part of their normal or routine activities as well as in response to requests by management.'[4]

So, to some extent at least, internal audit is presented as being able to determine whether it provides consulting services as set out in the charter – the agreement of management does not appear always to be required – even for formal consulting engagements. If consulting services may be provided as part of normal, routine internal audit activity this raises the question as to whether a recommendation made resulting from an assurance engagement means that the auditor is then working in consulting mode and the engagement is thereby to be regarded as a hybrid or blended one.

Even the use of internal auditors as firefighters confusingly appears to be regarded as 'consulting'. Practice Advisory 1000.C1–2 allows for 'emergency consulting engagements':

> 'Emergency consulting engagements – participation on a team established for recovery or maintenance of operations after a disaster or other extraordinary business event or a team assembled to supply temporary help to meet a special request or unusual deadline.'[5]

Practice Advisory 1000.C1.2 sees a potential for impairment of independence and objectivity if assurance services are provided within one year of a formal consulting engagement.[6] and the Advisory suggests ways in which this potential impairment can be managed. This risk to independence and objectivity is consistent with the Standards' guidance that assurance engagements should not be conducted by an internal auditor who has had operational responsibilities in that area of the business within the past twelve months. It does however leave us with a conceptual conundrum: if, in practice, all assurance engagements contain elements of consulting, then this impairment is omnipresent.

## A1.2.30  *Consulting activity by internal auditors*

**Checklist**

|  |  | Reference to Standards framework |
|---|---|---|
| **1. General** | | |
| 1.1 | Is it understood that the Attribute and Performance Standards relate to internal auditors performing both assurance and consulting engagements? | Practice Advisory 1000 C1–2 (Preamble) |
| 1.2 | Does the role of internal audit include a consulting role in addition to an assurance role? | Definition of internal auditing |
| 1.3 | If the role of internal audit includes a consulting role, has the chief audit executive confirmed that the board understands and approves the concept of providing these consulting services? | Practice Advisory 1000.C1–2, para 5. |
| 1.4 | Is the nature of consulting services defined in the audit charter? | 1000, 1000.C1–1 |
| 1.5 | Has the wording in the audit charter on internal audit consulting services been determined after considering that internal audit consulting services (a) may be formal (with written agreements) or informal, (b) may extend to some or all of process design, 'advice' and 'counsel', facilitation and training, and (c) should always have the expectation of adding value and improving the organization's operations? | Standards' Glossary definition of 'consulting services'; Practice Advisory 1000.C1–2 (Preamble) |
| 1.6 | Has consideration been given as to whether the execution of operational tasks or executive duties should be excluded from the scope of internal audit consulting, as set out in the Charter and in practice, except that 'emergency consulting engagements' by internal audit, for instance to recover or maintain operations after an extraordinary event, or to supply temporary help, are regarded as falling within the possible range of consulting services which internal audit may provide? | 1100, 1120, Practice Advisory 1000.C1–2, para 3, but see also para 8. |

|  | **Reference to Stand-ards framework** |
|---|---|
| **1. General** | |
| 1.7 Does the audit charter describe the nature of internal audit consulting activity as falling within the ambit of risk management, control and governance? | 2100, 2210.C1 |
| 1.8 Is the nature of consulting services defined in the audit charter, including the authority and responsibility of internal audit for consulting services; and are consulting engagements declined if prohibited by the charter? | 1000, 1000.C1, Practice Advisory 1000.C1–2, para 5 and 10. |
| 1.9 Does the audit charter explicitly or implicitly set out that internal audit consulting work may entail process design, 'advice' and 'counsel', facilitation and training; and should always have the expectation of adding value and improving the organization's operations? | Standards' Glossary definition of 'Consulting services' |
| 1.10 Has the possibility been considered that the internal audit activity may conduct hybrid engagements incorporating elements of both consulting and assurance activities, either in a blended or in a distinguishable way? | Practice Advisory 1000.C1–2, para 2. |
| 1.11 Is it acknowledged that special consulting engagements, such as participation in a merger or acquisition or in an emergency engagement (for example, a review of disaster recovery activities) may require departure from normal or established procedures for conducting internal auditing consulting engagements? | Practice Advisory 1000.C1–2 (Preamble) |
| 1.12 Has the chief audit executive determined the methodology for classifying different types of internal audit consulting engagement? | Practice Advisory 1000.C1–2, para 2. |
| 1.13 Is the execution of operational tasks or executive duties excluded from the scope of internal audit consulting, as set out in the Charter, and in practice? | 1100, 1120 |
| 1.14 Has the chief audit executive developed policies governing the custody and retention of consulting engagement records, as well as their release to internal and external parties; and are these policies consistent with the organization's guidelines and any pertinent regulatory or other requirements? | 2330.C1 |

|  |  | Reference to Stand-ards framework |
|---|---|---|
| **1. General** |  |  |
| 1.15 | Does the chief audit executive share information and coordinate activities with other internal and external providers of relevant consulting services to ensure proper coverage and minimize duplication of efforts? | 2050 |
| 1.16 | Is it the chief audit executive who decides whether to accept a consulting engagement? | 2010.C1 |
| 1.17 | Is it acknowledged by internal audit that the independence and objectivity of an assurance engagement may be impaired if it is conducted within one year after a formal consulting engagement, and are steps taken to minimise the effects? | Practice Advisory 1000.C1–2, para 7. |
| 1.18 | If there are potential impairments to internal audit independence or objectivity relating to a proposed consulting service, is disclosure made to the engagement client prior to accepting the engagement? | 1130.C1 |

|  |  | Reference to Standards framework |
|---|---|---|
| **2. Planning – general** |  |  |
| 2.1 | Are accepted consulting engagements included in the audit plan; and are the nature, extent and overall results of formal consulting engagements disclosed to management, the audit committee, board or other governing body along with other reports of internal auditing activities? | 2010.C1; 2060; Practice Advisory 1000.C1–2, para 17. |
| 2.2 | Before a consulting engagement is embarked upon, is it always clear how the results may, in a worthwhile way, improve management of risks, add value and improve the organization's operations? | 2010.C1 |
| 2.3 | Does the chief audit executive consider the scale of the risk before deciding whether to accept a consulting engagement? | 2010.C1 |
| 2.4 | Is there an effective process which leads to making reliable decisions as to whether to decline a consulting engagement or obtain competent advice and assistance, in cases where internal audit staff lack the knowledge, skills, or other competencies needed to perform all, or part of the engagement? | 1210.C1 |

| | | Reference to Standards framework |
|---|---|---|
| **2. Planning – general** | | |
| 2.5 | Does the internal audit activity effectively incorporate knowledge of risks gained from consulting engagements into the process of identifying and evaluating risk exposures of the organization? | 2110.C2 |
| 2.6 | Does the internal audit activity effectively factor into its assurance work the assurance which can be generated from the consulting engagements it has undertaken? | Practice Advisory 1000.C1–1 |

| | | Reference to Standards framework |
|---|---|---|
| **3. Engagement planning** | | |
| 3.1 | Has the internal audit activity developed appropriate policies and procedures for conducting consulting engagements? | Practice Advisory 1000.C1–2, para 5. |
| 3.2 | Are there clear consulting engagement objectives which address risks, controls, and governance processes to the extent agreed upon with the client? | 2210.C1 |
| 3.3 | Is it established that the engagement objectives of the consulting engagement are consistent with the overall values and goals of the organization? | 2130.C1 |
| 3.4 | For a consulting engagement in the area of governance, is it clear how the engagement results may improve in a worthwhile way the process through which (1) values and goals are established and communicated, (2) the accomplishment of goals is monitored, (3) accountability is ensured, and (4) values are preserved? | 2130 |
| 3.5 | Are internal audit consulting engagements 'agreed-upon', in nature and scope, between internal audit and the client? | Definition of 'consulting services' in the Glossary |
| 3.6 | How is it ensured that the intended scope of work will be sufficient to satisfy the agreed-upon objectives of the engagement? | 2220, 2220.C1 |

|  |  | Reference to Standards framework |
|---|---|---|
| **3. Engagement planning** | | |
| 3.7 | Does the client understand that the results of all consulting by internal audit may, at the judgment of the Chief Audit Executive, be presented to senior executives, board and audit committee members? | Practice Advisory 1000.C1–1 |
| 3.8 | How does the chief audit executive ensure that he or she retains the prerogative of setting the audit techniques to be used within a consulting engagement, and that there are no misunderstandings with respect to this between audit and the client? | Practice Advisory 1000.C1–1 |
| 3.9 | Have the internal auditors established an understanding with consulting engagement clients about objectives, scope, respective responsibilities, and other client expectations? For significant engagements, has this understanding been documented? | 2201.C1 |
| 3.10 | Is there a developed and recorded plan for the consulting engagement? | 2200 |

|  |  | Reference to Standards framework |
|---|---|---|
| **4. During a consulting engagement** | | |
| 4.1 | Is a disciplined, systematic evaluation methodology followed by internal audit in consulting work? | Practice Advisory 1000.C1–1 |
| 4.2 | How is it ensured that due professional care is exercised during a consulting engagement with respect to (a) the needs and expectations of clients, including the nature, timing, and communication of engagement results, (b) the relative complexity and extent of work needed to achieve the engagement's objectives, and (c) the cost of the consulting engagement in relation to potential benefits? | 1220.C1 |
| 4.3 | How is it ensured that during consulting engagements, internal auditors address risk consistent with the engagement's objectives and are alert to the existence of other significant risks? | 2110.C1 |

|  |  | Reference to Standards framework |
|---|---|---|
| **4. During a consulting engagement** | | |
| 4.4 | How is it ensured that during consulting engagements, internal auditors address controls consistent with the engagement's objectives and are alert to the existence of any significant control weaknesses? | 2120.C1 |
| 4.5 | When significant risk management, control and governance issues are identified during a consulting engagement, how does internal audit ensure they are communicated to senior management and the board? | 2440.C2 |
| 4.6 | When internal auditors develop reservations about the scope during the engagement, are these reservations discussed with the client to determine whether to continue with the engagement? | 2220.C1 |
| 4.7 | Do the internal auditors record relevant information to support the conclusions and engagement results? | 2330 |

|  |  | Reference to Standards framework |
|---|---|---|
| **5. Towards the end of the engagement** | | |
| 5.1 | Does the chief audit executive ensure the final results of consulting engagements are communicated to clients? | 2440.C1 |
| 5.2 | Are consulting engagement results communicated by internal audit promptly and in appropriate form and content having regard to the nature of the engagement and the needs of the client? | 2400, 2410.C1 |
| 5.3 | Does the internal audit activity monitor the disposition of results of consulting engagements to the extent agreed upon with the client? | 2500.C1 |
| 5.4 | In the case of consulting engagements, when the chief audit executive believes that senior management has accepted a level of residual risk that is unacceptable to the organization, does the chief audit executive discuss the matter with the client and, if the matter is not resolved, ensure that the matter is reported to the board for resolution? | 2600 |

---

[1]   As stated in each Practice Advisory, for instance Practice Advisory 1000.C1–1: 'Principles Guiding the Performance of Consulting Activities of Internal Auditors'.

[2]   'Risk management', 'control' and 'governance'.

3       Practice Advisory 1000.C1.2 (7 January 2002), para 10.
4       Practice Advisory 1000.C1.2 (7 January 2002), para 3.
5       Practice Advisory 1000.C1.2 (7 January 2002), para 3, last bullet point.
6       Practice Advisory 1000.C1.2 (7 January 2002), para 7.

## A1.2.31    An introduction to operational auditing

The term 'operational auditing' conjures up different images for internal auditors. It may be used to mean any of the following:

- The audit of *operating units* such as factories, subsidiary companies or overseas operations. With this meaning the scope of the audit may be limited to accounting and financial controls or it may be given a wider scope.
- The audit of accounting and financial control in *the functional areas of a business*, as distinct from the controls which are exercised within the accounting and financial functions of the business. These functional areas might be marketing, sales, distribution, production, etc, depending upon the nature of the business. This use of the expression *operational auditing* stresses that internal audit has a mission to review all operational areas of the business; it also implies, not necessarily correctly, that internal audit is an agent of the finance director or chief accountant who needs reassurance that appropriate financial and accounting controls are being applied in the operational areas of the business.
- The audit of *any part of the business* (operating unit, functional area, department, accounting department, treasury department, etc) where the audit objective corresponds to a review of the effectiveness and efficiency with which management are achieving their own objectives. This style of operational auditing may go beyond a review of internal control issues since management does not achieve its objectives simply by adhering to satisfactory systems of internal control. Alternatively the scope of the audit may be restricted to the internal control issues (financial and accounting controls and, often more significantly, operational controls) which contribute to the achievement of management's objectives in the operational area subject to review by internal audit.

Support for this style of auditing is given by leading management thinkers, eg:

'An effective tool of managerial control is the internal audit, or, as it is now coming to be called, the operational audit ... Although often limited to the auditing of accounts, in its most useful aspect operational auditing involves appraisal of operations generally ... Thus operational auditors, in addition to assuring themselves that accounts properly reflect the facts, also appraise policies, procedures, use of authority, quality of management, effectiveness of methods, special problems, and other phases of operations.

There is no persuasive reason why the concept of internal auditing should not be broadened in practice. Perhaps the only limiting factors are the ability of an enterprise to afford so broad an audit, the difficulty of obtaining people who can do a broad type of audit, and the very practical consideration that individuals may not like to be reported upon. While persons responsible for accounts and for the safeguarding of company assets have learned to accept audit, those who are responsible for far more valuable things – the execution of the plans, policies and procedures of a company – have not so readily learned to accept the idea.'[7]

## A1.2.32  *Scope*

A key issue for a business and its internal audit function to decide upon is whether the scope of internal audit work in an operational area of the business should be restricted to internal control issues or should be a comprehensive, general review of the operation.

The COSO view of internal control rightly sees one of the three objectives of internal control as being to give 'reasonable assurance' of 'effectiveness and efficiency of operations'. But internal control (ie management control) is only one of a number of facets of management – amongst others being planning, organising, staffing and leading. It is true that these facets overlap and an internal audit which is restricted to internal control issues may need to address planning, organising, staffing and/or leadership issues as deficiencies in these may weaken control. But there will be many aspects of planning, organising, staffing and leading which are neutral in their control effect but which contribute to the achievement of efficient and effective operations.

The key issue is whether internal audit may legitimately draw management's attention to deficiencies in planning, organising, staffing and leading which, while not weakening control, nevertheless impede the achievement of objectives. Internal audit is often defined as *the independent appraisal of the effectiveness of internal control*: control is not the whole of the management process. Should an enlightened enterprise restrict internal audit to internal control matters – or should internal audit be encouraged to review and report on *any matters* which may be commercially unsound? The jury is out on this! Differing positions are adopted in different enterprises. The middle-of-the-road enlightened approach is to encourage internal audit to interpret its mission as being the *appraisal of internal control* only (in all its component parts,[8] in all operational areas of the business and at all levels of management) and not to deliberately broaden its scope beyond this. However, if, during the course of audit work, other matters are noted incidentally which should be of management concern but do not directly have a control dimension, then internal audit should be encouraged to report to management on these matters even though they did not set out to embrace these matters within the scope of their audit work.

## A1.2.33  *Audit approach to operational audits*

Adopting the middle-of-the-road orientation to operational auditing, the following is an effective approach which has the merit that it strikes a chord with management as *management's objectives* are central to the audit throughout. It can be irksome to line management if the internal auditor only seems to be asking the question 'what might go wrong?' and rarely the question 'is management going to achieve their objectives?'. Motivated line management are not just charged with the responsibility to prevent unwanted exposures materialising – they have a mission to achieve objectives. An audit approach which acknowledges this will be both more useful and more acceptable. In this context, *some but not all* of management's objectives will relate to the prevention of unwanted outcomes.

## A1.2.34   *Example of the objectives-oriented audit approach*

An internal audit team based at Group HQ in New York is commencing an audit of an operating unit which is in Tokyo. As a fundamental part of their preparation for the fieldwork of this audit they meet with senior management who have overall responsibility for the Tokyo operation. There may be several senior managers, perhaps at director level, who share this responsibility for differing aspects of the Tokyo operation but, to keep this example more simple, let us assume that there is just one Group Production Director in New York to whom the head of the Tokyo operating unit reports for all purposes.

The audit team commences by establishing with the Group Production Director (**1**) **'what are his or her objectives for the Tokyo operation?'**. Right away the audit team may have significant findings for later inclusion in their audit report if it is apparent that the Director is unclear as to what the objectives are. Nevertheless, it is necessary for the audit team to establish what the objectives must be as the rest of the audit flows from this.

Having established the director's objectives for the Tokyo operation, the audit team then determines, in consultation with the director, (**2**) **'what information does the director need to receive so as to be in a position to know whether the operation is on course to achieve its set objectives?'**. Here again, the audit team may come up with findings for later inclusion in their audit report as audit investigation may reveal that the director is unclear as to what information he or she needs.

The audit team then checks on the available information at the director's disposal. This may lead to the following audit findings:

* the needed information *is not* being received:
  - at all;
  - in time;
  - in a helpful, useful format, etc;
* the director is not making use of some of the needed information which he or she is receiving;
* some unnecessary information *is* being prepared and received.

All of the above is done by the audit team *before* they leave their New York HQ to visit the Tokyo operation. Their approach in Tokyo is to confirm the validity of the information sent from Tokyo to New York and to determine whether there are is any other information which New York should be receiving (but are not) in the light of:

* what is actually happening in Tokyo;
* where it has a potential impact on the achievement of management's objectives for the Tokyo operation.

## A1.2.35   *The '3 E's' or the '6 E's'*

Internal auditors of operations need to understand the distinctive meanings of effectiveness, efficiency and economy.

- Effectiveness means 'doing the right things' – ie achieving objectives.
- Efficiency means 'doing them well' – for instance with good systems which avoid waste and rework.
- Economy means 'doing them cheap' – with, for instance, unit costs for labour, materials, etc being under control.

These three 'E's' can be related to each other in the following model:

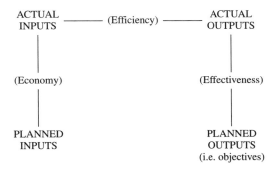

| Economy | the ratio between planned inputs and actual inputs in terms of unit costs |
| --- | --- |
| Efficiency | the ratio of actual inputs to actual outputs |
| Effectiveness | the ratio of actual outputs to planned outputs |

Internal auditors are now adding further 'E's' to their portfolio of matters of audit interest:

| Equity | Avoidance of discrimination and unfairness |
| --- | --- |
| Environment | Acting in an environmentally responsible way |
| Ethics | Legal and moral conduct by management and staff |

## A1.2.36  *VFM Auditing*

Value for money auditing is auditing which takes account of the '3 E's'. It frequently makes extensive use of performance indicators in the form of ratios and other statistics to give an indication of value for money – especially when trends are explored in these performance indicators over time, or variations in performance are identified and explained between different operating units.

## A1.2.37  *Environmental auditing*

Environmental auditing has been defined as:

> 'A management tool comprising a systematic, documented, periodic and objective evaluation of how well environmental organisation, management and equipment are performing with the aim of helping to safeguard the environment by:

- facilitating management control of environmental practices;
- assessing compliance with company policies which would include meeting regulatory requirements.'[9]

Where an enterprise has environmental considerations as some of their objectives it is entirely necessary and appropriate that internal controls should facilitate the assured achievement of those objectives. Hence environmental auditing becomes something which concerns internal auditors. Businesses may choose to have separate environmental audits conducted by others than internal audit; but internal audit should be in a position to provide this service to the business, and to take account of work which has been done by others which contributes to meeting this objective.

As with other issues which are subject to internal audits, the establishment of management's objectives (in this case relating to environmental responsibility) is not so much the remit of internal audit as is the appraisal of the extent to which internal controls provide management with an assurance of meeting those objectives. Specialist environmental auditors may take more naturally to commending to management what their environmental objectives should be. Nevertheless it is wise that internal auditors should be willing to give this advice to managements who seek it from internal audit.

Internal audit has long been concerned to advise management when regulatory requirements in general are not being met – one of the accepted [COSO] objectives of internal control is 'to provide reasonable assurance regarding the achievement of … compliance with applicable laws and regulations'. Where there are applicable laws and regulations relating to environmental matters, a scope for internal audit work which includes environmental considerations becomes mainstream for internal auditors – unless explicitly excluded by management and the Board.

## A1.2.38  *Quality audit*

Enterprises which have adopted total quality management principles (TQM) and have sought to develop (and perhaps to register) so-called quality systems (QS) under ISO, British or other similar standards may entrust to specialist quality auditors the task of reviewing the enterprise's performance with respect to TQM and QS. As with environmental auditing, it is not inappropriate for internal audit to take on this responsibility: if the business has objectives relating to TQM and QS it is appropriate for internal audit to review the business's internal controls which contribute to the achievement of those objectives.

---

7  H Koontz, C O'Donnell and H Weihrich: *Management* [McGraw-Hill, Singapore, 8th edition], pp 670–671.

8  The COSO *Internal Control – Integrated Framework* study [September 1992] identified the five components of internal control as being (1) control environment, (2) risk assessment, (3) control activities, (4) information and communication and (5) monitoring.

9  The International Chamber of Commerce [1989].

## A1.2.39   **Checklist on internal audit charter**

'**Audit Charter** – The audit charter of the internal audit activity is a formal written document that defines the activity's purpose, authority, and responsibility. The audit charter should (a) establish the internal audit activity's position within the organization; (b) authorize access to records, personnel, and physical properties relevant to the performance of engagements; and (c) define the scope of internal audit activities.'

| Issue | | Reference |
|---|---|---|
| **1. DEVELOPMENT AND APPROVAL OF THE CHARTER** | | |
| 1.1 | Is there a audit charter and is it in writing? | para 2 of PA1000–1 |
| 1.2 | Has senior management's approval of the audit charter been sought and obtained by the CAE? | para 1 of PA1000–1 |
| 1.3 | Has board approval and acceptance of the audit charter been sought and obtained by the CAE?[10] | Standard 1000; para 1 of PA1000–1 |
| 1.4 | Has the audit charter been signed and dated by the CAE, CEO and audit committee chair? | Per model audit charter available at http://www.theiia.org/ecm/guide-ia.cfm?doc_id=383 |
| **2. CHARTER REVIEW** | | |
| 2.1 | When was the audit charter last reviewed by the CAE?[11] | para 3 of PA1000–1 |
| 2.2 | When was the audit charter last reviewed by senior management?[12] | para 2 of PA1000–1 |
| 2.3 | Has the audit charter been reviewed and approved by the audit committee of the board within the last 12 months?[13] | para 2 of PA1000–1, para 5 of PA2060–2 |
| **3. COMMUNICATION ISSUES** | | |
| 3.1 | Is the audit charter communicated appropriately? | para 2 of PA1000–1 |
| 3.2 | Has the audit committee ensured that the audit charter, role, and activities of internal audit are clearly understood and responsive to the needs of the audit committee and the board? | para 3 of PA2060–2 |
| 3.3 | Was the result of the review of the charter by the CAE communicated to senior management and the board? | para 3 of PA1000–1 |
| **4. EVALUATING INTERNAL AUDIT PERFORMANCE** | | |
| 4.1 | Is the audit charter used as a basis for management and the board to evaluate the operations of the internal audit function? | para 2 of PA1000–1 |

| Issue | | Reference | Example IIA model audit charter wording http://www.theiia.org/ecm/ guide-ia.cfm?doc_id=383 | Example wording from other audit charters |
|---|---|---|---|---|
| **5. CONTENTS ON PURPOSE** | | | | |
| 5.1 | Is the purpose of the internal audit activity defined in the audit charter? | Standard 1000 | 'The mission of the internal audit department is to provide independent, objective assurance and consulting services designed to add value and improve the organization's operations. It helps the organization accomplish its objectives by bringing a systematic, disciplined approach to evaluate and improve the effectiveness of risk management, control, and governance processes.' | **'PURPOSE** The Group Internal Auditing Unit is responsible to advise all levels of management, and the Board through its Audit Committee, on the quality of the Group's operations with particular emphasis on systems of governance, risk management and internal control. It is a review activity which does not relieve line management of their responsibilities for effective governance, risk management and internal control. It functions by conducting independent appraisals leading to reports on its findings and recommendations addressed, as appropriate, to (a) |
| | | | | the levels of management who need to know and are capable of ensuring that appropriate action is taken, and (b) the Audit Committee of the Board.' |

| Issue | | Reference | IIA wording | Other wording |
|---|---|---|---|---|
| 5.2 | Does the audit charter define the scope of internal audit activities? | para 1 of PA1000–1 | 'The scope of work of the internal audit department is to determine whether the organization's network of risk management, control, and governance processes, as designed and represented by management, is adequate and functioning in a manner to ensure: | |
| | | | ● Risks are appropriately identified and managed | |
| | | | ● Interaction with the various governance groups occurs as needed. | |
| | | | ● Significant financial, managerial, and operating information is accurate, reliable, and timely. | |
| | | | ● Employees' actions are in compliance with policies, standards, procedures, and applicable laws and regulations. | |
| | | | ● Resources are acquired economically, used efficiently, and adequately protected. | |
| | | | ● Programs, plans, and objectives are achieved. | |
| | | | ● Quality and continuous improvement are fostered in the organization's control process. | |

| Issue | | Reference | IIA wording | Other wording |
|---|---|---|---|---|
| | | | • Significant legislative or regulatory issues impacting the organization are recognized and addressed appropriately. | |
| | | | Opportunities for improving management control, profitability, and the organization's image may be identified during audits. They will be communicated to the appropriate level of management.' | |
| 5.3 | Is the nature of assurance services provided by internal audit to the organization defined in the audit charter? | Standard 1000.A1 | | Consider adapting the wording of the new paragraph which The IIA's January 2003 Exposure Draft of proposed amendments to the *Standards* proposes to add to the Introduction part of the *Standards*. The first part of this paragraph reads: 'Assurance services involve the internal auditor's objective assessment of evidence for the purpose of providing an independent opinion regarding a process, system, or other subject matter. There are generally three parties involved in assurance services: (1) the person or group directly involved with the process or system – the process owner. |

| Issue | Reference | IIA wording | Other wording |
|-------|-----------|-------------|---------------|
| | | | (2) the person or group making the assessment – the auditor, and (3) the person or group using the assessment to make decisions – the user. Consulting services are advisory and other non-assurance activities delivered by the internal auditor generally at the specific request of an engagement client, while not assuming management responsibility for the engagement results.' |

| Issue | | Reference | IIA wording | Other wording |
|---|---|---|---|---|
| 5.4 | Is the nature of internal audit consulting services defined in the audit charter? | Standard 1000.C1 | 'The mission of the internal audit department is to provide independent, objective assurance and consulting services designed to add value and improve the organization's operations. It helps the organization accomplish its objectives by bringing a systematic, disciplined approach to evaluate and improve the effectiveness of risk management, control, and governance processes.' | Consider adapting the wording of the new paragraph which The IIA's January 2003 Exposure Draft of proposed amendments to the *Standards* proposes to add to the Introduction part of the *Standards*. The second part of this paragraph reads: 'Consulting services are advisory and other non-assurance activities delivered by the internal auditor generally at the specific request of an engagement client, while not assuming management responsibility for the engagement results. Consulting services involve two parties, the auditor and the client. Unlike assurance services engagements where the internal auditor determines the nature and scope, in consulting the nature and scope are subject to agreement with the client. Consulting services, like assurance services, are intended to add value and improve the organization's governance, risk management, and control processes.' |

| Issue | | Reference | IIA wording | Other wording |
|---|---|---|---|---|
| | | | | Alternatively: 'Subject to not prejudicing its assurance activity, the internal auditing unit may undertake consulting engagements the nature and scope of which are agreed upon with management and which are intended to add value and improve the organization's operations. Such consulting engagements will generally apply internal audit's competence in risk management, internal control and/or governance, and involve the provision of counsel, advice, facilitation, process design, and/or training.' |
| 5.5 | Is the internal audit role in governance matters covered adequately in the Charter? | The IIA's January 2003 Exposure Draft of proposed amendments to the Standards proposes an amended Standard 2130 on Governance, to read: 'The internal audit activity, consistent with the organization's structure, should contribute to the governance process by proactively assisting management and the board in fulfilling their responsibilities by: | | |
| | | • Assessing and promoting strong ethics and values within the organization. | | |

| Issue | | Reference | IIA wording | Other wording |
|---|---|---|---|---|
| | | ● Assessing and improving the process by which accountability is ensured. | | |
| | | ● Assessing the adequacy of communications about significant residual risks within the organization. | | |
| | | ● Helping to improve the board's interaction with management and the external and internal auditors. | | |
| | | ● Serving as an educational resource regarding changes and trends in the business and regulatory environment.' | | |
| **6. CONTENTS ON AUTHORITY** | | | | |
| 6.1 | Is the authority of the internal audit activity defined in the audit charter? | Standard 1000 | **'INDEPENDENCE** To provide for the independence of the internal auditing department, its personnel report to the chief audit executive, who reports functionally to the audit committee and administratively to the chief executive officer in a manner outlined in the above section on Accountability. It will include as part of its reports to the audit committee a regular report on internal audit personnel.' ... | 'AUTHORITY The Group Internal Auditing Unit derives its authority from senior management and from the Board to whose Audit Committee it has open access. The entity has also given the Group Internal Auditing Unit, for the purpose of its audit work, unrestricted access at any time to all the records, personnel, property and operations of the entity with strict responsibility for safekeeping and confidentiality. |

| Issue | Reference | | IIA wording | Other wording |
|---|---|---|---|---|
| | | | **AUTHORITY** The chief audit executive and staff of the internal audit department are authorized to: | The Audit Committee of the Board reviews the scope and nature of the work of the Group Internal Auditing Unit to confirm its independence, and receives and reviews its reports to the Committee. |
| | | | ● Have unrestricted access to all functions, records, property, and personnel. | The Group Internal Auditing Unit does not perform line tasks as this would impair its objectivity; neither has it any direct responsibility for, nor authority over, the activities it reviews.' |
| | | | ● Have full and free access to the audit committee. | |
| | | | ● Allocate resources, set frequencies, select subjects, determine scopes of work, and apply the techniques required to accomplish audit objectives. | |
| | | | ● Obtain the necessary assistance of personnel in units of the organization where they perform audits, as well as other specialized services from within or outside the organization. | |
| | | | The chief audit executive and staff of the internal audit department are not authorized to: | |
| | | | ● Perform any operational duties for the organization or its affiliates. | |

| Issue | | Reference | IIA wording | Other wording |
|---|---|---|---|---|
| | | | • Initiate or approve accounting transactions external to the internal auditing department. | |
| | | | Direct the activities of any organization employee not employed by the internal auditing department, except to the extent such employees have been appropriately assigned to auditing teams or to otherwise assist the internal auditors.' | |
| 6.2 | Does the audit charter establish the internal audit activity's position within the organization? | para 1 of PA1000–1 | | |
| 6.3 | Does the charter for the internal audit function clearly articulate both the functional and administrative reporting lines for the function as well as the principal activities directed up each line.'[14] | para 7 of PA 1110–2 | | |
| 6.4 | Does the audit charter authorize access to records, personnel, and physical properties relevant to the performance of engagements? | para 1 of PA1000–1 | | |

| Issue | | Reference | IIA wording | Other wording |
|---|---|---|---|---|
| 6.5 | If assurances are to be provided by internal audit to parties outside the organization, is the nature of these assurances defined in the audit charter? | Standard 1000.A1 | | |
| **7. CONTENTS ON RESPONSIBILITY** | | | | |
| 7.1 | Is the responsibility of the internal audit activity defined in the audit charter? | Standard 1000 | 'ACCOUNTABILITY The chief audit executive, in the discharge of his/her duties, shall be accountable to management and the audit committee to: | 'RESPONSIBILI-TIES The Group Head of Internal Audit is responsible for determining the Group Internal Auditing Unit's programme of work, so |
| | | | ● Provide annually an assessment on the adequacy and effectiveness of the organization's processes for controlling its activities and managing its risks in the areas set forth under the mission and scope of work. | that management and the Board can have assurance as to the objectivity of audit reports. To provide this reassurance to management and the Board, the scope of the Group Internal Auditing Unit's work includes ascertaining, at home and abroad |
| | | | ● Report significant issues related to the processes for controlling the activities of the organization and its affiliates, including potential improvements to those processes, and provide information concerning such issues through resolution. | and at all levels of the entity, that the assets of the Group are being safeguarded; that operations are conducted effectively, efficiently and economically in accordance with Group policies and procedures as well as with laws and regulations; and that records and reports of |

| Issue | | Reference | IIA wording | Other wording |
|---|---|---|---|---|
| | | | • Periodically provide information on the status and results of the annual audit plan and the sufficiency of department resources. | the Group are accurate and reliable. The review of systems under development is part of the Group Internal Auditing Unit's responsibilities. In |
| | | | • Coordinate with and provide oversight of other control and monitoring functions (risk management, compliance, security, legal, ethics, environmental, external audit).' ... | addition the Group Internal Auditing Unit may perform special reviews requested by management or the Board. The Group Internal Auditing Unit is not relieved of its responsibilities in |
| | | | **'RESPONSIBILITY** The chief audit executive and staff of the internal audit department have responsibility to: | areas of the Group's business which are subject to review by others; but should always assess the |
| | | | • Develop a flexible annual audit plan using an appropriate risk-based methodology, including any risks or control concerns identified by management, and submit that plan to the audit committee for review and approval as well as periodic updates. | extent to which it can rely upon the work of others and co-ordinate its audit planning with those other review agencies.' |
| | | | • Implement the annual audit plan, as approved, including as appropriate any special tasks or projects requested by management and the audit committee. | |

| Issue | | Reference | IIA wording | Other wording |
|---|---|---|---|---|
| | | | ● Maintain a professional audit staff with sufficient knowledge, skills, experience, and professional certifications to meet the requirements of this Charter. | |
| | | | ● Evaluate and assess significant merging/ consolidating functions and new or changing services, processes, operations, and control processes coincident with their development, implementation, and/or expansion. | |
| | | | ● Issue periodic reports to the audit committee and management summarizing results of audit activities. | |
| | | | ● Keep the audit committee informed of emerging trends and successful practices in internal auditing. | |
| | | | ● Provide a list of significant measurement goals and results to the audit committee. | |
| | | | ● Assist in the investigation of significant suspected fraudulent activities within the organization and notify management and the audit committee of the results. | |

| Issue | | Reference | IIA wording | Other wording |
|---|---|---|---|---|
| | | | Consider the scope of work of the external auditors and regulators, as appropriate, for the purpose of providing optimal audit coverage to the organization at a reasonable overall cost.' | |
| 7.2 | Does the audit charter set out the responsibility of internal audit to report to the audit committee on suspected frauds and assist in their investigation if significant? | para 5 of PA2060–2 | | |
| **8. CONTENTS ON IIA *STANDARDS*** | | | | |
| 8.1 | Is the audit charter consistent with the IIA *Standards*? | Standard 1000 | **'STANDARDS OF AUDIT PRACTICE** The internal audit department will meet or exceed the *Standards for the Professional Practice of Internal Auditing* of The Institute of Internal Auditors.' | 'The Board requires the Group Internal Auditing Unit to function professionally, adhering to the *Code of Ethics*, *Standards* and *Guidelines* of The Institute of Internal Auditors and meeting the requirements of regulatory authorities in those areas which are within the Group Internal Auditing Unit's responsibility.' |

10    Or acceptance of the audit committee or appropriate governing body.
11    Did the review assess whether the internal audit activity's purpose, authority, and responsibility, as defined in the audit charter, continue to be adequate to enable the internal audit activity to accomplish its objectives?
12    Did the review assess the adequacy of the internal audit activity's purpose?
13    Did the review assess the adequacy of the internal audit activity's purpose?
14    Para 7.

## A1.2.40    Internal audit charters

At A1.1.19 we reproduce the sample 'Charter' suggested by The Institute of Internal Auditors. Here we provide three further examples of charters for internal audit activities,15 giving effect to varying degrees to the requirement that the nature of consulting services provided by an internal audit activity should be defined in the 'Charter'.

Standard 1000 of The Institute of Internal Auditors on 'Purpose, Authority, and Responsibility' reads:

> 'The purpose, authority, and responsibility of the internal audit activity should be formally defined in a charter, consistent with the Standards, and approved by the board.'

Standard 1000.A1 reads:

> 'The nature of assurance services provided to the organization should be defined in the audit charter. If assurances are to be provided to parties outside the organization, the nature of these assurances should also be defined in the charter.'

and Standard 1000.C1:

> 'The nature of consulting services should be defined in the audit charter.'

The Glossary to these new Standards defines 'Charter' as:

> 'The charter of the internal audit activity is a formal written document that defines the activity's purpose, authority, and responsibility. The charter should (a) establish the internal audit activity's position within the organisation; (b) authorise access to records, personnel, and physical properties relevant to the performance of engagements; and (c) define the scope of internal audit activities.'

And 'Board' is defined to include audit committees working on behalf of boards and also sole individuals upon whom are vested the responsibilities more usually carried by directors collectively, viz.:

> 'A board is an organization's governing body, such as a board of directors, supervisory board, head of an agency or legislative body, board of governors or trustees of a non profit organization, or any other designated body of the organization, including the audit committee, to whom the chief audit executive may functionally report.'

## A1.2.41 *Example 1: sample 'Charter' for an internal auditing activity*

| **ABC Holdings plc** | |
|---|---|
| **CHARTER OF GROUP INTERNAL AUDIT** | |
| *In this Charter the following words and terms have these respective meanings:* | |
| 'The Entity' | The group of businesses within this plc; |
| 'The Board' | The Board of directors of the entity; |
| 'The Group' | All operations, investments and obligations which are the responsibility of the Board; |

| 'Audit Committee' | A committee of directors of the entity appointed by the Board as provided for in 'Terms of Reference of the Audit Committee' formally adopted by the Board; |
| --- | --- |
| 'Group Internal Audit' | The function which provides internal audit services to Group Management and to the Board through the Audit Committee. |

This charter identifies the purpose, authority and responsibility of the Group Internal Auditing Unit.

## PURPOSE

The Group Internal Auditing Unit is responsible to advise all levels of management, and the Board through its Audit Committee, on the quality of the Group's operations with particular emphasis on systems of control. It is a review activity which does not relieve line management of their responsibility for effective control. It functions by conducting independent appraisals leading to reports on its findings and recommendations addressed, as appropriate, to (a) the levels of management who need to know and are capable of ensuring that appropriate action is taken, and (b) the Audit Committee of the Board.

The Board requires the Group Internal Auditing Unit to function professionally, adhering to the *Code of Ethics*, *Standards* and *Guidelines* of The Institute of Internal Auditors and meeting the requirements of regulatory authorities in those areas which are within the Group Internal Auditing Unit's responsibility.

## AUTHORITY

The Group Internal Auditing Unit derives its authority from senior management and from the Board to whose Audit Committee it has open access. The entity has also given the Group Internal Auditing Unit, for the purpose of its audit work, unrestricted access at any time to all the records, personnel, property and operations of the entity with strict responsibility for safekeeping and confidentiality.

The Audit Committee of the Board reviews the scope and nature of the work of the Group Internal Auditing Unit to confirm its independence, and receives and reviews its reports to the Committee.

The Group Internal Auditing Unit does not perform line tasks as this would impair its objectivity; neither has it any direct responsibility for, nor authority over, the activities it reviews.

## RESPONSIBILITIES

The Group Head of Internal Audit is responsible for determining the Group Internal Auditing Unit's programme of work, so that management and the Board can have assurance as to the objectivity of audit reports. To provide this reassurance to management and the Board, the scope of the Group Internal Auditing Unit's work includes ascertaining, at home and abroad and at all levels of the entity, that the assets of the Group are being safeguarded; that operations are conducted effectively, efficiently and economically in accordance with Group policies and procedures as well as with laws and regulations; and that records and reports of the Group are accurate and reliable. The review of systems under development is part of the Group Internal Auditing Unit's responsibilities. In addition the Group Internal Auditing Unit may perform special reviews requested by management or the Board.

Subject to not prejudicing its assurance activity, the internal auditing unit may undertake consulting engagements the nature and scope of which are agreed upon with management and which are intended to add value and improve the organization's operations. Such consulting engagements will generally apply internal audit's competence in risk management, internal control and/or governance, and involve the provision of counsel, advice, facilitation, process design, and/or training.

The Group Internal Auditing Unit is not relieved of its responsibilities in areas of the Group's business which are subject to review by others; but should always assess the extent to which it can rely upon the work of others and co-ordinate its audit planning with those other review agencies.
**[Signed]**

15    Note that 'an internal audit' is no longer an internal audit 'activity', it is now an 'engagement'. New terminology uses 'activity' in a different context, dispensing with terms such as 'Unit' or 'Department' in favour of:

> **'Internal Audit Activity** – A department, division, team of consultants, or other practitioner(s) that provides independent, objective assurance and consulting services designed to add value and improve an organization's operations. The internal audit activity helps an organization accomplish its objectives by bringing a systematic, disciplined approach to evaluate and improve the effectiveness of risk management, control, and governance processes.' (*Glossary of Terms* to the new *Standards* of The Institute of Internal Auditors).

## A1.2.42   *Example 2: sample 'Charter' for an internal auditing activity*

---

**Internal audit charter**

1.  GROUP POLICY

    1.1   The Group Internal Audit Department is an independent, objective assurance and consulting activity designed to add value and improve the organisation's operations. It helps the organisation accomplish its objectives by bringing a systematic, disciplined approach to evaluate and improve the effectiveness of risk management, control and governance processes.

    1.2   The Department gives a service to the Group Board and all levels of management and is independent of all activities that it audits, to ensure the unbiased judgements essential to its proper conduct and impartial advice to management.

    1.3   The Department is empowered by the Board to carry out such a programme of audits as will enable the Department to review, appraise, and report on the above issues and to this end has a right of access to all activities undertaken in the organisation.

---

1.4 The Department assesses, together with management, risks that could have a significant impact on operations, and implements an audit plan, which encompasses the examination and evaluation of the adequacy and effectiveness of the organisation's system of internal control, and the quality of performance in carrying out assigned responsibilities.

1.5 The Group Internal Audit Department is an integral part of the organisation and functions under the policies established by management and the Group Board. It reports to the Audit Committee and the Group Chairman (who may delegate his responsibility to the Group Finance Director) and its ultimate responsibility is to the Group Board.

1.6 The Board requires the Group Internal Audit Department to function professionally, adhering to the *Code of Ethics* and *Standards* of The Institute of Internal Auditors.

1.7 Internal Audit staff shall observe all expected courtesies, confidentiality and statutory obligations while carrying out their responsibilities, and shall perform their tasks in a manner that is professional, objective and impartial.

2. AUTHORITY

2.1 The Internal Audit Department is authorised to carry out such audits as it considers necessary to enable it to report to the Group Finance Director in accordance with this Charter.

2.2 The Department shall have free and unrestricted access to the Group Chairman and Group Finance Director and to the Chairman of the Audit Committee.

2.3 Internal auditors shall have the right of unrestricted access to any and all of the organisation's records (manual and electronic), physical assets, property, and personnel relevant to the function, which is being reviewed. All employees are expected to assist Internal Audit as required.

3. INDEPENDENCE

3.1 The Internal Audit Department is independent from line management and has no direct responsibility for, or authority over, any of the activities under review.

3.2 Internal Audit shall not develop nor install systems and procedures, nor engage in any other activity which the Department may be required to review. It shall have an advisory role in determining and making recommendations on the methods, nature and standards of controls to be incorporated in any new system, or amendments to existing systems.

4. STRUCTURE

4.1 The Group Internal Audit Manager shall have overall responsibility for the effective and efficient functioning of the Internal Audit Department and will report accordingly to the Group Chairman, Group Finance Director and Chairman of the Audit Committee.

4.2 The Internal Audit Department shall be deemed to comprise all Audit Departments within the Group, whether constituted as a central function or as an in house department operating within one or more Group Subsidiary Companies.

4.3 Where an Audit Department operates solely within one Group Company or a group of Companies it will still be responsible to the Group Internal Audit Manager and not to the functional head of finance within that organisation.

5. ROLE AND SCOPE

5.1 Internal Audit provides assurance and consulting services to the organisation as detailed in this Audit Charter.

5.2 This service may include any or all of the following:

5.2.1 Identifying major problems and risk exposures.

5.2.2 Determining and reporting on the adequacy, reliability, and effectiveness of managerial controls and the integrity of information.

5.2.3 Suggesting improvements to business processes and controls.

5.2.4 Evaluating the economic, efficient, and effective use of resources.

5.2.5 Determining and reporting on the extent of compliance with relevant statutes, regulations, standards, and policies.

5.2.6 Reviewing the methods of safeguarding Group assets.

5.2.7 Monitoring controls designed to combat fraud; and investigating and reporting to the audit committee on significant frauds or suspected frauds.

5.2.8 Reviewing specific operations at the request of Group or company management, the Board or the Chairman of the Audit Committee.

5.2.9 Liaison with the external auditors to achieve the most efficient use of both resources.

5.2.10 Reviewing the integrity of individual company financial statements.

5.3 The main role of the Internal Auditing Department is to provide assurance. Internal audit assurance engagements entail an objective examination of evidence for the purpose of providing an independent assessment on risk management, control, or governance processes for the organisation. Examples may include financial, performance, compliance, system security, and due diligence engagements.

5.4 Subject to not prejudicing its assurance activity, the Internal Auditing Department may undertake consulting engagements the nature and scope of which are agreed upon with management and which are intended to add value and improve the organization's operations. Such consulting engagements will generally apply internal audit's competence in risk management, internal control and/or governance, and involve the provision of counsel, advice, facilitation, process design and/or training.

5.5   In practice, internal audit engagements frequently comprise elements of both assurance and consulting.

6.  AUDIT MANAGEMENT AND PLANNING

6.1   An audit plan shall be drawn up annually by the Group Internal Audit Manager for the Internal Audit Department and this will incorporate the plans for any in house audit departments. This plan will be presented by the Group Internal Audit Manager and approved by the Audit Committee.

6.2   Plans relating to individual Group Companies (or Groups of Companies) will be agreed with the respective Company's management, and will form part of the overall plan.

7.  REPORTING

7.1   A report will be submitted at the conclusion of each audit to the appropriate line manager who would be responsible for any action to be taken following the report.

7.2   A copy of all reports issued by the Internal Audit Department will be issued to, and retained by, the Group Internal Audit Manager, who shall report findings and management comment quarterly to the Group Chairman, Group Finance Director and the Audit Committee.

7.3   At the conclusion of each financial year the Group Internal Audit Manager will meet with the Chairman of the Audit Committee and submit to him a summary report setting out the audit opinion for the Group.

...........................................................

Group Internal Audit Manager

...........................................................

Group Finance Director

...........................................................

Group Chairman

...........................................................

Chairman of the Audit Committee

Dated        ...........................................................

## A1.2.43   *Example 3: sample 'Charter' for an Internal Auditing Activity*

*This charter has been contributed by Kelsey Walker, Business Assurance Director at Network Housing Association. Kelsey asks us to mention that she found much of the basis for this charter in articles written by other internal auditors. Kelsey can be contacted by e-mail at: kwalker@networkhg.org.uk; or by phone: 020 8903 1339.*

INTERNAL AUDIT CHARTER

## Purpose and scope of work

The purpose of the Internal Audit service is to provide independent, objective assurance and consulting services designed to add value and improve the organisation's operations. It helps the organisation accomplish its objectives by bringing a systematic, disciplined approach to evaluate and improve the effectiveness of risk management, control and governance processes.

The scope of work of the Internal Audit service is to determine whether the organisation's network of risk management, control and governance processes, as designed and represented by management is adequate and functioning in a manner to ensure:

- Risks are appropriately identified and managed.
- Significant financial, managerial and operating information is accurate, reliable and timely.
- Employees' actions are in compliance with policies, standards, procedures and applicable laws and regulations.
- Resources are acquired economically, used efficiently and adequately protected.
- Programmes, plans and objectives are achieved.
- Quality and continuous improvement are fostered in the organisation's control process.
- Significant legislative or regulatory issues impacting the organisation are recognised and addressed appropriately.
- Opportunities for improving management control, profitability and the organisation's image may be identified during audits. They will be communicated to the appropriate level of management.

## Accountability

The Head of Audit and Consultancy is accountable to management and the Group Audit Committee to:

- Provide annually an assessment on the adequacy and effectiveness of the organisation's processes for controlling its activities and managing its risks in the areas set forth under the Purpose and Scope of Work.
- Report significant issues related to the processes for controlling the activities of the Group, including potential improvements to those processes and provide information concerning follow up and implementation of agreed action.
- Periodically provide information on the status and results of the annual audit plan and the sufficiency of department resources.
- Co-ordinate with and provide oversight of other control and monitoring functions (risk management, external audit, internal quality auditing).

## Independence

To provide for the independence of the Internal Audit service, staff report to the Head of Audit and Consultancy, who in turn reports functionally and administratively to the Chief Executive, and periodically to the Group Audit Committee (see Accountability section). Included in the reporting is a regular report to the Group Audit Committee on internal audit staff resources.

## Responsibility

The Head of Audit and Consultancy and staff of the Internal Audit service have responsibility to:

● Develop a flexible annual audit plan using an appropriate risk-based methodology, including any risks or control concerns identified by management and submit that plan to the audit committee for review and approval as well as periodic updates.
● Implement the annual audit plan, as approved, including as appropriate any special tasks or projects requested by management and the audit committee.
● Maintain a professional audit staff with sufficient knowledge, skills, experience and training to meet the requirements of this Charter.
● Evaluate and assess significant new or changing services, processes, operations and control processes coincident with their development, implementation and/or expansion.
● Issue periodic reports to the Group Audit Committee and management summarising results of audit activities.
● Keep the Group Audit Committee informed of emerging trends and successful practices in internal auditing.
● Provide significant performance measurement targets and results to the Group Audit Committee.
● Assist in the investigation of suspected fraudulent activities within the organisation and notify management and the Group Audit Committee of the results.
● Consider the scope of work of the external auditors, internal quality auditors and regulators, as appropriate, for the purposes of optimal audit coverage, to the organisation at a reasonable overall cost.

## Authority

The Head of Audit and Consultancy and staff of the Internal Audit service are authorised to:

● Have unrestricted access to all functions, records, property and personnel.
● Have full and free access to the Group Audit Committee.
● Allocate resources, set frequencies, select subjects, determine scopes of work and apply the techniques required to accomplish audit objectives.
● Obtain the necessary assistance of personnel in departments of the organisation where they perform audits, as well as other specialised services from within or outside the organisation.

The Head of Audit and Consultancy and staff of the Internal Audit service are *not* authorised to:

● Perform operational duties inconsistent with the Audit and Consultancy role for the Association or the Group.
● Initiate or approve accounting transactions external to the Audit & Consultancy department.

## Standards of audit practice

The Internal Audit service will meet or exceed the Standards for the Professional Practice of Internal Auditing of The Institute of Internal Auditors and abide by the Code of Ethics.

| | |
|---|---|
| SIGNED | ...........................................................<br>Head of Audit & Consultancy |
| SIGNED | ...........................................................<br>Chief Executive |
| SIGNED | ...........................................................<br>Chair of Group Audit Committee |

# Understanding internal auditing – case studies

## A1.3.1   Case study on the place of consulting services in internal auditing

To use this case, participants are asked to read it and then debate the issues raised.

CONSULTING SERVICES BY INTERNAL AUDITORS: PRACTITIONER VIEWS
AND THE INSTITUTE OF INTERNAL AUDITORS' POSITION – A CRITIQUE OF
THE *AUDITWIRE* ARTICLE 'CONSULTING: FRIEND OR FOE'

*In its 25th year, AuditWire, a newsletter of The Institute of Internal Auditors Inc, is now available in electronic form, to IIA members only, on their website (www.theiia.org). It is the IIA's bimonthly membership newsletter. Each issue will also be available to members and subscribers via e-mail. The first electronic issue (Volume 25, Number 1, January-February 2003) leads with an interesting article on internal auditors as consultants by Christina Brune, the editor of AuditWire, titled 'Consulting: Friend or Foe'. At present the full path to this article is http://www.theiia.org/newsletter/aw_current.cfm?quickcode=B8JLjYX. Here we comment on that article.*

A survey in November 2002 by GAIN, The Institute of Internal Auditors' Global Auditing Information Network, found that 36% of respondents fully supported internal auditors doing consultancy work. 41% opted for the choice that 'consulting is usually the way to go, but you have to be careful; sometimes it is not a good idea'. 7% considered internal auditors should rarely or never do consulting work. 16% thought that in theory consulting sounded good, but in practice more often than not it is a bad idea. There were 341 responses to this survey.

The author of 'Consulting: Friend or Foe' draws attention to what The IIA's definition of internal auditing tells us about internal audit consulting:

> 'The IIA's definition of internal auditing affirms that it's internal auditors' duty to help the organization accomplish its objectives by evaluating and improving the effectiveness of risk management, control, and governance processes. Moreover, the definition gives equal consideration to both assurance and consulting activities.'

Indeed, the wording of the definition, which appears in the new Code of Ethics as well as the new Standards and was carefully developed before either of these, reads:

> 'Internal auditing is an independent, objective assurance and consulting activity designed to add value and improve an organization's operations. It

helps an organization accomplish its objectives by bringing a systematic, disciplined approach to evaluate and improve the effectiveness of risk management, control, and governance processes.'

We do not consider this definition is necessarily intended to give equal weight or importance to both the 'assurance' and the 'consulting' roles of internal auditors, if that is what Christina Brune's 'equal consideration' means. It is quite plausible that while internal audit may provide both 'assurance' and 'consulting' services, the former might be more fundamental than the latter. By 18 October 2001 there were 20 'consulting' *Standards* and 26 'assurance' *Standards* but a crude numeric comparison is not the way to weigh up the relative importance of the two internal auditing roles.

Richard Chambers, now vice-president of The IIA's Learning Centre, who was chairman of The IIA Standards Board when the 'consulting' *Standards* were developed, at least implies in the following quote that the internal auditor's 'assurance' role is the paramount role. We agree with that, though we do not agree with him that it should be the intention of internal audit to 'minimise risk to themselves':

> 'It's important for internal auditors to use care when selecting which consulting engagements to accept. My view is that auditors should always seek to minimize risk to themselves, meaning that they should avoid taking on engagements – such as designing and implementing an accounting system – that may damage their perceived objectivity or their reputation as auditors. The IIA also recommends that internal auditors put safeguards in place to ensure that they remain objective and that there is no perception of a conflict of interest. If there could be a perceived conflict, they may want to avoid the consulting engagement or – in the course of subsequent audit work – to clearly outline what their role was in the previous consulting work.'

Richard Chambers is also implying that it is the 'assurance' work which is auditing, and 'consulting' engagements are something else; but the new *Standards* framework regards both as aspects of internal auditing.

The IIA developed their new definition of internal auditing with very great care, carefully exposing it twice to comment before finalisation. The new *Standards Framework* (including the *Code of Ethics* and the *Standards* themselves) was then built on the foundations of the new definition of internal auditing which was regarded as having been accepted. Had internal auditors had prior sight of the new 'consulting' *Standards* which were subsequently to flow from the new definition, then the new definition might have been challenged more at the outset.

In practice, most if not all internal auditors have accepted that a result of 'assurance' auditing is (a) identification to management of areas where improvements can be made in risk management, control and governance and (b) indications as to how these may be achieved. Some internal auditors would add (c) internal audit persuasion of management to agree to the improvements, and (d) internal audit facilitation of their implementation. Many of these internal auditors would see all of this, or at least (a) and (b), as belonging to their 'assurance' role. Many internal auditors would have taken the view that they have the effect of 'improving' things (in the wording of the definition) when they are exercising their 'assurance' role. For instance, quoted in the *AuditWire* article is Peter Rodgers, vice president and general auditor of BISYS Group Inc in Columbus, Ohio:

'Auditors best add value to their organizations by auditing – by doing their own job, not management's job.'

Again, Rodgers is taking the perspective that 'consulting' services by internal auditors are not auditing services. We do not think that this quote from Rodgers takes us much further forward. After all, it is also 'management's job' to ensure that they have assurance and many managements delegate to internal audit much of the work involved in obtaining that assurance. It is not so much a matter of whether or not internal audit should be doing management's job, but which part, or parts, of management's job can at least to some extent be delegated by management to internal audit. Rodgers holds the following:

'The role of audit is to be the eyes and ears of the board and to identify problems. We're not necessarily responsible for fixing problems. That's what they're paying managers a very healthy salary to do. The more auditing does work that could just as easily be done by management or any competent third party, the more we blur our mission, obscure our focus, and weaken the power that we have to serve the corporation.'

The question is whether it is legitimate for management also to delegate to internal audit the delivery of 'consulting' services. Rodgers is specific here:

'When my audit team is approached by management for a consulting project, four red flags are raised in my mind:
- If management is asking the audit group for help, there must be a control concern. As an auditor, my first responsibility is to decide whether an audit or investigation is warranted.
- If there is no control concern, I must wonder whether the manager considers the project too risky for his or her own people to do or whether it's of too little value to engage a third party on the project.
- If it's too risky for the manager's own people to tackle, does this indicate that the manager has the wrong people on staff or not enough people? If the project has insufficient value to warrant hiring a third party, why would I want to associate our audit group with the project?
- Finally, I must ask myself whether I believe that I have been so successful in my assurance role that internal auditing has no other risk-based priorities to pursue. If so, the audit group must be overstaffed.'

In making the above assertions Rodgers is presuming that all 'consulting' services which an internal audit function might engage in will concern control. They often, perhaps invariably, will; but we should point out that IIA *Practice Advisories,* which give guidance on the *Standards,* do not circumscribe the nature of internal audit consulting services in this way. Now that we have the new 'consulting' *Standards,* we can see that The IIA has taken consulting much further – as will be clear from much of the rest of this article. Engagements devoid of an 'assurance' mission, often indistinguishable in purpose from those consulting engagements which might be conducted by external or internal management consultants, are now to be regarded as authentic internal auditing. While it is likely that most 'consulting' engagements undertaken by internal auditors will have a risk management, control and/or governance focus, that does not narrow down very much the nature of the consulting which internal auditors might undertake. There is also some indication in The

IIA's *Practice Advisories* that internal audit 'consulting' engagements may sometimes be undertaken in areas other than risk management, control and governance.

By agreeing to a new definition of internal auditing which described the nature of the work which internal auditors do, The IIA has accepted a pragmatic rather than principled view of internal auditing. In the late 1980s and early 1990s the feedback which The IIA was getting told them that the old *Standards* no longer reflected how internal auditors were spending much of their time. The mismatch was mainly to do with the use of internal auditors as internal consultants. Some, as with Rodgers, would say that internal auditors had allowed themselves to be borrowed by management to help in non-audit ways. It has to be a matter of judgement whether it was prudent to develop a pragmatic set of *Standards* based on actual, perhaps inappropriate, practice; or whether a more principled set of *Standards* would have been better. The IIA cast the die of their new definition of internal auditing in pre-Enron, more gung-ho, days when too many top management teams had too little regard for the need for reliable assurance. As Rodgers, in the *AuditWire* article, said:

> 'The Andersen debacle drove home the risks to maintaining our independence when we auditors neglect or stray from our primary mission, which should be providing internal control assurance.'

It is now a huge challenge to develop a principled set of *Standards* based on a pragmatic definition of internal auditing – not necessarily as it *should* be, but rather as it *is*.

In the article 'Consulting: Friend or Foe', Richard Chambers is quoted as follows:

> 'Internal auditing is really a continuum. At one end are the traditional services such as financial, performance, and compliance auditing. The other end includes consulting engagements such as providing management advice or facilitating discussions. Then there are extreme cases such as helping to fix problems.'

We are not told what is the substance of this continuum – just the character of its poles. We would not consider it to be a 'value' continuum with, at one extreme, traditional assurance engagements being of little value while, at the other extreme, 'fixing problems' is of high value. Neither should it be an 'independence' continuum, as the *Code of Ethics* and the *Standards* do not countenance selective application of the independence principle – even though Rodgers considers independence is at risk in consulting work:

> 'When auditing commits to a significant consulting engagement, management becomes the client – the boss. Management controls the project budget, schedule, and monitoring and declares the success or failure of the project team. Independence takes a vacation. ... When auditors run to management's side to pull on that end of the rope, the remaining auditors fall on their faces and management lands on its posterior.'

The article puts an opposite point of view from John Symonds, Internal Audit's Research & Development Manager at the UK's Ministry of Defence:

> 'Sometimes I think non-progressive auditors merely use the independence argument as an excuse for ducking out of consultancy. After all, it's

objectivity of mind that is key. However, it must also be recognized that some auditors are simply more comfortable doing routine, retrospective auditing.'

We feel a bit uncomfortable that Symonds is diminishing the importance of audit independence here. Objectivity is less likely if independence is lacking, and the perception of objectivity in the mind of the client is even less likely if independence is lacking. We would also not agree with the implication that 'assurance' auditing is necessarily 'routine' or 'retrospective'; nor with the implication that it is an easy option compared to consulting work. Indeed we consider that the reason many of today's internal auditors fight shy of 'assurance' auditing is that they find it too difficult to do successfully.

The *AuditWire* article gives us contrasting perspectives from experienced internal auditors. It is clear that there is disagreement on which 'consulting' services should be offered by internal auditors. Those in favour of 'consulting' services certainly include Geraldine Gail, Director of Internal Audit, the University of California, Santa Cruz:

> 'Consulting is one of the most important services we provide for management. We have found a direct correlation between our time spent on consulting and the decrease that we have in investigations. So, when I do my audit plan at the beginning of the year, I save a certain amount of time to do the consulting projects that aren't part of the risk-based audit program ...
>
> We have an incredibly wonderful, comfortable relationship [with management]. People see the audit staff as peers and feel very comfortable calling and asking them questions ...
>
> In the next couple of months, I'll be developing an online conflict-of-interest training course, which our federal researchers will be required to take. We'll be doing that with our new whistleblowers policy as well.'

Geraldine Gail would find Symonds a kindred spirit:

> 'The time is right for internal auditing to emerge as the ally of management. We're trying to become closer to the clients, helping them prevent and resolve problems and ensuring that they meet their primary business objectives.

But questions remain. First, might the 'incredibly wonderful, comfortable relationship [with management]' sometimes be counterproductive to the achievement of the audit 'assurance' objective? Secondly, is it sound to substitute consultancy work for assurance ('investigations') work – and what is the limit to this? Of course, it goes without saying that the more time internal audit spends on 'consulting' the less time is left for internal audit to spend on 'assurance' work. Thirdly, might the board of directors have the same perspective as management on the right balance between internal audit 'assurance' and 'consulting'? Fourthly, is it consistent with the new *Standards* to exclude the consulting projects from the risk-based audit plan, bearing in mind Standard 2010.C1:

> 'The chief audit executive should consider accepting proposed consulting engagements based on the engagement's potential to improve manage-

ment of risks, add value, and improve the organization's operations. Those engagements that have been accepted should be included in the plan.'

With respect to the third of our questions posed above, George Gulyas, Director of the Internal Audit Office at another university – the University of New South Wales, Sydney, Australia – again from the article in *AuditWire*, flags up the common different perspective of 'the board' compared to 'management':

> 'My Audit Committee of Council is guarded about consulting if it adversely impacts the completion of the approved annual audit program. However, senior management supports auditors doing consulting, because it provides a convenient source of expertise, usually at lower-than-commercial rates and, in the view of some senior managers, it keeps internal auditing gainfully occupied on issues other than auditing.'

Again, we see in the above quotation an experienced auditor taking the perspective that 'consulting' services by internal auditors are not auditing services – a view at odds with the new IIA *Standards.*

As with external auditors, perhaps internal auditors have allowed management rather than the board to call the tune. In the US in particular the CEO and the CFO call the shots to a greater extent than they do, for instance, in European companies where the board exercises more power, in our experience. Even if internal audit's primary mission were to be regarded as being a service to management (rather than the board) there is still the point that management also needs reliable, independent assurance. Chambers is quoted in the *AuditWire* article as siding with 'the board' as being the primary client of internal audit, and we would say that the new *Standards* of The IIA rightly does likewise:

> 'Most importantly, internal auditors are entrusted with the responsibility to take their cue from the board and to use their professional judgment when determining how and when to consult.'[1]

Practice Advisory 2060–2[2] reinforces this sentiment. It takes the view that there are two forms of reporting for internal audit – 'functional reporting' and 'administrative reporting'. While acknowledging the legitimacy of differing reporting practices for internal audit, The IIA believes that functional reporting should always be clearly distinct from administrative reporting and ideally with the former to the audit committee and the latter to the CEO.[3] PA 2060–2 defines the 'functional reporting' for internal audit as that which gives internal audit:

> 'the ultimate source of its independence and authority.'

and the Advisory states that The Institute of Internal Auditors (The IIA) recommends:

> 'the CAE report functionally to the "audit committee, board of directors, or other appropriate governing authority" '.

---

1       Richard Chambers quoted in 'Consulting: Friend or Foe'.
2       'Relationship with the audit committee', released by The Institute of Internal Auditors (The IIA) in December 2002, to be found at http://www.theiia.org/ecm/printfriendly.cfm?doc_id=4044. Practice Advisories are non-mandatory guidance. In this instance the guidance is on Standard 2060: 'Independence and Objectivity' which reads:

**2060 – Reporting to the Board and Senior Management**
'The chief audit executive should report periodically to the board and senior management on the internal audit activity's purpose, authority, responsibility, and performance relative to its plan. Reporting should also include significant risk exposures and control issues, corporate governance issues, and other matters needed or requested by the board and senior management.'

[3]   Para 3 of Practice Advisory 2060–2.

# Internal audit independence and objectivity – best practice guidance

**A2.1.1**   While we also refer to other important pronouncements, our main source of guidance for the parts of this Handbook which describe internal auditing best practice has been the *Professional Practices Framework* of The Institute of Internal Auditors. This *Framework* includes their *Definition* of internal auditing, *Code of Ethics*, *Standards*, and *Practice Advisories*. Of these, only the *Practice Advisories* are non-mandatory: they explain and elaborate upon best practice in most circumstances, and are important for practitioners and students. Readers can see the current complete list of *Practice Advisories* at www.theiia.org. Those current on 1 January 2005 are shown at APPENDIX 3 of this Handbook, including a useful topical classification. See APPENDIX 3.2.

In addressing this subject we have drawn more widely than those *Practice Advisories* classified by The Institute as applicable to this part of our Handbook, which are:

| **Practice Advisories, by Standard Number** | **Release date** |
|---|---|
| Practice Advisory 1100–1: Independence and Objectivity | 5 January 2001 |
| Practice Advisory 1110–1: Organizational Independence | 5 January 2001 |
| Practice Advisory 1110.A1–1: Disclosing Reasons for Information Requests | 5 January 2001 |
| Practice Advisory 1110–2: Chief Audit Executive (CAE) Reporting Lines | 3 December 2002 |
| Practice Advisory 1120–1: Individual Objectivity | 5 January 2001 |
| Practice Advisory 1130–1: Impairment to Independence or Objectivity | 5 January 2001 |
| Practice Advisory 1130.A1–1: Assessing Operations for Which Internal Auditors were Previously Responsible | 5 January 2001 |
| Practice Advisory 1130.A1–2: Internal Audit Responsibility for Other (Non-Audit) Functions | 1 February 2003 |

*Practice Advisories* carry the *Standard* number to which they principally refer. Readers are advised to consult the applicable *Standards* as we do not in every case reproduce them here. They are to be found at APPENDIX 2.

The overarching *Standard* is that:

> 'The internal audit activity should be independent, and internal auditors should be objective in performing their work.'[1]

A definition of independence appeared (see below) for the first time in the January 2004 Glossary to The Institute of Internal Auditors' *Standards*. The already existing objectivity definition then just saw the substitution of 'requires' by 'allows'. Internal audit functions are independent so that internal auditors can be objective.

> '**Independence** – The freedom from conditions that threaten objectivity or the appearance of objectivity. Such threats to objectivity must be managed at the individual auditor, engagement, functional and organizational levels.'

> '**Objectivity** – An unbiased mental attitude that allows internal auditors to perform engagements in such a manner that they have an honest belief in their work product and that no significant quality compromises are made. Objectivity requires internal auditors not to subordinate their judgment on audit matters to that of others.'

Whether an audit report is objective can be determined by considering the following:

> 'Objective communications are fair, impartial, and unbiased and are the result of a fair-minded and balanced assessment of all relevant facts and circumstances. Observations, conclusions, and recommendations should be derived and expressed without prejudice, partisanship, personal interests, and the undue influence of others.'[20]

The test for the chief audit executive is whether it is internal audit's professional judgment alone that has determined (a) the scope of internal audit work, (b) the execution of internal audit engagements, including unrestricted access to relevant information and personnel, and (c) the reporting of internal audit results. Of course, internal audit carefully weighs the views of others but the final determination should be that of internal audit. If this is so, then internal audit can be confident that the most senior point within the entity to whom internal audit reports, which is likely to be the board's audit committee, can place reliance upon internal audit.

> 'Internal auditors are independent when they can carry out their work freely and objectively. Independence permits internal auditors to render the impartial and unbiased judgments essential to the proper conduct of engagements. It is achieved through organizational status and objectivity.'[3]

The application of the auditor's professional judgement to determine scope, execution and reporting holds for both the assurance and the consulting services that the internal audit function might provide. The internal audit function should not compromise their professional judgements in either service. For instance, a chief audit executive would not accept a consulting engagement against his or her best professional judgement. Declining a consulting engagement may be on value for money grounds, or due to conflict of interest, or for lack of competence – and so on.

'The chief audit executive should consider accepting proposed consulting engagements based on the engagement's potential to improve management of risks, add value, and improve the organization's operations. Those engagements that have been accepted should be included in the plan.'[4]

However, there is one important distinction. The nature and extent of *consulting* engagements are 'agreed with the client' and so would not take place unless both parties were agreed, whereas the internal audit function, not the client, should be the judge of whether an *assurance* engagement takes place and what its scope should be.

'**Consulting Services** – Advisory and related client service activities, the nature and scope of which are agreed with the client and which are intended to add value and improve an organization's governance, risk management, and control processes without the internal auditor assuming management responsibility. Examples include counsel, advice, facilitation and training.'[5]

Some of the confusion around the concept of independence is due to a tendency to view independence in absolute rather than relative terms. In practice there is no such thing as total independence. It is a matter of degree. Arguably external auditors may be more independent than in-house internal auditors and indeed they are often termed 'the independent auditors'. However it is widely understood that external auditors also experience many threats to their independence. It has been said that as soon as internal auditors open their mouths they lose a degree of independence, since they become committed to, and associated with, what they have expressed. What we should aim for is sufficient internal audit independence so that internal auditors are able to be objective and will be perceived by others as objective.

In practice it is difficult for an audit committee to know whether, and the extent to which, the chief audit executive's professional judgement has been subordinated to that of others. This may happen, for instance, when management leans on internal audit to omit an embarrassing activity from the annual audit plan of audit engagements, or when management insists for political or other reasons that an activity should receive audit attention when the chief audit executive considers it to be of low risk. It may happen if management imposes a scope restriction upon the execution of an audit engagement. Or it may happen when management prevails upon the chief audit executive, against his or her professional judgement, to modify the way something it reported on to the audit committee. On its own, it is not enough for internal audit to have a direct reporting line through to the audit committee: the reporting line should be both direct and *not subject to management's oversight and control*.

When internal audit is unable to conduct itself independently, as set out above, it is important that those to whom internal audit reports are made aware of these constraints.

'When the chief audit executive believes that senior management has accepted a level of residual risk that may be unacceptable to the organization, the chief audit executive should discuss the matter with senior management. If the decision regarding residual risk is not resolved, the chief audit executive and senior management should report the matter to the board for resolution.'[6]

Even when *the audit committee itself* instructs the chief audit executive to deviate from his or her considered professional judgement, for instance with respect to the annual plan of audit engagements, the chief audit executive should ensure that it is placed on record to the audit committee that the internal audit function has been required to modify its approach and the likely consequences of this. Indeed the board itself may need to be informed by internal audit. Of course, we are referring here to extreme cases: it is likely that the chief audit executive will concur professionally with the steer that the audit committee gives.

'The chief audit executive should submit annually to senior management for approval, and to the board for its information, a summary of the internal audit activity's work schedule, staffing plan, and financial budget. The chief audit executive should also submit all significant interim changes for approval and information. Engagement work schedules, staffing plans, and financial budgets should inform senior management and the board of the scope of internal auditing work and of any limitations placed on that scope.'[7]

It is not just the audit committee that may need to know of constraints imposed upon internal audit which impact upon independence and objectivity. Senior levels of management also need to be informed when similar constraints have been imposed by more junior levels of management.

The Rules of Conduct within The Institute of Internal Auditors' *Code of Ethics* are intended to be obligatory commitments for internal auditors. One rule of conduct puts it like this:

'**2. Objectivity**
*Internal auditors:*

...

2.3 Shall disclose all material facts known to them that, if not disclosed, may distort the reporting of activities under review.'

where 'shall' represents a mandatory obligation.[8]

A key concern of an audit committee is to acquire and maintain confidence that internal audit is independent, as set out above. If a particular incident damages their confidence, it will be hard to restore. It is equivalent to a board of directors losing confidence in the quality and completeness of information it receives from the executive. Many of the measures that the audit committee takes are designed to provide substantial grounds for their confidence and to confirm that it is not misplaced. These measures include:

1. Using audit committee 'time alone' with the internal auditor to enquire whether there are any constraints impacting upon internal audit independence.

2.  Ensuring that the chief audit executive is made aware that the audit committee must be informed of any imposed scope restrictions or reporting restrictions.
3.  Challenging the make-up of the annual plan of audit engagements.
4.  Understanding the reasons for deviations in executing the annual audit plan.
5.  Ensuring that the chief audit executive has unrestricted access to the chair and members of the audit committee at all times.
6.  Requiring direct reports from internal audit to the audit committee.
7.  Discussing with the chief audit executive the results of internal audit work.
8.  Monitoring the adequacy of internal audit provision in terms of the quantum of internal audit resource, and the qualifications and experience of the internal auditors.
9.  Judging the personal qualities of independence inherent in the chief audit executive.
10. Enquiring into, and concurring with, the appointment, reappointment and dismissal of the chief audit executive.
11. Satisfying itself that the administrative and functional reporting arrangements for internal audit do not represent any significant challenges to internal audit independence or, if they do, understanding the nature of these and mitigating them.
12. In large organisations, perhaps with more than one internal audit function, satisfying itself that reporting mechanisms are sufficient to ensure that the audit committee would learn of all significant audit findings across the business.
13. Ensuring that protocols are in place which result in *timely* reporting of internal audit results to the audit committee.
14. Reserving the right to commission internal audit engagements to be conducted directly for the audit committee.
15. Reviewing the internal audit charter to ensure that it countenances no impediments to internal audit independence, rather the reverse.
16. Vigorously pursuing the matter when, for any reason, it is apparent that internal audit independence has been, or is being, compromised.

## A2.1.2   Organisational independence and reporting

Readers may also refer to B1.1.11 and B1.1.17.

Most auditors, whether internal or external, are contracted by the organisation they are auditing. This is not always the case – external auditors of governmental agencies might be chosen by, and contracted to, a separate audit commission. It would never be regarded as acceptable for an external auditor to be on the payroll of the entity to be audited, but to a lesser extent they experience similar threats to their independence by virtue of being the beneficiary of a service contract as distinct from an employment contract.

Internal auditing provision may be made by in-house internal auditors on the entity's payroll or it may be outsourced or a combination of both. Undoubtedly outsourced internal audit service providers experience fewer threats to their independence; yet, to where they report within the entity can constitute a significant risk to their independence – just as it can for in-house internal auditors. The client is whomsoever effectively grants or withdraws custom. However internal audit is sourced, the determination of the appointment, reappointment and dismissal of the internal auditor is a crucial factor of internal audit independence, which we discuss below.

In cases of partial outsourcing of internal audit, the chief audit executive has a responsibility to assess the competency, independence and objectivity of the internal audit service provider whenever the chief audit executive is to use or rely on the service provider's work and whether or not the service provider is appointed by the chief audit executive, by management or by the board. In the context of competence, we discuss this at A3.1. For independence and objectivity, the following is relevant:

> 'The chief audit executive should assess the relationship of the outside service provider to the organization and to the internal audit activity to ensure that independence and objectivity are maintained throughout the engagement. In performing the assessment, the chief audit executive should determine that there are no financial, organizational, or personal relationships that will prevent the outside service provider from rendering impartial and unbiased judgments and opinions when performing or reporting on the engagement.
>
> In assessing the independence and objectivity of the outside service provider, the chief audit executive should consider:
> - The financial interest the provider may have in the organization.
> - The personal or professional affiliation the provider may have to the board, senior management, or others within the organization.
> - The relationship the provider may have had with the organization or the activities being reviewed.
> - The extent of other ongoing services the provider may be performing for the organization.
> - Compensation or other incentives that the provider may have.'[9]

While The Institute of Internal Auditors would not regard it as best practice for internal audit services to be provided by the entity's external auditor (and indeed, under the US 2002 Sarbanes-Oxley Act, this, by and large is no longer permitted for US listed companies), there may be circumstances where this does occur. In such circumstances, The Institute advises:

> 'If the outside service provider is also the organization's external auditor and the nature of the engagement is extended audit services, the chief audit executive should ascertain that work performed does not impair the external auditor's independence. Extended audit services refers to those services beyond the requirements of auditing standards generally accepted by external auditors. If the organization's external auditors act or appear to act as members of senior management, management, or as employees of the organization, then their independence is impaired. Additionally, external auditors may provide the organization with other services such as tax and consulting. Independence, however, should be assessed in relation to the full range of services provided to the organization.'[10]

There is a downside to organizational independence for internal auditors. The more 'outside' the entity to be audited, the harder it will be for the internal auditor to understand the business, its risks, its controls and its governance processes. In groups of companies, group internal auditors may be just as remote from the activities to be audited as would be an outsourced internal audit service provider. This downside is, to some extent at least, counterbalanced by a likely better awareness than an 'inside' auditor of the challenges that other similar entities face and how they may be resolved.

Management teams need internal audit functions to assist them in their responsibilities for the review and improvement of risk management, internal control and governance processes. So it is appropriate that internal audit reports to management and that management oversees the adequacy of the internal audit provision. But internal audit today is not just an audit *for* management; it is also an audit *of* management *for the board*, usually via the board's audit committee. So it is appropriate that internal audit also reports to the audit committee on the results of its work and that the audit committee also oversees the adequacy of their internal audit provision. 'Reporting on the results of its work' might be termed *task reporting*. 'Oversight of the adequacy of audit provision' is to do with *functional reporting*. Beyond this, there is a third type of reporting – *administrative reporting* for pay and rations.

> 'The chief audit executive should have direct communication with the board, audit committee, or other appropriate governing authority. Regular communication with the board helps assure independence and provides a means for the board and the chief audit executive to keep each other informed on matters of mutual interest.
>
> Direct communication occurs when the chief audit executive regularly attends and participates in meetings of the board, audit committee, or other appropriate governing authority which relate to its oversight responsibilities for auditing, financial reporting, organizational governance, and control. The chief audit executive's attendance and participation at these meetings provide an opportunity to exchange information concerning the plans and activities of the internal auditing activity. The chief audit executive should meet privately with the board, audit committee, or other appropriate governing authority at least annually.'[11]

We can say that the highest level of functional reporting for internal audit should be to the audit committee of the board or, in the absence of an appropriate audit committee, to the board itself. And it should be *direct* functional reporting by internal audit to the audit committee, not via management. But it is also entirely legitimate that internal audit should be answerable for its professionalism to management as well – and so there is functional reporting at an executive level too. However, the audit committee should usually be the ultimate judge of the adequacy of the internal audit resource in terms of its professionalism, independence and coverage – which are the issues addressed in functional reporting. If functional reporting is not directly to the audit committee then the audit committee is seriously compromised in the extent that the committee can rely on the results of internal audit work.

Similarly, internal audit will also report audit results both to management and, in summary form, to the audit committee. Again, this should be *direct* reporting by internal audit to the audit committee.

It is not the board's job to manage. Thus it is also not the audit committee's job to manage. The audit committee is not an executive committee. The board sets direction and oversees that management implements it. Management should be left to manage. Administrative reporting by internal audit should therefore be to management. Thus, traditionally, it has been senior management to whom internal audit has been accountable for the stewardship of resources entrusted to internal audit. It has traditionally been management who have appointed, reappointed and dismissed internal auditors and determined their remuneration. This simple scenario is showing signs of breaking down as audit committees across the world are gradually assuming specific responsibilities previously held by management. One example would be the audit committee's approval of non-audit services provided by the external auditor. Another would be the US audit committee's responsibility to appoint the external auditor and decide the external auditor's fee. Consistent with these developments is the suggestion that the audit committee should appoint, reappoint and dismiss the head of internal audit and determine his or her remuneration and annual pay adjustment (see A2.2.11). More usual in practice is for the audit committee to review decisions made by management on these matters, and it is much to be preferred that prior concurrence of the audit committee should be obtained before any of these decisions are put into effect by management.

> 'Independence is enhanced when the board concurs in the appointment or removal of the chief audit executive.'[12]

A key issue is the positioning of internal audit within the entity with respect to its functional and administrative reporting relationships with management. Frequently internal audit reports to the same executive both functionally and administratively. While it is likely that the head of finance has a keener appreciation of the nature and requirements of internal audit than do other executives, it is not ideal that internal audit should belong to the finance function. It makes it harder for internal audit to objectively audit financial and accounting matters if internal audit belongs to the finance and accounting function. In implementing Section 404 of the US Sarbanes-Oxley Act (2002) re assessing and certifying to the effectiveness of internal control over financial reporting, many CFO's are turning to internal audit for assistance and this may be used as an additional justification for internal audit to belong to the finance and accounting function. But one of COSO's essential components of internal control is the monitoring of internal control and internal audit is an important part of that. Internal audit can do this better if internal audit has a considerable degree of independence from the activities it is monitoring. External auditors are likely to judge they can place less reliance on the work of internal audit in the areas of accounting and finance if internal audit belongs to the accountancy and finance function.

Belonging to this function also makes it harder for internal audit to audit effectively across the other areas of the business. For instance, an audit of marketing may not be welcomed by marketing if it is be done by an internal auditor from the finance function; and the presumption might be that such an audit engagement should be restricted to auditing how marketing *accounts* for its performance, rather than delving into operational aspects of marketing. Belonging to the finance function may also make it less likely and harder to staff the internal audit function in an interdisciplinary way.

Ideally, therefore, at an executive level, internal audit should report to the chief executive administratively and functionally.

> 'The chief audit executive should report to a level within the organization that allows the internal audit activity to fulfill its responsibilities.'[13]

> 'The chief audit executive should be responsible to an individual in the organization with sufficient authority to promote independence and to ensure broad audit coverage, adequate consideration of engagement communications, and appropriate action on engagement recommendations.'[14]

The chief executive has the ultimate managerial ownership of the results of internal audit work. If internal audit reports administratively to the chief executive rather than to the finance director, the generalist responsibilities of the chief executive will avoid the pitfalls set out immediately above.

> 'Ideally, the chief audit executive should report functionally to the audit committee, board of directors, or other appropriate governing authority, and administratively to the chief executive officer of the organization.'[15]

Where it is not practical for internal audit to report administratively to the chief executive, another executive who is not too closely associated with a specialist function should be sought. This might be the director of administration or the company secretary.

The seniority of the chief audit executive is also important to effective independence. To some extent it is a matter of to whom the chief audit executive reports administratively and functionally and in part also to whom he or she reports on the results of internal audit work. Authority is derived from the direct reporting lines. Considerable authority for internal audit is thus derived from the audit committee of the board. Partly this is a matter of the personal staff grade of the chief audit executive, and also a matter of his or her reputation. It is difficult for an in-house internal audit function to audit activities which are managed by executives who are as senior, or more senior, than the chief audit executive: in such cases it will always be impossible for the internal audit function to assign internal auditors who match the seniority of line management. It becomes more likely that internal audit will experience impairments to their independence and objectivity – such as a refusal to give the internal auditor access to staff or to information.

> 'The internal audit activity should be free from interference in determining the scope of internal auditing, performing work, and communicating results.'[16]

Of course, a good internal audit charter, well communicated, can be an antidote to this, to some extent.

Where internal audit is inappropriately positioned within the entity, an interest taken by the chief executive or by the top management team, perhaps through an internal audit committee mechanism, can assist in bolstering internal audit independence and objectivity:

> 'Internal auditors should have the support of senior management and of the board so that they can gain the cooperation of engagement clients and perform their work free from interference.'[17]

## A2.1.3  Independent determination of the scope of internal auditing, performance of work and communicating of audit results

It is particularly clear here that sufficient internal audit independence is a necessary prerequisite to an *objective* approach to determining the scope of internal auditing, to performing audit work and to communicating audit results, and that it is *objectivity* which is important if internal audit is to add most value.

The IIA *Code of Ethics* puts it like this:

> **'Objectivity**
> Internal auditors exhibit the highest level of professional objectivity in gathering, evaluating, and communicating information about the activity or process being examined. Internal auditors make a balanced assessment of all the relevant circumstances and are not unduly influenced by their own interests or by others in forming judgements.'

## A2.1.4  *Independent determination of the scope of internal auditing*

### The future plan of audit engagements

Senior management will rightly be consulted by the chief audit executive in drawing up the risk-based annual audit plan.

> 'The chief audit executive should establish risk-based plans to determine the priorities of the internal audit activity, consistent with the organization's goals.'[18]

and:

> 'The internal audit activity's plan of engagements should be based on a risk assessment, undertaken at least annually. The input of senior management and the board should be considered in this process.'[19]

It will be helpful if there has been established a pre-arranged basis to be used in developing the future plan of audit engagements; and that this basis has been agreed between the chief audit executive, senior management and the audit committee. A formulated risk assessment methodology can be the pre-arranged basis. Constructing this risk assessment methodology with care, applying it as objectively as possible, and documenting everything will make it less likely than an annual audit plan will be drawn up carelessly or with an unnecessarily high degree of subjectivity, notwithstanding that risk assessment always entails the exercise of judgement. At least judgement will be exercised largely in a consistent way and it will be clear what judgements are being made. This will provide a first and second line of defence when the chief audit executive considers it necessary for professional reasons to resist a management request to modify the proposed plan. First, the auditor can point out that management is asking internal audit to deviate from the agreed basis for determining what shall be audited. Secondly, if management persists, the chief audit executive may acquiesce but point out to management that it will be necessary to advise the audit committee that the previously agreed planning basis has not been applied on this occasion.

The chief audit executive should be mindful that senior management may be too inclined to believe their own propaganda and thus tend to overlook even very significant risks associated with their strategies. For instance, top management of a nuclear generator did not consider that cutting costs would lower morale of production workers, and that lower morale would become a serious safety risk. Even major risks of a business may not feature on top management's radar screen. There is therefore a risk in adopting a plan of audit engagements which is merely an accurate reflection of top management's perception of the major risks facing the entity. A proportion of audit time should be set aside to audit activities where there is no perception of major risk, in case these exist in a concealed way. Internal audit can 'look round corners' which top management does not have the time to do for themselves.

In drawing up the future plan of audit engagements, the chief audit executive will be dependent on the available internal audit resources. It is one thing to endeavour to be objective in allocating internal audit resources between different audit activities. It is another and more difficult matter to determine the optimum quantum of internal audit resources that the entity needs. Drawing up the future plan of audit engagements should be an opportunity for the chief audit executive to consider objectively whether the internal audit function is appropriately resourced, and to advise senior management and the audit committee accordingly. Budget conscious businesses may be inclined to salami slice the internal audit function progressively. Then there will be a tendency for internal audit to drop from their audit plan those audits judged to be of less importance. A consequence of this is that senior management may be unaware that internal audit coverage has become inadequate, since internal audit will continue to audit those activities which are perceived of greatest risk, which tend to be those for which senior management are responsible to manage.

It is not justifiable over time to spend much audit time on relatively unimportant business activities, nor vice versa. An objectively determined future plan of audits to be conducted will allocate auditor time to individual audit engagement *in proportion to relative risk*. This can be achieved by varying the size and/or experience of the audit team, varying the duration of the audit fieldwork and varying the interval between audit engagements.

The timing of an assurance audit will take account of the views of management of the activity to be audited, but the final decision should be with internal audit. The management of a business activity should not have the authority to decline to accept an assurance audit, nor for that matter to insist upon one.

## A2.1.5   The audit engagement plan

Broadly parallel issues apply when drawing up a plan for any individual audit engagement. We would stress the importance of background research and open discussion with management as a basis for identifying and assessing risks prior to drawing up the audit programme for the audit engagement.

Objectivity will be facilitated by hammering out an agreement with management as to their own objectives for the business activity which is the subject of the audit. Audit time should not be wasted on matters which are peripheral to the achievement of management's objectives.

## A2.1.6   *Independent performance of audit work*

Again, the stress here is on objectivity. There are innumerable ways in which lack of independence will contribute to a loss of objectivity during an audit engagement. Here are some examples:

1.    Management restricts auditor access to information and staff.
2.    Internal audit relies on explanations given by, or information prepared by, management – undertaking inadequate confirmatory testing.
3.    Inadequate audit time or inadequate auditor competence makes the internal auditor dependent on explanations given.
4.    Directed, judgement samples are used to draw unreliable audit conclusions.

Under Practice Advisory 1130–1, a scope limitation is a restriction placed upon the internal audit activity that precludes the audit activity from accomplishing its objectives and plans:

'Among other things, a scope limitation may restrict the:
- Scope defined in the charter.
- Internal audit activity's access to records, personnel, and physical properties relevant to the performance of engagements.
- Approved engagement work schedule.
- Performance of necessary engagement procedures.
- Approved staffing plan and financial budget.'

This Practice Advisory requires that a scope limitation along with its potential effect should be communicated, preferably in writing, to the board, audit committee, or other appropriate governing authority. Furthermore:

'The chief audit executive should consider whether it is appropriate to inform the board, audit committee, or other appropriate governing authority regarding scope limitations that were previously communicated to and accepted by the board, audit committee, or other appropriate governing authority. This may be necessary particularly when there have been organization, board, senior management, or other changes.'

## A2.1.7   *Independent communication of audit results*

Internal auditors should exercise their independent judgement in determining to whom audit results should be communicated. Communication should be to responsible management at the level who need to know and are capable of ensuring that appropriate action is taken. If, in the judgement of internal audit, appropriate action has not been taken, then internal audit should independently decide whether there is now a more senior level that needs to know.

Management should not seek to edit, restrict, emboss or otherwise modify what internal audit reports to the audit committee: the report should be prepared independently by internal audit and reported directly to the audit committee by the chief audit executive. Again, it is a matter of internal audit avoiding subordinating its judgement on professional matters to that of others.

## A2.1.8   Individual auditor objectivity

Much hinges on the individual internal auditor. Selection and development of internal auditors should place an accent on capacity to be objective:

> 'Internal auditors should have an impartial, unbiased attitude and avoid conflicts of interest.'[20]

Two rules of conduct within The Institute's *Code of Ethics* read:

> '**2.    Objectivity**
> *Internal auditors:*
>
> 2.1. Shall not participate in any activity or relationship that may impair or be presumed to impair their unbiased assessment. This participation includes those activities or relationships that may be in conflict with the interests of the organisation.
>
> 2.2 Shall not accept anything that may impair or be presumed to impair their professional judgement.'

Under Practice Advisory 1130–1, internal auditors are required to report to the chief audit executive any situations in which a conflict of interest or bias is present or may reasonably be inferred. The chief audit executive should then reassign such auditors.

The Institute of Internal Auditors' **Practice Advisory 1120–1 on Individual Objectivity is helpful:**

1.    Objectivity is an independent mental attitude that internal auditors should maintain in performing engagements. Internal auditors are not to subordinate their judgment on audit matters to that of others.
2.    Objectivity requires internal auditors to perform engagements in such a manner that they have an honest belief in their work product and that no significant quality compromises are made. Internal auditors are not to be placed in situations in which they feel unable to make objective professional judgments.
3.    Staff assignments should be made so that potential and actual conflicts of interest and bias are avoided. The chief audit executive should periodically obtain from the internal auditing staff information concerning potential conflicts of interest and bias. Staff assignments of internal auditors should be rotated periodically whenever it is practicable to do so.

4.  The results of internal auditing work should be reviewed before the related engagement communications are released to provide reasonable assurance that the work was performed objectively.

5.  It is unethical for an internal auditor to accept a fee or gift from an employee, client, customer, supplier, or business associate. Accepting a fee or gift may create an appearance that the auditor's objectivity has been impaired. The appearance that objectivity has been impaired may apply to current and future engagements conducted by the auditor. The status of engagements should not be considered as justification for receiving fees or gifts. The receipt of promotional items (such as pens, calendars, or samples) that are available to the general public and have minimal value should not hinder internal auditors' professional judgments. Internal auditors should report the offer of all material fees or gifts immediately to their supervisors.

## A2.1.9  Handling impairments to independence and objectivity

The *Standard* is set out like this:

> **'Impairments to Independence or Objectivity**
> If independence or objectivity is impaired in fact or appearance, the details of the impairment should be disclosed to appropriate parties. The nature of the disclosure will depend upon the impairment.
> – Internal auditors should refrain from assessing specific operations for which they were previously responsible. Objectivity is presumed to be impaired if an internal auditor provides assurance services for an activity for which the internal auditor had responsibility within the previous year.
> – Assurance engagements for functions over which the chief audit executive has responsibility should be overseen by a party outside the internal audit activity.
> – Internal auditors may provide consulting services relating to operations for which they had previous responsibilities.
> – If internal auditors have potential impairments to independence or objectivity relating to proposed consulting services, disclosure should be made to the engagement client prior to accepting the engagement.'[21]

We note that it is the *oversight* of assurance engagements for which the chief audit executive has responsibility which should be entrusted to another. This is not to say that every member of the audit team should be found from outside the internal audit function. This external oversight could be outsourced or it could be given to another employee within the business, preferably with past internal audit experience. Reporting through to the audit committee on the results of this engagement should be by whomsoever was assigned oversight of the engagement, and not by the chief audit executive.

Being realistic, internal auditors may be unable to attain high standards of independence and objectivity all the time. The Institute of Internal Auditors recognises this as a significant issue in Practice Advisory 1130.A1–2:[22]

> 'Some internal auditors have been assigned or accepted non-audit duties because of a variety of business reasons that make sense to management of the organization. Internal auditors are more frequently being asked to perform roles and responsibili-

ties that may impair independence or objectivity. Given the increasing demand on organizations, both public and private, to develop more efficient and effective operations and to do so with fewer resources, some internal audit activities are being directed by their organization's management to assume responsibility for operations that are subject to periodic internal auditing assessments.'

Clearly this trend is a major concern at a time when the independence of professional people generally is a large societal issue, and it is keenly appreciated that conflicts of interest should preferably be avoided or alternatively that safeguards should be introduced and full disclosure should be made to relevant parties. Practice Advisory 1130.A1–2[23] advises that internal auditors should consider the following factors in assessing the impact on independence and objectivity:

- 'The requirements of The IIA Code of Ethics and Standards for the Professional Practice of Internal Auditing (Standards);
- Expectations of stakeholders that may include the shareholders, board of directors, audit committee, management, legislative bodies, public entities, regulatory bodies, and public interest groups;
- Allowances and/or restrictions contained in the internal audit activity charter;
- Disclosures required by the Standards; and
- Subsequent audit coverage of the activities or responsibilities accepted by the internal auditor.'

The same Practice Advisory counsels that if on occasion management directs internal auditors to perform non-audit work, it should be understood that they are not functioning as internal auditors. Whether or not it is internal auditing work depends upon whether it falls within the definitions of assurance and consulting services *and* whether it is included within the scope of audit work as set out in the internal audit charter. The charter may be found to be an effective device to resist inappropriate encroachments upon internal audit independence through the assumption of non-audit work.

Note that:

'Engagement work schedules, staffing plans, and financial budgets should inform senior management and the board of the scope of internal auditing work and of any limitations placed on that scope.'[24]

Risk management is an example area where the internal audit activity may possibly trespass beyond what is legitimate as either an assurance or a consulting service:

'If requested, internal auditors can play a proactive role in assisting with the initial establishment of a risk management process for the organization. A more proactive role supplements traditional assurance activities with a consultative approach to improving fundamental processes. If such assistance exceeds normal assurance and consulting activities conducted by internal auditors, independence could be impaired. In these situations, internal auditors should comply with the disclosure requirements of the *International Standards for the Professional Practice of Internal Auditing (Standards)*.'[25]

The disclosure requirement is:

### 'Standard 1340 – Disclosure of Noncompliance
Although the internal audit activity should achieve full compliance with the Standards and internal auditors with the Code of Ethics, there may be instances in which full compliance is not achieved. When noncompliance impacts the overall scope or operation of the internal audit activity, disclosure should be made to senior management and the board.'

[1]    Standard 1100: 'Independence and Objectivity'.
[2]    Practice Advisory 2420–1: 'Quality of Communications', para 2.
[3]    Practice Advisory 1100–1: 'Independence and Objectivity'.
[4]    Standard 2010.C1.
[5]    Glossary to the IIA *Standards*.
[6]    Standard 2600: 'Resolution of Management's Acceptance of Risks'.
[7]    Practice Advisory 2020–1: 'Communication and Approval', para 1.
[8]    See definition of 'should' in the Glossary to the *Standards*.
[9]    Practice Advisory 1210.A1–1: 'Obtaining Services to Support or Complement the Internal Audit Activity', paras 6 and 7.
[10]   Practice Advisory 1210.A1–1: 'Obtaining Services to Support or Complement the Internal Audit Activity', para 8.
[11]   Practice Advisory 1110–1: 'Organizational Independence'.
[12]   Practice Advisory 1110–1: 'Organizational Independence'.
[13]   Standard 1110: 'Organizational Independence'.
[14]   Practice Advisory 1110–1: 'Organizational Independence'.
[15]   Practice Advisory 1110–1: 'Organizational Independence'.
[16]   Standard 1110.A1.
[17]   Practice Advisory 1110–1: 'Organizational Independence'.
[18]   Standard 2010: 'Planning'.
[19]   Standard 2010.A1.
[20]   Standard 1120: 'Individual Objectivity'.
[21]   Standards 1130, 1130.A1, 1130.A2, 1130.C1 and 1130.C2.
[22]   Internal Audit Responsibility for Other (Non-audit) Functions.
[23]   Internal Audit Responsibility for Other (Non-audit) Functions.
[24]   Practice Advisory 2020–1: 'Communication and Approval', para 2.
[25]   Practice Advisory 2100–4 (February 2004): 'The Internal Auditor's Role in Organizations Without a Risk Management Process', para 5.

# Internal audit independence and objectivity – supplementary guidance

## A2.2.1  Internal audit independence and professionalism

'Englishmen give themselves away every time they open their mouths'
George Bernard Shaw

'Internal auditors should not subordinate their judgement to that of others'
The IIA

The most senior point to which internal audit reports, which may be the audit committee of the board, needs to be confident that neither the scope of internal audit work nor the content and emphasis of internal audit report, has been unduly influenced by anything other than the internal auditor's best professional judgement.

The independence of auditors contributes to the effectiveness of the audit service by improving both the inherent objectivity of audit reports and the perception of their clients and others as to their reliability. While audit independence is not therefore an end in itself, it is an essential precondition for audit success. For it to be attained satisfactorily, it must be a quality which is justifiably prized by parts of the audit profession – by the professional bodies which represent auditors, by the functional units which conduct the audit service, by the universities which develop knowledge and understanding, and not least by individual auditors themselves. The arbiters of audit independence are not just the clients of the audit service but include as well others who may be impacted upon by audit as well as those who shape opinion and influence the regulatory framework.

With such a premium upon the need for audit independence it would be reassuring if it were possible clearly and simply to accredit an audit function as being independent. Yet it is mistaken to argue whether or not auditors are independent as if it were a matter of black or white. There can be no such thing as complete independence. Interdependence is a continuum between the two theoretical extremes of total dependence and total independence – neither of which are to be found in human affairs and certainly neither of which apply to audit. An audit function needs to be positioned at such a point along this continuum as to enable it to provide the service called for. That is not to say that such a positioning is a *guarantee* of audit success as success also crucially depends upon other factors.

The positioning of an audit function on the interdependence continuum is a matter of perceived judgement based upon the observance of a number of criteria. The valid criteria to use are not *all* the same – in nature or degree of relevance – for different types of audit. So, despite sometimes being called 'the independent auditors' it would be spurious to argue that external, statutory auditors were more independent than internal auditors.

Being a means to an end it is sometimes appropriate to trim the pursuit of independence when it runs counter to achieving audit objectives which for internal auditing relate to (a) giving reassurance to the organisation that systems of control are sound, and (b) timely and persuasive advice on improving them where appropriate.

For convenience we examine the criteria for independence according to whether they apply to the units providing the audit service, to the individual auditors or to the professional bodies concerned. There is some artificiality in attempting such a distinction. For instance, lack of knowledge and understanding impairs independence since with inadequate knowledge and understanding auditors *inter alia* have to depend upon other people to make judgements. The professional bodies, the units providing the service and the individual auditors each have an essential part to play in ensuring that auditors have adequate knowledge and understanding.

## A2.2.2   *The unit providing the audit service*

*Audit reporting* is at the heart of effective internal audit independence. The placing of the audit service organisationally is determined by 'to whom', and 'how', the head of audit reports for *administration* (to account for 'pay and rations'), for *function* (to account for the quality of the audit service) and on *assignments* (to communicate audit findings and recommendations). In practice audit reporting is usually very complex.

A litmus test of the real nature of audit reporting is to determine *who has the effective authority to appoint or dismiss the head of audit.*

For adequate independence to be achieved it must be tailored appropriately to the character of the particular enterprise and the agreed objectives and scope of the audit function. An audit scope which is too broad for the available audit resources jeopardises audit independence. It should be acknowledged however that restrictions upon the scope of internal audit may also of themselves impair audit independence: they may deflect internal audit from necessary areas of enquiry, and the potential for internal audit to be effective (even within those areas which are held to be within the scope of internal audit) is reduced.

Internal audit should not report administratively or functionally to an executive or director who also has functional responsibility for operations which may be within the scope of internal audit. Thus it would be unsound for internal audit to report to the head of finance or accounting if, as they should be, financial and accounting matters are to be included within the scope of the internal auditing function.

To illustrate this, from the perspective of the *external* auditor there would be less scope to rely upon the work of an internal auditing function which was closely linked to the accounting and financial processes of the business. The external auditor would question the objectivity of such an internal audit function in the latter's assessment of accounting and financial control as there would be a greater probability that the focus of internal audit activity in these areas, and the nature of internal audit reports, had been biased by a perceived or actual need to maintain the support of those to whom internal audit reported and of internal audit's close collateral associates. It would also be more likely that internal audit had been involved in the preparation of the financial results upon which the external auditor was required to give an opinion.

Internal auditing functions which report within accounting and finance may be so oriented in that direction as to interpret the scope of audit as being largely limited to accounting and financial matters, whereas it is in the operational areas of the business that key objectives are achieved and major opportunities exist to benefit from independent review.

Management outside the accounting area would themselves be likely to perceive that an internal auditing function located within the accounting and financial part of the business would approach the audit of their non-accounting operations in an slanted accounting-oriented mode, and those managers may therefore resist the audit process.

While it is fundamentally unsound it may be made to work tolerably well in practice for internal audit to report for *administration* within accounting and finance if its other reporting lines (*function* and *assignment*) are robustly arranged elsewhere, independently of accounting and finance. This generally calls for a strong working relationship with an audit committee of the main board where the arrangements correspond to those suggested in Table 2 below. To be guarded against is an intimate association between the audit committee and the head of audit – leading to a failure of that committee to properly evaluate the quality of the audit function's performance. It is essential that the audit committee performs this evaluation if the audit function's independence is to be maintained.

**Table 1: Internal Audit Independence**

1. Is internal audit organisationally distinct from any part of the enterprise in which it conducts audits?
2. Does internal audit derive its authority from the Board?
3. Does internal audit have a direct working relationship with the audit Committee of the Board, and does the Head of internal audit have a right of access to the Chair of that Committee?
4. Does the Head of Audit have direct access to the Chief Executive, and does the Chief Executive receive reports on audit assignments from the Head of Audit?
5. Does the Head of Audit have unrestricted access to the business's external auditors and to relevant regulatory authorities?
6. Is the recognised scope of internal audit consistent with the resources allocated to it?

7. Are there no operational areas or levels which are precluded from internal audit review?

8. Does internal audit have unrestricted access to personnel and information?

9. Is internal audit free of any responsibilities for conducting any operations other than independent reviews of internal control, and does internal audit avoid detailed involvement in systems design?

10. Is it clearly *management's* as distinct from *audit's* responsibility to accept and implement audit recommendations?

11. Are the audit assignments conducted, and their timing, consistent with the assessment of the Head of Audit as to relative audit need?

12. Is the content of audit reports entirely at the discretion of the Head of Audit?

13. Is the organisational status of the audit department, and the executive seniority of the head of the audit and its staff, sufficient to underwrite the above requirements?

14. Is it policy to staff the audit function with professionally competent and qualified personnel, and to require observance of the *Code of Ethics* and compliance with the *Standards* of The Institute of internal auditors?

15. Is the assignment of auditors to particular audit assignments done with due regard to the need to maintain effective independence?

16. Is there a *Charter* which sets out the distinctive rights and obligations of the audit function which is consistent with the above needs and is generally understood throughout the enterprise?

### Table 2: Audit Committee Relations with Internal Audit

1. Is there an Audit Committee, comprising only independent non-executive directors, which is a main committee of the Board?

2. Does the Audit Committee restrict its interest to auditing matters?

3. Is the Audit Committee required to approve the appointment and termination of employment of the Head of Internal Audit?

4. Does the Head of Internal Audit have direct access (at his or her discretion) to the chair of the Audit Committee?

5. Does the Audit Committee receive and consider reports from the Head of Audit summarising the main findings and recommendations of audit work?

6. Is the secretary of the Audit Committee the Company Secretary rather than the Head of Audit?

7. Does the Audit Committee regularly reassure itself as to the quality and scope of the audit function and its effective independence?

8. Are the above matters enshrined in the *Terms of Reference* of the Audit Committee and the *Charter* of the Internal Auditing function?

The Institute of Internal Auditors' policy is to recommend that businesses should have audit committees of the board. Where they are not present it is difficult to provide an adequate substitute in order to preserve audit independence. An *internal audit committee* comprising the most senior executives of the business can go some way to meeting the same need and in some businesses it exists alongside the audit committee of non-executive directors, the majority of whom should themselves be classified as 'independent' non-executive directors.

In the absence of either an audit committee of the board or an internal audit committee, greater reliance has to be placed on forging formally accepted direct lines of reporting to the board itself, the chief executive, the regulatory authorities and the external auditors. These reporting lines should be present even where there is an effective audit committee – with the exception that reporting to the board would, in that case, usually be via the audit committee.

It is important that the formal arrangements which reinforce internal audit's effective independence are codified in the *Terms of Reference* of the audit committee and a *Charter* for the internal audit function. There is an especial need for the audit function to have a *Charter* as its rights and obligations are significantly distinctive from other functions and would be neither understood nor accepted unless they were contained within a *Charter* approved by the board. Similarly the authority of the audit committee and its role vis-à-vis internal audit might be called to question without a similar policy statement.

These documents are important even in 'fair weather' days – and essential when concerns are being expressed or, in extreme cases, when a need for *whistleblowing* means the business is best served by well-established direct access between audit and the audit committee. In a very real sense, however, the arrangements for internal independence can be said to have at least partially failed if whistleblowing becomes an issue.

In practice the staff seniority profile of the audit function will also have a significant impact upon effective audit independence as this will both affect the confidence of its personnel to pursue lines of enquiry and also the level of cooperation which they receive from line staff in the course of their work. It is particularly important that the head of audit has considerable seniority – ideally one level below that of a main board executive director – and that the head of internal audit reports directly to a senior level. This will reflect upon the other staff in the audit function. It will also affect the level of management to which the audit function can audit effectively. In difficult audit situations it helps to maintain independence if the audit department can match the seniority of relevant line personnel with auditors of similar seniority.

The work that auditors do and the way they do it has a significant bearing upon audit independence. Auditors should be independent of the areas they review as they are less likely to review objectively their own work, or that of their audit colleagues. So auditors should not have routine responsibility for operating aspects of control systems, conducting reconciliations or administering other internal check tasks or general operational tasks.

A related issue is audit involvement in systems design. Audit recommendations whenever they are made usually amount to *some* involvement in systems design. The concern is that auditors on subsequent audit visits will find it harder to maintain their objectivity if procedures have been modified as a consequence of earlier audit recommendations. So auditors will have surrendered a degree of independence by conceding the need to make recommendations for improvements.

It is doubtful if any additional independence is surrendered if auditors are willing to make their recommendations at the initial design stage of a new system. We have said before that audit independence is a means to an end and not an objective in itself which should be adhered to in the face of all reason. It is clearly constructive to the business for the auditor to be willing to use his or her expertise in internal control to make recommendations for improvement, and it is much more constructive to make these recommendations, when the opportunity presents itself, at the initial design stage of a new system.

A workable degree of independence can be preserved in a variety of ways – for instance by impressing upon management that it is *their* decision whether to accept audit recommendations and that *they* have the responsibility for making arrangements for the detailed system design implications of accepted audit recommendations and for their implementation.

Rotation of auditors between audit visits also reduces the likelihood of the audit team being unable to take an objective view on a subsequent audit occasion. In general the assignment of auditors to audits should be done so as to avoid any likely actual or perceived compromise of audit objectivity. The special value, in terms of up-to-date knowledge and technical expertise, of assigning to an audit an auditor who worked in that operational area in the recent past needs to be weighed against the risk, if only perceived, of compromised independence.

At a 'macro' level, the way the internal audit unit is organised can also impinge upon independence issues if there is a likelihood of auditors becoming too familiar with the activities which they are auditing; but this too needs to be weighed against the independence advantages of having in-depth understanding of the topics under investigation.

## A2.2.3  *The individual auditor*

Aspiring to sufficient independence has both merits and demerits with regard to internal auditor esteem and job satisfaction; though on balance the association of independence with professionalism contributes positively and is thus likely to lead to better work performance by internal auditors. Yet this is of secondary significance compared to the importance of independence as a contributor to the inherent objectivity of audit reports and the perception of audit clients and others as to the reliability of audit.

No auditor, whether internal or external, can be completely independent. While the external auditor draws his fee from the client, the internal auditor receives perhaps his or her total remuneration from the business whose affairs are being audited. In this regard the monetary threat to independence is the greater for the internal auditor, though this is compensated for by the internal auditor having a deeper and broader grasp of the business to which he or she belongs.

### The individual auditor

1. Integrity?
2. High degree of understanding of the business in general?
3. Technical grasp of the audit subject?
4. Good professional auditing skills?
5. Resistance to accepting inadequate explanations?
6. Tact with firmness?
7. Avoidance of excessive 'authoritarianism'?
8. Avoidance of inappropriate social relationships?
9. Commitment to auditing?
10. Language skills as appropriate?
11. Understanding of the operating culture?

We do not consider that in general it is appropriate to restrict internal audit personnel from having social relationships with other colleagues employed by the same business. We recognise this may carry an implicit risk to audit independence. To a large extent this is counterbalanced by removing barriers between the auditor and other staff as this may lead to more productive working relationships between auditors and auditees. However, we consider it generally unrealistic to impose upon auditors social constraints of this sort and would recommend reliance upon other factors to safeguard effective independence.

As personal and technical qualities affect the degree of independence, as does personal behaviour, there is a need for most careful recruitment of appropriate staff to an audit function. While strongly authoritarian personalities might be expected to bolster an audit function's independence, the opposite can be the case and the disadvantages of an excess of authoritarianism are hard to exaggerate. The audit department has so much built-in formal authority that it can become overpowering and unacceptable if reinforced by authoritarian audit personalities. But the deciding factor is that adequate audit independence requires that *management* should have the option of accepting or rejecting audit recommendations on their merits: too much overt authority leads to unthinking emotional reactions – either of compliance or rejection – to audit recommendations.

A key required personality trait is *integrity* – a total though unobtrusive unwillingness to be 'bought off' with either inadequate explanations or by the temptations of collusion. Similarly this means an unwillingness to take advantage of the position of trust which comes from the auditor's knowledge of, and access to, the affairs of the business.

It is not just integrity which preserves the auditor from being unduly dependent upon inadequate explanations given to him or her. The quality of the audit function's methodologies and the availability of adequate audit time to enquire in sufficient depth are concomitant. A good understanding of local culture and a grasp of the languages in which business is conducted are also significant contributors to adequate independence in a growing number of audit departments.

In terms of technical qualities, the quality of understanding that the auditor has about the operation under review as well as the quality of his or her auditing skills are amongst the most effective safeguards against a personal loss of independence. This calls for departmental encouragement of continued professional development – which also has the indirect benefit of allowing audit staff the reassurance of meeting auditors from other businesses. It also suggests that it is a mistaken policy to staff internal audit units only with short-stay personnel.

## A2.2.4   *The professional bodies*

To the extent that a professional person has *external* authority and support, so independence is potentially enhanced. This is even more so if the professional person provides a service to several clients – a situation resembled in internal auditing only when it is contracted out or conducted by remotely located auditors in large groups of companies.

**Table 3: Professional Body's Contributions to Independence**

1.  Quality control of practitioners through:
    (a)   admission qualifications
    (b)   continued professional development
    (c)   research, development and publications
    (d)   quality assurance mechanisms
    (e)   professional discipline
2.  Representation on behalf of members on independence issues
3.  Representation of need for audit independence to legislators, regulators and others
4.  Avoidance of conflicting interests by the professional body

Nevertheless internal audit independence is increasingly being strengthened by the endorsements of regulators or statute. In the UK as well as in many other countries, internal auditing is thereby now virtually mandatory in central and local government, state financed agencies, banks, building societies and some other financial institutions.

The support the professional internal auditor receives from his or her professional body is also important. The professional body is a watchdog over many of the factors which contribute to independence and a buttress against threats to that independence. The profession needs mechanisms to reinforce the integrity of practitioners and to deal with lapses. It must be able to assist members whose independence is threatened. It has a major role to play to ensure that members have abundant opportunity and encouragement to improve their professional skills which, as we have seen, safeguard effective independence. It has a responsibility to society as a whole to, in effect, award 'kite marks' of proficiency to those who meet its standards with regard to independence and other attributes.

Of course the professional body itself needs to be independent to discharge its role effectively. In particular there must be no conflict of interest and it should be unambiguous as to the nature of its mission. It should certainly not be a 'trade association' as the service ideal should be paramount for a profession.

The Institute of Internal Auditors is fortunate in having an unambiguous mission as the only professional body dedicated to internal auditing. It is not our purpose here to 'knock' other professions but we do observe the ambiguity as to whether external auditors belong to an auditing or an accounting profession and we note that their professional bodies attend to other non-auditing occupational interests as well. Internal auditing also has the potential long-term advantage of not being fragmented into a number of representative bodies. Indeed The Institute of Internal Auditors enjoys an unrivalled degree of international integration and in this regard is excellently placed to ensure the objectivity of the increasing proportion of internal auditing which is conducted across national frontiers.

## A2.2.5   *Internal audit in groups of companies*

Groups of companies have to be careful to ensure that adequate internal auditor independence is assured. If a decentralised group of companies has a centralised audit function responsible for conducting all internal audits throughout the group of companies, then the recommendations we have made here (for reporting to the audit committee of the main board, and so on) may be just as readily followed in this group situation as in a single company case. Since those internal auditors will be group personnel their independence from subsidiary company management is more readily assured though this may be construed as remoteness and unresponsiveness to local needs. A lack of awareness of the local business and a shortage of appropriate language skills may balance out the other independence advantages, making the internal auditor more dependent upon explanations offered to him or her.

It is more common for internal audit to reflect the way the group is organised. So, in a decentralised group it is likely that internal audit will be decentralised. Then there will be a real challenge to the achievement of audit independence as it will require that a reporting line exists between internal audit in subsidiary companies through to the audit committee of the main holding company board. The mechanism for achieving this may be to arrange for some aspects of *functional* and *assignment* reporting by local internal audit functions to be through to group internal audit whose head will have access to the audit committee of the group board.

Heads of audit in subsidiary companies would have a right of access to the head of group internal audit and this would be safeguarded in their *Charter*. In this way group management and the group board can achieve higher levels of reassurance from their total internal audit provision.

This is not to say that local internal auditors would not also have access to their own chief executive, their local internal audit committees and to the audit committees of their subsidiary companies' boards – in a similar way to single company audit departments.

### A2.2.6  *Contracted-out internal auditing*

*Prima facie*, contracted-out internal auditing is more independent, but in practice this may not necessarily be the case. As part of the consideration which management and the board gives to the case for contracting out, it is suggested that they obtain satisfaction that the questions in Tables 1, 2 and 3 are answered satisfactorily before a decision on contracting out is taken.

Where a proportion of an in-house internal audit department's budget is made available for buying in certain audit services there is less of a threat to effective audit independence.

### A2.2.7  **Administrative, functional and engagement reporting for internal audit**

Many staff within businesses report in different directions for differing purposes. A reporting distinction is often made between 'line' and 'function' reporting. For instance, an accountant may be supplied by the group controller to act as the accountant of an operating unit. Functionally the accountant may report to the controller but he or she has a line reporting relationship to the operating unit's director for whom he or she supplies a service as a member of the operating unit's line management team. The controller is responsible for the professionalism of the accountant and that is the essence of the functional reporting relationship.

The reporting situation is usually more complex for internal audit.

The expression 'line reporting' is perhaps best avoided for internal audit, unless restricted in usage to the reporting lines *within* the internal auditing function. It could be misconstrued to imply that internal audit shared with line management responsibility for running the day-to-day affairs of the business. In fact internal audit is an independent review of the effectiveness of internal control on behalf of line management; internal audit should have no operating responsibilities other than the responsibilities associated with conducting internal audits. Of course, internal audit is part of the management team and there *is* a line through from internal audit ultimately to the chief executive and the Board.

If we adopt the position that internal audit is not part of line management but is a review on behalf of line management and the Board, it is appropriate to consider that three types of reporting apply to internal audit – the third since almost all internal audit engagements include the issuance of an audit report:

Administrative (for pay and rations)
Functional (to monitor internal audit professionalism)

Engagement or task (audit reports on audits).

The directions of these types of reporting may overlap and internal audit may report to more than one place for each of these purposes.

## A2.2.8   *Administrative reporting*

To whom internal audit 'belongs' may be usually regarded as mainly a matter of to which executive the head of internal auditing reports administratively to account for the stewardship of internal audit resources. This will usually be the same place as from which internal audit obtains its budgetary allocation and other resources. It is not ideal for internal audit to belong, and to be seen to belong, to the finance and accounting function of the business – for two principal reasons:

1.  Internal audits of financial and accounting operations and systems are usually an important part of the internal audit programme of audit engagements. If the head of internal auditing reports administratively to the head of finance or accounting there may be a significant risk that the necessary independence for effective internal auditing may not be present. Internal audit may be deflected away from reviewing certain accounting and financial areas against internal audit's better judgement, and candid comment by internal audit on the results of internal audit work in financial and accounting areas may not always come so easily. The independent, external auditors may consider they are less able to rely on internal work if internal audit reports to the senior executive who is responsible for preparing the year end financial statements.
2.  Executives working in other operational areas of the business (such as production, distribution, marketing, etc) may be less inclined to cooperate with an internal audit function which they perceive as being accounting and financially oriented, or may seek to limit its scope to a review of the accounting and financial aspects of operations. This will be especially so if they perceive of internal audit as being a review of their activities on behalf of a senior executive in finance and accounting. A key indicator of this is likely to be whether the person to whom the head of internal audit reports administratively is always copied with every internal audit engagement report.

One alternative to reporting administratively within finance and accounting would be to report for this purpose to the chief executive.

## A2.2.9   *Engagement/task reporting*

Even though reporting administratively within the finance and accounting function may impede internal audit independence and effectiveness, actual or perceived, it occurs in the majority of cases and can be made to work tolerably well in practice. It is less of a problem if internal audit also has other well developed reporting lines – which may include the following:

1. Summary reporting on internal control (a) to the chief executive, (b) to an internal audit committee comprising senior executives from the main operational areas of the business, (c) to the audit committee of the Board and (d) in the case of an internal audit function within a subsidiary, to group internal audit without the need for prior clearance from to whomsoever internal audit reports administratively. This is engagement reporting in high level summary form.
2. Functional reporting elsewhere than to whomsoever internal audit reports administratively – perhaps to an internal audit committee, to the audit committee of the Board and, in the case of an internal audit function within a subsidiary, to group internal audit.

Internal audit reports on audit engagements should generally be addressed to one person though they are likely to be copied to others. The person to whom an audit report is addressed should be the executive who needs to know and is capable of ensuring that appropriate action is taken. In essence, this is the person to whom the head of the audited unit reports as it is for that person primarily that the audit has been conducted. Those copied with audit reports should be kept to the minimum – they are likely to include the manager who heads up the unit which has been audited, the external auditor and group internal audit in the case of audits conducted by subsidiary company internal audit units. Circulating all audit reports in a routine way to the external auditor avoids the problem of deciding which reports to show the external auditor. The external auditor has a statutory right to have sight of all business documentation which may be relevant to the annual, statutory audit. The chief executive, who has top executive responsibility for internal control, may wish to see all internal audit reports – in detail or in summary form only. Similarly, internal audit committees and audit committees of Boards will require at least a summarisation of the most important internal audit findings and recommendations together with the status of the latter with respect to (a) acceptance by management, and (b) implementation.

## A2.2.10   *Functional reporting*

Functional reporting has the purpose of accounting for the professionalism of the internal auditing function. It includes provision of reassurance that internal audit is appropriately staffed, that there is an effective way of determining future programmes of internal audit work, and that there is effective execution of internal audit work.

## A2.2.11   Chief audit executive reporting lines – Practice Advisory

There is a Practice Advisory 1110–2, released in December 2002, on 'Chief Audit Executive (CAE) Reporting Lines' to be found at http://www.theiia.org/ecm/printfriendly.cfm?doc_id=4043. Practice Advisories are non-mandatory guidance – in this instance the guidance is on Standard 1110–2 'Organizational Independence' which reads:

**'1110 – Organizational Independence**
The chief audit executive should report to a level within the organization that allows the internal audit activity to fulfil its responsibilities.'

Although not referred to in this Advisory, there is a subordinate Assurance Standard which reads:

**'1110.A1** – The internal audit activity should be free from interference in determining the scope of internal auditing, performing work, and communicating results.'

Although 'non-mandatory', Practice Advisories reflect what is considered generally to be the best practice to be followed in order to fulfil the requirements of the Standards. The sentiment within the Practice Advisories is also regarded as being indicative of what would be correct answers in the professional examinations of The Institute of Internal Auditors.

While this Advisory refers to 'audit committee', the Standards make it clear that for some this may mean the board itself, or a single person who has the responsibilities usually held collectively by the board. Indeed, the Standards always use the term 'board' while defining this to include audit committees. So, if a chief audit executive reports to the board of directors rather than to an audit committee, it is not in violation of the advice contained within this Advisory.

This Advisory suggests that the reporting lines of internal audit should be appropriate to meet the increased needs of audit committees and other significant stakeholders as a stricter global climate of legislative, regulatory and financial reporting comes into force, and as internal audit plays a more significant role in the organization's governance and risk management activities.[1]

Internal audit reporting is complex. Other personnel in addition to the CAE may have multiplex reporting relationships, but it is unlikely that they would be more multiplex than those of the CAE. We have always taken the position that internal audit reports in three ways.

| | |
|---|---|
| Functional reporting: | to ensure that the professional service of the internal audit function is effective in meeting the entity's needs; |
| Administrative reporting: | for 'pay and rations' to ensure economic and efficient utilisation of internal audit resources; |
| Task reporting: | to communicate the results of audit engagements |

This Advisory takes the view that there are two forms of reporting for internal audit – 'functional reporting' and 'administrative reporting'. While acknowledging the legitimacy of differing reporting practices for internal audit, The IIA believes that functional reporting should *always* be clearly distinct from administrative reporting and *ideally* with the former to the audit committee and the latter to the CEO.[2]

We consider it is better to acknowledge a third type – reporting on audit work done – which we might call 'task reporting'; however, to the extent that this is covered in this Advisory, it is subsumed within functional reporting to the audit committee. But clearly internal audit also reports elsewhere on individual audit engagements – both in detail and in summary form. The Advisory relies on appropriate and effective functional and administrative reporting for internal audit to take care of what needs to be achieved by what we call 'task reporting', but we think the latter deserves a focus on its own:

> 'CAE reporting lines are also critical to ensuring that the appropriate flow of information and access to key executives and managers that are the foundations of risk assessment and reporting of results of audit activities. Conversely, any reporting relationship that impedes the independence and effective operations of the internal audit function should be viewed by the CAE as a serious scope limitation, which should be brought to the attention of the audit committee or its equivalent.'[3]

The Advisory defines the 'functional reporting' for internal audit as that which gives internal audit:

> 'the ultimate source of its independence and authority.'

While the Advisory states that The Institute of Internal Auditors (The IIA) recommends that:

> 'the CAE report functionally to the 'audit committee, board of directors, or other appropriate governing authority'

since the Advisory is referring to a reporting *line*, it could possibly be argued that the *end* of the functional reporting line should be the audit committee but that the CAE will first report functionally to others beneath this – perhaps to the chief executive or to the finance director. While the Advisory does recommend that:

> 'the functional reporting line should go directly to the Audit Committee or its equivalent to ensure the appropriate level of independence and communication'.[4]

this does not unambiguously state that the 'direct' line means that the CAE might not first report functionally to someone below the level of the audit committee. 'Directly' is not defined. What CAE does not feel accountable to the executive for the quality of service the internal audit function provides? Is it not often the case that the CAE reports to the same executive both administratively and functionally, while also reporting functionally to the audit committee? The Advisory does not explore this. The difficulty seems to us to reside in the fact that the audit committee is not, and should not be, an executive committee. The executive has a legitimate, strong functional interest in internal audit. After all, as an essential aspect of 'monitoring',[5] management is responsible for internal audit, which is acknowledged in this Advisory.[6]

This is not discussed directly in the Advisory, which does however state that The IIA's recommendation is for the audit committee (or other governing authority) to approve:

- the internal audit charter;
- the internal audit risk assessment and related audit plan;

- all decisions regarding the appointment or removal of the CAE; and
- the annual compensation pay adjustment of the CAE,

and to:

- receive from the CAE the results of CAE activities or other matters the CAE deems necessary, including private meetings with the CAE without management present;
- inquire of management and the CAE as to scope or budgetary limitations that impede the ability of internal audit to execute its responsibilities.

This Advisory therefore goes further than PA 2060–2,[7] which just requires the audit committee to review (rather than approve) the appointment, compensation, evaluation, retention, and dismissal of the CAE. Neither Advisory grasps the nettle of whether it is acceptable for these matters to be approved *after the event* – for instance after a CAE has been dismissed by the executive. However, this Advisory does recommend that the CAE should have access to the audit committee when the CAE deems determines it to be necessary. It is noteworthy that CAE remuneration approval is given to the audit committee, as also in Advisory 2060.

In the last of the bullet points above, there is reference in very general terms to certain aspects of what are required to oversee the professionalism and the degree of effectiveness of the internal audit function. We concur with this as a key responsibility of the audit committee – not least because the audit committee needs this sort of confidence in the internal audit function in order to be in a position to rely on what internal audit reports through to the audit committee on the results of internal audit work. But there is more to the oversight of the professionalism of internal audit than a consideration of internal audit 'scope' and 'budgetary limitations'. For instance, the independence, qualifications, experience, training and methods of the internal auditors are also relevant. It is true that, as we have seen, this Advisory also recommends that the audit committee approve the audit committee charter – but that is unlikely to be adequate to pick up on all of these matters sufficiently. The Advisory does say that:

> 'The charter for the internal audit function should clearly articulate both the functional and administrative reporting lines for the function as well as the principle [*sic*] activities directed up each line.'[8]

The Advisory sums up 'administrative reporting' as including, for internal audit:

- budgeting and management accounting;
- HR admin including personnel evaluations and compensation;
- internal communications and information flows; and
- administration of the organization's internal policies and procedures.

The Advisory recommends that:

> 'Budgetary controls and considerations imposed by the administrative reporting line should not impede the ability of the internal audit function to accomplish its mission.'[9]

To whomsoever internal audit reports administratively, the Advisory stresses that the CAE should have sufficient independence from that individual, such as the Chief Financial Officer, in order to be able to audit activities for which that individual is responsible:

> 'The internal audit function should be free to audit and report on any activity that also reports to its administrative head if it deems that coverage appropriate for its audit plan. Any limitation in scope or reporting of results of these activities should be brought to the attention of the audit committee.'[10]

The Advisory further recommends that the following should be key aspects of functional reporting for internal audit.

- Private meetings between the CAE and the audit committee.
- The audit committee to have final authority over the annual audit plan and major changes to it.
- The CAE to have open and direct access to the chair of the audit committee and its members.
- The audit committee at least once a year review the performance of the CAE and approve the annual compensation and salary adjustment.

The Advisory sees administrative reporting as not determining ultimate responsibility over audit scope or reporting of results, but needing to be appropriate to give internal audit sufficient authority and stature and to facilitate open and direct communications with any level of management.[11]

Finally, the Advisory appears to give internal audit a role in ensuring that the audit committee learns of material risk and control issues uncovered by other review agencies:

> 'CAEs should also consider their relationships with other control and monitoring functions (risk management, compliance, security, legal, ethics, environmental, external audit) and facilitate the reporting of material risk and control issues to the audit committee.'[12]

| | |
|---|---|
| 1 | Para 6. |
| 2 | Para 3. |
| 3 | Para 2. |
| 4 | Para 7. |
| 5 | COSO's Internal Control – Integrated Framework made 'monitoring' one of the essential components of an effective system of internal control. Although contentious, COSO also gave management, especially the CEO, 'ultimate responsibility' for internal control. |
| 6 | Para 8. |
| 7 | Practice Advisory 2060–2, also released in December 2002, on 'Relationship with the Audit Committee' to be found at http://www.theiia.org/ecm/printfriendly.cfm?doc_id=4044. |
| 8 | Para 7. |
| 9 | Para 7. |
| 10 | Para 5. |
| 11 | Para 7. |
| 12 | Para 8. |

## A2.2.12  Audit psychology

> 'We are too prone to assume that all behaviour stems from character, and there is insufficient appreciation that whatever the character of the individual may be, his

behaviour will be strongly influenced by the situation in which he finds himself.'
[Lord Brown, then Wilfred Brown, Chairman and Managing Director of Glacier
Metal]

## Introduction

'Psychology' is the science of the nature, functions and phenomena of the human mind and 'social psychology' focuses on the behaviour of minds in interactive situations. The two principal issues which concern us are the dynamics of effective internal auditing in situations which inevitably involve the auditor in social interactions, and secondly the selection and motivation of internal auditors. Both these issues are related to each other and to other secondary issues.

We must identify and characterize the various situations in which the internal auditor is placed and develop a better understanding of how behaviour is influenced by the characteristics of these situations. Behaviour is important as inappropriate behaviour may make the audit process ineffective or less effective.

It is not just the auditor's behaviour which bears upon whether the audit process is effective: there is hardly any aspect of auditing which does not entail interaction with people who are not auditors and so we cannot overlook the dynamics of the situation in which the non-auditor parties find themselves and the impact this has upon their reaction to the audit process. We shall be concerned, for instance, to explore how auditee response is affected both by the characteristics of the wider contexts of their various work situations and also by the more specific context of the way the audit itself is being conducted.

It will certainly invariably be the case that an appreciation by the internal auditor of the particular orientations of line managers is a necessary prerequisite to effective internal auditing as it should influence the auditor's own style of audit work. Auditor acceptability in the eyes of line management (and therefore, to a large extent, auditor effectiveness) hinges initially on communicating to line managers that the audit team has a keen and accurate appreciation of the total environment in which line management is working, their achievements to date and their short and long term objectives. Too often 'tunnel vision' characterizes the audit approach – understandable in view of the limited cognitive capacity of all people, but to be guarded against.

It is not just the interaction between internal audit and the auditee which is pertinent. Internal audit interacts with management in general, or should do so. It is possible that certain management cultures and styles fostered within some enterprises may be inimical to any effective internal audit, or at least to certain types of internal auditing. Certainly, 'internal audit is what internal auditors do' and that is defined in different ways by different top managements: top management calls the tune! In this context we use the term 'top management' to refer to levels of management instrumental in determining corporate policy, in particular in relation to internal audit practice within the business.

The relationship between internal audit and top management is crucially important. Other important relationships are those between internal audit and other management services (where the risk of conflict and professional jealousy may be considerable), between internal audit and external audit, and not least the relationships within the audit team itself.

Of course we do not discount the importance of personal character as a factor which influences behaviour and success. We have all met auditors who are square pegs in round holes even though their behaviour may still be a consequence, at least in part, of the situation they find themselves in. Nevertheless their formative situational circumstances may be outside the control of the director of internal auditing (relating, for instance, to their past or to their domestic circumstances).

A good manager will endeavour to understand the extent to which dysfunctional (that is 'abnormal, harmful, destructive') staff behaviour is a consequence of the work situation and the extent to which irritants in the work situation may be removed, but there are limits to how far a manager can go in remodelling his or her department's activity to fit the predilections of his or her staff. In the last analysis the conclusion might be that certain personnel are unsuitable for the auditing job and to all intents and purposes this may be a consequence of inflexible personal attributes.

Auditor selection procedures should be designed to make available within the internal auditing department a suitable psychological inventory of audit staff. The psychological make-up of applicants for audit jobs must be assessed during the selection process and related rather more to the nature of audit work in general than to the particular requirements of the different types of audit work to be undertaken, as each auditor will be assigned to a variety of widely differing audits.

It is true that different types of audit, as well as different roles within audit teams, demand from the auditor different mixes of psychological and behavioural qualities. For instance, systems-oriented auditing requires creativity in the development of recommendations for systems changes, whereas compliance auditing needs a frame of mind capable of attending to detail in audit work; the audit of payroll might require a determined commitment to tight control, whereas the audit of an oil exploration project in a third world country would require a perspective less preoccupied with the minutiae of control but uncompromisingly committed to more entrepreneurial, less structured and less programmed operational objectives.

Despite this, audit planning constraints and considerations of auditor job experience, auditor job satisfaction and audit objectivity will mean that auditors will be given, inevitably as well as intentionally, a wide variety of audit work experience. So, while 'psychological variety' within the staff inventory of any audit department is valuable there are limits at to how far this can be allowed for at the time of selection.

What should be looked for at time of selection, and developed thereafter, is character flexibility coupled with behavioural sensitivity: character flexibility indicative of ability and willingness to adjust to differing audit situations; and behavioural sensitivity to ensure that the human dimension of audit work is always prominent. Even compliance auditing should be seen as the audit of people and the way they behave, and systems-oriented audit work certainly requires user-friendly auditors tuned into needs of *user* staff. Internal auditing departments are now more aware that they are providing customers with services.

Selection processes must also reject those who would lack resoluteness, would not be personable, and who would be administratively disorganised. Recruitment of 'lame dogs' with the sole qualification of many years of experience within the enterprise must also be avoided.

Unsuitability for the audit job may express itself as engendering excessive aliena-tion of auditees due, for instance, to an abrasive personality. It may alternatively express itself as a low level of performance due to poor motivation and low levels of job satisfaction: while to some extent these are under the control of the director of internal auditing, there are undoubtedly some who are temperamentally unsuited to whatever internal audit work may be offered them. Some lack audit potential due to a disinclination or incapability to attend to detail. Others are driven by entrepreneurial flair which may have less scope for fulfilment in a function which involves checking the work of others, unless the scope of audit coverage includes significant audit coverage of the more entrepreneurial activities of the enterprise.

## A2.2.13 *Auditors' needs for acceptance and affiliation*

The auditor needs good working relationships with auditees in order to be able to do the auditing job effectively and to contribute to achieving a reasonable level of auditor job satisfaction. Hostility between auditor and auditee isolates and alien-ates the auditor exacerbating auditor job dissatisfaction. It also makes the audit less effective. Hostility is rarely the norm but milder forms of conflict are not uncom-mon.

Auditees may feel threatened by an audit visit. While few auditees are likely to be forcibly coerced as a result of the auditor's visit, it is the auditees' perception that matters and many auditees feel they have little or no choice but to acquiesce in the audit process. An auditee who feels threatened by an audit visit is less likely to cooperate wholeheartedly in the audit process: experienced auditors will acknowl-edge that many of their most useful audit findings and recommendations were suggested to them by forthcoming line staff, and might not have been identified if those staff had been less forthcoming. It is probable that most if not all the potential findings of an audit are already known to certain line staff. Failure to winkle out this information may be a consequence of auditor incompetence or auditee reluc-tance to divulge it (through fear of stepping out of line vis-à-vis his or her associates or superiors, or through fear of the consequences of an unfavourable audit report).

Some auditors are psychologically predisposed to bury themselves in documenta-tion and fail to talk enough to auditees. It is undoubtedly hard for an auditor to constantly reorientate from detailed vouching to meeting line staff and it is perhaps more cosy and less of a personal risk for an auditor to focus on auditing paperwork rather than on talking to line staff. Auditing may be an easy job in which to muddle along but it is a very difficult job to do well. A poorly done audit may not be noticed as such and, if noticed, the consequences for the auditors may not be severe.

It is perhaps for these reasons that some auditors have a bias towards avoiding interaction with auditees: while the personal risk would be greater if the auditor courted such exposure, the potential job satisfaction would be greatly enhanced as well – here is an area where, by leadership, an audit manager may improve auditor job satisfaction. Auditors need to develop the skill to interact with those auditees who are most likely to have something constructive to contribute, to listen carefully and critically, and to test the validity of the information so received.

Internal audit should resist being used for political reasons by weak line management as their shock troops. A request from a line manager to conduct an audit may be made so that the resulting audit report will give the line manager a pretext to take unpopular action the need for which is already obvious to the line manager before the audit commences. To conduct audits in such situations is to put internal audit and the audit report in the role of being instruments of punishment – which is counterproductive to effective internal auditing.

One of the greatest benefits which accrues from internal auditing comes when the internal auditor offers constructive advice rather that when merely highlighting defects. The auditor's recommendations are more likely to be accepted, and to be implemented successfully, if the auditor's relationship with the auditee is good. Of course the recommendations should be realistic as well. Internal audit should aim for 100% acceptance and implementation of audit recommendations.

Assuming the audit recommendations have been accepted, perhaps grudgingly, the task of implementing audit recommendations is left to the auditee excepting where participative styles of audit work prevail.[13] Unless the auditee is psychologically well disposed towards the auditor and the auditor's recommendations, it is likely that the recommendations will not be implemented wholeheartedly and most likely will fail: it will appear that the auditor's recommendations were inept when in reality their implementation was half-hearted. Sometimes there may be deliberate reneging by line staff on their agreement to implement audit recommendations. The possibility of follow-up audit work may increase commitment but risks alienation between audit and auditee on account of the inspectorial image which courts careless approaches to follow-up.

Where internal audit uses its formal authority, that is its legitimate power of influence, to force changes upon reluctant staff there are added risks: imposed changes have been shown to have very high risks of failure[14] and will tend also to further alienate line staff from the audit process, storing up problems in the future when cooperation will again be needed.

When change is recommended to auditees who are middle level managers with years of experience, by auditors who are fresh from college and are unconvincing in their audit approach – then the resistance to change is likely to be great. Sometimes this situation will be indicative of inept construction of the audit team by audit management, but most frequently it is not possible to avoid this imbalance entirely. In an audit interview situation the auditor is in the driving seat – regardless of relative staff grades. A policy of agreeing the composition of audit teams with line management increases the level of acceptability of the audit team and therefore reduces the risks associated with any incompatibility of staff grades.

While senior and middle management may be used to interacting with staff several grades more junior than themselves (the proverbial tea lady and the filing clerk spring to mind) they are not used to more junior staff *passing themselves off* as being in the dominant position. No normal manager likes to be dominated – certainly not by staff of a more junior grade. Yet this is so commonly the audit situation where an auditor straight from college, several staff grades more junior than the manager, demands the manager's time and the manager's explanations.

While it is good experience for the auditor to handle such sensitive situations and to gain experience of interacting with more senior staff, it is a very sensitive situation which must be handled with great tact and is one example of the need to select auditors with appropriate personal characteristics. It is also essential that the audit department has audit personnel of all staff grades and levels of experience so that the seniority and experience of line managers can be matched by representatives from the audit department if relationships between audit and auditee are breaking down or at risk of breaking down. This has implications for the seniority of the director of internal auditing whose seniority should be adequate to make room for appropriate seniority of all other audit personnel – both in order to match the seniority of auditor and auditee when necessary and also to provide adequate promotion opportunities within the audit department so as to motivate audit personnel. This should lead to retaining the services of some audit personnel so that the experience of the audit department is built up over the years.

We must recognise that there is sometimes a natural tendency to react more defensively to *major* audit findings and recommendations, that is to those audit points which are particularly important in operational terms. One of several reasons why it is much easier for line staff to concede an audit point if it is only of minor significance is that their ego is threatened less. Conversely, it is less likely that an impression of line management incompetence will result from an audit bereft of significant findings. It is a tenet of management theory that managers behave irrationally[15] and their reluctance to accept major audit points is an example. Of course this is not always the case, but where such a climate prevails it follows that auditors may be inclined to act roles which avoid most conflict, focusing attention on minor points of detail and not pursuing the potentially more important matters.

## A2.2.14   *Job satisfaction from internal auditing*

Internal auditors have been shown to enjoy less job satisfaction than either middle level managers or external auditors, though this is not inevitable and is probably not the case in many modern internal audit departments.[16] They may suffer in comparison with middle level managers due to the nature of their 'checking' work. They may suffer in relation to the external auditor on account of enjoying less autonomy: they do not, for instance, run their own business. They may also have less prestige: the job of the internal auditor has traditionally not had quite the image of statutory audit or public accountancy.

Job dissatisfaction probably accounts in part for the high turnover of staff in internal audit positions, though there are other influences such as the use of internal audit as a training ground for other positions within the enterprise. High levels of internal auditor job dissatisfaction are not unavoidable. The inspectorial approach to internal auditing brings less job satisfaction than an approach which also attempts to make constructive recommendations for improving efficiency, effectiveness and economy in all operational areas. It has also been shown that the so-called participative approach to internal auditing also improves auditor job satisfaction and reduces the hostility with which the auditor is received by the auditee, though many auditors doubt if this approach represents sensible audit practice.

The participative approach suggests that the auditor sits alongside the auditee until the latter's problems have been solved. The auditor might for instance become involved in the implementation of audit recommendations. Such an auditor might only make a visit if invited to do so, and might avoid issuing audit reports which could be interpreted as being critical. In short, it is likely that the 'participative' auditor has completely dropped the policing role of the auditor and has become merely an internal management consultant.

Recruitment policies mean that many internal auditors are in their first job with their company. This poses a special job satisfaction problem described graphically by Herzberg:

> 'Job attitude data suggests that after the glow of the initial year on the job, job satisfaction plummets to its lowest level in the work life of individuals. From a life time of diverse learning, successive accomplishment through the various academic stages, and periodic reinforcement of efforts, the entrant to our modern companies finds that, rather than work providing an expanding psychological existence, the opposite occurs; and successive amputations of his or her self-conceptions, aspirations, learning and talent are the consequence of earning a living.'[17]

There is much that an internal audit manager can do to improve internal audit staff job satisfaction – in particular by allocating staff to audit assignments so as to fully extend them, giving job variety, providing effective supervision, and fairly sharing the less popular assignments. In addition, twice-yearly formal assessments of audit personnel, followed by action to remedy noted weaknesses (by, for instance, closer supervision, special training, directed experience and so on), are means not only of improving the performance of audit personnel but also of communicating the importance of good quality work and achieving it.

Audit managers should build into the work programmes of their personnel opportunity for achievement, recognition of achievement, work with intrinsic interest, real responsibility and advancement. Herzberg considered these attributes, all of which relate closely to the job itself, to be *motivators* (that is, *satisfiers*) whereas other attributes which relate more to the surroundings of the job (such as working conditions, salary, supervision, company policy and administration) he designated *hygiene factors* (that is, *dissatisfiers*). Herzberg's view was that no amount of attention to the hygiene factors would positively motivate an employee although unsatisfactory hygiene factors would be a source of discontent. His was thus a two-factor hypothesis:

> 'Factors involved in producing job satisfaction were separate and distinct from the factors that led to dissatisfaction.'[18]

A personnel approach which concentrates upon creating satisfactory hygiene factors will never positively motivate personnel. Hygiene factors also have a much shorter *half life* than motivators: for instance, the favourable impact of a salary increase wears off very quickly (implying that a little and often is more effective) whereas the impact of achievement, recognition of achievement, or advancement last much longer.

A worthwhile way of motivating staff in an internal audit department is to introduce Management By Objectives (MBO), encouraging all members of staff to set their own objectives which should be measurable and attainable with a reasonable amount of effort. There are many measurable objectives applicable to internal auditing.[19] Clearly they should also be objectives which are appropriate in the sense that their achievement will enable the supervisor to attain his or her own objectives. The role of the supervisor is to help in the setting and achievement of objectives and to be restrained from exercising authority until after full discussion with subordinates. The subordinate should be the first rather than the last person to know whether or not personal objectives are being achieved, so it is important that he or she can measure his or her own progress.

### A2.2.15  *Internal audit roles and role conflicts*

All managers are acting many roles which are in conflict with each other. Mintzberg identified at least ten managerial roles, viz:[20]

**Interpersonal roles**
Figurehead
Leader
Liaison
**Informational roles**
Monitor
Disseminator
Spokesman
**Decisional**
Entrepreneur
Disturbance handler
Negotiator
Resource allocator

All managers, including internal auditors, to some extent act each of these roles as well as other roles such as the functional role, the expert role, the specialist role, the substitute operator role and the communication role. In addition they are acting roles outside their work situation, such as the role of father or mother.

All roles conflict with each other. A sign of maturity is the extent to which one can act all the necessary roles at different times or simultaneously and so satisfy all requirements. Empirical research has however shown that different people will interpret their jobs differently, emphasising the roles in which they feel most comfortable and either neglecting the other necessary roles or delegating them to subordinates.

Auditors have professional roles which include the following:

Inspector
Policeman
Inquisitor
Analyst
Judge
Reporter
Advisor
Comforter

While conflict may be creative, internal auditors have two roles which are in serious conflict with each other and require a high degree of professionalism to handle. The auditee may perceive the auditor to be a *policeman* whereas the auditor may emphasise an *advisory role*. The dilemma is that the internal auditor is, or should be, both a policeman *and also* an advisor. We define our use of the term 'policeman' in the next paragraph. Management expects the auditor to fill this policing role, and the auditee is inclined to see the auditor in this light – it often appears that the auditor merely comes in after the battle is over and bayonets the survivors; the auditor accentuates known failures; the auditor's reports are used as instruments for punishment by weak line managers who shelter behind these reports; and so on.

The auditee's perception of the auditor as a policeman is largely a consequence of the auditor's inspectorial role of checking form compliance with laid-down procedures, coupled with the auditor's considerable formal authority within the organization. A policeman has formal authority derived from the office the policeman holds and reinforced if necessary by coercive sanctions which tend to alienate – and all this is true of the auditor.

On the other hand, an advisor or consultant has little or no formal authority; the consultant's authority is based upon personal qualities rather than the office held by the consultant, and is reinforced only by the consultant's powers of persuasion – and there are elements of the advisor about the internal auditor.

This is not just a matter of differing perceptions about the auditor's role between the auditee and the auditor. although there are differing perceptions and these may have serious implications for audit effectiveness: at the root of this problem is the fact that the auditor actually *does* have these two conflicting roles – of 'policeman' and of 'advisor'.

The solution to this role conflict problem of internal auditors is not to drop either the policing or the advisory role but to develop effective ways of working both roles in harness. Generally this means the auditor should tone down the policing role whenever possible without actually failing in the inspectorial side of audit work.

## A2.2.16  *Understanding relationship stresses*

An important consideration bearing upon the causes of relationship stresses between the auditor and others is our general tendency to be intolerant of the imperfect rationality of people.

We tend to judge people, and we tend to judge ourselves, on the basis that all behave rationally as indeed people intend to do. Yet we actually work within the confines of our own 'mental sets' which oversimplify causality, stereotype, pigeon-hole and standardise in our attempts to cope with the complexity of the environment in which we function – or rather to avoid its complexity. We tend to think of ourselves and others as being adaptive and as being achievers with goals. Yet we are all imperfect in all respects mainly because we have only a limited capacity to endure cognitive strain.[21] We also make decisions based on imperfect and over-simplified information (sometimes known as 'satisficing' rather than 'optimising'), but even if our information were potentially perfect we would not use it perfectly as we have imperfect information processing capabilities. This is well illustrated by the following:

> 'It was Clark who invented the "mini-memo" so that Reagan could get home to his wife Nancy by 5.30 every afternoon. All issues for (his) attention had to be contained within a four-paragraph, one-page memorandum. As Clark explained: "He doesn't need long meetings to understand things. He really enjoys his free time." '[22]

We tend to process information sequentially rather than simultaneously, and to pursue goals in the same way (sequentially rather than simultaneously). Our reactions to situations are to a large extent governed by decisions we have taken with respect to earlier situations whereas better decisions might be taken if we were able to hold all the variables in our minds at the same time.

The generation of standard procedures is part of a similar process. We would not have the capacity to consider in detail how each business event and each transaction should be handled. If we were to do so we would do so imperfectly and act inconsistently. We would also act extremely slowly. So we pigeon-hole events so that they can be processed in accordance with standard procedures we have developed. The danger is that we may fail to notice variety and artificially interpret a business event as being similar to previous events for which we have developed a standard procedure. Our simplified models of causality ('stereotyping') encourage us to presume that history tend to repeat itself: we are prejudiced towards interpreting events and reacting to them in identical ways to previous occasions, and not so alert to the differences as we are to the similarities.

Auditors are not immune from these human limitations: how often are audit points overlooked through a failure within the audit team to correlate different items of data? Auditors find it hard to cope with the complexity of following up all their audit recommendations until each has been duly considered by appropriate levels of management and knowingly accepted and implemented, or rejected.

Auditors are also constantly confronted by auditees who, due to their inability to absorb the complexity or the implications of an audit recommendation, counter an audit recommendation on the basis of earlier decisions already taken or by inappropriately claiming, by reference to past experience, that the audit recommendation will not work. We mentioned earlier that auditees are sometimes inclined to resist major audit points. Major audit points may be too threatening to their mental framework, including their self esteem.

Although it is their relationships with auditees which are most crucial on a day-to-day basis, internal auditors also have important relationships with top management, with other management services, with the external auditors and with other internal auditors. Imperfect information processing is also at the root of much of the stress between internal audit and these other parties.

Top management may have a different, perhaps inappropriate, out-of-date perception of the role of internal audit within a modern organization: it is a responsibility of internal audit to try to influence top management to modify their perceptions.

The stresses between internal audit and other management services are often caused by a failure of all parties to appreciate both their respective distinctive roles and also the areas of overlap: conflict most frequently occurs at the area of overlap through failing to notice it or to handle it diplomatically. For instance, an audit finding that staff are inadequately trained impinges upon the responsibilities of the training department, and a finding that a system has design defects impinges upon the work of the systems analysts.

Similarly, conflict between internal and external audit can frequently be a consequence of a failure by either or both parties to understand the distinctive objectives and scope of the two audits. The result can be that external audit invalidly evaluates and criticises internal audit in terms of external audit objectives and scope, and vice versa. So there is a need for close collaboration between the two audits including discussion of, and agreement to, a joint programme or work.

Our understanding of group dynamics tells us that membership of a group meets important psychological needs of individuals who tend to adopt the norms and values of the group. Structuring our enterprises formally into functions, departments, sections and such like, while desirable and indeed inevitable, poses the problem that the constituent groups within an enterprise may develop *intra-group loyalties* to the detriment of inter-group affiliations. *Inter-group rivalries* are commonplace though frequently inimical to the achievement of overall enterprise objectives. Internal audit, with its special interest in control, must be aware that it will be more likely that there will be control problems at the interfaces of departments and groups than *within* a work group, particularly as a consequence of inadequate information transfer between groups.

A potentially fruitful area of audit recommendations is in the area of 'linking pins',[23] whereby key individuals, through their membership of two or more groups, provide effective links between these groups. There is scope for audit recommendations relating to linking pins. There is also scope for internal audit to address the problem of conflict between audit and other management services by applying the concept of linking pins to cross-membership between these different services, notwithstanding the need to preserve a reasonable degree of audit independence.

## A2.2.17  *Relationships within the internal audit work group*

It is a common if misinformed jibe against internal auditors that they obtain no exposure to the practice of management within their job situation. This is palpably incorrect. Internal auditing is in any case the independent review from within the organization of the management process in all its aspects, in all functional areas and at all levels. Then there is the internal audit department itself to be managed. Finally there is the conduct of the audit.

Some audits are conducted by sole auditors but wherever possible audit management should so plan their department's work programme that audits can be performed by two or three auditors with the fieldwork lasting for two or three weeks. We have earlier discussed the problem of the risk of alienation of the auditor from the auditee and this emphasises the need for each auditor to have an affiliate to sustain him. On the other hand, if the team is too large there is a risk that one or two auditors will feel it less important to perform well. Very short audits or excessively long ones are unsound as with the former there is not enough time to conduct in-depth work and with the latter the law of diminishing returns applies.

Audits are projects and audit team leaders must be as competent project managers as, for instance, those who manage construction projects or computerization projects. Audit team leaders should be trained in the dynamics of the work group. A work group is valued by its members because of its tendency to provide job satisfaction. Groups with high performance norms will achieve high output even in unsatisfactory surroundings, but low group performance norms depress individual performance. The more cohesive the group, the greater its power to perform well. This suggests that there should at least be some continuity of audit teams in order to build cohesiveness, and that team leaders and their superiors should emphasise the factors which contribute to job satisfaction, not neglecting the social aspects, as this will tend to create groups with high performance norms.[24]

It has been shown that groups which are run along participative lines, with group members participating democratically in decision-making, are more self-reliant especially during a boss's absence; and that the converse applies. While it may be true that audit team leaders are normally on-site with the team throughout an audit, this may not necessarily be so, and there are in any case other advantages in developing a self-reliant approach: in particular management skills are being nurtured in the team members.

This concept certainly puts a question mark on an excessively bureaucratic, standardised approach to the conduct of audits modelled around standard audit programme guides, standard internal control questionnaires and standard working paper and audit file techniques: in such an environment there is little opportunity for the team leader to develop in initiative, let alone the other members of the audit team to use their initiative. Participative teams have also been shown to be less apathetic and frustrated and to display less aggression towards the team leader. It has been shown that it is easier to change an individual's beliefs and behaviour when the change is a product of group discussion rather than an edict from a team leader.[25]

High morale within a team has been shown to lead to lower absenteeism and lower turnover.[26] Similarly, a considerate approach by the team leader has been shown to lead to higher productivity although there is not unanimity of agreement on this. We should not overlook the fact that a leader's style is often constrained to reflect the style of his or her boss: if a director of internal auditing is dissatisfied with the style of the audit managers, he or she should first examine his or her own approach.

Yet it must be mentioned that different personalities react differently to a group situation: authoritarian personalities are likely to react indifferently or negatively – another example of how certain personalities are more suited to audit work. The Freudian authoritarian personality, it is suggested, has been nurtured that way perhaps from early childhood. In that sense an auditors's personality is situational rather than genetic but it may be too ingrained for an audit manager to be able to modify it by an appropriate work environment. It would therefore be better to avoid selecting such people for audit positions.

This may appear paradoxical as a significant component of audit work avails itself of both the organizational authority vested in internal audit by top management and also of the authority which management vests in its laid-down procedures. Prima facie then, internal auditing *is* authoritarian and it might be considered that authoritarian personalities would be ideally suited to the work. However, the formal authority of the internal auditing department is so great that it will become overbearing if it is accentuated by authoritarian personalities in audit positions.

## A2.2.18   *The alienating and dysfunctional aspects of management control*

Not all auditees see *control* as being their principal priority, and so they are likely to feel the auditor is addressing the wrong issues, and it has been shown that excessively control-oriented approaches to management are often harmful in terms of achieving results. Audit should aim for agreement on audit scope with line management.

In many enterprises accountants and production people may tend to be *control-oriented* but marketing and R&D staff less so. Just as it is unlikely that the auditor will be effective if the auditor perceives the audit role to be one thing (perhaps that of an advisor) whereas the auditee sees the audit role as being another thing (perhaps that of policemen), so it is unlikely that audit will be very successful if the priorities of the area being audited are perceived differently by auditor and auditee.

There should really be no conflict here. The starting point of any audit is to determine management's objectives and the auditor should work in a way which is consistent with them. There should be no audit recommendations which make it harder for management to achieve their objectives.

That is not to say that all the attitudes the auditor will encounter in line management are necessarily appropriate. The internal auditor will encounter a variety of attitudes in the course of auditing – attitudes to work, resource stewardship, risk, equal rights, innovation etc. These attitudes need to be right, consistent with each other, understood and applied at all levels. Too often they are left to chance. It has been said that the most significant audit points and recommendations usually relate to matters of *organisation* rather than matters of *procedure*; often the greatest weaknesses of an enterprise are matters of *attitude* and the auditor should incorporate reviews of attitudes in the scope of audit work.

[13]  FE Mints 'Behavioural Patterns in Internal Audit Relationships' Research Report No 17 [1975], The Institute of Internal Auditors Inc, Florida, USA. See also G Morgan and B Pattinson 'The Role and Objectives of an Internal Audit – A Behavioural Approach' [1975], Chartered Institute of Public Finance and Accountancy, London.

[14]  T Burns and GM Stalker *The Management of Innovation* [1961] Tavistock, London.

[15]  H Simon *The New Science of Management Decision* [1960] Harper & Row, New York.

[16]  LW Porter 'A Study of Perceived Need Satisfaction in Bottom and Middle Management Jobs' [1961] *Journal of Applied Psychology,* Col 45; and JH Smith and WC Uecker 'Can Auditors Find Job Satisfaction?' [1976] *The Internal Auditor,* October.

[17]  F Herzberg *Work and the Nature of Man,* [1966] World, Cleveland, Ohio.

[18]  F Herzberg: *The Motivation to Work* [1959] John Wiley & Sons, New York.

[19]  AD Chambers *Internal Auditing – Theory and Practice* [1981] Pitman, pp 201–218.

[20]  H Mintzberg *The Nature of Managerial Work* [1973] McGraw-Hill, New York.

[21]  'Business News' (1981) Sunday Times, 8 February 1981, p8, cols 3–8.

[22]  R Likert *New Patterns of Management* [1961] McGraw-Hill, New York.

[23]  S Seashore *Group Cohesiveness in the Industrial Group* [1954] Institute for Social Research, Ann Arbor, Mich.

[24]  PN Khandwalla *The Design of Organizations,* [1977] Harcourt Brace Javanovich, New York, pp 186–187.

[25]  RL Kahn 'Productivity and Job Satisfaction' [Vol 13, 1970] *Personnel Psychology,* pp 257–286.

[26]  E Fleishman 'Leadership Climate, Human Resources Training, and Supervisory Behaviour' [1961] *Studies in Personnel and Industrial Psychology* (ed E Fleishman) Irwin, Homewood, Ill.

# Internal audit independence and objectivity – case studies

## A2.3.1 Self-test questions

1  Discuss the barriers to fostering good auditor/auditee relationships and say how they might be overcome.
2  Put yourself in the position of a newly appointed head of internal audit for a recently created audit function. You are required to produce a brief paper on how you intend to foster open and positive communications with auditee managers whilst protecting the independence of the audit function.
3  How would you deal with the differing role demands of the auditor as policeman and friendly advisor?
4  Which of these roles do you have, as an internal auditor?
   (a)  Punisher
   (b)  Judge
   (c)  Policeman
   (d)  Inspector
   (e)  Investigator
   (f)  Analyst
   (g)  Reporter
   (h)  Adviser
   (i)  Internal Consultant
   (j)  Counsellor

# Proficiency and care in internal auditing – best practice guidance

**A3.1.1**   While we also refer to other important pronouncements, our main source of guidance for the parts of this Handbook which describe internal auditing best practice has been the *Professional Practices Framework* of The Institute of Internal Auditors. This *Framework* includes their *Definition* of internal auditing, *Code of Ethics*, *Standards*, and *Practice Advisories*. Of these, only the *Practice Advisories* are non-mandatory: they explain and elaborate upon best practice in most circumstances, and are important for practitioners and students. Readers can see the current complete list of *Practice Advisories* at www.theiia.org. Those current on 1 January 2005 are shown at APPENDIX 3 of this Handbook, including a useful topical classification at APPENDIX 3.2.

In addressing this subject we have drawn more widely than those *Practice Advisories* classified by The Institute as applicable to this part of our Handbook, which are:

| **Practice Advisories, by Standard Number** | **Release date** |
| --- | --- |
| Practice Advisory 1200–1: Proficiency and Due Professional Care | 5 January 2001 |
| Practice Advisory 1210–1: Proficiency | 5 January 2001 |
| Practice Advisory 1210.A1–1: Obtaining Service to Support or Complement the Internal Audit Activity | 5 January 2001 |
| Practice Advisory 1210.A2–1: Identification of Fraud | 5 January 2001 |
| Practice Advisory 1210.A2–2: Responsibility for Fraud Detection | 5 January 2001 |
| Practice Advisory 1220–1: Due Professional Care | 5 January 2001 |
| Practice Advisory 1230–1: Continuing Professional Development | 5 January 2001 |

*Practice Advisories* carry the *Standard* number to which they principally refer. Readers are advised to consult the applicable *Standards* as we do not in every case reproduce them here. They are to be found at APPENDIX 2.

> **'Standard 1200 – Proficiency and Due Professional Care**
> Engagements should be performed with proficiency and due professional care.'

'Proficiency' and 'due professional care' are important terms used within the *Standards*. So is 'competency'. They are not defined in the Glossary to the *Standards*, but specific Standards in effect provide definitions of two of them:

### '1210 – Proficiency

Internal auditors should possess the knowledge, skills, and other competencies needed to perform their individual responsibilities. The internal audit activity collectively should possess or obtain the knowledge, skills, and other competencies needed to perform its responsibilities.'

### '1220 – Due Professional Care

Internal auditors should apply the care and skill expected of a reasonably prudent and competent internal auditor. Due professional care does not imply infallibility.'

'Proficiency' or 'professional proficiency' is a matter of possessing requisite competencies. 'Due professional care' is to do with applying these competencies appropriately. We could say that being able to apply the harder, technical competencies successfully is not just an act of will but is also to do with having professional insights and maturity which in themselves are softer forms of competency. Some of the softer, more intuitive competencies have to do with interpersonal skills:

> 'Internal auditors should be skilled in dealing with people and in communicating effectively. Internal auditors should understand human relations and maintain satisfactory relationships with engagement clients.
>
> Internal auditors should be skilled in oral and written communications so that they can clearly and effectively convey such matters as engagement objectives, evaluations, conclusions, and recommendations.'[1]

So, competency is a facet of both 'proficiency' and 'due professional care'. The *Code of Ethics* indicates this:

### 'Competency Principle

Internal auditors apply the knowledge, skills, and experience needed in the performance of internal auditing services.'

### 'Competency Rules of Conduct

Internal auditors:

Shall engage only in those services for which they have the necessary knowledge, skills, and experience.

Shall perform internal auditing services in accordance with the Standards for the Professional Practice of Internal Auditing.

Shall continually improve their proficiency and the effectiveness and quality of their services.'

It is interesting to assess from Standards 1210 and 1220 (above) whether The Institute of Internal Auditors is more forgiving of fallible performance if it is due to limitations of 'due professional care' than when it is due to lack of 'proficiency'. Certainly, the Institute has associated the concept of fallibility with the concept of 'due professional care' rather than with 'proficiency'. And it is true that individual internal auditors (as well as the chief audit executive with respect to the audit function as a whole) have solemn responsibilities to obtain and maintain the needed proficiencies. Incompetence is unjustifiable and work should not be undertaken without the requisite competence.

By definition, a professional person is one with the requisite competencies which enable him or her to do a professional job. Armed with these competencies, and having applied them with 'care and skill', it is still possible for the professional person to arrive at wrong or incomplete conclusions. It is often said that you can sue a professional person for being incompetent or negligent, but you will not succeed in suing a competent professional person who has applied his or her competence with reasonable care and skill (that is, has not been negligent) notwithstanding that the professional person can be shown, perhaps but not necessarily only in retrospect, to have come to inappropriate or incomplete conclusions. So, The Institute is right to associate the concept of 'fallibility' with 'due professional care' rather than with 'proficiency'.

## A3.1.2  Differing levels of competence

Any professional person needs a higher level and a different type of competence in the disciplines that are core to the profession. Commencing 2003, The Institute of Internal Auditors Inc, within their CIA content specification outlines (CSOs – which we would call 'syllabuses' (see APPENDIX 5)), have dropped the 'understanding' level and now distinguish just between 'proficiency' and 'awareness' levels:

> '**Proficiency** – Candidate is able to exhibit the competency in understanding and applying the subject matter in the workplace on a regular basis with skill and expertise.'

> '**Awareness** – Candidate exhibits awareness and knowledge. Candidate is able to define terms, recognise issues, and recall facts about the issues.'

Until 2003 the CSOs had also used 'understanding' defined as follows:

> '**Understanding** – Candidate exhibits sound understanding and ability to apply the competency. Candidates should understand relationships and problems involving the competency and apply the competency to new and different settings and the solution of problems.'

At a Practice Advisory level The Institute distinguishes between 'proficiency', 'understanding' and 'appreciation':

> 'Proficiency means the ability to apply knowledge to situations likely to be encountered and to deal with them without extensive recourse to technical research and assistance.

> ...

> An understanding means the ability to apply broad knowledge to situations likely to be encountered, to recognize significant deviations, and to be able to carry out the research necessary to arrive at reasonable solutions.

...

An appreciation means the ability to recognize the existence of problems or potential problems and to determine the further research to be undertaken or the assistance to be obtained.'[2]

Certainly, internal auditors need proficiency in auditing: internal auditors audit in accordance with internal auditing *Standards*. Internal auditors may also need other proficiencies – for instance:

'Proficiency in accounting principles and techniques is required of auditors who work extensively with financial records and reports.'[3]

An example of proficiency at an 'understanding' level could be of management principles:

'An understanding of management principles is required to recognize and evaluate the materiality and significance of deviations from good business practices.'[4]

'Appreciation' level competence would be likely to be needed across a wide front:

'An appreciation is required of the fundamentals of subjects such as accounting, economics, commercial law, taxation, finance, quantitative methods, and information technology.'[5]

On occasion The Institute of Internal Auditors uses the word 'qualified':

'The internal audit activity should [be] qualified in disciplines such as accounting, auditing, economics, finance, statistics, information technology, engineering, taxation, law, environmental affairs, and such other areas as needed to meet the internal audit activity's responsibilities.'[6]

## A3.1.3   Competence for assurance and consulting services

The stress in the *Standards* is upon the chief audit executive ensuring that the requisite competencies are available so that the internal audit function can fulfil its fundamental assurance role. It would be an admission of failure were the internal audit function to have to confess to being unable to undertake an assurance engagement on account of a lack of available competence. It is not the same with respect to the internal audit role in providing consulting services. By their nature, potential consulting services might call for a very broad range of skills, etc which might not reasonably be expected to be available to the internal audit function at all times. The *Standards* acknowledge this:

'1210.C1 – The chief audit executive should decline the consulting engagement or obtain competent advice and assistance if the internal audit staff lacks the knowledge, skills, or other competencies needed to perform all or part of the engagement.'

Nevertheless, it is an obligation of the chief audit executive to ensure that the internal audit function has the competence to be active in the categories of consulting services set out in the internal audit charter:

'**1000.C1** – The nature of consulting services should be defined in the audit charter.'

## A3.1.4  Ensuring individual and collective internal audit proficiency

Practical implications of this include:

- individual internal auditors should be aware of, and be frank about, the limitations of their personal competencies;
- internal auditors should be strongly committed to extending (where appropriate), deepening and updating their competencies;
- sub-standard work is unprofessional;
- competency requires adherence to the *Standards*;
- a lack of availability of applicable competencies may at times require the scope of internal audit work to be restricted, and this will need to be disclosed.

'Proficiency' is a responsibility of individual auditors as well as of the chief audit executive. It can only be the chief audit executive who can take care of ensuring that the internal audit function has the requisite competencies. It is not expected, nor is it feasible, for each internal auditor to be a polymath in terms of internal audit competencies:

> 'The internal auditing staff should collectively possess the knowledge and skills essential to the practice of the profession within the organization.'[7]

and:

> 'Each member of the internal audit activity, however, need not be qualified in all disciplines.'[8]

and:

> 'Professional proficiency is the responsibility of the chief audit executive and each internal auditor. The chief audit executive should ensure that persons assigned to each engagement collectively possess the necessary knowledge, skills, and other competencies to conduct the engagement properly.'[9]

An aspect of the professionalism of the chief audit executive is that he or she is systematic in specifying the competencies needed collectively by the internal audit function, and recruiting with care to this specification. This requires forward thinking with respect to how the internal audit function will need to change over time to meet the changing needs of the business going forward.

> 'The chief audit executive should establish suitable criteria of education and experience for filling internal auditing positions, giving due consideration to scope of work and level of responsibility. Reasonable assurance should be obtained as to each prospective auditor's qualifications and proficiency.'[10]

and:

'The chief audit executive should establish a program for selecting and developing the human resources of the internal audit activity. The program should provide for:
- Developing written job descriptions for each level of the audit staff.
- Selecting qualified and competent individuals.
- Training and providing continuing educational opportunities for each internal auditor.
- Appraising each internal auditor's performance at least annually.
- Providing counsel to internal auditors on their performance and professional development.'[11]

## A3.1.5  Due professional care

We have said that 'proficiency' or 'professional proficiency' is a matter of possessing requisite competencies. 'Due professional care' is to do with applying these competencies appropriately. We have also drawn attention to the inherent fallibility of auditing. In the context of 'due professional care' this is spelt out in Standard 1220.A3:

'The internal auditor should be alert to the significant risks that might affect objectives, operations, or resources. However, assurance procedures alone, even when performed with due professional care, do not guarantee that all significant risks will be identified.'

Other standards explain how the internal auditor may ensure he or she exercises due professional care in assurance and in consulting engagements:

'**1220.A1** – The internal auditor should exercise due professional care by considering the:
- Extent of work needed to achieve the engagement's objectives.
- Relative complexity, materiality, or significance of matters to which assurance procedures are applied.
- Adequacy and effectiveness of risk management, control, and governance processes.
- Probability of significant errors, irregularities, or noncompliance.
- Cost of assurance in relation to potential benefits.'

'**1220.C1** – The internal auditor should exercise due professional care during a consulting engagement by considering the:
- Needs and expectations of clients, including the nature, timing, and communication of engagement results.
- Relative complexity and extent of work needed to achieve the engagement's objectives.
- Cost of the consulting engagement in relation to potential benefits.'

In assessing whether due professional care has been exercised, the yardstick to use is what would be expected of a reasonably prudent and competent internal auditor in similar circumstances. The degree of care should be proportionate to the situation: for instance, when suspicions have been aroused it would be prudent to exercise extra care.

'Due professional care calls for the application of the care and skill expected of a reasonably prudent and competent internal auditor in the same or similar circumstances. Professional care should, therefore, be appropriate to the complexities of the engagement being performed. In exercising due professional care, internal auditors should be alert to the possibility of intentional wrongdoing, errors and omissions, inefficiency, waste, ineffectiveness, and conflicts of interest. They should also be alert to those conditions and activities where irregularities are most likely to occur. In addition, they should identify inadequate controls and recommend improvements to promote compliance with acceptable procedures and practices.

Due care implies reasonable care and competence, not infallibility or extraordinary performance. Due care requires the auditor to conduct examinations and verifications to a reasonable extent, but does not require detailed reviews of all transactions. Accordingly, internal auditors cannot give absolute assurance that noncompliance or irregularities do not exist. Nevertheless, the possibility of material irregularities or noncompliance should be considered whenever an internal auditor undertakes an internal auditing assignment.'[12]

## A3.1.6 Continuing professional development

As with professional people everywhere, internal auditors have a duty to maintain and develop their themselves professionally.

> **'1230 – Continuing Professional Development**
> Internal auditors should enhance their knowledge, skills, and other competencies through continuing professional development.'

Professional certification, which is 'encouraged', 'demonstrates proficiency' and also leads to an obligation to 'obtain sufficient continuing education to satisfy requirements related to the professional certification held'.[13]

## A3.1.7 Outsourcing internal audit

The rationale for outsourcing is when a better value for money service can be obtained by utilising an outside service provider. There is the additional advantage of making the employed staff establishment smaller and thus easier to manage. However, there is the challenge of managing contracts with outsourced service providers, and in particular specifying and ensuring adherence to service level agreements. Organisations must exercise great care in outsourcing activities which are strategically important to the entity – especially if they will be difficult to subsequently bring back in-house. Certain activities will also need to be kept in-house for security reasons.

'Outside service provider' is the phrase The Institute of Internal Auditors uses:

> 'An outside service provider is a person or firm, independent of the organization, who has special knowledge, skill, and experience in a particular discipline. Outside service providers include, among others, actuaries, accountants, appraisers, environmental specialists, fraud investigators, lawyers, engineers, geologists, security specialists, statisticians, information technology specialists, the organization's external auditors, and other auditing organizations.'[14]

Internal auditing is so-called not because it is necessarily undertaken by in-house staff on the entity's payroll but because it is primarily the audit of internal risk management, internal control and internal governance processes. More than 50% of internal auditing in the UK is now outsourced. This is done by entities of all sizes. Small entities, perhaps with a regulator-imposed obligation to have an internal audit, may outsource internal auditing especially if the requirement is for a number of auditor days which is less than one full-time member of staff. With careful choice of service provider, the small entity can access a range of competencies which could hardly be expected to be collectively possessed by just one or two in-house internal auditors. Large entities may outsource all their internal audit function perhaps to a 'Big 4' firm of public accountants; or the large entity may outsource just some of their internal audit function, for instance the audit of certain overseas operating units.

Where there is a regulator-imposed requirement for internal audit, which management and the board is reluctantly obliged to comply with, then there may be a special impetus to outsource internal audit. For instance, not all UK companies listed in the US, and therefore caught by Sections 302 and 404 of the 2002 Sarbanes-Oxley Act, are fervent believers in the merit of assessing and certifying to the effectiveness of internal control over financial reporting as set out in the Act. Many CEOs and CFOs of US listed companies are looking to their internal audit functions to undertake much of the legwork so that they can certify under Section 404. Some UK companies are muttering about delisting in the US. Where there is a perceived need for internal audit of a bureaucratic kind, which management would not wish to have done except for a legal and regulatory requirement, it is more likely that this internal auditing will be outsourced. This will especially be so if the risk would be that the in-house internal audit function would be deflected from meeting more important internal audit objectives, in order to meet the different requirements of law or regulation. Where there is a legal and or regulatory requirement, it can also be attractive to rely at least to some extent on outsourced service providers in view of their greater degree of independence. We can therefore expect that an effect of Sarbanes-Oxley will be to increase the extent of outsourced internal auditing of US listed companies.

Outsourcing internal audit does not, of course, only occur for negative reasons as set out above. There are many positive advantages of outsourcing internal audit – just as there are some demerits. We discuss these in A3.2.22.

Partial outsourcing of internal audit (or 'partnering' as it is termed) can be an attractive proposition. It is fair to say that the Institute of Internal Auditors places much more emphasis on partial outsourcing of internal audit than on total outsourcing.

### 'Standard 1210.A1

The chief audit executive should obtain competent advice and assistance if the internal audit staff lacks the knowledge, skills, or other competencies needed to perform all or part of the engagement.'

However, the Institute would aver that all internal auditing, whether outsourced, partially outsourced or in-house should be conducted in accordance with their

*Code of Ethics* and their *Standards* – see A1.1.7. Partial outsourcing may occur when the in-house chief audit executive is authorised to buy-in internal audit resources to supplement the in-house internal audit resource in terms of proficiency and quantum. The Institute gives the following as examples of this sort of outsourcing:

- 'Auditing activities where a specialized skill and knowledge are required such as information technology, statistics, taxes, language translations, or to achieve the objectives in the engagement work schedule.
- Valuations of assets such as land and buildings, works of art, precious gems, investments, and complex financial instruments.
- Determination of quantities or physical condition of certain assets such as mineral and petroleum reserves.
- Measuring the work completed and to be completed on contracts in progress.
- Fraud and security investigations.
- Determination of amounts by using specialized methods such as actuarial determinations of employee benefit obligations.
- Interpretation of legal, technical, and regulatory requirements.
- Evaluating the internal audit activity's quality improvement program in accordance with Section 1300 of the Standards.
- Mergers and acquisitions.'[15]

It may be at the discretion of the chief audit executive whether he or she expends the internal audit budget on in-house or outsourced staff resources. It is more likely that the chief audit executive will need to get the approval of management and of the audit committee to such decisions. When internal audit is partially outsourced, the usual responsibilities of the chief audit executive remain unchanged. This includes drawing up the annual plan of audit engagements and reporting through to the audit committee.

A considerable responsibility falls to the chief audit executive to 'assess the competency, independence, and objectivity of the outside service provider as it relates to the particular assignment to be performed'. (We discuss independence and objectivity in CHAPTER A2.2). This is analogous to an external auditor's obligation to assess the professionalism on any third party upon whom the external auditor intends to rely. It is also consistent with the responsibility of the chief audit executive to ensure that in-house internal auditors are competent to conduct their audit engagements. The assessment by the chief audit executive should also be made in cases where the outside service provider was appointed by management or the board and not by the chief audit executive – if 'the chief audit executive intends to use and rely on the outside service provider's work'.[16] Specific criteria for this assessment are given by The Institute of Internal Auditors:

- 'Professional certification, license, or other recognition of the outside service provider's competency in the relevant discipline.
- Membership of the outside service provider in an appropriate professional organization and adherence to that organization's code of ethics.
- The reputation of the outside service provider. This may include contacting others familiar with the outside service provider's work.
- The outside service provider's experience in the type of work being considered.
- The extent of education and training received by the outside service provider in disciplines that pertain to the particular engagement.

- The outside service provider's knowledge and experience in the industry in which the organization operates.'[17]

In addition to assessing competence, the chief audit executive is also required to assess the independence and objectivity of the outsourced internal audit service provider – which we discuss in A2.2.4.

Whoever is the chief audit executive has responsibility for all audit engagements, even when these are conducted by outside service providers:

> 'All internal auditing assignments, whether performed by or for the internal audit activity, remain the responsibility of the chief audit executive.'[18]

The audit committee of the board is likely to wish to avail itself of a direct reporting line from the partner in charge even of a partially outsourced internal audit provision, possibly to the extent of occasionally spending time alone with him or her. Not to do so would be to miss an obvious opportunity to enhance the total level of independent assurance that the audit committee receives. In essence this is not different from the audit committee sometimes wishing to meet with members of an in-house internal audit function other than the chief audit executive. In addition, the audit committee should require that chief audit executive to assess the competence of outsourced internal audit service providers and:

> 'the results of the assessment should be communicated to senior management or the board, as appropriate.'[19]

Audit committees should themselves be empowered by their terms of reference to take outside advice. Audit committees should also be empowered, by their terms of reference, to commission work to be done directly on the audit committee's behalf by the internal audit function. In such cases the internal audit report is addressed directly to the audit committee and is not given to management first, as would be usual for other audit engagements. When the audit committee is minded to commission internal audit work directly on the committee's behalf, depending on the circumstances the committee might opt for the work to be done by an outside service provider, rather than by the in-house internal audit function:

> 'An outside service provider may be engaged by the board, senior management, or the chief audit executive.'[20]

Even with an entirely in-house internal auditing function it is not easy for the audit committee of the board to determine whether the scope of internal audit work and the substance of internal audit reports to the audit committee have been determined solely by the exercise of the chief audit executive's professional judgement and without inappropriate pressure from management. We discussed this at A1.1.13. A good audit committee will also wish to confirm to its satisfaction that the internal audit function complies with internal auditing *Standards*. When internal audit is partially outsourced, the chief audit executive has similar challenges with respect to the outsourced service provision:

> 'The chief audit executive should obtain sufficient information regarding the scope of the outside service provider's work. This is necessary in order to ascertain that

the scope of work is adequate for the purposes of the internal auditing activity. It may be prudent to have these and other matters documented in an engagement letter or contract. The chief audit executive should review with the outside service provider:

- Objectives and scope of work.
- Specific matters expected to be covered in the engagement communications.
- Access to relevant records, personnel, and physical properties.
- Information regarding assumptions and procedures to be employed.
- Ownership and custody of engagement working papers, if applicable.
- Confidentiality and restrictions on information obtained during the engagement.

Where the outside service provider performs internal auditing activities, the chief audit executive should specify and ensure that the work complies with the Standards for the Professional Practice of Internal Auditing. In reviewing the work of an outside service provider, the chief audit executive should evaluate the adequacy of work performed. This evaluation should include sufficiency of information obtained to afford a reasonable basis for the conclusions reached and the resolution of significant exceptions or other unusual matters.'[21]

## A3.1.8 Internal auditors and fraud

There is undoubtedly an expectations gap for internal auditors in the area of fraud, just as there is for external auditors. Other parties expect both external auditors and internal auditors to be effective at detecting significant fraud. In the case of internal auditors, other parties may also expect internal audit to be effective at *preventing* significant fraud. Much effort is likely to be needed by the chief audit executive to explain internal audit's interface with fraud:

'Audit procedures alone, even when carried out with due professional care, do not guarantee that fraud will be detected.'[22]

However, in clarifying the limitations of internal audit in preventing and detecting fraud, the temptation should be avoided of adopting a position of zero responsibility for fraud. The prudent, middle way is set out as follows:

'The normal course of work for the internal audit activity is to provide an independent appraisal, examination, and evaluation of an organization's activities as a service to the organization. The objective of internal auditing in fraud detection is to assist members of the organization in the effective discharge of their responsibilities by furnishing them with analyses, appraisals, recommendations, counsel, and information concerning the activities reviewed.'[23]

and:

'A well-designed internal control system should not be conducive to fraud. Tests conducted by auditors, along with reasonable controls established by management, improve the likelihood that any existing fraud indicators will be detected and considered for further investigation.'[24]

Without suggesting that internal audit can be entirely effective in so doing, The Institute of Internal Auditors rightly gives internal audit more of a responsibility to prevent (deter) than to investigate or detect fraud:

'Deterrence of fraud consists of those actions taken to discourage the perpetration of fraud and limit the exposure if fraud does occur. The principal mechanism for deterring fraud is control. Primary responsibility for establishing and maintaining control rests with management.

Internal auditors are responsible for assisting in the deterrence of fraud by examining and evaluating the adequacy and the effectiveness of the system of internal control, commensurate with the extent of the potential exposure/risk in the various segments of the organization's operations. In carrying out this responsibility, internal auditors should, for example, determine whether:

- The organizational environment fosters control consciousness.
- Realistic organizational goals and objectives are set.
- Written policies (eg, code of conduct) exist that describe prohibited activities and the action required whenever violations are discovered.
- Appropriate authorization policies for transactions are established and maintained.
- Policies, practices, procedures, reports, and other mechanisms are developed to monitor activities and safeguard assets, particularly in high-risk areas.
- Communication channels provide management with adequate and reliable information.
- Recommendations need to be made for the establishment or enhancement of cost-effective controls to help deter fraud.'[25]

Internal auditing *Standards* require that, both in planning the programme of audit engagements and in planning the focus within each of these engagements, internal auditors should have regard to risk. The risk of fraud is part of this – but only part. In conducting audit work also, internal auditors should be mindful of the risk of fraud and alert to indications that fraud could, or might be occurring:

**'Standard 1210.A2**
The internal auditor should have sufficient knowledge to identify the indicators of fraud but is not expected to have the expertise of a person whose primary responsibility is detecting and investigating fraud.'

and

'In conducting engagements, the internal auditor's responsibilities for detecting fraud are to:

- Have sufficient knowledge of fraud to be able to identify indicators that fraud may have been committed. This knowledge includes the need to know the characteristics of fraud, the techniques used to commit fraud, and the types of frauds associated with the activities reviewed.
- Be alert to opportunities, such as control weaknesses, that could allow fraud. Some examples of indicators are unauthorized transactions, override of controls, unexplained pricing exceptions, and unusually large product losses. Internal auditors should recognize that the presence of more than one indicator at any one time increases the probability that fraud may have occurred.
- Evaluate the indicators that fraud may have been committed and decide whether any further action is necessary or whether an investigation should be recommended.
- Notify the appropriate authorities within the organization if a determination is made that there are sufficient indicators of the commission of a fraud to recommend an investigation.'

Certainly, this calls for what external auditors would term an appropriate degree of professional scepticism: things may not be how they at first appear!

Of course, if internal audit has been assigned the responsibility to be the entity's investigator of suspected fraud, then a requisite degree of expertise in fraud detection and investigation will be required to be available to the internal audit function:

'Investigation of fraud consists of performing extended procedures necessary to determine whether fraud, as suggested by the indicators, has occurred. It includes gathering sufficient information about the specific details of a discovered fraud. Internal auditors, lawyers, investigators, security personnel, and other specialists from inside or outside the organization are the parties that usually conduct or participate in fraud investigations.'[26]

'When conducting fraud investigations, internal auditors should:
- Assess the probable level and the extent of complicity in the fraud within the organization. This can be critical to ensuring that the internal auditor avoids providing information to or obtaining misleading information from persons who may be involved.
- Determine the knowledge, skills, and other competencies needed to carry out the investigation effectively. An assessment of the qualifications and the skills of internal auditors and of the specialists available to participate in the investigation should be performed to ensure that engagements are conducted by individuals having appropriate types and levels of technical expertise. This should include assurances on such matters as professional certifications, licenses, reputation, and the fact that there is no relationship to those being investigated or to any of the employees or management of the organization.
- Design procedures to follow in attempting to identify the perpetrators, extent of the fraud, techniques used, and cause of the fraud.
- Coordinate activities with management personnel, legal counsel, and other specialists as appropriate throughout the course of the investigation.
- Be cognizant of the rights of alleged perpetrators and personnel within the scope of the investigation and the reputation of the organization itself.

Once a fraud investigation is concluded, internal auditors should assess the facts known in order to:
- Determine if controls need to be implemented or strengthened to reduce future vulnerability.
- Design engagement tests to help disclose the existence of similar frauds in the future.
- Help meet the internal auditor's responsibility to maintain sufficient knowledge of fraud and thereby be able to identify future indicators of fraud.'

There is, of course, an obligation upon internal audit to report suspected fraud promptly:

'When an internal auditor suspects wrongdoing, the appropriate authorities within the organization should be informed.'[27]

and:

'Reporting of fraud consists of the various oral or written, interim or final communications to management regarding the status and results of fraud investigations. The chief audit executive has the responsibility to report immediately any incident of significant fraud to senior management and the board. Sufficient investigation should take place to establish reasonable certainty that a fraud has occurred before any fraud reporting is made. A preliminary or final report may be desirable at the conclusion of the detection phase. The report should include the internal auditor's conclusion as to whether sufficient information exists to conduct a full investigation. It should also summarize observations and recommendations that serve as the basis for such decision. A written report may follow any oral briefing made to management and the board to document the findings.'[28]

The *Standards* of the Institute of Internal Auditors are weakest in their coverage of internal audit's responsibilities with respect to the nature and extent of compliance and weakness testing, although the Practice Advisories are a bit more helpful. Internal auditors may detect a significant weakness of internal control when they assess the formal, laid down system or when compliance tests of that system uncover a failure to comply with a significant control procedure. Should internal auditors always conduct compliance tests of controls upon which they wish to rely – and to what degree? When a significant weakness of internal control *is* uncovered by internal audit, should internal auditors then conduct weakness tests designed to determine whether that weakness is being exploited, either accidentally or deliberately, and possibly fraudulently? Practice Advisory 1210.A2–1: 'Identification of Fraud', para 13 states:

'If significant control weaknesses are detected, additional tests conducted by internal auditors should include tests directed toward identification of other indicators of fraud.'

Or is it enough to tell management that there is a weakness and advise management to sort it out, without being able to advise management and the audit committee whether or not this weakness is leading to avoidable errors and losses? Internal auditors can communicate their findings with much more impact if they can express them not merely in hypothetical terms but in terms of actual consequences of poor control. And, of course, there is real value in uncovering significant frauds and other types of avoidable losses.

About six months before Barings Bank collapsed, their internal auditors reported that the Singapore front office was not segregated from the back office. Everyone knew this was a significant breach of a fundamental Barings control, but the internal auditors did not determine that this control weakness was being exploited fraudulently by Nick Leeson. Had they discovered the fraud at that juncture, it would probably have prevented the collapse of Barings. Nobody would say that would not have been a worthwhile use of internal audit time. Neither is it defensible to claim that looking for fraud is like looking for a needle in a haystack: when the internal auditor is aware of a significant control weakness, specific weakness tests can be designed that have a reasonable expectation of determining whether fraud is actually present.

Practice Advisory 1210.A2–1: 'Identification of Fraud' (paras 2 and 3) distinguishes between *management fraud* ('fraud designed to benefit the organization') and *employee and/or third party fraud* ('fraud perpetrated to the detriment of the organization'). The Advisory gives examples of both, which we reproduce at A3.2.12.

Management fraud poses a particular challenge to internal audit, especially when internal audit is in-house, as the internal auditors are then part of the management team though without line, executive responsibilities. Uncovering and reporting by internal audit of management fraud is an example of how, while modern internal audit is an audit *for* management, it is also an audit *of* management *for* the board. This stresses the importance of internal audit having a direct reporting line through to the audit committee of the board and of internal audit having the authority to report matters confidentially to the audit committee without needing to clear this with management first.

## A3.1.9  Internal auditors and information technology

Commencing 1 January 2004, the first two IT auditing standards were added. Both are assurance auditing standards[29], the first classified under 'Proficiency' (1210 standards) and the second under 'Due Professional Care' (1220 standards):

> '**1210.A3** – Internal auditors should have knowledge of key information technology risks and controls and available technology-based audit techniques to perform their assigned work. However, not all internal auditors are expected to have the expertise of an internal auditor whose primary responsibility is information technology auditing.'

and:

> '**1220.A2** – In exercising due professional care the internal auditor should consider the use of computer-assisted audit tools and other data analysis techniques.'

## A3.1.10  *Auditing in an IT environment*

Before the advent of IT there was no aspect of data processing which was a 'no go' area for auditors. Indeed it is only relatively recently that most internal auditors have surrendered the professional assessment of risk, control and governance of IT to others. As more and more business processes are IT-based, arguably most internal auditing should now be IT auditing. In Standard 1210.A3 The Institute of Internal Auditors is modestly calling for internal auditors to have 'knowledge' of key IT risks. While *knowledge* may be regarded as more than mere *awareness*, it is less than *understanding* and much less than *proficiency* or *expertise*. This is indicative of the extent to which internal audit has typically become relatively marginalised as the board's and management's provider of assurance on risk management, internal control and governance. The Institute clearly considers it impractical to pitch in a mandatory way for internal auditors to have a major role in IT auditing; but there is no reason why individual internal auditors and internal audit functions should not assume greater assurance responsibilities in this area than the Institute is confident to prescribe.

<ol>
<li>Practice Advisory 1210–1: Proficiency, paras 2 and 3.</li>
<li>Practice Advisory 1210–1: 'Proficiency', para 1.</li>
<li>Practice Advisory 1210–1: 'Proficiency', para 1.</li>
<li>Practice Advisory 1210–1: 'Proficiency', para 1.</li>
<li>Practice Advisory 1210–1: 'Proficiency', para 1.</li>
<li>Practice Advisory 1210.A1–1: 'Obtaining Services to Support or Complement the Internal Audit Activity', para 1.</li>
<li>Practice Advisory 1210–1: 'Proficiency', para 5.</li>
<li>Practice Advisory 1210.A1–1: 'Obtaining Services to Support or Complement the Internal Audit Activity', para 1.</li>
<li>Practice Advisory 1200–1: 'Proficiency and Due Professional Care', para 1.</li>
<li>Practice Advisory 1210–1: 'Proficiency', para 4.</li>
<li>Practice Advisory 2030–1: 'Resource Management', para 2.</li>
<li>Practice Advisory 1220–1: 'Due Professional Care', paras 1 and 2.</li>
<li>Practice Advisory 1230–1: 'Continuing Professional Development', paras 1–4.</li>
<li>Practice Advisory 1210.A1–1: 'Obtaining Services to Support or Complement the Internal Audit Activity', para 2.</li>
<li>Practice Advisory 1210.A1–1: 'Obtaining Services to Support or Complement the Internal Audit Activity', para 3.</li>
<li>Practice Advisory 1210.A1–1: 'Obtaining Services to Support or Complement the Internal Audit Activity', para 4.</li>
<li>Practice Advisory 1210.A1–1: 'Obtaining Services to Support or Complement the Internal Audit Activity', para 5.</li>
<li>Practice Advisory 2340–1: 'Engagement Supervision', para 3.</li>
<li>Practice Advisory 1210.A1–1: 'Obtaining Services to Support or Complement the Internal Audit Activity', para 4. Note that the use of the phrase 'the board' by The Institute of Internal Auditors should be taken to include the board's audit committee, as is apparent from the definition of 'Board' in the Glossary to the *Standards*.</li>
<li>Practice Advisory 1210.A1–1: 'Obtaining Services to Support or Complement the Internal Audit Activity', para 2. Note that the use of the phrase 'the board' by The Institute of Internal Auditors should be taken to include the board's audit committee, as is apparent from the definition of 'Board' in the Glossary to the *Standards*.</li>
<li>Practice Advisory 1210.A1–1: 'Obtaining Services to Support or Complement the Internal Audit Activity', paras 9 and 10.</li>
<li>Practice Advisory 1210.A2–1: 'Identification of Fraud', para 14.</li>
<li>Practice Advisory 1210.A2–2: 'Responsibility for Fraud Detection', para 1.</li>
<li>Practice Advisory 1210.A2–2: 'Responsibility for Fraud Detection', para 3.</li>
<li>Practice Advisory 1210.A2–1: 'Identification of Fraud', para 5.</li>
<li>Practice Advisory 1210.A2–1: 'Identification of Fraud', paras 7–9.</li>
<li>Practice Advisory 1210.A2–1: 'Identification of Fraud', para 6.</li>
<li>Practie Advisory 1210.A2–1: 'Identification of Fraud', para 10.</li>
<li>Denoted by the letter 'A' within the standard number.</li>
</ol>

# Proficiency and care in internal auditing – supplementary guidance

## A3.2.1  Tell-tale signs of fraud

It is a clichéd truism that business depends on trust, but a prudent interpretation of one aspect of this contention is that we should take abundant trouble to recruit trustworthy staff and business associates, and also abundant trouble to ensure that they then serve in a trustworthy way. We can say that while we must take infinite pains to recruit trustworthy people and to emphasise that our business depends upon their trustworthiness, nevertheless we should also ensure that we do not trust them!

This is as much in their interests as it is in the interests of the business. If we develop systems that prevent staff from conducting themselves in an untrustworthy way, then the finger of suspicion will not point in their direction. If our controls could confirm the honesty of their conduct, members of staff would be exonerated more or less automatically. Nobody benefits from a suggestion of personal dishonesty.

One can sympathise with the catering manager, the contracts manager or the purchasing officer who is so routinely suspected of dishonesty because it has not been possible to design systems which prevent backhanders being made to these people by suppliers, or which detect that these have been made. It would be much better for staff if it were possible to devise systems which prevented or detected this type of fraud. Indeed, in practice there are many measures we can take to reduce the likelihood that such fraud will occur, but usually we cannot entirely eliminate the risk.

One practical outworking of a policy of ensuring that our security and control do not depend excessively upon assumed trustworthiness of staff, is to foster a climate of mutual suspicion. Clearly, this must not be taken out of proportion, but there is much that can be done before that becomes a risk.

Business policy statements have an important place in fraud containment. Amongst other things, they can define an employee's responsibility in the case of suspected fraud. The progressive stance here is that employees should be charged with a duty, not merely a right, to report suspected wrongdoing, even if they are merely bystanding observers and not otherwise personally involved. The ways in which suspected wrongdoing should be reported, and then dealt with, also need to be clearly worked out and defined.

We can go a step or two further by encouraging staff to look for explanations of behaviour which could amount to tell-tale signs of wrongdoing, rather than ignoring these possible indicators. Of course, there will often be innocent explanations for apparently errant behaviour. But even innocent explanations may need to be known about by a caring, supportive employer.

The following are some of the typical tell-tale signs of fraud.

## A3.2.2  Altered attitudes

It is hard to generalise as to what these may be. It could be a change in the level of the individual's commitment to the business. This may be an apparently enhanced level of commitment which may either be a smokescreen for untrustworthy conduct in progress, or an excuse for the extra level of involvement which is needed, perhaps out of usual working hours, to perpetrate and conceal the fraud.

Or it may be a newly impaired level of commitment due to disillusionment with the employer. This sort of disillusionment can result from personal exploitation by the employer, whether actual or merely perceived; or it could be the result of some form of harassment. It could be a form of irrational self-justification for the fraudulent conduct which has been triggered perhaps by circumstances external to the business, thereby making it easier for the dishonest employer to square his or her conduct with their conscience.

Sometimes the tell-tale sign of a changed attitude may necessarily be a specific part of the process of concealing the fraud, as for example, with the previously prudent cashier who became a devotee of the betting shop.

## A3.2.3  Extravagant lifestyle

The employee who apparently lives beyond his or her means may have something to hide. Generally, explanations will be offered, such as betting winnings, inheritance, the wealth of a partner and so on. We take these at face value at our peril.

The author recalls one blatant case where a clerk dressed more smartly, acquired a toupee and an expensive partner, moved to a better home and even acquired the same model of car as the directors had. Amazingly, nobody thought it their business to query or confirm the clerk's explanations for this newly extravagant lifestyle, nor the clerk's decision to stay in that modestly remunerated job.

## A3.2.4  Questionable friendships

A close friendship is questionable if it is with a contractor or another party with whom the member of staff routinely, or even just occasionally, represents the business. It is important that these friendships are not secretive. The finger of suspicion will reasonably start pointing if the employee is not completely open about these relationships, so that management can ensue that no excessive risks to the business ensue.

Habitually mixing with people known or suspected of having criminal connections will also need to be explained, as will known friendships which appear to be strikingly unusual for a person in the employee's position.

## A3.2.5 *Self-contained behaviour*

Secretiveness can be a form of aid to concealment of fraud. Excessively self-contained behaviour can also be indicative of personal values and orientations which could indicate a compromised loyalty to the business. Excessively self-contained behaviour can point to personal circumstances or personality qualities which should be causes of concern. For instance, the employee who is preoccupied with a personal problem, such as an unsharable financial need, may seek to alleviate the problem deceitfully at the business's expense. Or the person with a personality under strain may be at risk of behaving irrationally in a dishonest way. Key positions of trust are best filled by employees of robust temperaments, all other things being equal.

## A3.2.6 *Excessive private phone calls and internet access*

Excessive private phone calls during working hours should be addressed as a specific cause of concern by a supervisor. Some businesses have policies to regulate private phone calls; others provide pay phones for employees to use for private calls; most leave it to the discretion of supervisors to ensure that the opportunity to make private calls is not abused by employees. Eavesdropping on an employee's private calls is now regarded as a breach of the employee's rights to privacy, though it can be acceptable where it is required for business monitoring and control purposes, so long as employees know about it.

While excessive making of private calls may be a fraud issue in itself, it may also point to the on-going conduct of another more serious fraud, such as the running of a private business during work time. Certainly, it needs to be explained and understood.

Again, business policies vary with respect to internet access during working hours and via business IT equipment. Some businesses encourage it, whether or not the access is work-related, on the grounds that they wish their staff to become internet-literate for today's e-commerce world. Other businesses outlaw personal internet access via the businesses' IT systems: their main concern is usually not so much a matter of the line access costs but the cost of staff time consumed in this way during working hours. Web-based chat lines can be particularly addictive for some staff.

There is also the matter of staff access to undesirable websites which can be a form of harassment for other staff as well as tainting the business ethically for their permissive or negligent attitude to such access.

Similar challenges apply to personal internet access as to the making of private phone calls. We would certainly recommend that a business should have a specific internet access policy rather than leaving it to the discretion of supervisors to determine what is acceptable. Software can bar access to websites which are regarded as not permissible and can record attempts to visit those sites for management review.

## A3.2.7 *Irregular private life*

As with altered attitudes, an irregular private life could be suggestive of behaviour associated with the perpetration or concealment of fraud, or with the difficulty of living a personal life when one's nearest and dearest are aware or suspicious of the person's wrongdoing. So an irregular private life could be an effect of dishonest conduct at work. It could also be a cause of it; by placing the individual under mental or financial strain so that they may be more inclined to behave dishonestly.

Businesses need to have a good record of helping staff resolve their personal difficulties. Some staff will then be less likely to contemplate fraudulent ideas and the business will be in a better position to know where are the fraud risks.

## A3.2.8 *Poor job performance*

Preoccupation with the perpetration and concealment of fraud can divert an employee from the demands of the job, leading to observable poor work performance. It may be a matter of the time-consuming nature of the fraud or it may be a matter of the worry that the fraud is causing the perpetrator, so that he or she is diverted from focussing on the work at hand. Poor performance may also be indicative of fraud in the sense that targets are not met due to the diversion of company income for personal gain, or to the diversion of personal expenses so that they are accounted for as business operating costs.

## A3.2.9 *Appearance of being under pressure on the job*

This tell-tale sign overlaps considerably with 'poor job performance' as well as with 'unclear explanations for exceptions' (see A3.2.10). Creating an aura or a reality of indispensability, drive and energy can be a smokescreen for ongoing fraud or even a necessary prerequisite for its perpetration or concealment. Undertaking the fraud on top of performing one's normal duties will undoubtedly add to the pressure the individual experiences and projects.

Appearance of excessive pressure on the job needs to be attended to by management, even apart from any concerns that it may be indicative of fraud: excessive pressure is counterproductive to efficient and effective operations. Excessive pressure is often caused by insensitive, perhaps autocratic, top management imposing unrealistic targets upon staff: in itself this creates a fraud risk as it can lead to staff alienation and compromised levels of staff loyalty. It can also lead to creative accounting.

## A3.2.10  *Unclear explanation for exceptions*

Auditors in particular quickly learn that when they do not understand an explanation it may be because the explanation is not genuine. Independent confirmation of implausible explanations will often be needed. Not appearing to have time to provide satisfactory explanations for exceptions and showing irritation at being approached for explanations can be conscious tactics by the defrauder to put enquirers off the scent.

## A3.2.11  *Conclusions*

Of course, nobody is saying that these tell-tale signs are entirely reliable signposts of dishonest conduct, or even of the risk of dishonest conduct developing in the future. But they should not be overlooked. As we have indicated, apart from the possibility of fraud, they often need to be followed up for reasons of operational efficiency and effectiveness as well as of good human resource management.

In today's business culture all members of staff have empowered roles to play 'outside their narrow box'. We have all known examples where observed, possible wrongdoing has not been reported. In the empowered business culture no member of staff should be able to claim that it is 'not my business'. In practical terms the challenge may be that the observer has the merest suspicion but no hard evidence of wrongdoing and the concern is that the observed conduct may be entirely innocent. Good whistleblowing policies can come into play here.

Then again, fraud may occur with no revealing tell-tale signs of fraud. Nevertheless, many frauds are discovered by accident, often through the carelessness of the defrauder and the vigilance of observers. The carelessness of the defrauder often leaves behind a trail of highly visible tell-tale signs, which it is wise to formally try to capture.

## Areas vulnerable to fraud

**A3.2.12**  The Institute of Internal Auditors distinguishes between fraud perpetrated for the benefit of or to the detriment of the organisation.

'Fraud encompasses an array of irregularities and illegal acts characterized by intentional deception. It can be perpetrated for the benefit of or to the detriment of the organization and by persons outside as well as inside the organization.

Fraud designed to benefit the organization generally produces such benefit by exploiting an unfair or dishonest advantage that also may deceive an outside party. Perpetrators of such frauds usually accrue an indirect personal benefit. Examples of frauds designed to benefit the organization include:
- Sale or assignment of fictitious or misrepresented assets.
- Improper payments such as illegal political contributions, bribes, kickbacks, and payoffs to government officials, intermediaries of government officials, customers, or suppliers.

- Intentional, improper representation or valuation of transactions, assets, liabilities, or income.
- Intentional, improper transfer pricing (eg, valuation of goods exchanged between related organizations). By purposely structuring pricing techniques improperly, management can improve the operating results of an organization involved in the transaction to the detriment of the other organization.
- Intentional, improper related-party transactions in which one party receives some benefit not obtainable in an arm's-length transaction.
- Intentional failure to record or disclose significant information to improve the financial picture of the organization to outside parties.
- Prohibited business activities such as those that violate government statutes, rules, regulations, or contracts.
- Tax fraud.

Fraud perpetrated to the detriment of the organization generally is for the direct or indirect benefit of an employee, outside individual, or another organization. Some examples are:

- Acceptance of bribes or kickbacks.
- Diversion to an employee or outsider of a potentially profitable transaction that would normally generate profits for the organization.
- Embezzlement, as typified by the misappropriation of money or property, and falsification of financial records to cover up the act, thus making detection difficult.
- Intentional concealment or misrepresentation of events or data.
- Claims submitted for services or goods not actually provided to the organization.'[1]

It has been shown that 75 per cent of frauds involving theft also involve negotiable instruments of which, of course, cash is an obvious example. The defrauder is attracted to the opportunity which negotiable instruments provide to convert the theft into value of a different form, so making traceability more difficult. In principle, the more liquid (convertible) the commodity, the more potentially attractive it becomes to a defrauder and the tighter the controls therefore need to be. Forged inputs are often the means by which frauds are set up, and so inputs to cash payment routines need to be particularly closely controlled and monitored.

Most frauds involving theft also involve personal account manipulation. There are a number of different sorts of personal accounts which may offer fraud potential.

- An account of an employee. This may be an account of an employee who is a customer or a supplier of the business that employs him or her. Every employee has at least one account with the employer; their payroll account.
- A fictitious or unauthorised account. Pay particular attention to the risk that a genuine account which should be closed is in fact modified so that it can be used for fraudulent purposes. An example would be the payroll account of an employee who leaves which is not removed or terminated from the computer. An allied risk is the new employee who declines to start employment but whose payroll record has already been set up.
- An account of an unwitting customer or supplier, or of a number of customers or suppliers. The teeming and lading fraud is an example of this. Another example would be the application of a balance on an apparently dormant account for fraudulent purposes, perhaps with the intention of using part of

the proceeds of fraudulent activity to replenish the dormant account before anyone notices that it has been raided.

- Account of outside accomplice. For instance, a genuine account can be set up to be used by an inside employee as a channel to divert funds which are then withdrawn by the outside accomplice.
- Another example is the proper opening of a new customer account with a low credit limit. The customer manages the account immaculately and then applies for a larger credit limit which is granted on the strength of the customer's track record. The customer then quickly runs up debts for the full credit amount and absconds.
- Account of employer of outside accomplice. An example would be the use of this account to charge for goods or services enjoyed by the accomplices who, through their respective employments, may be in a position to initiate the accounting entries and approvals involved.

Other areas vulnerable to fraud include purchasing, catering, and contracts. These come in various forms and are particularly pernicious since it is not possible by means of internal controls and internal checks to eliminate the possibility of backhanders being offered by suppliers or their agents to the employees with whom they deal.

Sales frauds are of course another problem area. It may be a matter of short deliveries, made possible by a failure to check at the point of delivery. Or it may be a matter of sales ledger frauds of which there are several types, including:

- unauthorised file or program amendment;
- low price for accomplice;
- altered credit limits;
- induced rejection and resubmission after false alteration;
- improper write-offs; and
- teeming and lading.

## A3.2.13  *Information which has been the object of fraud*

It is unlikely that there is any information in possession of a business which would not be of interest and value to outsiders who do not have a right of access to it. So all information is potentially vulnerable to fraud. The box gives a not exhaustive summary of some of the different sorts of business information which are known to have been the object of frauds.

The *Data Protection Act 1998* forces standards of conduct and security over personal data which businesses hold. It may be wise for a business to apply equivalent standards to all the data the business holds, whether it is personal data or not. First, this will ensure that no personal data is overlooked and not subjected to the regime which should apply to it. Secondly, all corporate data will benefit from the application of the data protection principles.

### A3.2.14   Information which has been the object of fraud

Payroll, trade secrets, patent applications, market research, sales analyses, complaints letters, forecasts, financial data, accounts, new products, pricing, tenders, customers, shareholders, proprietary programs, other software, engineering data, manuals and policies.

## A3.2.15   E-fraud

> '... in the e-world everything changes fast so the opportunities for fraud change at least as fast. ... The remoteness of many of the fraudsters ... may reduce the perceived chances of being caught. If it is true that about 5% of e-transactions are fraudulent, how will an organisation that does not know its customers make any money on increasingly tight margins? ... we have often seen a possibly unwitting increase in the risk appetite.'

A few years ago we noted that an increasing proportion of computer-based frauds, and then an increasing proportion of those frauds were related to real-time systems. On reflection, this was not surprising as, first, most business systems had become computer-based and, secondly, most computer systems had become online and real-time.

Now we are experiencing the rise and rise of e-fraud, which is a reflection of the increasing rôle of e-commerce in business today. Even if e-fraud is unsurprising, this does not allow us to dismiss e-fraud as of no consequence.

### A3.2.16   *E-fraud facilitators*

It is of course true that many traditional types of fraud are now being given a new lease of life by the opportunities that the internet affords. Advance fee frauds are nothing new, but pose an extra risk in e-commerce. Likewise, the so-called 'pump and dump equity schemes', which utilise internet chat lines to deliberately talk up share prices, are a novel manifestation of what is in essence a traditional fraud. Recently, fictitious, misleading company announcements on websites have had dramatic impact on their share prices. These frauds have been all too successful on account of:

- the new remoteness of many customers and suppliers;
- the undue plausibility afforded to web-based information;
- the speed with which business is conducted over the internet, encouraging a less thorough approach to client authentication; due diligence of customers and suppliers is still important;
- the relative difficulty of seeking subsequent redress for breach of terms negotiated by e-mail.

The distinctive characteristics of e-commerce need to be understood as they provide the new means for perpetrating often traditional frauds in highly distinctive ways. New approaches to countering e-fraud are therefore necessary.

### A3.2.17   *E-fraud countermeasures*

Generally, the key to effective countermeasures is to harness the technology which is the basis of contemporary commercial systems so as to apply the same technology in the service of control and security. For instance:

- online and real time data processing needs online, real time auditing responses;
- e-commerce credit card transactions require online authentication by World-pay, Europay or similar;
- website firewalls are essential; and
- embedded programming designed to detect fraudulent transactions is an important way ahead and so on.

The breakneck speed with which dotcom companies have been set up has often meant that dotcom companies and companies with e-business operations have neglected to put in place an appropriate control framework. Control frameworks tend to be established over time and 'time' is what has been in short supply. When there is major change, effective controls are even more important. For instance, internal audit is a comparative rarity in dotcom companies, but is vitally important:

> 'from the point of view of the internal auditor – as an expert in risk management – the issues are to ensure that the organisation is performing the fundamentals correctly and to facilitate the discussion of risk management with the right people.'

## A3.2.18  *E-fraud costs and risks*

One estimate is that internet fraud cost UK banks and retailers an estimated $15 million in 2000. We believe this is probably a significant underestimate. The consultancy, Retail Decisions, has concluded that fraud on the internet is running at 5–10 per cent of all internet credit card transactions. Experian, the credit and business information company, has claimed that while most websites currently report less than 1 per cent of fraudulent transactions, in some cases these losses are as high as 40 per cent.

The *Financial Times* reported that credit card fraud in general now costs $(US)4 billion *per annum*, worldwide, or $2 per credit card issued, rising annually by one-third. An increasing proportion of credit card fraud will migrate to become e-fraud as e-commerce becomes more ubiquitous and as banks introduce security measures which promise to be quite effective in combatting fraud in traditional credit card transactions. Europay recently estimated that 6 per cent of credit card fraud was already internet-based in 2000, and that this type of fraud is rapidly becoming more common. Richard Fiddis, chief operating officer of Experian, has put it simply:

> 'the internet is becoming the first choice for thieves.'

An issue of concern is the extent to which the potential of e-fraud is attracting both criminal elements as well as those with a record of sharp business practice. Kroll Associates, on the basis of their usual investigations of the backgrounds of executives and directors, has found that 39 per cent of dotcom executives and directors have 'unsavoury backgrounds', compared to a norm of about 10 per cent. Pre-employment screening standards should not be compromised; but they are of course no antidote to the risk of fraud in e-commerce operations which are being set up by untrustworthy people.

Apart from the senior executives and directors of dotcom companies, most of the other dotcom employees are too young to have much of a background either way, whether straight or unsavoury. So, we have a new sector staffed by young, inexperienced technical people balanced by older more experienced people at senior levels said to be disproportionately skewed towards being untrustworthy, compared to business in general. This is a recipe for fraud. It also augers badly for the future as young, inexperienced, high-flying dotcom personnel serve their business apprenticeships under less trustworthy management teams.

The crash in dotcom stocks is a further warning sign: the field of business history is littered with examples of management teams which have become engaged in fraud (especially, but not exclusively, fraudulent financial reporting) when the tide has turned against them and it is becoming harder to report results up to market expectations. The temptations are particularly acute in highly geared companies.

The breathtaking pace of the e-business revolution has often meant that basic controls, especially over the hiring of staff at all levels, have been overlooked:

> 'the whole effort has been to move at internet speed, which has meant not stopping to do careful checks on employees, or putting in place internal auditing or security.'

At present, the most costly type of internet fraud for banks is card theft and misuse. It is one manifestation of electronic impersonation (or 'identify theft') and is achieved in a variety of ways.

The fraud risks of traditional face-to-face credit card usage are well known. In New York some department store employees were caught illegally swiping customer credit cards into hand-held 'scanners'. The scanners captured the personal information from the 'strip' and this information was then illegally used to create fraudulent credit cards. A solution to this would be for the customer to request to swipe the card personally, but few customers are likely to insist on this on account of the embarrassment factor and also because most of the risk to customers is generally covered by the bank and the retailer. The initiative would need to be taken by the retailer to insist that customers swiped their cards personally.

Similar precautions are not available to reduce the risk of fraud in e-commerce credit card transactions, but there are promising alternative developments. The Secure Electronic Transaction (SET) scheme uses digital signatures to authenticate the identities of both cardholder and electronic retailer.

In July 2000, the Electronic Signatures in Global and National Commerce Act became law in the US. It gives digital signatures the same legal standing as conventional ink-on-paper ones, and is seen as an essential step in the evolution of the internet.

## A3.2.19  *A useful source*

www.FraudIndex.com: a weekly e-newsletter about fraud, with solutions to fraud scams and schemes making the news.

---

[1]   Practice Advisory 1210.A2–1: 'Identification of Fraud', paras 1, 2 and 3.

## A3.2.20 Using knowledge within internal audit effectively

*We suggest this article should be read in conjunction with* A3.2.21 'Wise internal auditors manage knowledge well'. *Mary Hardy wrote this article when she was Group Audit Director at Diageo where the experiences recounted in this article were then taking place. Mary is now Internal Audit Director for Transport for London and can be contacted at Windsor House, 42–50 Victoria Street, London SW1H 0TL. Tel: +44 (0) 20 7941 4087. Fax +44 (0)20 7941 4434. E-mail: maryhardy@tfl.gov.uk.*

Before we can consider how to use knowledge effectively in any context, we need to have a working definition. For the purpose of this paper I am defining knowledge as:

> 'An accumulation of information about:
> - Business strategies, operations and risks that is of relevance to enable the internal audit function to plan its work in a focused manner; and
> - Audit processes and procedures to enable audit work to be carried out efficiently and effectively.'

It is very important to differentiate between 'knowledge', 'data', and 'information'. The amount of data available to us in this technological age is substantial and it is very tempting to build spreadsheets and databases and analyse this data to the ninth degree because we have the technology available to do it. However, we must constantly challenge whether the data is a mere collection of ciphers or whether it is information that is indeed adding to our knowledge and enabling us to do our job more effectively.

### Business knowledge

The key elements of knowledge that an internal auditor requires about the business are the strategic plans and objectives and the risks associated with those strategic plans. As companies' compliance with the Combined Code and Turnbull improves, the management and mitigation actions for risks as well as the sources of assurance should be documented and these will also be key pieces of knowledge for the internal auditor.

So armed with the above knowledge of the business, what does the internal auditor do next?

### Audit knowledge

The following example is based on how we manage knowledge in group audit in Diageo plc. At the moment these knowledge databases are on a variety of spreadsheets and linked Lotus Notes databases. We are, however, in process of installing an integrated software package, which will pull them together more effectively and give us search functionality, which will make the knowledge much more accessible and, therefore, valuable.

In order to understand what knowledge means to us in Diageo, I need to briefly introduce the group to you. Diageo was formed in December 1997 from a merger between Guinness and Grand Metropolitan. We have many, many well-known brands amongst which the key ones are Johnnie Walker, Smirnoff, Baileys, Guinness, Haagen-Dazs and Burger King. The Group operates in over 150 countries worldwide with two of the businesses headquartered in the US (Pillsbury and Burger King) and two in the UK (UDV and Guinness), along with the corporate headquarters. Annual revenues for the year ended 30 June 1999 were in the order of £12 billion.

As I write this article the group audit function is being decentralised so that each business will have its own business risk assurance team headed by a business risk assurance director with a central team who will have an ongoing coaching, quality assurance and co-ordination role. Prior to this decentralisation, the group audit function consisted of 45 staff based in five offices around the world. A similar number and distribution are anticipated once decentralisation has been completed.

In a group of this size and diversity, it is vitally important that the internal audit function has access to the right knowledge to enable it to operate effectively; it would be extremely easy to spend all the time analysing data!

There are eight segments to the knowledge databases within group audit in Diageo:

1.   standards database;
2.   audit universe;
3.   audit planner;
4.   skills database;
5.   electronic workpapers;
6.   audit reports;
7.   good practice database; and
8.   discussion database.

The contents and use of the each of these databases are described below.

## Standards database

In order to ensure consistency of quality of work throughout the audit group, we have a number of agreed standards that are followed on a worldwide basis.

| | |
|---|---|
| **Audit methodology** | This sets out the philosophy behind the audit approach as well as walking through the audit process from start to finish. |

| Master risk matrices | These are *not* audit checklists! However, they take each standard business process and identify the most common risks to those processes. They are only intended as a starting point to enable auditors to do their own thinking as the risks to any process will vary significantly depending on which of the four businesses are being audited and which part of the world the auditor is in. Alongside the common risks are the common controls you might expect to see. The auditor develops both the risk and the control aspects of this matrix before performing audit work. The matrix will then carry a summary of the audit work completed, and weaknesses identified which need to be included in the report will also be highlighted. |
|---|---|
| Reporting templates | We have a standard report format that is used by all of the auditors around the world. This is particularly important to ensure consistency of presentation for those people based at the corporate centre who receive copies of all reports issued. We also have standard wordings for conclusions with definitions included in the reports so there can be no misunderstanding of what the conclusions mean. |
| Distribution lists | Whilst this may seem a trivial point, in a group of 77,000 with constant turnover of staff and reorganisations, trying to keep track of who requires reports, where they are and what their current job title is can be something of a nightmare! By having the standard distribution lists on the database we can be sure that auditors use the current version and report distribution is accurate. |

## Audit universe

For every auditable entity in Diageo we have an entry on the audit universe. This does not incorporate an audit risk ranking and scoring system, which is what most people take an audit universe to mean. What it does contain is background information on the entity including business size, organisation charts and key players, major business/systems/personnel changes, major risks and then information on the entity's location and useful data on hotels, restaurants, bars, cinemas etc. Note that an auditable entity is not necessarily just a business unit, but it could be the functions within a large business unit, or possibly a major project.

## Audit planner

This is simply the forward schedule of staff and job planning. We always aim to have the planning fixed for the next three months and provisional for the three months afterwards.

## Skills database

On joining the department each member of staff is asked to fill in a skills database form which is updated annually. This gives us information on work experience, language skills and IT knowledge as well as career aspirations. The search functionality included in this enables managers to identify the individuals with the appropriate skills for the job they are trying to plan as well as to ensure that the planning, as far as is possible, meets career aspirations.

## Electronic work papers

The software package we are installing will enable all work papers to be reviewed remotely by managers and directors and so cut down on travel time, and improve response times should audit issues arise. There is also a capacity to scan documents into the work papers so that a complete file is available. The software will produce the detailed findings section of the audit report so that only the executive summary will need to be an original document.

## Audit reports

Copies of all audit reports will be maintained on the system. In the new system the important addition will be search functionality so that we will be able to analyse reports by business, risk category or finding.

## Good practice database

As we perform audits and identify examples of good business practice we not only highlight these in the executive summary of the audit reports to give credit to local management for the work they are doing, but we also add them to the good practice database.

## Discussion database

This is a free form Lotus Notes database which allows the audit staff to raise questions or start discussion topics as well as to put on to the system information that they believe will be of use to others in the department. Quite often this information will be a summary of a conference they have recently attended or maybe of some articles they have read in an industry magazine. At the end of each week an automatic e-mail is sent to all staff informing them what has been added to the discussion database during the course of that week to both encourage them to read the additions and remind them that the discussion database is there.

I hope the above outline of how we manage knowledge in Diageo Group Audit has been of interest and will help you to think about how you can use knowledge effectively within your internal audit department.

# Wise internal auditors manage knowledge well

**A3.2.21**   *We suggest this article should be read in conjunction with A3.2.20 'Using knowledge within internal audit effectively'. Jeffrey Ridley wrote this article. Jeffrey is professor of auditing, attached to London South Bank University l. He can be contacted as follows. Tel: +44 (0) 1526 354472. E-mail: profridley@btopenworld.com.*

Those who study and advise on knowledge management have written well on this subject over the past few years; both as a product of learning and as an important management tool to motivate and stimulate innovation. Knowledge management is a means of developing, capturing and communicating information. It is also about searching information to improve strategic thinking and decision-making processes. Most good knowledge management processes now use electronic methods to ensure all information available is being used to best advantage for the organisation and its entire staff.

Bill Gates of Microsoft discusses the value of the 'electronic library' of knowledge in all organisations:

> '... to gather and organize information, disseminate the information to people who need it, and constantly refine the information through analysis and collaboration ...'

His simplified definition of knowledge management is:

> '... nothing more than managing information flow ...'.

But is management of information enough and can it ever be simplified? In most organisations management of information is one of its most difficult tasks, too often disorganised and not used wisely.

All organisations have seen explosions of information. Storing and searching that information to achieve an organisation's two key objectives, its aims and improved performance, is not that easy. It requires good planning, efficient methods and a commitment to share knowledge. How often are all your information flows tested for the knowledge requirements of these two key objectives? Do you ever do this in your internal auditing function, your auditee's function or for the whole organisation? Such tests are becoming more and more important as volumes of information continue to grow. Internal auditors have a clear responsibility to address and evaluate knowledge management in their own functions and in all other areas of their organisations.

Auditing, as practised by internal auditors or any other type of auditor, is based on established principles that have been tested and developed over many years. It has its own 'scientists' who have explored and developed better methods and opened up new boundaries of knowledge for those that practise its art. Committed practitioners have driven its development, either individually or in groups. Its principles have a universal acceptance. Its standards are continually being developed and revised to meet new demands by both practitioners and those who rely on its

167

services. There is a continuous programme of research and development at academic and practitioner levels that documents and influences what is practised.

The IIA's 1941 Certificate of Incorporation sowed the seeds for a science of internal auditing. This stated that The IIA's then purpose as a profession was:

> 'To cultivate, promote and disseminate knowledge and information concerning internal auditing and subjects related thereto; to establish and maintain standards of integrity, honor and character among internal auditors; to furnish information regarding internal auditing and the practice and methods thereof to its members, and to other persons interested therein, and to the general public; to cause the publication of articles relating to internal auditing and practices and methods thereof; to establish and maintain a library and reading rooms, meeting rooms and social rooms for the use of its members; to promote social intercourse among its members; and to do any and all things which shall be lawful and appropriate in furtherance of any of the purposes hereinbefore expressed.'

The IIA has researched a common body of knowledge for internal auditing since the 1970s. Its knowledge framework, researched and published in the early 1990s, has this to say about internal auditing knowledge:

> '... internal auditors must possess skills and knowledge from several different disciplines. They must be excellent communicators, both orally and in writing. They must be well versed in computers and technology to be proficient in the new Information age. They must be logical thinkers. They must possess accounting, economics, finance, and other types of management knowledge to understand business and the context in which organisations operate. They must also have numerous other types of support knowledge, such as human relations, sampling, quantitative methods, and fraud detection abilities. Indeed, it appears that the knowledge required to be an effective internal auditor almost demands that one be "superhuman" – an expert in numerous disciplines.'

Detail supporting this research was used to update the syllabus for The IIA Inc Certified Internal Auditor (CIA®) examination programme as it is today. Further research by The IIA in the late 1990s resulted in a new competency framework for internal auditing. Created from global research this framework identifies knowledge areas vital to internal auditing. Its guidance is now impacting much of the teaching and training in internal auditing today across the world. Its influence will grow, placing new demands on knowledge requirements for all internal auditors.

O'Regan (2001) recently studied the current professional status of internal auditing and recognises The IIA as:

> '... the driving force behind the increasing professionalisation of internal auditing over the last half-century.'

He lists amongst other attributes of The IIA:

> '... a defined body of examined and certified knowledge ...'

This attribute, more than any other, has driven the development of the profession and the science of internal auditing as we know it today. That defined body of knowledge is clearly stated in the current syllabi of The IIA Certified Internal

Auditor (CIA) examination programme and the new international standards for the professional practice of internal auditing. Both are available in electronic form and provide a bank of knowledge that will grow, adding significant value worldwide to all internal auditing functions. Good knowledge management skills will be needed by internal auditors for these to be used to create best professional internal auditing practices. They should impact all internal auditors and provide continuous opportunities for performance improvement.

This year has seen a number of case studies being published showing how internal auditors are contributing to knowledge management in the organisations they serve. Four such studies developed by The IIA-UK (2001) demonstrate how internal auditors in Lex Services, Bank of England, Central Bank of Ireland and HM Customs & Excise have embraced knowledge management. Each is using electronic methods to store, manage and spread knowledge about their internal auditing to all audit staff and others in their organisations. Each is using their auditing to review how knowledge in their organisations is being managed.

A recent issue of the Institute of Internal Auditor's newsletter Auditwire (2001) also outlines how other North American based internal auditors are '... getting involved and shaping key roles ...' in effective knowledge management. The article demonstrates how internal auditors in General Motors Corporation, Ford Motor Company, Xerox Corporation and Tosco Corporation are developing their knowledge management strategies and skills, as well as contributing to the dissemination of knowledge about control and risk across their organisations. All use databases linked to electronic communication systems to communicate their knowledge, both globally within their internal auditing functions and across their organisations. Each sees this as an added value to the services they provide. It improves the quality of audits and increases management awareness of best practices. For those internal auditing functions with a high turnover rate their planned and structured sharing of knowledge is seen to continuously improve the performance of all levels of staff, whether new or experienced, contributing to better teamwork, supervision and management of all resources.

It is not only large internal auditing functions that embrace the challenges of Intranet to spread knowledge throughout their services. The internal audit manager of Network Housing Association, London, has used her organisation's Intranet to establish a 'home site' for internal auditing. This site spreads up-to-date knowledge of its staffing, charter, audit planning, risk assessments, auditing procedures and quality assurance measures for all the organisations it serves. Capturing such knowledge, and keeping it up-to-date, provides an important stimulus and challenge for its internal auditing staff, as excellent learning processes.

But it is not just in-house Intranet knowledge that internal auditors should manage. Worldwide websites now provide large databases of knowledge with powerful search engines. There can be few internal auditing activities that could not benefit from knowledge freely available on websites set up outside the organisations they serve. All internal audits, risk assessments and consultancy activities need to manage and search this external knowledge. Any internal auditors today that do not reference into internet websites are weakened by a less than complete understanding of the knowledge available for the services they provide.

The IIA has also published guidance on the use of the internet by internal auditors. Written by an internal auditor this book provides:

> '... options for accessing the Internet, useful Internet tools and services for audit professionals, a comprehensive list of available resources, and case studies of how internal auditors use the Internet for audit-related work.'

The author, Jim Kaplan, has his own website (www.auditnet.org) providing useful references for all internal auditors seeking to increase their knowledge and the value of their services.

Creating frameworks for the implementation of good knowledge management practices has occupied many consultants over the past few years. Bain & Company's research lists knowledge management requirements as:

- 'Catalog and evaluate the organisation's current knowledge base;
- Determine which competencies will be key to future success and what base of knowledge is needed to build a sustainable leadership position therein;
- Invest in systems and processes to accelerate the accumulation of knowledge;
- Assess the impact of such systems on leadership, culture, and hiring practices;
- Codify new knowledge and turn it into tools and information that will improve both product innovation and overall profitability.'

Lloyd sees:

> '... a close link among data, information, knowledge and wisdom ...'

He argues that:

> '... we start with wisdom and that provides the framework within which to manage knowledge ...'

His definition of wisdom is the combination of knowledge and values. It is the use to which knowledge is put that is critical in all knowledge management processes. Being wise after the event is frequent. The art of good internal auditing must always be to be wise before the event. Being wise about knowledge before the event is a key to success in all internal auditing services.

Knowledge management will always be key to innovation and creativity in all sciences. Whether you view internal auditing as a profession, science or art, or none of these, there is no doubt that it requires well-managed knowledge to add value in all the services it provides. Knowledge not just of the organisation but also knowledge that is available outside the organisation. There are many roles for internal auditors to occupy in knowledge management; as a user, as a communicator and a provider of assurance. Roles that now require wise internal auditors to have the knowledge to be not only good auditors, but also to be good teachers and consultants.

# A3.2.22   **Controlling the outsourced internal auditing contract**

*Geoffrey Clark has contributed this article. He is a director of Internal Audit Services Limited, which offers a particularly interesting approach to the provision of outsourced internal auditing services. Internal Audit Services maintains a large database of skilled internal auditors and in our experience usually has been able to meet the needs of businesses for contracted out internal auditing using locally or semi-locally based internal auditors with the appropriate sector-specific backgrounds. This approach to outsourced internal audit provision very often results in mature internal auditors, perhaps early-retired people, being matched to client needs at very reasonable cost. It is surprising how much internal auditor expertise there is 'out there' which Internal Audit Services database is able to access.*

*These are intended as practical tips to purchasers on how to manage an outsourced contract. The perspective is that of a niche provider putting himself into the shoes of prospective purchasers. This is not an academic approach and there are no statistics. This article is based purely on personal experience and belief. For soundly based academic research, the right starting point would be 'The Outsourcing Dilemma: What's Best for Internal Auditing', by Larry E Rittenberg and Mark Covaleski, published in 1997 by The Institute of Internal Auditors Research Foundation (USA): ISBN 0–89413-384–5.*

## *Background*

Our experience is that the internal audit market is expanding steadily. It seems that with each passing year, more people can claim to be internal auditors; and there is a shortage of internal audit skills. Clearly, this is a very positive environment for all internal auditors. In terms of outsourced internal audit, the expansion is more uneven and is subject to flux.

The reasons for the steady expansion overall are well known. One is the stricter regulatory environment that has grown up over the last ten years. The same causes also may be attributed to the expansion of outsourced internal auditing; but outsourced internal auditing owes its development to other factors as well. One is the new wider availability; there are now a broader range of providers and more modes of provision existing in the marketplace. Providers range from 'one person bands' through to the very large firms of accountants, and down again to smaller specialist niche firms.

An increasing amount of marketing is being undertaken by all these providers. Although this marketing expenditure primarily is intended to feed opportunities through to individual firms, the expanded marketing effort has had the general effect of encouraging the take-up of internal audit, for the benefit of everyone engaged in this activity.

## *Options*

As regards mode of provision, the range of options has increased for purchasers. These are not restricted to a straight choice between in-house provision and a total outsourcing of the service. There are now many hybrids available, such as the outsourcing of certain skills, languages, countries, trading divisions or subsidiaries; or of particular parts of the work plan; or of the assessment of risk; or of the assessment of the performance of the internal auditing activity itself.

Some purchasers have outsourced the work of all except the head of audit, who remains as the only direct employee of the organisation. There are also examples of splitting higher level strategic work from field audit work: that is, outsourcing one while retaining the other in-house.

Thus the possible permutations have expanded greatly. Alongside all of these changes, the culture and attitudes of purchasers have changed. There is a great deal less reticence about hiring in whatever additional resources are needed on an *ad hoc* basis. This might be to catch up with a work plan that has fallen behind or to provide maternity leave cover, and so on.

All of these changes appear to have occurred mainly over the last ten years and they thus indicate a sea-change in attitudes and behaviour over that time.

## Outsourcing drivers

We can sum up the drivers behind the expansion of outsourcing in general, as distinct from internal audit in particular, as being the following:

- import the culture of casual labour from other activities eg dock labour; legal, accountancy and other professions; building industry;
- external pressures eg legislative pressures such as the Employment Protection Act (1974);
- internal pressures eg the cost of internal resources needs to be reduced; or the size of the organisation is too small for internal auditing to be in-house;
- precedent; or trend set by others in other areas eg in manufacturing by Marks & Spencer since the 1930s; facilities management from the 1980s; IT from the 1990s;
- a need for a flexible resource or a different mix of skills; and
- the increasing availability of supply eg Brook Street Bureau formed in late 1940s; Manpower from the USA in 1964; Capita, sold off by CIPFA in 1988; and many others entering the market since then.

Most of the drivers imply that it is essentially labour that is being outsourced. However, in some instances it is know-how which is the sought after resource. Most of these drivers apply as much to the growth in outsourcing of internal audit as to the outsourcing of other activities.

Further factors specifically driving the expansion of outsourcing of internal audit have included:

- compulsion eg local government compulsory competitive tendering (1994), best value (1999); directives to NHS trusts to form audit committees; directives to housing associations by the Housing Corporation making internal audit mandatory (1995); other changes in the regulatory framework;

- as regards quoted companies, coercion or changes in best practice eg Cadbury (1992), the Combined Code (1999), the Turnbull Committee (1999), Smith (2003), Higgs (2003), Sarbanes-Oxley (2002, USA); the appointment of non-executive directors; the formation of audit committees; the need for improved internal controls;
- elevation in importance of corporate governance matters generally to the wider audience eg to bankers, suppliers, customers, regulators, shareholders, prospective investors/venture capitalists;
- 'bad news' events eg Barings, Maxwell, Enron, WorldCom etc;
- perceptions of new risks and the need for an outside perspective;
- insufficient skills, or a need for a different mix of skills;
- a growing need for a truly independent view;
- a greater 'ability to let go': that is, the ability of purchasers to trust and have confidence in an alternative mode of supply, as manifested for instance by the esteem in which the provider is generally held, the quality of references from other clients, the quality of the tender submission (if applicable), adherence to standards and guidelines, adherence to quality standards (eg ISO 9001), membership of professional institutes and adherence to codes of professional ethics;
- supply availability eg from external auditors, from the 'Big Four' firms, from smaller and local accountancy practices, from specialist/niche providers, from consortium arrangements (common in the NHS), and from in-house departments seeking third party clients; and
- growth of joint ventures.

All of these drivers have worked powerfully together to build momentum to a point where expansion is now inevitable and unstoppable. However that expansion is not steady and rapid, but is rather characterised by a state of flux around a cycle.

## Advantages and disadvantages of outsourcing

Dennis Cox from Prudential Fund Managers, who gave the April 1999 Internal Auditing Moorgate Lecture, listed some advantages as being:

- introduces new skills;
- third party knowledge;
- resources when required; and
- total independence.

Note that these skills imply the provision of know-how rather than labour.

Cox listed these disadvantages:

- integration with suppliers;
- service level may fluctuate;
- loss of key skills;
- change to corporate culture; and
- price.

'Integration with suppliers' means there is a danger in treating the outsourced internal audit provider as just another supplier. We would not treat the statutory auditors or other professionals in this way, but rather as strategic advisers who provide important know-how and ongoing support.

Some of the disadvantages Cox mentions can also be advantages, for example bringing change to corporate culture, or a price advantage.

## Approaches to outsourcing

Various approaches can be adopted by a purchaser, some of which have already been referred to. We can sum up the options with respect to approach as being:

- a work plan totally devolved on the provider to carry out;
- a work plan partially devolved on the provider; and
- secondments of staff to existing (perhaps reduced) in-house departments on a call-off basis.

The preparation of a work plan itself can be devolved on the provider, or can be produced prescriptively by the client. A consensus approach is preferable whereby the provider independently produces a draft work plan based on an assessment of risk, and then produces a definitive plan that takes into account the stated desires of the client including the client's audit committee.

As regards the composition of the plan, or the assignment brief, clients naturally do have their own agenda, even if sometimes that agenda is hidden. Motives differ, and may include that:

- the client seeks a good image for its corporate governance, perhaps above all else;
- the client has a minimalist approach, to be able to say 'we have internal audit' is enough!; or
- the client seeks ongoing comfort on very specific controls only – eg takings to bank, computer audit, etc.

These differing motives will inevitably affect the approach of the provider.

## Key features and principles of a contract

In the contract itself it is better to err on the side of formality if in doubt. Of course, that requires a written contract. Whether this should be a document entitled 'contract', a written tender, or merely an exchange of correspondence is for the parties to determine. Apart from the actual selection process, these are some of the key points to consider and to cover when constructing a contract:

- an outsourced business is still your business;
- define the level(s) in the hierarchy at which the provider is to report;
- define the degree of autonomy to be granted to provider in assessing risk, compiling the work plan, setting objectives, and commencing audits;

- identify which skills are to be outsourced;
- define deliverables like audit reports, etc;
- monitor supplier activity and performance;
- ensure there is a corrective mechanism for when things go wrong;
- ensure there is a cessation mechanism for when things go very wrong; and
- there must also be charging and invoicing mechanisms, including submission of detailed time sheets and expense claims.

## Controlling the internal audit contract

There are particular key control mechanisms to be used when controlling a contract, once it is activated. For instance:

- fix audit committee and other periodic review meetings, including dates;
- check invoices to time sheets and expenses claims;
- keep copies of all correspondence, faxes and e-mails;
- get feedback from audited entities on performance;
- complete customer satisfaction questionnaires when requested by the provider; it is helpful feedback to the provider;
- institute a formal annual performance appraisal including a written report.

## Summary

Internal auditing is expanding. Outsourcing of internal audit is expanding along with outsourcing generally. However, this is not 'mono-directional'; the mode of supply will change and go through cycles. Outsourcing is primarily a matter of outsourcing the provision of know-how, not just of labour. Of course, there are advantages and disadvantages; and the range of options and permutations available to purchasers is increasingly sophisticated. Invariably, the contract should be written; while it may take various forms, there are a number of key factors to remember and include when constructing a contract, and there are also certain important control mechanisms to help control the contract.

Internal Audit Services can be contacted at Hornefield House, David Street, Meopham, Kent, DA12 0BT (tel: +44 (0)1474 813052; fax: +44 (0)1474 812498; email: RGC@internalaudit.co.uk).

## A3.2.23    Computer-assisted auditing techniques – automating the audit

Here we introduce the different opportunities to automate the audit, approaching the subject topic by topic. 'Automating the audit' is an expression of the late 1980s which has been used to 'label' particular types of computer-based methodologies which are becoming available to auditors. Of course, audit software has been available since the early 1960s and so the more recent expression 'automating the audit' has tended to be loosely applied to the more recent developments whereas the older expressions, 'computer-assisted auditing techniques' (CAATs) and 'generalised audit software', are terms now often used to refer only to the earlier techniques (most notably audit interrogation software) although these expressions are really interchangeable with 'automating the audit'.

Originally (late-1960s and 1970s) computer-based auditing techniques fell into two categories, and these two traditional categories still provide a useful insight into audit software to assist in the technical aspects of an audit. These two categories were:

- Techniques for the review of systems controls;
- Techniques for the review of real data.

There is also audit-related software for administrative purposes, such as:

- Departmental administration, such as automating administration at the internal audit function/activity level. An example is time reporting (recording and analysis) software.
- Audit administration, such as automating administration at the level of an individual audit. Examples are project management software and electronic audit working papers.
- Departmental technical support, such as decision support on matters of audit judgment which have to be determined at departmental level. An example would be audit needs assessment software.
- Audit technical support, such as automated assistance in the performance of technical as opposed to administrative steps which are part of the conduct of an audit. One example would be frisk assessment software. Another example would be audit interrogation software such as IDEA or ACL.
- For security and control. Strictly this is not audit software but may sometimes be useful for auditors. Examples would be software to analyse journal logs of terminal activity, or software to eavesdrop on terminal activity.

No classification is entirely watertight between the various categories and in this case, for instance, it may be rather arbitrary as to whether an available technique is classified as an administrative or a technical audit aid.

## A3.2.24   *Techniques for the review of systems controls*

Techniques for the review of systems controls focus on the procedures of the system rather than on the data. These techniques are intended to confirm to the auditor that the programmed procedures of the system are effective. By implication, if the procedures are sound the auditor obtains some *indirect* confirmation that the data held on the computer files is also sound. These techniques used to be widely used by external auditors, but more recently external auditors have tended to make more use of *techniques for the review of real data* since these latter techniques provide *direct* confirmation that data is valid – and thus provide direct audit reassurance about the correctness of the year-end financial statements which are being audited. Since these techniques concentrate on control procedures they are important to internal auditors who have an obligation to reassure management that internal control is sound – including the controls built into computer-based systems.

An example of a technique for the review of systems controls is the test data method. Originally this was commonly a pack of punched cards of input data to a client system, designed by the auditor to contain within the pack as many conditions of potential audit interest as possible. Strictly speaking this is not an audit software technique as the software the auditor is using is the software that management is using to run their computer applications – more literally it is an *audit data technique*. The auditor would process this audit input through the client's application software and check from the output that everything had been processed correctly. In that way the auditor could obtain reassurance on the adequacy of the programmed controls built into the application programmes. Another use of this technique, especially favoured by external auditors, was to process through the client's system the same test pack annually: if the output was unchanged from the year before, the auditor would obtain some reassurance that the client had not significantly modified the system in respect of the conditions contained within the auditor's test pack. As punched cards were superseded, the auditor's test data came to be held on other media – especially magnetic tape and diskettes.

To be effective, this audit technique requires care to ensure that the programs which are used to process the auditor's test data are the same programs that management uses to process their transactions. This cannot be automatically assumed as, to be safe, it is generally necessary to set up a special run to process the auditor's test data. Mixing the auditor's test data with real, live data is generally too risky in terms of corrupting the output of the system.

A limitation of this technique is that it can only be a test of the control and other procedures of which the auditor is aware. It cannot be regarded as a 100% test of all routines built into the computer programs of the application. For instance, if a fraudulent programmer had coded a program so that a double payment was made when an asterisk appeared in a particular input field, the test data method would never notice this as the auditor would never think of putting an asterisk in that field.

### A3.2.25 Integrated test facility (ITF)

A development of the test data method, it entails incorporation into management's computer-based applications of a built-in test facility which the auditors can use. For instance, if a sales ledger application were divided into twelve sections, a thirteenth section could be provided for. The auditor could maintain dummy accounts in Section 13, processing dummy transactions against those accounts so as to test that the programmed procedures of the application functioned satisfactorily. It is a more effective audit tool that the traditional test data method as it allows for a more continuous audit testing. The test data method has the audit limitation that it is a test of the computer-based procedures which were current at the time of the test only.

No audit testing method gives 100% audit reassurance: one of the limitations of the integrated test facility is that the application programs have to be coded so as to be able to distinguish audit test data from real, live data – which means that there is some risk that the auditor's data receives special treatment by the computer programs.

Since this method usually requires audit specification at the design stage of the system, it is more likely to be driven by internal audit; but external auditors may make use of the facility. There is sometimes a problem with multiple use of the same facility by auditors and others (such as the system development group).

### A3.2.26   Other techniques for the review of systems controls

Auditors may make use of many other software tools to provide audit reassurance about procedures of a computer-based system. For instance:

- Code comparison software to compare two versions of a program.
- Flowchart generation software.
- Mapping software to trace the logical path taken through a computer program when it is used (especially useful to identify programmed routines which are not being accessed).

## A3.2.27   *Software for the review of real data*

This is software targeted at management data held on computer files. It provides *direct* audit assurance on validity of data held on computer files. *Indirectly* it indicates to the auditor whether the procedures of the system have been working properly – as invalid data may indicate deficient controls. Generalised audit software, sometimes termed 'audit interrogation software', is the commonest example of this. This can be instructed to look for conditions on computer files, for example:

- customers whose credit limits have been exceeded;
- large or slow moving items;
- negative balances;
- duplicate records;
- incomplete records;
- etc.

Generalised audit software can also be instructed to:

- provide totals of file amounts;
- provide totals of error conditions detected on files;
- perform an aged analysis of a file;
- select a sample for further audit investigation;
- perform debtors and creditors circularisations;
- etc.

An attraction of generalised audit software for the auditor is that it is the auditor's own software. Whether or not other users make use of the same audit interrogation software, it is software *outside* the software of the application. It can therefore provide powerful confirmation that the application software has performed properly.

### A3.2.28   Embedded audit monitors and real-time auditing

Variously known as 'integrated audit monitors', 'embedded audit software', 'resident audit programs' etc, these are a sophisticated variant of generalised audit software. They represent audit programming resident in an on-line, real-time system, continuously monitoring transactions as they are being processed. When conditions are detected by the monitor which fit a profile indicating potential audit interest, details are recorded to an auditor's disk file – available only to the auditor via the auditor's terminal. In a sense, the auditor is collecting his or her own audit trail and is not dependent upon the trail left by the system.

Undoubtedly the incorporation of audit software into the IT applications of an enterprise, or into their operating system software, represents a sophisticated approach to automated auditing. It usually requires the internal audit function to specify its requirements at the design stage of a new system and preferably to program the audit software independently. Then the audit software, embedded into the production system or into its operating system software, conducts audit monitoring on behalf of the auditor of transactions while they are being processed. Items of audit interest are recorded to a special audit file which the auditor reviews via his or her terminal at a later stage. In this way the auditor is creating audit trail and is not dependent upon records left behind by the system after processing in order to find evidence of events of audit interest. Protagonists of this approach to auditing point out that it is logical for the audit department to use real-time, online auditing techniques as these are likely to be necessary for effective auditing of real-time, online systems which management are now using.

Unlike the traditional generalised audit software method, this method is not dependent on evidence being left behind on computer files after processing is completed. Neither is it a 'point-in-time' audit technique as the monitoring can be continuous except when it has been switched off by the auditor.

Since this method requires specification of audit software at the design stage of the system, it is more likely to be a feasible technique for internal rather than external auditors.

### A3.2.29   *Digital analysis tests and 'Benford's Law'*

'In any large database of naturally occurring numerical information, such as a list of cities ranked by population or islands ranked by surface area, the number "one" will probably be the first digit of 30.1 per cent of the database's numbers (1, 15, 199, 1003, and so on). A "two" will probably occur in 17.6 per cent of the numbers (2, 27, 200 and so on); and the probability reduces to 4.6 per cent for a "nine" appearing as the first digit.'

'Digital analysis is being used by listed companies, large private companies, professional firms and government agencies in the US and Europe – and by one of the world's biggest accounting firms.' (*Mark Nigrini*)

Benford was a physicist working for General Electric when he discovered this 'first-digit phenomenon' in 1938. But as far back as 1881 one Simon Newcomb wrote a note to the American Journal of Mathematics pointing out that he had noticed that early pages of books of logarithms were more grubby than later pages, undoubtedly due to their more frequent use. More recently, Mark Nigrini showed how it could be applied to detecting fraud in his PhD thesis published in 1992. He is author and publisher of 'Digital Analysis Tests and Statistics'.

Benford's Law holds because 'large things are made up of lots of little things', to quote Nigrini. For instance, there are thousands of small islands but only a few continents; thousands of tributaries but fewer rivers. Looked at another way, the 'gap' between 'one' and 'two' is greater than the gap between 'eight' and 'nine' in that, for instance, growing a business from a turnover of £1 million to a turnover of £2 million entails doubling its size, which is not the case with the incremental growth from £8 million to £9 million.

The law applies most faithfully when there is no natural limit to what is being measured, as there is with, for instance, the height or weight of people. It may not apply if numbers are, quite legitimately, rounded up or down. In business it can be expected to apply, for instance, to stock market prices, sales figures, payments, census data, ragbags of figures extracted from documents, declared income, suspicious data in clinical trails, suspicious data in quality assurance test results, data in laboratory notebooks, etc. Sometimes it may be possible to apply Benford's Law to optimising the use of space in warehouses, or storage space in computer systems.

Logic exists within ACL (Audit Command Language) to check quickly a large database for conformity to Benford's Law. ACL is one of the two leading generalised auditing packages, the other being IDEA (Interactive Data Extraction and Analysis). One group of auditors who are pursuing this approach is the North Yorkshire Audit Partnership based at Scarborough Borough Council where James Ingham is the audit manager involved. The technique is quite widely used, for instance within Proctor & Gamble, Colgate-Palmolive and American Airlines. In the US, The Institute of Internal Auditors Inc now runs training courses on applying Benford's Law in fraud investigations, and have claimed it to be the biggest advance in the field for years.

References and contact details on Benford's Law:

- ACL Services Ltd, 575 Richards Street, Vancouver BC, V6B 2Z5, Canada (tel: +1 604 669 4225; www.acl.com).
- Robert Matthews (10 July 1999): 'The Power of One' (New Scientist).
- Mark Nigrini: mark_nigrini@email.msn.com. Author of 'Digital Analysis Tests and Statistics'. He is professor of accountancy at Southern Methodist University, Dallas.
- James Ingham: jringham@ukonline.co.uk who is using the technique in audit contexts.
- Eric Weisstein: 'Treasure Troves of Science'.

## A3.2.30   *Electronic audit working papers*

The heart of automating the audit is to develop a system of electronic audit working papers to replace the paper-based files of completed standard audit working paper forms which still characterise so much auditing work. No longer do pads of standard forms have to be carried to audit locations. No longer is it so necessary for an audit manager to visit auditors 'in the field' in order to review completed audit working paper files – these can now be transmitted to the audit manager at Audit HQ or at home for his or her review. This can be done from the auditor's laptop computer via a modem to the audit manager's equivalent computer.

Standard word processing and spreadsheet software is all that is needed to develop and use a reasonably satisfactory system of electronic audit working papers for internal audit purposes. Standard audit working paper forms can be designed to be called up and completed on the computer screen. Of course the same word processing software will have other audit uses, notably for drafting the audit report preferably towards the end of the audit field work. Tailor-made audit working paper software may have special advantages as it can be designed to allow logical steps to be automated, eg:

- Automated checking of electronic working papers for completeness:
    - Is there evidence of supervision and review on each schedule?
    - Is there an audit conclusion on each lead schedule?
    - Have all points raised by the auditors on 'audit point sheets' been answered?
- Automated checking of electronic working papers for accuracy:
    - Do all numeric data foot and cross foot?
    - Do numeric totals carry forward accurately to lead schedules?
- Automated processing:
    - Footing and cross footing (but note that standard word processing software can do this).
    - Carry forward of numeric data to lead schedules.
    - Highlighting of unsatisfactory findings for audit management review.
    - Highlighting of proposed audit recommendations for audit management review.
    - Consolidation and reformatting of material contained within the audit working papers in order to prepare the draft audit report.

# Proficiency and care in internal auditing – case studies

## A3.3.1 Not just a matter of early recognition of sales – the twisted yarn at a carpet retailer

'The Board has thoroughly investigated the circumstances surrounding the early recognition of sales and a detailed report was released on 26 August 1998, and is being made available to all shareholders with the report and accounts. Whilst the practice was widespread, it did not result in any personal financial gain or direct loss of cash or property to the Group. The underlying strength of the Group's operations and its balance sheet remain, and its future profit earning ability is unimpaired.'

So the chairman reported. But it resulted in the resignation or dismissal of two main board directors as well as a senior manager, the collapse of the share price and the suspension of the shares by the Stock Exchange; and then, inexorably, in the takeover of XYZ plc at a knock down price by an overseas company. And all because of a problem with sales cut off – or did it go deeper than that?

The chairman did indeed apologise to the shareholders:

'I preface my review with an apology to all our shareholders. I deeply regret that the error took place in the timing of the recognition of sales and the impact it has had on our Company.'

In what seems to have been a classic case of whistleblowing, an XYZ plc employee informed the external auditors who in turn, after conducting their own investigation, informed the board – not all of whom, as we shall see, were entirely unaware of the matter. In an implied admission of an autocratic management style ruled by fear, the directors were later to report that:

'the Company will develop a culture which encourages staff to report concerns and potential improvements in operating practice'.

The absence of such a culture must have been the main reason why the malpractice continued so long. Indeed, it is our belief that every company should have a whistleblowing policy, and every company of significant size should have a whistle-blowing statement.

We can expect the external auditor to pay close attention to the treatment of sales cut-off at the end of the financial year. Getting it wrong can overstate or understate sales. It is usually when sales are *overstated*, as in this case, that the alarm bells start ringing. It can also lead to double counting of goods as being in stock and also being in sales, fictitiously strengthening the balance sheet as well as the profit.

It took several years and a tip off to the external auditors to catch up with it. We can only assume that there must have been a suggestion of deliberately hoodwinking the auditors – and there was so little point in it. But once a malpractice has been started, it can be so difficult to back out of it.

It all started as a temporary expedient several years earlier. The board had approved excessively tough sales targets which could only be met by 'borrowing' sales from the start of the following year and treating them as if they had been sales in the old year. 'Met', the targets were; and so sales targets were raised for the following year. Of course they were harder to achieve because sales which rightly belonged to that year had already been accounted for as sales of the previous year. So the temporary expedient became a permanent practice which tended to escalate as one year faded into the next with only a hazy cut-off between the two; and the company became immersed in an ever increasing fraud which was bound to be discovered but was very difficult to extricate itself from without drawing attention to it. It was a *management* fraud as distinct from an employee fraud and must have required collusion on a wide scale – in both its perpetration and in its concealment.


## THE CHRONOLOGY

| | |
|---|---|
| May 98: | XYZ plc issued the first of two profits warnings. |
| 6 July 98: | The external auditors informed the board about the matter. |
| 13 July 98: | The board asked the Stock Exchange to suspend dealings in its shares. |
| 19 August 98: | The Group Finance and Management Information Systems Director tendered his resignation. |
| 26 August 98: | The shares were relisted |
| by 26 August 98: | The Senior Operations Manager had been suspended and had then resigned |
| 26 August 98: | The directors published a report on the matter at the same time as releasing the year end results. XYZ plc Group Managing Director had originally hoped that the special review of the matter, commissioned from the external auditors, would have been completed within two weeks so that the annual results could have been announced at the end of July as planned. |
| 23 April 99: | The Group Managing Director was dismissed |
| mid-August: | Brown & Jackson make an indicative offer to acquire XYZ plc at 50.5p a share. |
| end of August: | Wassall makes an offer to acquire XYZ plc. |
| 8 September 99: | XYZ plc agree an £84.2m cash bid (93p/share) from ABC, a French carpet company, nine minutes after belatedly announcing that it was again being investigated for fraud, this time by the Department of Trade and Industry. |

| 8 September 99: | Wassall withdrew and made about £20m. Wassell had built up a 24% stake, just under 15% of which was acquired at an average of 53p a share, and the rest at 80p a share. |
| --- | --- |

| Chairman: | He had been the non-executive chairman since XYZ plc came onto the market in 1996 on the back of a prospectus signed off by the external auditors. He was an accountant, who used to work for the external auditors – a fact which XYZ plc 1997/98 annual report did not mention. |
| --- | --- |
| Group managing director: | He had been XYZ plc's founder and was dismissed as group managing director in April 1999. |
| Senior operations manager: | Not a member of the board, he resigned apparently because he knew all about the malpractice. |
| Group finance and management information systems director: | He resigned apparently because he did not know about the malpractice. |

## NON-COMPLIANCE WITH THE GROUP'S STATED ACCOUNTING POLICY

The point 'when a sale becomes a sale' is when legal title passes from the supplier to the customer. Possibly it would have been defensible to regard a sale to a customer just before the end of the year as belonging to that year even if the carpet were not in stock and could not be delivered for a month or two – particularly as in most cases the customer, we are told, had paid up front. The trouble was that XYZ plc's annual report regularly misled shareholders with words to the effect that:

> 'Group turnover comprises the value of sales excluding VAT and intra-group transactions. Turnover is recognised when the goods have been delivered to the customer's home or collected from the store.'

For five years, sales in all of XYZ plc's 258 stores had been recorded early for goods still in the stockrooms of the stores and which had been ordered by customers and in most cases fully paid for (called 'pre-dispatching'). In the latter years this practice applied to interim (half-year) results too. Had it not done so, interim results would have looked particularly poor. So there was an early recognition of profit.

There was clearly a risk that the goods were also counted as still being in stock. It seems that this was so, especially in view of the size of the accounting adjustment which had to be made when the practice came to light. The directors' report of 26 August 1998 on the practice acknowledged that they were improving stocktaking procedures which suggests that 'double counting' was indeed an element of this affair. The company operated a perpetual inventory system with periodic stock counts. There had been a full stock count in March 1998, four months before the board were told by the external auditors about the problem, and indeed stock in some stores had been counted again in May/June 1998. A perpetual inventory system should have safeguarded against double counting of stock in both sales and in inventory, as the system would take out of inventory the carpets which the system regarded as sales. Perhaps the physical counts of stock towards the 27 June 1998 year end were relied upon to provide the year-end stock figures, meaning that adjustments would have been made of the stock balances per the perpetual inventory records to reflect what was actually present in the warehouses. If this was so, it is a salutary reminder that the physical count is not necessarily the figure to rely upon.

On the positive side, the directors were able to report that there had been no loss of goods or cash, and there was no evidence of personal financial gain. But we do not know the extent to which past bonuses had been related to performance which had been inflated by 'pre-dispatching'.

## THE INFORMATION ANGLE

'Pre-dispatching' resulted in incorrect information in relation to delivery dates and fitting, and, as a consequence, the early recognition of sales. Insufficient information regarding prior years prevented reliably establishing the effect of early recognition of sales in those years.

XYZ plc had one director who was responsible for finance, accounting and management information. The company said he was unaware of the practice and as a consequence he resigned when the practice came to light. The implication, which carries a warning for all finance directors with these responsibilities, is that his focus on group issues meant that he was out of touch with the 'detail' of accounting at the level of the stores – perhaps not surprising with such a broad scope of responsibility. It is of course at the level of the basic inputs to the accounting records that the figures must be right if the management accounts are to be dependable and the financial statements are to be true. Today's typical board is smaller than it used to be, but there is a risk in vesting too much responsibility in one person.

## THE FINANCIAL CONSEQUENCES

We know that sales for the year which ended on 27 June 1998 were overstated by £6.4m in respect of goods not delivered as at 27 June 1998. Sales for that year must have been *understated* in respect of goods delivered at the start of the year but regarded as sales of the previous year. The published accounts showed an exceptional item of £3m with the note:

> 'The net cumulative effect of the error at 27 June 1998 amounting to sales of £6,400,000 and an operating profit charge of £3,000,000, has been recognised in the current year since it is not possible to quantify reliably the element relating to 1997 and prior years. The charge includes associated costs of £900,000 which are included in operating expenses. Therefore the directors recorded an exceptional item of £3m which reduced profits for the year ended 27 June 1998 by £3m to £11.2m. The adjustment comprised £2.1m relating to early recognition of sales and £900,000 being the costs (inquiry: £348,000; management changes: £377,000; professional costs for re-listing £175,000).'

Note how much of the hit to the accounts – almost one third of the total – was down to the direct costs of sorting out the problem. Of course that overlooks the other costs associated with staff morale and the low level of confidence which manage-ment must have felt they could place in the management accounts. When the dishonesty of senior staff is known of or suspected it encourages the development of fraudulent ideas in the minds of more junior staff.

A year later, early in September 1999, XYZ plc reported a pre-tax loss of £4.25m for their 1998–99 year compared to the previous year's profit (after the exceptional item) of £11.2m. This was a loss per share of 4.36p compared to earnings per share of 8.53p. The final dividend was passed leaving the total at 0.5p compared to the previous year of 7.75p. One wonders what the board had in mind when it declared the interim dividend of 0.5p.

We can see the impact of this affair on the movements in XYZ plc share price, though there were also other influences at work. In particular XYZ plc were to be criticised for a lack of a credible top management with a clear strategy. XYZ plc had floated in July 1997 at 215p, hitting a high of 320p in January 1998, but in May 1998 the first of two profits warnings wiped 50p off share price. By April 1999, when the unfavourable publicity about the malpractice had had its full effect, the shares had collapsed to 36.5p, and continued to trade at below 40p until reports of a possible bid. On August 19, 1999 they rose to 48p after an indicative bid, rising to 61.5p a day later and 70.5p on 24 August. It was reported that 'XYZ plc is certainly trying to raise the share price in order to escape the offer altogether or make sure it is not taken on the cheap'. In the event, on 8 September 1999 XYZ plc agreed to a 93p per share bid from ABC, the French carpet company.


REPUTATIONAL LOSS

In today's business environment, building and cherishing the reputation of the company is the most important trust that top management and the board have. The relentless scrutiny of companies' affairs by analysts, media and others means that there are now no dark corners where dubious practices can be concealed for long. In today's designer-conscious world the corporate brand and its product brands determine market success and can be damaged beyond repair by unfavourable publicity. Consumers and investors quickly dessert in droves. On the other hand, a crisis handled quickly, firmly and appropriately can enhance the reputation of the management team. But in this case it was the opposite of that with the group managing director only being fired nine months after the crisis broke.

Here are some of the negative media comments at the time:

> 'Assuming the current management can deliver on its promises, the theoretical upside in the share price is higher than what any bidder would offer today.'

> 'Restoring the company's threadbare credibility is bound to take more time than will be pledged in the excitement of a looming bid battle.'

> 'For us, the main attraction of the company was its price.'

> 'Shareholders have seen their investment crumble in the past two years because of poor management and accounting irregularities.'

When the new group managing director took over in July 1999 he said:

'People have got to decide whether [I am the same as my predecessor] who over-promised and under-delivered constantly … I am not here to apologise for [him] and his team, but I am having trouble getting rid of the bad taste. I understand that. When I arrived and asked to see [his] three-year strategy, there wasn't one. There was an over-optimistic budgeting in the belief that the market would come along and save them.'


CORPORATE GOVERNANCE ANGLES

When the malpractice became known, the Stock Exchange demanded a detailed report on XYZ plc's internal controls. This was commissioned by the company from their external auditor and a summary was sent out with the 1997–98 annual report to the shareholders. It was a sound approach that the auditors' special report was addressed to the chairman and to the non-executive directors, implying that it was they who insisted on the inquiry, and acknowledging the special role of the non-executive directors in resolving issues of this sort. It is a good illustration of the need for non-executive directors, some or all of whom should be independent, on the board.

The chairman's statement in that report included the following:

### 'Code of Best Practice
The Board reports on its compliance with the Code of Best Practice of the Cadbury Committee on page 19. During the year there was a breakdown of financial controls in respect of sales recognition procedures in branches. A thorough review has taken place to ensure, so far as possible, that such an event cannot recur. Specific actions to be taken as a result of this review are set out in the Directors' report. As chairman, I have overall responsibility for ensuring appropriate implementation of these changes and for continued monitoring of the Group's compliance with its internal policies and procedures. Otherwise I am satisfied that we continue to follow best practice in all areas of corporate governance.'

and on page 19 the Directors' report on internal control described the matter in these words:

'During the year a breakdown of financial controls in respect of sales cut-off procedures in branches was discovered. A thorough review of the Group's financial reporting procedures has been completed in order to ensure, so far as possible, that such an event cannot recur. Specific actions to be taken as a result of this review include:
(i)    strengthened director presence in operations;
(ii)   outsourcing of internal audit;
(iii)  modification of management accounting;
(iv)  improved stock-taking procedures; and
(v)   the development of a company culture which encourages staff to report concerns and potential improvements in operating practice.

The Chairman will have overall responsibility for ensuring appropriate implementation of these changes and for continued monitoring of the Group's compliance with its policies and procedures.'

We wonder why the audit committee as well as the board itself were not given a key role in monitoring compliance.

In reporting in this way, the company was complying with the Rutteman guidance on the Cadbury Code provision that directors should report on the effectiveness of internal control. At that time, it was the Rutteman guidance rather than the new Turnbull guidance which applied, and Rutteman required that material breakdowns in internal financial control should be addressed in the directors' report on internal control, specifying the actions taken or to be taken to prevent a recurrence, or why the directors considered no action was needed. Of course, it was the former in this case.

This Code provision has been modified in the new Combined Code so that directors in compliance with the equivalent Code provision now have to report on *all* aspects of internal control. It is no longer just internal financial control which has to be reported but operational and compliance (legal and regulatory) control as well, as well as risk management.

Arguably this XYZ plc affair was as much a breakdown of internal operational control as it was of internal financial control and this will often be so in such cases. The XYZ plc directors' internal control report draws attention to the changes being made in operational control as well as to the changes in internal financial control – both of which together were designed to prevent the problem continuing.

The new Turnbull guidance uses the same test of materiality to determine whether the directors need to address a breakdown in operational control or compliance control as Rutteman gave for breakdowns in internal financial control. The test is that if the event(s) was so serious that it was mentioned somewhere within the annual report and accounts (and it occurred because of a breakdown in internal control) then the control aspects of it should also be addressed in the directors' internal control report. The snag is that directors have more discretion as to whether they refer to a material breakdown in operational or compliance control than they do with respect to breakdowns in internal financial control. This is a consequence of accounting and auditing standards prescribing quite precisely what has to be disclosed in the annual financial statements. So if the material problem was operational in nature, to which there was no obligation to refer in the financial statements, then the directors could avoid having to refer to the matter in their internal control report by simply making sure that there was no reference to the matter anywhere else in the annual report.

We also consider that had the new Turnbull guidance been in force at the time of the XYZ plc affair, the directors would not have needed to be specific about the actions they were taking to prevent a recurrence of the reported problem but could have restricted themselves to describing in general terms the process they follow to deal with breakdowns in internal control. This view of ours is based on our interpretation of a change in phraseology between the draft and the final Turnbull reports. The draft wording (now replaced by para 38) was consistent with the old Rutteman guidance and read:

> 'Where weaknesses in internal control have resulted in material losses or contingencies which require disclosure in the annual report and accounts, the board should describe what corrective action it has taken or intends to take; or explain why no changes are considered necessary.'

The amended, final Turnbull guidance (para 38, p11 of the Turnbull report) now reads:

'In relation to Code provision D.2.1, the board should summarise the process it (where applicable, through its committees) has applied in reviewing the effectiveness of the system of internal control. It should also disclose the process it has applied to deal with material internal control aspects of any significant problems disclosed in the annual report and accounts.'

It is to be hoped, and indeed expected, that companies will continue the practice which XYZ plc followed, notwithstanding that now it would be permissible for them to be less transparent.

As an aspect of corporate governance it is interesting that the directors' report of 26 August 1998 acknowledged that:

'The Chairman has overall responsibility to ensure the appropriate imple-mentation of these changes and for continued monitoring of the Group's compliance with its policies and procedures.'

Chairmen, even non-executive chairmen as in this case, *do* have overall responsi-bility for the functioning of the board and to ensure that each member of the board is executing the policy of the board. It is also commendable that the board immediately investigated after the external auditor had informed the board of the matter, but this promptness pales not a little when one recollects that some of the board members were already aware of the practice. The board had little choice as the annual results would be published in about six weeks' time and clearly there was a major discrepancy to be investigated. Not being able to quantify the effect quickly, a week after the external auditors informed them, the board asked the Stock Exchange to suspend dealings in the shares from 13 July 1998.

Prompt action at a time of crisis can enhance a board's image, but is unlikely to have done so in this case. Being unable to quantify a loss, suspending shares, and then incurring £175,000 disclosed professional costs of re-listing, would have seriously dented shareholder confidence in the board.

The directors' report of 26 August 1998 blamed XYZ plc's senior operations manager: it said that the '"pre-dispatching" system was directed by the senior operations manager' who had been suspended shortly after the directors' inquiry commenced and had resigned by 26 August 1998 with a £156,000 payoff payable in instalments. Clearly he knew all about the fraud. So the board targeted for retribu-tion a non-board member and had the gall to rely on the results of their external auditors' inquiry to deflect blame from the board itself, saying:

'In their report to the Company in connection with the inquiry, [the external auditors] have advised the Board that no evidence has come to their attention which indicates that any member of the Board of the Company was involved in, or aware of, this practice.'

As far as the group finance and management information systems director was concerned, the media said he was:

'... just the sacrificial lamb. They had to have a main board director shot, although the problem is in fact on the retail operation side.'

It is true that this director, who was on a 12-month rolling contract, also tendered his resignation on 19 August 1998 and received an immediate £221,000 pay-off. The ground for his resignation was the opposite of that of the senior operations manager: the finance director is said to have known nothing about the fraud, but should have known; and the directors' report referred to:

'... specific actions to be taken as a result of this [including] strengthened Finance Director presence in operations.'

The disparity of treatment between the two people who resigned is interesting. Instalment payments tend to secure confidentiality. These payments were determined, on advice, by the non-executive directors acting as the Remuneration Committee, as 'being in the best interests of the Company'. What could that have meant?

The bloodletting was not yet complete. As part of their response to the crisis, the directors' report of 26 August 1998 had reported that:

'The Group Managing Director has now taken over direct responsibility for retail operations.'

But he was to be dismissed without compensation just eight months later in April 1999, following the discovery that he had misled the board about his knowledge of accounting errors in 1998. In contrast to statements made to the board at the time, he had been aware of the accounting irregularities. On 3 September XYZ plc were to report that he had 'played an integral part in the practice known as pre-dispatching'.

Clearly those who build up private companies are vulnerable following a listing. It would be interesting to know how his deception came to light – was this another example of whistleblowing? We note that the practice of 'pre-dispatching' had been going on for several years and so would have had a misleading effect on the financial statements at the time of the listing which would have shown performance better than it really was.

The chairman was to say:

'I had always thought I had known [him] quite well, but clearly I didn't. He told the board he had no idea about the goings-on. I was extremely surprised and shocked to learn that this was not the case.'

Although he went without compensation, a few months later he was in line to collect £1.3m by selling his 1.54m XYZ plc shares.


## INVESTIGATIONS

On 8 September 1999, XYZ plc announced belatedly that they were the subject of a Section 447 inquiry which their chairman believed related to false accounting in breach of company law and allegedly misleading the auditors who resigned over the affair. Nine minutes later they announced they had agreed the £84.2m cash bid (93p per share) from ABC Saint-Maclou, who said at the time that they would terminate their offer if the DTI upgraded its probe to a public inquiry under section 432 of the Companies Act, which they did not. The Serious Fraud Office had also looked at accounting irregularities at XYZ plc and decided not to do anything.

## MANAGEMENT AND BUSINESS CHANGES

To fill an important gap, an interim finance director was appointed temporarily, having served elsewhere as an interim finance director since, in 1997, he had ceased being finance director for Meyer International. As we have said, the plan was that the new finance director was to have a strengthened presence in operations. Management reporting was to be modified and stocktaking procedures improved. It would not have been easy to find a permanent finance director quickly in these circumstances, but it is to be wondered whether an interim director would have had the weight to implement the board's stated intention.

Early in September 1999 the new group managing director announced a three-year plan to revitalise XYZ plc – which a commentator described 'very impressive, but all too late.' He said XYZ plc's difficulties had resulted from 'a lot of own goals' rather than problems in the market. He intended to revive staff morale, concentrate on higher value goods, target the right customers and get pricing right. 2000 was to have seen the launch of three concept stores where bedding, furniture and floor coverings would be put together in three categories: traditional, contemporary and mass appeal. He said the brand had been looking tired.

## THE AUDIT ANGLES

By 1998, the auditors had been in post for eight years but had not reported the problem. It is hard to avoid the conclusion that they must have been deliberately misled. When they had completed their special inquiry for the board, costing £348,000, they informed the Board of their intention not to seek re-appointment at the forthcoming Annual General Meeting.

A general issue is raised in this. Is it appropriate for the annual statutory audit to be performed by a firm for whom the chairman of the company once worked? In favour of going along with this is the undoubted fact that chairmen of companies, especially non-executive chairmen as in this case, sleep better at night if they have confidence that a high quality audit is being conducted. And the mutual confidence that the auditor and the chairman are likely to have in these circumstances may assist the external auditor, to some extent, to gain a measure of audit assurance. On the other hand, as shown in our extract from the Combined Code below, the audit committee needs to keep under review the independence and objectivity of the company's auditors. One thing is sure, this illustrates the wisdom of XYZ plc ensuring that the chairman of the company is not also the chairman of the audit committee.

THE THEN 1998 COMBINED CODE ON AUDIT COMMITTEES AND
EXTERNAL AUDITORS

### D.3  Audit Committee and Auditors

| Principle | The board should establish formal and transparent arrangements for considering how they should apply the financial reporting and internal control principles and for maintaining an appropriate relationship with the company's auditors. |
|---|---|

### Code Provisions

**D.3.1** The board should establish an audit committee of at least three directors, all non-executive, with written terms of reference which deal clearly with its authority and duties. The members of the committee, a majority of whom should be independent non-executive directors, should be named in the report and accounts.

**D.3.2** The duties of the audit committee should include keeping under review the scope and results of the audit and its cost effectiveness and the independence and objectivity of the auditors. Where the auditors also supply a substantial volume of non-audit services to the company, the committee should keep the nature and extent of such services under review, seeking to balance the maintenance of objectivity and value for money.

It was decided that internal audit should be outsourced, as the external auditors had recommended in their report to the board on their investigation. We do not know why they judged the in-house internal audit to be inappropriate for the future. Perhaps they were exercised about a lack of internal audit independence. We would generally expect sales cut-off to be an important matter to be scrutinised carefully by the external auditor rather than by the internal auditor as there is a need to co-ordinate and avoid unnecessary overlap between the two audits.

## A3.3.2    Desk-based exercise in designing an audit interrogation

PART 1

On the attached sheets you have a description of a simple computer-based fixed assets register. Please put down on the form provided your ideas on what an auditor might use audit interrogation software to achieve, making use of data and evidence present, or likely to be present on the computer-based file for fixed assets.

### Introduction

This is an introductory case study on specifying the tests to be performed by an enquiry program. The file to be interrogated is a fictionalised, simplified FIXED ASSETS FILE designed for training purposes. Details of the file are set out here. The exercise excludes any consideration of file comparison techniques.

## Case study

Participants are asked to make a schedule of test, analysed by class of test under the heading shown in Table 1.

### Table 1: Classification of test

| Field name | Audit samples | Reperform-ance of calculations | Items not conforming to system rules | Items conform-ing but of audit interest | Totals and analy-ses | Com-ments |
|---|---|---|---|---|---|---|
|  |  |  |  |  |  |  |

NB Some tests will involve a combination of fields on the file.

### Fixed assets master file
1.   The file is maintained on an annual basis and keeps all records for sold or scrapped goods until the end of the year of scrapping. For the purpose of simplicity, in this case study participants are to assume that all additions are created as new, discrete records.
2.   In reality, the contents of such a file would be considerably more complex but the file described in Table 2 is sufficient to demonstrate the principles involved in specifying an enquiry.

### Table 2: Fixed-assets master file

| Field name | Mne-monic | Comment |
|---|---|---|
| STATUS INDICATOR | SI | A = addition this year, E = existing asset S = scrapped asset |
| ASSET NUMBER | AN | 6 digits, plus a check digit |
| ASSET DESCRIPTION | AD |  |
| ASSET LOCATION | AL | 3 digits, (location code = cost centre) |
| ASSET CLASSIFICATION | AC | FH = Freehold property LL = Long leasehold (over 50 years) SL = Short leasehold (under 50 years) PM = Plant and machinery FF = Fixtures and fittings MV = Motor vehicles |
| DEPRECIATION RATE | DR | 5 digits nn.nnn% |
| DEPRECIATION BASIS | DB | N = not depreciated S = straight line R = reducing balance |
| DATE IN USE | DU | 6 digits, ddmmyy (mm = accounting period number) |

| Field name | Mne-monic | Comment |
|---|---|---|
| ORIGINAL COST | OC | 9 digits, n,nnn,nnn.nn |
| REVALUED COST | RC | 9 digits, n,nnn,nnn.nn |
| DATE OF REVALUATION | RD | 6 digits, ddmmyy (only made at period 01) |
| DATE OF DISPOSAL | DD | 6 digits, ddmmyy (mm = accounting period number) |
| DISPOSAL PROCEEDS | DP | 9 digits, n,nnn,nnn.nn |
| CUMULATIVE DEPRECIATION BROUGHT FORWARD | CD | 9 digits, n,nnn,nnn.nn |
| DEPRECIATION CHARGE THIS YEAR | DC | 9 digits, n,nnn,nnn.nn |

**Accounting Policies**

1.   Depreciation is calculated each accounting period on the status of the asset as at the end of that period (ie no depreciation in period of disposal).
2.   Monthly depreciation is accumulated in the 'depreciation charge this year' field.
3.   Table 3 shows rates and bases.
4.   Depreciation is calculated until residual value is $0.

**Table 3: Rates and bases**

| Asset classification | Depreciation rate(s) (per cent) | Basis |
|---|---|---|
| FH | Nil | - |
| LL | Nil | - |
| SL | 2 | S |
| PM | 20 | R |
| FF | 25 | S |
| MV | 33.333 | R |

PART 2

## Answer form

| Field name | Audit sam-ples | Reperform-ance of calculations | Items not conforming to system rules | Items con-forming but of audit interest | Totals and analyses | Com-ments |
|---|---|---|---|---|---|---|
|  |  |  |  |  |  |  |
|  |  |  |  |  |  |  |
|  |  |  |  |  |  |  |
|  |  |  |  |  |  |  |
|  |  |  |  |  |  |  |
|  |  |  |  |  |  |  |
|  |  |  |  |  |  |  |

PART 3

## Suggested solution

| Field name (Mne-monic) | Audit sam-ples | Re-perfor-mance of calcu-lations | Items not con-forming to sys-tem rules | Items con-forming but of audit interest | Totals and analyses | Comments |
|---|---|---|---|---|---|---|
| SI | A (1 in n) E (1 in n) S (1 in n) |  | Not A, E, S |  | Cost (or valua-tion) and accumu-lated depre-ciation (CD + DC) | Analyses for Compa-nies Acts Notes to Accounts. Samples for tests to additions (perhaps related to cost). Samples for physical verifica-tion. Samples of scrappings (perhaps related to cost, or odd disposal value). |

| Field name (Mnemonic) | Audit samples | Re-performance of calculations | Items not conforming to system rules | Items conforming but of audit interest | Totals and analyses | Comments |
|---|---|---|---|---|---|---|
| AN | | Check digit calculation | Not numeric, duplicate | | | |
| AD | | | Blank | | | |
| AL | | | Blank | | Analysis of depreciation charge by cost centre | If detailed table of cost centres available then a more sophisticated test could be performed. |
| AC | | | Not FH, LL, SL, PM, FF, MV | | Cost (or valuation) and accumulated depreciation (CD + DC) | Analyses for Companies Acts Notes to Accounts |
| DR | | | Not in accordance with AC per table | | | |
| DB | | | Not in accordance with AC per table. | | | |
| DU | | | Invalid or future date. Not current year if SI = 'A' | | | |
| OC | | | Negative, zero | Large items | | |
| RC | | | Negative, zero if RD ≠blank | Large items | | |

| Field name (Mnemonic) | Audit samples | Re-performance of calculations | Items not conforming to system rules | Items conforming but of audit interest | Totals and analyses | Comments |
|---|---|---|---|---|---|---|
| RD | Current year | | Blank if RC ≠0 | Re-valuations varying by x% from OC | Total of this year's revalued items | |
| DD | | | Invalid or future date. Blank if SI = 'S' | Date in use and date of disposal in the same year. | | |
| DP | | | | Selection of large profits/losses on disposal (with cost or revaluations as appropriate) | Aggregate profit/ loss on disposal | For checking to profit and loss account |
| CD | | | Not 0 if SI = 'A'. Negative or zero. CD + DC greater than cost or revaluation. | | Total | For checking to previous years accounts |
| DC | | Recalculate DC with reference to appropriate dates and fields (on cost or valuation) | Not numeric ≠0 unless disposed in period 01 | | Total for the year | For checking to profit and loss account |

NB The above tests are not exhaustive but indicate the types of tests that can be performed.

# Quality assurance and improvement programme – best practice guidance

**A4.1.1** While we also refer to other important pronouncements, our main source of guidance for the parts of this Handbook which describe internal auditing best practice has been the *Professional Practices Framework* of The Institute of Internal Auditors. This *Framework* includes their *Definition* of internal auditing, *Code of Ethics*, *Standards* and *Practice Advisories*. Of these, only the *Practice Advisories* are non-mandatory: they explain and elaborate upon best practice in most circumstances, and are important for practitioners and students. Readers can see the current complete list of *Practice Advisories* at www.theiia.org. Those current on 1 January 2005 are shown at APPENDIX 3 of this Handbook, including a useful topical classification at APPENDIX 3.2.

In addressing this subject we have drawn more widely than those *Practice Advisories* classified by The Institute as applicable to this part of our Handbook, which are:

| Practice Advisories, by Standard Number | Release date |
| --- | --- |
| Practice Advisory 1300–1: Quality Assurance and Improvement Program | 25 May 2004 |
| Practice Advisory 1310–1: Quality Program Assessment | Rev 25 May 2004 19 December 2001 |
| Practice Advisory 1311–1: Internal Assessments | Rev 25 May 2004 19 Dec 2001 |
| Practice Advisory 1312–1: External Assessments | Rev 25 May 2004 19 Dec 2001 |
| Practice Advisory 1312–2: External Assessment – Self Assessment with Independent Validation | 25 May 2004 |
| Practice Advisory 1320–1: Reporting on the Quality Program | Rev 25 May 2004 5 Jan 2001 21 Feb 21 2003 revised |

*Practice Advisories* carry the *Standard* number to which they principally refer. Readers are advised to consult the applicable *Standards* as we do not in every case reproduce them here. They are to be found at APPENDIX 2.

'External and internal assessments of an internal audit activity should be performed to appraise and express an opinion as to the internal audit activity's compliance with the Standards and, as appropriate, should include recommendations for improvement. These reviews can have considerable value to the organization's governance processes, the chief audit executive CAE, and other members of the internal audit activity. Only qualified persons should perform these reviews.'[1]

Mastering the subject of the quality assurance and improvement programme is relatively straightforward as there is quite a close match between the Practice Advisories and each of the Standards in this area:

| Stand-ard | Subject | Practice Advisory | Handbook reference |
|---|---|---|---|
| 1300 | The quality assurance and improvement programme, in general | PA1300–1: Quality Assurance and Improvement Program | A4.1.1 and A4.1.3 |
| 1310 | Monitoring and assessing the overall effectiveness of the quality assurance and improvement programme | PA 1310–1: Quality Program Assessments | A4.1.4 |
| 1311 | Ongoing internal assessments | PA 1311–1: Internal Assessments | A4.1.5 |
| 1311 | Periodic internal assessments | PA 1311–1: Internal Assessments | A4.1.6 |
| 1312 | External assessments | PA 1312–1: External Assessments | A4.1.7 |
| 1312 | External assessments by self assessment with independent validation | PA 1312–2: External Assessments Self Assessment with Independent Validation | A4.1.8 |
| 1320 | Reporting on the quality programme | PA 1320–1: Reporting on the Quality Program | A4.1.9 |
| 1330 | Use of 'Conducted in accordance with the *Standards*' | PA 1330–1: 'Use of Conducted in Accordance with the *Standards*' | A4.1.10 |
| 1340 | Disclosure of Noncompliance | | |

Rules of Conduct within The Institute of Internal Auditors' *Code of Ethics* are mandatory. One requires that internal auditors:

'shall continually improve their proficiency and the effectiveness and quality of their services.'[2]

Another, which specifies the principal benchmark to be used to assess internal audit performance, is that internal auditors:

'shall perform internal auditing services in accordance with the Standards for the Professional Practice of Internal Auditing.'[3]

for which readers should also refer to A1.1.6.

The relative importance The Institute attaches to quality assurance can perhaps be illustrated by observing that the *Standards* themselves have over 200 words on this subject, compared with much fewer on, for instance, audit testing. The leading Standard is as follows:

> **'1300 – Quality Assurance and Improvement Program**
> The chief audit executive should develop and maintain a quality assurance and improvement program that covers all aspects of the internal audit activity and continuously monitors its effectiveness. This program includes periodic internal and external quality assessments and ongoing internal monitoring. Each part of the program should be designed to help the internal auditing activity add value and improve the organization's operations and to provide assurance that the internal audit activity is in conformity with the Standards and the Code of Ethics.'

A key purpose of the quality assurance and improvement programme is to '**ensure**'[4] that the scope of work of an internal audit activity:

> 'includes all the activities in the Standards and in The Institute of Internal Auditors' definition of internal auditing'[5]

which reads:

> 'Internal auditing is an independent, objective assurance and consulting activity designed to add value and improve an organization's operations. It helps an organization accomplish its objectives by bringing a systematic, disciplined approach to evaluate and improve the effectiveness of risk management, control, and governance processes.'[6]

The secondary purpose of the quality assurance and improvement programme is:

> 'to provide reasonable **assurance**[7] to the various stakeholders of the internal audit activity'[8]

on the above matters, which the Practice Advisory 1300–1 classifies as being that the internal audit activity:
- 'Performs in accordance with its charter, which should be consistent with the International Standards for the Professional Practice of Internal Auditing and Code of Ethics,
- Operates in an effective and efficient manner, and
- Is perceived by those stakeholders as adding value and improving the organization's operations.'[9]

and which Practice Advisory 1310–1 elaborates upon as follows:
- 'Compliance with the Standards and Code of Ethics, including timely corrective actions to remedy any significant instances of non-compliance,
- Adequacy of the internal audit activity's charter, goals, objectives, policies, and procedures,
- Contribution to the organization's governance, risk management, and control processes,
- Compliance with applicable laws, regulations, and government or industry standards,
- Effectiveness of continuous improvement activities and adoption of best practices, and

- Whether the auditing activity adds value and improves the organization's operations.'[10]

## A4.1.2 Timing requirement for implementation

External assessments should be made at least once every five years. The Practice Advisories use the phrase 'internal audit activities' to refer to the function that provides the internal auditing service, and we do so throughout this chapter. If internal audit activities have a firm intention to conduct an external assessment within five years of the date that the requirement for internal and external assessments came into force (1 January 2002), then they may regard themselves as in compliance with the Standards in this respect even if no external assessment has yet taken place.

Periodic internal assessments should take place at least annually to be compliant with the *Standards*, except that the requirement may be waived in the year in which an external assessment is made:

> 'The requirement that internal audit activities conduct ongoing and periodic internal assessments became effective as of January 1, 2002. In addition, at least one external assessment is required during the five years commencing on that date and at least once during each five-year period thereafter. The requirement for a periodic internal assessment may be waived for the year in which an external assessment is performed.'[11]

While an external assessment is required within five years of 1 January 2002, an earlier external review is highly recommended. Organizations that had had external reviews prior to 1 January 2002 are encouraged to have their next external review within five years of their last review – and so on. However, we should not overlook that the Practice Advisories, to which we are referring here with respect to timing, are discretionary not mandatory.

## A4.1.3 Chief audit executive responsible for the quality assurance and improvement programme

Where there is a responsibility, there should be a matching accountability obligation. The Institute of Internal Auditors makes it the responsibility of the chief audit executive to:

> 'develop and maintain a quality assurance and improvement program'[12]

and thus also states that the chief audit executive:

> 'should be accountable for implementing [the quality assurance and improvement] processes [which] should include appropriate supervision, periodic internal assessments and ongoing monitoring of quality assurance, and periodic external assessments.'[13]

and:

'**Communicating Results** – To provide accountability and transparency, the CAE should share the results of external, and, as appropriate, internal quality program assessments with the various stakeholders of the activity, such as senior management, the board, and external auditors.'[14]

Assigning the responsibility to the chief audit executive is quite significant. There is wide support for the notion that quality assurance functions within entities are better if they are independent of the activities over which they provide assurance, notwithstanding that the management who are responsible for functions also have primary responsibility for their quality. It is widely accepted that much of the assessment of quality on behalf of both responsible management and stakeholders is generally done better if entrusted to an independent party – such as an internal quality assurance section. The Institute of Internal Auditors takes a different view with respect to the review of internal audit's quality assurance:

'The QA&IP processes should be performed by or under direct supervision of the CAE. Except in small internal audit activities, the CAE would usually delegate most QA&IP responsibilities to subordinates. In large or complex environments (eg, numerous business units and/or locations), the CAE should establish a formal QA&IP function independent of the audit and consulting segments of the internal audit activity. This independent function should be headed by an audit executive. This executive (and limited staff) would not normally perform all of the QA&IP responsibilities, but would administer and monitor these activities.'[15]

The Institute takes the line that the results of periodic internal reviews should be reported directly to the chief audit executive:

'The Chief Audit Executive (CAE) should establish a structure for reporting results of periodic reviews that maintains appropriate credibility and objectivity. Generally, those assigned responsibility for conducting ongoing and periodic reviews should report to the CAE while performing the reviews and should communicate their results directly to the CAE.'[16]

The Institute also takes the line that the primary responsibility for selecting the external assessor should be with the chief audit executive:

'**Approval by Management and the Board** – The CAE should involve senior management and the board in the selection process for an external reviewer and obtain their approval.'[17]

Again, we are uncomfortable with this: it is analogous to the financial director (or chief financial officer) choosing the external auditor of the entity – which would not be approved of.

When it comes to communicating the final results of the external assessment, the Institute does commend that there should preferably be direct reporting by the assessor to senior management and the board. 'Direct' reporting means that the communication of the report is directly from the assessor and its contents have been determined exclusively by the assessor.

'The preliminary results of the [external] review should be discussed with the CAE during and at the conclusion of the assessment process. Final results should be communicated to the CAE or other official who authorized the review for the organization, preferably with copies sent directly to appropriate members of senior management and the board.'[18]

It is not entirely clear why The Institute has adopted the policy of placing the chief audit executive centre stage in the assessment of the internal audit activity. It could be an example of a tendency by The Institute to elevate the role of internal audit. Another example of this being the enhanced role for internal audit that The Institute gives in respect to internal audit's relationship with audit committee where the policy of The Institute is that the chief audit executive should be the secretary to the audit committee (see 'Internal audit relationship with the audit committee – Practice Advisory' B1.1.17). It could be that, since internal audit is an intricately specified function within the business, it is considered too difficult for a general quality assurance function internal to the business to satisfactorily oversee the assessment of internal audit quality. It might also be held to be inappropriate to rely on a general quality assurance function within the entity to assess internal audit quality when at other times the internal audit activity would be auditing that quality assurance function. It could be that internal audit is seen as a special case in view of its expertise in conducting independent reviews. Whatever the reason(s) it is problematic in view of the vested interest that internal audit has in the results of the quality assurance and improvement programme over internal audit, and sits uneasily alongside Standard 1130.A2:

'Assurance engagements for functions over which the chief audit executive has responsibility should be overseen by a party outside the internal audit activity.'

It would be particularly problematic in situations where internal audit has been outsourced completely.

Although it is a valid point to make, we consider it misses the main point for The Institute to stress that:

'These [external] reviews can have considerable value to the chief audit executive (CAE) and other members of the internal audit activity.'

Indeed, that is true, but their principal purpose must surely be to provide reassurance to senior management and to the board, via their audit committee, on the quality of their internal audit activity. Hence:

'These reviews can have considerable value to the organization's governance processes, the chief audit executive CAE, and other members of the internal audit activity. Only qualified persons should perform these reviews.'[19]

## A4.1.4   Monitoring and assessing the overall effectiveness of the quality assurance and improvement programme

The risk associated with allocating responsibility to the chief audit executive for the internal quality assurance and improvement programme is, to some extent, mitigated by the requirement for external assessments by independent and competent parties (see below – A4.1.7–8) and also by the requirement that the board or its audit committee should learn of the results of the external assessments. However, under the Standards[20], the chief audit executive is given the responsibility to ensure that all this happens.

### 'Standard 1310 – Quality Program Assessments

The internal audit activity should adopt a process to monitor and assess the overall effectiveness of the quality program. The process should include both internal and external assessments.'

and:

### 'Standard 1320 – Reporting on the Quality Program

The chief audit executive should communicate the results of external assessments to the board.'

Practice Advisory 1300–1 lists a number of 'key elements' which may be considered for inclusion within the quality assurance and improvement programme 'under the direction of the chief audit executive' and to be administered (etc) by an internal auditor or auditors working in the quality assurance and improvement programme function who:

> 'to the extent practicable, [are independent] of the functions and activities being reviewed.'[21]

The work, which should cover 'the entire spectrum of audit and consulting work',[22] could be assigned, either ad hoc for particular tasks or on a longer-term basis, to other internal audit executives and staff; but would be overseen, administered, etc through the quality assurance and improvement programme function within the internal audit function.

Readers should consult the Practice Advisory[23] for the detail of the important list of key elements – which correspond to the most important determinants of internal audit activity quality. In summary, these are the internal auditing topic areas covered, but this list should not be regarded as exhaustive:

- policies and procedures;
- budgeting and financial management;
- the audit risk universe and long-range planning;
- coordination with other review agencies;
- scheduling engagements;
- audit tools;
- recruitment, training and development;
- keeping current with the *Standards*;
- internal audit metrics;
- information gathering and periodic summary reports to senior management and to the audit committee;
- database of audit recommendations and action plans;
- quality assurance activities themselves.

## A4.1.5　Ongoing internal assessments

The stress here is on 'routine'. Sometimes termed 'internal review', 'ongoing monitoring' and 'self-assessments',[24] these:

> 'are usually incorporated into the routine policies and practices used to manage the internal audit activity and should be conducted by means of such processes and tools as:
> - Engagement supervision as described in Practice Advisory 2340–1 Engagement Supervision,
> - Checklists and other means to provide assurance that processes adopted by the internal audit activity (eg, in an audit and procedures manual) are being followed,
> - Feedback from audit customers and other stakeholders,
> - Project budgets, timekeeping systems, audit plan completion, cost recoveries, and
> - Analyses of other performance metrics, (such as cycle time and recommendations accepted).'[25]

In other words, we are referring here to the routine ways in which internal quality is assessed during the course of internal audit work, which should be:

> 'an integral part of the day-to-day supervision, review, and measurement of the internal audit activity'[26]

The principal challenge for most internal audit functions will be to ensure that:

> 'Conclusions should be developed as to the quality of ongoing performance, and follow-up action should be taken to assure appropriate improvements are implemented.'[27]

This will be more straightforward for some measures of on-going performance than others. For instance, how many internal audit activities develop metrics for the extent that completed checklists provide assurance that adopted internal audit processes are being followed?

## A4.1.6　Periodic internal assessments

These are:

> 'periodic reviews performed through self-assessment or by other persons within the organization, with knowledge of internal audit practices and the Standards.'

as distinct from the other type of internal assessments which are:

> 'Ongoing reviews of the performance of the internal audit activity.'[28]

Periodic assessments are usually not routine: rather, they are special-purpose reviews and will usually involve compliance testing.

> 'They should be designed to assess (a) compliance with the internal audit activity's charter, the International Standards for the Professional Practice of Internal

Auditing, and the Code of Ethics, and (b) the efficiency and effectiveness of the activity in meeting the needs of its various stakeholders.'[29]

The outputs of a periodic internal assessment are (a) conclusions as to the quality of performance of the internal audit activity and (b) appropriate action initiated to achieve improvements and conformity to the *Standards,* as necessary.

An internal assessment is, if you like, an internal audit of the internal audit activity. It may be undertaken as a self-assessment by members of the internal audit activity, or by competent audit professionals (CIAs and similar) currently assigned elsewhere in the organization, or a mix of these:

> '[Internal assessments may] encompass a combination of self-assessment and preparation of materials subsequently reviewed by CIAs, or other competent audit professionals, and include benchmarking of the internal audit activity's practices and performance metrics against relevant best practices of the internal auditing profession. The IIA's Quality Assessment Manual, or a comparable set of guidance and tools, should serve as the basis for periodic internal assessments. [They may] include more in-depth interviews and surveys of stakeholder groups.'[30]

Note the predictable US-oriented stress upon performing the assessment against a recognised framework designed for the purpose.

## A4.1.7  External assessments

**'Standard 1312 – External Assessments**
External assessments, such as quality assurance reviews, should be conducted at least once every five years by a qualified, independent reviewer or review team from outside the organization.'

and:

> '… external assessments of the internal audit activity, by an individual or team having a high level of competence and experience in the internal audit profession.'[31]

The thrust of the external review is to assess ('appraise and express an opinion of') whether the *Standards* have been complied with and to make recommendations for improvement.[32] The scope of the external assessment, which is an important part of the quality assurance and improvement programme, is given as:

- 'Compliance with the Standards, The IIA's Code of Ethics, and the internal audit activity's charter, plans, policies, procedures, practices, and applicable legislative and regulatory requirements,
- Expectations of the internal audit activity expressed by the board, executive management and operational managers,
- Integration of the internal audit activity into the organization's governance process, including the attendant relationships between and among the key groups involved in that process,
- Tools and techniques employed by the internal audit activity,

- Mix of knowledge, experience, and disciplines within the staff, including staff focus on process improvement, and
- Determination as to whether or not the audit activity adds value and improves the organisation's operations.'[33]

Qualified persons to act as external assessors might be found from amongst:

> 'IIA quality assurance reviewers, regulatory examiners, consultants, external auditors, other professional service providers, and internal auditors from outside the organization whose internal audit activity is the subject of the external assessment.'[34]

They should have integrity, objectivity and competence (each of which are defined in Practice Advisory 1312–1) and be:

- Independent of the organisation and of the internal audit activity;
- Competent in the professional practice of internal auditing;
- Competent in the external assessment process.

The criteria for competence given in Practice Advisory 1312–1 will significantly narrow the gene pool from which external assessors can be found:

> '**Competence** – Performing and communicating the results of an external assessment require the exercise of professional judgment. Accordingly, an individual serving as an external assessor should:
> - Be a competent, certified audit professional (eg, CIA, CPA, CA, or CISA), who possesses current, in-depth knowledge of the Standards.
> - Be well versed in the best practices of the profession.
> - Have at least three years of recent experience in the practice of internal auditing at a management level.
> - External assessment team leaders and independent validators (New Practice Advisory 1312–2 – [see A4.1.7 below]) should have an additional level of competence and experience, such as that gained from working previously as a team member on an external quality assessment, successful completion of The IIA's quality assessment training course or similar training, and CAE or comparable senior internal audit management experience.
>
> The review team should include members with information technology expertise and relevant industry experience. Individuals with expertise in other specialized areas may assist the external review team. For example, specialists in enterprise risk management, statistical sampling, operations monitoring systems, or control self-assessment may participate in certain segments of the review.'[35]

Practice Advisory 1312–1 goes into some detail on the criteria for independence.[36] With respect to one popular way of resourcing the external assessment, that of the 'reciprocal peer review', this section of the Practice Advisory states that, for instance:

> 'Reciprocal peer reviews between two organizations would not pass the independence test.'

(more than two organisations must be in the frame) and:

'Individuals who are in another department of that subject organization or in a related organization, although organizationally separate from the internal audit activity, are not considered independent for purposes of conducting an external assessment. A related organization may be a parent organization, an affiliate in the same group of entities, or an entity with regular oversight, supervision, or quality assurance responsibilities with respect to the organization whose internal audit activity is the subject of the external assessment.'

A useful practical expedient in particular cases is offered:

'To overcome concerns that there may be an appearance or reality of impairment of independence [in instances such as 'reciprocal peer reviews' or 'related organisations'] one or more independent individuals could be part of the external assessment team, or scheduled to participate subsequently, to independently validate the work of that external assessment team.'

Essential components of the report on the external assessment include:

- An opinion on the internal audit activity's compliance with the *Standards* based on a structured rating process;[37]
- an assessment and evaluation of the use of best practices, recommendations for improvement where appropriate; and
- responses from the CAE that include an action plan and implementation dates.[38]

The Institute advises that a periodic *internal* assessment, performed within a short time prior to an external assessment, can serve to facilitate and reduce the cost of an external assessment.

## A4.1.8  *External assessments by self-assessment with independent validation*

Late in May 2004 the Institute introduced a concession targeted at smaller internal audit activities for whom the conventional approach of the external assessment may be regarded as too onerous. We consider the concession could also be useful even in multinationals for the assessment by group internal audit of internal audit activities located within operating units. Under this concession, the self-assessment part of the external assessment, which is to be fully documented, is undertaken by a team under the direction of the chief audit executive *in a way which emulates the external assessment process*, at least with respect to evaluation of compliance with the *Standards*. So, to this extent it is similar to a periodic internal review performed by self-assessment *except that its terms of reference are as for an external review*. However, unlike a periodic internal review, there is then an independent on-site validation by a qualified reviewer who should be similarly qualified as the external assessor per Practice Advisory 1312–1 and cannot be an insider:

'Individuals who are in another department of that subject organization or in a related organization, although organizationally separate from the internal audit activity, are not considered independent for purposes of conducting an external assessment. A related organization may be a parent organization, an affiliate in the same group of entities, or an entity with regular oversight, supervision, or quality assurance responsibilities with respect to the organization whose internal audit activity is the subject of the external assessment.'[39]

The independent validation is to include a rigorous review of the self-assessment team's own evaluation of compliance with the *Standards* and the *Code of Ethics*.

It is not clear from this whether this concession of 'self-assessment' as part of the external review allows the self-assessment to be conducted by competent audit professionals currently assigned elsewhere in the organisation, as is permissible for periodic internal assessments; or whether the intention is that it should always be undertaken by current members of the internal audit activity. The phrase 'self-assessment' would seem to infer the latter. But Practice Advisory 1312–2 merely requires that the team should be 'under the direction of the chief audit executive' without specifying that it should necessarily comprise current internal auditors. Although the phrase 'under the direction of the chief audit executive' is not used in Practice Advisory 1312–1 (in the context of periodic internal reviews conducted by competent audit professionals currently assigned elsewhere in the organisation) we consider it is clear from PA1312–1 that periodic internal reviews are to be under the direction of the chief audit executive. So we would infer that it is legitimate for competent audit professionals currently assigned elsewhere in the organisation to be used for an external review by self-assessment, notwithstanding that this is not specifically stated in PA1312–2. This interpretation is lent weight by:

'If the external assessment takes the form of a self-assessment with independent validation (New Practice Advisory 1312–2), the periodic internal assessment can serve as the self assessment portion of this process.'[40]

The Institute sounds a note of caution:

'... insofar as possible, in order to achieve optimum quality assurance and process-improvement benefits, an internal audit activity should consider the self-assessment with independent validation as an interim measure and endeavour to obtain a full assessment during subsequent periods.'[41]

## A4.1.9   Reporting on the quality programme

It is only with respect to external assessments of the internal audit activity that there is a Standard (ie mandatory) requirement for internal audit to ensure that the results are reported to the board:

**'Standard 1320 – Reporting on the Quality Program**
The chief audit executive should communicate the results of external assessments to the board.'

But at the non-mandatory level of the Practice Advisories there is abundant guidance that most aspects of the quality assurance and improvement programme should be reported not just to the board but to senior management, external auditors and perhaps to other stakeholders of internal audit:

'To provide accountability and transparency, the CAE should share the results of external, and, as appropriate, internal quality program assessments with the various stakeholders of the activity, such as senior management, the board, and external auditors.'[42]

'The CAE should share the results of internal assessments, necessary action plans, and their successful implementation with appropriate persons outside the activity, such as senior management, the board, and external auditors.'[43]

'The preliminary results of the [external] review should be discussed with the CAE during and at the conclusion of the assessment process. Final results should be communicated to the CAE or other official who authorized the review for the organization, preferably with copies sent directly to appropriate members of senior management and the board.'[44]

'The CAE should communicate the results of the [external] review to appropriate members of senior management and to the board, if not already copied directly, as well as the specifics of planned remedial actions for significant issues and subsequent information as to accomplishment of those planned actions.'[45]

## A4.1.10   Use of 'Conducted in accordance with the *Standards*'

In CHAPTER A1.1 we discussed the *Code of Ethics* obligation to perform internal audit services in accordance with the *Standards*:

'[Internal auditors] shall perform internal auditing services in accordance with the Standards for the Professional Practice of Internal Auditing.'[46]

One of the purposes of the quality assurance improvement programme (A4.1) is to provide assurance that the internal audit activity is in conformity with the *Standards* and the *Code of Ethics*.[47]

The Institute of Internal Auditors' *Standards* are intended to be mandatory for all internal auditors and all internal audit activities which are providing an internal audit service consistent with the Institute's definition of internal auditing as contained within the preamble to both their *Code of Ethics* and *Standards*. It is therefore odd, even ambiguous, that the main Standard pertinent to this section (A4.1.10) is expressed as a discretionary matter. In all other respects, discretionary approaches are set out in the Practice Advisories, not in the *Standards* themselves.

**'1330 – Use of "Conducted in Accordance with the Standards"**

Internal auditors are encouraged to report that their activities are "conducted in accordance with the International Standards for the Professional Practice of Internal Auditing". However, internal auditors may use the statement only if assessments of the quality improvement program demonstrate that the internal audit activity is in compliance with the Standards.'

There may be occasions when the internal audit activity is unable to conduct its work in full accord with the *Standards* and internal auditors with the *Code of Ethics*. This may occur when, for instance, the scope of the engagement is effectively constrained by management or when the report by internal audit to the audit committee is unduly influenced by management against the better professional judgement of the chief audit executive. In such cases, disclosure of noncompliance should be made appropriately:

> **'1340 – Disclosure of Noncompliance**
>
> Although the internal audit activity should achieve full compliance with the Standards and internal auditors with the Code of Ethics, there may be instances in which full compliance is not achieved. When noncompliance impacts the overall scope or operation of the internal audit activity, disclosure should be made to senior management and the board.'

Practice varies between internal audit activities as to whether reports of every audit engagement include a routine reference to compliance by the internal audit activity with the *Standards*; and compliance by both the internal audit activity and also by individual internal auditors with the *Code of Ethics*. Note that the *Code of Ethics* states that:

> 'This Code of Ethics applies to both individuals and entities that provide internal auditing services.'

An alternative approach is to include, within the internal audit activity's annual or more frequent overall reports to the audit committee of the board, reference to whether or not internal audit has been in compliance with the *Code of Ethics* and *Standards*. However, it is mandatory to disclose within an audit engagement report when non-compliance has impacted upon the specific engagement:

> **'Standard 2430 – Engagement Disclosure of Noncompliance with the Standards**
>
> When noncompliance with the Standards impacts a specific engagement, communication of the results should disclose the:
> - Standard(s) with which full compliance was not achieved,
> - Reason(s) for noncompliance, and
> - Impact of noncompliance on the engagement.'

The practice of drawing attention to enforced non-compliance with the *Code of Ethics* and *Standards* can be an effective way of drawing management's and the audit committee's attention to ways in which internal audit is being inhibited from following best practice. It provides an external, authoritative reference source to support internal audit's expression of concern. It is no longer merely management's word and opinion against those of the chief audit executive.

It is only permissible for an internal audit ativity to claim compliance with the *Code of Ethics* and *Standards* if the quality assurance and improvement programme has been applied in accordance with the *Standards* and this has revealed:

> '[no] instances of noncompliance that impact the overall scope or operation of the internal audit activity'.[48]

One such instance would be the failure to undertake an external assessment by 1 January 2007, that is within five years of 1 January 2002:

'The requirement that internal audit activities conduct ongoing and periodic internal assessments became effective as of January 1, 2002. In addition, at least one external assessment is required during the five years commencing on that date and at least once during each five-year period thereafter.'[49]

Practice Advisory 1330–1 guides that:

'Any significant instances of noncompliance should be remedied before the internal audit activity uses the compliance phrase. Noncompliance that has been disclosed by a quality assessment (internal or external) or covered by related recommendations should be adequately remedied and the remedial actions should be reported and documented by the board, and senior management as appropriate, prior to the internal audit activity s use of the compliance phrase.'[50]

## A4.1.11   Engagement records and the quality assurance programme

External reviews, such as peer reviews of external audit firms or external assessments of internal audit activities, as discussed above, have as a pre-requisite a reasonable record of performance. Hence, a major justification for quality internal audit engagement records is that they facilitate external assessments of the internal audit activity.

'Working papers that document the engagement should be prepared by the internal auditor and reviewed by management of the internal audit activity. The working papers should record the information obtained and the analyses made and should support the bases for the observations and recommendations to be reported. Engagement working papers generally:
- Provide the principal support for the engagement communications.
- Aid in the planning, performance, and review of engagements.
- Document whether the engagement objectives were achieved.
- Facilitate third-party reviews.
- Provide a basis for evaluating the internal audit activity's quality program.
- Provide support in circumstances such as insurance claims, fraud cases, and lawsuits.
- Aid in the professional development of the internal auditing staff.
- Demonstrate the internal audit activity's compliance with the Standards for the Professional Practice of Internal Auditing.'[51]

We discuss internal audit engagement records in more detail in B4.1.10.

[1]   Practice Advisory 1330–1: 'Use of Conducted in Accordance with the *Standards*', para 1.
[2]   *Code of Ethics*, Rule of Conduct 4.3.
[3]   *Code of Ethics*, Rule of Conduct 4.2.
[4]   Bolding is ours.
[5]   Practice Advisory 1300–1: 'Quality Assurance and Improvement Program', para 1.
[6]   Taken from the Preamble to both the *Code of Ethics* and the *Standards*. Discussed in depth at the start of this chapter.
[7]   Bolding is ours.
[8]   Practice Advisory 1300–1: 'Quality Assurance and Improvement Program', para 2.
[9]   Practice Advisory 1300–1: 'Quality Assurance and Improvement Program', para 2.
[10]   Practice Advisory 1310–1: 'Quality program Assessments', para 3.
[11]   Practice Advisory 1310–1: 'Quality program Assessments', para 2.
[12]   Practice Advisory 1300–1: 'Quality Assurance and Improvement Program', para 1.

| | |
|---|---|
| 13 | Practice Advisory 1300–1: 'Quality Assurance and Improvement Program', para 2. |
| 14 | Practice Advisory 1310–1: 'Quality Program Assessments', para 5. |
| 15 | Practice Advisory 1300–1: 'Quality Assurance and Improvement Program', para 3. |
| 16 | Practice Advisory 1311–1: 'Internal Assessments', para 8. |
| 17 | Practice Advisory 1312–1: 'External assessments', para 10. |
| 18 | Practice Advisory 1312–1: 'External assessments', para 10. |
| 19 | Practice Advisory 1330–1: 'Use of Conducted in Accordance with the *Standards*', para 1. |
| 20 | Standard 1320. |
| 21 | Practice Advisory 1300–1: 'Quality Assurance and Improvement Program', para 3. |
| 22 | Practice Advisory 1310–1: 'Quality Program Assessments', para 1. |
| 23 | Practice Advisory 1300–1: 'Quality Assurance and Improvement Program', para 4. |
| 24 | Practice Advisory 1310–1: 'Quality Program Assessments', para 2. |
| 25 | Practice Advisory 1311–1: 'Internal Assessments', para 2. |
| 26 | Practice Advisory 1310–1: 'Quality Program Assessments', para 2. |
| 27 | Practice Advisory 1311–1: 'Internal Assessments', para 3. |
| 28 | Standard 1311 and Practice Advisory 1311–1: 'Internal Assessments'. |
| 29 | Practice Advisory 1311–1: 'Internal Assessments', para 4. |
| 30 | Practice Advisory 1311–1: 'Internal Assessments', para 5. |
| 31 | Practice Advisory 1310–1: 'Quality Program Assessments', para 2. |
| 32 | Practice Advisory 1312–1: 'External assessments', para 2. |
| 33 | Practice Advisory 1312–1: 'External assessments', para 11. |
| 34 | Practice Advisory 1312–1: 'External assessments', para 5. |
| 35 | Practice Advisory 1312–1: 'External assessments', para 8 & 9. |
| 36 | Practice Advisory 1312–1: 'External assessments', para 6. |
| 37 | Per Practice Advisory 1312–1, para 13, the term 'compliance' means that the practices of the internal audit activity, taken as a whole, satisfy the requirements of the *Standards*. 'Noncompliance' means that the impact and severity of the deficiencies in the practices of the internal audit activity are so significant that they impair the internal audit activity's ability to discharge its responsibilities. The degree of partial compliance with individual *Standards*, if relevant to the overall opinion, should also be expressed in the report on the independent assessment. |
| 38 | Practice Advisory 1312–1: 'External assessments', para 13. |
| 39 | Practice Advisory 1312–1: 'External assessments'. |
| 40 | Practice Advisory 1311–1: 'Internal Assessments', para 6. |
| 41 | Practice Advisory 1312–2: 'External assessments Self Assessment with Independent Validation', para 6. |
| 42 | Practice Advisory 1310–1: 'Quality Program Assessments', para 5. |
| 43 | Practice Advisory 1311–1: 'Internal Assessments', para 9. |
| 44 | Practice Advisory 1312–1: 'External assessments', para 12. |
| 45 | Practice Advisory 1312–1: 'External assessments', para 14. |
| 46 | *Code of Ethics*, Rules of Conduct para 4.2. |
| 47 | Standard 1300. |
| 48 | Practice Advisory 1330–1: 'Use of Conducted in Accordance with the *Standards*', para 2. |
| 49 | Practice Advisory 1310–1: 'Quality program Assessments', para 2. |
| 50 | Practice Advisory 1310–1: 'Quality program Assessments', para 3. |
| 51 | Practice Advisory 2330–1: 'Recording Information', para 1. |

# Quality assurance and improvement programme – supplementary guidance

## A4.2.1 Raising the standard – research into best practice internal audit in housing associations

Internal auditing has been part of good corporate governance practices in the housing association sector for many years. The development of these practices has been and still is by its regulator The Housing Corporation, working closely with the National Federation of Housing Associations (the employers' representative body) and the Housing Association Internal Audit Forum (representing internal auditors working in housing associations and affiliated to the Institute of Internal Auditors – UK & Ireland).

During 2003, Professor Jeffrey Ridley researched internal auditing in housing associations, on behalf of the Housing Association Internal Audit Forum (www.haiaf.org.uk). The results of that research were published in a report, *Raising the Standard*. This report contains 24 internal auditing best practice benchmarks and references that are reproduced, by permission, below. Although some of the references are to housing association requirements they could equally apply to internal auditing requirements in all sectors. Like all 'best practices, those shown are dynamic and will change in time, introducing new challenges for all internal auditors. At the end of each best practice there are three numbered boxes that can be ticked by the reader wishing to score their internal audit activity against the best:

**Score**
1. ☐ = **needs improvements**
2. ☐ = **meets best practice**
3. ☐ = **exceeds best practice**

A score between 48–72 and the activity is doing very well. The closer to 72 the more excellent it is. Below 48 there is action to take to identify the 'gaps' that require targets and measures for improvements. But remember, the best scores are team scores that include at least one of internal audit's customers!

BEST PRACTICE 1

To be effective boards must establish policies to achieve their objectives. This applies to all boards in all sectors. In HAs such policies should enable the implementation of the National Housing Federation ten principles of good governance (as defined in its publication *Competence and Accountability – Standards, Accountability, Openness, Equality, Review, Clarity, Control, Information, Structures, Audit*, 2000). The NHF recommends that these should be communicated to all HA employees, other stakeholders and interested parties. IAAs should review all the policy information published in its organisation to ensure that it is up to date and meets the requirements of good governance. The IIA *Standards* state that 'The internal audit activity should contribute to the organisation's governance process by evaluating and improving the process through which (1) values and goals are established and communicated (2) the accomplishment of goals is monitored, (3) accountability is ensured and (4) values are preserved'. Internal auditors have a role to play in ensuring that appropriate policies are approved and communicated by the board to ensure effective governance of all HA operations and relationships with other organizations

| 1. ☐ needs improvements | 2. ☐ meets best practice | 3. ☐ exceeds best practice |
|---|---|---|

BEST PRACTICE 2

The IAA should be fully conversant with its audit committee's terms of reference and provide guidance on its content. The IIA *Professional Practices Framework* recommends that internal audit should encourage the audit committee to review its activities and practices compared with best practices and to meet with the chairperson to discuss whether the material and information being furnished to the committee meets its needs. A list of relevant material and information is a useful starting point for such a discussion. Internal audit should develop such a list and review it at audit committee level.

| 1. ☐ needs improvements | 2. ☐ meets best practice | 3. ☐ exceeds best practice |
|---|---|---|

BEST PRACTICE 3

There is an opportunity for internal audit, particularly in the smaller HA, to promote itself as capable of carrying out special assignments/projects for the audit committee as part of its programme of work. The IIA *Professional Practices Framework* provides useful guidance for encouraging and carrying out such assignments/projects. Each should be a formal engagement approved at audit committee level.

| 1. ☐ needs improvements | 2. ☐ meets best practice | 3. ☐ exceeds best practice |
|---|---|---|

BEST PRACTICE 4

Research by the IIA-UK & Ireland, *Benchmarking Survey*, 2000, reported that the average number of internal audit staff in 'not for profit' organisations with turnover between £7–28M and total employees between 87–800 was 4. (The increased focus on governance, risk management and internal audit activities since that time may well have increased that average.)

HA boards and audit committee members must be satisfied that they have the right level of resources and competences to ensure adequate internal audit reviews of internal control. The right time for deciding this level is when a process of risk assessment is linked into development of annual internal and external audit plans. The audit committee has a vital role to play in ensuring a satisfactory risk assessment process is in place and this considers resources for internal audit.

Circular 25/01 states that an internal audit needs assessment should be conducted to calculate the resource level required taking into account the existence of other forms of assurance. This assessment should be formal and be both a quantitative and qualitative measure. The ICAEW guidance for audit committees, *The effective audit committee: a challenging role*, 2001, which is referred to in 25/01, recommends that the audit committee should question whether the IAA is adequately resourced.

The IIA Standards state that the head of internal audit also has a vital role to ' ... assist the audit committee in evaluating the adequacy of the personnel and budget and the scope of results of the internal audit activities, to ensure that there are no budgetary or scope limitations that impede the internal audit activity to execute its responsibilities.'

| 1. ☐ needs improvements | 2. ☐ meets best practice | 3. ☐ exceeds best practice |
|---|---|---|

**Best Practice 5**

The IIA Attribute Standards require that ' ... all internal auditors should possess the knowledge, skills, and other competencies needed to perform their individual responsibilities. The internal audit activity collectively should possess or obtain the knowledge, skills, and other competencies needed to perform its responsibilities.'

Circular 25/01 requires the IAA in an HA to be ' ... appropriately resourced ...', stating that this should be kept under review by the audit committee. Such a review should take place annually whether the internal audit activity is in-house or out-sourced. The review should include the size of the activity and the knowledge, skills and other competencies of the internal audit staff, both individually and collectively.

| 1. ☐ needs improvements | 2. ☐ meets best practice | 3. ☐ exceeds best practice |
|---|---|---|

**BEST PRACTICE 6**

Since 1999 The IIA has defined internal auditing as ' ... an independent, objective assurance and consulting activity designed to add value and improve an organisation's operations. It helps an organisation accomplish its objectives by bringing a systematic, disciplined approach to evaluate and improve the effectiveness of risk management, control and governance processes.' This definition is clearly set out in the model internal auditing charter in Circular 25/01. Achieving the independence and objectivity required by this definition needs an approved direct line of reporting to both the HA board and if it exists an audit committee of the board. IAAs and boards/audit committees should ensure that any involvement by IAAs in the operating practices in their HAs, at management or other levels, does not adversely impact their independence and objectivity. Boards/audit committees should require IAAs to state formally in their internal audit activity reporting any adverse influences on their independence and objectivity.

| 1. ☐ needs improvements | 2. ☐ meets best practice | 3. ☐ exceeds best practice |
|---|---|---|

BEST PRACTICE 7

All IAAs should maintain an up to date library of appropriate governance guidance publications and use these in the services they provide. A good understanding of relevant literature and guidance for audit, risk, control and governance is essential for all internal auditors, in their assurance and consultancy roles. The IIA in its recently published *Practice Advisory 2060–2: Relationship with the Audit Committee* also recommends that internal audit should meet periodically with the chairperson of the audit committee '... to discuss whether the materials and information being furnished to the audit committee members are meeting their needs.' This guidance requires a good understanding by internal auditors of the information and materials available to audit committee members in the fulfillment of their board responsibilities.

| 1. ☐ needs improvements | 2. ☐ meets best practice | 3. ☐ exceeds best practice |
|---|---|---|

BEST PRACTICE 8

The IIA recommends that the 'purpose, authority and responsibility' of an internal audit activity should be formally defined in a charter, consistent with its standards and approved by the board.' The nature of both assurance and consulting services should be defined in the charter. The Housing Corporation model charter is appropriate for all IAAs in HAs. The IIA states in its guidance that 'a key criterion against which an internal audit activity should be measured is its charter'. This suggests that the content of the charter should be clearly linked to measures, the results of which should be reported to the board/audit committee. Although no specific interval is given by The IIA for a charter to be reviewed and re-approved at board level, best practice would dictate that this should be at least annually, linked to the approval of planning and resources for the activity.

| 1. ☐ needs improvements | 2. ☐ meets best practice | 3. ☐ exceeds best practice |
|---|---|---|

BEST PRACTICE 9

All internal audit charters should give IAAs unrestricted access to all operations and require all internal audit engagements to be linked to the organisation's objectives and the measures used to evaluate the performance of those objectives. This will require all the primary objectives of control, in particular efficiency and effectiveness, to be part of every internal audit engagements.

| 1. ☐ needs improvements | 2. ☐ meets best practice | 3. ☐ exceeds best practice |
|---|---|---|

## BEST PRACTICE 10

It is important that the perception of roles internal auditors undertake in an HA is clear and measured to ensure that they reflect the purpose, authority and responsi-bilities of the internal audit activity, as approved by the board/audit committee. Also, that they meet their customers' expectations and satisfaction (if not delight!). *The IIA Professional Practices Framework* provides useful guidance for the development of the various roles practiced by internal auditors, assurance, consultancy, facilitation, educational etc. Not all will apply in every HA but many will and should be considered.

| 1. ☐ needs improvements | 2. ☐ meets best practice | 3. ☐ exceeds best practice |
|---|---|---|

## BEST PRACTICE 11

The IIA *Standards* recommend that the IAA should always confirm that the board/ audit committee understand and approve the concept of internal auditors providing consultancy services and the implications of these on its independence and objectivity. 'Once approved the internal audit charter should be amended to include the authority and responsibilities for consulting activities and the internal audit activity should develop appropriate policies and procedures for conducting such engagements.' Such policies and procedures should always address the issues of internal audit independence and objectivity.

| 1. ☐ needs improvements | 2. ☐ meets best practice | 3. ☐ exceeds best practice |
|---|---|---|

## BEST PRACTICE 12

All HAs should have a published code of conduct that applies to all its employees. The National Housing Federation, *Integrity at Work: model code of conduct for employees of registered landlords,* 2000, provides guidance on the introduction of such a code. It draws on the seven principles of public life developed by the Nolan Committee. Since this guide was first issued in 1996, the focus on good governance in all organisations has increased the importance of publishing a code of conduct in an organisation: not just for employees, but also for all that interact with the organisation. The GoodCorporation Standard – www.goodcorporation.com – pro-vides a good 2003 benchmark for a code of conduct in all types of organisation, demonstrating accountability to all an organisation's stakeholders. The IIA pub-lished its first *Code of Ethics* in 1968 and the more recent revision was published in 1999. The IIA requires all internal auditors who state that they use its *Standards* to comply with its *Code of Ethics.* All HA audit committees and boards should be aware of The IIA code and require their internal audit staff (whether internal or outsourced) to comply with its principles and rules.

| 1. ☐ needs improvements | 2. ☐ meets best practice | 3. ☐ exceeds best practice |
|---|---|---|

BEST PRACTICE 13

There will always be a need for internal audit staff to continue their professional education if the level of competence in an IAA is to be maintained and improved. This is essential for the achievement of quality in internal audit work. Training plans are essential at both individual internal auditor and activity levels. Such plans should be shared with the audit committee and subsequently reviewed for completion and benefits. The IIA-UK & Ireland publication *Learning for the longer term,* 2000, provides a formal continuing professional development programme that is appropriate for all internal audit staff. It is competency based, covering both cognitive and behavioural skills. It starts with a self-analysis and leads the individual into planning knowledge and skills development. Every IAA and internal auditor should use such a guide for planning and monitoring continuing professional development.

| 1. ☐ needs improvements | 2. ☐ meets best practice | 3. ☐ exceeds best practice |
|---|---|---|

BEST PRACTICE 14

The planning of audit and consultancy engagements linked to an organisation's risk and exposures is an essential process for every IAA. The IIA in its *Standards* recommends an annual process for planning, linked to an organisation's risk management process, with the incorporation of components from the organisation's strategic plans into the IAA plan. (By doing so the '… audit universe will consider and reflect the overall business plan objectives …'.)

| 1. ☐ needs improvements | 2. ☐ meets best practice | 3. ☐ exceeds best practice |
|---|---|---|

BEST PRACTICE 15

The IIA Standards recognise that small internal audit activities may be managed informally, such staff '… being directed and controlled through daily close supervision and written memorandum. In a large internal audit activity, more formal and comprehensive policies and procedures are essential to guide the audit staff in the consistent compliance with the internal audit activity's standards of performance'. Consistency in audit work and the need to demonstrate a high level of quality and due professional care, both during an engagement and afterwards, suggest that it is advisable to have a manual that describes the procedures to be followed for all types of internal audit engagements (assurance and consultancy). Such a manual is essential for any quality assurance and improvement programme established in an IAA.

| 1. ☐ needs improvements | 2. ☐ meets best practice | 3. ☐ exceeds best practice |
|---|---|---|

BEST PRACTICE 16

Co-ordination of assurance activities and liaison of activities and the performance monitoring of each should be included in the terms of reference for both audit committees and IAAs. This has always been recognised and recommended in both internal audit and external audit professional *Standards*. Recently the National Audit Office and HM Treasury published *Co-operation Between Internal and External Auditors*, 2000. This sets out a useful checklist for both internal and external audit co-operation. The list of areas for co-ordination, liaison and evaluation is based on recommended guidelines in The IIA *Standards*. Evaluation of external audit by IAAs has been a recommendation in The IIA *Standards* since 1987. Such an evaluation should take place annually whether the IAA is in-house staffed or outsourced.

The Public Audit Forum (www.public-audit-forum.gov.uk) was established in 1998 by the National Audit Office, Northern Ireland Audit Office, Audit Commission, National Health Service in England & Wales and the Accounts Commission for Scotland to provide a focus for developmental thinking about public audit. Its publication *What Public Sector Bodies can expect from their Auditors*, 2000, contains the following guidance for close working relationships between internal and external audit:

> 'Co-operation between external and internal auditors should be a two-way process. Internal audit should not become simply an agent of external audit. Working relationships should involve:
> – periodic meetings to discuss matters of mutual interest;
> – access to each other's high level plans and systems notes and findings;
> – mutual consultation on audit plans and visits, which gives sufficient advance notice; and
> – common understanding on audit techniques, methods and terminology.'

The IIA *Standards* require internal audit to take a lead in ensuring that such co-ordination takes place:

> 'The chief audit executive should share information and co-ordinate activities with other internal and external providers of relevant assurance and consulting services to ensure proper coverage and minimize duplication of efforts.'

> '... the board may request the chief audit executive to assess the performance of external auditors.'

> 'Provide information (to the audit committee) on the co-ordination with and oversight of other control and monitoring functions (eg risk management, compliance, security, business continuity, legal, ethics, environmental, external audit).'

HM Treasury guidance is based on the following principles being implemented into both the internal and external audit practices. The same principles can be applied to all assurance services:

1. Both parties are committed to developing co-ordinated and effective audit services.
2. Regular consultation takes place between both parties.
3. Regular and open communication takes place between both parties.
4. Mutual confidence exists, based on the work of each party being conducted within relevant professional standards.
5. All information exchanged is treated professionally and with integrity.

| 1. ☐ needs improvements | 2. ☐ meets best practice | 3. ☐ exceeds best practice |
|---|---|---|

BEST PRACTICE 17

One of the world's largest utilities recently advertised for UK internal audit staff, stating that responsibilities include 'promoting UK internal audit as a center of excellence for best practice risk and controls advice'. Such responsibilities are now becoming part of the responsibilities of many internal audit activities across all sectors, including those in HAs.

The IIA Standards provide a useful benchmark for internal audit involvement in the risk management process. 'Risk management is a key responsibility of management. To achieve its business objectives, management should ensure that sound risk management processes are in place and functioning. Boards and audit committees have an oversight role to determine that appropriate risk management processes are in place and that these processes are adequate and effective. Internal auditors should assist both management and the audit committee by examining, evaluating, reporting, and recommending improvements on the adequacy and effectiveness of management's risk processes. However, internal auditors acting in a consulting role can assist the organisation in identifying, evaluating, and implementing risk management methodologies, and controls to address those risks.'

The Housing Corporation in its recently published Risk Management Topic Paper No.4 Risk Mapping – Dilemmas and Solutions, April 2003, supports the above. 'It is important to note that this risk assessment is the responsibility of management. It forms a part of the controls assurance framework set out in the Housing Corporation Circular on Internal Controls Assurance. It is a form of self-certification. Despite this being self-assessment, other assurance processes will test the validity of the controls evaluation. Internal audit will provide independent assurance that the controls can be relied upon and on the management assurances. In addition the risk management process will be subject to internal audit in the same way as any other process.'

The IIA-UK & Ireland Professional Briefing Note 10 Managing Risk, 1998 lists the following appropriate roles for internal audit in the process of assessing and identifying risk (these roles are repeated in Circular 25/01):

(a) as facilitators enabling and guiding managers and staff through the process;
(b) as team members who are part of the broader-based multi-disciplinary and multi- skilled groups, providing internal audit expertise to the group;
(c) as risk and control analysts, providing advice to managers on business risk; and
(d) as providers to management of tools and techniques used to analyse risks and controls; and

(e)    as a centre of expertise for managing risk, for example in managing databases or maintaining corporate risk files.

| 1. ☐ needs improvements | 2. ☐ meets best practice | 3. ☐ exceeds best practice |
|---|---|---|

## BEST PRACTICE 18

The HAIAF, A Practical Guide to Risk Management, 1999, recognised that control risk self-assessment (CRSA) programmes '... are being widely used now in industry by internal audit activities, who must provide assurance on an increasing range of complex controls. This route is open to all HAs and a number have implemented such programmes. When linked to risk management, these initiatives support one another to provide a depth of assurance for management and internal audit.'

The IIA Inc offers a learning programme and certificate in control self-assessment knowledge and techniques – *Certification in Control Self-Assessment* (*CCSA*) – see www.theiia.org for details of its syllabus and examinations. Use these as a benchmark. This is an international certification programme. At least one UK government department has qualified some of its staff in the use of CRSA using this certificate. The IIA-UK & Ireland also includes CRSA knowledge and skills techniques in its training and examination programmes – see www.iia.org.uk.

| 1. ☐ needs improvements | 2. ☐ meets best practice | 3. ☐ exceeds best practice |
|---|---|---|

## BEST PRACTICE 19

Circular 25/01 recommends that:

'... internal audit should give the board (or audit committee) an annual report, including an:

...

e)    overview of the systems of internal control reviewed.'

The IIA Standards recommend that such a report '... should emphasise the critical role played by the control processes in the quest for the organisation's objectives, and it should refer to the major work performed by internal audit and to other important sources of information that were used to formulate the overall assurance judgment ... the report should be clear, concise and informative and targeted to meet their (management and the audit committee/board) needs.'

| 1. ☐ needs improvements | 2. ☐ meets best practice | 3. ☐ exceeds best practice |
|---|---|---|

## BEST PRACTICE 20

The IIA Standards require the IAA to '... contribute to the organisation's governance process by evaluating and improving the process through which (1) values and goals are established and communicated (2) the accomplishment of goals is monitored (3) accountability is ensured, and (4) values are preserved.'

Such a contribution should require that internal audit provide the audit committee/ board with an annual opinion statement on governance, accountability and probity, covering the ten principles in the National Housing Federation Competence and Accountability, 2000:

**Standards: Accountability: Openness: Equality: Review: Clarity: Control: Information: Structures: Audit.**

| 1. ☐ needs improvements | 2. ☐ meets best practice | 3. ☐ exceeds best practice |
|---|---|---|

BEST PRACTICE 21

The IIA *Standards* provide the framework and guidance for quality systems covering both assurance and consultancy engagements. The *Standards* require a quality assurance and continuous programme to be implemented by an IAA claiming it is using its guidance. Such a programme should include the following elements:

'Supervision

Internal assessments

External assessments'

Qualified persons who are independent of the organisation should perform external quality assessments. It is recommended that these should be carried out at least once every five years. ISO 9000 provides a good benchmark for all the quality assurance and continuous improvement requirements of The IIA *Standards*. It is important that the board/audit committee is aware that a quality assurance and continuous programme has been established in an IAA and assessments of its quality performance are reported to the board/audit committee.

| 1. ☐ needs improvements | 2. ☐ meets best practice | 3. ☐ exceeds best practice |
|---|---|---|

BEST PRACTICE 22

In most industry sectors there has been a development of internal audit contribution to the establishment of quality/improvement programmes. Circular 25/01 recognises quality management systems as a form of assurance for management and the boards of HAs. The Housing Corporation and Audit Commission both encourage the contribution internal audit can make to Best Value reviews. The government in its Modernising Government *Guide to Quality Schemes and Best Value*, 2000, recognises the support quality schemes can give to the achievement of Best Value. The Cabinet Office, *Getting it Together*, 2001, focuses on how quality schemes can help the public sector to deliver efficient, high quality services. Its advice is appropriate for all HAs and is being followed by many. How each quality scheme links into the other and impacts risk, control and governance is important for HA boards, audit committees and all those who provide assurance services. Internal audit activities can provide advice and guidance on how quality schemes are implemented.

The IIA new definition of internal auditing provides opportunities for internal audit to offer its knowledge and skills to add value to the development and implementation of all quality/programmes, in both its assurance and consultancy roles. This can be through internal audit or consultancy engagements. Whichever role is used The IIA strongly advises that the terms of reference for such contributions should be approved at board/audit committee level and any adverse impact on the independence and objectivity of internal audit clearly understood. When carrying out a consultancy engagement to add value to a quality programme, The IIA recommends that the internal audit activity should understand:

- 'Needs of management officials, including the nature, timing and communication of engagement results.
- Possible motivations and reasons for those requesting the service.
- Extent of work needed to achieve the engagement's objectives.
- Skills and resources needed to conduct the engagement.
- Effect on the audit plan previously approved by the audit committee.
- Potential impact on future audit assignments and engagements.
- Potential organisational benefits to be derived from the engagement.'

| 1. ☐ needs improvements | 2. ☐ meets best practice | 3. ☐ exceeds best practice |
|---|---|---|

## BEST PRACTICE 23

Recommendations for internal audit best practice involvement in information technology were published in previous research covering internal audit in housing associations. These recommended the following checklist of questions that all internal auditors should ask and audit:

### 1. SYSTEMS:

- **How computer systems are developed?**
- **How computer systems first operate when implemented?**
- **How established computer systems are maintained?**

### 2. COMPUTERS OPERATIONS

- **Where are computers located?**
- **What power do computers have in the operations they control?**
- **How secure are their operations?**
- **How well are they managed?**
- **What contingency plans exist for their replacement?**

### 3. AUDIT TECHNIQUES

- **What programmes exist to improve internal audit work?**
- **What computer output can be used to improve internal audit work?**

Also mentioned was the fourth edition of the CIPFA Computer Audit Guidelines, which at that time covered:

COMPUTER AUDIT MANAGEMENT
THE MANAGEMENT OF IT
INSTALLATION CONTROLS
APPLICATION CONTROLS
AUDITING THE TECHNOLOGY
COMPUTER ASSISTED AUDITING
COMPUTER AUDIT AND LAW

Since then these guidelines have been revised and are now in a recently published sixth edition, endorsed by the IIA-UK & Ireland as appropriate for all its members. 'Aimed at both established and budding auditing practitioners, the Guidelines focus firmly on computer auditing as a top level management responsibility. Adding a wealth of new material to the timeless principles of the previous editions, the publication focuses on the duty of top management to install the most effective controls and security measures to protect the computer environment they now depend upon and the vital information it supports.'

Past research concluded with an IT best practice framework for internal audit linked to The IIA, *Systems Auditability and Control® (SAC)* 1997 framework. This framework is still appropriate today. The IIA has now published an *eSAC model®* that focuses on how the risks resulting from rapid technology and e-business changes can be managed and controlled. These risk and controls are now becoming important to many HAs.

| 1. ☐ needs improvements | 2. ☐ meets best practice | 3. ☐ exceeds best practice |
|---|---|---|

BEST PRACTICE 24

The following is an appropriate benchmark for the importance of developing an internal audit strategy, agreeing this at board and audit committee level, embedding it in all internal audit processes and marketing it throughout the organisation/s in which an internal activity provides its services.

**Internal audit marketing:**
- starts with a strategic business plan
- agrees a vision statement for the next three years
- creates a marketing plan for today
- relates all its objectives to organisation objectives
- demonstrates commitment to satisfy all its customers
- demonstrates its professionalism and ethics
- demonstrates competence and experience
- covers all its activities and relates these to organisation activities
- is supported by quality systems
- demonstrates how it delivers best value to the organisation
- is well documented
- is measured to assess its success
- justifies its cost
- is communicated throughout the organisation it serves
- is used by organisation management to demonstrate commitment to control

| 1. ☐ needs improvements | 2. ☐ meets best practice | 3. ☐ exceeds best practice |

*Part B*

# Performing internal audit

# Managing the internal audit activity – best practice guidance

**B1.1.1**   While we also refer to other important pronouncements, our main source of guidance for the parts of this Handbook which describe internal auditing best practice has been the *Professional Practices Framework* of The Institute of Internal Auditors. This *Framework* includes their *Definition* of internal auditing, *Code of Ethics*, *Standards*, and *Practice Advisories*. Of these, only the *Practice Advisories* are non-mandatory: they explain and elaborate upon best practice in most circumstances, and are important for practitioners and students. Readers can see the current complete list of *Practice Advisories* at www.theiia.org. Those current on 1 January 2005 are shown at APPENDIX 3 of this Handbook, including a useful topical classification at APPENDIX 3.2.

In addressing this subject we have drawn more widely than those *Practice Advisories* classified by The Institute as applicable to this part of our Handbook, which are:

| Practice Advisories, by Standard Number | Release date |
|---|---|
| Practice Advisory 2000–1: Managing the Internal Audit Activity | 5 January 2001 |
| Practice Advisory 2010–1: Planning | 5 January 2001 |
| Practice Advisory 2010–2: Linking the Audit Plan to Risk and Exposure | 7 March 2001 |
| Practice Advisory 2020–1: Communication and Approval | 5 January 2001 |
| Practice Advisory 2030–1: Resource Management | 5 January 2001 |
| Practice Advisory 2040–1: Policies and Procedures | 5 January 2001 |
| Practice Advisory 2050–1: Coordination | 5 January 2001 |
| Practice Advisory 2050–2: Acquisition of External Audit Services | 7 February 2002 |
| Practice Advisory 2060–1: Reporting to Board and Senior Management | 5 January 2001 |
| Practice Advisory 2060–2: Relationship with the Audit Committee | 3 December 2002 |

*Practice Advisories* carry the *Standard* number to which they principally refer. Readers are advised to consult the applicable Standards as we do not in every case reproduce them here. They are to be found at APPENDIX 2.

Internal audit managers share with other managers a need for diverse management skills and competencies. Here we focus on those which are specific to the context of internal auditing; they are those alluded to within the *Standards* of the Institute of Internal Auditors and elaborated upon within their *Practice Advisories*. For those for whom the *Standards* are mandatory (see A1.1.4), compliance with *Practice Advisories* is nevertheless optional. However, the content of Practice Advisories is generally regarded as representing best practice and thus to be the best way of ensuring that the *Standards* are adhered to. The content of the *Practice Advisories* can often point to what are regarded as the correct answers to questions within the professional examinations of The Institute of Internal Auditors.

Throughout the *Standards* and the *Practice Advisories*, The Institute generally uses the phrase 'internal audit activity' to refer to the function that provides the internal audit service. While we tend to refer to the internal audit activity's relationship with the audit committee (of the board), pronouncements of The Institute of Internal Auditors consistently refer to the internal audit activity's relationship with the *board*. However, their definition of 'Board' allows that it might in practice be the audit committee of the board:

> '**Board** – A board is an organization's governing body, such as a board of directors, supervisory board, head of an agency or legislative body, board of governors or trustees of a non profit organization, or any other designated body of the organization, including the audit committee, to whom the chief audit executive may functionally report.'[1]

The frequent criticism that internal auditors do not understand management should be completely unfounded. Surveys of internal auditing, in comparison with other activities within entities, have consistently found that internal auditing activities are stronger at planning, a key managerial function, than are most other activities. Managing the internal audit activity successfully is itself an in-depth exercise in the art of management. Each individual audit project is itself an exercise in project management – and project management is a complex and increasingly important managerial skill. Leadership and quality are other key managerial attributes essential for effective internal auditing. We should not overlook that the internal audit activity is a review of the management process at work across the entity. There can be no doubt that chief audit executives and individual internal auditors gain very significant managerial experience while they work within internal audit.

The three overarching managerial responsibilities of chief audit executives are to manage so that:

- 'Audit work fulfills the general purposes and responsibilities described in the charter, approved by senior management, and accepted by the board.
- Resources of the internal audit activity are efficiently and effectively employed.
- Audit work conforms to the Standards for the Professional Practice of Internal Auditing.'[2]

Arising from the above, chief audit executives also have responsibilities with respect to (a) the *content* and *communication* of the charter of the internal audit activity, (b) the *quality* of internal audit resources, and (c) ensuring that all the activities set out within the *Standards* and within the definition of internal auditing are covered within the scope of work which is implemented. It is not generally appreciated that there is a professional obligation to ensure that *all*[3] the activities set out within the *Standards* are covered within the scope of internal audit work:

(a)

> 'There are three areas of activities that are key to an effective relationship between the audit committee and the internal audit function, chiefly through the Chief Audit Executive (CAE):
> …
> ● Ensuring that the charter, role, and activities of internal audit are clearly understood and responsive to the needs of the audit committee and the board.'[4]

(b)

> 'Professional proficiency is the responsibility of the chief audit executive and each internal auditor. The chief audit executive should ensure that persons assigned to each engagement collectively possess the necessary knowledge, skills, and other competencies to conduct the engagement properly.'[5]

(c)

> 'The Chief Audit Executive (CAE) is responsible for establishing an internal audit activity whose scope of work includes all the activities in the Standards and in [The Institute of Internal Auditors'] definition of internal auditing.'[6]

and:

> 'The chief audit executive should periodically assess whether the purpose, authority, and responsibility, as defined in the charter, continue to be adequate to enable the internal audit activity to accomplish its objectives. The result of this periodic assessment should be communicated to senior management and the board.'[7]

## B1.1.2 Policies and procedures to guide the internal audit activity

The extent to which an internal audit activity needs a formal management approach supported by written policies and procedures is likely to be related to its size and the complexity of its work:

> 'Formal administrative and technical audit manuals may not be needed by all internal auditing entities. A small internal audit activity may be managed informally.'[8]

The objective here is:

> 'to guide the audit staff in the consistent compliance with the internal audit activity's standards of performance.'[9]

The form and content of written policies and procedures should be appropriate to the size and structure of the internal audit activity and the complexity of its work. Formal administrative and technical audit manuals may not be needed by all internal auditing entities. A small internal audit activity may be managed informally. Its audit staff may be directed and controlled through daily, close supervision and written memoranda. In a large internal audit activity, more formal and comprehensive policies and procedures are essential to guide the audit staff in the consistent compliance with the internal audit activity's standards of performance.[10]

In the smallest of internal audit activities it may be enough to depend upon the activity's charter and the *Code of Ethics* and *Standards* of The Institute of Internal Auditors supplemented by reference to those parts of the Practice Advisories with which the chief audit executive has exercised his or her discretion to apply or not. In a small internal audit activity, past audit working papers and reports – and especially the past plans for individual audit engagements – may also be a valuable substitute for technical guidance on performing particular audit engagements.

In larger internal audit activities a greater emphasis on developing and following audit policies and procedures will be both more necessary as well as more affordable. The objective is:

- to ensure consistently high standards of work;
- to codify the experience of the internal audit function in order to make it available to all;
- to progressively enhance audit policies and procedures so as to improve quality of audit performance;
- to facilitate supervision (direction, oversight and review).

Affordability comes from the more extensive opportunities to apply formal policies and procedures in the larger internal audit activity, and also from their contribution to the quality in audit work. They are better value for money in the larger internal audit activity.

Internal auditing activities of any size may need a degree of formal policies and procedures, beyond their charters etc, when external regulatory requirements so require.

B4.1.10 explores the value of standardised engagement records and the importance of ensuring that audit engagement records are addressed sufficiently within the policies and procedures of the internal auditing activity. With respect to audit engagement records, Practice Advisory 2330.A1–2 advises:

> 'Internal department policies should be developed in regard to the operation of the internal audit activity. These written practices should cover, among other matters, what should be included in engagement records, how long should departmental records be retained, how outside requests for access to department records should be handled, and what special practices should be following in handling an investigation with legal counsel.'[11]

## B1.1.3 Planning

Planning for the internal audit activity should be consistent with both its charter and with the goals of the organization.[12] We should not overlook the need for there to be congruence between the internal audit plan and *both* the internal audit charter *and* the goals of the entity. Neither the goals for the internal auditing activity nor an annual audit plan of audit engagements consistent with the internal audit charter could be established appropriately without reference to the annual business plan of the entity as well as to its longer term goals:

> 'The audit universe can include components from the organization's strategic plan. By incorporating components of the organization's strategic plan, the audit universe will consider and reflect the overall business objectives.'[13]

At all levels of audit planning the internal audit activity should factor in a keen awareness of management's goals and objectives. Thus, for an individual audit engagement, the audit starting point is to clarify the objectives that management have for the activity to be audited; then the focus of audit effort should be on matters germane to the achievement of these objectives. It is unlikely that there is justification to include within an audit report any finding or recommendation which is not relevant to the achievement of management's objectives. Similarly, when drawing up the plan of audit engagements to be conducted, the chief audit executive should have clearly in mind the overall goals and objectives of the entity: allocation of audit resources across the different potential auditable units within the audit universe should be proportionate to the risks that each unit presents to the achievement of the entity's overall goals and objectives – with the most important goals and objectives meriting proportionately more auditor attention.

The Institute of Internal Auditors has identified four areas in which there are distinctive features of the internal auditing planning process to be established:

1.  Internal audit activity goals.
2.  Internal audit engagement work schedules.
3.  Internal audit staffing plans and financial budgets.
4.  Internal audit activity reports.[14]

We consider there is a fifth important area which The Institute and most internal auditors overlook. That is, forward planning for the necessary future changes in an internal audit activity so that the internal audit activity will be well placed to meet the changing needs of the entity for internal audit going forward – perhaps using a time horizon of three to five years forward. Too often internal audit activities find they are poorly placed to provide the internal audit service being asked for as of today – and the reason is often that the internal audit activity had previously failed to anticipate the need for future change in the composition, structure and competencies of the internal audit activity on a timely basis. We would call this 'strategic planning for internal audit'. That the UK's HM Treasury applies the phrase 'strategic planning' to conducting the audit needs assessment in order to determine the future plan of audit engagements over the next twelve months or so, is indicative that long term planning for change in the internal audit activity is largely being overlooked. We cover what we term 'strategic planning for internal audit' in B1.2.1. Put another way:

●   Does the chief audit executive have a sound appreciation of how the goals and objectives of the entity are likely to change over the next three to five years?

- Has the chief audit executive assessed how these changes are likely to impact upon the necessary character of the internal audit activity going forward?
- Has the chief audit executive, after negotiation with senior management and after reference to the audit committee, instigated measures which will reform the internal audit activity appropriately, going forward?

### B1.1.4  *Internal audit activity goals*

In practical terms, the achievement on budget and on time of the planned programme of audit engagements is an important, if not *the most important*, operational target for the internal audit activity. The Institute of Internal Auditors calls this programme 'the audit engagement work schedules'. There may be other goals for the internal audit activity which are set, such as:

- Contribute to the achievement of the overall goals of the business (as defined in the corporate business plan);
- Achieve a target level of client acceptance of the internal audit service;
- Through coordination with the external auditor, to avoid unnecessary duplication of audit work and to contain the external audit fee (see B1.1.15);
- To achieve internal audit proficiency in particular specialist internal audit area(s) – such as environmental, IT, contracts, etc;
- To achieve a particular level of audit reporting success (eg percentage of accepted audit recommendations which are implemented successfully);
- etc

The more objective the measurability of goal attainment, the better:

> 'The goals of the internal audit activity should be capable of being accomplished within specified operating plans and budgets and, to the extent possible, should be measurable. They should be accompanied by measurement criteria and targeted dates of accomplishment.'[15]

### B1.1.5  *Risk assessment as a component of audit planning*

There is a presumption that audit plans should be risk-based:

> '**Standard 2010.A1** – The internal audit activity's plan of engagements should be based on a risk assessment, undertaken at least annually. The input of senior management and the board should be considered in this process.'

Practice Advisory 2010–2: 'Linking the Audit Plan to Risk and Exposures' endorses Standard 2010.A1 that the audit activity's plan of engagements should be based on a risk assessment undertaken at least annually:

> 'Changes in management direction, objectives, emphasis, and focus should be reflected in updates to the audit universe and related audit plan. It is advisable to assess the audit universe on at least an annual basis to reflect the most current strategies and direction of the organization. In some situations, audit plans may need to be updated frequently (eg, quarterly) in response to changes in the organization's environment of management activities.'[16]

Until 2004, most if not all official pronouncements on risk had focussed exclusively on the management of uncertainties and risks which might *negatively* affect the organisation. The impression given had been that management's responsibility was to identify and assess the affect of future events which, if they occurred, might negatively impact upon the achievement of objectives – and to design and implement satisfactory mitigation responses. Now there has emerged an awareness that a comprehensive (we term it a 360°) approach to risk management should also set out to identify and assess the effect of future events not anticipated within the organisation's strategic plan which, *if they occurred and could be exploited by the organisation, would impact positively upon the organisation's performance.* So risk management is not just about managing 'downside risk'. It is about managing what might be termed 'upside risk' as well. 'Upside risks' represent extra potential opportunities.

While The Institute of Internal Auditors acknowledges what we term, inelegantly, as 'upside risk' (B2.1.3), they nevertheless, even as recently as 2004,[17] associate the internal audit activity, mainly or even exclusively, with 'downside risk':

> 'The internal audit activity's audit plan should be designed based on an assessment of risk and exposures that may affect the organization. Ultimately, key audit objectives are to provide management with information to mitigate the negative consequences associated with accomplishing the organization's objectives'[18]

and:

> 'Audit work schedules should be based on, among other factors, an assessment of risk priority and exposure. Prioritizing is needed to make decisions for applying relative resources based on the significance of risk and exposure.'[19]

Practice Advisory 2010–2 recognises that risk modelling may assist the chief audit executive to develop a risk-based audit plan.[20] An issue which is often debated is whether the annual plan of audit engagements to be conducted should correspond to top management's and the board's assessment of major risks. The Institute's position is not necessarily so:

> 'Developing assessments and reports on the organization's risk management processes are normally a high audit priority. Evaluating management's risk processes is different than the requirement that auditors use risk analysis to plan audits. However, information from a comprehensive risk management process, including the identification of management and board concerns, can assist the internal auditor in planning audit activities.'[21]

The determination of the annual plan of audit engagements should be consistent with the best professional judgement of the chief audit executive; when this is not so, senior management and the board, through its audit committee, should be made aware of the disparity. It is quite likely that the chief audit executive does not consider the assessment of risk undertaken by senior management and the board to be satisfactory basis, unamended, to determine the audit engagements to be conducted. One reason for this is that top management tend to believe their own propaganda and overlook the downside risks associated with some of the policy initiatives they are committed to. Another reason is that the major risks of a business may be 'buried in the woodwork' – unknown to top management but amenable to identification by internal audit in the course of routine audit work. So a proportion of total available internal audit time should be allocated to auditing across the business, including within the audit plan areas of the business where there is no perception that there is major risk. Major risk could be concealed within those areas; and a lack of internal audit attention to perceived 'low risk' areas could encourage management, staff and others to develop business practices, fraudulent or otherwise, which could create major risks to the business.

## B1.1.6  Communication and approval of internal audit activity plans

We have said that achievement, on budget and on time, of the planned programme of audit engagements is an important target for the internal audit activity. The Institute of Internal Auditors calls this programme the 'engagement work schedules',[22] 'engagement work schedule priorities',[23] 'audit work schedules'[24] or simply 'the internal audit activity's audit plan'.[25] The chief audit executive, senior management and the audit committee all need to be committed to an agreed schedule of internal audit engagements and should monitor its progress:

> 'The chief audit executive should submit annually to senior management for approval, and to the board for its information, a summary of the internal audit activity's work schedule, staffing plan, and financial budget. The chief audit executive should also submit all significant interim changes for approval and information. Engagement work schedules, staffing plans, and financial budgets should inform senior management and the board of the scope of internal auditing work and of any limitations placed on that scope.'[26]

(See B1.1.10 'Internal audit activity reports'.)

The approved engagement work schedule, staffing plan, and financial budget, along with all significant interim changes, should contain sufficient information to enable the board to ascertain whether the internal audit activity's objectives and plans support those of the organization and the board.

## B1.1.7  Internal audit resource management

**Table 1** is a minimal layout for an annual plan of audit engagements. In **Table 1** we provide the information for the chief audit executive, senior management and the audit committee to approve and then to monitor progress as information in the vacant columns is entered.

Practice Advisory 2010–1 requires that:

> 'Engagement work schedules should include the following:
> * What activities are to be performed;
> * When they will be performed; and

- The estimated time required, taking into account the scope of the engagement work planned and the nature and extent of related work performed by others.'[27]

Note that planned audit engagements of a 'consulting services' variety, as well as those which are 'assurance services', should be included in the annual audit plan, and progress should be reported for them:

**'Standard 2010.C1**
The chief audit executive should consider accepting proposed consulting engagements based on the engagement's potential to improve management of risks, add value, and improve the organization's operations. Those engagements that have been accepted should be included in the plan.'

Note too that follow-up audit engagement should also be included within the annual audit plan:

'The chief audit executive is responsible for scheduling follow-up activities as part of developing engagement work schedules. Scheduling of follow-up should be based on the risk and exposure involved, as well as the degree of difficulty and the significance of timing in implementing corrective action.'[28]

To the extent possible, it may be desirable to 'draw the boundaries' around an audit engagement so that it can be allocated a reasonable but not excessive number of auditor days – and preferably by a team rather than by a sole auditor. An audit duration of, say, ten to fifteen days allows some in-depth work to be undertaken between the planning and end phases of the audit. The planning phase of the audit usually can take place some time before the fieldwork. A team rather than a sole auditor can be helpful in terms of mutual support.

## TABLE 1: AUDIT ENGAGEMENTS WORK SCHEDULE (IE PLANNED ANNUAL PROGRAMME OF AUDIT ENGAGEMENTS)

**Example**

| Company name |
| --- |
| Annual Internal Audit Plan 2006 |

Audit Resource scheduled in this audit plan: 332 days representing 70% of one full-time Internal Audit Manager's time and 90% of 0.9 of a Senior Auditor's time for the year.

| SYSTEM (ie AUDIT ENGAGEMENT) | 2006 Planned (auditor days) | 2006 Actual (auditor days) | Planned report issue date | Actual report issue date |
|---|---|---|---|---|
| **CORPORATE SYSTEMS** | | | | |
| Corporate Governance | 5 | | November 2006 | |
| External Relations | 5 | | May 2006 | |
| Management Information and Statistics | 5 | | September 2006 | |
| Business Continuity Planning | 5 | | October 2006 | |
| Risk Management | 5 | | June 2006 | |
| **Sub Total** | **25** | | | |
| ... | | | | |
| OTHER | | | | |
| VFM Studies | 4 | | | |
| Project Management reviews | 7 | | | |
| Recommenda-tion Tracking and Follow-up | 7 | | | |
| Audit Management (incl. Audit Committee work) | 30 | | | |
| Consultancy/ Advice | 20 | | | |
| Planning | 10 | | | |
| Sub Total | **78** | | | |
| **GRAND TOTAL** | **332** | | | |

Although most of the following are unlikely to be shown on the face of the planned programme of audit engagements, they are matters to be considered in establishing engagement work schedule priorities:

- 'The dates and results of the last engagement;
- Updated assessments of risks and effectiveness of risk management and control processes;

- Requests by senior management, audit committee, and governing body;
- Current issues relating to organizational governance;
- Major changes in enterprise's business, operations, programs, systems, and controls;
- Opportunities to achieve operating benefits; and
- Changes to and capabilities of the audit staff.'[29]

## B1.1.8 *Internal audit staffing plans and financial budgets*

In addition to the planned programme of audit engagements, there will be a plan which shows the assignment of audit staff of different levels to each audit engagement. Calendar dates can be associated with this, but it will usually be unwise to develop and publish a firm staff plan more than between three to six months forward – as it is unsettling for staff if travel and other plans, once announced, have to be changed except rarely. It is also inefficient to develop plans which are almost certainly going to need to be modified. Apart from the knowledge, skills and other competencies required[30, 31] for each audit engagement, audit management will also take into account such matters as:

- Restricted availability of audit staff to travel, or to travel to particular locations;
- The desirability of achieving some continuity of audit team members between audit engagements;
- The need to develop audit staff through variety of audit experience;
- Inter-personal relationships;
- Special needs for supervision.

Apart from being appropriate for the audit engagements planned, staffing plans and financial budgets must reflect:

> 'administrative activities, education and training requirements, and audit research and development efforts'.[32]

The budgeted costs of each audit can be calculated and actual costs monitored. Usually the staff cost element of budgeted costs can be based on the standard cost of an auditor day and this can also include an apportionment of the internal audit activity's overheads: it is unlikely to worthwhile calculating the exact costs of each individual auditor's time having regard to their pay rates, etc. Travel and subsistence costs can be charged to an audit engagement as direct costs.

In determining the resources necessary to perform an audit engagement, evaluation of the following is important, as well as consideration of the use of external resources in instances where additional knowledge, skills, and other competencies are needed:

- 'The number and experience level of the internal auditing staff required should be based on an evaluation of the nature and complexity of the engagement assignment, time constraints, and available resources.
- Knowledge, skills, and other competencies of the internal auditing staff should be considered in selecting internal auditors for the engagement.

- Training needs of internal auditors should be considered, since each engagement assignment serves as a basis for meeting developmental needs of the internal auditing activity.'[33]

### B1.1.9  Charging for audit work

Some internal auditing activities recharge audit costs to those parts of the business that have been audited. Opinions vary as to the merit of this. It results in a more accurate indication of the true costs of running the different departments (etc) of the business. A close approximation to this can however be achieved by a year-end allocation of total audit costs across the cost centres of the business.

One principle is that costs should be borne by line managers who are able to control those costs, and it is not the case that managers of audited activities should have a veto over whether or not their activities are audited by internal audit; nor, if so, how much internal audit resource should be allocated to those audits. This veto would only apply to the provision of consulting services by internal audit (see A1.1.11 and A1.1.13), not the provision of assurance services.

Charging out audit costs to audited units can, however, make responsible management more aware of the need to benefit from the results of the audit. However, much the same can be achieved if the audit report of the engagement indicates how much the audit has cost – without necessarily charging that cost against the budgets of audited management. Highlighting the cost of an audit in this way can also be a valuable incentive to the audit team to use their best endeavours to ensure that the results of the audit justify its cost.

Treating audit costs as a central overhead to be allocated across the cost centres of the business at the end of the year can assist in holding the chief audit executive more to account for total audit costs and for budgetary control: if it is too easy to transfer audit costs to operating divisions, it may not be so apparent how much internal audit is costing. On the other hand, charging cost-conscious line managers for internal audit services can make internal audit more conscious of the need to provide evident value-for-money. But value-for-money from internal auditing does not just come from specific cost savings arising from audit conclusions: it can be counterproductive to the requirement for internal audit to 'add value' if internal auditors are always expected to justify themselves in terms of cost savings resulting from internal audit work. An obvious example is the unknown but conceivably large avoidable loss or fraud that was prevented as a result of an implemented audit recommendation.

## B1.1.10  Internal audit activity reports

The sample audit plan we show in *Table 1* (above) achieves flexibility by scheduling significantly fewer than all of the budgeted future audit time availability. The Institute puts it like this:

> 'The work schedules should be sufficiently flexible to cover unanticipated demands on the internal audit activity.'[34]

In this way, it is realistic to hold the internal audit activity to account to complete this planned programme of audits whilst having time available for unanticipated audit engagements and other unanticipated audit activity. The audit committee should monitor this carefully, and the chief audit executive should report progress against plan clearly to the audit committee, as well as to senior management. Reporting progress against plan is an important part of what The Institute of Internal Auditors calls 'activity reporting'. Sometimes this has been called task reporting. There are many different facets of activity reporting, for instance:

- A report from the chief audit executive to the audit committee on progress against plan in terms of completing scheduled audit engagements;
- A report to the audit committee on the principal results of audit work conducted over the past period;
- An annual report to the audit committee, perhaps including the chief audit executive's overall opinion on the effectiveness of risk management, internal control and governance processes;
- Any or all of the above, but addressed to senior general management;
- Audit reports on individual audit engagements completed.

## B1.1.11  *Reporting to the board to senior management*

While the internal audit activity is primarily an audit *for* management, it is also in effect an audit *of* management *for* the board. We discuss this at A2.1.2.

Senior management and the audit committee will be particularly interested in whether the planned programme of audit engagements is being completed on budget and on time. Variations need to be identified and explained to the audit committee: reasons for variations are almost certainly informative to the audit committee. Variations may indicate that , for instance:

- The internal audit activity is under-staffed or wrongly resourced compared to the agreed levels and competencies;
- Internal audit has experienced obstacles to the performance of some audit engagement(s) contained within the agreed audit plan;
- Some audit engagement(s) have consumed more of different audit resources due to problems encountered after the audit plan was drawn up;
- Management has diverted internal audit to assist in areas of the business and in ways not covered in the audit plan, for instance to 'fire-fighting assign-ments'.

In practice, senior management and audit committees need crystal clear reporting by the chief audit executive of progress against the plan of audits to be conducted – so that they can understand whether progress is to plan and the reasons of variations – and the root causes of those reasons. The reasons for variations in progress against plan are likely to be very informative for senior management and the audit committee as they are likely to draw attention to other matters of importance to them. Variations in progress against plan could be due to any of the four factors listed immediately above.

The audit committee of the board will wish to obtain a clear insight into whichever of the above circumstances apply.

The chief audit executive has the managerial responsibility to report on internal audit activities ('activity reports') to both senior management and the board. While these reports may, rarely, be as infrequent as once a year, they will usually be much more frequent. Many audit committees receive such reports at each audit committee meeting. The chief audit executive's activity reports highlight major findings and recommendations as well as reporting progress against the audit plan:

> 'The chief audit executive should submit activity reports to senior management and to the board at least annually. Activity reports should highlight significant engagement observations and recommendations and should inform senior management and the board of any significant deviations from approved engagement work schedules, staffing plans, and financial budgets, and the reasons for them.'[35]

## B1.1.12  *Level of detail in audit activity reports*

It will be necessary to determine the appropriate level of detail within reports to different parties on the results of audit engagement. Too much detail can obscure the results which need to be communicated. While audit reports should be concise they should not be too brief to communicate what is needed.

Typically, audit committees have too much information to assimilate, within their available time, to be able to cope with more than one or two paragraphs on each audit engagement completed. One or two paragraphs should usually give the chief audit executive the scope to communicate the main issues which need to be drawn to the audit committee's attention without diverting them into a consideration of unnecessary detail. The audit committee can always ask for the full version of an audit engagement report if, in the circumstances, that is needed.

The likely practice will therefore be that the chief audit executive prepares for each meeting of the audit committee a report which contains:

- an introduction;
- highlights;
- (an overall conclusion);
- a paragraph or two on each audit completed;
- advance notice of critical issues arising from audits not yet completed;
- a schedule of progress against the planned (annual) programme of audits.

Not all chief audit executives are required to provide to the audit committee an overall conclusion on the effectiveness of risk management, control and governance processes. Where there is such a requirement, which we commend, it may not be expected to appear within every activity report to the audit committee. It is more likely to be a requirement for the chief audit executive's annual report to the audit committee, or possibly a six-monthly requirement.

The annual report of the chief audit executive to the audit committee is therefore likely to contain the following:

- an introduction;
- overall conclusion;
- summary of key issues arising from internal audit work over the past year;
- a schedule of progress against the planned (annual) programme of audits;
- discussion of emerging risks;
- discussion of adequacy of audit resources;
- proposed audit plan for the following year.

Where boards are approximately balanced numerically between executive and non-executive directors, the practice may be followed of each non-executive director 'shadowing' a particular executive director. The shadow takes a particular interest in the work of that executive director and the rest of the board relies to some extent on this. The shadow is also a point of reference that the executive director can consult when needed. Where shadowing of this sort applies, it could be that the non-executive shadow of the finance director (or another director) is the only member of the audit committee who routinely receives a copy of each full audit engagement report.

As with the audit committee, some senior management do not need the full detail contained within typical audit engagement reports. A practical approach is to commence an audit engagement report with a high level summary spreading over a page or two and containing the following:

- introduction;
- scope and objectives of the audit;
- conclusion;
- summary of main issues arising from the audit.

Only this high level summary needs to be circulated to senior management – unless they have asked for the supporting detail or unless the chief audit executive considers on occasion that it is necessary that they should have the supporting detail. It should be the professional determination of the chief audit executive as to whom the results of audit work are communicated and to what level of detail.

## B1.1.13   Managing coordination with other assurance and consulting services

While the emphasis in our following discussion is on coordination between internal audit and external audit, there should also be an awareness that the chief audit executive has a responsibility to manage so that there is effective coordination with other internal and external review services. These might include, for instance:

**Internal**
Quality assurance
Risk management
Technical audit
Corporate social responsibility

The compliance function
Internal management consultants

External
Regulators and inspectors
Environmental auditors
Management consultants

The pertinent Standard is as follows:

> **'Standard 2050 – Coordination**
> The chief audit executive should share information and coordinate activities with other internal and external providers of relevant assurance and consulting services to ensure proper coverage and minimize duplication of efforts.'

When internal auditors assist external auditors and others they should do so in full observance of their obligations under the *Code of Ethics* and *Standards* of The Institute of Internal Auditors:

> 'Work performed by internal auditors to assist external auditors in fulfilling their responsibility is subject to all relevant provisions of the Standards for the Professional Practice of Internal Auditing.'[36]

In most contexts the principal coordination to be achieved is between external and internal audit. The chief audit executive should regard it as one of his or her managerial responsibilities to achieve this coordination and to report thereon to senior management and the board (through its audit committee):

> 'Oversight of the work of external auditors, including coordination with the internal audit activity, is generally the responsibility of the board. Actual coordination should be the responsibility of the chief audit executive.'[37]

## B1.1.14   *Audit risk for external and internal auditors*

This coordination must be put in the context of the different audit objectives that these two audit services set out to achieve.

Considered in terms of risk, 'audit risk' for the external auditor is the risk that audit processes fail to uncover significant misstatements in the financial results of the company that are being audited. Financial results would be significantly misstated if they misled the reader. The external auditor's audit planning emphasis is to minimise this external audit risk.

'Audit risk' for the internal auditor is the risk that internal audit fails to uncover significant weaknesses in risk management, control and governance processes. Risk-based internal audit planning together with the approaches adopted to conduct audit engagements are designed to minimise this risk. We should add that 'audit risk' for an internal auditor is not just the risk of failing to discover significant weaknesses, but is also the risk of failing to persuade management and the board as to the need for remedies. So the communication of audit results is an important part of the internal audit process which contributes to minimising internal audit risk.

The Institute puts the contrast between internal and external audit like this:

> 'The scope of internal auditing work is described within Section 2100 of the Standards. On the other hand, the external auditors' ordinary examination is designed to obtain sufficient evidential matter to support an opinion on the overall fairness of the annual financial statements. The scope of the work of external auditors is determined by their professional standards, and they are responsible for judging the adequacy of procedures performed and evidence obtained for purposes of expressing their opinion on the annual financial statements.'[38]

## B1.1.15   *Internal audit coordination with external audit*

We have introduced the subject of coordination between internal and external audit in terms of 'audit risk' in order to illustrate the potential for, and limitations of, coordination between 'the two audits'. Internal auditing activities in general should avoid undertaking work on behalf of the external auditor if it is work that internal audit would not otherwise undertake in order to meet internal audit objectives. There may be minor exceptions as when external audit finds it particularly difficult to access relevant information required to perform an audit test: in such cases it may be more cost-effective for internal audit to undertake that supernumerary task on behalf of the external auditor. However, care must be taken to ensure that by working on behalf of the external auditor, the internal audit activity is not being deflected from meeting its own internal audit objectives.

It is unlikely that there will be a 'one for one' saving in audit time and cost when internal audit assists the external auditor. The external auditor will need to confirm the quality of internal audit work upon which the external auditor wishes to rely and to evaluate the results. Caution must be exercised to ascertain that the external auditor is not asking the internal auditor to undertake a larger quantum of work (such as testing a larger sample) than would be the case if the external auditor did this work directly.

It is therefore appropriate that:

> 'The chief audit executive should make regular evaluations of the coordination between internal and external auditors. Such evaluations may also include assessments of the overall efficiency and effectiveness of internal and external auditing functions, including aggregate audit cost.'[39]

Enquiry should also be made as to whether the external auditor intends to rely (wholly or partially) on *the detail of the work done* by the internal auditor, or on *the summary results of that work*, or on the internal auditors' *conclusions and audit opinion* based on the work and results. It is, for instance, the lowest degree of reliance if the external auditor is only prepared to regard the internal auditor's contribution as partially meeting the requirements of an audit test – and then only after the external auditor has checked that the work was undertaken appropriately.

Under external auditing standards there are circumstances when an external auditor, after assessment, is entitled to rely upon the opinion of another professional, but usually this will be a professional in another field – such as an actuary or a property valuer. It is much less likely that the external auditor will place reliance upon the opinion of an internal auditor – not least because the internal auditor is employed by the external auditor's client. For instance, the US PCAOB's Auditing Standard No 2 makes it clear that the external auditors' attestation to the CEO's and CFO's certification of the effectiveness of internal control over financial reporting[40] (which requires the external auditors to be satisfied that the CEO and CFO have followed a due process, and also requires the external auditors to determine and report whether or not they concur with the CEO's and CFO's opinion as to effectiveness) must not place any reliance on work done on their behalf by the internal auditor.

Now that it is less frequently acceptable for external auditors to provide internal audit services to the same client, it follows that external auditors will generally be less willing to rely on work done on their behalf by internal auditors.

While we have focussed on external auditor reliance upon the internal audit activity, the internal audit activity may wish to place reliance upon the external auditor. This may create a requirement for internal audit access to external audit working papers:

> '*Access to each other's audit programs and working papers.* Access to the external auditors' programs and working papers may be important in order for internal auditors to be satisfied as to the propriety for internal audit purposes of relying on the external auditors' work. Such access carries with it the responsibility for internal auditors to respect the confidentiality of those programs and working papers. Similarly, access to the internal auditors' programs and working papers should be given to external auditors in order for external auditors to be satisfied as to the propriety, for external audit purposes, of relying on the internal auditors' work.'[41]

and:

> 'It is common practice for internal and external auditors to grant access to each other's audit working papers. Access to audit working papers by external auditors should be subject to the approval of the chief audit executive.'[42]

'Circular' mutual reliance is a risk and does of course need to be avoided; this is one of the management responsibilities of the chief audit executive:

> 'In coordinating the work of internal auditors with the work of external auditors, the chief audit executive should ensure that work to be performed by internal auditors ... does not duplicate the work of external auditors which can be relied on for purposes of internal auditing coverage.'[43]

## Advantages of coordination between external and internal audit
- May contain the external audit fee.
- Fosters mutual respect, understanding and openness between the two audits.
- Assists in developing audit staff.

**Disadvantages of coordination between external and internal audit**
- May detract the internal auditing activity from meeting important internal audit objectives.
- May increase the total time taken to audit in the areas where there is coordination.

## B1.1.16 Internal audit advice on external audit provision

> 'The internal auditor's participation in the selection, evaluation, or retention of the organization's external auditors may vary from no role in the process, to advising management or the audit committee, assistance or participation in the process, management of the process, or auditing the process.'[44]

It is usual for audit committees to consult their external auditors for their view on the adequacy and professionalism of the internal audit function. Audit committees would be missing a valid opportunity were they not to similarly consult the chief audit executive on the adequacy and professionalism of the external audit. The audit committee should annually reconsider the continued appointment of the external audit firm and that consideration can be better informed by a report from the chief audit executive.

> 'Since IIA Standards require internal auditors to "share information and coordinate activities with other internal and external providers of relevant assurance and consulting services," it is advisable for internal auditors to have some role or involvement in the selection or retention of the external auditors and in the definition of scope of work.'[45]

The closer the chief audit executive works with the audit committee of the board, the more likely it is that internal audit will have a significant role in assessing the performance of the external auditor and in the selection process. We discuss internal audit's relationship with the audit committee in B1.1.17 below.

In the context of the desirability that internal audit has unlimited scope to audit all the affairs of the entity, the entity's approach to its oversight of the external audit is a legitimate area for internal audit coverage:

> 'Internal auditors should determine how the organization monitors ongoing service activities from external auditors. Compliance with the terms of service contracts and other agreements should be assessed on a periodic basis. Assessment of the independence of the external auditors should include internal audit participation, be performed at least annually, and be communicated to the audit committee.'[46]

## B1.1.17 Internal audit relationship with the audit committee

Practice Advisory 2060–2 'Relationship with the audit committee' was released by The Institute of Internal Auditors in December 2002 and can be found at http://www.theiia.org/ecm/printfriendly.cfm?doc_id=4044. Practice Advisories are non-mandatory guidance – in this instance the guidance is on Standard 2060 'Independence and Objectivity' which reads:

### '2060 – Reporting to the Board and Senior Management

The chief audit executive should report periodically to the board and senior management on the internal audit activity's purpose, authority, responsibility, and performance relative to its plan. Reporting should also include significant risk exposures and control issues, corporate governance issues, and other matters needed or requested by the board and senior management.'

Although 'non-mandatory', Practice Advisories reflect what is considered generally to be the best practice to be followed in order to fulfil the requirements of the Standards. The sentiment within the Practice Advisories is also regarded as being indicative of what would be a correct answers in the professional examinations of The Institute of Internal Auditors.

This Advisory refers to a model charter for an internal audit function, available at http://www.theiia.org/ecm/guide-ia.cfm?doc_id=383 and reproduced at A1.1.19.

In keeping with the new Standards of The Institute of Internal Auditors, this Practice Advisory allows that the term 'audit committee' should be regarded also as referring to any other 'governance body that is charged with oversight of the organization's audit and control functions'47 and thus the Advisory is offered as having applicability more broadly than just to relationships between internal audit and audit committees. In place of the audit committee, it could, for instance, be the board itself if the board has not delegated some aspects of audit and control oversight to an audit committee. It could also be the chief executive of a government agency if that individual had responsibilities which in other entities would be collectively borne by a board of directors and its audit committee.

The Advisory is not bashful in promoting the role of internal audit with respect to audit committees. In places it even creates the impression that internal audit may be in effective charge of the audit committee. For instance, the Advisory suggests that the chief audit executive (CAE) should be responsible for determining the content of the internal audit charter48 and it gives the CAE a likely major role with respect to the charter of the audit committee itself:

'The CAE should assist the committee in ensuring that the charter, role and activities of the committee are appropriate for it to achieve its responsibilities.'49

The CAE is also given the role to review the completeness and accuracy of the information the audit committee receives – not just the information pertinent to its oversight of internal audit. This role for internal audit is more justifiable if, as in the Advisory, it is accepted that the CAE should be secretary of the audit committee.

The Advisory certainly gives internal audit the committee secretarial role. A contrary view would be that this is unsound in that the audit committee, being a committee of the board, should receive its secretarial support from the same source as the board itself. In the UK, this would mean that the company secretary would therefore usually be the secretary to the audit committee. If the CAE is secretary to the audit committee, it may make it more difficult for the audit committee to form an objective view of the professionalism, etc of the internal audit function since most committees develop a 'cosy' relationship with their secretary. It is also helpful for the secretary of the audit committee to be present at the board meeting when the chairperson of the audit committee speaks to the board on the audit committee's report to the board – this would happen naturally if the secretary to the audit committee were also the secretary of the board.

The Advisory classifies its content into:

> 'three areas of activities [which] … are key to an effective relationship between the audit committee and the internal audit function, chiefly through the Chief Audit Executive:
> - Assisting the audit committee to ensure that its charter, activities, and processes are appropriate to fulfil its responsibilities.
> - Ensuring that the charter, role, and activities of internal audit are clearly understood and responsive to the needs of the audit committee and the board.
> - Maintaining open and effective communications with the audit committee and the chairperson.'[50]

The first of these three, which is tantamount to advising that the CAE should be the committee's secretary, is elaborated upon in the Advisory as follows (which we set out here in abbreviated form):[51]

- Annually advise the audit committee on its charter (terms of reference).
- Maintain a planning agenda (pro forma agenda for committee meetings) for the audit committee.
- Draft meeting agendas, facilitate distribution of materials to committee members and write up audit committee minutes.
- Encourage the audit committee to benchmark itself against leading practices.
- Meet the committee chairman to discuss the informational needs of the committee.
- Find out if committee members need special presentations or training.
- Inquire whether the committee considers its frequency of meetings and their duration are sufficient.

The Advisory puts the second of these three areas of audit committee activity in the context that:

> 'the CAE's relationship to the audit committee should revolve around a core role of the CAE that the audit committee understands, supports, and receives all assistance needed from the internal audit function. The IIA supports the concept that sound governance is dependent on the synergy generated among the four principal components of effective corporate governance systems: boards of directors, management, internal auditors, and external auditors. In that structure, internal auditors and audit committees are mutually supportive. Consideration of the work of internal auditors is essential for the audit committee to gain a complete understanding of an organization's operations. A primary component of the CAE's role with the committee is to ensure this objective is accomplished and the committee views the CAE as their trusted advisor.'[52]

This is elaborated upon in the Advisory as follows (which we set out here also in abbreviated form):[53]

- Ask the committee to review and approve the internal audit charter, annually. (IIA's sample charter is reproduced at A1.1.19).
- Review with the audit committee that the functional and administrative reporting lines of internal audit allow adequate independence.
- Incorporate in the audit committee's charter the review of (a) the appointment, compensation, evaluation, retention, and dismissal of the CAE, and (b) review and approval of proposals to outsource any internal audit.
- Assist the committee to evaluate the scope, resources and results of internal audit activities.
- Inform the committee of internal audit coordination with, and oversight of, other control and monitoring functions (eg management, compliance, security, business continuity, legal, ethics, environmental, external audit).
- Report to the committee significant control issues and opportunities for improvement across the organisation.
- Report progress against the approved annual audit plan and results; advise on the sufficiency of internal audit resources.
- Incorporate into the internal audit charter the responsibility of internal audit to report to the committee on suspected frauds and assist in their investigation if significant.
- Make the committee aware that quality assessment reviews of the internal audit function should be done every five years.

The essential elements of communication by the CAE to the audit committee are given as:

- regular private meetings between the CAE and the committee;
- an annual summary report and assessment of internal audit results;
- periodic reports to the committee of internal audit results;
- keeping the committee informed of emerging internal audit trends and practices;
- discussing with the committee its informational needs; and
- reviewing the completeness and accuracy of the information the committee receives.

The last could be construed as being a candidate to become a standard internal audit engagement included within the annual audit plan subject to qualifying for this attention as a result of an audit needs assessment.

## B1.1.18  *Not explored*

This Advisory is certainly not intended to be a comprehensive treatise on audit committees. It states that:

> 'The Institute acknowledges that audit committee responsibilities encompass activities that are beyond the scope of this advisory, and in no way intends it to be a comprehensive description of audit committee responsibilities.'[54]

But within its own more limited remit, to be useful guidance the Advisory needs more detail both with respect to the issues covered and the treatment of some of the issues which are referred to.

Internal audit/audit committee relationship issues not addressed include whether it is sufficient for just the CAE to have access to the audit committee: some would say that it is necessary for *all* the internal auditors in the function to have direct access to the chair of the audit committee, since there have been occasions when the CAE has sought to bury audit findings, perhaps in order not to embarrass a top management team with whom the CAE has a (too) close working relationship. Another matter not covered in this Advisory is whether the CAE should have a right to request that items be placed on the agenda of the audit committee. We know that some chairs of audit committees make it a practice to spend perhaps a day or two a year within the internal audit function – in order to break down barriers and to get a better 'feel' of the risk and control issues of the organisation as well as the degree of freedom of the internal audit function to conduct itself independently: again there is no suggestion of this in the Advisory. Incidentally, 'risk' gets little attention in this Advisory. We would also have liked to see a recommendation that internal audit might report to the audit committee on the efficiency and effectiveness of the external audit, not just on the extent to which there is coordination between external audit and others. Practice Advisory 2050–1 also ordinarily restricts the chief audit executive's assessment of external audit to this limited context:

> 'In exercising its oversight role, the board may request the chief audit executive to assess the performance of external auditors. Such assessments should ordinarily be made in the context of the chief audit executive's role of coordinating internal and external auditing activities, and should extend to other performance matters only at the specific request of senior management or the board. Assessments of the performance of external auditors should be based on sufficient information to support the conclusions reached. Assessments of the external auditors' performance with respect to the coordination of internal and external auditing activities should reflect the criteria described in this Practice Advisory.'[55]

However, that Practice Advisory does set out a possible broader remit for the assessment:

> 'Assessments of the performance of external auditors extending to matters beyond coordination with the internal auditors may address additional factors, such as:
> * Professional knowledge and experience.
> * Knowledge of the organization's industry.
> * Independence.
> * Availability of specialized services.
> * Anticipation of and responsiveness to the needs of the organization.
> * Reasonable continuity of key engagement personnel.
> * Maintenance of appropriate working relationships.
> * Achievement of contract commitments.
> * Delivery of overall value to the organization.'[56]

Matters which could usefully have been discussed in more detail include aspects of committee secretariat support. We are referring not to the routine provision of secretarial services, but the need for audit committees and their members individually to have access to full secretariat support between meetings. Then there is the failure of the Advisory to do more than mention the need for audit committee to review the appointment and dismissal of the CAE. Practice Advisory 2060–2[57] goes further with the IIA's recommendation that the audit committee should:

'Approve all decisions regarding the appointment or removal of the CAE'

but neither Advisory is clear as to whether the *prior approval* of the audit committee should be obtained. Although 'special tasks or projects requested [of internal audit] by the audit committee' are mentioned, there is no further elaboration of the challenges associated with internal audit undertaking special engagements directly on behalf of the audit committee, with the engagement report going direct to the audit committee rather than to management as well. Finally, there was no discussion of the occasions when the CAE should *not* be present at audit committee meetings.

1   As defined in the Glossary to the Institute's *Standards* – a revised definition commencing 1 January 2004.
2   Practice Advisory 2000–1: 'Managing the Internal Audit Activity', para 1.
3   Practice Advisory 1300–1, 'Quality Assurance and Improvement Program', para 1.
4   Practice Advisory 2060–2: 'Relationship with the Audit Committee', para 3.
5   Practice Advisory 1200–1: 'Proficiency and Due Professional Care', para 1.
6   Practice Advisory 1300–1, 'Quality Assurance and Improvement Program', para 1.
7   Practice Advisory 1000–1: 'Internal Audit Charter', para 1.
8   Practice Advisory 2040–1: 'Policies and Procedures', para 1.
9   Practice Advisory 2040–1: 'Policies and Procedures', para 1.
10  Practice Advisory 2040–1: 'Policies and Procedures', para 1.
11  Practice Advisory 2330.A1–2: 'Legal Considerations in Granting Access to Engagement Records', para 5.
12  Practice Advisory 2010–1: 'Planning', para 1.
13  Practice Advisory 2010–2: 'Linking the Audit Plan to Risk and Exposures', para 3.
14  Practice Advisory 2010–1: 'Planning', para 1.
15  Practice Advisory 2010–1: 'Planning', para 2.
16  Practice Advisory 2010–2: 'Linking the Audit Plan to Risk and Exposures', para 4.
17  Practice Advisory 2010–2 was revised in February 2004.
18  Practice Advisory 2010–2: 'Linking the Audit Plan to Risk and Exposures', para 2.
19  Practice Advisory 2010–2: 'Linking the Audit Plan to Risk and Exposures', para 5.
20  Practice Advisory 2010–2: 'Linking the Audit Plan to Risk and Exposures', para 5.
21  Practice Advisory 2100–4 (February 2004): 'The Internal Auditor s Role in Organizations Without a Risk Management Process', para 2.
22  Practice Advisory 2010–1: 'Planning', para 3.
23  Practice Advisory 2010–1: 'Planning', para 4.
24  Practice Advisory 2010–2: 'Linking the Audit Plan to Risk and Exposures', para 5.
25  Practice Advisory 2010–2: 'Linking the Audit Plan to Risk and Exposures', para 2.
26  Practice Advisory 2020–1: 'Communication and Approval', para 1.
27  para 3.
28  Practice Advisory 2500.A1–1: 'Follow-up Process', para 6.
29  Practice Advisory 2010–1: 'Planning', para 4.
30  Such as language skills.
31  Practice Advisory 2030–1: 'Resource Management', para 1.
32  Practice Advisory 2030–1: 'Resource Management', para 1.
33  Practice Advisory 2230–1: 'Engagement Resource Allocation', para 1.
34  Practice Advisory 2010–1: 'Planning', para 4.
35  Practice Advisory 2060–1: 'Reporting to Board and Senior Management', para 1.
36  Practice Advisory 2050–1: 'Coordination', para 4.
37  Practice Advisory 2050–1: 'Coordination', para 2.
38  Practice Advisory 2050–1: 'Coordination', para 1.
39  Practice Advisory 2050–1: 'Coordination', para 5.
40  Under Sarbanes-Oxley Act (2002), Section 406; applicable to US issuers.
41  Practice Advisory 2050–1: 'Coordination', para 10.
42  Practice Advisory 2330.A1–1: 'Control of Engagement Records', para 3.
43  Practice Advisory 2050–1: 'Coordination', para 3.
44  Practice Advisory 2050–2: 'Acquisition of External Audit Services', para 1.

45    Practice Advisory 2050–2: 'Acquisition of External Audit Services', para 1.
46    Practice Advisory 2050–2: 'Acquisition of External Audit Services', para 12.
47    Para 1.
48    Penultimate bullet point in para 5.
49    Para 4 and third bullet point in para 5.
50    Para 3.
51    Para 4.
52    Para 5.
53    Para 5.
54    Para 2.
55    Practice Advisory 2050–1: 'Coordination', para 6.
56    Practice Advisory 2050–1: 'Coordination', para 7.
57    Practice Advisory 1110–2, also released in December 2002, on 'Chief Audit Executive (CAE) reporting lines' to be found at http://www.theiia.org/ecm/printfriendly.cfm?doc_id=4043.

# Managing the internal audit activity – supplementary guidance

## B1.2.1    Strategic planning for internal audit

This technique uses three progressive worksheets (that is, one after the other) which allow the head of internal auditing, with his or her senior internal audit colleagues and with senior general management, to get to grips with the issues at stake in determining how the internal auditing unit should develop in the medium to long term – without getting lost in the complexities of this planning task.

'Medium to long term' can be set at three to seven years – depending upon what is regarded as a realistic planning horizon. It is suggested that this technique is revisited annually at which time the planning assumptions made previously will be reconsidered for continuing appropriateness and the plan will be rolled forward for a further 12 months.

It has often been said that the only certainty about the future is that the future is uncertain. Some managements consider it a waste of time, indeed positively harmful, to endeavour to plan long term. In the context of internal auditing this would not appear to be so. Long-term future plans for internal audit will certainly need regular adjustment as circumstances change, often significantly, in an unpredictable way. Long-term plans for internal audit must always be treated with caution. Yet the propensity for internal auditing functions to be unable to meet the current needs of their businesses (due often to their earlier failure to plan on a timely basis for the necessary changes to be made) leads to the conclusion that long-term planning for internal auditing functions is important. Fundamental changes to internal auditing cannot always be made 'at the drop of a hat overnight'. Without long-term planning for internal audit, the head of internal auditing is likely to be springing surprises upon management and the Board when pointing out that the audit function is not well placed to meet current needs. Had management and the Board (through its audit committee) been involved in this long-term planning process for internal audit, these problems would come as no surprise and indeed the business as a whole would either have knowingly avoided them occurring or would have knowingly shouldered the associated risks.

Relatively few internal auditing functions have planned strategically for long term change. Most heads of internal auditing think of 'audit planning' as relating exclusively to 'tactical planning' – that is determining which auditable units within the audit universe will be audited and how much auditor resource will be allocated to each. It is tempting to think of long-term planning as a luxury to be indulged in only if spare time becomes available: of course it never does. It is understandable that day-to-day pressures on an overworked audit function are given full attention to the exclusion of everything else. Yet those pressures will be the greater, and the function will become more overworked and less effective, if it is not working within the context of a carefully considered long-term strategic plan. Internal auditors are knowledgeable proponents of the need for economy, efficiency and effectiveness: none of these will apply to the internal audit function which has not troubled to design and implement its strategic plan.

Worksheet 1 is a simple form which allows the work of the internal auditing function to be divided into categories and for each of these categories to be explored in the rows of the matrix form. The categories of work should be those which occupy audit time now, and those which may do so in the future.

The classification into categories could be according to the split of time within audits – such as time spent fact finding, time spent writing audit reports, and so on. Alternatively it could be according to the type of audits conducted by the internal auditing function. Of course the breakdown into categories can be done in a variety of ways, and users of this technique should be imaginative and probably run through the technique several times using a different classification each time, in order to obtain a more detailed picture of the changes which are needed in the internal auditing function over the future planning period.

Commencing with the top row of Worksheet 1, each row should be completed sequentially. The penultimate row ('medium-term scope for re-sourcing this as work of the Unit') should be completed consistent with the currently agreed policies which are to apply to the internal auditing function over the planning period. The final row ('strategic importance of this activity') is the perceived importance of the activities which head the columns of this worksheet *to the enterprise as a whole,* not just to the internal auditing function.

As the planning project develops (that is, as the worksheets of this technique are completed) it may become necessary to return to Worksheet 1 and alter some of the planning assumptions entered upon it if they prove to have unacceptable consequences and lead, for instance, to top management agreeing to modify the policies (and therefore their reflection on Worksheet 1) which shall govern internal audit over the future planning period.

The next step is to transfer to Worksheet 2A the data from rows 1, 4 and 5 of Worksheet 1. Worksheet 2 allows several dimensions of the planning problem to be represented simply, clearly and attractively so that all participants in this planning exercise are focusing on the same issues. The transfer is done by inserting red circles in the appropriate boxes, the size of the circles corresponding to the percentages in row 1 of Worksheet 1. If the percentage had been 0%, a blue circle of 'average' size should be used.

It creates a better impact if overhead projector transparencies are used for Worksheet 2A (and also for the other worksheets). Worksheet 2B provides the rubric for Worksheet 2A and should be introduced as a transparency underlay to Worksheet 2A.

In a series of brainstorming sessions within the internal auditing department and with appropriate senior general management, the adjustments of audit effort will be determined and entered on Worksheet 2A (with Worksheet 2B present as an underlay) as '++', '+', '-' or '-'. These are the adjustments which are necessary to move the internal auditing function from where it is now to where it needs to be by the end of the planning period.

Worksheet 3 simply records the alternative courses of action which could be taken in order to make these necessary adjustments, and some of these must be selected to be the basis of the plan of change which will be implemented during the planning period.

The strategic planning process for the long term development of the auditing function should be a joint exercise between internal audit management and representatives of general management and the Board. If the technique we are recommending here is used, then it should be worked through by a planning team comprising these parties. Internal audit is a service to the business and it is essential that the business as a whole determines the sort of internal auditing it should have. It is essential that the business as a whole shoulders the responsibility for any limitations in the audit service which are the result of either policy constraints imposed upon the audit function or the failure to establish appropriate policies.

The audit function would first be advised to have a 'dry run' applying this technique to their function. The plan should then be worked through again with a broader team. Depending upon the nature of the business and the positioning of internal audit within it, this team might comprise:

- the head of internal audit;
- the deputy head of internal audit;
- the chairperson of the audit committee of the Board;
- the chief executive;
- the person to whom the head of internal audit reports administratively;
- the head of group internal audit if the plan is being developed for a subsidiary's internal audit function.

We have earlier recommended that transparency-based versions of the worksheets are used with the aid of an overhead projector with the planning team sitting around a table. Suitable fine pens to use with these transparencies would be Staedtler Lumocolor Fine (Code number 316 – washable). It is essential to use washable pens as you will need to make changes as the planning assignment progresses. A black, red and blue pen will be required.

One of the strengths of the technique is that it represents visually, attractively and simply the key issues which have to be addressed. It removes unnecessary complexity. It ensures that each member of the planning team is focusing on the same issues and is thinking about them in the same way at the same time. It largely avoids the problem of certain team members suggesting that the task should be approached in a different way from a different starting point. It will also be found that members of the planning team will be attracted to the technique which they will quickly understand and will greatly enjoy using. The plan will be the better for the pleasure that the team members experience in working out the plan: they will be motivated to participate in the assignment which they will enter into with energy and enthusiasm. In practice possibly the greatest challenge will be to convene meetings attended by the right people.

The technique is used by completing the supplied transparency versions of the suite of three worksheets commencing with the first which is shown as Worksheet 1. It is best that this is done during a 'round table' discussion between those who are contributing to the planning exercise, though some preparatory work gathering data will be necessary. Since the work can only be focused appropriately when initial planning parameters have been decided upon, it is necessary to have an initial meeting of the planning team before proceeding with the data gathering task. For instance, we shall see that data relating to the first data rows of Worksheet 1 should be objectively determined by reference to audit department records but the data which will be required is only known when the appropriate column headings of Worksheet 1 have been agreed. It is also unrealistic to expect the main planning meeting to complete the planning assignment, so the programme for the planning project should be as follows:

| | |
|---|---|
| First | Dry run within the auditing department (one to four meetings corresponding to 'second', 'third', 'fourth' and 'fifth' below). |
| Second | Planning team meets for the first time to decide column titles for Worksheet 1. |
| Third | Planning team meets for the second time to complete Worksheets 1 and 2 (some prior data collection will be necessary). |
| Fourth | Head of audit identifies possible courses of action (Worksheet 3). |
| Fifth | Planning team meets for the third and final time to select from possible alternative courses of action. |
| Sixth | Head of audit implements the agreed plan. |

It is likely to be appropriate to complete the suite of worksheets several times taking a different subject each time. For instance, where the subject is *Productive Assignments of the Audit Department* and these have been categorised into:

EXAMPLE 1: USE OF PRODUCTIVE AUDIT TIME BY *AUDIT SUBJECT*
1. Accounting and financial auditing.
2. Operational and value-for-money (VFM) auditing.
3. Audit of advanced computer systems.
4. Auditing for regulatory compliance.
5. Environmental auditing.
6. Assisting the external auditor.
7. Other non-internal audit work (such as operating internal checks, fire-fighting assignments, etc).

Of course it is not obligatory that this breakdown is used, or that seven categories are identified.

Users of this technique will find that audit activity sometimes defies precise categorisation. The most common problem is that a particular activity or audit resource could be recorded in more than one column of Worksheet 1. For instance, in the above example a particular operational audit may be of a business activity which is making use of an advanced computer system. Such an audit could be classified in column 2 or 3 of Worksheet 1 and a rule has to be agreed upon, and thereafter followed, to determine how such audit work should be treated on Worksheet 1. The rule options would include:

1.  Classifying any audit which entails a review of an advanced computer system in column 4 even if the audit topic could fit into another column.
2.  Accounting for such as audit in more than one column according to the proportions of audit time which can reasonably be attributed to the different columns.

The output of this technique will be an indication of where adjustments need to be made in the relative commitment of audit resources to each of these categories of audit work, between now and the planning horizon. It is likely that an exploration should be made as to how commitment to *other* categories of audit activity and resources should be changed over the planning period. For instance, further examples are given here:

EXAMPLE 2: USE OF PRODUCTIVE AUDIT TIME BY *AUDIT STEP*
1.  Audit preparation
2.  Familiarisation and fact finding
3.  Audit interviewing
4.  Compliance testing
5.  Substantive or weakness testing
6.  Audit reporting
7.  Audit follow-up

EXAMPLE 3: *NON-AUDITING* PRODUCTIVE WORK
1.  Recruitment
2.  Planning
3.  Audit procedures development
4.  Summary reporting to the audit committee, etc
5.  Training
6.  Professional activities
7.  Audit client support and relations

EXAMPLE 4: *UNPRODUCTIVE* WORK
1.  Travel time
2.  Idle time
3.  Holidays
4.  Sickness
5.  Social time
6.  Compassionate leave

For each of the audit subjects given in the above four examples it is unlikely that the categorisation into columns given above will be exactly applicable for particular audit departments for whom this technique is applied. The planning team should think carefully as to what the *subjects* should be and how each subject should be broken down into *categories*.

Returning to the case study that we are using, our example of Worksheet 1 shows a scenario where the subject is *Productive Assignments of the Audit Department* completed using the breakdown given in Example 1 (above):

1.  The first row gives the breakdown of the investment the audit department is currently making in each of the three categories of work. In this case it is appropriate that the breakdown is based upon an analysis of *audit time*, but in other examples it might be more appropriate to use *monetary value* as the criterion. This information can be objectively determined and can be gathered before the planning meeting commences which completes this form.
2.  The second row should be a matter of fact: it is simply an indication of the trend in investment of audit time in the category of work to which the column refers. It should be completed according to *relative* rather than *absolute* audit time – in other words 'is a particular type of audit work consuming a greater or lesser *proportion* of the audit department's time?'
3.  The third row is a matter of judgement which will be based on considerations such as the level of experience of audit personnel in this category of work and their willingness to engage upon it.
4.  The 'medium term scope for resourcing this as audit department work' row requires the planning team to judge whether, through to the end of the planning period (perhaps five years forward), the audit department is likely to be able to perform this sort of work. In making this decision the planning team should be open to the possibility of transferring resources between columns. Thus, for instance, if a category of work could be done so long as the audit department scaled down their attention to another category of audit work, then the score might be 'Good'.
    In completing this row, the planning team should assume that the known policy framework which relates to internal audit will remain unchanged. Thus, for instance, if it has already been established that enhanced salaries may be offered to internal auditors commencing 12 months hence, then this can be borne in mind in determining whether to score 'The Audit of Advanced Computer Systems' as 'Good', 'Fair' or 'Poor'. The planning team is not entitled to speculate as to how policies might be changed sometime in the future unless it has already been agreed that they shall be changed.
5.  The key to completing the last row is to do it in the context of the likely strategic importance of the activity *to the business as a whole* (not to the internal auditing department) by the end of the planning period.

It will be clear from our discussion about completing the first Worksheet that involvement of senior management in the planning assignment is essential. Senior management and the Board have the authority to decide the policy framework which will be apply to internal audit (row 4) and senior management should understand what is likely to be of strategic importance to the business in the future.

It is also apparent that this planning exercise should dovetail into the long-term plans of the business as a whole if possible.

Three dimensions of the planning assignment as now contained within Worksheet 1, namely the data in rows 1, 4 and 5, can now be transferred to Worksheet 2 (using part 2A) where it is then available for further consideration in a clear, attractive form.

(The second and third rows of information on Worksheet 1 are *not* carried forward to Worksheet 2 and no further use is usually made of this data: however, it is considered that completing rows 2 and 3 of Worksheet 1 will have been helpful in marshalling the thoughts of the planning team – even though completion of those rows was not strictly essential).

Worksheet 2 consists of the basic transparency (Worksheet 2A) and an underlay to it which is introduced later (Worksheet 2B). Even if the user is not making use of an overhead projector, both Worksheets 2A and 2B must be prepared as transparencies so that the underlay will be revealed. Of course, if the user is using an overhead projector, both Worksheets 2A and 2B must be prepared as transparencies so that the projector light will shine through them both at once.

We discussed earlier that a comprehensive planning exercise will entail using Worksheet 1 several times, each time with a different subject. Each different use of Worksheet 1 will subsequently lead to the creation of an additional copy of Worksheet 2A, but it is unnecessary to have more than one copy of the underlay worksheet (Worksheet 2B).

Before introducing the underlay (Worksheet 2B), the user should draw circles with a fine overhead projector pen on the transparency which is Worksheet 2A – one circle for each column of Worksheet 1. The large box in which each circle should be drawn is determined by the specification of the vertical and horizontal axes of Worksheet 2A which correspond to the description of rows 4 and 5 of Worksheet 1. The size of the circle that is drawn should correspond approximately to the percentage score given in row 1 of Worksheet 1.

Use a fine red pen for the circles except where it is a zero percentage. To represent zero a circle of infinitely small size cannot be drawn and so we recommend drawing a circle of a 'standard' size using a different colour (blue). It is essential to use washable pens as later the user is likely to need to be able to relocate circles as the planning assignment progresses. It is worthwhile using a Uno or equivalent stencil to make the circles neat and to improve the opportunity of observing the scaling by size which we are recommending.

The Worksheets are shown at the end of B1.2.1 in the form of a case study. Each circle has been numbered to identify its column of origin from Worksheet 1, and the percentage score (row 1 of Worksheet 1) has been attached to reinforce the visual impression given by the varied size of the circles.

Since we are restricted to a single colour for the purpose of this material we are unable to use blue to highlight zero percentage circles so we have shown them as dots.

When the circles have been drawn and labelled the underlay (2B) can be introduced so that Worksheet 2 is complete with parts 2A and 2B. This has been done for our case study. This has introduced a rubric for each box. The rubric represents advice as to the likely appropriate planning adjustments that need to be achieved between now and the end of the planning period for any category of activity present in the associated box. It is advice which the planning team is not obliged to follow but the team should be clear as to why it intends to diverge from that advice. The rubric is necessarily cryptic and opposites also apply: for instance 'reduce if large' also means 'increase if small'. The given rubric leaves the team to make their own assessments on such matters as what constitutes 'large'.

Experience shows that the planning team usually has a lively session on Worksheet 2, aided by a strong focus by all team members of the same issues. The team records what they consider to be the needed broad level of adjustment by putting a +, ++,-or-against each circle. Where no adjustment is proposed, nothing is entered against the circle.

The team must decide whether they are thinking in terms of the *proportional* allocation of resource in each of these categories. If so, their adjustment entries in Worksheet 2 make no allowance for *absolute* increases or decreases in total audit resources due perhaps to future planned expansion or an awareness by management of the need to invest more heavily in internal audit in view of increased general levels of business risk. If the team completes Worksheet 2 *proportionally only*, it must nevertheless discuss and decide upon absolute levels of adjustment of total audit resources.

The alternative approach is for the planning team to indicate adjustments on Worksheet 2 which allow both for changes in proportional and absolute allocation of audit resources to the categories of audit activity being addressed. This allows the Worksheet to reveal not only required adjustments between categories but overall adjustment in the total provision – ie to the size of the audit department over the planning period.

The bottom right box of Worksheet 2 has the rubric 'No Internal Audit Department solution'. The rationale for this is that if an activity will be of high strategic importance to the business it should not be entrusted to a group who will be badly placed to conduct that work. In such a case the planning team will explore the reasons for the audit department being poorly placed to carry out this work. The team will return to Worksheet 1 and consider whether it is possible to free up the policy constraints which led to a 'P' in Row 4. Confronted with the implications indicated on Worksheet 2, management may now be more amenable to improving the policy framework. It could be, for instance, that management has been resolutely opposed to paying premium salaries to IT auditors with a consequence that internal audit is going to be poorly placed to audit advanced computer systems until that policy constraint is removed. On the other hand there may be alternative ways of solving this problem, such as seconding personnel from the Information Services section of the business to strengthen the Internal Audit department's computer auditing competence.

It is conceivable that management may still resist any constructive policy changes to improve internal audit's competence even where that competence is low and the strategic importance to the business of that particular category of activity is high. Then management either needs to make alternative arrangements, such as retaining outside consultants to do this work, or management knowingly takes the risk to be vulnerable in this area. It is unlikely that internal audit should plan to invest time in this area as that time will be wasted if internal audit is going to be poorly placed to do that work.

Adjustments have been indicated for our case study using +, + +,-or-. If these adjustments reflect both proportionate *and* absolute changes in audit resource then the overall conclusion must be that in this case future audit needs in these categories of audit activity will be satisfied without an overall increase in audit resources. What remains to be done is to determine how the shifts between these categories are to be achieved. But if these adjustments reflect only the needed change in *proportionate* allocation of audit resources, then the planning team needs to consider separately how the total availability of audit resources may need to change as, for instance, the business expands in the future or takes greater risks.

Our case study shows that the planning team has decided that the internal audit department will not have responsibility for auditing advanced computer systems. We do not know what, if any, alternative arrangements the planning team are proposing to cover this activity. In general this would be regarded, certainly by internal audit, as an unfortunate decision.

The planning tool takes the user one stage further though, as we shall see, there are stages beyond which are also essential. The case study shows the transfer of our Case Study data from Worksheet 2 to Worksheet 3. Worksheet 3 needs to show only those activities which will require an adjusted focus by the end of the planning period. Although we show only *one* Worksheet 3, in practice this part of the planning assignment would run to several sheets – at least one sheet for each activity which has to be adjusted.

Within the planning meeting and outside it brainstorming sessions should be convened to identify as many possible alternative courses of action which might contribute to moving the audit department from where it is now to where it needs to be by the end of the planning period. Contributors will not only be planning team members. The contribution of other internal auditors is likely to be particularly valuable as well as having the indirect but important quality of involving staff in the development of their own functional area. Contributors should be encouraged to be imaginative and should never be ridiculed for thinking laterally and for suggesting possibilities which may seem bizarre. Most of the options identified will be discarded eventually. However, those options eventually selected may include some which represent radical departures from conventional thinking, if appropriate. Some of the options selected may have been suggested initially by the consideration of other options which were ultimately discarded.

A senior member of the audit department, perhaps the head of audit, should supervise the preparation of lists of alternative courses of action in the format of Worksheet 3. They could for instance include some of the following:

- retraining;
- transfer of some staff out of internal audit;
- internal recruitment to internal audit from operational areas of the business;
- external recruitment;
- development of audit methodologies;
- early retirement;
- audit assistance from consultants;
- out-sourcing/contracting out all or part of internal audit;
- control self-assessment by management;
- emphasis on client service;
- risk analysis approaches to planning audits;
- redundancies;
- etc.

The final meeting of the planning team selects from these possible courses of action those which they consider should be adopted and which, if adopted, will move the audit department from where it is now to where it is thought it will need to be by the end of the planning period.

As far as the planning team is concerned, their involvement has now ended – though the team will be reconvened in twelve months time, with some new membership, to revise and roll forward the strategic plan. The planning assignment is not however completed as far as the audit department is concerned.

The head of audit must do the following:

1. Design an implementation programme for the selected courses of action with target dates of accomplishment and measurable performance targets to be achieved by interim and final stages.
2. Proceed with implementation.
3. Measure implementation performance and take corrective action as necessary.
4. Throughout, report to responsible management and to the audit committee of the Board on progress against plan.

## Using the technique in other areas of the business

Although designed originally for internal audit planning, this tool works excellently for other areas of the business. On occasion auditors might wish to use the tool during the course of an audit of a business area in order to develop recommendations for future change, to be included in their audit report. This would represent a level of involvement in long term planning which would usually be beyond the scope of any audit. More frequently auditors will wish to recommend the tool to line management and explain its use to them.

*Worksheet 1*

| ASSESSMENT OF THE UNIT'S SCOPE, DEPLOYMENT & STRENGTH | | | | | | | |
|---|---|---|---|---|---|---|---|
| Type of work/category of resource | | | | | | | |
| | 1 | 2 | 3 | 4 | 5 | 6 | 7 | 8 |
| % of Unit's productive time spent now (Total = 100%) | | | | | | | | |
| Trend in type of work<br>G=Growing<br>S=Static<br>D=Declining | | | | | | | | |
| Ability to do work well with current resources<br>S=Strong<br>M=Medium<br>W=Weak | | | | | | | | |
| Medium-term scope for re-sourcing this as work of the Unit*<br>G=Good<br>F=Fair<br>P=Poor | | | | | | | | |
| Strategic importance of this activity<br>L=Low<br>M=Medium<br>H=High | | | | | | | | |

\* Allowing for possibilities of altering the staffing profile of the Unit

## Case study: Worksheet 2A

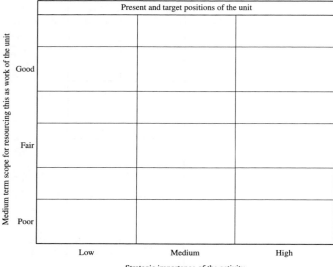

**Strategic importance of the activity**

### Instructions
1.  Draw appropriately-sized RED circles for Unit Time spent now on each type of work. BLUE circle if 0%. Label circles with type of work and %age.

## Case study: Worksheet 2B

| | | |
|---|---|---|
| Reduce if large | Develop plan to expand now if small: reduce if too large | Develop plan to expand now if small |
| | | |
| Minimise this work | Aim for some involvement by the unit | Develop plan to expand if small |
| | | |
| Drop this work – if any | Develop plan to expand if small | No unit solution |
| | | |

2.  Put +, ++, -, or-against a circle to indicate needed adjusted in involvement by the Unit.

*Worksheet 3*

| STRATEGIC PLAN FOR THE UNIT | |
|---|---|
| Category of Activity/Resource | Alternative courses of action to change future position |
| | |

## B1.2.2  Published reports on internal control by internal audit

It is not new for internal auditors to report publicly in the annual reports of entities. Here we reprint a set of such reports which appeared as early as the 1970s. We are missing just one of these. We are grateful to Neville de Sppretter, the current Audit Manager at Anglian Water, for permission to reprint these.

It was Allan Legg who was head of internal audit at Anglian Water from 1974–76. He went on to head up internal audit respectively at British Gas, British Telecom and then at The World Bank in Washington. His successor as head of Anglian Water's internal audit was Graeme Ward, both a qualified engineer and a qualified accountant who subsequently became head of internal audit at Abbey National, President of The Institute of Internal Auditors-UK, and a captain of hi-tech industry. It was Graeme who started the annual Compacs conference. Fortune favours the brave!

These internal audit reports, which appeared in the annual reports of Anglian Water during the 1970s, have many points of interest. Clearly internal audit was primarily an audit of accounting and financial matters, under the direction and control of the director of finance (1974–75). But, as we shall see, its financial and accounting 'home base' was not allowed to be a significant restriction upon internal audit scope.

*Internal audit coverage*

Three years after being set up, internal audit was able to report that it had reviewed all financial systems in operation (1977–78) – not a bad achievement although, admittedly, by the start of 1975 the department had its full complement of as many as 17 audit staff (1974–75) – even though they regarded internal audit resources as being 'scarce' (1974–75). It is interesting to speculate how many internal auditors would be in post today in an equivalent but downsized function.

It is unlikely that the contemporary downsizing of internal audit can be attributed reasonably to either a more optimal allocation of internal audit resources to the areas of greatest relative need, nor to a better use of IT to assist in internal audit work by automating aspects of it.

## Risk assessment

With regard to the former, it looks as if internal audit in Anglian Water in the 1970s applied rather similar risk assessment methods in audit planning as we would today – take, for instance, their statements that:

> 'A formal system of audit planning and control has been instituted to ensure that the scarce audit resources are allocated to the best advantage of the Authority'
>
> (1974–75)

## IT auditing

With regard to the latter it is striking that the internal audit function recruited a computer professional into it from its inception (1974–75). By 1977–78 the internal audit function had a computer audit terminal connected to Anglian Water's new mainframe and by then there is a clear suggestion that audit software was being built into the new IT systems being developed. The policy was:

> 'Wherever possible, use is made of the computer to aid audit work.'

A year later they were able to report in similar terms, this time that:

> 'Considerable use is made of the computer installation to aid audit work and one notable example was the audit software built into their new direct billing applications.'

## A multi-disciplinary function

Despite its financial and accounting orientation, it was clearly considered that internal audit should be a multi-disciplinary function – capable, for instance, of making a positive contribution in the areas of contracting and IT. Internal audit staff 'were recruited from a wide variety of sources'. Apart from an IT specialist, another internal auditor was an engineer (1974–75).

## Internal audit's mission

The first of this set of reports had outlined the role and responsibilities of internal audit (1974–75). As we have pointed out, its accounting and financial vantage point did not appear to have narrowed its scope significantly. Its mission, *inter alia*, was:

'to detect fraud, misappropriation, irregular expenditure and losses due to waste or extravagance' and 'to review the monitoring procedures in use … which ensure the physical security of assets and the privacy and confidentiality of information.'

## Scope of internal audit work

This must have allowed it a broad role. In 1977–78 they were starting to audit information relating to demand forecasting and to the formulation of the Authority's capital development programme.

In 1978–79 we note an internal audit focus on (a) 'information systems that lead to decision making' and to (b) internal audit involvement at the development stage of an improved project appraisal system and in (c) the development of new controls over capital expenditure.

In 1976–77 internal audit had reported they conducted comprehensive examinations of capital spending and had also completed internal audits on 'energy' and 'research'. In 1976–77 internal audit was involved in the planning for the introduction of Anglian Water's new mainframe computer.

In 1978–79 we find them appraising every new IT application 'to ascertain whether all basic control requirements have been met'. As early as 1976–77 they make it clear that internal audit is concerned that Anglian Water's procedures and policies lead to 'best possible value for money'.

## 'External' internal control

An organisation's internal control often extends to the systems in place within outside businesses, and that management and auditors should therefore consider the extent to which these should be reviewed before coming to an opinion on internal control. A foretaste of this appears in the 1976–77 internal audit report which describes a number of audits conducted by Anglian Water of District Councils, who had an agency relationship with Anglian Water.

## Proactive role

Although internal audit is described as having a protective role (1976–77), it is also seen as being proactive in assisting in promoting improvements – whether financial, administrative or operational.

## The 'total audit'

Commencing 1974–75, reference is made to the close liaison and co-operation between internal and external audit particularly with regard to the elimination of duplication (1977–78) and in 1978–79 the very modern concept of the 'total audit coverage' is introduced within internal audit's public report.

## *The opinion on internal control*

Perhaps it is particularly interesting to see how internal audit expresses overall opinion on internal control in these published reports. Understandably, for a newly established function, it takes a few years before internal audit expresses such an opinion which first features in the 1977–78 report using the words:

> 'The standard of financial administration achieved throughout the Authority is now considered by the Chief Internal Auditor to be generally satisfactory'.

Internal audit points out that it had not expressed this opinion until they had been able to report that they had by then reviewed all financial systems in operation.

The following year (1978–79) the opinion was fleshed out:

> 'The standard of financial administration achieved is considered to be generally satisfactory. This opinion has been formed following reviews of all major financial systems, carried out in each division and at headquarters designed to ensure that systems, controls and procedures were effective, remained relevant in the light of changing circumstances and were adhered to in practice.'

It was in 1978–79 that the very modern phrase 'reasonable assurance' was used in connection with the objectives of internal control, as it is currently in both the COSO[1] and Rutteman[2] reports and thus in directors' internal control reports following the COSO or Rutteman guidance.

By 1979–80 there had been a refinement of emphasis in that the wording of the opinion joined internal audit and management together as endorsing the sentiment expressed:

> 'During the year all major financial systems have been audited sufficiently to satisfy management on the soundness, adequacy and application of controls, and that the assets and interests of the organisation have been accounted for and protected from serious losses due to any reason, including fraud and poor value for money.'

As with 1990s reports on internal control, these opinions from Anglian Water were not 'point of time' opinions as of the year end date but rather related to the whole of the year being reported though perhaps without expressly stating so. They also, as with 1990s reports, tended to imply a *current* and even future assurance rather than merely assurance relating to the old year which was being reported. While they overtly focused upon internal *financial* control, arguably they were broader than that.

Unlike so many 1990s published reports on internal control, undoubtedly these statements included expressions of opinion on internal control in various terms – 'generally satisfactory', 'effective', 'relevant', 'adhered to', 'sound', 'adequate', 'applied', 'protected from serious losses' and 'value for money'.

# *Conclusion*

So we have observed a thoroughly modern internal audit function in place a generation ago. Indeed in certain respects it was not only ahead of its time, but in advance of contemporary practice at the turn of the millennium.

INTERNAL AUDIT

Under the Accounts and Audit Regulations 1974 the Authority was required to carry out, under the direction and control of the Director of Finance, an internal audit of the accounts of the Authority and of its officers.

At its meeting in November 1974 the Authority agreed that the role and responsibilities of internal audit should be:

(a)   to secure the installation of soundly based systems of control within each area of directorate or divisional responsibility;

(b)   to review and where necessary make recommendations for the improvements of systems, controls and procedures in order to ensure that they are both efficient and effective, that they remain adequate in the light of changing circumstances and that they are adhered to in practice;

(c)   to assist in protecting the assets and interests of the Authority by carrying out a continuous examination of activities in order to detect fraud, misappropriation, irregular expenditure and losses due to waste or extravagance;

(d)   to review the monitoring procedures in use within the Authority which ensure the physical security of assets and the privacy and confidentiality of information

Internal audit is an integral part of the Finance Directorate, but to ensure its objectivity and independence in reviewing, appraising and reporting on systems and procedures it does not have any responsibility for developing and installing procedures, preparing records or engaging in any activity which will subsequently be subject to audit review and appraisal. The Chief Internal Auditor is directly responsible and reports to the Director of Finance personally, while all internal audit staff based either at Headquarters or at four area offices located in various parts of the region are responsible to the Chief Internal Auditor and not to the Headquarters' directorates or divisions whose work they review and appraise.

A very close liaison has been maintained by internal audit with the Authority's external auditors, Price Waterhouse & Co, since the start.

Although recruitment of internal audit staff did not begin until a late stage, by 1 January 1975 all 17 audit staff were in post, and by the end of the financial year each division had been the subject of an audit visit, although inevitably the initial coverage could not be as extensive as would have been desired following the considerable changes which occurred at and after the 1st April 1974. Considerable emphasis has been placed on the internal training of audit staff, who were recruited from a wide variety of sources, and it is believed that this will provide to be a very sound investment for the future.

A formal system of audit planning and control has been instituted to ensure that the scarce audit resources are allocated to the best advantage of the Authority.

An unusual feature has been the recruitment of two non-accountants – an engineer and a computer professional – to ensure that the necessary expertise is available to enable internal audit to make a positive contribution in the vital areas of contract procedures and administration and of data processing.

**Anglian Water Annual Report 1974–75.**


INTERNAL AUDIT

The Authority's internal audit staff carry out a continuous independent appraisal of accounting, financial and related processes to ensure that in all aspects of the Authority's work adequate internal controls are operating, and that where such controls are considered not to be operating effectively management are informed and appropriate action is taken. Internal auditors are expected to adopt a positive attitude and assist in promoting improvements to financial, administrative and operational procedures and policies so that the Authority may obtain the best possible value for the money it spends. This requirement to promote improvements arises out of internal audit's prime protective role and is not in substitution for it.

In addition to audits of divisional and headquarters activities, teams of internal audit and divisional staff carried out audits of expenditure incurred by district councils as agents of the Authority under Sections 7 and 15 of the Water Act 1973. In many cases these audits have resulted in the negotiation of substantial reductions in the amounts claimed from the Authority by the agent councils.

Other internal audit work during the financial year included planning for the introduction of the Authority's new computer, a comprehensive examination of capital spending and audits of spending on energy and research.

**Anglian Water Annual Report 1976–77. Part 6 – Finance**


INTERNAL AUDIT

The Authority's internal audit staff carry out a comprehensive and independent appraisal of accounting, financial and related processes as a service to management. Internal audit is a managerial control which functions by measuring and evaluating the effectiveness of other controls. By the end of the financial year all financial systems in operation throughout the Authority had been reviewed and, in many cases, recommendations had been made and accepted for improvements to systems, controls and procedures to ensure that they remained both efficient and effective. The standard of financial administration achieved throughout the Authority is now considered by the Chief Internal Auditor to be generally satisfactory. Without losing sight of internal audit's prime protective role, increasing effort was devoted to appraising and evaluating information systems that lead to decision making in the Authority. A start was made in auditing the information relating to demand forecasting and the formulation of the Authority's capital development programme.

During the year, the internal audit headquarters team moved from Diploma House to Brook House, Huntingdon, and took delivery of the computer audit terminal connected to the new mainframe. This move was aimed at ensuring that the development of audit techniques in relation to the new systems, particularly direct billing, went in hand with the development of those systems themselves. Wherever possible, use is made of the computer to aid audit work.

Close co-operation between the Authority's internal auditors and the external auditors, Price Waterhouse and Co, has continued throughout the year, particularly in respect of the elimination, as far as has been possible, of duplication of work by the various teams.

**Anglian Water Annual Report 1977–78. Part 6 – Finance**

INTERNAL AUDIT

The Authority has a system of internal control to provide reasonable assurance that its transactions are appropriately recorded and reported, its assets are protected, established policies are followed and costs are properly controlled and managed. This system is prescribed by the Financial Regulations, written delegation of duties to responsible officers and other clearly defined procedures. These are supplemented by a comprehensive internal audit appraisal of all accounting, financial and related processes.

The standard of financial administration achieved is considered to be generally satisfactory. This opinion has been formed following reviews of all major financial systems, carried out in each division and at headquarters designed to ensure that systems, controls and procedures were effective, remained relevant in the light of changing circumstances and were adhered to in practice.

Internal audit effort continued to be devoted to appraising and evaluating the information systems that lead to decision making. During the year a contribution was made to the introduction of an improved project appraisal system and to the development of controls over capital expenditure. With the publication of divisional revenue output measures a start was made on inter-divisional comparisons of performance.

Considerable use is made of the computer installation to aid audit work, and during the year an important innovation in the form of a special reports feature was developed jointly by the computer audit staff and Honeywell. This system is now operating on all direct billing applications. In addition, each new computer application is independently appraised by internal audit to ascertain whether all basic control requirements have been met.

The internal auditors liaise with the external auditors, Price Waterhouse and Co, to ensure that total audit coverage is adequate and to eliminate any unnecessary duplication of work.

**Anglian Water Annual Report 1978–79. Part 6 – Finance**

INTERNAL AUDIT

The scale and complexity of the Authority's organisation is recognised by the framework of control which is set down in Financial Regulations, Rules of Contract and the Schemes of Delegations. Within that structure management is responsible for ensuring that detailed systems of control exist to safeguard the Authority's assets, ensure reliability of records, promote operational efficiency and monitor adherence to policies and directives.

Management in turn relies on an effective internal audit to review, appraise and report on these systems of control.

During the year all major financial systems have been audited sufficiently to satisfy management on the soundness, adequacy and application of controls, and that the assets and interests of the organisation have been accounted for and protected from serious losses due to any reason, including fraud and poor value for money.

**Anglian Water Annual Report 1979–80. Part 6 – Finance**

1       'Internal control – integrated framework' (September 1992) Committee of Sponsoring Organizations of the Treadway Commission (COSO), American Institute of Certified Public Accountants.
2       'Internal control and financial reporting: guidance for directors of listed companies registered in the UK' (December 1994) 'The Rutteman Report', ICAEW.

## B1.2.3   Internal audit relationship with the audit committee – comment on the new Practice Advisory

*Practice Advisory 2060–2 on 'Relationship with the audit committee', was released by The Institute of Internal Auditors (The Institute of Internal Auditors) in December 2002. Practice Advisories are non-mandatory guidance – in this instance the guidance is on Standard 2060 – 'Independence and Objectivity' which reads:*

> **'Standard 2060 – Reporting to the Board and Senior Management**
> The chief audit executive should report periodically to the board and senior management on the internal audit activity's purpose, authority, responsibility, and performance relative to its plan. Reporting should also include significant risk exposures and control issues, corporate governance issues, and other matters needed or requested by the board and senior management.'

*Although 'non-mandatory', Practice Advisories reflect what is considered generally to be the best practice to be followed in order to fulfil the requirements of the Standards. The sentiment within the Practice Advisories is also regarded as being indicative of what would be a correct answers in the professional examinations of The Institute of Internal Auditors.*

*This Advisory refers to a model charter for an internal audit function, reprinted in this Handbook at A1.1.19.*

In keeping with the new *Standards* of The Institute of Internal Auditors, this Practice Advisory allows that the term 'audit committee' should be regarded also as referring to any other 'governance body that is charged with oversight of the organization's audit and control functions'[3] and thus the Advisory is offered as having applicability more broadly than just to relationships between internal audit and audit committees. In place of the audit committee, it could, for instance, be the board itself if the board has not delegated some aspects of audit and control oversight to an audit committee. It could also be the chief executive of a government agency if that individual had responsibilities which in other entities would be collectively borne by a board of directors and its audit committee.

The Advisory is not bashful in promoting the role of internal audit with respect to audit committees. In places it even creates the impression that internal audit may be in effective charge of the audit committee. For instance, the Advisory suggests that the chief audit executive (CAE) should be responsible for determining the content of the internal audit charter[4] and it gives the CAE a likely major role with respect to the charter of the audit committee itself:

> 'the CAE should assist the committee in ensuring that the charter, role and activities of the committee are appropriate for it to achieve its responsibilities.'[5]

The CAE is also given the role to review the completeness and accuracy of the information the audit committee receives – not just the information pertinent to its oversight of internal audit. This role for internal audit is more justifiable if, as in the Advisory, it is accepted that the CAE should be secretary of the audit committee.

The Advisory certainly gives internal audit the committee secretarial role. A contrary view would be that this is unsound in that the audit committee, being a committee of the board, should receive its secretarial support from the same source as the board itself. In the UK, this would mean that the company secretary would therefore usually be the secretary to the audit committee. If the CAE is secretary to the audit committee, it may make it more difficult for the audit committee to form an objective view of the professionalism, etc of the internal audit function since most committees develop a 'cosy'; relationship with their secretary. It is also helpful for the secretary of the audit committee to be present at the board meeting when the chairperson of the audit committee speaks to the board on the audit committee's report to the board – this would happen naturally if the secretary to the audit committee were also the secretary of the board.

The Advisory classifies its content into:

> 'three areas of activities [which] ... are key to an effective relationship between the audit committee and the internal audit function, chiefly through the Chief Audit Executive:
> - Assisting the audit committee to ensure that its charter, activities, and processes are appropriate to fulfil its responsibilities.
> - Ensuring that the charter, role, and activities of internal audit are clearly understood and responsive to the needs of the audit committee and the board.
> - Maintaining open and effective communications with the audit committee and the chairperson.'[6]

The first of these three, which is tantamount to advising that the CAE should be the committee's secretary, is elaborated upon in the Advisory as follows (which we set out here in abbreviated form):[7]

- Annually advise the audit committee on its charter (terms of reference).

- Maintain a planning agenda (pro forma agenda for committee meetings) for the audit committee.
- Draft meeting agendas, facilitate distribution of materials to committee members and write up audit committee minutes.
- Encourage the audit committee to benchmark itself against leading practices.
- Meet the committee chairman to discuss the informational needs of the committee.
- Find out if committee members need special presentations or training.
- Inquire whether the committee considers its frequency of meetings and their duration are sufficient.

The Advisory puts the second of these three areas of audit committee activity in the context that:

> 'the CAE's relationship to the audit committee should revolve around a core role of the CAE that the audit committee understands, supports, and receives all assistance needed from the internal audit function. The Institute of Internal Auditors supports the concept that sound governance is dependent on the synergy generated among the four principal components of effective corporate governance systems: boards of directors, management, internal auditors, and external auditors. In that structure, internal auditors and audit committees are mutually supportive. Consideration of the work of internal auditors is essential for the audit committee to gain a complete understanding of an organization's operations. A primary component of the CAE's role with the committee is to ensure this objective is accomplished and the committee views the CAE as their trusted advisor.'[8]

This is elaborated upon in the Advisory as follows (which we set out here in abbreviated form):[9]

- Ask the committee to review and approve the internal audit charter, annually. (IIA's sample charter is reproduced at A1.1.19).
- Review with the audit committee that the functional and administrative reporting lines of internal audit allow adequate independence.
- Incorporate in the audit committee's charter the review of (a) the appointment, compensation, evaluation, retention, and dismissal of the CAE, and (b) review and approval of proposals to outsource any internal audit.
- Assist the committee to evaluate the scope, resources and results of internal audit activities.
- Inform the committee of internal audit coordination with, and oversight of other control and monitoring functions (eg management, compliance, security, business continuity, legal, ethics, environmental, external audit).
- Report to the committee significant control issues and opportunities for improvement across the organisation.
- Report progress against the approved annual audit plan and results; advise on the sufficiency of internal audit resources.
- Incorporate into the internal audit charter the responsibility of internal audit to report to the committee on suspected frauds and assist in their investigation if significant.
- Make the committee aware that quality assessment reviews of the internal audit function should be done every five years.

The essential elements of communication by the CAE to the audit committee are given as:

- Regular private meetings between the CAE and the committee.
- An annual summary report and assessment of internal audit results.
- Periodic reports to the committee of internal audit results.
- Keeping the committee informed of emerging internal audit trends and practices.
- Discussing with the committee its informational needs.
- Reviewing the completeness and accuracy of the information the committee receives.

The last could be construed as being a candidate to become a standard internal audit engagement included within the annual audit plan subject to qualifying for this attention as a result of an audit needs assessment.

## Not explored

This Advisory is certainly not intended to be a comprehensive treatise on audit committees. It states that:

> 'The Institute acknowledges that audit committee responsibilities encompass activities that are beyond the scope of this advisory, and in no way intends it to be a comprehensive description of audit committee responsibilities' [10]

But within its own more limited remit, to be useful guidance the Advisory needs more detail both with respect to the issues covered and the treatment of some of the issues which are referred to.

Internal audit/audit committee relationship issues not addressed include whether it is sufficient for just the CAE to have access to the audit committee: some would say that it is necessary for *all* the internal auditors in the function to have direct access to the chair of the audit committee, since there have been occasions when the CAE has sought to bury audit findings, perhaps in order not to embarrass a top management team with whom the CAE has a (too) close working relationship. Another matter not covered in this Advisory is whether the CAE should have a right to request that items be placed on the agenda of the audit committee. We know that some chairs of audit committees make it a practice to spend perhaps a day or two a year within the internal audit function – in order to break down barriers and to get a better 'feel' of the risk and control issues of the organisation as well as the degree of freedom of the internal audit function to conduct itself independently: again there is no suggestion of this in the Advisory. Incidentally, 'risk' gets little attention in this Advisory. We would also have liked to see a recommendation that internal audit might report to the audit committee on the efficiency and effectiveness of the external audit, not just on the extent to which there is coordination between external audit and others.

Matters which could usefully have been discussed in more detail include aspects of committee secretariat support. We are referring not to the routine provision of secretarial services, but the need for audit committees and their members individually to have access to full secretariat support between meetings. Then there is the failure of the Advisory to do more than mention the need for audit committee to review the appointment and dismissal of the CAE. Practice Advisory 2060–2[11] goes further with The Institute of Internal Auditors's recommendation that the audit committee should:

'Approve all decisions regarding the appointment or removal of the CAE'

but neither Advisory is clear as to whether the *prior approval* of the audit committee should be obtained. Although 'special tasks or projects requested [of internal audit] by the audit committee' are mentioned, there is no further elaboration of the challenges associated with internal audit undertaking special engagements directly on behalf of the audit committee, with the engagement report going direct to the audit committee rather than to management as well. Finally, there was no discussion of the occasions when the CAE should *not* be present at audit committee meetings.

| | |
|---|---|
| 3 | Para 1. |
| 4 | Penultimate bullet point in Para 5. |
| 5 | para 4 and third bullet point in Para 5. |
| 6 | Para 3. |
| 7 | Para 4. |
| 8 | Para 5. |
| 9 | Para 5. |
| 10 | Para 2. |
| 11 | Practice Advisory 1110–2, also released in December 2002, on 'Chief Audit Executive (CAE) reporting lines', discussed at A2.2.11 of this Handbook. |

## B1.2.4  Issues impacting audit committee effectiveness

| | |
|---|---|
| 1. | The composition of the board |
| 2. | The board committees and their duties |
| 3. | The means of appointing audit committee members, and the term of their appointment |
| 4. | The experience and independence of audit committee members |
| 5. | The training and development of audit committee members |
| 6. | The means of appointing a chair for the audit committee, and the term of this appointment |
| 7. | The terms of reference of the audit committee, in particular the committee's responsibilities and authorities |
| 8. | Appropriateness of the responsibilities of the audit committee and the responsibilities of other board committees |
| 9. | The means of reporting by the audit committee to the board |
| 10. | General administration of the committee's business |
| 11. | The servicing of the committee's needs (secretarial etc) |
| 12. | Access by others to audit committee members between meetings |
| 13. | Audit committee members' involvement between meetings |

| 14. | The number, timing and duration of audit committee meetings |
|---|---|
| 15. | The timeliness within the company's year of the committee's agenda items |
| 16. | Regularity of attendance of audit committee members at committee meetings |
| 17. | Whether appropriate non-committee members are in attendance at audit committee meetings when required. |
| 18. | Quality of audit committee agenda, agenda papers and minutes |
| 19. | The degree of correspondence between the committee's responsibilities and the record of its meetings |
| 20. | The committee's approach to its scrutiny of the financial statements |
| 21. | The committee's approach to its review of the effectiveness of management's internal control |
| 22. | The committee's approach to the oversight of the external audit |
| 23. | The committee's approach to oversight of the internal audit. |
| 24. | The committee's approach to meeting the requirements of regulators |
| 25. | The thoroughness of the board's approach to its oversight responsibilities generally |
| 26. | Whether the committee has the authority to seek professional advice from outside the company, and whether the committee exercises such a right appropriately |
| 27. | The approach to setting up and running audit committees in groups of companies, where each subsidiary may have an audit committee |
| 28. | Determining the membership of subsidiary company audit committees |
| 29. | Effective relationships between subsidiary audit committees and the main audit committee |

## B1.2.5  Audit committee *inputs* for assessing internal control effectiveness

After the year end, but shortly before finalising the Annual Report, the audit committee should meet to consider internal control. In some cases, their scope may be limited to internal *financial* control.

The committee's formal review of internal control will benefit from a number of inputs to it. To a small extent what will be appropriate will depend upon whether the audit committee's review of internal control is restricted to just internal *financial* control or whether it also covers the other aspects of internal control (control for *operational efficiency and effectiveness* and control for *legal and regulatory compliance*). However, in practice it is hard to separate these out.

Companies have considerable discretion in their approach which is likely to make use of some of the following inputs (ie evidence on internal control for the committee to consider[12]).

## *Intelligence gathered as board members during the year*

Many of the agenda items of board meetings, and of the meetings of other board committees over the previous year, will have informed the audit committee members about matters which have internal control implications. Indeed, many board decisions will have had impact upon internal control. Of course audit committee members would be unlikely to exclude this intelligence from their deliberations on internal control, but we are suggesting that a written summary of these matters should be prepared for the audit committee, most probably by the finance director or by the company secretary. It should also cover matters aired at board committees which have no non-executive representation.

## *Confirmation that key line managers are clear as to their objectives*

Contemporary definitions of internal control acknowledge that internal control is intended to provide reasonable assurance of the achievement of objectives. It follows that to assess whether internal control has been effective, management should be clear as to their objectives and whether they have been achieved. Failure to achieve objectives might not be a consequence of defective internal control; for instance it may be due to external events. Succeeding in achieving objectives might not be a consequence of effective internal control since control weaknesses might not have been exploited. So it is wise to consider both the extent to which objectives have been achieved as well as to framework of internal control in coming to an opinion on the effectiveness of internal control.

## *A report from the Executive on key risks*

Internal control must be proportionate to relative risk. It is important that the business has a clear idea of the risks it faces – risks of failing to achieve objectives; and risks of unwanted outcomes. The audit committee needs this to be clear when its considers the effectiveness of internal control.

## *A report from the Executive on the key procedures which are designed to provide effective internal control*

A summary of this had to be included in the internal control report for publication in order to comply with the old Rutteman guidance, now superseded by the Turnbull guidance. Here we are looking for something more detailed. Clearly the arrangements the business has in order to achieve effective internal control are absolutely crucial to determining whether or not there has been, and will be, effective internal control. So the audit committee needs to be clear about them. The audit committee may have recommendations to make to management.

Common examples are:

- the audit committee itself;
- a code of business conduct;

- the budgetary control system:
  - – a formal process of risk assessment;
  - – internal audit;
  - – a credit committee;
  - – control (and risk) self-assessment.

## *The committee's assessment of the effectiveness of internal audit*

COSO (US) and Rutteman/Turnbull (UK) rightly elevated the monitoring of internal control to the status of, respectively, an essential component of internal control and an essential criteria for assessing internal control effectiveness. It follows that this traditional interest of the audit committee becomes an important input to their assessment of internal control effectiveness. The committee will be concerned to satisfy itself that the internal audit function is properly resourced. Also of concern will be the scope of internal audit work, which should be at least as broad as the committee's own review of the effectiveness of internal control. The committee will wish to monitor the completion of internal audit's planned programme of audits against their earlier approved plan.

The committee's assessment of internal audit should (a) be done carefully, (b) lead to a definite conclusion and (c) be documented. Internal auditing Standards[13] guide that periodically the internal audit function should audit itself and also that external reviews should be conducted of internal audit: these can be valuable sources for the committee's assessment of internal audit effectiveness.

## *Reports from internal audit on scheduled audits performed*

During the year most audit committees receive a summary report on each internal audit performed. Taken separately and together these reports help the audit committee build a picture of the effectiveness of internal control within the business. Some audit committees nominate one of their members to 'shadow' the head on internal audit and this person may receive a full copy of each detailed internal audit report. An agenda item of most audit committee meetings will be a report from the head of internal audit, and perhaps at the end of each meeting the committee should arrange to meet this person without any other member of the executive being present.

## *Reports on special reviews commissioned by the committee from internal audit or others*

In the UK the Cadbury Report stipulated that the audit committee should be empowered to take independent professional advice. Before going outside, the committee may consider commissioning internal audit to conduct specific assignments on the committee's behalf, reporting to directly to the committee. Survey data shows this is happening occasionally – perhaps once a year on average. This goes further than merely influencing the content of internal audit's planned programme of work.

## Internal audit's overall summary opinion on internal control

If the audit committee of non-executive directors is expected to come to an opinion on the effectiveness of internal control – either for publication or for confidential transmission to the board, then it is not unreasonable for the committee to expect the head of internal audit to formally express in writing his or her opinion on this. Usually it will be unacceptable for this opinion to be qualified by protestations about inadequate internal audit resources and coverage – the audit committee itself will not wish to qualify its opinion on internal control in these ways.

## The overall results of a control self-assessment process

If the business has put in place a process of control and risk self-assessment by management and staff, then the results of this should be a valuable additional monitoring of internal control effectiveness available to the audit committee over and above the inputs they receive from internal audit. Internal audit's own opinion of the effectiveness of the CSA programme should also be obtained. The audit committee will be particularly interested in the most significant outputs from the CSA programme and will need to know of any limitations in its coverage, with explanations.

## Letters of representation ('comfort letters') on internal control from line management

A minimalist approach to CSA will be to rely on letters of representation about internal control from line managers. Even with a full CSA programme in place, these can be a useful supplement. It would not be usual for these to be addressed to the audit committee, but the audit committee should receive a report upon this process and the matters arising therefrom.

## The external auditors' management letter

The report from the external auditors on internal control now becomes centre stage as an important part of the audit committee's deliberation of the effectiveness of internal control. Of course it should not be regarded as comprehensive and would, in any case, major on internal *financial* control. It now needs to be available no later than the audit committee meeting which formulates the directors' internal control report for publication.

## A losses report from the CEO or FD

Losses are likely to be indicative of ineffective internal control. If the audit committee does not ask for a regular report on losses from the Executive, then this may be the reason why the committee does not learn of control breakdowns. It is best not to call this an 'avoidable losses' report as the committee should not risk the

Executive holding back information about an event on the grounds that the Executive does not think it could have been avoided. What should be covered in this report are:

- an account of losses which were exceptional in size;
- an account of losses which were exceptional in character;
- an account of any other losses of which the Executive should understand that the audit committee would wish to be told.

## An Executive report on any material developments since the b/s date and the present

Rutteman stipulated that any such events should be taken into account when the internal control report for publication is being formulated.

## The Executive's proposed wording of the internal control report for publication.

It is much better not to undertake initial drafting in committee, although the committee is likely to wish to adapt the wording which the Executive suggests.

What is essential is that the audit committee, on behalf of the board, makes a carefully considered judgement about internal control. The more comprehensive the array of inputs available, the more likely that the committee will not come to faulty judgements about internal control quality and thus not mislead either the directors or readers of published accounts. Of course, the inputs need to be of high quality.

---

[12]    For the UK, in general these inputs should relate to the period under review. US guidance is that the published report on internal control relates only to control in place *at a point in time* whereas, since Rutteman ('Internal Control and Financial Reporting – Guidance to Directors of Listed Companies Registered in the UK', ICAEW, December 1994), the UK requirement has been that:

> 'The directors' statement should cover the period of the financial statements and should also take account of material developments between the balance sheet date and the date upon which the financial statements are signed.'

[13]    *Standards for the Professional Practice of Internal Auditing* (1995) Institute of Internal Auditors Inc, Altamonte Springs, Florida.

---

## B1.2.6    Audit committee *processes* for assessing internal control effectiveness

The board is responsible for setting overall policy and strategy and for monitoring the performance of management. Management themselves are responsible for internal control and one essential aspect of internal control is that it should be monitored. 'Internal control' is synonymous with 'management control'. So management is responsible for internal control. Yet, in an overall sense, the board rather than management is responsible to ensure that the business has effective systems of internal control: indeed Rutteman[14] requires that the directors' internal control statements for publication should acknowledge the responsibility of the board for this.

## A matter for management and the board

So here is a challenge: with respect to internal control, how to determine where to draw the line between the responsibilities of the audit committee of the board and the responsibilities of the audit committee? In reality, the line cannot be drawn with great clarity. For instance, a survey by the author of this handbook of the largest multinational health care companies[15] found that most audit committees commission assignments, for instance assignments to be conducted by internal audit directly on behalf of the committee and reporting to the committee. The survey found that typically such a commission only comes internal audit's way about once a year. The Cadbury Report[16] stipulated that the audit committee should be empowered to take independent professional advice – and indeed that individual directors, whether executive or non-executive, should be similarly empowered.

## General principles

Allowing that the lines cannot be drawn with great clarity between what management should do about internal control and what the audit committee of the board should do, nevertheless there are general principles that should apply which can be summed up as follows.

- Management should be seen to be responsible for internal control and for making sufficient arrangements for its monitoring.
- The audit committee is the board's first line in *reviewing* the performance of management in discharging their responsibility for internal control, including its monitoring. The audit committee does not usurp management's own responsibilities for internal control.
- Whether or not the Board publicly discloses its opinion on internal control effectiveness,[17] it should *have* an opinion, and is likely to rely on its audit committee to do the groundwork for arriving at such an opinion.
- It follows that the audit committee will wish to come to an opinion about the effectiveness of internal control.
- Many audit committees are more confident dealing with financial and accounting matters than with operational matters and in some cases the scope of the committee's review of internal control may be so circumscribed.
- Beyond internal *financial* control there is control over *operations* and internal control to provide reasonable assurance of compliance with *laws and regulations*. There is no escaping that the board is responsible to ensure that management has effective internal control of these non-financial reporting aspects since the viability and success of the enterprise depends at least as much upon them as upon effective internal financial control. Indeed it is not possible to distinguish neatly between internal *financial* control and other internal control.

- Every board needs to decide whether to delegate to its audit committee a consideration of the non-financial aspects of internal control in addition to a consideration of internal *financial* control; or to reserve this for detailed review at main board meetings, or to deal with it effectively in some other way(s).
- Board review of the effectiveness of the non-financial aspects of internal control should be tackled at least as systematically and as diligently as its oversight of internal financial control.

## *The approach to take*

Let us assume that it is to be the audit committee which fronts the board's review of the effectiveness of *all* aspects of internal control. In a business which makes other arrangements, most of the advice we offer below will still apply, though with adaptation to allow for the transfer of responsibilities away from the audit committee.

The general process can be summed up as follows:

- Ensure adequate committee time is set aside to review internal control and enough advance notice is given to prepare and study the relevant agenda papers. In practice the main pitfall is to combine on the same agenda another substantive item: so, for instance, it is unwise for the committee to make its detailed review of the effectiveness of internal control in the same meeting which considers the draft financial results for publication. Both these agenda items are substantial. Both have to be deliberated upon after the end of the financial year, just before the publication of the annual results.[18] It is better to hold two separate audit committee meetings at about the same time, perhaps each lasting for half a day, in order to avoid one of these two agenda items not being dealt with adequately.
- Bring forward to mid-year meetings of the audit committee as much as possible of the committee's consideration of internal control, away from the pressure of the year end deadlines, and allowing more time for any necessary remedial action. B1.3.3 gives illustrative timings and agenda for audit committee meetings throughout the year.
- Review all the evidence about the effectiveness of internal control which has been brought before the audit committee. We reiterate that it is important that the external auditor's report to management on internal control is available to an audit committee meeting before the preparation of the directors' report on internal control. However, there are many other inputs which the audit committee will need to consider.
- Take oral advice from management, internal and external audit and others in attendance at the audit committee meeting.
- Draw conclusions as a committee. Whether or not the directors are going to *publish* their opinion about internal control effectiveness, they should intend to come to their own conclusion about it, and will rely on their audit committee to advise them. It is possible that in some cases the audit committee will take the view that they are unable to conclude as to whether or not internal control is effective. If that is the case, the committee should

ensure that it is not placed at that disadvantage in the following year. If the audit committee is unable to conclude on the effectiveness of internal control, it is likely that internal control is ineffective.

- Carefully document the committee's consideration about internal control. This means:

    - develop and retain comprehensive committee agendas capable of indicating retrospectively the scope of the committee's consideration of internal control;

    - develop and retain detailed agenda papers on the internal control agenda items;

    - record detailed minutes which should be retained of the committee's consideration of the internal control agenda items, capable of demonstrating retrospectively the nature of the debate which took place, the views expressed and the basis for the judgements taken;

    - make sure the minutes indicate clearly the decisions arrived at about internal control.

This approach will be valuable if, at some future date, the board is challenged about the quality of its oversight of internal control.

[14] 'Internal Control and Financial Reporting – Guidance for directors of listed companies registered in the UK', Report of the Working Group chaired by Paul Rutteman, (1994) ICAEW, London.

[15] '1997 Survey of Internal Auditing in the Health Care Sector' (1997) Spilsby, England.

[16] 'The Financial Aspects of Corporate Governance', Report of the Committee chaired by Sir Adrian Cadbury (1992) Gee & Co.

[17] Hampel introduced a revision to the relevant item of the Cadbury Code to remove the word 'effectiveness'. However, this Provision of the Cadbury Code had been implemented, following the Rutteman Guidance, with no requirement for directors to disclose their opinion as to internal control effectiveness, although Rutteman allowed that directors might choose to do so. This state of affairs continued with the 2003 Combined Code.

[18] This is because the annual results carry both the financial statements and the directors' report on internal control.

## B1.2.7   Audit committee *outputs* from assessing internal control effectiveness

Clearly the Board has overall responsibility to ensure that the business has effective internal control. In this regard the Board monitors the performance of executive management. In practice the Board is likely to rely upon, at least to a considerable extent, the audit committee to assist its consideration of the quality of risk management and internal control. So we have no hesitation in claiming that the principal output of the audit committee on internal control is its report to the Board. Of secondary importance is the wording the audit committee will suggest for the directors report on internal control for publication.

The Board needs assurance that risk management and internal control are effective, or advice that it is not. The Board is overall oversight responsibility for all aspects of internal control – not just internal financial control. The Board should be at least as concerned about (a) controls for operational efficiency and effectiveness and (b) controls for compliance with laws and regulations, as for (c) controls over the reliability of financial reporting. So the audit committee's reports to the board about internal control need to cover *all* aspects of internal control and to comment on internal control's effectiveness. If the audit committee narrows the scope of its reports on internal control to the Board, then the Board will need to obtain other advice from other sources.

The scope and wording varies of directors' reports on internal control for publication. Surrogates for the word 'effective' have been used as boards grapple with the meaning of that term – for instance 'served its purpose' or 'are appropriate to the business'.

We conclude this section with suggested summaries of likely audit committee outputs on internal control.

## *Outputs – for transmission to the Board prior to going to print with the Annual Report*

- Endorsement of the key control procedures (note: since Rutteman, in the UK these are for the *directors* to have established) as being satisfactory.
- Committee opinion on internal (financial) control effectiveness – probably for internal use only and not for publication.
- Committee's proposed draft internal control report for publication.
- Any Committee concerns about internal control of sufficient importance for the Board.

## *Outputs – for transmission to senior executive management*

- Outstanding committee concerns about internal control.
- The committee's recommended revisions of approach for the future.

# Case study: Worksheet 1

USE OF PRODUCTIVE AUDIT TIME BY *AUDIT SUBJECT*

Type of work/category of resource

| | 1 | 2 | 3 | 4 | 5 | 6 | 7 | 8 |
|---|---|---|---|---|---|---|---|---|
| | Accounting & financial auditing | Operational & VFM auditing | Audit of advanced computer systems | Auditing of regulatory compliance | Environmental auditing | Assisting the external auditor | Other non-internal audit work | |
| % of Unit's productive time spent now (Total = 100%) | 40 | 10 | 0 | 10 | 0 | 20 | 20 | |
| Trend in type of work<br>G=Growing<br>S=Static<br>D=Declining | S | G | S | G | S | G | S | |
| Ability to do work well with current resources<br>S=Strong<br>M=Medium<br>W=Weak | S | W | W | S | W | S | M | |
| Medium-term scope for re-sourcing this as work of the Unit*<br>G=Good<br>F=Fair<br>P=Poor | G | F | P | G | F | F | P | |
| Strategic importance of this activity<br>L=Low<br>M=Medium<br>H=High | M | H | H | L | M | L | M | |

\*   Allowing for possibilities of altering the staffing profile of the Unit

## Case study: Worksheet 2A

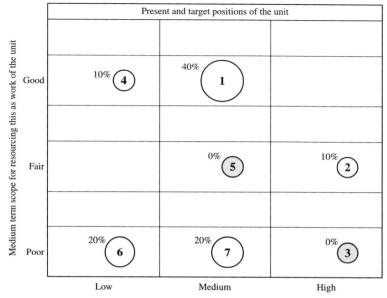

## Case study: Worksheet 2B

## Case study: Worksheet 3

| STRATEGIC PLAN FOR THE UNIT | |
| --- | --- |
| Category of Activity/Resource | Alternative courses of action to change future position |
| 1  Accounting & financial audits (-) | |
| 2  Operational & VFM audits (++) | |
| 3  Regulatory compliance audits (+) | |
| 4  Environmental audits (+) | |
| 5  Assisting the external auditor (-) | |
| 6  Other non-internal audit work (-) | |

# Managing the internal audit activity – case studies

## B1.3.1 Self evaluation questions on audit committees

1. What aspects of the audit committees are most challenging for your organisation to implement?
   - For what reasons?
   - How might problems be overcome?
2. Does your organisation have sufficient non-executive resource to adopt best practice guidance for audit committees?
   - If not, what actions can improve the situation?
3. Are your non-executives suitably trained for their role?
   - If not, what is lacking and how might this be addressed?
4. How does your audit committee's terms of reference compare with the model terms of reference?
   - If there are inappropriate material differences, are there any barriers to 'closing the gap'?
   - How might these barriers be addressed?
5. How might small organisations most effectively achieve/enhance appropriate objectivity of the audit committee without creating a disproportionate overhead?
6. Does your audit committee's activity encompass all the areas it should?
   - If not, what actions might be undertaken to 'close the gap'?
7. How does your audit committee engage in 'constructive challenge'?
   - In what ways might this be made more productive?
8. Do you think that your audit committee has an effective relationship with the external audit function?
   - How might the situation be improved?
9. Do you think your audit committee has an effective relationship with the internal audit function?
   - How might the situation be improved?
10. What role does your audit committee have in relation to the statement on internal control?
    - Are there any ways in which this could be improved?

## B1.3.2 Case studies for course on meeting the requirements of your audit committee

CASE 1

### Building an effective working relationship between internal audit and the audit committee

Which of the following two points of view do you think is nearer the mark – and why? They are quoted from the first electronic issue of *AuditWire* (Volume 25, Number 1, January-February 2003). Now in its 27th year, *Auditwire*, a newsletter of The Institute of Internal Auditors Inc, is available in electronic form, to IIA members only, on their website (http://www.theiia.org). It is The IIA's bimonthly membership news-letter. Each issue will also be available to members and subscribers via e-mail. The quotes appeared in the lead article by Christina Brune, the editor of *AuditWire*, titled 'Consulting: Friend or Foe': at present the full path to this article is http://www.theiia.org/newsletter/aw_current.cfm?quickcode=B8JLjYX.

#### Point of view No 1 of Peter Rodgers, vice president and general auditor of BISYS Group Inc in Columbus, Ohio:

'The Andersen debacle drove home the risks to maintaining our independ-ence when we auditors neglect or stray from our primary mission, which should be providing internal control assurance. ...

When my audit team is approached by management for a consulting project, four red flags are raised in my mind:

- If management is asking the audit group for help, there must be a control concern. As an auditor, my first responsibility is to decide whether an audit or investigation is warranted.
- If there is no control concern, I must wonder whether the manager considers the project too risky for his or her own people to do or whether it's of too little value to engage a third party on the project.
- If it's too risky for the manager's own people to tackle, does this indicate that the manager has the wrong people on staff or not enough people? If the project has insufficient value to warrant hiring a third party, why would I want to associate our audit group with the project?
- Finally, I must ask myself whether I believe that I have been so successful in my assurance role that internal auditing has no other risk-based priorities to pursue. If so, the audit group must be overstaffed.'

#### Point of view No 2 of Geraldine Gail, Director of Internal Audit, the University of California, Santa Cruz:

'Consulting is one of the most important services we provide for manage-ment. We have found a direct correlation between our time spent on consulting and the decrease that we have in investigations. So, when I do my audit plan at the beginning of the year, I save a certain amount of time to do the consulting projects that aren't part of the risk-based audit program. ...

We have an incredibly wonderful, comfortable relationship [with management]. People see the audit staff as peers and feel very comfortable calling and asking them questions. …

In the next couple of months, I'll be developing an online conflict-of-interest training course, which our federal researchers will be required to take. We'll be doing that with our new whistleblowers policy as well.'

## CASE 2

### Satisfying the audit committee's need to assess internal audit quality

The audit committee intends to get on top of evaluating the quality of the internal audit of the entity. It has not done this before. The committee is likely to ask you, the chief audit executive, for advice; and you intend to prepare yourself to give good advice. What will be the main points that you will wish to get across to the committee?

## CASE 3

### Internal audit assistance in keeping the independent audit under review

What advice would you give to the audit committee on how they should approach their evaluation of the quality of the external audit, and how might internal audit be able to assist in this?

## CASE 4

### Internal audit serving the board/audit committee in the 'top-down' and 'embedded' assessment of risk and control

As chief audit executive, what do you consider your role should be with respect to enterprise risk management?

## CASE 5

### Emerging, new demands on audit committees and internal auditors

What will be the major challenges to your audit committee to meet the recommendations of the Higgs Committee?

## CASE 6

### Avoiding audit committee overload

Is this a problem. If so, how will your organisation address it?

CASE 7

The audit committee of the board has for some time been expressing concern about the level and quality of internal audit resources available to the enterprise. Certain non-executive directors on the audit committee think that the executive is not placing adequate stress upon internal audit. Over the past three years internal audit has been cut back as the business has downsized in response to declining turnover. Now the efforts of the executive are paying off and the company is expanding in terms of both turnover and new ventures. The executive is reluctant to increase fixed overheads to the level they were in 'the bad old days'. The executive reassures the audit committee that they are confident that internal audit coverage is sufficient in both quantity and quality. They offer that a senior executive should perform a special review of internal audit, reporting his conclusions to the audit committee; this senior executive fully understands the nature of internal auditing as he had, a few years before, been head of the enterprise's internal audit function.

What should the audit committee do?

**The solution**

The audit committee decided to accept the offer of the special review. In addition they indicated their intention to commission an external review of the internal audit function by someone, or a firm, competent to perform the review. While this might be the enterprise's external auditors, the committee was concerned that (a) they might not be sufficiently independent of the executive to be entirely objective, and (b) they might assess the quality of internal audit in terms of how useful internal audit was in meeting external audit objectives – which was not the point of the review. The audit committee decided to consult the Institute of Internal Auditors to properly resource this quality assurance review. The committee is particularly concerned that at a time of expansion, the enterprise's systems of internal control should be strong, and so an effective internal audit function is particularly needed at this time.

CASE 8

The enterprise has been approached to be one of 15 participating in a benchmark study of internal auditing. For a variety of reasons they decided not to participate on this occasion, but used this opportunity to formulate their policy on participation in such a survey in the future.

**The solution**

This is what they decided:

- The enterprise does not compete with other enterprises on the strength of their internal audit function and so, in principle, there is no reason why internal audit should not be benchmarked.
- The most useful benchmarking of their internal audit will be against other internal audit functions in similar businesses of approximately similar size.
- They identified the following as being matters of particular interest to be gleaned from a benchmarking exercise:
  - Comparative levels of internal audit resources (quantity and quality);

- Comparative practices with respect to outsourcing internal audit, control and risk self-assessment, etc;
- Comparative costs of internal audit, distinguishing between payroll, travel and other costs;
- Comparative scope of internal audit programmes;
- Career profiles in internal audit;
- Best practice benchmarks in the cohort covered by the survey.
- On cost grounds, being a relatively small business, they had a preference for utilising *GAIN* (the Institute of Internal Auditors' benchmarking service) rather than participating in a special exercise led by consultants.

## B1.3.3   Case 9: Timing and content of audit committee meetings, showing the committee's consideration of internal control

The Head of Internal Audit was asked to advise the audit committee on the timing and content of their meetings. The company year end is 31 December. It is a small listed company.

*This is the essence of the advice which the Head of Internal Audit developed:*

Notwithstanding that Cadbury allows the committee to meet only twice a year, at a minimum this committee will need to meet four times a year. We are showing the agenda for the February meeting as dealing, *inter alia*, with the financial statements for publication as well as with the assessment of the effectiveness of internal control. With two heavy items like this it is likely that one will be dealt with inadequately unless adequate committee time is safeguard. Accordingly we are suggesting a full day meeting but an alternative would be two separate meetings at approximately the same time during February. Further meetings should be arranged as required.

In each case we recommend that the audit committee's meeting is scheduled 8–10 days before the associated board meeting so that its draft minutes may be tabled at the board meeting and the Board spoken to by the chair of the audit committee.

These are the meetings we suggest, together with their principal agenda items:

### July meeting (8–10 days before the associated Board)
1   Interim results
2   Summary reports on internal audit work done
    (i)   Including internal auditor time alone with the committee
3   Consideration of anticipated impact of changes in accounting standards and in accounting treatment upon the next set of annual financial statements, including s simulated set of financial statements

### November (8–10 days before the associated board meeting)
1   Summary reports on internal audit work done
    (i)   Including internal auditor time alone with the committee
2   Discussion and approval of the internal audit plan of work to be conducted in the coming financial year

**February** (*likely to be a full day's meeting, or preferably two separate half day meetings, ideally about 8 days before the associated Board*).

**Part 1**
1    Final results
    (i)    Consideration of external auditor's report of audit now completed
2    External audit time alone with the committee
3    Committee's recommendation, for transmittal to the board, on the appointment of the external auditors for the current year's audit

**Part 2**
4    Summary reports on internal audit work done
    (i)    Including committee time alone with the internal auditor
5    Concluding the committee's review of internal control
    (i)    External auditor's draft management letter
    (ii)    Committee's consideration of the Executive's Losses Report
    (iii)    Committee's review of internal audit's overall summary opinion on internal control
6    Formulation and adoption of the committee's opinion of the effectiveness of internal control over the year under review, and their draft internal control report for publication (both for communication the board).

**April, May or June** (*8–10 days before the associated board meeting*)
1    The committee's review of its own terms of reference
2    Consideration of planned external audit approach
3    Preliminary review of whether to consider appointing alternative external auditors for the *following* financial year
4    Summary reports on internal audit work done.
    (i)    Including committee time alone with the internal auditor.
5    Receive a report on an external quality assurance review of the internal audit function (once every three years).
6    Committee conclusions on the present and planned future adequacy of the internal audit function.
    (i)    Including time *without* the internal auditor being present.
    (ii)    Including review of the internal audit function's 'charter' or 'terms of reference'

# Nature of work – best practice guidance

**B2.1.1**   While we also refer to other important pronouncements, our main source of guidance for the parts of this Handbook which describe internal auditing best practice has been the *Professional Practices Framework* of The Institute of Internal Auditors. This *Framework* includes their *Definition* of internal auditing, *Code of Ethics*, *Standards*, and *Practice Advisories*. Of these, only the *Practice Advisories* are non-mandatory: they explain and elaborate upon best practice in most circumstances, and are important for practitioners and students. Readers can see the current complete list of *Practice Advisories* at www.theiia.org. Those current on 1 January 2005 are shown at APPENDIX 3 of this Handbook, including a useful topical classification at APPENDIX 3.2.

In addressing this subject we have drawn more widely than those *Practice Advisories* classified by The Institute as applicable to this part of our Handbook, which are:

| Practice Advisories, by Standard Number | Release date |
|---|---|
| Practice Advisory 2100–1: Nature of Work | 5 January 2001 |
| Practice Advisory 2100–2: Information Security | 1 February 2001 |
| Practice Advisory 2100–3: Internal Audit's Role in the Risk Management Process | 7 March 2001 |
| Practice Advisory 2100–4: Internal Audit's Role in Organizations Without a Risk Management Process | 7 March 2001 |
| Practice Advisory 2100–5: Legal Considerations in Evaluating Regulatory Compliance Programs | 28 March 2001 |
| Practice Advisory 2100–6: Control and Audit Implications of e-Commerce Activities | 12 June 2003 |
| Practice Advsory 2100–7: The Internal Auditor's Role in Identifying and Reporting Environmental Risks | 12 June 2003 |
| Practice Advisory 2100–8: The Internal Auditor's Role in Evaluating An Organization's Privacy Framework | 12 February 2004 |
| Practice Advisory 2110–1: Assessing the Adequacy of Risk Management Processes | 7 March 2001 |
| Practice Advisory 2110–2: The Internal Auditor's Role in the Business Continuity Process | 12 June 2003 |
| Practice Advisory 2120.A1–1: Assessing and Reporting on Control Processes | 18 June 2001 |

| | |
|---|---|
| Practice Advisory 2120.A1–2: Using Control Self-Assessment for Assessing the Adequacy of Control Processes | 18 June 2001 |
| Practice Advisory 2120.A1–3: The Internal Auditor's Role in Quarterly Financial Reporting, Disclosures, and Management Certification | 20 February 2003 |
| Practice Advisory 2120.A1–4: Auditing the Financial Reporting Process | 12 June 2003 |
| Practice Advisory 2120.A4–1: Control Criteria | 5 January 2001 |
| Practice Advisory 2130–1: Role of the Internal Audit Activity and Internal Auditor in the Ethical Culture of an Organization | 1 February 2001 |

*Practice Advisories* carry the *Standard* number to which they principally refer. Readers are advised to consult the applicable *Standards* as we do not in every case reproduce them here. They are to be found at APPENDIX 2.

In this discussion of best practice with respect to the nature of internal work we restrict ourselves to interpreting the mandatory *Standards* themselves as well as touching on other important developments (such as COSO on enterprise risk management and HM Treasury on the principles and concept of risk management). Readers will also find material germane to the nature of internal auditing within other best practice sections of this handbook – in particular CHAPTER A1.1 – and our supplementary guidance (CHAPTER B2.2) is also very extensive.

The October 2001 release of the new *Standards* described internal auditing as:

> **'Standard 2100 – Nature of Work**
> The internal audit activity evaluates and contributes to the improvement of risk management, control and governance systems.'

The January 2004 release of the *Standards* made this modification to reflect wording within the definition of internal auditing which appears in the preamble to both the *Code of Ethics* and the *Standards*:

> **'Standard 2100 – Nature of Work**
> The internal audit activity should evaluate and contribute to the improvement of risk management, control, and governance **processes using a systematic and disciplined approach.'**

This still leaves open the question as to whether the 'systematic approach' is applied to planning the programme of audit engagements so that internal audit covers the affairs of the entity in a rational way over time; or whether a 'systematic approach' refers to a need to plan and conduct each audit engagement in a systematic way. We would say both. We do however note that too many internal audit activities display a lack of a systematic approach in one or both respects, so that it is hard to discern that the future plan of audit engagements has been drawn up in a systematic and disciplined way – rather it seems too random, ad hoc and reactive to circumstances – and too there may be little of a standard, systematic approach followed within individual audit engagements.

## B2.1.2 Risk management, control and governance

These three conceptual frameworks (risk management, control and governance) overlap very considerably and it is untidy for The Institute to treat each in their *Standards* in separate but heavily overlapping ways. We have already discussed this at A1.1.12. The new COSO framework for enterprise risk management (see B2.2.28) incorporates all of the internal control framework and not very much more, as COSO acknowledges:

> **'Encompasses Internal Control**
> Internal control is an integral part of enterprise risk management. This enterprise risk management framework encompasses internal control, forming a more robust conceptualization and tool for management. Internal control is defined and described in Internal Control – Integrated Framework.'[1]

The emphasis placed by The Institute of Internal Auditors upon internal audit's role with respect to the *internal* aspects of corporate governance increases the overlap between (a) the 'governance processes' pertinent to the internal audit role (b) internal control and (c) risk management. With respect to 'governance processes' this is illustrated in this extract from a Practice Advisory, especially if, as we believe, 'measures of accountability' is intended to refer to accountability *within* the entity rather than to public reporting:

> '... internal auditing evaluations, in the aggregate, provide information to appraise the overall management process. All business systems, processes, operations, functions, and activities within the organization are subject to the internal auditors' evaluations. The comprehensive scope of work of internal auditing should provide reasonable assurance that management's:
> - Risk management system is effective.
> - System of internal control is effective and efficient.
> - Governance process is effective by establishing and preserving values, setting goals, monitoring activities and performance, and defining the measures of accountability.'[2]

We suggest that, almost by stealth and without sufficient recognition by The Institute, in fact internal audit is moving more and more towards a role with respect to the external aspects of corporate governance – for instance as shown in B2.1.7 below.

## B2.1.3 *Risk management*

At A1.1.12 we discussed the appropriate interface of the internal auditing activity with the risk management process. Undoubtedly, the risk management process is an important process about which senior management and the board will require assurance:

> 'Boards and audit committees have an oversight role to determine that appropriate risk management processes are in place and that these processes are adequate and effective. Internal auditors should assist both management and the audit committee by examining, evaluating, reporting, and recommending improvements on the adequacy and effectiveness of management's risk processes. Management and the

board are responsible for their organization's risk management and control processes. However, internal auditors acting in a consulting role can assist the organization in identifying, evaluating, and implementing risk management methodologies and controls to address those risks.'[3]

If internal audit is a key player in the provision of the risk management service, then it makes it more difficult for internal audit to provide this assurance. We discussed this, in the context of risk management, in A2.1.9 'Handling impairments to independence and objectivity'.

The Institute acknowledges that there may be a wide variation in the roles that the internal audit activity may play in the risk management process:

'The internal audit activity's role in the risk management process of an organization can change over time and may be found at some point along a continuum that ranges from:
- No role, to
- Auditing the risk management process as part of the internal audit plan, to
- Active, continuous support and involvement in the risk management process such as
- Participation on oversight committees, monitoring activities, and status reporting, to
- Managing and coordinating the risk management process.'[4]

If the internal audit activity has any responsibility for the risk management process, the oversight of the internal audit of it should be entrusted to another (see A2.1.9):

**'Standard 1130.A2**
Assurance engagements for functions over which the chief audit executive has responsibility should be overseen by a party outside the internal audit activity.'

Until 2004, most if not all official pronouncements on risk had focussed exclusively on the management of uncertainties and risks which might *negatively* affect the organisation. The impression given had been that management's responsibility was to identify and assess the affect of future events which, if they occurred, might negatively impact upon the achievement of objectives – and to design and implement satisfactory mitigation responses. Now there has emerged an awareness that a comprehensive (we term it a 360°) approach to risk management should also set out to identify and assess the effect of future events not anticipated within the organisation's strategic plan which, if they occurred *and could be exploited by the organisation* to impact *positively* upon the organisation's performance.

'All entities face uncertainty, and the challenge for management is to determine how much uncertainty to accept as it strives to grow stakeholder value. Uncertainty presents both risk and opportunity, with the potential to erode or enhance value. Enterprise risk management enables management to effectively deal with uncertainty and associated risk and opportunity, enhancing the capacity to build value.'[5]

We are uncomfortable with COSO's assertion that unplanned opportunities should necessarily be responded to through the entity's strategic planning processes as the opportunity may well have passed before these processes can get a grip on the opportunity:

'Opportunities are channelled back to management's strategy or objective-setting process.'[6]

So risk management is not just about managing 'downside risk'. It is about managing what might be termed 'upside risk' as well. Upside risks represent extra potential opportunities.

While The Institute of Internal Auditors acknowledges what we term, inelegantly, as 'upside risk', they nevertheless associate the internal audit activity mainly or exclusively with 'downside risk' as these two extracts from Practice Advisory 2010–2: 'Linking the Audit Plan to Risk and Exposures' illustrate:

'Any organization faces a number of uncertainties and risks which can both negatively or positively affect the organization. Risk can be managed in a number of different ways, including acceptance, avoidance, transfer, or control. Internal controls are a common method for reducing the potential negative impact of risk and uncertainty.'[7]

and:

'The internal audit activity's audit plan should be designed based on an assessment of risk and exposures that may affect the organization. Ultimately, key audit objectives are to provide management with information to mitigate the negative consequences associated with accomplishing the organization's objectives, as well as an assessment of the effectiveness of management's risk management activities. The degree or materiality of exposure can be viewed as risk mitigated by establishing control activities.'[8]

We consider this to be an unsatisfactory current limitation in the profession's theory and practice. Failure to grasp an unanticipated opportunity should be regarded as as much a failure of control as failure to avoid the consequences of an exposure. Another prevalent limitation in the theory and practice of risk management is a failure to factor into risk assessments a consideration of the likelihood and probably impact if several uncertain events, which may constitute either negative exposures or positive opportunities, were to occur simultaneously. Risks may be said to be like London buses – they tend to come all at once. Too rarely do our risk registers or other methodologies for assessing risk, make allowance for this. It is when there is a conjunction between several risk events that the impact is likely to greatest.

There is common ground, though different terminology, on the different available means to manage risk, as shown in Table 1. The UK's HM Treasury has added a '5th T' to reflect the concept of 'upside risk': they define and illustrate 'Take the opportunity' as:

'This option is not an alternative to those above; rather it is an option which should be considered whenever tolerating, transferring or treating a risk. There are two aspects to this. The first is whether or not at the same time as mitigating threats, an opportunity arises to exploit positive impact. For example, if a large sum of capital funding is to be put at risk in a major project, are the relevant controls judged to be good enough to justify increasing the sum of money at stake to gain even greater advantages? The second is whether or not circumstances arise which, whilst not generating threats, offer positive opportunities. For example, a drop in the cost of goods or services frees up resources which can be re-deployed.'[9]

Some organisations have added a '6th T' – 'Track'. 'Track' corresponds, broadly, to COSO's final essential component of internal control, which is 'monitoring' (see B2.2.10).

**Table 1: Terms applied to ways of managing risk**

**Different ways of managing risk**

| IIA (PA 2010–2), 2004[10] | COSO ERM, 2004[11] | HM Treasury (UK), 2004[12] |
|---|---|---|
| Acceptance | Acceptance | Tolerate |
| Control | Reduction | Treat |
| Transfer | Sharing | Transfer |
| Avoidance | Avoidance | Terminate |
| | | Take the opportunity |

HM Treasury usefully point out that the option of 'treat' in addressing risk can be further analysed into four different types of controls:[13]

> Detective controls
> Directive controls
> Preventative controls
> Corrective controls

We provide HM Treasury's definitions of these later in this section under Internal Control.

**B2.1.4   COSO on enterprise risk management**

Readers should refer to B2.2.25 for a full critique on this 2004 framework. There are eight COSO (2004) components for effective enterprise risk management whereas there were only five COSO (1992) internal control components. But largely the extra components have been created by separating out content from some of the 1992 internal control components – particularly the risk assessment component – and labelling them separately. Perhaps the most significant expansion from the 1992 to the 2004 frameworks is that ERM is fourth category of objectives – strategic – has joined the three categories of internal control objectives:

> 'This enterprise risk management framework is geared to achieving an entity's objectives, set forth in four categories:
> ● Strategic – high-level goals, aligned with and supporting its mission
> ● Operations …
> ● Reporting …
> ● Compliance …'[14]

and it follows therefore that one of the new components of enterprise risk management is 'objective setting'.

While these represent significant extensions from the 1992 internal control framework, that was more to do with inappropriate limitations to the 1992 framework rather than being to do with intrinsic limitations to the concept of internal control. We have always accepted that there needs to be effective internal control over the setting and achievement of the entity's strategic objectives.

The 1992 and 2004 studies both make the point that the essential components of internal control and of enterprise risk management are also criteria for assessing the effectiveness of internal control and enterprise risk management. Put simply, for example, this means that an audit committee should assess the effectiveness of each of the components in coming to a view as to whether internal control/ enterprise risk management is effective. So should internal audit activities – both for the entity as a whole and within each audit engagement. This is what we call the 'process approach' to assessing internal control or enterprise risk management effectiveness. A second approach is the 'outputs approach' which requires an evaluation of results in order to assess whether internal control or enterprise risk management has been effective. The UK Rutteman and Turnbull reports are very clear that conclusions on internal control effectiveness are only justified if both 'process' and 'outputs' have been assessed.

## B2.1.5 *Internal control*

We cover internal control in depth in B2.2.1 to B2.2.24.

The generally accepted definition of internal is the COSO (1992) one:

> 'Internal control is broadly defined as a process, effected by the entity's board of directors, management and other personnel, designed to provide reasonable assurance regarding the achievement of objectives in the following categories:
> - Effectiveness and efficiency of operations.
> - Reliability of financial reporting.
> - Compliance with applicable laws and regulations.'

The Institute of Internal Auditors adds a fourth category – safeguarding of assets – and broadens the compliance category:

> **'Standard 2120.A1**
> Based on the results of the risk assessment, the internal audit activity should evaluate the adequacy and effectiveness of controls encompassing the organization's governance, operations, and information systems. This should include:
> - Reliability and integrity of financial and operational information.
> - Effectiveness and efficiency of operations.
> - Safeguarding of assets.
> - Compliance with laws, regulations, and contracts.'

The Institute defines a control as:

> '*Control* is any action taken by management to enhance the likelihood that established objectives and goals will be achieved. Controls may be preventive (to deter undesirable events from occurring), detective (to detect and correct undesirable events which have occurred), or directive (to cause or encourage a desirable

event to occur). The concept of a system of control is the integrated collection of control components and activities that are used by an organization to achieve its objectives and goals.'[15]

HM Treasury classify the methods of 'treating' (or 'reducing' or 'controlling') into four categories of control:[16]

'DETECTIVE CONTROLS: These controls are designed to identify occasions of undesirable outcomes having been realised. Their effect is, by definition, "after the event" so they are only appropriate when it is possible to accept the loss or damage incurred. Examples of detective controls include stock or asset checks (which detect whether stocks or assets have been removed without authorisation), reconciliation (which can detect unauthorised transactions), and "Post Implementation Reviews" which detect lessons to be learnt from projects for application in future work.

DIRECTIVE CONTROLS: These controls are designed to ensure that a particular outcome is achieved. They are particularly important when it is critical that an undesirable event is avoided – typically associated with Health and Safety or with security. Examples of this type of control would be include a requirement that protective clothing be worn during the performance of dangerous duties, or that staff be trained with required skills before being allowed to work unsupervised.

PREVENTIVE CONTROLS: These controls are designed to limit the possibility of an undesirable outcome being realised. The more important it is that an undesirable outcome should not arise, the more important it becomes to implement appropriate preventive controls. The majority of controls implemented in organisations tend to belong to this category. Examples of preventive controls include separation of duty, whereby no one person has authority to act without the consent of another (such as the person who authorises payment of an invoice being separate from the person who ordered goods prevents one person securing goods at public expense for their own benefit), or limitation of action to authorised persons (such as only those suitably trained and authorised being permitted to handle media enquiries prevents inappropriate comment being made to the press).

CORRECTIVE CONTROLS: These controls are designed to correct undesirable outcomes which have been realised. They provide a route of recourse to achieve some recovery against loss or damage. An example of this would be design of contract terms to allow recovery of overpayment. Insurance can also be regarded as a form of corrective control as it facilitates financial recovery against the realisation of a risk. Contingency planning is an important element of corrective control as it is the means by which organisations plan for business continuity/recovery after events which they could not control.'

One of the COSO categories of objectives of internal control, and also of enterprise risk management, is 'compliance'. Compliance has several meanings in an internal audit context, each overlapping with each other. One use of the word is in the context of 'compliance tests' which are tests that an auditor conducts to ascertain whether there is compliance with specific control procedures – in contrast to 'weakness tests' (sometimes known as 'substantive tests') which are designed to measure the effect of a control weakness. A second use of the word is as in 'compliance programme' or 'regulatory compliance programme' – a programme which exists to assess whether compliance, usually with external regulations, pertains. We can illustrate this use of the term by reproducing a multi-choice CIA question here:

> 'PA 2100–5/6 Internal audit should review the compliance programme in an organisation to determine whether it can be improved. As part of such a review internal audit should seek input from:
> a.   The board only.
> b.   Management only.
> c.   The external auditors only.
> **d.   Employees (correct answer).**'

The COSO use of the term refers to one of the objectives of a system of internal control which is to provide reasonable assurance of compliance with (a) laws and (b) regulations (as well as compliance with (c) covenants entered into within contracts, (d) the policies of the board, and (e) internal procedures).

### B2.1.6   Control self-assessment (CSA), or control risk self-assessment (CRSA)

We explore CSA in more detail in B2.2.39 to B2.2.61.

Although the approach has been with us for many, many years, CSA as it is now termed, developed in the 1980s and 1990s. It is the review of risk and control by line management and staff for themselves, rather than relying on an independent review by internal audit. The format for these reviews may be workshop-based or survey-based. The internal audit activity may facilitate the CSA programme, facilitate the CSA workshops and report to the audit committee on the results of the CSA programme. There are several significant differences between CSA and the traditional internal audit approach. First, CSA rarely generates a file of working papers containing objective evidence to support the results, as does traditional internal auditing: instead, participants bring to the workshop what they subjectively know or believe from their own experience. Secondly, CSA encounters challenges in authoritatively run entities where line managers and staff may be reluctant to be candid about weaknesses and opportunities for improvement. Thirdly, the report of a CSA workshop is the report of the workshop participants, not of the internal audit activity who may have facilitated the workshop.

CSA takes advantage of participative non-threatening, non-hierarchical styles of management where 'downsizing', 'delayering' and 'empowerment' have become realities. Arguably in such cultures, line management and staff are better placed, and are empowered to review risk management, control and governance processes for themselves rather than depending upon internal audit to do it for them.

CSA is rarely an alternative for a traditional internal audit function, but the two approaches may co-exist well. Some internal audit activities follow a hybrid approach, perhaps commencing and ending the fieldwork of an otherwise conventional audit engagement with a CSA workshop.

## **B2.1.7** *Governance processes*

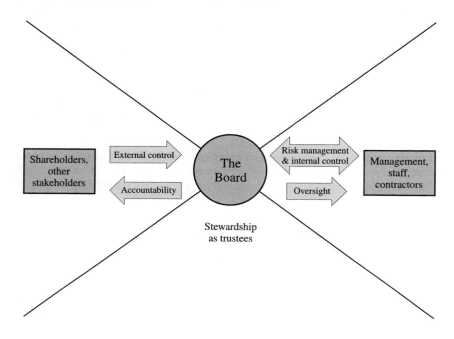

See also B2.2.90.

Corporate governance is to do with external as well as internal control – as illustrated in the above diagram. It comprises the processes of accountability to, and oversight by, stakeholders – which provide the means by which external control can be exercised. And it comprises the processes of accountability to and oversight by the board – which are necessary if risk management and internal control are to be effective so that corporate objectives can be achieved.

The Hampel Committee's 1998 Combined Code's Principle on Internal Control first stated:

> 'The board should maintain a sound system of internal control to safeguard shareholders' investment and the company's assets.'

(This wording is continued in the 2003 Combined Code, Principle C.2)

While this is a non-standard statement as to the objectives of internal control, and gives the *board* a 'maintenance' responsibility which we would prefer to attribute to *management,* nevertheless it makes the point that internal control is central to the responsibilities of the board.

The 1999 Turnbull Report expressed much better than the Hampel Committee the respective responsibilities for internal control of the board, management and other personnel, viz:

'The board of directors is responsible for the company's system of internal control. It should set appropriate policies on internal control and seek regular assurance that will enable it to satisfy it that the system is functioning effectively. The board must further ensure that the system of internal control is effective in managing risks in the manner which it has approved.'[17]

and:

'It is the role of management to implement board policies on risk and control. In fulfilling its responsibilities, management should identify and evaluate the risks faced by the company for consideration by the board, and design, operate and monitor a suitable system of internal control which implements the policies adopted by the board.'[18]

and:

'All employees have some responsibility for internal control …'.[19]

The Turnbull Report, which has now been included by the Financial Reporting Council as part of the 2003 Combined Code publication, is in the process of being revised.

So the board is at the pivotal point of corporate governance. Internal control is an essential part of corporate governance and thus internal auditors are important players in corporate governance. Internal auditors, in their assessment of risk management and internal control, largely focus on the internal dimensions of corporate governance – but not exclusively so.

## HOW INTERNAL AUDITORS MAY CONTRIBUTE TO THE EXTERNAL SIDE OF CORPORATE GOVERNANCE

- Assisting the board in formulating their published reports on internal control under the UK Turnbull guidance
- Under the Sarbanes-Oxley Act (Section 302), assisting CEOs and CFOs in their groundwork to be able to certify that each annual or quarterly report does not contain any untrue statement of a material fact or omit to state a material fact necessary in order to make the statements made, in light of the circumstances under which such statements were made, not misleading – ie *internal control over disclosures.*
- Under the Sarbanes-Oxley Act (Section 404) assisting CEOs and CFOs in the groundwork necessary to certification of the effectiveness of *internal control over financial reporting.*
- Contributing to the reliability of financial statements through some of the routine work that internal auditors do
- Contributing to the reliability of financial statements through the results of fraud investigations undertaken by the internal audit activity – see below
- Involvement in environmental/sustainability audit and reporting
- Assurances to the board on other operational analyses which are published, especially those not subject to other independent attestation
- Advising audit committee on the quality of external audit
- Providing secretarial services to the audit committee

Practice Advisory 1210.A2–1: 'Identification of Fraud' draws attention to the fact that the results of a fraud investigation may indicate that fraud has had a previously undiscovered significant adverse effect on the financial position and results of operations of an organization for one or more years on which financial statements have already been issued:

> 'Internal auditors should inform senior management and the board of such a discovery.'[20]

| | |
|---|---|
| 1 | Framework volume, chapter 1 on 'Definition', p33 and also Executive Summary, p25. |
| 2 | Practice Advisory 2100–1: 'Nature of Work', para 8. |
| 3 | Practice Advisory 2100–4 (February 2004): 'The Internal Auditor's Role in Organizations Without a Risk Management Process', para 1. |
| 4 | Practice Advisory 2100–3: 'The Internal Auditor's Role in the Risk Management Process', para 6. |
| 5 | Enterprise Risk Management, COSO, (2004): Executive Summary, p1. |
| 6 | Framework volume, chapter 1 on 'Definition', p22. |
| 7 | Para 1. |
| 8 | Para 2. |
| 9 | *Management of risk – Principles and concepts* (2nd edition, 2004) known as 'The Orange Book' (HM Treasury Assurance, Control and Risk Team, London). |
| 10 | Practice Advisory 2010–2: 'Linking the Audit Plan to Risk and Exposures', para 1. |
| 11 | *Enterprise Risk management – Integrated Framework* (September 2004) The Committee of Sponsoring Organization of the Treadway Commission (COSO). |
| 12 | *Management of risk – Principles and concepts* (Revised edition, 2004), known as 'The Orange Book', (HM Treasury Assurance, Control and Risk Team, London). |
| 13 | *Management of risk – Principles and concepts* (Revised edition, 2004), known as 'The Orange Book' (HM Treasury Assurance, Control and Risk Team, London), para 6.2. |
| 14 | 'Enterprise Risk Management' (2004) COSO, Executive Summary, p5. |
| 15 | Practice Advisory 2100–1: 'Nature of Work', para 6. |
| 16 | *Management of risk – Principles and concepts* (Revised edition, 2004) known as 'The Orange Book' (HM Treasury Assurance, Control and Risk Team, London), para 6.2. |
| 17 | The Turnbull Report, para 16. |
| 18 | The Turnbull Report, para 18. |
| 19 | The Turnbull Report, para 19. |
| 20 | Practice Advisory 1210.A2–1: 'Identification of Fraud', paras 11 and 12. |

# Nature of work – supplementary guidance

## B2.2.1   Developments in internal control concepts and definitions over time

Internal control is a complex, carefully thought-out concept. We tend to take its meaning for granted. Here, we explore the development of the definition and framework of internal control over the last century. A summary table at B2.2.24 gives an overview.

'Control' divides into 'external control' by the stakeholders of an entity (such as the shareholders, debenture holders, creditors) and 'internal control' by the board, management and other personnel.

Internal control has often been seen as synonymous with 'management control' – control by management of the internal affairs of the entity. Now it is more clearly understood that the board has overall oversight and monitoring responsibilities for internal control and that all members of staff, especially in empowered entities, have roles to play in achieving effective internal control.

## B2.2.2   *The meaning of internal control*

Some important concepts can contribute to our understanding of internal control. We can summarise them as follows.

- Control consists of *external* as well as *internal* control.
- Internal control is broadly synonymous with *management control*, subject to oversight by the board and inputs from other members of staff.
- Management is primarily responsible for internal control.[1]
- Internal audit is the independent appraisal of the effectiveness of internal control on behalf of management.[2]
- Management control is achieved by the judicious application of *all* of the elements of management – planning, organising, directing, staffing, controlling and coordinating.

Control is analogous to the process of a central heating or air conditioning thermostat, which:

- has a planned temperature (eg 24°C);
- takes measurements of actual performance;
- compares actual against plan;

- notes the variance between actual and plan; and
- makes a decision whether to switch on the pump (or fan) to keep actual performance within a tolerable range of planned performance.

With this model of control it is clear that first there is a need for a plan against which to control. The development of policies on business conduct and the design of detailed procedures are both aspects of planning. Secondly, control entails monitoring. Thirdly, control requires decision taking: decision taking is usually associated with planning but it is also right at the heart of controlling – an indication that it is impossible neatly to unravel planning from controlling.

## B2.2.3 *The first definition of internal control (AICPA)*

A seminal definition of internal control dates back to 1948 though it has now been generally replaced by the Committee of Sponsoring Organizations (COSO) definition which we look at later. In 1948, AICPA defined internal control in a way which they acknowledged was 'broader than the meaning sometimes attributed to the term', as follows:

> 'Internal control comprises the plan of organisation and the co-ordinate methods and measures adopted within a business to safeguard its assets, check the accuracy and reliability of its accounting data, promote operational efficiency, and encourage adherence to prescribed managerial policies.'[3]

Two key points to note about this definition are first that it identified planning, organisational arrangements and procedures as being basic to internal control, and secondly that it gave four objectives of internal control which were to do with:

- safeguarding assets;
- reliability of accounts;
- operational efficiency; and
- effectiveness (achievement of policies).

The definition also characterised internal control more as a 'state of affairs' than as a 'process' (which is the emphasis in the more recent COSO definition).

## B2.2.4 *Administrative and accounting control*

A significant milestone in the development of conventional wisdom about internal control came in 1958 when AICPA divided internal control into (a) administrative control, and (b) accounting control.[4] This distinction has been with us ever since.[5] The motivation for the distinction was an awareness on the part of public accountants acting as external auditors that their primary concern was with the controls which contribute to the reliability of the accounts (or published financial statements) and that they as external auditors were not so concerned with so-called 'administrative controls' over operations. Dividing internal control into administrative and accounting controls was intended to allow external auditors to largely restrict their interest in internal control to the accounting controls only.

AICPA made the distinction as follows:

> 'Accounting control comprises the plan of the organisation and the procedures and records that are concerned with the safeguards of assets and the reliability of financial records'

and

> 'Administrative control includes, but is not limited to, the plan of organization and the procedures and records that are concerned with the decision processes leading to management's authorization of transactions. Such authorization is a management function directly associated with the responsibility for achieving the objectives of the organization and is the starting point for establishing accounting controls of transactions.'[6]

## B2.2.5  *Traditional UK definitions of internal control*

In the UK a broadly similar understanding about the nature of internal control emerged. The generally accepted UK definition of internal control was:

> 'the whole system of controls, financial and otherwise, established by the management in order to carry on the business in an orderly and efficient manner, ensure adherence to management policies, safeguard the assets and secure as far as possible the completeness and accuracy of the records.'[7]

At about that time, an alternative UK definition of internal control (which did not replace the above definition) was:

> 'The regulation of activities in an organisation through systems designed and implemented to facilitate the achievement of management objectives.'[8]

## B2.2.6  *IIA definitions of internal control*

We must make reference to the position of The Institute of Internal Auditors. Until the adoption of their new Standards in 2002, The IIA had a straightforward definition of internal control which could be reconciled to the definitions we have already used. The IIA identified five objectives of control in contrast to the four explicit in the AICPA/CCAB pronouncements we have already considered and the three objectives in the COSO framework to which we turn our attention shortly. Until 2002 The IIA continued to adhere to their position that internal control exists to achieve these five objectives in contrast to COSO's three objectives[9] notwithstanding that The IIA was one of the five COSO bodies. By 2002 The IIA had come into line with COSO except that it continues to show 'safeguarding of assets' as a separate objective of internal control. It is generally regarded as to have been a mistake by COSO not to have done so.

Until the adoption of the new IIA Standards, The IIA definition of internal control was as follows:

'The overall system of internal control is conceptual in nature. It is an integrated collection of controlled systems used by an organization to achieve its objectives and goals.'[10]

Now, their definition has become more complex (see Row 12 of the table at B2.2.24, and also APPENDIX 2 which is the new IIA Standards):

'**Control** – Any action taken by management, the board, and other parties to enhance risk management and increase the likelihood that established objectives and goals will be achieved. Management plans, organizes, and directs the performance of sufficient actions to provide reasonable assurance that objectives and goals will be achieved.'

And The IIA's old five objectives of control, which were:
(a)   'the reliability and integrity of information;
(b)   compliance with policies, plans, procedures, laws and regulations;
(c)   the safeguarding of assets;
(d)   the economical and efficient use of resources; [and]
(e)   the accomplishment of established objectives and goals for operations or programmes.'[11]

have now been rejigged to four.
- 'Reliability and integrity of financial and operational information.
- Effectiveness and efficiency of operations.
- Safeguarding of assets.
- Compliance with laws, regulations, and contracts.'

## B2.2.7   *Treadway, COSO and the UK equivalents*

During the 1980s five US bodies[12] known as COSO (Committee of Sponsoring Organizations) invited Treadway to head a commission of enquiry in the wake of concern about fraudulent financial reporting. The so-called Treadway Report[13] was published in 1987 and even today can be downloaded from the web (www-.coso.org). Treadway recommended that management should include a report on internal control with their published financial statements. Adoption of this proposal was initially deferred pending clarification of the meaning of internal control and the form and process of any such report by management: it never became mandatory in the US though it is a practice frequently followed. To provide this clarification, COSO funded a further project, the fieldwork of which was conducted by Coopers & Lybrand, which led to the publication in 1992 of 'Internal Control – Integrated Framework'[14] (known as 'The COSO Report'). This gave us a new definition of internal control which is supplanting the 1948 AICPA definition and its derivatives. COSO also gives guidance on how internal control is achieved by means of five interrelated control components. Finally, COSO gave guidance on the process and form of public reports by management on internal control. One limitation of the 1992 COSO internal control framework was that within the COSO definition itself there was no acknowledgment that today's outsourcing means that so much of what contributes to an organisation's effective internal control now occurs within the activities of business partners (see B2.2.76 on internal control when activities are outsourced).

## B2.2.8 *The COSO definition of internal control*

'Internal control is broadly defined as a process, effected by the entity's board of directors, management and other personnel, designed to provide reasonable assurance regarding the achievement of objectives in the following categories:
- Effectiveness and efficiency of operations.
- Reliability of financial reporting.
- Compliance with applicable laws and regulations.'

COSO recognises that the three objectives of control are 'distinct but overlapping categories [which] address different needs and allow a directed focus to meet the separate needs'. It is easier to reconcile these three categories of objectives with the four objectives of control in the 1948 definition if one bears in mind that the drafters of the COSO definition intended that safeguarding of assets against unauthorised use (etc) should be regarded as part of the effectiveness and efficiency of operations objective, whereas in the UK Rutteman was to classify this as part of internal financial control.

The COSO definition puts stress on 'process' though this is a largely cosmetic change of nomenclature from the earlier uses of the expressions 'methods and measures' and 'system' which we referred to earlier. (The UK continues to use the expression 'system'.)

'Internal control is not an event or circumstance, but a series of actions that permeate an entity's activities. These actions are pervasive, and are inherent in the way management runs the business.'[15]

The COSO definition also usefully stresses that internal control cannot *guarantee* the achievement of control objectives – but can give reasonable assurance of doing so.

## B2.2.9 Approximate matching of principal classifications of stated objectives of internal control

| | Old AICPA/CCAB | IIA (1978 to 2001) | COSO (1992) | IIA (2002) |
|---|---|---|---|---|
| 1 | Safeguarding assets | The safeguarding of assets | (COSO intended this to be subsumed within row 3) | Safeguarding of assets |
| 2 | Reliability of accounts | The reliability and integrity of information | Reliability of financial reporting | Reliability and integrity of financial and operational information |
| 3 | Operational efficiency | The economical and efficient use of resources | Effectiveness and efficiency of operations | Effectiveness and efficiency of operations |
| 4 | Effectiveness | The accomplishment of established objectives and goals for operations or programmes | ('Effectiveness' is included in Row 3 above) | ('Effectiveness' is included in Row 3 above) |

| | Old AICPA/CCAB | IIA (1978 to 2001) | COSO (1992) | IIA (2002) |
|---|---|---|---|---|
| 5 | | Compliance with policies, plans, procedures, laws and regulations | Compliance with applicable laws and regulations | Compliance with laws, regulations, and contracts |

## B2.2.10   *Components of internal control*

COSO goes on to provide a classification of the ways in which internal control is achieved which they term the five interrelated control 'components' and COSO's extensive discussion of the nature of these components is extremely useful.

| | |
|---|---|
| • Control environment | for instance, the ethical tone set by the Board |
| • Risk assessment | for instance, it is necessary for management to assess relative risk as a prerequisite for developing and maintaining commensurate effective internal control |
| • Control activities | for instance, segregation of duties |
| • Information and communication | for instance, exception reports |
| • Monitoring | for instance, by internal audit |

## B2.2.11   *The Rutteman Report on internal control*

A parallel development took place in the UK. The Cadbury Report[16] recommended that directors of listed companies should report publicly on internal control, and guidance was prepared on this.[17]

This guidance defined internal control as:

> 'The whole system of controls, financial and otherwise, established in order to provide reasonable assurance of:
> 1.   effective and efficient operations;
> 2.   internal financial control; and
> 3.   compliance with laws and regulations.'

The UK therefore perpetuated the 1972 suggestion that it is possible and helpful to distinguish between financial and other controls whereas COSO really makes the distinction only at the level of the *objectives* of control, not the *process* of control. In other words COSO is saying internal control can give reasonable reassurance of the achievement of three categories of objectives, whereas Rutteman agreed that there are these three aims but suggested further that there are also at least two sub-sets of internal controls (one of which comprises the internal financial controls), and that control over the reliability of financial statements is achieved by the internal financial controls subset.

COSO does not go so far as to claim there are two sub-sets of internal control. COSO only goes as far as to recognise, with regard to the three categories of objectives of control, that:

> 'these distinct but overlapping categories address different needs and allow a directed focus to meet the separate needs'.[18]

Until the Turnbull Report, the UK also placed less emphasis upon *process*.

Rutteman replaced the five US components by which control is achieved by five similar *criteria,* taking exception to the word *components.* The criteria were:

- control environment;
- identification and evaluation of risks, and control objectives;
- information and communication;
- control procedures; and
- monitoring and corrective action.

Rutteman described these as 'criteria' in order to emphasise that the quality of these internal control components should be assessed in order to evaluate the effectiveness of internal control. In other words, it is not enough to consider whether there have been any significant breakdowns in internal control as a means of concluding on internal control effectiveness, although this must be done. Even if there have been no breakdowns in internal control, the system of internal control may still be defective – it may be just that its weaknesses have not yet been exploited.

## B2.2.12 *The Turnbull Report on internal control*

The Turnbull guidance, which replaced the Rutteman guidance, gives us a new definition of internal control:

> 'An internal control system encompasses the policies, processes, tasks, behaviours and other aspects of a company that, taken together:
> - facilitate its effective and efficient operation by enabling it to respond appropriately to significant business, operational, financial, compliance and other risks to achieving the company's objectives. This includes the safeguarding of assets from inappropriate use or from loss and fraud, and ensuring that liabilities are identified and managed;
> - help ensure the quality of internal and external reporting. This requires the maintenance of proper records and processes that generate a flow of timely, relevant and reliable information within and outside the organisation;
> - help ensure compliance with applicable laws and regulations, and also with internal policies with respect to the conduct of business.'

Turnbull also carries forward the COSO/Rutteman components/criteria of internal control, though for a reason which is not very clear, Turnbull has combined two of the five so that we now have:

- risk assessment;
- control environment and control activities;

- information and communication; and
- monitoring.

The author does not consider it wise for committees convened for a particular purpose to redefine an important concept which has been meticulously considered by another committee with that specific remit. COSO remains the authoritative definition of internal control, and is widely accepted throughout the world as such.

## B2.2.13 *Would a more modest paradigm of internal control be better?*

The generally accepted COSO definition of internal control states that internal control is the process that gives reasonable assurance of the achievement of objectives. COSO gave three categories of objectives – effectiveness and efficiency of operations, reliability of financial reporting, and compliance with applicable laws and regulations.

Does this mean that internal control comprises *all* of the processes that management applies to achieve the organisation's objectives, or just those processes which are designed to *assure* (ie confirm, attest) that management are doing what is necessary to achieve objectives? If so, how can one distinguish between the two? The external audit profession uses the word 'assurance' in the latter sense of 'confirming' or 'attesting' – they talk about 'assurance services'; might we not also do so when we are defining the scope of internal control? Would this not help to keep the concept of internal control more modestly confinable and practical – rather than making it appear to be *all*, or at least *most*, of management? Indeed, what did COSO mean the scope of internal control to be regarded as? How could we apply a more modest concept of the boundaries of internal control while still holding to the COSO framework?

### B2.2.14 How COSO described the overlap between 'management' and 'internal control'

In the final COSO Report, the authors stated:

> 'Some respondents [to the COSO exposure draft] said that internal control is only a part, albeit an important part, of the management process, and that the exposure draft incorrectly defines internal control in a way that encompasses or appears to encompass the entire management process. They believe this implies that internal control can ensure management's achievement of the entity's objectives, which implication could continue or aggravate the existing expectation gaps.

> To address these comments, the final report more clearly distinguishes internal control from other aspects of the management process. It makes it clear that many management responsibilities such as establishing objectives, making business decisions, executing transactions and carrying out plans are among the management activities that are integrated with, but not a part of, the internal control system.'[19]

COSO went on to state that:

'Internal control can be judged effective in the case of each of the three categories[20] respectively, if the board of directors and management have reasonable assurance that:

- They understand the extent to which the entity's operations objectives are being achieved.
- Published financial statements are being prepared reliably.
- Applicable laws and regulations are being complied with.'[21]

and:

'Even effective internal control can only help an entity achieve [the basic business objectives]. It can provide management information about the entity's progress, or lack of it, toward their achievement. But internal control cannot change an inherently poor manager in to a good one. And, shifts in government policy or programs, competitors' actions or economic conditions can be beyond management's control. Internal control cannot assure success, or even survival.'[22]

and:

'achievement of operations objectives – such as a particular return on investment, market share or entry into new product lines – is not always within the entity's control. Internal control cannot prevent bad judgements or decisions, or external events that can cause a business to fail to achieve operations goals. For these objectives, the internal control system can provide reasonable assurance only that management and, in its oversight role, the board are made aware, in a timely manner, of the extent to which the entity is moving toward those objectives.'[23]

COSO accepted that not everything management does is an element of internal control. Establishment of objectives, for example, while an important management responsibility is not part of internal control, but is a precondition to internal control. Similarly, many decisions and actions by management do not represent internal control.

COSO considered that establishing objectives was a prerequisite to effective internal control, objectives providing measurable targets toward which the entity moves in conducting its activities.[24] However, although an entity should have reasonable assurance that certain objectives are achieved, COSO pointed out that that might not be the case for all objectives.

On the other hand, COSO suggested that an effective internal control system should provide reasonable assurance that an entity's financial reporting objectives are being achieved. Similarly, there should be reasonable assurance that compliance objectives are being achieved. This is because both of these categories are primarily based on external standards established independently of the entity's purposes, and achieving them is largely within the entity's control.

COSO pointed out:

'there is a difference when it comes to operations objectives. First, they are not based on external standards. Second, an entity may perform as intended, yet be out-performed by a competitor. It could also be subject to outside events – a change in government, poor weather and the like – that it cannot control. It may even have considered some of these events in its objective-setting process and treated them as low probability, with a contingency plan in case they occurred. However, such a plan only mitigates the impact of outside events. It does not ensure that the objectives are achieved. Good operations consistent with the intent of objectives do not ensure success.

The goal of internal control in this area focuses primarily on: developing consistency of objectives and goals throughout the organization, identifying key success factors and timely reporting to management of performance and expectations. Although success cannot be ensured, management should have reasonable assurance of being alerted when objectives are in danger of not being achieved.'

COSO provided a useful table, reproduced here, which sought to show how internal control was not all of management.

### B2.2.15  Internal control and the management process

| Management Activities | Internal Control |
|---|---|
| Entity-level objective setting – mission, value statements | |
| Strategic planning | |
| Establishing control environment factors | ✔ |
| Activity-level objective setting | |
| Risk identification and analysis | ✔ |
| Risk management | |
| Conducting control activities | ✔ |
| Information identification, capture and communication | ✔ |
| Monitoring | ✔ |
| Corrective actions | |

While this limits internal control to something less than all of management, it is not so clear whether it limits internal control to 'assurance' activities. Indeed, it is a challenge to separate those activities of management which are assurance activities from other things which managers do.

The Canadian CoCo programme (see B2.2.51) excludes decisions from internal control, thus making internal control certainly less than *all* of what management does. The classic work on management control by Anthony (1965)[25] defined management control as 'the process by which managers assure that resources are obtained and used effectively and efficiently in the accomplishment of the organization's objectives'. So CoCo and Anthony both lend weight to the suggestion that internal control is an 'assuring' or supportive process or processes. If this is so, then the challenge is to logically demarcate the assurance processes from the other processes within the business – or perhaps this cannot be done.

### B2.2.16  *Risk assessment*

COSO also made a distinction between risk assessment, which COSO classified as part of internal control, and the resulting plans, programmes or other actions deemed necessary by management to address the risks. COSO regarded the actions undertaken to be a key part of the larger management process, but not an element of the internal control system.[26]

Topical today, in the light of Turnbull, COSO regarded risk analysis not as a theoretical exercise but as often critical to the entity's success, and most effective when it includes identification of all key business processes where potential exposures of some consequence exist. The COSO report suggested that risk analysis might involve process analysis, such as identification of key dependencies and significant control nodes, and also the establishment of clear responsibility and accountability. COSO suggested that effective process analysis directs special attention to cross-organisational dependencies, identifying, for example, where data originate, where they are stored, how they are converted to useful information and who uses the information; and that large organisations usually need to be particularly vigilant in addressing intra-company and inter-company transactions and key dependencies. These processes can be positively affected by quality programmes which, with a 'buy-in' by employees, can be an important element in risk containment.

### B2.2.17   *A directed focus*

COSO also accepted that the COSO definition of internal control accommodated subsets of internal control, so that those who wish to can focus separately, for example on controls over financial reporting or on controls related to compliance with laws and regulations, are able to do so. Similarly, a directed focus on controls in particular units or activities of an entity can be accommodated.[27]

### B2.2.18   Recent UK perceptions

*Rutteman*

UK perceptions have not been entirely consistent. Rutteman's definitions of internal control[28] and of internal *financial* control left open the possibility that his working party was restricting the scope of internal control to those elements which provided *assurance* of the achievement of objectives, viz.

Internal control:

> 'The whole system of controls, financial and otherwise, established in order to provide reasonable assurance of:
> 1.  effective and efficient operations.
> 2.  internal financial control.
> 3.  compliance with laws and regulations.'

Internal financial control:

> 'The internal controls established in order to provide reasonable assurance of:
> (a)  the safeguarding of assets against unauthorised use or disposition; and
> (b)  the maintenance of proper accounting records and the reliability of financial information used within the business or for publication.'

## B2.2.19   *Hampel*

The Hampel Report was even more ambiguous on the matter:

> 'The board should maintain a sound system of internal control to safeguard shareholders' investment and the company's assets.'

## B2.2.20   *Turnbull*

On the other hand, the most recent UK report to attempt a definition of internal control, the Turnbull Report,[29] perhaps almost unwittingly comes down unambiguously on the side of internal control being all those things that management does to ensure the achievement of objectives, not just those things which provide reassurance that objectives are being achieved:

> 'An internal control system encompasses the policies, processes, tasks, behaviours and other aspects of a company that, taken together:
> * facilitate its effective and efficient operation by enabling it to respond appropriately to significant business, operational, financial, compliance and other risks to achieving the company's objectives. This includes the safeguarding of assets from inappropriate use or from loss and fraud, and ensuring that liabilities are identified and managed;
> * help ensure the quality of internal and external reporting. This requires the maintenance of proper records and processes that generate a flow of timely, relevant and reliable information within and outside the organisation;
> * help ensure compliance with applicable laws and regulations, and also with internal policies with respect to the conduct of business.'

### B2.2.21   Internal control in the context of management theory

It is difficult to separate out internal control from the other elements or functions of management, viz.[30]

* Planning.
* Organising.
* Staffing.
* Directing and leading.
* Controlling.
* Co-ordinating.

These functions interact, overlap and coalesce. Control is an important set of threads woven through the tapestry of management. It is beguiling but misleading to consider internal control to be *all* of management.[31]

The arguments in favour can be summed up as follows.

1. Many of the definitions of internal control are very broad so as apparently to leave little space for any other managerial functions.
2. Control depends upon each of the other functions of management. There is no control without:
   * Planning:

- For instance, design of the right procedures (which is part of planning) is essential for effective control.
        - There has to be a plan against which to exercise control. Without a plan there can be no control.
- Organising:
        - For instance, structuring the business into subdivisions and determining reporting arrangements[32]
- Directing and leading:
        - Few would question that the quality of leadership impacts upon control.
- Staffing:
        - Too few or too many staff can lead to things getting out of control – as can incompetent, disloyal, dishonest or lazy staff.
- Coordinating:
        - The art of ensuring that happenings occur in harmony with each other – without which things will be out of control.

Despite these beguiling arguments, it is more prudent to acknowledge that whilst planning, organising and the other functions of management are mechanisms by which the board and management achieves control, managers also achieve other objectives apart from control by the judicious application of these elements of management. For instance, they may develop effective long-term plans; or they may make excellent staffing arrangements so that not only control but other elements of management are better handled.

## B2.2.22   Implications for internal audit scope

If internal auditors interpret their mission as to conduct an independent appraisal of the effectiveness of internal control, it is true that they may be drawing management's attention to weaknesses in planning, organising, directing, staffing and co-ordinating which may account for control weaknesses. It would not therefore be beyond the scope of internal auditing to raise audit points which relate to weaknesses in planning, staffing, directing and so on. Conventionally this would be done when these weaknesses provide an explanation for actual or potential breakdowns of control. There may be other weaknesses in planning, staffing and so on which do not impinge directly upon control and would therefore be beyond the scope of internal audit to detect or comment upon – if we define internal auditing as being the review of internal control.

On the other hand the terms of reference of many internal auditors require them to draw management's attention to *anything* they detect during the course of their internal auditing work which is commercially unsound and so not too much ceremony may be attached to whether an audit finding is, or is not, a control point.

Nevertheless the generally accepted emphasis of internal audit is the review of internal control so it is perhaps less likely that internal audit will detect weaknesses in the other elements of management which do not have a significant control impact.

## B2.2.23 *Enterprise risk management (COSO)*

In B2.2.25 we draw attention to the SEC's Rule on implementing section 404 of the US Sarbanes-Oxley Act (2002) recognises three internal control frameworks for the review of internal control effectiveness – CoCo, Turnbull and COSO (1992). We can expect the new COSO Enterprise Risk Management framework to be accorded similar recognition – both on merit and because of the statement (see above) that:

> 'The entirety of *Internal Control – Integrated Framework* is incorporated by reference into this framework [ie into COSO's new enterprise risk management exposure draft].'

In time, we suggest that directors' reports on internal control will be superseded by directors' reports termed 'reports on risk management' or 'reports on risk management and internal control'. They will include but not be limited to internal control. The UK's *Combined Code* Provision on directors internal control reviews (C.2.1 in the 2003 *Code*) has, since 1998, included risk management within the scope of those reviews. The rewording of this provision as it appears in the 2003 UK Code, from 'risk management' to 'risk management systems' gives a better indication of what it is that the directors are reviewing.

### B2.2.24  How definitions of internal control have developed over the years

|   | Date | Source | Definition of internal control |
|---|------|--------|-------------------------------|
| 1. | 1916 | Henri Fayol: *Administration Industrielle et Générale.* | Control as one of the elements of management. |
| 2. | 1948 – publication 1949 | American Institute of Certified Public Accountants: *Internal Control – Elements of a Co-ordinated System and its Importance to Management and the Independent Public Accountant*, New York. | 'Internal control comprises the plan of organisation and the co-ordinate methods and measures adopted within a business to safeguard its assets, check the accuracy and reliability of its accounting data, promote operational efficiency and encourage adherence to prescribed managerial policies.' |
| 3. | 1980 and 1992 | Consultative Committee of Accounting Bodies, Auditing Practices Committee: *Auditing Guideline* [1980, s3]; and Chartered Institute of Management Accountants: *A Framework for Internal Control* [1992]. | 'the whole system of controls, financial and otherwise, established by the management in order to carry on the business in an orderly and efficient manner, ensure adherence to management policies, safeguard the assets and secure as far as possible the completeness and accuracy of the records.' |

| | Date | Source | Definition of internal control |
|---|---|---|---|
| 4. | 1972 and 1988 | AICPA, 1972 and AICPA: *Professional Standards, Volume 1* (June 1, 1988). | 'Accounting control comprises the plan of the organisation and the procedures and records that are concerned with the safeguards of assets and the reliability of financial records' 'Administrative control includes, but is not limited to, the plan of organization and the procedures and records that are concerned with the decision processes leading to management's authorization of transactions. Such authorization is a management function directly associated with the responsibility for achieving the objectives of the organization and is the starting point for establishing accounting controls of transactions.' |
| 5. | 1983 | IIA Inc: *Control: Concepts and Responsibilities* [Statement on Internal Auditing Standards (SIAS), No. 1 [July 1983]], and Standard 305. | 'The overall system of internal control is conceptual in nature. It is an integrated collection of controlled systems used by an organization to achieve its objectives and goals.' 'The primary objectives of internal control are to ensure: <br><br>(a)   the reliability and integrity of information; <br><br>(b)   compliance with policies, plans, procedures, laws and regulations; <br><br>(c)   the safeguarding of assets; <br><br>(d)   the economical and efficient use of resources; <br><br>(e)   the accomplishment of established objectives and goals for operations or programmes.' |
| 6. | 1990 | CCAB: Auditing Guideline 308: *Guidance for Internal Auditors* (Glossary of Terms section) [1990]. | 'The regulation of activities in an organisation through systems designed and implemented to facilitate the achievement of management objectives.' |
| 7. | September 1992 | *Internal Control – Integrated Framework*, published by The Committee of Sponsoring Organizations of the Treadway Commission, obtainable from American Institute of Certified Public Accountants, Harborside Financial Center, 201 Plaza III, Jersey City, NJ 07311–3881. Their website: www.coso.org | 'Internal control is broadly defined as a process, effected by the entity's board of directors, management and other personnel, designed to provide reasonable assurance regarding the achievement of objectives in the following categories: <br><br>●   Effectiveness and efficiency of operations; <br><br>●   Reliability of financial reporting; <br><br>●   Compliance with applicable laws and regulations.' |

|     | Date | Source | Definition of internal control |
| --- | --- | --- | --- |
| 8. | December 1994 | *Internal Control and Financial Reporting* ('The Rutteman Report') (ICAEW). | **Internal control:** 'The whole system of controls, financial and otherwise, established in order to provide reasonable assurance of: |
|     |      |        | 1.    effective and efficient operations. |
|     |      |        | 2.    internal financial control. |
|     |      |        | 3.    compliance with laws and regulations.' |
|     |      |        | **Internal *financial* control:** 'The internal controls established in order to provide reasonable assurance of: |
|     |      |        | (a)    the safeguarding of assets against unauthorised use or disposition; and |
|     |      |        | (b)    the maintenance of proper accounting records and the reliability of financial information used within the business or for publication.' |
| 9. | November 1995 | Guidance on Control, Control and Governance – Number 1, ('The CoCo programme'), The Canadian Institute of Chartered Accountants, ISBN 0–88800–436–1. | 'Control comprises those *elements* of an organization (including its resources, systems, processes, culture, structure and tasks) that, taken together, support people in the achievement of the organization's objectives. These objectives fall into one or more of the following categories: |
|     |      |        | ●   **Effectiveness and efficiency of operations** includes objectives related to an organization's goals, such as customer service, the safeguarding and efficient use of resources, profitability and meeting social obligations. This includes the safeguarding of the organization's resources from inappropriate use or loss and ensuring that liabilities are identified and managed. |
|     |      |        | ●   **Reliability of internal and external reporting** includes objectives related to matters such as the maintenance of proper accounting records, the reliability of information used within the organization and of information published for third parties. This includes the protection of records against two main types of fraud: the concealment of theft and the distortion of results. |
|     |      |        | ●   **Compliance with applicable laws and regulations and internal policies** includes objectives related to ensuring that the organization's affairs are conducted in accordance with legal and regulatory obligations and internal policies.' |
| 10. | 1997/1998 | The Hampel Report and The Combined Code. | 'The board should maintain a sound system of internal control to safeguard shareholders' investment and the company's assets.' |

| | Date | Source | Definition of internal control |
|---|---|---|---|
| 11. | September 1999 | Internal Control – Guidance for Directors on the Combined Code, ('The Turnbull Report'), the Institute of Chartered Accountants in England & Wales, ISBN 1–84152-010–1. | 'An internal control system encompasses the policies, processes, tasks, behaviours and other aspects of a company that, taken together:<br><br>● facilitate its effective and efficient operation by enabling it to respond appropriately to significant business, operational, financial, compliance and other risks to achieving the company's objectives. This includes the safeguarding of assets from inappropriate use or from loss and fraud, and ensuring that liabilities are identified and managed;<br><br>● help ensure the quality of internal and external reporting. This requires the maintenance of proper records and processes that generate a flow of timely, relevant and reliable information within and outside the organisation;<br><br>● help ensure compliance with applicable laws and regulations, and also with internal policies with respect to the conduct of business.' |
| 12. | Effective January 2002 | Standards for the Professional Practice of Internal Auditing (Standards), the Institute of Internal Auditors Inc, available on their website: www.theiia.org | **New Standard 2110.A2**<br>'The internal audit activity should evaluate risk exposures relating to the organization's governance, operations, and information systems regarding the<br><br>● Reliability and integrity of financial and operational information.<br><br>● Effectiveness and efficiency of operations.<br><br>● Safeguarding of assets.<br><br>● Compliance with laws, regulations, and contracts.'<br><br>**New Standard 2120.A1:**<br>'Based on the results of the risk assessment, the internal audit activity should evaluate the adequacy and effectiveness of controls encompassing the organization's governance, operations, and information systems. This should include:<br><br>● Reliability and integrity of financial and operational information.<br><br>● Effectiveness and efficiency of operations.<br><br>● Safeguarding of assets.<br><br>● Compliance with laws, regulations, and contracts.' |

|  | Date | Source | Definition of internal control |
|---|---|---|---|
|  |  |  | **From the Glossary to the new *Standards*:**<br>'Control – Any action taken by management, the board, and other parties to enhance risk management and increase the likelihood that established objectives and goals will be achieved. Management plans, organizes, and directs the performance of sufficient actions to provide reasonable assurance that objectives and goals will be achieved.'<br>'Adequate Control – Present if management has planned and organized (designed) in a manner that provides reasonable assurance that the organization's risks have been managed effectively and that the organization's goals and objectives will be achieved efficiently and economically.'<br>'Control Environment – The attitude and actions of the board and management regarding the significance of control within the organization. The control environment provides the discipline and structure for the achievement of the primary objectives of the system of internal control. The control environment includes the following elements: |
|  |  |  | • Integrity and ethical values.<br><br>• Management's philosophy and operating style.<br><br>• Organizational structure.<br><br>• Assignment of authority and responsibility.<br><br>• Human resource policies and practices.<br><br>• Competence of personnel.'<br><br>**'Control Processes** – The policies, procedures, and activities that are part of a control framework, designed to ensure that risks are contained within the risk tolerances established by the risk management process.' |
| 13. | September 2004 | Enterprise Risk Management Framework, published by The Committee of Sponsoring Organisations of the Treadway Commission obtainable from www.coso.org | 'Enterprise risk management is a process, effected by an entity's board of directors, management and other personnel, applied in strategy setting and across the enterprise, designed to identify potential events that may affect the entity, and manage risks to be within its risk appetite, to provide reasonable assurance regarding the achievement of entity objectives.' |

| | Date | Source | Definition of internal control |
|---|---|---|---|
| 14. | March 2004 | Public Company Accounting Oversight Board (PCAOB) Auditing Standard No 2 on 'An audit of internal control over financial reporting performed in conjunction with an audit of financial statements' (www.pcaobus.org)) | 'Internal control over financial reporting is defined as follows: A process designed by, or under the supervision of, the company's principal executive and principal financial officers, or persons performing similar functions, and effected by the company's board of directors, management, and other personnel, to provide reasonable assurance regarding the reliability of financial reporting and the preparation of financial statements for external purposes in accordance with generally accepted accounting principles and includes those policies and procedures that: |

(1)  Pertain to the maintenance of records that, in reasonable detail, accurately and fairly reflect the transactions and dispositions of the assets of the company;

(2)  Provide reasonable assurance that transactions are recorded as necessary to permit preparation of financial statements in accordance with generally accepted accounting principles, and that receipts and expenditures of the company are being made only in accordance with authorizations of management and directors of the company; and

(3)  Provide reasonable assurance regarding prevention or timely detection of unauthorized acquisition, use or disposition of the company's assets that could have a material effect on the financial statements.'

(Note: This definition is the same one used by the SEC in its rules requiring management to report on internal control over financial reporting, except the word 'registrant' has been changed to 'company' to conform to the wording in the Public Company Accounting Oversight Board's Auditing Standard No 2. (See Securities Exchange Act Rules 13a–15(f) and 15d–15(f) see 17 C.F.R. 240, 13a–15(f) and 15d–15(f)).)

---

[1]    In the UK, the 1990 CCAB: Auditing Guideline 308: Guidance for Internal Auditors put it like this:

'It is a management responsibility to determine the extent of internal control in the organisation's systems which should not depend on internal audit as a substitute for effective controls. Internal audit, as a service to the organisation, contributes to internal control by examining, evaluating and reporting to management on its adequacy and effectiveness. Internal audit activity may lead to the strengthening of internal control as a result of management response.'

[2]    This conveniently concise definition of internal auditing now has to give way to the new definition of The Institute of Internal Auditors:

'Internal auditing is an independent, objective assurance and consulting activity designed to add value and improve an organization's operations. It helps an organization accomplish its objectives by bringing a systematic, disciplined approach to evaluate and improve the effectiveness of risk management, control, and governance processes.'

3   American Institute of Certified Public Accountants: Internal Control – Elements of a Co-ordinated System and its Importance to Management and the Independent Public Accountant, AICPA, New York, 1948, pub 1949.

4   American Institute of Certified Accountants: Statement on Auditing Procedure No 29, AICPA, New York, October 1958.

5   Vide, eg American Institute of Certified Public Accountants: SAP 54 (Statement on Auditing Procedure, No. 54), November 1972; also AICPA SAS No. 1 and No. 55 ; and more recently the distinction is continued in the US COSO report, Internal Control – Integrated Framework [1992] and in the Rutteman Report [1994].

6   AICPA, 1972 and AICPA, Professional Standards, Volume 1 (1 June 1988).

7   Consultative Committee of Accounting Bodies, Auditing Practices Committee: Auditing Guideline [1980, para 3]; and Chartered Institute of Management Accountants: A Framework for Internal Control [1992].

8   CCAB: Auditing Guideline 308: Guidance for Internal Auditors (Glossary of Terms section) [1990].

9   This was discussed and agreed at the mid-year meeting of the Internal Auditing Standards Board off IIA Inc (December 1993).

10  IIA Inc, Control: Concepts and Responsibilities, Statement on Internal Auditing Standards (SIAS), No. 1 [July 1983].

11  IIA Inc, Standard 305.

12  American Institute of Certified Public Accountants, American Accounting Association, The Institute of Internal Auditors, The Institute of Management Accountants, The Financial Executives Institute.

13  Report of the National Commission on Fraudulent Financial Reporting, National Commission on Fraudulent Financial Reporting, New York, 1987 ('The Treadway Commission Report').

14  Internal Control – Integrated Framework, known as 'The COSO Report' (September 1992), Framework volume (published by The Committee of Sponsoring Organizations of the Treadway Commission, obtainable from American Institute of Certified Public Accountants, Harborside Financial Center, 201 Plaza III, Jersey City, NJ 07311–3881, p111. Their new (1999) website: www.coso.org. (Committee of Sponsoring Organizations of the Treadway Commission, AICPA, September 1992).

15  Internal Control – Integrated Framework, Framework volume, p10.

16  Report of the Committee on the Financial Aspects of Corporate Governance, Gee, December 1992 ('The Cadbury Report').

17  Internal Control and Financial Reporting, 'The Rutteman Report', (ICAEW, December 1994).

18  Eg by auditors.

19  Internal Control – Integrated Framework, p111.

20  The three categories are: effectiveness and efficiency of operations; reliability of financial reporting; Compliance with applicable laws and regulations.

21  Internal Control – Integrated Framework COSO, Executive Summary, p4.

22  Internal Control – Integrated Framework, Executive Summary, p4.

23  Internal Control – Integrated Framework, Framework volume, p12.

24  Internal Control – Integrated Framework, Framework volume, p35.

25  Anthony, R.N. (1965): 'Planning and Control Systems: A Framework for Analysis'; Division of Research Graduate School of Business Administration, Harvard University; see, for instance, pp 10–15.

26  Internal Control – Integrated Framework, Framework volume, p39.

27  Internal Control – Integrated Framework, Framework volume, p10.

28  Internal Control and Financial Reporting, December 1994, 'The Rutteman Report', (ICAEW).

29  Internal Control – Guidance For Directors On The Combined Code, (September 1999) ('The Turnbull Report'), The Institute of Chartered Accountants in England & Wales, ISBN 1–84152-010–1.

30  Henri Fayol first described the elements or functions of management in 1916 in his classic book Administration Industrielle et Générale and he was the first to identify 'controlling' as a function of management. His book did not appear in English until published in Geneva in 1929 by the International Institute of Management – but this was a limited edition and it only became widely read in English with the Pitman (London) edition of 1949. Fayol, who then became

acknowledged as the father of management theory described the functions of management in terms which to us now appear dated:

- Planning
- Organising
- Commanding
- Co-ordinating
- Controlling

Had Fayol been widely read soon after he wrote his book, perhaps the concepts of internal control would have been established much sooner – and perhaps the Institute of Internal Auditors would have been established earlier than 1941.

31 Chambers AD, GM Selim and G Vinten: Internal Auditing, [Pitman, London, 2nd edition, 1987], vide Chapter 4, also in first edition (1981).

32 To illustrate the proximity between organising and controlling it is illuminating to remember that Fayol used the label 'span of control' to describe the issue of how many subordinates one boss might supervise – yet this is clearly a matter of organisation as well as of control.

## B2.2.25   COSO's Enterprise Risk Management Framework and Application Guidance

'The main goal of a management science must be to enable business to take the right risk. Indeed, it must be to enable business to take greater risks – by providing knowledge and understanding of alternative risks and alternative expectations; by identifying the resources and efforts needed for desired results; by mobilizing energies for contribution; and by measuring results against expectations; thereby providing means for early correction of wrong or inadequate decisions. All this may sound like mere quibbling over terms. Yet the terminology of risk minimization does induce a hostility to risk-taking and risk-making – that is, to business enterprise.'[32]

'All entities face uncertainty, and the challenge for management is to determine how much uncertainty to accept as it strives to grow stakeholder value. Uncertainty presents both risk and opportunity, with the potential to erode or enhance value. Enterprise risk management enables management to effectively deal with uncertainty and associated risk and opportunity, enhancing the capacity to build value.'[33]

COSO's 'Enterprise Risk Management' was eventually published in September 2004.[34] The exposure draft period had ended on October 14, 2003. It comes in two volumes:

- Executive Summary and Framework
- Application Techniques

In 1992 COSO, an affiliation of five US-based professional bodies,[35] published their internal control framework[36] which was destined to become the global 'bible' on internal control for a more than a decade. It sought to address the issues raised by the Treadway Commission's recommendation that companies should report publicly on their internal control.[37] For the UK, the 1992 COSO study came to underpin both the Rutteman[38] and Turnbull[39] guidance – especially with respect to the definition, objectives and components of internal control – though the Turnbull Working Party, interpreting as it did the internal control provisions within the UK's Combined Code,[40] took things a stage further with an additional emphasis on risk management.

COSO has caught up and has taken the lead with this new Enterprise Risk Management study for which PricewaterhouseCoopers initially committed approximately 10,000 hours of professional time. This new framework is likely to replace the COSO internal control framework, upon which it builds, to become the new guiding star in this area for the next decade, although the earlier 1992 framework will continue in parallel since it has become built into laws and regulations across the world. It will be worthwhile any practitioner familiarising him or herself with this new framework as quickly as possible as it is likely to underpin professional practice for many years to come.

The US SEC's new 2003 rule on reports on internal control[41] requires that the certified reviews of internal control over financial reporting to be based upon a recognised framework. While not intending to be prescriptive as to the framework to be used, the SEC mentions three acceptable frameworks – the 1992 COSO internal control framework, The Canadian Chartered Accountants' CoCo framework and the Turnbull approach. Specifically the SEC requires that management bases its evaluation:

> 'on a suitable, recognized control framework that is established by a body or group that has followed due-process procedures, including the broad distribution of the framework for public comment.'[42]

> 'The Guidance on Assessing Control published by the Canadian Institute of Chartered Accountants and the Turnbull Report published by The Institute of Chartered Accountants in England & Wales are examples of other suitable frameworks.'[43]

It is inconceivable that the new COSO Enterprise Risk Management framework will be anything less than acceptable to the SEC – not least because COSO regards their 1992 framework as being fully incorporated into their new enterprise risk management framework:

> 'the entirety of that framework [Internal Control – Integrated Framework] is incorporated by reference into this one [Enterprise Risk Management – Integrated Framework].'[44]

Now that we have this new COSO ERM Study as well as the US Sarbanes-Oxley requirements, the UK's 1999 Turnbull Report already looks rather inadequate. The UK has also had 2003 Combined Code developments in areas earlier covered by Turnbull. It has been suggested that, while the SEC mentions Turnbull as an acceptable framework to use for Sarbanes-Oxley certification purposes, it is no oversight that no mention of Turnbull was made by PCAOB in their new Auditing Standard No 2 or the audit of CEO's and CFO's Sarbanes-Oxley internal control reports.[45] So the suggestion that the UK needs a new Turnbull-type report has gathered momentum. As a consequence, in 2003 the Financial Reporting Council established the Turnbull Review Group under the chairmanship of Douglas Flint, Group Finance Director of HSBC: their target is draft revised guidance by mid-2005 to take effect, after finalisation, for accounting periods commencing on or after 1 January 2006.

An interesting question is whether we can expect that regulators may in the future replace the requirements for published internal control statements by requirements for enterprise risk management statements. However, we should note that since 1999 UK internal control statements have a scope which covers risk management as well as all the three COSO objectives of internal control (which are also three of the four objectives given by COSO for enterprise risk management).[46]

A somewhat convincing, though slightly cynical argument can be advanced that fundamentally all that has changed between the old (1992) and new (2004) COSO studies is that:

- The fourth COSO objective of enterprise risk management has been added to the three 1992 COSO objectives of internal control. It is 'Strategic – high-level goals, aligned with and supporting the entity's mission'.[47]
- 'Objective setting' is given as an essential component of enterprise risk management whereas, perhaps inappropriately,[48] it was not a COSO component of internal control;
- The 'risk assessment' component of internal control has been formally split into three parts ('risk identification', 'risk assessment' and 'risk response'); an effective 'risk response' may also involve the application of any of the 1992 internal control components;
- The narrative of the report is in the contemporary idiom with much more specific mention of the term 'risk' and of contemporary risk management techniques;
- The title 'enterprise risk management' has been selected rather than 'internal control' since the former is the contemporary language of management gurus and consultants.

Indeed, since the COSO definitions of internal control and enterprise risk management, as well as the categorisation of the objectives of each, are so similar to each other, it is apparent that we are dealing with the same or a closely similar concept though with a different title.

## B2.2.26  *Building on Internal Control – Integrated Framework*

So, COSO's new *Enterprise Risk Management* framework builds upon their 1992 internal control framework. This is helpful as it allows a graceful transition by practitioners from the old to the new with minimal reorientation. Certainly, if the old *Internal Control – Integrated Framework* concepts were sound, it would have been unconvincing to jettison them in favour of a brand new model. This has not been done: we have the impression that as little has been changed from the old *Internal Control – Integrated Framework* as was necessary, even down to the look and feel of the two publications, the typeface, the sections within corresponding chapters and the wording of text within them. There is nothing in the new enterprise risk management framework which alters the old internal control framework – rather it only extends it. Furthermore, it is not intended for the moment to supersede the old internal control framework by the new enterprise risk management one:

'Because that framework [Internal Control – Integrated Framework] has stood the test of time and is the basis for existing rules, regulations and laws, that document remains in place as the definition of and framework for internal control. While only portions of the text of Internal control – Integrated Framework are reproduced in this [ERM] framework, the entirety of that framework is incorporated by reference into this one.'[49]

## B2.2.27  *Defining 'enterprise risk management'*

| COSO: Internal Control – Integrated Framework (1992) | COSO: Enterprise Risk Management (2002/3) |
|---|---|
| 'Internal control is broadly defined as a process, effected by the entity's board of directors, management and other personnel, designed to provide reasonable assurance regarding the achievement of objectives in the following categories:<br><br>– Effectiveness and efficiency of operations;<br><br>– Reliability of financial reporting<br><br>– Compliance with applicable laws and regulations.' | 'Enterprise risk management is a process, effected by an entity's board of directors, management and other personnel, applied in strategy setting and across the enterprise, designed to identify potential events that may affect the entity, and manage risks to be within its risk appetite, to provide reasonable assurance regarding the achievement of entity objectives.'[50]<br>This definition is purposefully broad. It captures key concepts fundamental to how companies and other organizations manage risk, providing a basis for application across organizations, industries and sectors. It focuses directly on achievement of objectives established by a particular entity and provides a basis for defining enterprise risk management effectiveness.[51] |

The common ground between 'enterprise risk management' and 'internal control' is evident from the COSO definitions of both, above. Unlike the old pre-1992 definitions of internal control,[52] each is regarded as a 'process' rather than as a 'state of affairs' – a means to an end, not an end in itself.

Although the three categories listed at the end of the internal control definition (as the objectives of internal control) are no longer presented as being formally part of the new enterprise risk management definition, the new COSO study says that:

'Within the context of an entity's established mission or vision, management establishes strategic objectives, selects strategy and sets aligned objectives cascading through the enterprise. This enterprise risk management framework is geared to achieving an entity's objectives, set forth in four categories:
- Strategic – high-level goals, aligned with and supporting its mission
- Operations – effective and efficient use of its resources
- Reporting – reliability of reporting
- Compliance – compliance with applicable laws and regulations.

This categorization of entity objectives allows a focus on separate aspects of enterprise risk management. These distinct but overlapping categories – a particular objective can fall into more than one category – address different entity needs and may be the direct responsibility of different executives. This categorization also allows distinctions between what can be expected from each category of objectives. Another category, safeguarding of resources, used by some entities, also is described.'[53]

and:

'Objectives are set at the strategic level, establishing a basis for operations, reporting and compliance objectives. Every entity faces a variety of risks from external and internal sources, and a precondition to effective event identification, risk assessment and risk response is establishment of objectives. Objectives are aligned with the entity's risk appetite, which drives risk tolerance levels for the entity's activities.'[54]

The categorisation of the objectives of internal control (and now of enterprise risk management) has varied over time, as illustrated in the following table. Indeed the new *Standards* of The Institute of Internal Auditors are not entirely consistent with the 2004 COSO categorisation, although it is possible to reconcile to the two. The COSO categorisation has changed between 1992 and 2004.

**Approximate matching of principal classifications of stated objectives of internal control and enterprise risk management**

| | Old AICPA/ CCAB | IIA (1978 to 2001 old *Standards*) | COSO (1992) – *Internal Control – Integrated Framework* | IIA (2002 new *Standards*) | COSO (2004) – *Enterprise Risk Management*[55] |
|---|---|---|---|---|---|
| 1 | Arguably not covered at all, or at least not explicitly so. | | | | 'Strategic – relating to high-level goals, aligned with and supporting the entity's mission.' |
| 2 | Operational effectiveness | The accomplishment of established objectives and goals for operations or programmes. | ('Effectiveness' is included in Row 3 below.) | ('Effectiveness' is included in Row 3 below.) | ('Effectiveness' is included in Row 3 below.) |
| 3 | Operational efficiency | The economical and efficient use of resources. | Effectiveness and efficiency of operations. | Effectiveness and efficiency of operations. | 'Operations – relating to effective and efficient use of the entity's resources.' |
| 4 | Safeguarding assets | The safeguarding of assets. | (COSO intended 'safeguarding of assets' to be subsumed within row 3 – above)[56] | Safeguarding of assets | (COSO intends this to be subsumed within row 3 – above) |
| 5 | Reliability of accounts | The reliability and integrity of information. | Reliability of financial reporting. | Reliability and integrity of financial and operational information. | 'Reporting – Relating to the reliability of the entity's reporting.' |

| | Old AICPA/ CCAB | IIA (1978 to 2001 old *Standards*) | COSO (1992) – *Internal Control – Integrated Framework* | IIA (2002 new *Standards*) | COSO (2004) – *Enterprise Risk Management* [55] |
|---|---|---|---|---|---|
| 6 | | Compliance with policies, plans, procedures, laws and regulations. | Compliance with applicable laws and regulations. | Compliance with laws, regulations, and contracts. | 'Compliance – relating to the entity's compliance with applicable laws and regulations.' |

## B2.2.28   *How the COSO ERM framework has been developed*

A 'framework' is a structure or model which describes a process in general terms. The intention is that it should become widely accepted so as to facilitate understanding, communication between practitioners and enhancement.

The pyramid shows the five essential components of an effective internal control process, as given in 1992's *Internal Control – Integrated Framework*; and the first cube shows COSO's understanding of the relationships between these components and the objectives of internal control. The second cube shows the equivalent for enterprise risk management, taken from the 2004 COSO report.

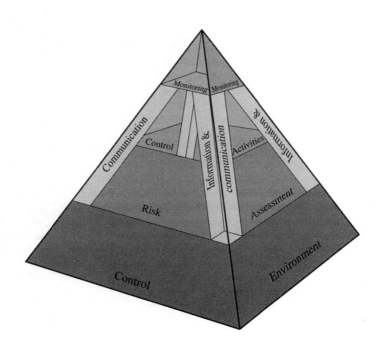

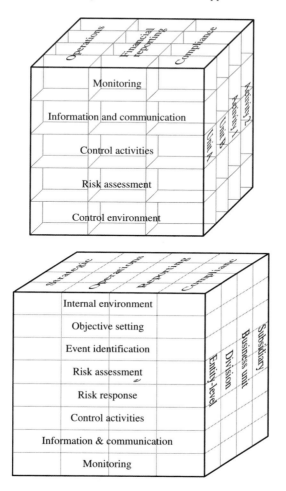

Key to the cube:

The four objectives categories – strategic, operations, reporting and compliance – are represented by the vertical columns. The eight components are represented by horizontal rows. The entity and its units are depicted by the third dimension of the cube.[57]

It is difficult to adequately represent the concept of enterprise risk management even in COSO's three-dimensional cube, as is acknowledged by COSO:

'Each component row "cuts across" and applies to all four objectives categories. For example, financial and non-financial data generated from internal and external sources, which is part of the information and communication component, is needed to set strategy, effectively manage business operations, report effectively and determine that the entity is complying with applicable laws.

Similarly, looking at the objectives categories, all eight components are relevant to each. Taking one category, effectiveness and efficiency of operations, for example, all eight components are applicable and important to its achievement.

Enterprise risk management is relevant to an entire enterprise or to any of its individual units. This relationship is depicted by the third dimension, which represents subsidiaries, divisions and other business units. Accordingly, one could focus on any one of the matrix's cells. For instance, one could consider the top right back cell, representing the internal environment as it relates to compliance objectives of a particular subsidiary.

It should be recognized that the four columns represent categories of an entity's objectives, not parts or units of the entity. Accordingly, when considering the category of objectives related to reporting, for example, knowledge of a wide array of information about the entity's operations is needed. But in that case, focus is on the right-middle column of the model – the reporting objectives – rather than the operations objectives category'.[58]

## B2.2.29  *The components of internal control and of enterprise risk management*

The 'eight interrelated components' of enterprise risk management are the criteria for effectiveness:

'The criteria for effectiveness – the presence and effective functioning of each component – remain in the final document. It was concluded that the principle developed in the internal control framework, and carried forward to the enterprise risk management framework, is logical and best serves users' needs – that when the eight components are deemed present and functioning effectively (and no material weaknesses exist), the result or outcome is that management and the board gain reasonable assurance regarding achievement of the stated objectives. The final document retains that principle, and also highlights that bringing risk within the entity's risk appetite is a necessary element of effective enterprise risk management. The concept of a subjective judgment as to the presence and functioning of the eight components has been removed, on the basis that the judgment can be objective, based on the principles in this framework'.[59]

The eight components of enterprise risk management are:

- internal environment;
- objective setting;
- event identification;
- risk assessment;
- risk response;
- control activities;

- information and communication; and
- monitoring.

Note the significant overlap with COSO's 1992 internal control components. We give the COSO definitions of these components in the table below. While we understand the desire to separate out 'risk response' so that it becomes a distinct component (although COSO accepts that the components are 'interrelated'), there is some ambiguity as to whether COSO regards 'responses' as 'controls'. We are not clear that 'responses' deserves to be highlighted as a distinct component of enterprise risk management. The following quotes from the new COSO study should throw light on this:

**'Separate Evaluations**

While ongoing monitoring procedures usually provide important feedback on the effectiveness of other enterprise risk management components, it may be useful to take a fresh look from time to time, focusing directly on enterprise risk management effectiveness. This also provides an opportunity to consider the continued effectiveness of the ongoing monitoring procedures.'

**'Scope and Frequency**

Evaluations of enterprise risk management vary in scope and frequency, depending on the significance of risks and importance of the risk responses and related controls in managing the risks. Higher-priority risk areas and responses tend to be evaluated more often. Evaluation of the entirety of enterprise risk management – which generally will be needed less frequently than the assessment of specific parts – may be prompted by a number of reasons: major strategy or management change, acquisitions or dispositions, changes in economic or political conditions, or changes in operations or methods of processing information. When a decision is made to undertake a comprehensive evaluation of an entity's enterprise risk management, attention should be directed to addressing its application in strategy setting as well as with respect to significant activities. The evaluation scope also will depend on which objectives categories – strategic, operations, reporting and compliance – are to be addressed.'[60]

and:

'... management has the ability to override the enterprise risk management process, including risk response decisions and control activities.'[61]

| Comparing COSO's Internal Control and Enterprise Risk Management components | | |
| --- | --- | --- |
| **Component** | **COSO: Internal Control – Integrated Framework (1992)** | **COSO: Enterprise Risk Management (2004)** |
| **Environment** | '**Control environment** – The control environment sets the tone of an organization, influencing the control consciousness of its people. It is the foundation for all other components of internal control, providing discipline and structure. Control environment factors include the integrity, ethical values and competence of the entity's people; management's philosophy and operating style; the way management assigns authority and responsibility, and organizes and develops its people; and the attention and direction provided by the board of directors.'[62] | '**Internal Environment** – Management sets a philosophy regarding risk and establishes a risk appetite. The internal environment sets the basis for how risk and control are viewed and addressed by an entity's people. The core of any business is its people – their individual attributes, including integrity, ethical values and competence – and the environment in which they operate.'[63] 'The internal environment encompasses the tone of an organization, influencing the risk consciousness of its people, and is the basis for all other components of enterprise risk management, providing discipline and structure. Internal environment factors include an entity's risk management philosophy; its risk appetite; oversight by the board of directors; the integrity, ethical values and competence of the entity's people; and the way management assigns authority and responsibility, and organizes and develops its people.'[64] |
| **Objective setting** | [not within the concept of the COSO internal control framework] | '**Objective Setting** – Objectives must exist before management can identify potential events affecting their achievement. Enterprise risk management ensures that management has in place a process to set objectives and that the chosen objectives support and align with the entity's mission/vision and are consistent with its risk appetite.'[65] 'Objectives are set at the strategic level, establishing a basis for operations, reporting and compliance objectives. Every entity faces a variety of risks from external and internal sources, and a precondition to effective event identification, risk assessment and risk response is establishment of objectives. Objectives are aligned with the entity's risk appetite, which drives risk tolerance levels for the entity.'[66] |

| Comparing COSO's Internal Control and Enterprise Risk Management components | | |
|---|---|---|
| **Component** | **COSO: Internal Control – Integrated Framework (1992)** | **COSO: Enterprise Risk Management (2004)** |
| **Event Identification** | [Included in 'Risk assessment' – see next row] | '**Event Identification** – Potential events that might have an impact on the entity must be identified. Event identification involves identifying potential events from internal or external sources affecting achievement of objectives. It includes distinguishing between events that represent risks, those representing opportunities, and those that may be both. Opportunities are channeled back to management's strategy or objective-setting process.'[67] <br> 'Management identifies potential events that, if they occur, will affect the entity, and determines whether they represent opportunities or whether they might adversely affect the entity's ability to successfully implement strategy and achieve objectives. Events with negative impact represent risks, which require management's assessment and response. Events with positive impact represent opportunities which management channels back into the strategy and objective-setting processes. When identifying events, management considers a variety of internal and external factors that may give rise to risks and opportunities, in the context of the full scope of the organization.'[68] <br> 'Enterprises operate in environments where factors such as globalization, technology, restructurings, changing markets, competition and regulation create uncertainty. Uncertainty emanates from an inability to precisely determine the likelihood that events will occur and the associated impacts. Uncertainty also is presented and created by the entity's strategic choices. For example, an entity has a growth strategy based on expanding operations to another country. This chosen strategy presents risks and opportunities associated with the stability of the country's political environment, resources, markets, channels, workforce capabilities and costs.'[69] |

| Comparing COSO's Internal Control and Enterprise Risk Management components | | |
|---|---|---|
| **Component** | **COSO: Internal Control – Integrated Framework (1992)** | **COSO: Enterprise Risk Management (2004)** |
| **Risk assessment** | 'Every entity faces a variety of risks from external and internal sources that must be assessed. A precondition to risk assessment is establishment of objectives linked at different levels and internally consistent. Risk assessment is the identification and analysis of relevant risks to achievement of objectives, forming a basis for determining how risks should be managed. Because economic, industry, regulatory and operating conditions will continue to change, mechanisms are needed to identify and deal with the special risks associated with change.'[70] | '**Risk Assessment** – Identified risks are analyzed in order to form a basis for determining how they should be managed. Risks are associated with objectives that may be affected. Risks are assessed on both an inherent and a residual basis, with the assessment considering both risk likelihood and impact.'[71] 'Risk assessment allows an entity to consider the extent to which potential events have an impact on achievement of objectives. Management assesses events from two perspectives – likelihood and impact – and normally uses a combination of qualitative and quantitative methods. The positive and negative impacts of potential events should be examined, individually or by category, across the entity. Risks are assessed on both an inherent and a residual basis.'[72] |
| **Risk response** | [Arguably covered in 'Risk assessment' and 'Control activities' – see rows above and below] | '**Risk Response** – Personnel identify and evaluate possible responses to risks, which include avoiding, accepting, reducing and sharing risk. Management selects a set of actions to align risks with the entity's risk tolerances and risk appetite.'[73] 'Having assessed relevant risks, management determines how it will respond. Responses include risk avoidance, reduction, sharing and acceptance. In considering its response, management assesses the effect on risk likelihood and impact, as well as costs and benefits, selecting a response that brings residual risk within desired risk tolerances. Management identifies any opportunities that might be available, and takes an entity-wide, or portfolio, view of risk, determining whether overall residual risk is within the entity's risk appetite.'[74] |

| Comparing COSO's Internal Control and Enterprise Risk Management components | | |
|---|---|---|
| Component | COSO: Internal Control – Integrated Framework (1992) | COSO: Enterprise Risk Management (2004) |
| Control activities | 'Control activities are the policies and procedures that help ensure management directives are carried out. They help ensure that necessary actions are taken to address risks to achievement of the entity's objectives. Control activities occur throughout the organization, at all levels and in all functions. They include a range of activities as diverse as approvals, authorizations, verifications, reconciliations, reviews of operating performance, security of assets and segregation of duties.'[75] | 'Control Activities – Policies and procedures are established and executed to help ensure that the risk responses management selected are effectively carried out.'[76] 'Control activities are the policies and procedures that help ensure that management's risk responses are carried out. Control activities occur throughout the organization, at all levels and in all functions. They include a range of activities –as diverse as approvals, authorizations, verifications, reconciliations, reviews of operating performance, security of assets and segregation of duties.'[77] |

| Comparing COSO's Internal Control and Enterprise Risk Management components | | |
|---|---|---|
| Component | COSO: Internal Control – Integrated Framework (1992) | COSO: Enterprise Risk Management (2004) |
| **Information and communication** | 'Pertinent information must be identified, captured and communicated in a form and timeframe that enables people to carry out their responsibilities. Information systems produce reports, containing operational, financial and compliance-related information, that make it possible to run and control the business. They deal not only with internally generated data, but also information about external events, activities and conditions necessary to informed business decision-making and external reporting. Effective communication also must occur in a broader sense, flowing down, across and up the organization. All personnel must receive a clear message from top management that control responsibilities must be taken seriously. They must understand their own role in the internal control system, as well as how individual activities relate to the work of others. They must have a means of communicating significant information upstream. There also needs to be effective communication with external parties, such as customers, suppliers, regulators and shareholders.'[78] | '**Information and Communication** – Relevant information is identified, captured and communicated in a form and timeframe that enable people to carry out their responsibilities. Information is needed at all levels of an entity for identifying, assessing and responding to risk. Effective communication also occurs in a broader sense, flowing down, across and up the entity. Personnel receive clear communications regarding their role and responsibilities.'[79] 'Pertinent information is identified, captured and communicated in a form and timeframe that enable people to carry out their responsibilities. Information systems use internally generated data, and information from external sources, providing information for managing enterprise risks and making informed decisions relative to objectives. Effective communication also occurs, flowing down, across and up the organization. All personnel receive a clear message from top management that enterprise risk management responsibilities must be taken seriously. They understand their own role in enterprise risk management, as well as how individual activities relate to the work of others. They must have a means of communicating significant information upstream. There is also effective communication with external parties, such as customers, suppliers, regulators and shareholders.'[80] |

| Comparing COSO's Internal Control and Enterprise Risk Management components | | |
|---|---|---|
| Component | COSO: Internal Control – Integrated Framework (1992) | COSO: Enterprise Risk Management (2004) |
| Monitoring | 'Internal control systems need to be monitored – a process that assesses the quality of the system's performance over time. This is accomplished through ongoing monitoring activities, separate evaluations or a combination of the two. Ongoing monitoring occurs in the course of operations. It includes regular management and supervisory activities, and other actions personnel take in performing their duties. The scope and frequency of separate evaluations will depend primarily on an assessment of risks and the effectiveness of ongoing monitoring activities. Internal control deficiencies should be reported upstream, with serious matters reported to top management and the board.'[81] | 'Monitoring – The entire enterprise risk management process is monitored, and modifications made as necessary. In this way, it can react dynamically, changing as conditions warrant. Monitoring is accomplished through ongoing management activities, separate evaluations of the enterprise risk management processes or a combination of the two.'[82] 'Enterprise risk management is monitored – assessing the presence and functioning of its components over time. This is accomplished through ongoing monitoring activities, separate evaluations or a combination of the two. Ongoing monitoring occurs in the normal course of management activities. The scope and frequency of separate evaluations will depend primarily on an assessment of risks and the effectiveness of ongoing monitoring procedures. Enterprise risk management deficiencies are reported upstream, with serious matters reported to top management and the board.'[83] |

COSO stresses the interrelatedness of the objectives and components of enterprise risk management in various places, eg:

> 'This categorization of entity objectives [into Strategic, Operations, Reporting and Compliance] allows a focus on separate aspects of enterprise risk management. These distinct but overlapping categories – a particular objective can fall into more than one category – address different entity needs and may be the direct responsibility of different executives. This categorization also allows distinctions between what can be expected from each category of objectives. Another category, safeguarding of resources, used by some entities, also is described.'[84]

and:

> 'This categorization of entity objectives allows a focus on separate aspects of enterprise risk management. These distinct but overlapping categories – a particular objective can fall under more than one category – address different entity needs and may be the direct responsibility of different executives. This categorization also allows distinctions between what can be expected from each category of objectives.'[85]

and:

'Although some control activities relate solely to one category, there often is overlap. Depending on circumstances, a particular control activity could help satisfy entity objectives in more than one of the categories. For example, certain operations controls also can help ensure reliable reporting, reporting control activities can serve to effect compliance, and so on.'[86]

and:

'Information is needed at all levels of an organization to identify, assess and respond to risks, and to otherwise run the entity and achieve its objectives. An array of information is used, relevant to one or more objectives categories.

Operating information from internal and external sources, both financial and non-financial, is relevant to multiple business objectives. Financial information, for instance, is used in developing financial statements for reporting purposes, and also for operating decisions, such as monitoring performance and allocating resources. Reliable financial information is fundamental to planning, budgeting, pricing, evaluating vendor performance, assessing joint ventures and alliances, and a range of other management activities.'[87]

## B2.2.30   *Stated rationale of enterprise risk management*

Underpinning this new COSO study is their stated, fundamental purpose of enterprise risk management – to create, preserve and realise value for stakeholders:

'An underlying premise of enterprise risk management is that every entity, whether for-profit, not-for-profit, or a governmental body, exists to provide value for its stakeholders. All entities face uncertainty, and the challenge for management is to determine how much uncertainty the entity is prepared to accept as it strives to grow stakeholder value. Uncertainty presents both risk and opportunity, with the potential to erode or enhance value. Enterprise risk management enables management to effectively deal with uncertainty and associated risk and opportunity and thereby enhance the entity's capacity to build value.'[88]

## B2.2.31   *Marrying the Enterprise Risk Management Framework with The IIA Standards*

COSO's three objectives of internal control (1992), which are also three of the four COSO objectives of enterprise risk management, are not identical to the four objectives of internal control and of risk management given in The IIA *Standards*. (The five-fold categorisation in the old IIA Standards has, of course, been superseded.) It is an anomaly that The IIA, as the most active of the five COSO bodies, is not entirely in line with COSO. The new COSO study refers to part of this difference:

'Some entities use another category of objectives, "safeguarding of resources", sometimes referred to as "safeguarding of assets". Viewed broadly, these deal with prevention of loss of an entity's assets or resources, whether through theft, waste, inefficiency or what turns out to be simply bad business decisions – such as selling product at too low a price, failing to retain key employees or prevent patent infringement, or incurring unforeseen liabilities. These are primarily operations objectives, although certain aspects of safeguarding can fall under other categories. Where legal or regulatory requirements apply, these become compliance issues. When considered in conjunction with public reporting, a narrower definition of safeguarding of assets often is used, dealing with prevention or timely detection of unauthorized acquisition, use, or disposition of an entity's assets that could have a material effect on the financial statements.'[89]

COSO defines internal audit's responsibility for risk management in a narrower way than is allowed for in the new IIA *Standards Framework*. Here, we reproduce what the COSO study says, and then the more broadminded guidance of a Practice Advisory within The IIA Standards framework:

COSO:

**'Internal Auditors**
Internal auditors play a key role in evaluating the effectiveness of –and recommending improvements to – enterprise risk management. Standards established by the Institute of Internal Auditors specify that the scope of internal auditing should encompass risk management and control systems. This includes evaluating the reliability of reporting, effectiveness and efficiency of operations and compliance with laws and regulations. In carrying out their responsibilities, internal auditors assist management and the board of directors or audit committee by monitoring, examining, evaluating, reporting on, and recommending improvements to the adequacy and effectiveness of the entity's enterprise risk management.'[90]

Practice Advisory 2100–3 on *Internal Audit's Role in the Risk Management Process*, puts it in non-prescriptive terms like this:

'The internal audit activity's role in the risk management process of an organization can change over time and may be found at some point along a continuum that ranges from:
- No role; to
- Auditing the risk management process as part of the internal audit plan; to
- Active, continuous support and involvement in the risk management process such as participation on oversight committees, monitoring activities, and status reporting; to
- Managing and coordinating the risk management process.'[91]

COSO is thus endorsing the conventional 'assurance' internal audit role with respect to risk management (the second of the above four bullet points on The IIA's 'continuum') and gives no encouragement for internal audit to get more deeply involved perhaps as part of the consulting services which internal audit may provide consistent with The IIA *Standards*. In this Practice Advisory The Institute is endorsing the provision of consulting services by internal audit and defining these in such a way that, for instance, acting as the risk manager of the entity would not be an inappropriate role for the internal audit activity. But it is only at the lesser level of this Practice Advisory that The IIA specifically refers to internal audit as legitimately being the risk manager of the entity. The *Standards* themselves give no such encouragement – either in what we quote below or in the consulting *Standards* which are subsidiary to Standard 2100. It is possible that COSO more closely corresponds to The IIA's policy for internal auditing than does The IIA's own Practice Advisory 2100–3.

**'Standard 2100 – Nature of Work**
The internal audit activity evaluates and contributes to the improvement of risk management, control and governance systems.'

Nevertheless there are many cases in practice where internal auditors have been given by management the role to manage and coordinate the risk management process. So the question is whether, from COSO's perspective, in such cases internal audit is wearing a 'non-auditing hat' or whether the service that internal audit is providing here fits into the consulting role of internal audit as covered by The IIA *Standards* framework – including their Code of Ethics and the Practice Advisories.

One interpretation of COSO would be that COSO believes that supporting, managing or coordinating the risk management process is *not* part of internal audit's *assurance* role, and that it is their assurance role which should be regarded as the primary role of an internal audit function.

## B2.2.32 *Responsibilities of the board and others for enterprise risk management*

While COSO cedes to management the primary responsibility for enterprise risk management it is as well to note that 'the board' is also put centre stage by COSO:

'Although directors primarily provide oversight, they also provide direction and approve strategy and certain transactions and policies. As such, boards of directors are an important element of enterprise risk management.'[92]

and:

'Management is accountable to the board of directors or trustees, which provides monitoring, guidance, and direction. By selecting management, the board has a major role in defining what it expects in integrity and ethical values, and through its oversight activities can determine whether its expectations are being met. Similarly, by reserving authority in certain key decisions, the board plays a role in setting strategy, formulating high-level objectives, and broad-based resource allocation.

The board provides oversight with regard to enterprise risk management by:
- Knowing the extent to which management has established effective enterprise risk management in the organization
- Being aware of and concurring with the entity's risk appetite
- Reviewing the entity's portfolio view of risk and considering it against the entity's risk appetite
- Being apprised of the most significant risks and whether management is responding appropriately.'[93]

So we are uneasy with COSO's assertion that:

'The chief executive officer is **ultimately responsible** [for enterprise risk management]'[94]

though, since day-to-day ownership of risk may be assigned downwards, we are comfortable that COSO is right that:

'The chief executive officer ... should assume "ownership".'[95]

Indeed, despite COSO's unambiguous assertion about where ultimate responsibility is vested, COSO by no means excludes the board from enterprise risk management:

> 'Among the most critical communications channels is that between top management and the board of directors. Management must keep the board up-to-date on performance, risk and the functioning of enterprise risk management, and other relevant events or issues. The better the communications, the more effective a board will be in carrying out its oversight responsibilities – acting as a sounding board on critical issues, monitoring its activities, and providing advice, counsel and direction. By the same token, the board should communicate to management its information needs to management, and provide feedback and direction.'[96]

This is not an unimportant issue. Since the 1977 US Foreign Corrupt Practices Act indicated that the board is responsible for internal control there have been repeated attempts to pass the buck back to management. For instance, the Treadway recommendation for public reports on internal control led to the 1992 COSO internal control framework study which advised that the report be signed by the CEO and the CFO. Now the SEC's implementation of Sarbanes-Oxley with respect to certifying and reporting on internal control over financial reporting also lays this responsibility at the feet of these two executives. There is not the same buck-passing in the UK where, under the Combined Code and the Turnbull Report, it is *the board as a whole* who are ultimately responsible for internal control and risk management, who must review its effectiveness and who should report publicly on it. Perhaps this is a tacit US acknowledgment that their boards are often 'unbalanced': though often comprised of a large majority of non-executive directors, they frequently have an all-powerful, dominant CEO who is also chairman of the board. Gradually this is breaking down in the wake of Enron, Tyco and so on. It is not surprising that the non-executives, and indeed the US board as whole, are more beholden to the executive and perhaps not so keen to be given ultimate responsibility for internal control.

It appears that when the US, but not the UK, refers to 'board oversight responsibility', something less than 'ultimate responsibility' is intended. Were it not for the questionable practices of some senior executives of US listed companies, it would seem to be more congenial and less risky to be a non-executive director in the US than in the UK, but more risky to be an executive director in the US.

The position being taken by COSO on this issue could be construed as suggesting that the board is answerable to the chief executive officer in that the latter who is regarded as 'ultimately responsible' for enterprise risk management: many US boards do appear to have been answerable to their CEO – especially when the CEO has also been the chairman.

The 2003 Higgs Report and the new UK 2003 Combined Code counsels that a significant portion of a UK board should be executive, while also counselling that 50% of the board, *excluding the chairman*, should be independent non-executive directors.

'**A.3    Board balance and independence**
*Main Principle*
The board should include a balance of executive and non-executive directors (and in particular independent non-executive directors) such that no individual or small group of individuals can dominate the board's decision taking.

*Supporting Principles*
... To ensure that power and information are not concentrated in one or two individuals, there should be a strong presence on the board of both executive and non-executive directors.

*Code provisions*
...

A.3.2 Except for smaller companies,[97] at least half the board, excluding the chairman, should comprise non-executive directors determined by the board to be independent. A smaller company should have at least two independent non-executive directors ...'[98]

In addition to COSO setting out the responsibilities of internal auditors for enterprise risk management,[99] which we touched on earlier, COSO points out that other parties are also involved (bolding added):

'**Everyone** in an entity has some responsibility for enterprise risk management. The **chief executive officer** is ultimately responsible [for the entity's enterprise risk management] and should assume "ownership". Other **managers** support the risk philosophy, promote compliance with the risk appetite and manage risks within their spheres of responsibility consistent with the risk tolerances. Other **personnel** are responsible for executing in accordance with established enterprise risk management directives and protocols. The **board of directors** provides important oversight to enterprise risk management. A number of **external parties** often provide information useful in effecting enterprise risk management, but they are not responsible for the effectiveness of the entity's risk management.'[100]

While we consider this understates the role of the board of directors, we also consider it is to understate the role of 'other personnel' by implying that their role is just to 'execute'. Where control self assessment is effectively embedded within the business, the role of other personnel is much more profound that mere execution. Indeed, elsewhere, COSO acknowledges this:

'Personnel identify and evaluate possible responses to risk, including avoiding, accepting, reducing and sharing risk.'[101]

## B2.2.33    *Meaning of the 'portfolio' approach*

A legitimate criticism of most approaches to risk management which have been developed recently is that they offer concepts and tools which are applied more readily at business sub-unit or activity level, rather than for the entity as a whole across activities, functions and sub-units. We might call this a 'silo mentality'. In reaction, we have seen the arrival of terms such as 'enterprise-wide risk management', 'entity-wide risk management', 'portfolio view', 'built-in' or 'embedded risk management'. The latter is to be found in the Turnbull Report; and the other terms in the COSO report, which has grasped the interrelatedness of risk management:

> 'Management needs to not only manage individual risks, but also understand interrelated impacts.'[102]

and:

> 'Enterprise risk management requires an entity to take a portfolio view of risk. This might involve each manager responsible for a business unit, function, process, or other activity developing an assessment of risk for the activity. The assessment may be quantitative or qualitative. With a composite view at each succeeding level of the organization, senior management is positioned to make a determination whether the entity's overall risk portfolio is commensurate with its risk appetite.'[103]

and:

> 'Enterprise risk management is most effective when these mechanisms are built into the entity's infrastructure and are part of the essence of the enterprise. By building in enterprise risk management, an entity can directly affect its ability to implement its strategy and achieve its mission.'[104]

COSO claims that their enterprise risk management framework accommodates taking this 'portfolio view':

> 'The definition reflects certain fundamental concepts. Enterprise risk management is:
> * A process, ongoing and flowing through an entity
> * Effected by people at every level of an organization
> * Applied in strategy setting
> * Applied across the enterprise, at every level and unit, and includes taking an entity level portfolio view of risk [etc]...'[105]

COSO correctly point out that the portfolio view concept was absent from COSO's 1992 *Internal Control – Integrated Framework*:

> 'A concept not contemplated in the internal control framework is the portfolio view of risk. In addition to focusing on risk in considering achievement of entity objectives on an individual basis, it is necessary to consider composite risks from a "portfolio" perspective.'[106]

'Portfolio view' is a phrase used many times by COSO. However, we did not feel we obtained much guidance in the *Framework* volume on the methods to be applied in taking a holistic view of risk across the enterprise. This guidance is to be found mainly in the *Application Techniques* volume.

The guidance counsels a need to consider 'aggregate effect' in the context of 'risk responses':

> 'Having considered responses to risk on an individual or a group basis, management considers the aggregate effect of its risk responses across the entity.'[107]

COSO claims that enterprise risk management provides enhanced capabilities to achieve seven results, the last four of which in particular suggest an enterprise-wide orientation, viz:

- 'Aligning risk appetite and strategy ...
- Enhancing risk response decisions ...
- Reducing operational surprises and losses ...
- Identifying and managing cross-enterprise risks – Every enterprise faces a myriad of risks affecting different parts of the organization. Management needs to not only manage individual risks, but also understand interrelated impacts. ...
- Providing integrated responses to multiple risks – Business processes carry many inherent risks, and enterprise risk management enables integrated solutions for managing the risks. ...
- Seizing opportunities – By considering a full range of potential events, rather than just risks, management identifies events representing opportunities. ...
- Improving deployment of capital – Obtaining robust information on risk allows management to effectively assess overall capital needs and enhance capital allocation. ...'[108]

## B2.2.34 *Assessing the effectiveness of enterprise risk management, with reasonable assurance*

At a macro level, the COSO judgement of effectiveness of enterprise risk management corresponds quite closely to their 1992 criteria for judging internal control effectiveness:

> 'Determining whether enterprise risk management is "effective" is a judgment resulting from an assessment of whether the eight components are present and functioning effectively. Thus, the components are also criteria for effective enterprise risk management. For the components to be present and functioning properly there can be no material weaknesses, and risk needs to have been brought within the entity's risk appetite.

> When enterprise risk management is determined to be effective in each of the four categories of objectives, the board of directors and management have reasonable assurance that:
> - They understand the extent to which the entity's strategic objectives are being achieved
> - They understand the extent to which the entity's operations objectives are being achieved
> - The entity's reporting is reliable
> - Applicable laws and regulations are being complied with.'[109]

and:

> 'Because objectives relating to reliability of reporting and compliance with laws and regulations are within the entity's control, enterprise risk management can be expected to provide reasonable assurance of achieving those objectives. Achievement of strategic objectives and operations objectives, however, is subject to external events not always within the entity's control; accordingly, for these objectives, enterprise risk management can provide reasonable assurance that

management, and the board in its oversight role, are made aware, in a timely manner, of the extent to which the entity is moving toward achievement of the objectives.'[110]

and (COSO, 1992):

'Internal control can be judged effective in each of the three categories, respectively, if the board of directors and management have reasonable assurance that:
- They understand the extent to which the entity's operations objectives are being achieved.
- Published financial statements are being prepared reliably.
- Applicable laws and regulations are being complied with.'[111]

We are not convinced that it is helpful for COSO in 2004 to characterise the achievement of two of their four objectives of enterprise risk management as being within an entity's control whereas the other two are not (though one was in 1992). External or errant events beyond management's control may lead to an entity's failure to achieve *any* of these four objectives. For instance, carefully concealed fraud may make financial statements unreliable. This COSO publication acknowledges that collusion, failures of judgment, breakdowns and management overrides are limitations of enterprise risk management:

'Achievement of objectives is affected by limitations inherent in all management processes. These include the realities that human judgement in decision-making can be faulty and that breakdowns can occur because of such human failures as simple error or mistake. Additionally controls can be circumvented by the collusion of two or more people, and management has the ability to override the enterprise risk management process, including risk response decisions and control activities.'[112]

Collusion, failures of judgment, breakdowns and management overrides are all so often significant factors in fraudulent financial reporting. It does not seem entirely reasonable that COSO is setting such a significantly higher level of attainment expectation for the reporting and compliance objectives than for the strategy and operations objectives, not least because of the severe criminal sanctions which the CEO, CFO and others face under Sarbanes-Oxley for failure to measure up in respect of reporting.

Good internal control and good enterprise risk management can give reasonable assurance, though not an absolute guarantee of the achievement of each of these four of these objectives. At most, it is only a difference of degree which marks out the operational and strategic objectives as being generally greater management challenges. Recent US corporate governance debacles have certainly not indicated that 'reliable financial reports' is an objective more readily achieved than strategic or operational objectives.

The illogicality of COSO so circumscribing the potential of enterprise risk management to give reasonable assurance that strategic and operational objectives may be achieved, but not being so modest about the potential of enterprise risk management with respect to the ERM reporting and compliance objectives, is further illustrated by the artificiality of discriminating between these four objectives. Helpful though it is to categorise the objectives of enterprise risk management into four (and of internal control into three) categories, it is an artificial construct. For instance, there is no doubt that reliable financial reporting should be a strategic objective of a modern enterprise, and the accounting/reporting process is as much an operation as production or distribution. Similarly with the compliance objective.

It has become customary to set about the assessment of internal control effectiveness by (a) treating the internal control components as 'criteria' for that assessment, while also considering (b) whether ineffectiveness is indicated because of a known, significant breakdown. The rationale for this approach is that (b) on its own would not be enough as the absence of any known, significant breakdowns would not necessarily mean that there had been none of these – just that they had not been discovered; and even if there had been no significant breakdowns caused by ineffective internal control, that would not on its own be enough to allow a conclusion that internal control had been effective – it might just have been a matter of the weaknesses in the internal control systems not having been exploited, either deliberately or by chance. COSO has placed the main emphasis on (a) whereas in the UK the emphasis has been on (a) and also (b).[113]

The 1992 and 2003 COSO approach further differs from the UK approach in that 'effectiveness' is regarded in the UK as applying to the whole of the period under review and also to the subsequent period up to the date of the effectiveness report, whereas for COSO (1992 and 2003) effectiveness is taken 'at a point in time':

'While enterprise risk management is a process, its effectiveness is a state or condition at a point in time.'[114]

COSO (1992) took the same approach:

'While internal control is a process, its effectiveness is a state or condition of the process at one or more points in time.'[115]

This means that a published internal control statement under the COSO 1992 guidance will apply to the effectiveness of internal control as of the date of the review. Unlike the UK, earlier ineffectiveness, rectified by the year-end, need not therefore be construed as ineffectiveness to be reported. It does appear to us that this is another example of a rules-based US orientation leading to the possibility that misleading reports may be made. Furthermore, we question whether it is meaningful to assess a *process* as effective at a point in time rather than over a duration.

As we have just discussed, the old and new COSO studies allow that internal control, and now enterprise risk management, may not have been ineffective just because *operational* objectives have not been achieved, but ineffectiveness will usually have to be presumed if *financial reporting* and *compliance* objectives have not been achieved. That is because operational objectives may fail to be achieved due to external events beyond the company's control.

'Effective enterprise risk management provides reasonable assurance that an entity's reporting objectives are being achieved. Similarly, there should be reasonable assurance that compliance objectives are being achieved. Achieving reporting and compliance objectives is largely within the entity's control. That is, once the objectives have been determined, the entity has control over its ability to do what's needed to meet them.

But there is a difference when it comes to strategic and operations objectives, because their achievement is not solely within the entity's control. An entity may perform as intended, yet be outperformed by a competitor. It is subject to external events – such as a change in government, poor weather and the like – where an occurrence is beyond its control. It may even have considered some of these events in its objective-setting process and treated them as having a low likelihood, with a contingency plan in case they occurred. However, such a plan only mitigates the impact of external events. It does not ensure that the objectives are achieved.

Enterprise risk management over operations focuses primarily on developing consistency of objectives and goals throughout the organization; identifying key success factors and risks; assessing the risks and making informed responses; implementing appropriate risk responses and establishing needed controls; and timely reporting of performance and expectations. For strategic and operations objectives, enterprise risk management can provide reasonable assurance that management and, in its oversight role, the board are made aware, in a timely manner, of the extent to which the entity is moving toward these objectives.'[116]

and:

'In considering limitations of enterprise risk management, three distinct concepts must be recognised:
- First, risk relates to the future, which is inherently uncertain.
- Second, enterprise risk management – even effective enterprise risk management – operates at different levels with respect to different objectives. For strategic and operations objectives, enterprise risk management can help to ensure that management, and the board in its oversight role, is aware, in a timely manner, only of the extent to which the entity is moving toward the achievement of these objectives. But it cannot provide even reasonable assurance that the objectives will be achieved.
- Third, enterprise risk management cannot provide absolute assurance with respect to any of the objectives categories.'[117]

A key concept that has emerged during the 1990s is that of 'reasonable assurance' as distinct from 'certainty' or 'absolute assurance' that internal control, and now enterprise risk management, are effective. The COSO study gives the following reasons for convictions about effectiveness always being limited to a level of 'reasonable assurance':[118]

- Human judgement in decision-making can be faulty;
- Breakdowns can occur because of human failures such as simple errors or mistakes;
- Controls can be circumvented by collusion of two or more people; and
- Management has the ability to override enterprise risk management decisions.

There is also the additional reason that external events may be unpredictable in character and scale.

**B2.2.35** *'Internal control' and 'enterprise risk management' – which belongs to which, or are they the same?*

It is clear that COSO now regards internal control as being part of enterprise risk management, albeit a large part, rather than enterprise risk management being part of internal control. All the five components of internal control per *Internal Control – Integrated Framework* are carried forward to become five of the eight components of enterprise risk management. This position is confirmed by COSO within the study:

> **'Encompasses Internal Control**
>
> Internal control is an integral part of enterprise risk management. This enterprise risk management framework encompasses internal control, forming a more robust conceptualization and tool for management. Internal control is defined and described in Internal Control – Integrated Framework. Because Internal Control – Integrated Framework is the basis for existing rules, regulations and laws, and has stood the test of time, that document remains in place as the definition of and framework for internal control. While only portions of the text of Internal Control – Integrated Framework are reproduced in this framework, the entirety of Internal Control – Integrated Framework is incorporated by reference into this framework. Appendix C describes the relationship between enterprise risk management and internal control.'[119]

The 2004 COSO report has an appendix which describes how enterprise risk management is more encompassing than internal control.[120] For many this COSO position invites a reorientation. Gleim certainly considered it to be the other way round:

> 'Risk management is the process of assessing the risks faced by an organization and developing strategies to minimize their effects. Consequently, risk assessment and management are part of the control function.'[121]

*Internal Control – Integrated Framework* regarded 'risk assessment' as one of the five essential components of internal control, and defined risk assessment as:

> 'Risk assessment is the identification and analysis of relevant risks to achievement of the objectives, forming a basis for determining how the risks are managed.'[122]

The 1992 COSO concept of internal control specifically embraced both the 'identification' and 'assessment' of risk – which are shown in the 2004 COSO study as being two of the eight essential components of an effective enterprise risk management process – within the single component 'risk assessment'. The above definition of 'risk assessment' from the 1992 COSO internal control study stated that risk assessment:

> 'form[s] a basis for determining how the risks are managed'.

That 'basis' is to be found in other components of the COSO internal control framework (such as 'control environment', 'control activities', 'information and communication', and 'monitoring').

## B2.2.36 Which is bigger – 'internal control' or 'enterprise risk management'?

We consider on balance that *'Internal Control – Integrated Framework'* intended to describe internal control as comprising the processes applied *in order to achieve* the entity's objectives, not just those processes designed to *assure* (ie confirm, attest) that management etc are doing what is necessary to achieve objectives. The most recent UK report to attempt a definition of internal control, the Turnbull Report,[123] comes down unambiguously on the side of 'broadly defining' (to use COSO's phrase) internal control as being all those things that management does to ensure the achievement of objectives, not just those things which provide assurance that objectives are being achieved:[124]

> 'An internal control system encompasses the policies, processes, tasks, behaviours and other aspects of a company that, taken together:
> - facilitate its effective and efficient operation by enabling it to respond appropriately to significant business, operational, financial, compliance and other risks to achieving the company's objectives. This includes the safeguarding of assets from inappropriate use or from loss and fraud, and ensuring that liabilities are identified and managed;
> - help ensure the quality of internal and external reporting. This requires the maintenance of proper records and processes that generate a flow of timely, relevant and reliable information within and outside the organisation;
> - help ensure compliance with applicable laws and regulations, and also with internal policies with respect to the conduct of business.'

We do however have a slight hesitancy in concluding that on balance *'Internal Control – Integrated Framework'* intended to describe internal control as comprising the processes applied in order to achieve the entity's objectives, not just those processes designed to assure (ie confirm, attest) that management etc are doing what is necessary to achieve objectives. We consider the COSO framework (whether 1992 or 2004) is not worked out clearly in this respect. Wording in the new COSO study carries forward sentiment from the 1992 study (when similar wording was used), appearing to indicate that internal control in the context of *operational objectives* is limited in scope to what provides assurance (most of which we have quoted earlier in a different context):

> 'Effective enterprise risk management provides reasonable assurance that an entity's reporting objectives are being achieved. Similarly, there should be reasonable assurance that compliance objectives are being achieved. Achieving reporting and compliance objectives is largely within the entity's control. That is, once the objectives have been determined, the entity has control over its ability to do what's needed to meet them.

> But there is a difference when it comes to operations objectives, because their achievement is not solely within the entity's control. An entity may perform as intended, yet be outperformed by a competitor. It is subject to external events – such as a change in government, poor weather and the like – where an occurrence is beyond its control. It may even have considered some of these events in its objective-setting process and treated them as having a low likelihood, with a contingency plan in case they occurred. However, such a plan only mitigates the impact of external events. It does not ensure that the objectives are achieved.

Enterprise risk management over operations focuses primarily on developing consistency of objectives and goals throughout the organization; identifying key success factors and risks; assessing the risks and making informed responses; implementing appropriate risk responses and establishing needed controls; and timely reporting of performance and expectations. For these objectives, enterprise risk management can provide reasonable assurance that management and, in its oversight role, the board are made aware, in a timely manner, of the extent to which the entity is moving toward these objectives.'[125]

While it is true that COSO's five essential internal control components have been incorporated into the eight enterprise risk components, our discussion has sought to show that this would not of itself make enterprise risk management a broader concept that internal control, were it not for the new focus on applying enterprise risk management at the strategy formulation stage.

## B2.2.37   *Enterprise risk management as something less than all of the management process*

If the concept of 'enterprise risk management' has integrity, it must be possible to show how it fits into the management process as a whole. The new COSO study says:

Exposure draft wording, omitted from the final version, said:

'Enterprise risk management ... is interrelated with corporate governance by providing information to the board of directors on the most significant risks and how they are being managed. And it interrelates with performance management by providing risk-adjusted measures, and with internal control, which is an integral part of enterprise risk management.'[126]

Final exposure draft wording introduced some confusion:

'Because enterprise risk management is part of the management process, the enterprise risk management framework components are discussed in the context of what management does in running the business. Not everything management does, however, is an element of enterprise risk management. For example, the process of establishing objectives is a critical component of enterprise risk management, but the particular objectives selected by management, while an important management responsibility and an important link to an entity's strategy, is not part of enterprise risk management. Similarly, responding to risks, based on an assessment of the risks, is a part of enterprise risk management, but which specific risk responses are selected is not. These are a matter of business judgement applied in decision-making, among many decisions and actions by management that are not part of enterprise risk management.'[127]

The wording in the final COSO framework is:

**'Enterprise Risk Management and the Management Process**
Because enterprise risk management is part of the management process, the enterprise risk management framework components are discussed in the context of what management does in running a business or other entity. But not everything management does, however, is a part of enterprise risk management. Many

judgments applied in management's decision making and related management actions, while part of the management process, are not part of enterprise risk management. For example:

- Ensuring there is an appropriate process for objective setting is a critical component of enterprise risk management, but the particular objectives selected by management are not part of enterprise risk management.
- Responding to risks, based on an appropriate assessment of the risks, is a part of enterprise risk management, but the specific risk responses selected and the associated allocation of entity resources are not.
- Establishing and executing control activities to help ensure the risk responses management selects are effectively carried out is a part of enterprise risk management, but the particular control activities chosen are not....'[128]

In the last of the above examples, by excluding 'control activities' from enterprise risk management, there is a suggestion that enterprise risk management does not embrace all of internal control, since 'control activities' is an essential COSO internal control component. 'Control activities' is also one of the eight COSO enterprise risk management components.

## B2.2.38  *Risk responses*

As we would expect, there is a rough correspondence between the risk response categories which COSO uses and those of HM Treasury in the UK (which are also used by Shell International Petroleum) – see the following table:

**Risk responses[129]**

| Comparing COSO (2004) with HM Treasury (2000) | | | | |
|---|---|---|---|---|
| **COSO – Enterprise Risk Management** | | | **HM Treasury** | |
| **Response** | **Meaning** | **Example** | **Response** | **Meaning** |
| *Avoidance* | 'Exiting the activities giving rise to risk.' | Providing a referral service. | *Terminate* | 'Some risks will only be treatable, or containable to acceptable levels, by terminating the activity.' |
| *Acceptance* | 'No action is taken to affect risk likelihood or impact, or both.' | Do nothing | *Tolerate* | 'Ability to do anything about risks may be limited, or the cost of taking any action may be disproportionate to the potential benefit gained. In these cases the response may be toleration.' |

| Comparing COSO (2004) with HM Treasury (2000) | | | | |
|---|---|---|---|---|
| **COSO – Enterprise Risk Management** | | | **HM Treasury** | |
| **Response** | **Meaning** | **Example** | **Response** | **Meaning** |
| *Reduction* | 'Action is taken to reduce the risk likelihood or impact, or both.' | Invest in IT to reduce the risk of system failure. | *Treat* | 'By far the greater number of risks will belong to this category. The purpose of treatment is not necessarily to obviate the risk but more likely to contain the risk to an acceptable level. The actions that an organisation takes in treating risk are called "internal control" – they are actions instigated from within the organisation (although their effects may be felt outside of the organisation) which are designed to contain risk to acceptable levels.' |
| *Sharing* | 'Reducing risk likelihood or impact by transferring or otherwise sharing a portion of the risk.' | A university outsourced dorm management to a property management company. | *Transfer* | 'For some risks the best response may be to transfer them. This might be done by conventional insurance or it might be done by paying a third party to take the risk in another way.' |

32    PF Drucker *Management: Tasks, Responsibilities, Practices* (Pan UK edition, 1979) p 433.

33    Enterprise Risk Management (COSO, 2004) Executive Summary, p1.

34    The two-volume set is available as item # 990015 from www.cpa2biz.com.

35    American Institute of Certified Public Accountants, American Accounting Association, The Institute of Internal Auditors, Institute of Management Accountants, Financial Executives International.

36    Committee of Sponsoring Organizations Of The Treadway Commission (COSO), (September 1992): *Internal Control – Integrated Framework*, (about $(US)50 from AICPA , Harborside Financial Centre, 201 Plaza Three, Jersey City, NJ 07311–3881, http://www.aicpa.org).

37    Report of the Committee on Fraudulent Financial Reporting ('The Treadway Report') (1987), Committee Of Sponsoring Organizations Of The Treadway Commission, (COSO). This 200 page report can be downloaded from the COSO website: www.coso.org. It was the first of several reports published by COSO.

38    Internal Control and Financial Reporting – Guidance for Directors of Listed Companies Registered in the UK (December 1994); known as 'The Rutteman report'.

39    *Internal Control – Guidance for Directors on the Combined Code* (September 1999) ISBN 1 84152 010 1), ICAEW, Chartered Accountants' Hall, PO Box 433, Moorgate Place, London, EC2P 2BJ, also available in pdf format at www.icaew.co.uk/internallcontrol; known as 'The Turnbull report'.

40    *The Combined Code* (1998), an appendix to 'The Purple Book' – the listing rules of the Financial Services Authority, (FSA). 'The Combined Code' can be downloaded in pdf format from: http://www.fsa.gov.uk/pubs/ukla/lr_comcode.pdf

41    The US Securities and Exchange Commission's Final Rule on 'Management's Reports on Internal Control Over Financial Reporting and Certification of Disclosure in Exchange Act Periodic Reports' was published on 11 June 2003. It interprets Section 404 (and also 302) of the Sarbanes-Oxley Act (2002), having made modifications from an earlier exposure draft. It can be downloaded from http://www.sec.gov/rules/final/33–8238.htm.

42    SEC Rule, p13 of 93.

43 SEC Rule, pp 85 of 93: endnote 67.

44 Executive Summary, p8.

45 Public Companies Accounting Oversight Board (PCAOB), (9 March, 2004) Auditing Standard No 2 '*An audit of internal control over financial reporting performed in conjunction with an audit of financial statements*'. Auditing Standard No. 2 can be downloaded from www.praobus.org. It runs to 185 pages and 25 pages of preamble.

46 The Provision in the UK's 2003 Combined Code of best practice for corporate governance reads:

> 'The directors should, at least annually, conduct a review of the effectiveness of the group's system of internal controls and should report to shareholders that they have done so. The review should cover all **material** controls, including financial, operational and compliance controls and risk management **systems**.'

The two words in bold have been added to the 2003 Code, not having been present in the 1998 Code and therefore not subject to the 1999 Turnbull guidance, but hopefully to be elaborated upon in the mid-2005 Flint guidance which is to replace the Turnbull guidance, and which is due to apply for UK listed companies' reports of years commencing on or after 1 January 2006.

47 Executive Summary, p5.

48 Inappropriately because, for instance, objective setting at lower levels is a means by which an entity obtains 'reasonable assurance' that it will achieve overall entity objectives.

49 Executive Summary, p8.

50 Executive Summary, p4.

51 Conceptual Framework volume, Chapter 1 on 'Composition', p4.

52 Eg American Institute of Certified Public Accountants: Internal Control – Elements of a Co-ordinated System and its Importance to Management and the Independent Public Accountant, New York:

> 'Internal control comprises the plan of organization and the co-ordinate methods and measures adopted within a business to safeguard its assets, check the accuracy and reliability of its accounting data, promote operational efficiency, and encourage adherence to prescribed managerial policies.'

53 Executive Summary, p5.

54 Framework volume, chapter summary to chapter 3 on 'Objective Setting, p35.

55 Conceptual Framework volume, Chapter 1 on 'Composition', p9.

56 In contrast to the UK Rutteman Report which regarded the safeguarding of assets as part of internal financial control.

57 Conceptual Framework volume, Chapter 1 on 'Definition', p23.

58 Conceptual Framework volume, Chapter 1 on 'Definition', p24.

59 Appendix E (Consideration of Comment Letters), p117; see also Executive Summary, p7; and Chapter 1 on 'Definition', p24–5.

60 Framework volume, chapter 9 on Monitoring, p77.

61 Framework volume, Chapter Summary to chapter 11 on 'Limitations of Enterprise Risk Management', p93.

62 July 1994 Edition, Vol 1, p4 – Executive Summary.

63 Framework, chapter 1 on 'Definition', p22.

64 Framework volume, chapter summary to chapter 2 on 'Internal Environment', p27.

65 Framework volume, Chapter 1 on 'Definition', p34.

66 Framework volume, chapter summary to chapter 3 on 'Objective Setting, p35.

67 Framework volume, Chapter 1 on 'definition', p22.

68 Framework volume, chapter summary to chapter 4 on 'Event identification', p41.

69 Framework volume, chapter 1 on 'Definition', p13.

70 July 1994 Edition, Vol 1, p4 – Executive Summary.

71 Framework volume, Chapter 1 on 'definition', p22.

72 Framework volume, chapter summary to chapter 5 on 'Risk Assessment', p49.

73 Framework volume, Chapter 1 on 'Definition', p22.

74 Framework volume, chapter summary to chapter 6 on 'Risk Response', p55.

75 July 1994 Edition, Vol 1, p4 – Executive Summary.

76 Framework volume, Chapter 1 on 'Definition', p22.

77    Framework volume, chapter summary to chapter 7 on 'Control Activities', p61.
78    July 1994 Edition, Vol 1, pp 4–5 – Executive Summary.
79    Framework volume, Chapter 1 on 'Definition', p22.
80    Framework volume, chapter summary to Chapter 8 on 'Information and Communication', p67.
81    July 1994 Edition, Vol 1, pp 4–5 – Executive Summary.
82    Framework volume, Chapter 1 on 'Definition', p22.
83    Framework volume, chapter summary to Chapter 9 on 'Monitoring', p75.
84    Executive Summary, p5.
85    Framework volume, Chapter 1 on 'Definition', p21.
86    Framework volume, Chapter 7 on 'Control activities', p61.
87    Framework volume, Chapter 8 on 'Information and communication', p67.
88    Framework volume, Chapter 1 on 'Definition', p13.
89    Framework volume, Chapter 1 on 'Definition', p21.
90    Framework volume, Chapter 11 on 'Roles and Responsibilities', p88.
91    Practice Advisory 2100–3 on 'Internal Audit's Role in the Risk Management Process', para 6.
92    Framework volume, Chapter 1 on 'Definition', p18.
93    Framework volume, Chapter 10 on 'Roles and Responsibilities', pp 83–4.
94    Executive Summary, p8; and Framework volume, chapter summary of Chapter 10 on 'Role and Responsibilities, p83.
95    Executive Summary, p8; and Framework volume, chapter summary of Chapter 10 on 'Role and Responsibilities, p83.
96    Framework volume, Chapter 8 on 'Information and Communication', p73.
97    A smaller company is one that is below the FTSE 350 throughout the year immediately prior to the reporting year.
98    2003 UK Combined Code, (23 July 2003), Financial Reporting Council (http://www.frc.org.uk/publications/).
99    Framework volume, Chapter 10 on 'Roles and Responsibilities', p88.
100   Framework volume, Chapter 10 on 'Roles and Responsibilities', p83.
101   Framework volume, Chapter 1 on 'Definition', p22.
102   Framework volume, Chapter 1 on 'Definition', p15.
103   Framework volume, chapter 1 on 'Definition', p19.
104   Framework volume, Chapter 1 on 'Definition', p17.
105   Executive Summary, p4.
106   Framework volume: Appendix B – Relationship Between Enterprise Risk Management – Integrated Framework and Internal Control – Integrated Framework, p110.
107   Framework volume: Appendix B – Relationship Between Enterprise Risk Management – Integrated Framework and Internal Control – Integrated Framework, p111.
108   Framework volume, Chapter 1 on 'Definition', p15.
109   Framework volume, Chapter 1 on 'Definition', p24.
110   Executive Summary, p5
111   Executive Summary to Internal Control – Integrated Framework, p4.
112   Framework volume, chapter summary to Chapter 11 on 'Limitations of enterprise risk management', p93.
113   *Vide,* Rutteman and now Turnbull.
114   Framework volume, Chapter 1 on 'Definition', p24.
115   Executive Summary to Internal Control – Integrated Framework, p4.
116   Framework volume, Chapter 3 on 'Objective Setting', p39.
117   Framework volume, Chapter 11 on 'Limitations of enterprise risk management', p93.
118   Framework volume, Chapter 10 on 'Limitations of enterprise risk management', p94.
119   Framework volume, Chapter 1 on 'Definition', p33 and also Executive Summary, p25.
120   Appendix C – Relationship Between Enterprise Risk Management Framework and Internal Control – Integrated Framework
121   IN Gleim *Management Control and Information Technology* CIA Review Part III (10th edition, December 2001) p142.
122   Internal Control – Integrated Framework, chapter Summary to Chapter 3, p33.
123   *Internal Control – Guidance For Directors On The Combined Code*, (September 1999) ('The Turnbull Report'), The Institute of Chartered Accountants in England & Wales, ISBN 1–84152–010–1

124      The Canadian CoCo programme excluded decisions from internal control, thus making internal control certainly less than *all* of what management does. The classic work on management control by Anthony (1965) defined management control as 'the process by which managers assure that resources are obtained and used effectively and efficiently in the accomplishment of the organization's objectives'. So CoCo and Anthony both lend weight to the suggestion that internal control is an 'assuring' or supportive process or processes. If this is so, then the challenge is to logically demarcate the assurance processes from the other processes within the business – or perhaps this cannot be done.

125      Framework volume, Chapter 3 on 'Objective Setting', p39.

126      Executive Summary, p3.

127      Conceptual Framework volume, pp 17–18.

128      Framework volume, Chapter 1 on 'Definition', p26.

129      HM Treasury (September 2000): Management of Risk – A Strategic Overview -'The Orange Book', p9; and COSO (2004) Framework volume, Chapter 6 on 'Risk Response', pp 55–56.

## B2.2.39   Control risk self assessment

A strong programme of control risk self assessment (CRSA) can contribute significantly to the confidence that the board may have that the risk management and internal control arrangements within the business are sound so as to give reasonable assurance that corporate objectives are being achieved, and that there are strong risk management processes embedded within the business, per the Turnbull guidance.

## B2.2.40   *Introducing CRSA*

CRSA (or control self assessment (CSA) as it often termed) is highly packaged by consultants. It can be difficult to break through the hype to understand its essential nature and whether it can be of continuing value within a business. Just to ask this question risks the wrath of those who promote CRSA! Now, coming through as a new wave promoted equally heavily by management consultants, is an approach labelled 'enterprise-wide risk management'.

## B2.2.41   **Defining CRSA**

So what *is* CRSA? We can describe it as simply the assessment of risk, and controls over risk by staff at all levels for themselves. Beyond that, CRSA has been dressed up with protocols and magic tricks which have become the preserve of a small cognoscenti and are serving to exclude the uninitiated – just what is not required if CRSA is to gain ground. It is a shame that the mysteries of CRSA are too often, and too much, shrouded behind issues of intellectual property rights rather than being in the same open domain as most other professional concepts and approaches.

In a broad sense, any approach to the self assessment of risk and internal control is CRSA – it may range from occasional completion by line managers of a business controls certificate, through to the use of letters of representation on risk and control or the completion of questionnaires – all the way up to participative workshops using anonymous voting approaches. Towards the end of this section (B2.2.52) we provide a sample business controls certificate, a standard 'boilerplate' form of wording for a letter of representation on risk management and internal control and an example of a questionnaire.

## B2.2.42 *Letters of representation on risk management and internal control*

The use of letters of representation or questionnaires has its limitations, but then so do all other approaches to self assessment. The concept is that all managers with key responsibilities for risk management and internal control make a return on their awareness and performance, usually once a year. The content of the return is then assessed by more senior management and/or by internal audit in order to identify areas of probable relative risk and control weaknesses where further investigative and remedial work appears to be needed – perhaps by way of internal audit 'fieldwork'. Summaries of the returns are fed through to the audit committee of the board, usually by internal audit, and serve to add to the degree of confidence that the board attains with respect to its oversight of risk management and internal control.

Some managers are likely to refuse to return a letter of representation, claiming there is no way they can commit themselves to the sentiments they are being asked to express, or claiming to be perplexed by the terminology of the return. It should be made clear to managers that they should modify the wording of their return to make it consistent with what they feel they can confidently associate themselves with. Other managers are likely to wish to clear their in-trays as quickly as possible and may not take the exercise sufficiently seriously. But the majority will enter into the spirit of things in a responsible way, with most of the rest of the managers resolving to put themselves into a better position to be able to approach the exercise more responsibly the following year. Top management support for the approach is essential if it is to work in a valuable way.

Undoubtedly, as with so many other things, with the support of the board and the audit committee, top management must champion CRSA, and staff at all levels and in all areas may engage in it. It is likely that internal audit will need to facilitate and monitor CRSA if it is to survive and prosper. 'Facilitation' is one of the forms of consultancy that the new internal auditing *Standards* regard as authentic internal auditing (see the Glossary to the new Standards at the end of APPENDIX 2, and the discussion on internal audit consulting in at A1.2.29 to A1.2.30). CRSA is not a sufficient substitute for traditional internal auditing of the 'assurance' variety, but the mix of internal audit work will change dramatically in a CRSA-oriented enterprise.

## B2.2.43 *Why CRSA?*

What is new about CRSA? Line management have always been responsible for internal control. Indeed self assessment programmes have been in place in some corporations[132] for many, many years – and these have often embraced an assessment of issues beyond a narrow view of control – such as quality, safety, equity, environmental management, etc.

Contemporary paradigms of internal control all avow that the monitoring of internal control is an essential part of internal control itself, as is the process of risk assessment (see B2.2.10). In the past, management has often found that the monitoring of internal control has been done best when it has been delegated on their behalf to an internal audit function. An internal audit function has the specialist skills to conduct reviews objectively. Its relative freedom from other duties means that the monitoring of internal control is not so likely to be put on the back burner.

So, can the monitoring of internal control be left to line management and staff? Or, put another way, what has changed which makes CRSA attractive today? As we have said, CRSA is unlikely to flourish without internal audit to give it a helping hand. An important issue can be the degree to which internal audit is independent enough of the CRSA programme so as to be able to provide top management and the audit committee with objective reassurance about the CRSA programme's effectiveness. Too much internal audit independence from the CRSA programme may mean CRSA is likely to fail; too little and CRSA is just a tool for internal audit. Indeed, a hybrid approach, combining both internal audit and CRSA, is sometimes applied: in this approach the fieldwork of an internal audit engagement commences, and perhaps also ends, with a CRSA workshop.

Top management and the audit committee will want advice from internal audit as to where to first introduce CRSA. In its participative workshops form, CRSA works best in non-threatening, non-hierarchical parts of the business. Top management and the audit committee will ask for periodic reports from internal audit on CRSA's effectiveness. So CRSA is more likely to run in parallel with internal audit in all but the smallest enterprises that may not have internal audit.

CRSA is very much a response to, some would say an essential component of, the modern re-engineered business. Downsized, delayered businesses have empowered staff to control the destinies of their business activities. They have more authority as well as more responsibility. It is in keeping with empowerment that they should monitor their own risk and control arrangements, and that control should be tightly focused on the achievement of key objectives. Nowhere is this more important than in the re-engineered business where the development and implementation of new management processes can, of itself, have such a detrimental effect on risk and control.

Certainly it ill behoves anyone to denigrate this new enchantment with assessing the effectiveness of internal control. Introducing CRSA through participative workshops, perhaps aided by anonymous voting, which is fun and can be an important and regular way of giving practical substance to the re-engineered, empowered and participative business.

## B2.2.44 *The role of internal audit in control risk self assessment*

Embedding the review of control and risk within the business, as Turnbull stipulates, is giving a new impetus to control risk self assessment in many enterprises. Turnbull's guidance on implementing the Combined Code provision on internal audit is also putting the spotlight on internal auditing generally. So it is not inappropriate to review the relationship between internal audit and control risk self assessment.

The prudent corporate approach is not to see CRSA as an alternative to internal audit, but rather to co-ordinate CRSA with the internal audit process and see them as complementary ways of assessing risk and control. Conventional internal auditing has the advantage that audit findings are supported by evidence which internal auditing standards require to be contained within the records of the audit engagement. 'Evidence' in CRSA programmes is, in the main, vested in the knowledge and experience which the participants bring to the CRSA workshops – which has its own advantage as their 'know-how' is likely to exceed that which can be acquired by a sole internal auditor or by an internal audit team during the brief fieldwork of an audit assignment.

The closeness of the CRSA participants to the activities they are considering has the possible disadvantage, compared with conventional internal auditing, of a relative lack of objectivity perhaps because of excessive familiarity or because of a reluctance to admit to weaknesses. Internal auditors also have the edge in the quality of their professional skills in conducting reviews of activities. Furthermore, summary reports on internal auditing engagements to the audit committee from a properly constituted internal auditing function will be perceived by the audit committee as being more independent of management and thus potentially more dependable than those which are generated through the CRSA programme.

Internal audit can facilitate the CRSA process in a number of important ways. A successful CRSA programme can also provide valuable reassurance to internal audit.

## B2.2.45   *Internal audit as a facilitator of control risk self assessment*

Internal audit should be a respected advisor to management and the board on risk, control and governance matters. It is natural that management will turn to internal audit for assistance in the following ways with respect to CRSA.

- Advice as to which parts of the organisation CRSA should be introduced into first. CRSA works best in non-hierarchical, non-threatening parts of the entity where the culture is open to the acknowledgment, without penalty, of control weaknesses. There are also likely to be some parts of the entity which have a greater need for CRSA in the sense that conventional internal audit review is difficult – perhaps because of the highly technical nature of the activity – but nevertheless risk is believed to be high and internal control is believed to be weak.
- Advice on the preparation of the training sessions for those who will be involved in CRSA. Internal audit involvement may go beyond an advisory role, to become the sole or principal provider of this training. Training will be needed in the principles of internal control and risk management as well as the approach to be followed in the CRSA programme.

- Review of the CRSA work completed by individual line managers and emerging from CRSA workshops.
- Facilitation of the CRSA workshops themselves.
- Guidance on the consolidation upwards of the results of CRSA, and possibly an active role in making these consolidations through to top management and the audit committee of the board.
- Advice to top management and to the audit committee as to the effectiveness of CRSA, so that they receive reliable advice on the extent to which they can rely upon the CRSA programme.
- Review of the follow up of agreed actions to be taken resulting from CRSA, though ideally responsibility for the follow up process should be with management, not with internal audit.

Management and administration of the CRSA programme by internal audit threatens a conflict of interest for internal audit. Internal auditing standards require internal audit to be independent of the activities they audit. For executive responsibility to be given to internal audit for the CRSA programme challenges internal audit independence and hence internal audit objectivity. For instance, there is the problem of the reliability of internal audit advice to top management and to the audit committee as to the effectiveness of the CRSA process if internal audit have, in effect, been championing and managing it.

### B2.2.46   Control risk self assessment as reassurance to internal audit

The results of the CRSA can be utilised by internal audit where the head of the internal auditing unit is satisfied that the quality of CRSA work means that it can be relied upon. Internal audit has always had a professional obligation to avoid duplication of audit work where the work of others can be relied upon to meet internal audit objectives at least in part. Involvement of internal audit as an advisor in the CRSA process will provide internal audit with the confidence to draw conclusions as to the effectiveness of CRSA and the extent to which it can be relied upon to meet internal audit objectives.

### B2.2.47   *Dealing with concerns about CRSA*

The concerns about CRSA are best resolved if we allow that CRSA should be an additional and *not* an alternative approach (to internal audit) to the monitoring on risk management and internal control. It is hard to be confident that management and staff, who have never been busier, can be relied upon exclusively as the mechanism for monitoring risk and control arrangements effectively.

Senior managers in several businesses have said there is no way they could entertain the introduction of CRSA if this were to involve training sessions followed by annual, participative workshop sessions. They consider their managers and staff are either too busy, or could not safely take their eyes off of real time problems for the duration, or both. For them, CRSA has to be implemented in a less demanding way – through letters of representation on internal control or through self assessment questionnaires possibly completed online through the company's network and returned to internal audit for review.

Of course, as we suggested in B2.2.42, internal control comfort letters and questionnaires may not be taken seriously – there is always a risk that they are just another document to get off the desk (or screen) as quickly as possible.

CRSA gurus propound an annual cycle for CRSA although it is not entirely clear why necessarily this should be so. Certainly, conventional forms of internal audit rarely work to a one-year cycle. Is there not a risk that staff at all levels will resent the time it takes as CRSA quickly recycles a second and a third time? If they do not resent it, they will surely find it harder to take it so seriously. On the other hand, they will become more adept at working CRSA.

It was striking that a March 1994 survey of internal auditing in the pharmaceutical sector found that eight of the twenty-two respondent companies had by then introduced CRSA with a further six then planning to set it up. A repeat survey in 1997 found CRSA present in only five surveyed companies – some indication that CRSA is not always standing the test of time.

## B2.2.48   *Objectivity*

There is also the challenge of objectivity. To what extent will managers and staff be candid about control deficiencies? Certainly CRSA works best in a culture where acknowledgment of deficiencies incurs brownie points rather than black marks. A participative workshop approach to CRSA makes it harder for a more senior member of staff to avoid unwelcome candour – particularly if the workshop is enabled by anonymous voting.

Possibly managers and staff, even with the best wills in the world, may be too close to their responsibilities to be able to assess their affairs with a high degree of objectivity or to have a clear view of their control interfaces with other business activities. But nobody would surely suggest that that they should not endeavour to do so. Here again the participative workshop approach to CRSA scores heavily over the more pedestrian letter or questionnaire-based approaches – especially if members are chosen who cut across departmental frontiers and levels.

The determination of each activity to be the subject of a participative workshop must also be done imaginatively so that it is not a mere reflection of the way the business is structured. Control is usually relatively strong within a group of people put together to work on a common or a series of closely related tasks: they very often have well developed formal procedures reinforced by informal ones as well as by a strong sense of group commitment. Control is usually weakest where there is a need for co-ordination between separate parts of the business. We need to be sure that CRSA addresses this issue – in particular through the determination of the workshops which will take place and their membership. Traditional internal auditing is also quite well placed to address this issue as internal auditors have the rare authority and opportunity to step across departmental frontiers to explore control issues wherever they spread. Even so, internal auditors prefer to audit business activities which correspond to the work responsibilities of a formal sub-division of the business – they know where to go to do the audit and which manager will take ownership of the issues raised as a result of the audit. CRSA is ideally suited to be applied to a business process which cuts across departmental frontiers, as the members of the CRSA workshop can be carefully selected to be representative of the different facets of that activity.

### B2.2.49   *The CRSA workshop*

Our preference is for a workshop to take a short working day – perhaps commencing mid-morning and ending mid-afternoon. Those invited to attend will be the key players in the different facets of the activity which is the subject of the CRSA. This does not necessarily mean that only senior staff and managers will be present – it all depends on how crucial to the activity is the work of more junior members of staff.

Anonymous voting hardware and software may be used. This can comprise of cordless key pads which allow the workshop members to vote anonymously on issues which arise during the workshop. This makes for more candid expressions of view – especially when otherwise a junior member of staff might otherwise be constrained by his or her perception of the expectations of others present at the workshop. Anonymous voting breaks through log jams and enables the workshop to make progress more quickly. But it is a mistake to believe that it allows consensus views to gel – instead it implies that the majority view prevails.

Where the cordless keypads are connected to a peripheral device of a computer which accepts the voting signals, the computer software can be organised to immediately display the results of voting anonymously using a computer projector, and to store the results so that the report of the workshop can be generated quickly and attractively after the workshop has ended.

It is likely that one or two internal auditors will facilitate the CRSA workshop – one as the main facilitator and the other to take notes.

The approach to the conduct of the workshop may entail these stages:

- brainstorm on what are the objectives for the activity which is the subject of the CRSA;
- brainstorm on what are the perceived major risks to attaining these objectives (and also the perceived major risks of unwanted consequences possibly occurring in parallel with the achievement of these objectives);
- consider whether the risk profile can be improved by, for instance, risk avoidance or risk transfer
- consider the adequacy of controls and where and how they can be improved; and
- develop an action plan to implement to proposed changes to risk and control.

A variant of this approach is to utilise a standard set of questions as the agenda of the workshop. In our experience this leads to similar workshop outcomes. A suggested list of questions was developed by CoCo and is given below at B2.2.51.

After the conclusion of the workshop, the report of the workshop is written, including the action plan. The action plan then has to be approved by senior management and it then usually falls to those who attended the CRSA workshop to implement the changes outlined in the action plan. The CRSA may be repeated 12 months later to review progress and to repeat the process.

## B2.2.50 *Conclusion*

CRSA, like the quality circles of perhaps a decade ago, has caught the mood of the times. If we dissect it we discover an amalgam of traditional practices often overlaid by modern technology. It may not last for ever. It is likely to reinvent itself – perhaps now in the form of enterprise-wide risk management. Despite the pros and cons, it is easier to espouse CRSA in principle than to give it ensuring substance in practice. But then, the effective monitoring of internal control has never been straightforward.

## B2.2.51   CoCo's Sample Assessment Questions

This is copyright of the Canadian Institute of Chartered Accountants and is reproduced with their kind permission. It formed Exhibit C of their 'Guidance on Control' [November 1995] which was Number 1 in their 'Control & Governance' series. CICA offers this, together with Number 2 'Guidance for Directors – Governance Processes for Control' [December 1995], a binder and a subscription to subsequent exposure drafts and guidance issued by their Criteria for Control (CoCo) Board.

SAMPLE ASSESSMENT QUESTIONS

To assess the effectiveness of control, an organization may find it helpful to express the criteria as questions tailored to its circumstances. The following is a simple example of questions a group might use to conduct a self assessment. They have been tailored by drawing on some of the explanatory material in this guidance ('Guidance on Control', Control and Governance No 1, (Toronto, CICA, November 1995). In each case, the answer to the question would be followed up by 'How do we know' to trigger identification and discussion of the control processes.

**Purpose**
- Do we clearly understand the mission and vision of the organization?
- Do we understand our objectives, as a group, and how they fit with other objectives in the organization?
- Does the information available to us enable us to identify risk and assess risk?
- Do we understand the risk we need to control and the degree of residual risk acceptable to those to whom we are accountable for control?
- Do we understand the policies that affect our actions?
- Are our plans responsive and adequate to achieve control?
- Do we have manageable performance targets?

**Commitment**
- Are our principles of integrity and ethical values shared and practised?

- Are people rewarded fairly according to the organization's objectives and values?
- Do we clearly understand what we are accountable for, and do we have a clear definition of our authority and responsibilities?
- Are critical decisions made by people with the necessary expertise, knowledge and authority?
- Are levels of trust sufficient to support the open flow of information and effective performance?

**Capability**
- Do we have the right people, skills, tools and resources?
- Is there prompt communication of mistakes, bad news and other information to people who need to know, without fear of reprisal?
- Is there adequate information to allow us to perform our tasks?
- Are our actions coordinated with the rest of the organization?
- Do we have the procedures and the processes to help ensure achievement of our objectives?

**Monitoring and learning**
- Do we review the internal and external environment to see whether changes are required to objectives or control?
- Do we monitor performance against relevant targets and indicators?
- Do we challenge the assumptions behind our objectives?
- Do we receive and provide information that is necessary and relevant to decision-making?
- Are our information systems up to date?
- Do we learn from the results of monitoring and make continuous improvements to control?
- Do we periodically assess the effectiveness of control?

## B2.2.52 *Business controls certificate – example wording*

**To:**     The Director of Internal Audit
            The Finance Director – Operating Group

We confirm to the best of our knowledge and belief that operations at ............................... comply with the business controls set out in the attached self-certification questionnaire except as noted. Additionally, we are not aware of any fraudulent transactions or any irregularities involving management or employees who have significant roles in the system of internal control.

General Manager/Chief Executive     Finance Director

## B2.2.53 *Letter of representation on risk management and internal control – standard form of wording*

From:   A Line Manager
To:     Internal Audit, or to: ...........................................................................

Line Manager immediately senior (copy Internal Audit), or to: ........................
The Audit Committee (copy Internal Audit) in the case of the most senior
executive management
Re.:      Representations on internal control
Date:     ..............................................................................................................

I confirm that the objectives I am responsible for achieving are clearly defined. I
acknowledge that the identification, assessment and control of risks to the achievement of these objectives, and the maintenance of effective internal control to
provide reasonable assurance of the achievement of these objectives, are amongst
my key managerial responsibilities. I am confident I understand what this entails
and have been given the necessary authority to achieve these outcomes.

I have agreed with responsible management the risk appetite which should be
applied to my area of responsibilities, and I believe I am managing operations
within these parameters.

Having monitored achievement of my objectives and the functioning of the risk
management and internal control arrangements in place within my area of responsibilities I consider that throughout 20XX risks have been satisfactorily managed
and internal control has been adequate to provide reasonable assurance of effective
and efficient operations, of internal financial control, and of compliance with laws
and regulations; and that these arrangements have been complied with in all
material respects throughout this period.

I have communicated to my staff the essential elements of an effective system of
risk management and internal control and have ensured that: (a) they are aware of
their responsibilities especially in areas of potential critical risk; and (b) they have
been empowered to operate appropriate control procedures effectively.

All staff within my area of responsibility, at all levels, have been appraised of their
duty to report upwards unresolved matters of concern about risk and control and to
deal expeditiously and effectively with such matters reported to them. In reporting
upwards, staff have been empowered, without risk of victimisation, to by-pass
intermediate levels of management where they consider this to be necessary. I have
taken appropriate steps to confirm that no matters remain unresolved as a result of
this process. All such matters drawn to my personal attention by staff have been
dealt with to my satisfaction.

No issues remain outstanding related to risk or control in my areas of my
responsibility, which have been communicated to me by internal or external audit
or by others.

I have considered whether significant changes have been made to business practices in my area of responsibility which may have impacted upon risk or weakened
internal control and believe that this is not the case. Furthermore our plans for
future change have been appraised in the context of their potential risk and internal
control impacts and I believe these issues have been addressed satisfactorily.

I am unaware of any weaknesses in risk management and internal control or irregularities in accounting practices which should be drawn to your attention.

## B2.2.54 *Self-check questionnaire on internal control for managers to use*

The questionnaire which ends this section was included in a guide to internal control for management and staff of a multinational company. We reproduce here both the guide and the questionnaire.

### B2.2.55 Internal control – a guide for management and staff

*Why internal control?*
- Four in five organisations in the UK have suffered a breakdown in their IT systems during the past two years at an annual cost of £1.2 billion and increasing. A quarter of the incidents led to serious losses.
- Age Concern, the UK's leading charity for the elderly, ground to a halt after theft of computer chips.
- In February 1995 the UK's oldest merchant bank, Barings, collapsed. When Leeson had joined Barings, he had two outstanding County Court judgments against him. Because of this record, Barings had failed to get Leeson a trading licence in the UK, but they had not disclosed his record to the Singaporean authorities. An ignored internal audit report in August 1994 had concluded that there was 'a significant general risk that the controls could be over-ridden by Nick Leeson as he is the key manager in the front and the back office'. He was also not only trading but was supervising the trading function (ie the 'front room') as well.
- On 26 September 1995, criminal complaints were filed against a rogue trader, Mr Iguchi, for running up £700m losses over 11 years in the New York trading arm of Daiwa Bank (Japan's tenth biggest commercial bank), through unauthorised trading of American Treasury bonds and falsification of the bank's books and records to conceal the losses. Mr Iguchi had been in charge of front and back office operations.

At least half of large companies are victims of fraud more than once a year, and in most cases an employee is involved. Fraud is avoidable loss due to an inadequate system of internal control. Other avoidable losses, including accidental errors or omissions, may be even more damaging, for example flood.

Internal control is not designed just to prevent these sorts of unwanted consequences. Internal control, probably designed and observed, provides *reasonable assurance* of the achievement of objectives – not an *absolute guarantee* as a business may be thrown off course by external events. Without effective internal control no enterprise is likely to achieve its objectives.

### B2.2.56 *What is internal control?*

Internal control is control by management of what happens within the business. It is *management control*.

Internal control is broadly defined as a process, effected by the entity's board of directors, management and other personnel, designed to provide reasonable assurance regarding the achievement of objectives in the following categories:

- effectiveness and efficiency of operations;
- reliability of financial reporting;
- compliance with applicable laws and regulations.

'Effectiveness and efficiency of operations' includes the safeguarding of assets, that is the prevention or timely detection of unauthorised acquisition, use or disposition of the entity's assets.

Internal control is much more than internal (cross) check. It is the totality of methods that management has introduced to provide reasonable assurance of the achievement of objectives and the avoidance of unwanted outcomes. As such, internal control is the essence of good management. The classic view of management is that it comprises effective planning, organising, staffing, directing and controlling. Each of these must be done well if there is to be effective internal control.

We can distinguish between (a) *preventative controls* designed to avoid the non-achievement of objectives or to avoid the occurrence of unwanted outcomes and (b) *detective controls* to inform management and others when things have gone wrong.

**B2.2.57**   *Practical advice on internal control*

Internal control should assist management to achieve their objectives. These objectives must be clear when an internal control framework is established.

There is no such thing as 100 per cent effective control. The allocation of additional resources to improve control may have inadequate marginal benefit. Whether that is so is a matter of management judgement in the light of:

- the importance of the objectives, and the degree of risk of not achieving them;
- the seriousness of the potential exposures, and the degree of risk of them occurring; and
- the cost, if any, of additional control measures.

Control must be cost-effective – tailored to a realistic assessment of need and appropriate for the purpose. Control will be more cost-effective if:

- complex controls are rejected in favour of simple ones which have the same control effect;
- redundant controls are jettisoned;
- compensating controls are rationalised; and
- checks are performed on *samples* where appropriate.

Much can be done in a well controlled way with no additional use of resources. For instance, dividing work between two members of staff will not necessarily be costly.

It is best to place control as early as possible within the system. Until control has been established there is a greater possibility of error or loss which may go undetected.

Where control depends upon a reconciliation of figures, the reconciliation should be performed or supervised by someone who is (a) competent and (b) independent of the generation of any of the figures which are to be reconciled.

Where control depends upon supervision it is important that this is taken seriously. Delegation is an important and valid management approach but it should not be abdication. Authority, rather than responsibility, is delegated.

A well designed system of internal control is worse than worthless unless it is complied with, since the semblance of control may lead to a false assurance. Senior management should set a good example with regard to control compliance.

While control serves a much broader purpose than the prevention and detection of fraud, this is nevertheless an important aspect. But fraud often involves the circumvention of controls through deception and/or collusion. Management and staff must be encouraged to watch out for tell-tale signs of both fraud and error.

Broadly, a 25–50–25 per cent rule applies. 25 per cent will be honest in all circumstances. 25 per cent dishonest whenever circumstances permit. 50 per cent are easily swayed. Few will be able to resist the temptation to defraud if they have an unsharable financial problem, there is opportunity and very little risk of detection, and the consequences upon detection would be modest.

We should take a lot of trouble to recruit trustworthy staff. But thereafter systems of internal control should confirm they are working in a trustworthy way. This is in the interests of staff themselves – otherwise the finger of suspicion is likely to start pointing at them. A good system of internal control reduces the opportunity for fraud and makes detection more likely. It has been said that the best form of prevention (of fraud) is detection.

*Key controls which should be in place*

**B2.2.58**    There are five necessary components of a system of internal control.

Control environment
- Commitment to competence and integrity.
- Communication of ethical values and control consciousness.
- Appropriate organisational structure.
- Appropriate delegation of authority with accountability.

Risk assessment
- Identification of key business risks in a timely manner.
- Consideration of the likelihood of risks crystallising and their likely impact.

- Prioritising allocation of resources for control.

Control activities
- Procedures to ensure completeness and accuracy of transactions, accounting, data processing and information reports.
- Appropriate authorisation limits.
- Controls to limit exposure to loss of assets or to fraud.
- Procedures to ensure compliance with laws and regulations.

Information and communication
- Performance indicators to monitor activities, risks and progress in meeting objectives.
- Systems which communicate relevant, reliable and up-to-date information.

Monitoring
- A monitoring process to give reasonable assurance to the Board of appropriate control procedures in place.
- Identification of business change which may require modification of the system of internal control.
- Formal procedures for reporting weaknesses and for ensuring appropriate corrective action.

In the following table at B2.2.61 is a checklist of some of key control issues likely to be relevant in most contexts.

**B2.2.59**   *Control risk self assessment*

Contemporary management approaches risk effective internal control. De-layering broadens the *span of supervisory control* of remaining management layers and empowers staff to make more decisions; replacing hierarchical management by project-based management may have the effect of increasing individual authority and weakening reporting.

Any process of business re-engineering must preserve the essential internal control framework both *during* the process of re-engineering (when the attention of staff to internal control matters may be diverted) and *after* processes have been re-engineered (when essential controls may have been superseded inadvertently).

In an environment of empowered staff management and staff may assume more responsibility for identifying risks and improving internal control – through a process of control risk self assessment – especially where delegation of this to internal audit results in only incomplete coverage on an annual basis.

(Also see B2.2.39 to B2.2.50.)

**B2.2.60**   *Internal control for the smaller operating unit*

In a small business there is less opportunity to rely on forms of segregation to achieve internal control at minimal or no cost. On the other hand the closeness to operations of the small unit's senior management means that they may be more sensitive to control problems as they develop. Where control cannot be achieved by segregation it has to be achieved by supervision. Parts of the supervisory control process may be automated using the computer.

It is the control risk rather than the number of staff employed which should determine the controls which are appropriate even for the operating unit which employs few people.

## B2.2.61    The questionnaire

*Key control issues*

|  |  | Yes | No |
|---|---|---|---|
| 1. | Is there shared responsibility for all important parts of the accounting system – so that absolute and independent control by any one person is avoided? |  |  |
| 2. | Have you avoided giving any one person custody or control of (a) assets (such as cash or stock), or (b) operations (such as Purchasing) – where that person *also* has involvement in accounting for those assets or operations? |  |  |
| | 2.1    If this is unavoidable, is there frequent, independent review of the accounting records? |  |  |
| 3. | Is authorisation of (a) the acquisition, use or disposal of an asset, or (b) the initiation of any operation or programme – segregated from those who have custodial or operational responsibilities for these matters? |  |  |
| 4. | Do two people always work together when handling significant qualities of cash and other attractive assets? |  |  |
| 5. | Where control depends upon a reconciliation of accounting and other data, is it always conducted by someone independent of the generation of any of the data being reconciled? |  |  |
| 6. | Have you avoided situations where a single person or department inappropriately is allowed to handle all or several phases of a transaction or operation? |  |  |
| 7. | Wherever possible is the work of one employee complementary to (ie serves as a check upon) that of another so that a continuous audit is made of the details of the business? |  |  |
| 8. | Do staff who have been assigned to segregated duties also use adequately segregated office facilities (such as office, telephone, filing cabinet, email)? |  |  |
| 9. | Do you successfully avoid staff standing in for other staff when their respective duties are meant to be segregated for control purposes? |  |  |

|  | Yes | No |
|---|---|---|
| 10.   Are authorisation limits and methods of authorisation (sole, dual, by committee, etc) appropriate to the risks involved in every case? |  |  |
| 10.1   Is 'third level' authorisation applied where risks of collusion are greatest? |  |  |
| 10.2   Is 'after the event' authorisation applied where prior authorisation may not be effective? (For instance, changes to computer-based customer credit limits may require prior authorisation; but additionally it may be helpful for a changed credit limit *not* to be applied by the computer until an appropriate manager has had it displayed on his or her screen and has approved the new value. This acts as an additional safeguard against unauthorised or invalid computer input.) |  |  |
| 11.   Is full use made of the potential of exception reports, and are these reports followed up? |  |  |
| 12.   Are physical security controls applied wherever necessary and are they satisfactory in the light of the risks involved? |  |  |
| 13.   Do personnel controls maximise the opportunities for recruiting and retaining trustworthy staff? |  |  |
| 13.1   Are procedures upon dismissal adequate to minimise the security risks associated with terminated staff? |  |  |
| 14.   Are all managers capable of supervising effectively the number of staff for which they are directly responsible? |  |  |
| 14.1   Is the supervision of contractors, suppliers etc similarly effective? |  |  |
| 15.   Are adequate records created and retained in accessible form for a sufficient period of time? |  |  |
| 16.   Is all information necessary for management control available promptly (eg no later than one-third of way thru' the next period so that timely corrective action is possible)? |  |  |
| 17.   Is there satisfactory control over who can add, delete, amend and interrogate computer-based corporate data? |  |  |
| 18.   Where appropriate, as a last resort to achieve satisfactory internal control, is certain knowledge segregated on a need to know basis? |  |  |
| 19.   Are there effective procedures to ensure the validity of payments? |  |  |
| 20.   Is there effective physical and accounting control over returns from customers, and over the payment of refunds? |  |  |
| 21.   Is there effective custody and control (including accurate accounting for) all promotional vouchers (and other 'accountable documents' with potential value)? |  |  |
| 22.   Is the control over non-standard transactions effective? |  |  |

|  | | Yes | No |
|---|---|---|---|
| 23. | Are all staff required to take their holidays? | | |
| | 23.1 Do all staff take at least one holiday of at least two weeks' duration each year? | | |
| | 23.2 Are duties re-assigned to other staff when staff are on holiday? | | |
| 24. | Is excessive dependence upon key members of staff avoided? | | |
| | 24.1 In every case are there substitute staff ready to step in promptly to perform competently the duties of staff who become unavailable? | | |
| 25. | Are duties rotated where appropriate? | | |
| 26. | Is original documentation (such as expenses vouchers) required to support claims – to avoid the risk of multiple presentation? | | |
| 27. | Is all documentation stamped appropriately – eg with 'Date Received' or with a cancellation stamp? | | |
| 28. | Are there adequate arrangements to protect corporate data and data processing? | | |
| | 28.1 Where appropriate, are they tested? | | |
| 29. | Are there adequate arrangements to protect corporate data and data processing? | | |
| | 29.1 Where appropriate, are they tested? | | |
| 30. | Are all important procedures fully documented? | | |
| | 30.1 Are the procedures known to those who apply them? | | |
| | 30.2 Is the documentation of procedures kept up-to-date? | | |
| 31. | Is there an effective internal audit with unrestricted scope and unrestricted rights of access? | | |

[132] Vide, eg IBM, BP.

# B2.2.62 Balancing 'control by segregation' with 'control by supervision'

With so much focus on developing new and better approaches to management, there is always a risk that we jettison more traditional approaches which were serving essential purposes. Our contemporary fascination with enterprise risk management has given us an excuse to move away from systematic, detailed control of the affairs of our organisations. Even auditors, with their risk-based approaches, have moved away from obtaining audit assurance through the detailed verification of transactions. Whether in the application of control procedures within businesses or in the detailed testing of transactions by auditors – both are now too boring to be expected of staff or auditors. We have moved away from the suggestion that internal auditors should, over time, systematically audit all the operations of an entity in case major risks might be concealed in what appear to top management to be low risk areas. In making this move we are introducing a new risk. Of course the spin is that there are now new and better ways of mitigating risk

– whether to the achievement of corporate objectives or to the completion of high quality audits – and that risk assessment and risk mitigation can itself be systematic.

Conventional wisdom is now that everything has its price. It is argued that it is reasonable to knowingly and intentionally leave a level of residual risk within any system if the cost of so doing will not be too great. We design and market new products and services having factored into the price of the products or services an overhead charge to cover the cost of the frauds and other avoidable losses which we have calculated will occur. We now have only an overall and sweeping rather than a detailed commitment to control. We also create a moral hazard for our staff, our business partners and those who interface with us as suppliers or customers, and a situation where the cost of fraud and avoidable losses is escalating to become a significant part of GDP. When people have more opportunity to behave unethically, unethical behaviour becomes more attractive and commonplace. It is our belief that entities should be required by regulation to undertake a fraud and loss stress test on new products and services before launch. Where there is a responsibility there should be matching accountability – otherwise irresponsibility creeps in. So we also believe that entities should be required to report of their anti-fraud measures and their control philosophy and approach. We do not consider that the current requirements to report on internal control go far enough in this regard.

Contemporary attitudes to risk presume we can calculate the future costs of going live with incompletely controlled systems. It also presumes that better controls mean more cost – which need not be the case.

Risk assessment is shot through with subjective, unreliable judgements. It is almost always largely a matter of judgement whether we identify and measure risks correctly. Important though contemporary approaches to enterprise risk management are, too much confidence is being placed upon them. We need to get back to basics.

In the context of fraud prevention and fraud detection but also from the perspective of every other objective of internal control, it is helpful to consider that satisfactory control arrangements are likely to comprise an appropriate amalgam of different forms of what we may call 'segregation' (or 'separation') on the one hand, and different forms of 'supervision' on the other hand. If effective control cannot be achieved by taking advantage of opportunities for segregation, then more resort must be made to supervisory controls. Usually both will be needed, depending upon the circumstances.

Fraud is, in one sense, a form of breakdown in the system of control, a deliberate form of avoidable error and loss. Segregation and supervision controls will bear down upon accidental breakdowns in the system as well as fraudulent ones.

Segregation controls have the advantage that they are often, but not always, *preventative* rather than *detective* in nature, they prevent or deter frauds from occurring rather more than detecting them after they have occurred. Supervisory controls are preventative and detective in nature; preventative because the fact of supervision encourages staff to undertake their duties responsibly; detective because the act of supervision should detect errant performance by staff. Of course, supervision should be timely so that detection occurs before it is too late to achieve rectification.

Segregation and supervisory control approaches do much more than prevent or detect avoidable losses (whether fraudulent or not) by mitigating the likelihood and impact of these unwanted outcomes. They should also always be part of the approach that an entity adopts to give it reasonable assurance of the achievement of goals and execution of strategies successfully. Of course, serious losses can impact drastically on the achievement of objectives: the failure of Barings to segregate their back office from their front office, which led to the collapse of Barings, illustrates how this may be so. But objectives and strategies are not achieved merely by the avoidance of unwanted outcomes: every entity needs to be geared up to perform positively in order to achieve intended outcomes. Segregation and supervisory controls can aid in this significantly. Some forms of segregation are associated with specialisation in the division of work, which is often a more productive way of organising work. Of course, quality supervision also contributes to the achievement of objectives by inspiring and developing staff.

Segregation controls may not cost anything to administer, it may be just a matter of organising how tasks are performed so that segregation controls are standard aspects of working practices. So it is not necessarily true that control has to be costly. Certainly the absence of control is likely to be more costly. It is too simplistic to argue that internal control must be cost effective; it is often impossible to quantify the costs and benefits of control; it is often impossible to anticipate the damage that may ensue from a breakdown in internal control. Effective control in some contexts, such as within the nuclear industry, has to be a *sine qua non* almost regardless of what it costs.

While segregation controls may not be costly, on the other hand supervisory controls invariably entail an overhead as they represent an extra task (or tasks) to be performed. They also have the disadvantage of being no more effective that the diligence of those entrusted to undertake the supervision. Too often 'delegation' is interpreted as 'abdication' and staff are just left to get on with things in an unsupervised way. Supervision entails conscious, defined activity. While authority can be delegated, to staff who therefore acquire their own responsibilities, it is sound to consider that responsibility is never delegated, only shared. So a failure by a junior member of staff to whom authority has been delegated is a failure of more senior staff who retain the overall responsibility even though the execution of the task has been delegated. It should rarely be regarded as acceptable for senior staff to attempt to avoid responsibility for an operational failure on the grounds that they are responsible for 'policy' not 'operations'.

Segregation and supervision controls may depend upon people to execute them, or they may be incorporated into IT systems. One person's work may be reconciled to another person's work manually or by using IT. Two segregated IT systems may produce output which is reconciled by a third IT system, or manually. Often segregation and supervisory controls are part IT-based and part people-based. For instance software may produce an exception report which must be followed-up by a supervisor.

Where resort has to be made to supervision to achieve control, it is usually necessary to ensure that the supervisory function has a sufficient degree of independence from the execution of the task being supervised.

Applying segregation and supervision approaches to the achievement of control can assist in the achievement of financial, operational and compliance control objectives. Financial control is the control over the reliability of financial information used within the business and for publication. Operational control is to do with assurance that operations are executed efficiently and effectively. Compliance control objectives are to do with ensuring adherence to regulations and laws.

In the table at B2.2.75 we provide a classification of different available forms of segregation, and we offer a few further words of explanation here.

## B2.2.63   *Segregation of duties*

Sometimes our 'segregation of operations' (see B2.2.65) is alternatively termed 'segregation of duties'. Here, by 'segregation of duties' we mean that some very sensitive tasks will be better controlled if they are shared between more than one person, so that one person acts as an observer of, and a semi-automatic check over, the work of the other person. This also has the benefit of the business avoiding becoming excessively dependent upon one key member of staff. The 'downside' of this sort of control is that the business is entrusting control sensitive knowledge to a wider spread of staff.

### B2.2.64   Segregation of fundamental responsibilities

Control will be improved if certain original operations are segregated from authorisation and both of these should be segregated from accounting. We call this a matter of making sure that fundamental responsibilities are segregated. Some of these original operations will be custodial in nature, such as the cashier function which keeps custody over cash, or the storekeeper who is custodian of stores. Other original operations are not custodial, for instance 'purchasing'. Control will be strengthened, for instance, if the person who authorises a purchase is different from the person who places the purchase order with the supplier, and both of these people should have nothing to do with accounting in the books of account for any aspect of the purchase. If this fundamental segregation is not followed, control will be weaker unless compensated by other appropriate segregation or supervision controls. One of the most frequent breaches of this segregation control is where managers have the authority to incur expenditure up to certain limits, so long as it is within their budget, without recourse to a purchasing officer to place the purchase with a supplier.

### B2.2.65   Segregation of operations

Some other operations are incompatible with each other in the sense that they should not be undertaken by the same person or section. For instance, it is widely held that control is improved if selling is segregated from credit control; or if IT systems development is segregated from IT operations. If this is not done, then supervisory controls will need to be relied upon more. For instance, one company allows sales staff to flex the levels of credit advanced to customers in order to maximise sales and because of the sales staff's local knowledge of their clients. But to compensate for the control weakness thereby created, the credit decisions of the sales staff are reviewed regularly (ie 'supervised') by a credit committee. Many companies have risk committees which review the levels of risk being taken by operational management.

### B2.2.66   Segregation of staff

This means of control refers to the need to ensure that the control effect of segregating operations is not negated by the reality of the situation. For instance, do staff engaged in segregated operations inappropriately share the same office, the same telephone or the same filing cabinet or computer, or inappropriately overhear what is happening in another operation which should be segregated from their work? Does one member of staff substitute for another during the latter's absence, and thereby engage in a task incompatible with their main operational tasks? Does one member of staff have a special personal relationship with another member of staff who is mainly engaged in other operations which should be segregated? And so on. It is not always possible to avoid these sorts of control weaknesses, but they should be identified and compensated for, by other segregation controls or by supervision, or both.

### B2.2.67   Segregation of data

Centralised databases require software walls to be built to restrict who is able to add, change, delete or merely use each item of data. This applies within a business and also to prevent hacking from outside, for which firewalls are important. Within a business it is necessary to define at the design stage of a database who needs the authority to add, change, delete or use each item of data to be held on the database and then to design the controls of the system to achieve these restrictions. Principally, control is achieved via a secure system of password access which restricts the access that individuals have to computer programs and to parts of the corporate database. Protocols should restrict the access of computer program modules to those parts of the database which those program modules should be expected to need to access, and should also restrict what activity the program modules can engage in with respect to the parts of the database which they are authorised to access. Individual computers on a network can be restricted to which computer programs on the network they can use, so, for instance, a computer in the payroll department would be barred from accessing computer-based customer records.

### B2.2.68   Segregation of bookkeeping steps

Control will be improved if certain bookkeeping steps are segregated from other bookkeeping steps. An example might be the posting of a credit from the posting of a debit on a personal account.

PC-based accounting systems often make the segregation of bookkeeping steps a matter which is honoured more in the breach than in the observance. Where this is the case, businesses need to be aware of the risks they are running and to endeavour to compensate through the application of alternative segregation and supervisory controls.

### B2.2.69 Segregation of data entry

This is similar to segregating bookkeeping steps, but applicable to an IT environment.

For instance, an example might be the posting of an original entry from the posting of a correcting entry. It has been shown that many IT frauds involve the submission of fraudulent input data and that this fraudulent data is often incorporated into input data which has earlier been rejected as invalid and which is then 'corrected' for resubmission in a fraudulent way. Many businesses have tighter controls over the initial generation and submission of input data than over the correction and resubmission of input data which had earlier been rejected.

Sometimes a deliberate but innocent-looking error in input data can induce its rejection in order to facilitate its fraudulent alteration prior to resubmission. The risk of this can be avoided if the posting of an original entry is segregated from the posting of a corrected entry of that type. This also serves as a check on the quality of work of the staff who generated this data in the first place.

### B2.2.70 'Segregation' of authority to commit the business

If authority to commit the business is vested in a sole individual, control will not be so strong as if it is dual authority (vested in two people). Control may be stronger still if authority to commit is vested in one person but has to be reviewed *ex post* by a supervisor or an independent person. Where authority to commit is vested in a committee it is likely to be stronger still. The best controlled situation is where nobody has authority to commit the business!

Applying the appropriate means to commit the business is not enough on its own to achieve effective control. What is also needed are established and applied authority limits coupled to the appropriate means of authority to commit the business.

### B2.2.71 'Segregation' of time

Intelligent use of time, especially by building in considered delays, can improve control. For instance, it may be satisfactory to delay delivery of goods or services until a cheque has cleared. Computer terminal 'log off after time out' is another example. Time locks on safes or on access to other secure areas is yet another example. Barring client computers from accessing a server outside anticipated working hours may assist in preventing unauthorised activity on a computer network, and so on.

Rotating duties deters fraud if it is known to be company policy, as it makes it more likely that it will be detected. Closely related to this is a policy of transferring supervisors and managers between operating units every two or three years, where feasible.

Where staff work in pairs, as for instance in some delivery contexts, periodic changes in the pairing can be expected to enhance control as it reduces the risk of collusion occurring or continuing.

It is notable that many frauds come to light when the defrauding employee is absent, making the point that it is wise to insist that employees take at least one holiday of two weeks' duration each year. While they are away, their duties should be undertaken by a substitute. We should be wary of the employee who always comes in during their annual vacation on the pretext that they are indispensable, or 'just to check up that everything is okay'.

### B2.2.72   Segregation of knowledge

As a last resort, restricting knowledge on 'a need to know basis' will reduce the number of people who are informed about the control weaknesses within our systems, and thus who potentially are able to exploit those weaknesses. This may be both necessary and acceptable if we know that our systems in certain respects are inherently vulnerable to dishonesty in ways that cannot be rectified easily or at all, or at least have not been rectified.

But restricting knowledge often has unacceptable dysfunctional effects, and should therefore be regarded as a last resort when other forms of satisfactory control are not available. One dysfunctional effect is that staff are less able to use their initiative if they are restricted in what they know and understand. Another is the de-motivational impact.

### B2.2.73   Segregation of 'operation' from 'review'

The monitoring (review) of control is an essential part of internal control, and needs to be done objectively. Independence of review from operations (as with a properly set up internal audit function) facilitates the achievement of this. Internal auditors cannot review with sufficient objectivity the operation of tasks which fall within their own remit to execute. One of the insidious mistakes that management often makes is to entrust to internal audit the execution of particularly control sensitive tasks, on the basis that internal auditors may be regarded, not always correctly, as trustworthy and as having sufficient independence to be able to conduct those important control-sensitive tasks objectively. This is counter-productive as it deprives those tasks from being audited effectively by internal audit.

The test to apply is whether internal audit is charged with the responsibility to execute anything which needs to be done for the business to function satisfactorily on a routine basis. If such is the case then, by definition, internal audit has responsibility for a task which is incompatible with its audit role. This would also be counter-productive as it would dilute management's own sense of responsibility for administering key controls, on the basis that they could leave it to the internal auditors, which of course they cannot safely do.

## B2.2.74 Postscript on segregation

Empowerment, downsizing and delayering have all made inroads into the traditional approaches to control set out in this article. Businesses today are more willing to take risks with control, often with calamitous results, in pursuit of enhanced performance. They do not see it as a matter of taking undue risks: they rationalise their approach as being a matter of establishing a control regime which is risk-based. The challenge is to make a realistic assessment of risk, and not to use the risk assessment as a pretext for cutting the investment in control to unacceptable levels.

## B2.2.75 Table: Control by segregation (ie 'separation')

| | Type of segregation | Comments | Examples |
|---|---|---|---|
| 1. | **Duties** | Ensuring that control sensitive tasks are shared by two people who act as a cross check on each other, and excessive dependence on one member of staff is avoided. | Issuance of new passwords; or database administration; or credit control. |
| 2. | **Fundamental responsibilities** | Originating operations *from* authorisation of acquisition or use *from* accounting. | Cashier function *from* authorising use or replenishment of cash *from* accounting for cash; or storekeeping *from* authorising use; or replenishment of stores *from* accounting for cash; or (eg) purchasing *from* accounting *from* authorisation. |
| 3. | **Operations** | Separating out organisationally the execution of other incompatible activities which are incompatible with each other from a control perspective. | Sales *from* credit control; or IT programming *from* IT operations; etc. |
| 4. | **Staff** | Making sure that the impact of segregating 'fundamental responsibilities' and 'operations' is not invalidated by staffing arrangements. | For instance when staff engaged on segregated operations share the same office/phone/filing cabinet/computer; or staff are substituted by others who are usually engaged on segregated activities; or staff are transferred to segregated tasks. |

|  | Type of segregation | Comments | Examples |
|---|---|---|---|
| 5. | **Data** | Centralised databases require electronic walls between different parts of the corporate database to prevent unauthorised access by staff and outsiders which might violate other segregation controls. | No staff should be able to access their payroll record. |
| 6. | **Bookkeeping** | Internal control will be improved by segregating certain bookkeeping operations. | Posting of debits *from* posting of credits on personal accounts. |
| 7. | **Data entry** | Consider whether the authority that individuals have to enter computer data has the effect of violating any of the segregation controls which are being replied upon. | Since many IT frauds are instigated by modifying data which has been rejected due to error, make sure that the correction and resubmission of rejections is performed by someone other than the staff member who entered the original data which was rejected. |
| 8. | **Means of authority to commit the company** | Authority to commit the entity is under progressively stronger control, as follows:<br><br>• vested in a sole individual;<br>• dual authority;<br>• sole authority, with prior approval at a higher level; and<br>• by committee. | Capital investments above a certain level are approved by a committee of the board on the recommendation of the executive. |
| 9. | **Time** | Time delays within processes may improve control if defects may possibly reveal themselves after a short time.<br>Rotation of duties means that the work of one person will, in time, be subjected to the attention of another, making it less likely that fraud will be concealed, and thus deterring its perpetration.<br>A compulsory holiday of a fortnight's duration at least once a year, with duties being understudied by another member of staff during the absence on holiday. | Delay delivery until the cheque has cleared; or one clerk looks after one set of customer accounts for a month or two before exchanging these accounts with those of another clerk. |
| 10. | **Knowledge** | Segregation of knowledge on a 'need to know basis'. This should be a last resort when other forms of control are not available, since it restricts the extent that staff can take an intelligent interest in the affairs of the business and tends to reduce job satisfaction and motivation. | Access to IT program documentation. Security code to activate a process. |

|  | Type of segregation | Comments | Examples |
|---|---|---|---|
| 11. | **Review from operations** | Those responsible for review should not have operational responsibilities for what they review. | Internal audit should not design or operate systems. |

## B2.2.76 Internal control when activities are outsourced

Outsourcing means business objectives are more dependent on suppliers and service providers than ever before. Investment institutions rely on custodians; businesses rely on internet service providers; environmentally managed businesses depend on the responsibility of their suppliers – and so on.

Throughout the 1990s standard-setting and other bodies have been active in defining internal control and its necessary components, its evaluation and its reporting. Undoubtedly this has enhanced our appreciation of internal control in the contemporary environment.

One major contribution has been to develop approaches to reviewing and reporting upon internal control. At a more fundamental level has been the development of definitions of internal control and explanations of its characteristics which have been more in harmony with modern business needs and practices. It is not that the older definitions and insights were wrong – just that they did not overtly refer to matters which became important since those definitions and insights were developed.

### B2.2.77 An altered definition for changing times

B2.2.1 to B2.2.24 traces the development of internal control concepts and definitions. The replacement of the 1948 AICPA definition of internal control by the 1992 COSO definition in particular has had a profound impact. This impact has particularly been felt in the more acute appreciation that risk assessment (while COSO termed this 'risk assessment', the Rutteman guidance (commendably succinct in other respects) preferred 'identification of risks and control objectives') is an essential component of any system of internal control. The subsequent contemporary and ubiquitous development of business risk consulting groups in most large professional firms has been a direct consequence. Of equal impact has been the overt recognition that monitoring (the Rutteman guidance termed this 'monitoring and corrective action') is also an essential component of internal control – a focus which could be claimed to be closely linked to the developing interest in controls assurance reports and control opinion assignments.

The COSO definition has also captured for the first time the sense that internal control is a dynamic 'process' rather than an inert state of affairs; that it is a collaborative responsibility not just of management but also of the board and other personnel; and that it provides reasonable assurance, though not an absolute guarantee, of the achievement of objectives.

Clearly, these sentiments, encapsulated within the COSO internal control definition, have caught the mood of the times, but the phrasing of the definition in this way has also arguably contributed to giving these sentiments more expression in reality. We are suggesting that the wording of definitions can influence, not merely reflect, practice. For instance there has been considerable post-1992 stress on the overall responsibilities of the board for internal control. There is now also more emphasis in practice upon the contribution that members of staff other than management can and should make to the development of more effective systems of internal control – for instance through their participation in control risk self assessment workshops.

## B2.2.78   *Post-1992 COSO*

Whether in the past the evolution of internal control definitions has given the impetus to the development of new practices or *vice versa* is a mute point. In reality it has probably been a bit of both. The new pronouncements have caught the tide of events and shaped them. The same will happen again.

Now, there is a need for a further evolution, beyond COSO, in internal control definition and emphasis – which will lead to a further wave of developments – including the development of professional pronouncements to take account of this new focus and perhaps a fresh orientation and designation for internal control specialists in the large professional firms (the 'business risk' designation becoming passé already).

It was remarkable that the AICPA internal control definition of 1948 survived for 44 years. It is true that it was modified a little before its passing. It does seem that the life of the 1992 COSO definition will be shorter, very influential though it has been.

COSO and Rutteman overlooked *external* internal control – the need to control what happens 'outside' the entity which contributes to the achievement of the entity's objectives. The COSO text which supports the COSO internal control definition similarly overlooks the externalities of internal control.

Take, for instance, these abstracts from COSO:

> 'Internal control is effected by a board of directors, management and other personnel in an entity. It is accomplished by the people of an organization, by what they do and say. People establish the entity's objectives and put control mechanisms in pace.' (*Internal Control – Integrated Framework* ('The COSO Report'), 'Framework' volume, p11.)

> 'Control environment – The core of any business is its people – their individual attributes, including integrity, ethical values and competence – and the environment in which they operate. They are the engine that drives the entity and the foundation on which everything rests.' (COSO, 'Framework' volume, p12.)

> 'The control environment sets the tone of an organisation, influencing the control consciousness of its people. It is the foundation for all other components of internal control, providing discipline and structure. Control environment factors include the integrity, ethical values and competence of the entity's people; management's philosophy and operating style; the way management assigns authority and

responsibility, and organises and develops its people; and the attention and direction provided by the board of directors.' (COSO, 'Framework' volume, p19.)

It is not that the COSO definitions are inconsistent with the fact that some internal control is 'external' to the entity. The same can be said of Rutteman. It is more a matter that the COSO and Rutteman definitions and discussions largely or completely overlook that such is the case and therefore do not address the issue. For instance, companies' codes of business conduct and, where applicable, codes of ethical (or scientific) conduct should enjoin contractors and other business partners to observe the same principles and approaches as those that apply to in-house personnel.

There is increasing reliance on external providers contributing to the achievement of an entity's objectives and the internal control implications of this need to be addressed openly.

## B2.2.79   *What is 'external' internal control?*

By external control we mean the internal control which takes place, at least in part, outside the entity itself. A key issue is whether controls within supplier organisations can be regarded as either (a) outside an entity's system of internal control as they function within the supplier organisation, or (b) of no concern to the entity for other reasons. This would be likely to be the case if one or more of the following applies:

- the goods or services supplied did not contribute to the achievement of the entity's objectives – which would be very unlikely;
- the goods or services being supplied were commodities whose quality is always standard or readily discernible before supply;
- alternative sources of supply were readily available which would be satisfactory with regard to quality, delivery, etc;
- internal control mechanisms within the entity were a satisfactory alternative to internal control procedures within the supplier organisation with respect to safeguarding the quality of goods or services being supplied, in that they permit or ensure the detection and rectification (without significant disruption or cost, and without significant impediment to the achievement of the entity's objectives) of substandard provision.

It is entirely mistaken to regard the controls within the supplier organisation as *external* controls. 'External control' is control by the stakeholders – often principally the shareholders – over management. Internal control is management control – the arrangements that management puts in place and operates to give the entity reasonable assurance of the achievement of objectives.

From an outsourced supplier's perspective, the control that their client exercises over their affairs may be regarded as external control over the supplier; but from the client's perspective it is part of their internal control. This may apply to some extent even to the supply of what may appear, *prima facie*, to be commodity products. For instance, B&Q, Marks and Spencer, Bodyshop and others are famous for their monitoring of what happens within their suppliers' businesses as it impacts upon the achievement of their own objectives. In reality these are not commodity supplies as their special characteristics cannot be relied upon without client involvement which is likely to include supplier monitoring by the client.

Many corporate objectives are planned, direct commercial outcomes. Other objectives are indirect: stories are rife of western multinationals whose images and even businesses have been tarnished by exploitative labour practices within their supplier organisations.

### B2.2.80   JIT

JIT (just in time management) makes businesses more dependent on internal controls in their suppliers' businesses, and the integration of those controls with the entity's own controls.

### B2.2.81   Outsourcing

The allure of outsourcing is hard to resist. It makes the entity smaller at its core, easier for it to change direction, easier in many other respects to manage, often easier for management to vary production to match demand, and with a smaller fixed overhead cost. In addition, there is the presumption that outsourcing will be to a specialist provider who can offer better value for money than the in-house alternative, and thus contribute to the bottom line.

Against the allure of outsourcing must be set the overhead, and sometimes the impracticality, of putting in place mechanisms to monitor the internal controls within the supplier entities. Where these mechanisms are impractical, the entity has, in effect, lost control and for security reasons the activity should not have been outsourced.

There is a general trend towards outsourcing anything that is not 'core'. We would define 'core' as being the business activities which should be kept in-house because they can be done better (more economically, efficiently or effectively) in-house, or because they need to be kept in-house for security reasons. Security considerations include the long term viability of outsourcing a service, the future difficulties of bringing it back in-house, and the extent to which outsourcing weakens the entity for instance by stripping out in-house systems, staff resources and skills. Anything else is a candidate to be outsourced to a provider who can perform the service more economically or more effectively – often because the provider specialises in that provision. It is a major challenge for a business to determine what is 'core' – what it can do as well as or better than outside providers. To continue to keep in-house what is not 'core' is a recipe for medium to long term decline.

The issue of outsourcing is of course not new: businesses have always had suppliers. But what is new is the *extent* of outsourcing of many non-core activities which have traditionally been regarded as being close to the heart of the business; and the *extent* to which many basic business service functions (such as accounting, IT services, internal auditing) have become candidates for outsourcing. There are internal control implications here as more and more of the essential internal controls of an entity may be designed, operated and monitored by new-style suppliers who may be providing similar services to many other entities.

### B2.2.82 Outsourcing checklist

- Do the tender document and the subsequent contract specify an adequate minimum standard of service, and ensure that unanticipated contingencies will be serviced effectively?
- Are the contracting procedures for outsourcing adequate to ensure the contractor is selected objectively, and are these procedures followed?
- Is it evident that contracted out services are value-for-money?
- Has management considered, and are management managing, the security risk associated with utilisation of outsiders for contracted out work?
- Is contracted out work periodically market tested so as to ensure the service is provided competitively?
- Are all services currently performed by in-house personnel considered on an impartial basis for market testing?
- Has management and the board a clear strategic grasp of what is its core activity/ies which are not to be regarded as candidates for outsourcing?
- Is partial outsourcing (whereby contract staff work alongside in-house staff) rationally considered as an option wherever it may be applicable?
- Is contracting-out leading to excessive dependence on one supplier, and does management and the board regularly consider this risk?
- Does management review the discharge of contracts for outsourced services with a view to learning lessons from cost overruns, etc?

### B2.2.83 *Internal auditing for the outsourced entity*

In a highly outsourced entity it may be more likely that internal auditing along with many other key business activities has been outsourced. The entity then needs to consider whether it has lost control. There may be special vulnerabilities in outsourcing the review of internal control over other outsourced activities.

Through the outsourcing of so many non-core processes we are seeing the transfer of more of the internal control system to outside the core business. Third party reviews of internal control, arranged by outsourced suppliers on behalf of their clients, will become more important, but are often inadequate. Amongst the potential defects of third party reviews are that they may be conducted at an inappropriate time from the perspective of the party that needs to rely on the third party review. They are likely to be conducted with inadequate awareness on the part of the reviewer of the controls which are important to a particular entity that needs to rely on the third party review: this being so because the entity may have considerable discretion as to the extent to which it achieves internal control in-house (via the inputs to, and outputs from, the service provider) or relies on internal controls within the service organisation.

An entity must negotiate rights of audit access to a service provider at the pre-contract stage. The wording and content of service level agreements becomes very important. The development of collaborative systems which integrate the businesses of the entity with that of the service provider may be an effective way of addressing many of the internal control challenges of reliance upon service providers. Of course, collaborative systems have to be designed with care as they need to integrate in a controlled way with the already existing systems of the various parties.

As a last resort, the risks associated with making significant use of service providers may be covered by insurance. Care should be taken to ensure that necessary insurance cover is in place. It is all too easy to assume without checking that a service provider has appropriate classes of sufficient insurance cover in place.

## B2.2.84 *Contractors and joint ventures*

Much outsourcing is to do with the provision of services which, while often important, are ancilliary to the main mission of the entity. The provision of inputs, such as materials or sub-assemblies would be examples. Even the outsourcing of IT and accounting services might fall into this category.

Other outsourcing occurs when the entity entrusts to another the responsibility of interfacing with the customer. For instance, a financial institution might entrust the administration of a mortgage book, including collections, to another. UK Training & Enterprise Councils usually subcontracted with training companies and others to deliver many of the training programmes which the TECs were under contract with government to deliver.

Where the performance and management of key relationships with 'end clients' is entrusted to outsourced service providers, it is usually particularly important that the monitoring of internal control within the service providers' businesses is not neglected. Thus, for instance, TECs instituted a special FAM (Financial Appraisal and Management) audit to evaluate the standard of service provision of their contractors.

Joint ventures are a special case. A useful publication by the Institute of Internal Auditors Research Foundation ('Internal audit involvement in the joint-venture process'[133]) points out that reporting and review mechanisms such as internal audit or independent auditor review should be specified within the terms of the legal agreement of the joint venture, and might cover the following.

- What areas or activities are to be audited?
- What are the record-retention guidelines, including audit working papers retention?
- Type and timing of notice required prior to the start of the audit.
- Communication channel for audit status and subsequent audit findings.
- Statement on use of auditing standards (eg the Institute of Internal Auditors).
- Responsibility assignment for corrective action of audit findings.

An SRI International Report[134] drew attention to *two* critical areas for joint venture monitoring:

- the joint venture activities; and
- the partner(s) in the joint venture.

## B2.2.85  *The importance of customers*

Here we have been assuming that 'external' internal control is within the supplier organisations of the entity. Thought should be given to whether the internal control within the customer organisations of the entity may not also be relevant. Where vertical integration is quite complete then sources of supply and outlets for products and services may be more under control – though often at a cost. Even where there is no vertical integration, the entity should be concerned about the reliability of all organisations in the chain.

Entities may also need to be concerned about the quality of internal control in organisations which are not, directly or indirectly, suppliers or customers of the entity.

## B2.2.86  *Millennium risk*

At the time of the 'millennium challenge' there were concerns about the possible breakdown of public infrastructure systems. We would generally characterise these types of risk as being external, but they are nevertheless risks to the achievement of corporate objectives; and systems of internal control are intended to provide reasonable assurance of the achievement of objectives.

The reliance that entities had upon software and hardware suppliers with regard to 'millennium compliance' was an example of how businesses achieve their objectives, or fail to do so, through dependence upon control within supplier entities; and the difficulties of assessing the compliance characteristics of supplied hardware and software. The millennium challenge was much broader than this, and illustrated vividly the extent to which the achievement of corporate objectives is dependent upon what happens external to the entity – in telecoms, electricity supply, public transport systems and so on (vide, eg The Year 2000 Issue – Supplementary Guidance for Auditors, The Auditing Practices Board, June 1998).

## B2.2.87  *Internal control in cyberspace*

With the galloping development of the use of the internet for business purposes, how we develop satisfactory monitoring of our internal control arrangements which exist within cyberspace now represents a particularly acute challenge. Just as with in-house computer systems, we are sure a 'black box' approach of auditing around the internet system will not be adequate. The 'black box' approach to monitoring depends upon matching output with input so as to conclude that nothing has gone wrong within the system. It is a tempting approach when it is difficult to review the system itself. The best the 'black box' approach can achieve is to indicate that nothing observable has gone wrong *to date*: it provides virtually no assurance that the system is sufficiently controlled to prevent things from going wrong tomorrow. The 'black box' approach may therefore have the potential to provide more audit assurance for the external auditor of historical financial statements than for the internal auditor of internal control as it is operating currently and can be expected to operate in the future. The Institute of Internal Auditors has produced a useful guide to internet security[135].

### B2.2.88   *Scope of directors' public reports on internal control when internal control is outsourced*

A related issue is whether controls within supplier organisations are beyond the scope of the directors' public reports on internal control. For the UK, the current scope requirement is to report on internal control over the *whole* of the business for the *whole* of the period under review, though in the US, under the SEC interpretation of Sarbanes-Oxley, it is 'point of time' reporting. It is idiosyncratic if a policy of outsourcing should radically alter the scope of the directors' report – but this issue has not been tackled head-on in the guidance which has been developed.

### B2.2.89   *Conclusions*

A root and branch revamp of our definitions and expositions of internal control is needed. To date, standard setting and other bodies are addressing 'external' internal control in a piecemeal way. For instance, ICAEW's Audit Faculty has revised its guidance on reporting on the internal controls of investment custodians to third parties.[136]

The APB's excellent briefing paper on providing assurance on internal control[137] described a framework for forming an opinion on the effectiveness of internal control suitable for reporting to third parties on internal control adequacy. The framework illustrated the separate elements of an engagement to provide assurance on internal control, the range of considerations that apply to each process, and, consequently, the inherent complexity of engagements to provide assurance about the effectiveness of internal control. APB's publication on audit evidence considerations when an entity uses a service organisation was useful but entirely from the external audit angle.[138]

---

133   'Internal audit involvement in the joint-venture process', (1990): The Institute of Internal Auditors' Research Foundation, 249 Maitland Avenue, Altamonte Springs, Florida 32701–4201; ISBN 0–89413-208–3.

134   Marina Gorbis and Karen York *Strategic partnerships: a new corporate response* 'SRI International' Report 730, Winter 1985–86.

135   Kaplan, Jim, (2000): 'The auditor's guide to internet resources', 2nd edition; The Institute of Internal Auditors Inc, USA; 'www.theiaa.org'.

136   *Reports on Internal Controls of Investment Custodians Made Available to Third Parties, Audit Faculty Technical Release* FRAG 21/94 (Revised); available from The Audit Faculty, Chartered Accountants' Hall, PO Box 433, Moorgate Place, London, EC2P 2BJ (Tel: 0171 920 8526; Fax: 0171 638 6009). The Audit Faculty of the Institute of Chartered Accountants in England and Wales issued this revised 17-page Technical Release in September 1997 to assist reporting accountants who are requested to report in accordance with the framework for reporting which is set out in this Release. The Release points out that increased usage of reports on internal controls in this area has resulted in the recipients identifying more precisely the information they need, and that at the same time reporting accountants have gained experience in assessing

the risks to them of issuing reports that relate to what are often very significant levels of customer assets. The Release provides an illustrative report and also an attachment of illustrative tests performed by the reporting accountants. While the Release stresses that the latter should not be regarded as a specimen work programme, both the latter and the former will undoubtedly be valuable for those who need to construct their own internal control review programmes to cover this important area.

[137] Providing assurance on the effectiveness of internal control (July 2001), The Auditing Practices Board, £5.50 each, post-free from ABG Professional Information, PO Box 21375. London, WC1N 1QP. Tel: +44 (0)20 7920 8991. Fax: +44 (0)20 7920 8992. E-mail: info@abgpublications.co.uk.

[138] Audit evidence when an entity uses a service organisation, Statement on Auditing Standards No. 480, The Auditing Practices Board, April 1998, 15 pps, £5, Accountancy Books, PO Box 620, Central Milton Keynes, MK9 2JX. Tel: + 44 (0)1908 248000.

## B2.2.90    The scope of corporate governance and the role of internal audit in corporate governance

The board of directors is at the heart, or the pivotal point, of corporate governance.

Looking one way, the board is appointed by the shareholders to be trustees of their interests. So the accountability of the board to the shareholders is an essential prerequisite if they are to exercise control from outside ('external control') over their stakes in the company. In turn, an essential concomitant with accountability is the outside audit – without which there can be no assured accountability. In this respect it is regrettable that so few of the published corporate governance assertions of directors are subject to independent audit.

Looking the other way, the board has oversight responsibility for what is happening within the business. In particular the board's responsibility is to formulate policies and oversee their faithful implementation. The quality of information that the board receives, and the board's commitment (in terms, for instance, of the frequency of board and board committee meetings) are important here.

While it is management that has responsibility for internal control, the board has oversight responsibility for internal control. In essence, this means that the board needs to know whether the company has effective internal control. Where it is ineffective, the board will need to take action; and in extreme cases if management is unable to rectify significant inadequacies of internal control, the board may need to use its powers to effect changes in the top management team. It was unfortunate that the Hampel Report and the resultant UK *Combined Code* described the board's responsibility for internal control as being a 'maintenance' responsibility – maintenance is a management responsibility. But this was symptomatic of the Hampel committee's fairly general failure to differentiate the responsibilities of the board from those of management.

For several years, the internal auditing profession has been defining itself as having a significant role in 'corporate governance'. As we shall see, this is not just because 'internal control' is an essential part of corporate governance, though it is largely for this reason. As far back as December 1997, The Institute of Internal Auditors amended the strap line below the title of their bi-monthly journal, *The Internal Auditor*, so that it read 'Global perspectives on risk, control and governance' whereas it had previously read, rather pedestrianly, 'Journal of The Institute of Internal Auditors'. In the UK, commencing October 1995, the Institute of Internal Auditors adopted the strap line 'The corporate governance and internal control magazine' for their monthly journal *Internal Auditing*: it had previously read 'Journal of the Institute of Internal Auditors – United Kingdom'. Now, controversially, there is no strap line and the UK journal title reads just 'Internal Auditing and Business Risk' with the last three words in smaller text.

These harbingers of formal change were to become enshrined within the new definition of internal auditing which is now contained within both the new *Code of Ethics* and the new *Standards* of The Institute of Internal Auditors, viz:

> 'Internal auditing is an independent, objective assurance and consulting activity designed to add value and improve an organization's operations. It helps an organization accomplish its objectives by bringing a systematic, disciplined approach to evaluate and improve the effectiveness of risk management, control, and governance processes.'

If there were any doubt about internal audit's locus within corporate governance, that must be dispelled by the provision (C.3.5) within the UK's *Combined Code* which, as elaborated upon by the Turnbull Report, requires boards at least once a year to consider whether their companies have appropriate internal auditing arrangements.

Traditionally internal audit has been involved in governance due to its role as providing assurance about the quality of internal control to management and especially to the board. Now, internal audit is involved in two additional though closely related ways. The first is risk management, and the second is the accountability of the board to its shareholders and other stakeholders.

The *Standards* for internal auditing give equal stress to internal audit's role in risk management and in internal control, though it is probably true to say that the internal auditing profession is still feeling is way towards a definitive position of its role in risk management. The UK Turnbull Report in particular has stressed the importance of risk management as an aspect of corporate governance, for instance in order that boards can implement satisfactorily *Combined Code* provision C.2.1 on the board reviewing and reporting on internal control and risk management. Many boards are looking to their internal audit function to assist the board in the board's top-down assessment of risk and control, and also to assist the board is evaluating the adequacy of the company's embedded processes for the review of risk and control (both being set out within the Turnbull Report as necessary for boards who are claiming to be adhering to Code Provision C.2.1). Practice Advisory 2100–3: 'Internal Audit's Role in the Risk Management Process', paragraph 6, states:

> 'The internal audit activity's role in the risk management process of an organization can change over time and may be found at some point along a continuum that ranges from:
> – No role; to
> – Auditing the risk management process as part of the internal audit plan; to

- Active, continuous support and involvement in the risk management process such as participation on oversight committees, monitoring activities, and status reporting; to
- Managing and coordinating the risk management process.'

If, as is often the case today, internal audit is significantly involved in the process of risk management, then the *Code of Ethics* and the *Standards* come into play with respect as follows:

'**Objectivity** – Internal auditors shall not participate in any activity or relationship that may impair or be presumed to impair their unbiased assessment' [New Code of Ethics 2.1 – see APPENDIX 1]

and

'Assurance engagements for functions over which the chief audit executive has responsibility should be overseen by a party outside the internal audit activity.' [New Standard 1130.A2 – see APPENDIX 2]

To date, it is probable that few chief audit executives have so far arranged for another party to audit the organisation's risk management process, as they should do if they are significantly involved in the risk management process. Nobody would suggest it is an unimportant process not warranting serious assurance auditing.

While internal audit's roles in internal control and in risk management stake out internal audit's claims to be active players in corporate governance, it goes further than that. As we have seen, the accountability of the board to the stakeholders is an essential part of corporate governance and internal audit is becoming a progressively bigger player in this.

Internal audit findings often relate to issues which may impact the reliability of financial statements which will be published – and this is not new: internal audit may draw the attention of the audit committee to inadequate accounting which impacts upon the reliability of financial statements. Internal audit may assist the external audit in the statutory audit of the published financial statements. Internal audit is now assisting the board and the audit committee in formulating its public report on internal control and risk management. Then, internal audit is more frequently becoming involved in environmental auditing and reporting under, for instance ISO14000 or the European 'Eco-Management and Audit Scheme' (EMAS). More generally, internal auditing is giving assurances to the board on other operational analyses which are published, especially those not subject to other independent attestation. Internal audit sometimes also now has direct relationships with regulators.

On 9 April 2001 *The Wall Street Journal Europe* said, in its leading page one article 'European Companies Shy Away From Issuing Profit Warnings':

'Faced with a sudden cooling of the economy, North American companies have been churning out profit warnings. In Europe, however, only a few companies have admitted they won't live up to analysts' expectations.

Why the ominous silence in Europe? The short answer is denial. Many companies seem to be hoping to avoid the global slowdown. Others appear unwilling to show their hands before regularly scheduled releases of results.

Investors aren't waiting. These days, they dump shares on the mere suspicion that a profit warning is due, reasoning that if US competitors are issuing them, the Europeans must be sharing their pain. "It often seems that companies should have known their problems much earlier," grumbles Markus Straub of SdK, a shareholder-rights group in Germany. **"At best, you can say they need to improve their internal auditing; at worst it could be criminal." '**

The bolding is ours. The interesting point here is that at least one corporate governance pressure group considers internal auditors have a role to influence the reliability of disclosures to the market, and to prevent fraudulent financial reporting.

# Nature of work – case studies

## B2.3.1  Reputational crisis – case

Read the following account and be prepared to discuss the reputational management issues touched on in this case.

Even though in June 1999 Interbrand made Coca-Cola, at $83.8bn or 60% of the
company's market value, the most highly valued of all brands, there is clearly much
to learn from the way Coca-Cola handled a crisis at that time which, when it was
announced on 15 June 1999, led to an immediate fall in their share price by over $1,
down to $63 on the New York Stock Exchange (a fall which continued further) and an
estimated loss of £37m in sales[1] though it was not made clear whether this was the
size of the loss in France alone or throughout the world. The lesson is that, to occupy
the moral high ground following a product contamination crisis, the following are
essential:

- early disclosure;
- prompt acknowledgment of responsibility;
- full acknowledgment of likely consequences (eg health effects);
- fulsome apology;
- a convincing account of how it happened;
- clear proposed account with suppliers (and others) whose confirmation is
  necessary for its credibility;
- a convincing account of how rectification will be achieved;
- up front public involvement from the top of the company (usually the chairman).

In comparison, Perrier in 1990 did quite well to limit the damage when their product
was contaminated with benzene, even though the event was estimated to have cost
Perrier $200m (£125m) and, arguably, allowed competing mineral waters to take
market share.

In an example of how 'brand association' can extend the damage to reputation,
Coca-Cola Beverages, the London-listed Coke bottler for eastern and central
Europe, reported that they were being punished by the hit to consumer confidence
from the withdrawal of Coke in Belgium and France, even though it was not a
supplier to either country.[2] Their shares, which had been floated in London in 1998
at 160p fell a further 7% to 128p on disappointing trading results for the half year to
2 July 1999. The company attributed this to further factors in addition to the
contamination scare – especially trading conditions in Russia and the war in
Kosovo.

Of course, a brand as strong as Coca-Cola tends to bounce back from reputational
crises, but if they repeat themselves the damage can be long term and even

permanent. In particular, two of Interbrand's factors are particularly strong for the Coca-Cola brand: it is *established*, being almost 120 years old; and it has a wide *geographical spread,* being sold in 200 countries.

The 1999 Coca-Cola crisis can be summed up as follows. In June 1999 a health scare forced the withdrawal of Coca-Cola products from four northern European countries (Belgium, Luxembourg, France and the Netherlands). It was damaging that the media coverage indicated that only in the case of the Netherlands did Coca-Cola take the initiative to insist on the withdrawal. In France the authorities introduced a blanket ban on the sale of Coca-Cola, Coca-Cola Light, Fanta and Sprite but allowed sales to restart on 23 June when their own analysts confirmed that French Coke showed 'no anomalies' – a verdict which supported the analysis of Coca-Cola France. If there is an obvious lesson to be learnt from this it is that a more convincing initial reaction from Coca-Cola might have headed off the public actions which the French authorities took and the public anxieties which evidenced themselves. The main headline article in the *Financial Times* on 16 June[3] reported that the Belgian Health Ministry on 15 June reported that 100 people, mainly schoolchildren, had fallen ill within the previous week suffering from stomach upsets, nausea and headaches, with eight being in hospital, and that 15m cans and bottles were involved. A similar number were affected in France.

When the Belgian Health Ministry first broke the news, it took Coca-Cola a crucial five or six hours to react even though they must have been in contact with the Belgian health authorities on this matter for at least a few days previously. While it was appropriate that Coca-Cola's statement came from their Atlanta headquarters, it would have been more convincing if their chairman had made the statement: it was not until the evening of 16 June, following the *FT* headline, that Coca-Cola's chairman apologised. And it was very unconvincing to many that Coca-Cola blamed two separate chemical problems at different plants and claimed 'no health or safety problems were found'. It was not until almost a week after the events themselves that the chairman of the US parent, Douglas Ivester, apologised and he had still not appeared on television. Luc Van den Bossche, Belgian Health Minister, was quoted as saying:

> 'It's a bit disturbing that a big firm with worldwide fame ... did not take far reaching measures more spontaneously.'

So the die was cast for consumers to blame the brand. This was not improved by the unconvincing explanations and Coca-Cola's protestations on 17 June that no link had been established between the illnesses and the allegedly contaminated Coke. First, it emerged that Aga had supplied the alleged bad (or 'sub-standard' as Coca-Cola put it) $CO_2$ to the Coke bottling plant in Antwerp, but Aga claimed to have kept samples of what they had despatched which showed that it had *not* been bad. Secondly, it had been claimed that wooden pallets had been sprayed in France with what was reported to be a fungicide, but industry experts claimed never to have heard of this practice and France's consumer affairs minister, Marylise Lebanchu, also cast doubt on this, saying:

> 'I cannot see how a fungicide present on a pallet and seeping onto cans can contaminate the consumer to such a degree ... Toxicologists tell us that if in fact it's a case of contamination of the outside of the can, illness is practically impossible.'[4]

Apparently, most of the contaminated cans had been sent from their Dunkirk bottling plant to Belgium. An estimated 800 pallets out of the 150,000 sent to Belgium were said to have been affected. A spokesman for Coca-Cola Europe admitted the contamination but said that of the affected pallets, only 20 cans per unit of 2,460 would have been directly contaminated. Coca-Cola said the contamination had been by phenol, sometimes used as a form of rat poison.

Without a convincing explanation, consumers were left to be concerned about the true nature and extent of the problem. They were likely to conclude that the company had something serious to hide. What might have been a minor issue became a major crisis through hesitation and inaction. The sentiment expressed by a Coca-Cola France spokesman became merely retrospective wishful thinking:

'This is not a scandal. It is not an "affaire". It is simply an issue.'[5]

The risk is in part not just of withdrawal of custom for companies about whose products a sceptical public has doubts; it is also a matter of withdrawal by investors of their confidence that the management team is capable of handling these sorts of issues and thus capable of safeguarding their investment.

[1]  Martin Baker 'Coca-Cola calms consumers' fears over poisoning' (1999) *Sunday Business*, 27 June, p15.
[2]  John Willman 'Coke bottler hit by Kosovo and Russia' (1999) *Financial Times*, 14 July, p20; and Nelson Fraser 'Coca-Cola hit by war in Kosovo' (1999) *The Times*, 14 July, p26.
[3]  Neil Buckley and Betty Liu 'Coca-Cola hit by drinks health scare in Europe' (1999) *Financial Times*, 16 June, p1; also 'Coca-Cola drinks recalled' (1999) *Financial Times*, 15 June, p3.
[4]  John Williams and Nicholas George 'Explanation met with scepticism' (1999) *Financial Times*, 18 June, p3.
[5]  Martin Baker 'Coca-Cola calms consumers' fears over poisoning' (1999) *Sunday Business*, 27 June, p15.

# Engagement planning – best practice guidance

**B3.1.1**   While we also refer to other important pronouncements, our main source of guidance for the parts of this Handbook which describe internal auditing best practice has been the *Professional Practices Framework* of The Institute of Internal Auditors. This *Framework* includes their *Definition* of internal auditing, *Code of Ethics, Standards*, and *Practice Advisories*. Of these, only the *Practice Advisories* are non-mandatory: they explain and elaborate upon best practice in most circumstances, and are important for practitioners and students. Readers can see the current complete list of *Practice Advisories* at www.theiia.org. Those current on 1 January 2005 are shown at APPENDIX 3 of this Handbook, including a useful topical classification at APPENDIX 3.2.

In addressing this subject we have drawn more widely than those *Practice Advisories* classified by The Institute as applicable to this part of our Handbook, which are:

| Practice Advisories, by Standard Number | Release date |
|---|---|
| Practice Advisory 2200–1: Engagement Planning | 5 January 2001 |
| Practice Advisory 2210–1: Engagement Objectives | 5 January 2001 |
| Practice Advisory 2210.A101: Risk Assessment in Engagement Planning | 5 January 2001 |
| Practice Advisory 2230–1: Engagement Resource Allocation | 5 January 2001 |
| Practice Advisory 2240–1: Engagement Work Program | 5 January 2001 |
| Practice Advisory 2240.A1–1: Approval of Work Program | 5 January 2001 |

*Practice Advisories* carry the *Standard* number to which they principally refer. Readers are advised to consult the applicable *Standards* as we do not in every case reproduce them here. They are to be found at APPENDIX 2.

In most tasks in life, the preparatory and concluding stages are crucially important; so it is with the internal audit engagement. The performance of the engagement is likely to go so much better if the engagement has been thoroughly planned. The results of performing the engagement, if they are to be useful, will then depend upon what happens after the end of the audit fieldwork – communicating results, monitoring progress and resolving management's acceptance of risks. That The Institute of Internal Auditors acknowledges this is illustrated by a simple comparison of word counts between the different parts of their *Standards*, as shown in this table:

| Stage of the audit | Word count within the *Standards* (Jan 2004) |
|---|---|
| Engagement planning | 504 |
| Performing the engagement | 199 |
| Communicating results | 344 |
| Monitoring progress | 78 |
| Resolution of management's acceptance of risks | 66 |

(In our view, The Institute is very lightweight in the rigour of its Standards and guidance on *performing* audit engagements (CHAPTER B4.1). For instance there is too little guidance on the circumstances in which internal auditors should conduct compliance and weakness (substantive) tests and to what extent.

We have come to the conclusion that planning an audit engagement is so important that it is best to regard it as a project in its own right – to be planned carefully and to be undertaken at a timing separate from the time scheduled to perform the audit fieldwork and to be commenced well in advance of the dates scheduled for the audit fieldwork. Sometimes a distinct survey will need to be undertaken as part of the planning phase.[1] Audit management should allow that the planning phase will usually be a significant consumer of internal audit resources. While audit fieldwork usually requires undivided focus by an audit team for a finite amount of time, the earlier planning phase of the audit can be done in parallel with other audit activities – such as planning other audit engagements. It is preferable to allow plenty of time between the start of planning an audit and the date by which the planning has to be completed. As with other research projects there are likely to be delays in obtaining feedback during the planning process and it is difficult to predict how long it will take to plan the audit engagement. On the other hand, a thorough plan for the audit engagement makes it easier to predict how much time will be needed to perform the audit (ie for the audit fieldwork).

Some internal audit activities tend to gloss over the need to plan each audit engagement. It is not an optional extra. Indeed the results of the plan, including the engagement programme and subsequent amendments to it of an audit engagement are to be authorized and documented:

> **'Standard 2200 – Engagement Planning**
> Internal auditors should develop and record a plan for each engagement.'

and:

> 'Planning should be documented.'[2]

and:

> 'In obtaining approval of the engagement work plan, such plans should be approved in writing by the chief audit executive or designee prior to the commencement of engagement work. Adjustments to engagement work plans should be approved in a timely manner. Initially, approval may be obtained orally, if factors preclude obtaining written approval prior to commencing engagement work.'[3]

They may also gloss over the need to allocate time to conclude an audit after the fieldwork has been completed. For instance, internal auditors may travel over a weekend from the fieldwork of one audit to the fieldwork of their next audit and are expected to 'hit the ground running' at each location with little or no prior planning and no discrete time allowed for communicating results and for follow-up. This can only be acceptable if (a) the field auditors are working to audit programmes which are the result of careful engagement planning by other, perhaps more senior, internal auditors, and (b) other, probably more senior, internal auditors take on the responsibility for communicating audit results and for subsequent follow-up. However, there will always be the need for coordination between the field auditors and those who, within this scenario, plan the audits and handle the results of the fieldwork. This coordination will require an allocation of field auditor time. The best approach is that the field auditors are actively involved in the planning of their audits and in handling the results of their audits.

Ideally, the auditors who will perform the audit engagement should also plan it, and the requirement for supervision at the planning stage should not be overlooked:

> 'The internal auditor is responsible for planning and conducting the engagement assignment, subject to supervisory review and approval.'[4]

and:

> 'The chief audit executive is responsible for assuring that appropriate engagement supervision is provided. Supervision is a process that begins with planning and continues throughout the examination, evaluation, communicating, and follow-up phases of the engagement. Supervision includes:
> * Ensuring that the auditors assigned possess the requisite knowledge, skills, and other competencies to perform the engagement.
> * Providing appropriate instructions during the planning of the engagement and approving the engagement program …
> * Providing opportunities for developing internal auditors' knowledge, skills, and other competencies.'[5]

## B3.1.2   The audit engagement planning process

Standard 2201 sets out a logical process of planning considerations which internal auditors will readily understand, as shown in the following diagram. While all of the elements within this diagram should be addressed to the extent practical at the planning stage of the audit, those elements towards the start of the continuum are more likely to be addressed more fully during the planning phase.

*Planning considerations continuum*

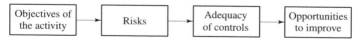

The engagement planning process should be designed to give the internal auditors the best possible understanding of these four matters – and generally the focus should be on each of these in turn, starting with management's objectives:

**'Standard 2201 – Planning Considerations**
In planning the engagement, internal auditors should consider:

- The objectives of the activity being reviewed and the means by which the activity controls its performance.
- The significant risks to the activity, its objectives, resources, and operations and the means by which the potential impact of risk is kept to an acceptable level.
- The adequacy and effectiveness of the activity's risk management and control systems compared to a relevant control framework or model.
- The opportunities for making significant improvements to the activities risk management and control systems.'

## B3.1.3   Dialogue with responsible management as part of the engagement planning process

*Understanding management's objectives for the activity to be audited*

The starting point should be to obtain an understanding of management's objectives for the activity to be audited. It is not possible to undertake a successful audit unless it is set firmly in the context of management's objectives. This will entail a dialogue at the planning stage between internal audit and management with overall responsibility for the activity. The results of this dialogue should be documented:

> 'A summary of matters discussed at meetings and any conclusions reached should be prepared, distributed to individuals, as appropriate, and retained in the engagement working papers.'[6]

It is important to determine correctly to whom within the management team to enter into this dialogue at the planning phase of the audit. Generally, the main client is responsible management at the level above the management who manage the activity to be audited. Internal audit could be said to be an extension of his or her eyes and ears – looking round corners which that manager is unable to do so for him or herself or does not have the time to do so. As has been said: 'Internal auditors do what management would do if management had the time and knew how.' Eventually, the communication of the results of the audit will be to the same manager. Audit results should be communicated to the level of management who needs to know and can ensure that appropriate action is taken on those results.

> 'The chief audit executive is responsible for determining how, when, and to whom engagement results will be communicated. This determination should be documented and communicated to management, to the extent deemed practical, during the planning phase of the engagement. Subsequent changes which affect the timing or reporting of engagement results should also be communicated to management, if appropriate.'[7]

If management are unclear as to their objectives, then audit results are starting to emerge even at the planning stage of the audit, which will warrant inclusion within the eventual audit report. Note, however, that significant audit findings should be communicated promptly.

## B3.1.4 *Understanding the risks of the activity to be audited*

Planning the audit cannot proceed until a meeting of minds has been achieved between internal audit and responsible management as to management's objectives for the activity to be audited. Internal audit should also establish to their satisfaction that management's objectives are consistent with the overall goals and objectives of the entity. Once management's objectives are clear, audit planning can proceed to identifying and assessing the risks to the achievement of those objectives.

> 'The purpose of the risk assessment during the planning phase of the engagement is to identify significant areas of activity that should be examined as potential engagement objectives.'[8]

Management should be clear about these risks and, again, future audit results may start to emerge even at this planning stage if it is apparent that management is vague about risks. Further insights about risk are also likely to emerge during the fieldwork of the audit.

## B3.1.5 *Understanding the controls of the activity to be audited*

Conversations with responsible management at the planning phase of the audit should also identify the principal controls upon which management is relying to inform management as to whether their objectives are being achieved and the associated risks being mitigated. If management are unclear as to the controls they rely upon, then important audit results may be emerging during this planning phase of the audit. Where the controls involve the provision of information to responsible management, the auditors planning the audit can ask to see the information. During the planning phase, internal audit should be able to assess, to some extent, whether the controls in place have the potential to be effective, whether further controls appear to be needed, and indeed whether the controls in place are being applied by senior responsible management.

## B3.1.6 *Keeping management informed of progress in planning*

Towards the end of the planning phase the internal auditors should consider whether each of the following, where applicable, has been discussed with responsible management:

- 'Planned engagement objectives and scope of work.
- The timing of engagement work.
- Internal auditors assigned to the engagement.
- The process of communicating throughout the engagement, including the methods, time frames, and individuals who will be responsible.
- Business conditions and operations of the activity being reviewed, including recent changes in management or major systems.
- Concerns or any requests of management.
- Matters of particular interest or concern to the internal auditor.
- Description of the internal auditing activity's reporting procedures and follow-up process.'[9]

## B3.1.7   Surprise audit engagements

It will be apparent that there are issues with respect to the 'surprise audit' in regard to the dialogue approach with management we have outlined above. It may still be possible to preserve an element of surprise while still engaging in meaningful, confidential dialogue with more senior management. However, significant elements of planning an audit engagement should usually involve line management running the activity to be audited. The element of surprise is unnecessary and counter-productive in most audit contexts. Frequently, where an element of surprise is needed, the internal audit activity should examine whether the purpose of the audit indicates that internal audit is undertaking a role which management should be undertaking for themselves. For instance, the effective operation of many controls may require an element of surprise, but it is not an internal audit responsibility to take over from management the operation of controls. The audit role includes to review that controls are operating effectively.

## B3.1.8   Other sources of information to use in the planning phase of an audit engagement

During the planning phase the internal auditor will discuss with management and utilise other sources so as to obtain a good understanding of the operations to be audited – so as to be able to develop an informed and detailed audit programme to be followed during the fieldwork of the audit. Other sources might include previous audit working papers, procedures manuals of the activity to be audited, and audit research materials:

> 'Background information should be obtained about the activities to be reviewed. A review of background information should be performed to determine the impact on the engagement. Such items include:
> - Objectives and goals.
> - Policies, plans, procedures, laws, regulations, and contracts which could have a significant impact on operations and reports.
> - Organizational information, eg, number and names of employees, key employees, job descriptions, and details about recent changes in the organization, including major system changes.
> - Budget information, operating results, and financial data of the activity to be reviewed.
> - Prior engagement working papers.
> - Results of other engagements, including the work of external auditors, completed or in process.
> - Correspondence files to determine potential significant engagement issues.
> - Authoritative and technical literature appropriate to the activity.'[10]

## B3.1.9   Surveys at the planning phase of an engagement

Sometimes it will be necessary, as part of planning the engagement, to undertake a distinct survey which may entail a visit to the activity during the planning phase of the audit:

'A survey is a process for gathering information, without detailed verification, on the activity being examined. The main purposes are to:
- Understand the activity under review.
- Identify significant areas warranting special emphasis.
- Obtain information for use in performing the engagement.
- Determine whether further auditing is necessary.'[11]

A survey may involve use of these procedures:
- 'Discussions with the engagement client.
- Interviews with individuals affected by the activity, eg, users of the activity's output.
- On-site observations.
- Review of management reports and studies.
- Analytical auditing procedures.
- Flowcharting.
- Functional "walk-through" (tests of specific work activities from beginning to end).
- Documenting key control activities.'[12]

## B3.1.10  The audit engagement programme

Working through the above continuum of planning considerations during the planning phase of the audit will highlight areas for audit enquiry during the fieldwork of the audit, and allow an audit engagement programme for the field-work to be developed which is tightly focused on management's objectives, risks and controls. During the planning phase it should also be possible to determine the audit procedures to be followed within the audit fieldwork, and this should be done:

'Engagement procedures, including the testing and sampling techniques employed, should be selected in advance, where practicable, and expanded or altered if circumstances warrant.'[13]

Note the importance of documenting the audit plan and the distinction between 'management's objectives' and the 'engagement's objectives':

'Planning should be documented. Engagement objectives and scope of work should be established. Engagement objectives are broad statements developed by internal auditors and define what the engagement is intended to accomplish. Engagement procedures are the means to attain engagement objectives. Engagement objectives and procedures, taken together, define the scope of the internal auditor's work. Engagement objectives and procedures should address the risks associated with the activity under review.'[14]

At the start of the planning phase, internal audit would have had a general impression as what those audit objectives would be, but the planning phase itself should have provided the opportunity to modify and refine the audit objectives so as to increase the potential of the audit engagement to add value to the business.

The engagement programme should:
- 'Document the internal auditor's procedures for collecting, analysing, interpreting, and documenting information during the engagement.

- State the objectives of the engagement.
- Set forth the scope and degree of testing required to achieve the engagement objectives in each phase of the engagement.
- Identify technical aspects, risks, processes, and transactions that should be examined.
- State the nature and extent of testing required.
- Be prepared prior to the commencement of engagement work and modified, as appropriate, during the course of the engagement.'[15]

[1]     Practice Advisory 2210.A1–1: 'Risk Assessment in Engagement Planning', paras 3–6.
[2]     Practice Advisory 2210–1: 'Engagement Objectives', para 1.
[3]     Practice Advisory 2240.A1–1: 'Approval of Work Programs', para 1.
[4]     Practice Advisory 2200–1: 'Engagement Planning', para 1.
[5]     Practice Advisory 2340–1: 'Engagement Supervision', para 1.
[6]     Practice Advisory 2200–1: 'Engagement Planning', para 4.
[7]     Practice Advisory 2200–1: 'Engagement Planning', para 1.
[8]     Practice Advisory 2210–1: 'Engagement Objectives', para 2.
[9]     Practice Advisory 2200–1: 'Engagement Planning', para 1.
[10]    Practice Advisory 2210.A1–1: 'Risk Assessment in Engagement Planning', para 1.
[11]    Practice Advisory 2210.A1–1: 'Risk Assessment in Engagement Planning', para 3; see also paras 4–6.
[12]    Practice Advisory 2210.A1–1: 'Risk Assessment in Engagement Planning', para 5.
[13]    Practice Advisory 2240–1: 'Engagement Work Program', para 1.
[14]    Practice Advisory 2210–1: 'Engagement Objectives', paras 1 and 2.
[15]    Practice Advisory 2200–1: 'Engagement Planning', para 1.

# Engagement planning – case studies

## B3.2.1 Engagement planning [Practice Advisories 2200–1 and 2240–1]

CASES FOR CONSIDERATION
1.      To what extent do your 'engagement programmes':
        A.      Define the scope of the internal auditor's work, by:
                ● stating the objectives of the engagement;
                ● documenting the auditor's procedures for collecting, analysing, interpreting, and documenting information during the engagement.

                *Engagement objectives* are broad statements which define what the engagement is to accomplish.

                *Engagement procedures* are the means to attain engagement objectives. Engagement procedures, including the testing and sampling techniques employed, should be selected in advance, where practicable, and expanded or altered if circumstances warrant.' [PA 2240–1].

                *Engagement objectives and procedures together* define the *scope of* the internal auditor's *work*.
        B.      Set forth the scope and degree of testing to achieve the engagement objectives in each phase of the engagement.
        C.      Identify technical aspects, risks, processes, and transactions that should be examined.
        D.      State the nature and extent of testing required.
and are they:
        E.      Prepared prior to the commencement of engagement work and modified, as appropriate, during the course of the engagement.
2.      PA 2200–1 states that 'all those in management who need to know about the engagement should be informed. Meetings should be held with management responsible for the activity ... A summary of matters discussed at meetings and any conclusions reached should be prepared, distributed to individuals, as appropriate, and retained in the engagement working papers'. In your organisation, does this happen, and which of the following may be included (as per PA 2200–1):
        ● Planned engagement objectives and scope of work?
        ● The timing of engagement work?
        ● Internal auditors assigned to the engagement?
        ● The process of communicating throughout the engagement, including:
                – methods;

- time frames;
- individuals responsible.
- Business conditions of activity being reviewed, including recent changes in management or major systems
- Concerns or requests of management
- Matters of particular interest or concern to the internal auditor
- Description of the internal auditing activity's reporting procedures and follow-up process.

3. Is your engagement planning documented [PA 2210–1]?

# Performing the engagement – best practice guidance

'All internal auditing assignments, whether performed by or for the internal audit activity, remain the responsibility of the chief audit executive. The chief audit executive is responsible for all significant professional judgments made in the planning, examination, evaluation, report, and follow-up phases of the engagement. The chief audit executive should adopt suitable means to ensure that this responsibility is met.'[1]

**B4.1.1**    While we also refer to other important pronouncements, our main source of guidance for the parts of this Handbook which describe internal auditing best practice has been the *Professional Practices Framework* of The Institute of Internal Auditors. This *Framework* includes their *Definition* of internal auditing, *Code of Ethics, Standards*, and *Practice Advisories*. Of these, only the *Practice Advisories* are non-mandatory: they explain and elaborate upon best practice in most circumstances, and are important for practitioners and students. Readers can see the current complete list of *Practice Advisories* at www.theiia.org. Those current on 1 January 2005 are shown at APPENDIX 3 of this Handbook, including a useful topical classification at APPENDIX 3.2.

In addressing this subject we have drawn more widely than those *Practice Advisories* classified by The Institute as applicable to this part of our Handbook, which are:

| **Practice Advisories, by Standard Number** | **Release date** |
|---|---|
| Practice Advisory 2300–1: The Internal Auditor's Use of Personal Information in Conducting Audits | 12 February 2004 |
| Practice Advisory 2310–1: Identifying Information | 5 January 2001 |
| Practice Advisory 2320–1: Analysis and Evaluation | 5 January 2001 |
| Practice Advisory 2330–1: Recording Information | 5 January 2001 |
| Practice Advisory 2330.A1–1: Control of Engagement Records | 5 January 2001 |
| Practice Advisory 2330.A1–2: Legal Considerations in Granting Access to Engagement Records | 28 March 2001 |
| Practice Advisory 2330.A2–1: Retention of Records | 5 January 2001 |
| Practice Advisory 2340–1: Engagement Supervision | 5 January 2001 |

*Practice Advisories* carry the *Standard* number to which they principally refer. Readers are advised to consult the applicable *Standards* as we do not in every case reproduce them here. They are to be found at APPENDIX 2.

## B4.1.2   Identifying information

Identifying information is a matter of determining the requisite information to be obtained in order to assist in meeting the objective(s) of the audit engagement, and determining from where and how the information can be obtained.

Managers understand that there is a type of circular process as illustrated in the following diagram. From available data, information may be drawn. The information is analysed and the analysis provides a basis for decision taking. Decisions lead to actions and data is collected on the results of those actions. And so it cycles round.

**Management's information processing cycle**

Some entities have a surfeit of data but inadequate information drawn from that data. Some have abundant information but inadequate analysis made using that information. Some entities suffer from abundant analysis but a relative inability to make decisions based upon that analysis. Others may be quite good at making decisions but poor at ensuring that the requisite action flows from the decisions that had been made. If action is not taken well, then results are unlikely to be up to expectations. Certainly all of these elements need to be present proportionately to each other in the interests of economy, efficiency and effectiveness; and each should be a sound basis for the element which follows it.

Internal auditors experience a broadly similar process. When they plan an audit engagement they determine the information they will need in order to meet the engagement's objective(s). Even as early as the planning phase of the engagement they will collect much of this information. As they perform audit work they derive further relevant information from basic data. The data may be physical 'data' which the auditor observes; or it may be disclosed during meetings which take place during the audit engagement; or it may be present within records which the auditor reviews. Information, either presented by management or put together by the auditors, should provide the auditor the opportunity to make meaningful analyses and from these to draw relevant conclusions – which are the equivalent of the 'decisions'.

## The internal auditing activity's information processing cycle

Internal audit conclusions are actioned by internal audit and by management. Internal audit endeavours to 'get a sale' on every audit finding and recommendation; but whether or not this is achieved depends on management as well. Since the internal activity has no executive authority[2], internal audit only advises and tries to persuade, but cannot insist.

The contemporary phraseology is that 'agreed actions' should arise from 'audit conclusions'. However, management may choose to accept a level of residual risk which the chief audit executive considers to be unacceptable: we discuss this at CHAPTER B7.1. It is important that agreed action is taken and that it is successful. The results should be monitored. Internal audit should know the status of each audit recommendation – whether it has been accepted, the date set by management to implement the change, whether management has made the change – and so on.

As with management generally, so it is with the internal audit activity that all of the elements within the diagram are present in proportion to each other, and each should be a sound basis for the element which should flow from it. Most auditors will recognise from their experience occasions when too much time has been spent in gathering information, for instance, to the extent that it has not been possible to make effective use of much of that information – and so on. It will help to avoid spending audit time disproportionately if the engagement objective(s) are clearly kept in mind:

> 'Internal auditors should consider the factors listed below in determining the extent to which analytical auditing procedures should be used. After evaluating these factors, internal auditors should consider and use additional auditing procedures, as necessary, to achieve the engagement objective.
> - The significance of the area being examined.
> - The adequacy of the system of internal control.
> - The availability and reliability of financial and nonfinancial information.
> - The precision with which the results of analytical auditing procedures can be predicted.
> - The availability and comparability of information regarding the industry in which the organization operates.
> - The extent to which other engagement procedures provide support for engagement results.'[3]

## B4.1.3 Analysis and Evaluation

During the planning phase of an audit engagement, much of the requisite information will be gathered[4] with the rest being collected during the fieldwork of the audit. Auditors are skilled in the analysis of information in order to uncover matters of audit interest.

'Analytical auditing procedures may include:
- Comparison of current period information with similar information for prior periods.
- Comparison of current period information with budgets or forecasts.
- Study of relationships of financial information with the appropriate nonfinancial information (for example, recorded payroll expense compared to changes in average number of employees).
- Study of relationships among elements of information (for example, fluctuation in recorded interest expense compared to changes in related debt balances).
- Comparison of information with similar information for other organizational units.
- Comparison of information with similar information for the industry in which the organization operates.'[5]

'Analytical auditing procedures provide internal auditors with an efficient and effective means of assessing and evaluating information collected in an engagement. The assessment results from comparing information with expectations identified or developed by the internal auditor. Analytical auditing procedures are useful in identifying, among other things:
- Differences that are not expected.
- The absence of differences when they are expected.
- Potential errors.
- Potential irregularities or illegal acts.
- Other unusual or nonrecurring transactions or events.'[6]

Auditors should not overlook that when analytical auditing procedures reveal results which the auditor cannot sufficiently explain, there is an audit obligation to ensure that these are communicated to management:

'When analytical auditing procedures identify unexpected results or relationships, internal auditors should examine and evaluate such results or relationships. The examination and evaluation of unexpected results or relationships from applying analytical auditing procedures should include inquiries of management and the application of other engagement procedures until internal auditors are satisfied that the results or relationships are sufficiently explained. Unexplained results or relationships from applying analytical auditing procedures may be indicative of a significant condition such as a potential error, irregularity, or illegal act. Results or relationships from applying analytical auditing procedures that are not sufficiently explained should be communicated to the appropriate levels of management. Internal auditors may recommend appropriate courses of action, depending on the circumstances.'[7]

Internal auditors must be careful not to be content with unclear explanations. In general and auditor should pursue a matter until it is sufficiently explained. If an auditor does not understand an explanation, it is quite likely to be because it has not been explained. It may be because there is attempted concealment of wrongdoing or a failure on the part of management to fully grasp the issue. Auditors should similarly be cautious of being intimidated by managers who are 'too busy' to give the auditor sufficient time.

Note that:

> 'Detection of fraud consists of identifying indicators of fraud sufficient to warrant recommending an investigation. These indicators may arise as a result of controls established by management, tests conducted by auditors, and other sources both within and outside the organization.'[8]

We discuss the internal auditor's responsibility for prevention and detection of fraud at A.1.1.16.

In considering accessing information, internal auditors will need to be aware of burgeoning data protection legislation which defines and protects individual rights to privacy of personal data:

> 'It is important that the internal auditor understands and complies with all laws regarding the use of personal information in their jurisdiction and those jurisdictions where their organization conducts business.'[9]

> 'The internal auditor must understand that it may be inappropriate, and in some cases illegal, to access, retrieve, review, manipulate, or use personal information in conducting certain internal audit engagements.'[10]

## B4.1.4 *Audit testing*

We discuss audit testing in more detail within B4.2.1 to B4.2.18 and at B4.3.1 to B4.3.4.

The Institute of Internal Auditors' Standards and Practice Advisories are not at all prescriptive of the nature and extent of audit testing which should be undertaken during audit engagements, leaving the matter wide open to the judgment of the auditor. Of course, this is an important judgement area which should be supervised.

Because of the important of quality in communicating audit engagement results, the Institute has this to say:

> 'Accurate communications are free from errors and distortions and are faithful to the underlying facts. The manner in which the data and evidence is gathered, evaluated, and summarized for presentation should be done with care and precision.'[11]

Audit testing is time consuming and needs to be determined according to need.

> 'In conducting audit engagements, methods and techniques for testing and validating exposures should be reflective of the risk materiality and likelihood of occurrence.'[12]

Auditors generally discriminate between the three following types of audit test.

### B4.1.5   Walk through tests

These are tests of perhaps just one or two transactions, walking them sequentially through all the processing stages of the system. The purposes of walk through tests may be (a) to confirm the auditor's understanding of the system, and (b) to highlight key controls which the auditor may need to evaluate further, perhaps in compliance and/or weakness tests. Since audit testing can be very time-consuming, it can be helpful to make further use of the very small walk through test sample so that it becomes part of the larger sample needed for compliance testing.

### B4.1.6   Compliance tests

These are tests designed to determine the extent to which a control procedure is being complied with. There is no point in conducting a compliance test of a procedure that the internal auditor has already concluded does not have the potential to be an effective control.

### B4.1.7   Weakness, or substantive, tests

These are tests designed to measure the impact, if any, of a control weakness. A control weakness may exist due to an absence of appropriate control procedures or due to the control procedures not being applied as they should be, or not being entirely effective – or a combination of these reasons.

### B4.1.8   *Statistical sampling in internal auditing*

We discuss statistical sampling in more detail in B4.2.1 to B4.2.18 and at B4.3.1 to B4.3.4, contrasting it with 'directed' or 'judgemental' sampling.

Internal auditors should be familiar with the techniques of statistical sampling, be able to apply them in audit engagements, and be able to provide consultancy advice on the use of statistical sampling in business situations.

Statistical sampling usually entails working with sample sizes which are too large for the audit time available, so most internal auditors rely upon 'judgemental' sampling most of the time. When it is possible to automate audit testing using the computer, then statistical sampling is more likely to be practical. On occasions, however, automated audit testing can avoid the need to base audit conclusions of the results of a statistical or judgmental sample, since it may be practical for software to give the auditor an exact answer after an automated review of 100% of the population on the computer database.

### B4.1.9   *Audit interviewing*

'Audit interviewing' is a pretentious expression which perhaps inappropriately stresses an authoritarian image for internal audit. Nevertheless, meeting with people to find out information, to gain access to other individuals or to further information, or to gauge opinions is an important component of performing audit work. It gets very little coverage in the *Standards Framework* of The Institute of Internal Auditors. We cover it at B4.2.20 to B4.2.32.

## B4.1.10   Engagement records

The phrase 'audit working papers' still has wide currency even though audit records may be computer-based. If the latter, the inelegant phrase 'electronic audit working papers' is sometimes used. The phrase 'audit working papers' is not used within the *Standards* themselves, having been replaced by 'engagement records'; but it still appears several times within the *Practice Advisories*. We believe the phrase 'audit working papers' has been avoided in the *Standards* since it implies the medium of paper, and that in time it will be edited out of the *Practice Advisories*. Of course, internal audit records need not be paper-based:

> 'Engagement working papers may be in the form of paper, tapes, disks, diskettes, films, or other media. If engagement working papers are in the form of media other than paper, consideration should be given to generating backup copies.'[13]

The fundamental essential, the minimum requirement, of internal audit engagement records is that they contain the evidence that sufficiently supports the conclusions and results of the audit engagement – and especially the contents of the engagement report:

> 'Engagement working papers should be complete and include support for engagement conclusions reached.'[14]

It is arguable that the need for comprehensive engagement records is less for internal audit than for external audit. It is less likely that an internal auditor will need to produce a comprehensive set of engagement records in order to defend in depth his or her audit performance subsequently as might the external auditor – in court, or by the profession or internally within the firm. However, both external and internal audit share the need for their engagement records to be sufficient to contribute to the quality of their audit work and to facilitate effective supervision. Furthermore, third parties (such as external auditors, regulators, external assessors, group internal audit functions) may need to refer to internal audit engagement records:

> 'Engagement working papers generally ... facilitate third-party reviews.'[15]

It is preferable that the style of work in planning and performing an audit engagement should generate audit engagement records as an automatic by-product:

> 'The working papers should record the information obtained and the analyses made and should support the bases for the observations and recommendations to be reported.'[16]

So, for instance, a schedule will be prepared to assist the auditor to conduct a detailed test of a sample of transactions and to record the results. That schedule then becomes part of the engagement records. Some internal audit activities follow the practice of requiring the auditor who prepared the schedule to write a conclusion on the schedule.

Note that working papers should be titled, signed, dated, indexed, etc:

> 'The following are typical engagement working paper preparation techniques:
> - Each engagement working paper should identify the engagement and describe the contents or purpose of the working paper.
> - Each engagement working paper should be signed (or initialled) and dated by the internal auditor performing the work.
> - Each engagement working paper should contain an index or reference number.
> - Audit verification symbols (tick marks) should be explained.
> - Sources of data should be clearly identified.'[17]

Every aspect of the audit process, from planning to follow-up, should be reflected within the engagement records:

> 'The organization, design, and content of engagement working papers will depend on the nature of the engagement. Working papers for an audit should document the following aspects of the engagement process:
> - Planning.
> - The examination and evaluation of the adequacy and effectiveness of the system of internal control.
> - The engagement procedures performed, the information obtained, and the conclusions reached.
> - Review.
> - Communicating.
> - Follow-up.'[18]

Engagement records should achieve the following:
> - 'Provide the principal support for the engagement communications.
> - Aid in the planning, performance, and review of engagements.
> - Document whether the engagement objectives were achieved.
> - Facilitate third-party reviews.
> - Provide a basis for evaluating the internal audit activity's quality program.
> - Provide support in circumstances such as insurance claims, fraud cases, and lawsuits.
> - Aid in the professional development of the internal auditing staff.
> - Demonstrate the internal audit activity's compliance with the Standards for the Professional Practice of Internal Auditing.'[19]

It is strongly desirable that a common approach to internal audit engagement records should be followed by all internal auditors within the entity, so that each auditor can quickly understand the work recorded by each other auditor. This is a prerequisite of efficient supervision. It also facilitates one auditor continuing the work started by another auditor. Finally it enables the internal audit activity to implement improvements in approach, over time.

> 'The chief audit executive should establish working paper policies for the various types of engagements performed. Standardized engagement working papers such

as questionnaires and audit programs may improve the efficiency of an engagement and facilitate the delegation of engagement work'[20]

Areas where standardisation of engagement records is practical will include:

- indexing system of engagement records;
- style of audit programmes;
- style of audit points sheets;
- style of internal control questionnaires;
- style of flowcharting;
- style of write-ups of interview conducted;
- style of schedules recording the conduct and results of detailed tests.

In addition to standardisation *within* engagement records, there will be a need to standardise the organisation of engagement records into principal files – which may be paper-based or electronic, or both. One effective approach is for each auditable unit within the audit universe to have a *permanent file* of information being of continuing significance.

> 'Some engagement working papers may be categorized as permanent or carry-forward engagement files. These files generally contain information of continuing importance.'[21]

There will also be a *current file* of schedules applicable to the last, or current, audit engagement. The permanent file evolves over time: schedules superseded from the permanent file may be transferred into a special section of the current file. We recommend that current files are retained until the completion of the next audit following the audit when that file was current – at which point they can be destroyed. Keeping the current file until then is helpful to the next audit team as they can then see how the previous audit team approached their task. The permanent file is never destroyed; it just develops over time. Some internal auditing activities also maintain a correspondence file for each audit engagement, whereas others divide correspondence between the permanent and current audit files.

> 'Record retention requirements should be designed to include all engagement records, regardless of the format in which the records are stored.'[22]

Almost all audit engagements include the preparation and issuance of an audit report. Since audit reports will be retained indefinitely, they should either be filed separately or a copy may be kept in the permanent file. The file which was the current file at the time is also likely to hold a copy of the audit report.

Policies and procedures for security over engagement records and for controlled access thereto need to be addressed.

> 'Departmental policies should explain who in the organization is responsible for ensuring the control and security of departmental records, who can be granted access to engagement records, and how requests for access to those records are to be handled.'[23]

The Institute states the general, unexceptional, principle that:

'Engagement working papers are the property of the organization. Engagement working paper files should generally remain under the control of the internal audit activity and should be accessible only to authorized personnel.'[24]

and goes on to say:

'Management and other members of the organization may request access to engagement working papers. Such access may be necessary to substantiate or explain engagement observations and recommendations or to utilize engagement documentation for other business purposes. These requests for access should be subject to the approval of the chief audit executive.'[25]

and:

'It is common practice for internal and external auditors to grant access to each other's audit working papers. Access to audit working papers by external auditors should be subject to the approval of the chief audit executive.'[26]

and:

'There are circumstances where parties outside the organization, other than external auditors, request access to audit working papers and reports. Prior to releasing such documentation, the chief audit executive should obtain the approval of senior management and/or legal counsel, as appropriate.'[27]

In CHAPTER B1.1 we explored the general place of policies and procedures in internal auditing.

## B4.1.11   Engagement Supervision

Every aspect of the planning and performance of the audit engagement should be supervised by more senior internal audit management:

'The chief audit executive is responsible for assuring that appropriate engagement supervision is provided. Supervision is a process that begins with planning and continues throughout the examination, evaluation, communicating, and follow-up phases of the engagement.'[28]

'The extent of supervision required will depend on the proficiency and experience of internal auditors and the complexity of the engagement. The chief audit executive has overall responsibility for review but may designate appropriately experienced members of the internal audit activity to perform the review. Appropriately experienced internal auditors may be utilized to review the work of other less experienced internal auditors.'[29]

An element of supervision of the performance of an audit engagement is that:
- 'Working papers that document the engagement should be ... reviewed by management of the internal audit activity.'[30]

Supervision includes:
- 'Seeing that the approved engagement program is carried out unless changes are both justified and authorized.

- Determining that engagement working papers adequately support the engagement observations, conclusions, and recommendations.
- Ensuring that engagement communications are accurate, objective, clear, concise, constructive, and timely.
- Ensuring that engagement objectives are met.
- Providing opportunities for developing internal auditors' knowledge, skills, and other competencies.'[31]

An important purpose of supervision during the fieldwork of an audit engagement is to ensure that auditor objectivity is preserved. Field auditors can get so close to the detail that they may find it hard to preserve sufficient objectivity without the assistance of effective supervision:

'The process of collecting, analyzing, interpreting, and documenting information should be supervised to provide reasonable assurance that the auditor's objectivity is maintained and engagement goals are met.'[32]

Unlike external auditing *Standards*, the mandatory internal auditing *Standards* do not impose an obligation that supervision should be documented, but this is covered at the level of a discretionary Practice Advisory:

'Appropriate evidence of supervision should be documented and retained.'[33]

'All engagement working papers should be reviewed to ensure that they properly support the engagement communications and that all necessary auditing procedures have been performed. Evidence of supervisory review should consist of the reviewer initialing and dating each working paper after it is reviewed. Other review techniques that provide evidence of supervisory review include completing an engagement working paper review checklist and/or preparing a memorandum specifying the nature, extent, and results of the review.'[34]

'Reviewers may make a written record (review notes) of questions arising from the review process. When clearing review notes, care should be taken to ensure that the working papers provide adequate evidence that questions raised during the review have been resolved. Acceptable alternatives with respect to disposition of review notes are as follows:
- Retain the review notes as a record of the questions raised by the reviewer and the steps taken in their resolution.
- Discard the review notes after the questions raised have been resolved and the appropriate engagement working papers have been amended to provide the additional information requested.'[35]

The supervisory responsibility includes a responsibility to approve variations from the previously agreed engagement work plan:

'In obtaining approval of the engagement work plan, such plans should be approved in writing by the chief audit executive or designee prior to the commencement of engagement work. Adjustments to engagement work plans should be approved in a timely manner. Initially, approval may be obtained orally, if factors preclude obtaining written approval prior to commencing engagement work.'[36]

---

[1]   Practice Advisory 2340–1: 'Engagement Supervision', para 3.
[2]   Except to run the internal auditing activity.
[3]   Practice Advisory 2320–1: 'Analysis and Evaluation', para 4.

4    Practice Advisory 2320–1: 'Analysis and Evaluation', para 3:

'Internal auditors should use analytical auditing procedures in planning the engagement in accordance with the guidelines contained in Section 2200 of the Standards (Practice Advisory 2210-1).'

5    Practice Advisory 2320–1: 'Analysis and Evaluation', para 2.
6    Practice Advisory 2320–1: 'Analysis and Evaluation', para 1.
7    Practice Advisory 2320–1: 'Analysis and Evaluation', para 5.
8    Practice Advisory 1210.A2–1: 'Identification of Fraud', paras 11 and 12.
9    Practice Advisory 2300–1: 'The Internal Auditor's Use of Personal Information in Conducting Audits', para 4.
10   Practice Advisory 2300–1: 'The Internal Auditor's Use of Personal Information in Conducting Audits', para 5.
11   Practice Advisory 2420–1: 'Quality of Communications', para 1.
12   Practice Advisory 2010–2: 'Linking the Audit Plan to Risk and Exposures', para 5.
13   Practice Advisory 2330–1: 'Recording Information', para 4.
14   Practice Advisory 2330–1: 'Recording Information', para 3.
15   Practice Advisory 2330–1: 'Recording Information', para 1.
16   Practice Advisory 2330–1: 'Recording Information', para 1.
17   Practice Advisory 2330–1: 'Recording Information', para 7.
18   Practice Advisory 2330–1: 'Recording Information', para 2.
19   Practice Advisory 2330–1: 'Recording Information', para 1.
20   Practice Advisory 2330–1: 'Recording Information', para 6.
21   Practice Advisory 2330–1: 'Recording Information', para 6.
22   Practice Advisory 2330.A2–1: 'Retention of Records', para 1.
23   Practice Advisory 2330.A1–2: 'Legal Considerations in Granting Access to Engagement Records', para 7.
24   Practice Advisory 2330.A1–1: 'Control of Engagement Records', para 1.
25   Practice Advisory 2330.A1–1: 'Control of Engagement Records', para 2.
26   Practice Advisory 2330.A1–1: 'Control of Engagement Records', para 3.
27   Practice Advisory 2330.A1–1: 'Control of Engagement Records', para 4.
28   Practice Advisory 2340–1: 'Engagement Supervision', para 1.
29   Practice Advisory 2340–1: 'Engagement Supervision', para 2.
30   Practice Advisory 2330–1: 'Recording Information', para 1.
31   Practice Advisory 2340–1: 'Engagement Supervision', para 1.
32   Practice Advisory 2240–1: 'Engagement Work Program', para 2.
33   Practice Advisory 2340–1: 'Engagement Supervision', para 2.
34   Practice Advisory 2340–1: 'Engagement Supervision', para 5.
35   Practice Advisory 2340–1: 'Engagement Supervision', para 6.
36   Practice Advisory 2240.A1–1: 'Approval of Work Programs', para 1.

# Performing the engagement – supplementary guidance

## B4.2.1 Audit testing

The Auditor's Operational Standard of the Chartered Association of Certified Accountants, while directed primarily at external auditors, is also applicable to internal auditors. Other professional accounting bodies have closely similar auditing standards, viz:

> 'The auditor should obtain relevant and reliable audit evidence sufficient to enable him (sic) to draw reasonable conclusions therefrom.'

> 'If the auditor wishes to place reliance on any internal controls, he (sic) should ascertain and evaluate those controls and perform compliance tests on their operation.'

While the external auditor may have ways of obtaining audit reassurance that the client's financial statements are true and fair *other than* by placing reliance on internal controls, the internal auditor cannot avoid making an assessment of internal control as the mission of the internal auditor is to reassure management that their systems of internal control are sound. Compliance testing is therefore an important component of almost all internal audit assignments. Compliance tests (and other types of audit test) must be arranged so that the evidence they provide is:

- relevant;
- reliable; and
- sufficient.

## B4.2.2 *Types of audit test*

There are three principal types of audit test:

- walk through tests;
- compliance tests; and
- weakness, or substantive, tests.

Walk through tests usually involve taking a very small number of transactions, perhaps half a dozen, and tracing their processing – perhaps by observation. The purpose of walk through tests is to confirm the auditor's understanding of the characteristics of the system and can therefore be classified as part of the fact-finding stage of the audit.

Compliance tests are designed to confirm whether or not (and the extent to which) control procedures are being followed by management and staff. While walk through tests contribute to providing this reassurance, compliance tests are likely to involve audit examination of larger samples in order to provide the level of audit reassurance required. The smaller sample used earlier in the audit as a walk through test may often be regarded as forming part of the larger compliance test.

Where non-compliance with controls is established (either by talking with staff, by observation as part of the walk through process, or by conducting compliance tests of these controls) there may be an audit requirement to 'drill down in depth' to establish one or both of the following:

- Has non-compliance with the control led to avoidable errors and losses? Alternatively, non-compliance with this control may not have caused any actual unwanted outcomes.
- If avoidable errors and losses have occurred, how many, and to what cost?

We call these 'weakness tests' because they are designed to measure the impact, if any, of a control weakness. Alternatively, external auditors usually call these 'substantive tests' as they are designed to substantiate completeness, existence, valuation, ownership and/or disclosure. Weakness or substantive tests may be appropriate not just when a laid down control has not been fully complied with but also when there is a control weakness due to an essential control procedure not being laid down as a requirement.

## B4.2.3 *Objectives of 'weakness' or 'substantive' tests*

The issues of completeness, existence, valuation, ownership and/or disclosure are *prima facie* of interest to the external auditor conducting an audit of the financial statements, but they are also often applicable to internal auditors. External auditors (in the Operational Standard referred to above) define them as follows:

| | |
|---|---|
| Completeness | Assets, liabilities and transactions have been completely recorded. |
| Existence | The recorded assets and liabilities exist and the recorded transactions actually took place. |
| Valuation | The recorded assets and liabilities have been correctly valued and the recorded transactions correctly measured. |
| Ownership | The recorded assets are owned by the company, the liabilities have been properly incurred by the company and the transactions were properly undertaken by the company. |
| Disclosure | The financial statements are drawn up in accordance with statutory and professional requirements and are not misleading. |

Similar interests apply to internal auditors whose work is not, however, so oriented towards the financial statements of the company. Internal auditors would add the following interests which also might be the subject of audit testing:

Availability      Company resources were appropriately available to the business at all times.

Economy      Input costs were minimised.

Efficiency      Activity was conducted in the right ways so as to maximise output per unit of input.

Effectiveness      Objectives (planned outputs) were achieved.

## B4.2.4   *General testing principles*

Making use of the computer, for instance with audit interrogation software, it is sometimes practical to obtain exact answers by testing every unit within the audit universe (ie population). For instance, an audit interrogation package might be able to quickly go through a customer file and identify every customer whose credit limit had been exceeded, specifying how many were in that position and the total amount of excess credit. Otherwise, auditors are likely to have to work with samples taken from the population. The results obtained from samples are at the best only reliable estimates, not exact answers. Audit interrogation software can often be used to select a sample for further work by the auditor – this is particularly useful if the items within the universe resist identification manually – perhaps because they are not numbered, or are not held in a manually kept file in numeric sequence.

If the auditor wishes to be able to draw reliable conclusions about the population as a whole, the sample selected must be representative of the population sampled from. It must also give results which can be objectively measured. There is an obvious premium on the sample size not being excessive as this would entail extra audit work, and much of the development work in devising modern sampling plans has been inspired by a desire to reduce sample size. A sampling plan is a method of statistical sampling suitable for a particular purpose, and we introduce these in the final part of this session.

## B4.2.5   *Sample selection – by judgement or randomly*

Auditors select samples by judgement or randomly. Random sampling is appropriate for the selection of samples for scientific (ie statistical) sampling work. Judgement (ie 'directed') sample selection is subjective and does not allow reliable conclusions to be drawn on the population as a whole based on one's analysis of the sample. Judgement sampling does have the advantage of allowing the auditor to determine sample size according to the time available for the audit test. It also allows the auditor to select items which he or she considers to be of special audit interest. For instance, a few large items may comprise the larger part of the value of a ledger: if they are within the auditor's judgement sample they enable a larger amount of the total value of the ledger to be covered by a test of a smaller number of transactions. Judgement sampling also allows the use of the so-called 'auditor's nose' to home in on items of audit interest.

On the other hand, random samples are representative of the population as a whole. Prerequisites of random selection are:

- know the population; and
- ensure each item has an equal chance of selection.

## B4.2.6   Random number selection

A sample may be selected at random in a variety of ways. Random number tables can be used to determine the items to be selected, or software can be used to generate the random numbers. The table should be entered at random and proceeded through in a predetermined order. If a selected number does not exist in the population, the table should be proceeded with in the usual way rather than picking out the next item in the population after the missing item (which could create significant bias in sample selection).

## B4.2.7   Interval selection

If the population is unnumbered or its numbering resists identification a modification to random selection can be used. One modified approach is called 'interval selection'. Once again, each item should have an equal chance of being selected and the population must be 'known' – for instance there should be no items missing from the population. The first item in the population is picked at random and the population is then passed through selecting every 'nth' item. Inapplicable items should be selected but ignored – the immediately adjacent item to an inapplicable item should not be selected so as to avoid the risk of bias in the sample selected. Excess selections should be randomly excluded. If the population is patterned, then more than one pass should be made from new random starting points.

## B4.2.8   Cluster selection

If it is difficult to access all of a population in order to select a sample, a compromise can be made – with a small sacrifice on reliability as it can be argued that under this method each item in the universe does not truly have an equal chance of being selected. We call this 'cluster sampling' although the expression 'cluster selection' is a less confusing expression as this technique relates only to sample selection and does not refer to a sampling plan. Under this method of sample selection, a cluster is selected at random. It may be a filing cabinet at a particular location. All of the items in the selected cluster become the selected sample and are examined by the auditor. If a sample is then selected from the selected cluster we call this 'multi-stage' sampling – which certainly has a reduced degree of reliability.

## B4.2.9   Stratified selection

It is sometimes helpful to divide a population into more than one sub-population, grouping into each sub-population items which are most closely similar. Many audit populations lend themselves to this process of stratification. For instance, an inventory might divide into two or three classes, eg:

Class A: 15% of the different items held in stock account for 65% of the total investment in stock.

Class B: 20% of the different items held in stock account for 20% of the total investment in stock.

Class C: 65% of the different items held in stock account for 15% of the total investment in stock.

Once again, in order to stratify a population, you must first know your population! Separation into more than one stratum can be done by judgement or by mathematics. A sample is then taken from each stratum (using random number selection, interval selection or cluster selection). The results of the audit tests on each stratum must be interpreted separately and then combined by judgement to allow overall subjective conclusions to be drawn about the population as a whole. Since each stratum has less variability than the population as a whole (a concept we discuss below) this technique often allows smaller samples to be worked with or a higher degree of reliability to be obtained – the two are trade-off against each other.

## B4.2.10  *Determining required sample size*

If the auditor is using judgemental sampling as distinct from statistical sampling, sample size is likely to be determined by the auditor's judgement of the time available for the task. Required sample size for scientific/statistical sampling is influenced by:

- under audit control:
  - required *confidence*;
  - required *precision*;
- not under audit control:
  - population *variability*;
  - population *size* (to a limited extent).

## B4.2.11  **Confidence and precision**

'Confidence' is a matter of how confident we are that the sample results are representative of the population as a whole within the precision limits we have set. 'Precision' means 'tolerance'. Combining these two related concepts, we might settle for:

'95% confident that the value of discounts is $3m ± 2%'.

Another way of putting this is to say that 19 samples out of 20 would produce results within 2% of each other.

While that level of confidence and precision might be suitable for the external auditor, it is unlikely that the internal auditor will generally work to such high levels of confidence and precision as this would usually result in sample sizes being uncomfortably large.

### B4.2.12   Variability

Required sample size is very sensitive to the variability of the population. Since all people have two feet, a very small sample would be adequate to determine the average number of feet that people had. On the other hand, a larger sample would be required to reliably determine the average size of a foot – since the size of feet is more variable. A population of similar objects, such as feet, arranged by size will tend to be bell shaped in that the majority will tend towards the mean (or average). The shape of the bell curve depicts the variability of the population and this can be measured mathematically using the idea of the *standard deviation.*

The standard deviation of a population is the square root of the average of the squared deviations from the mean. 68% of the items within the population will be within one standard deviation of the mean, 95.5% within two standard deviations and 99.7% within three standard deviations. One can be 68% confident that each item selected in a sample will be ± one standard deviation of the mean.

To be able to interpret the reliability of sample results it is therefore often necessary to know the standard deviation of the population as a whole. Unfortunately this is often unknown as the auditor has not examined the whole population and wishes to avoid doing so by working with a sample only. To meet this difficulty, many sampling plans make use of the principle of an assumed standard deviation – if the assumed deviation is exceeded in the sample tested, then the auditor can have less confidence in the results or, alternatively, the auditor must select additional items so as to work with a larger sample until the required level of confidence is attained.

### B4.2.13   *Sampling plans*

Sampling plans are methods of statistical sampling designed to be appropriate for particular types of audit testing. Each method allows the requisite sample size to be determined and the results of the test on the sample to be evaluated. Selection of the sample of given size should be at random using one of the methods referred to earlier in these notes.

It is beyond the scope of this introduction to deal with each sampling plan in detail. We introduce only the principal ones.

### B4.2.14   Estimation sampling

'Attribute sampling' is an example of a sampling plan which is usually used to test internal control. It allows 'how many' answers to be obtained – such as the determination of the number of errors in the population as a whole. It could, for instance, estimate the number of invoices sent out late, but not 'how late', nor their value, which would be the task of 'variables sampling'.

Attribute sampling makes use of tables or a formula to determine sample size after determining population size, desired confidence level and precision and the expected error rate.

### B4.2.15  Stop-or-go sampling

This is a variant of attribute sampling suitable if it is possible to work with small samples from 'clean' (ie almost error free) populations. First the user determines the number of errors in a small sample. Then the user reads from a table the possible maximum error rate for the desired level of confidence. If that error rate is satisfactory, the auditor ends his or her test. If not, a further sample is added to the original sample and the results re-evaluated, and so on until the desired confidence level has been reached. If the sample size gets too large, the user can switch to normal attribute sampling.

### B4.2.16  Discovery sampling

A variant of attribute sampling. It is suitable to discover at least one example of an error when the auditor suspects there is more than one error, and is willing to specify an assumed number of errors and will not pass an opinion on the population as a whole. For instance, in a population of 5,000, the auditor might be content with fewer than 100 errors. If the auditor examines 150 items and finds no error amongst them, the auditor can be 95.4% confident that the population has fewer than 100 errors.

### B4.2.17  Variables sampling

This is usually used to estimate values, but can be used to estimate volumes or other units. Monetary unit sampling is a refinement of this. Tables are used after determining population size, desired confidence and precision and standard deviation.

## B4.2.18  *Sample evaluation*

Don't forget that sample results are reliable estimates – not exact answers. Sample results are also data which must be interpreted. The auditor needs to ask:

- Are the results significant/material?
- What is the reason(s) for these results?
- What is the root cause?
- What are the effects?

## B4.2.19  Audit Interviewing

Here we consider the differing interviewing situations that the auditor may be in, and the appropriate approaches to take at each stage of an interview. Our purpose is to provide practical advice to assist the auditor in what is, for many, one of the most vexing parts of the audit job.

To start with it is as well to realise that an audit interview is not an isolated happening. The nature of the social interaction which will occur within an audit interview depends to a large extent upon the context in which the interview occurs. One aspect of this background is the general credibility of the internal auditing department. Another is the image of the internal auditing department – for instance, whether it is seen as an unwelcome spy and snoop, or as a constructive aid to management.

Certainly, the very word 'interview' betrays the unequal roles of the two actors involved: it is an activity in which the interviewer tends to dominate, and few like to be dominated. So there is an inherent risk of conflict even before the interview commences.

Auditors must balance the advantages of having more than one auditor present at an interview with the risks of weight of audit numbers intimidating the interviewee. If the meeting includes several line staff representatives then it can be matched by a similar number of auditors, subject to audit team size, without engendering intimidation. The advantages are that the auditors present can perform different roles, one or more concentrating on directing the meeting (in particular ensuring that subject matter is covered and all questions are asked), another making the essential record of the meeting, and perhaps another studying body language.

A related aspect is the extent to which audit staff are generally encouraged to cultivate friendly relationships with auditees. A survey of almost 350 internal audit managers found that 57% claimed to encourage their audit staff to make specific attempts to cultivate friendly relationships with the individuals responsible for the work they were reviewing, although in a majority of cases this extended only occasionally to contact outside office hours. A friendly relationship is one of the social enablers which facilitate effective communication; so, to the extent that it may be absent, the auditor will have additional problems in the interview situation.

The auditor should be aware of entering the interview situation with the distinct possibility that the interviewee is at the least wary of the auditor and perhaps even hostile. Mints[1] found that the inspection-oriented auditor (who tended to report all violations and whose reports were often used as instruments of punishment) triggered hostile reactions in the majority of auditees: the effect was partly that they were unwilling to talk frankly with the auditor as they felt threatened, and partly that they were less likely to accept the auditor's findings. At the other extreme, the participative auditor (whose approach was to assist the auditee in the implementation of the auditor's recommendations and who went to great lengths to ensure that no blame attached to any auditee as a result of the audit work) was not met by a hostile response.

The participative approach is not, however, one which most internal auditing departments follow. The most common audit approach was found by Mints to be somewhere between the inspection and the participative styles, with the auditor trying to carry the roles of both policeman and friendly advisor. Not surprisingly Mints found that the typical auditee was still wary and suspicious of such an auditor, and this is the reception we are likely to encounter even if it is masked by the subtleties of politeness.

## **B4.2.20** *Types of audit 'interview'*

### The initial meeting

When an operation is to be audited for the first time, as with a newly acquired subsidiary company, initial contact must be made between internal audit and line management. The initiative invariably rests with internal audit as it is usually they who will initiate the audit. Face-to-face contact is much to be preferred.

Where line management of the operating unit to be audited are of a senior level it is likely to be appropriate for this initial contact to be arranged between the director of internal auditing and the head of the operation to be audited. Although there will be times when this meeting will take place between people of unmatched seniority (one of the attractions of internal audit is that it enables young people to become accustomed to meeting and dealing with people at more senior levels) this is a potential cause of tension which may lead to a strained relationship between internal audit and line management. It is sound practice to match the seniority of the auditor with the seniority of the line manager as closely as possible. Managers are used to dealing with other managers of equivalent, or nearly equivalent, seniority and are unlikely to react favourably if confronted by a much more junior auditor. This is especially the case as it must be realised that in some respects the auditor is acting the dominant role and no manager takes kindly to being dominated by a more junior person. This is one reason why it is important that the status of senior members of the internal auditing department is senior enough.

The purpose of this initial meeting is to explain the objectives and methods of working of the internal auditing department. As the internal auditing department's function is carefully worked out and not easily understood, many internal auditing departments have found it useful to produce a booklet which sets out clearly their function. A copy of this is left behind after the meeting for the line manager to study at leisure.

We have considered the initial meeting prior to an audit which is to be conducted for the first time. On subsequent occasions it is less important for the director of internal auditing, or an immediate deputy, to be present at the initial meeting which takes place at the commencement of the audit – indeed it will probably be impractical for this person to attend. On these occasions the auditing department should do the best it can to match the seniorities of the auditor and the line manager. A wide disparity of seniority is less serious if the auditor is already known to the line manager from an earlier audit visit. If it is to be a new auditor a suitable introduction should be arranged.

### **B4.2.21** The tour of the premises

The tour of the premises at the commencement of an audit should be regarded as an interview situation with as much at stake as at any other interview. The auditors involved should be well-prepared and should behave carefully. Initial impressions are hard to change and unfavourable impressions of the audit team made at this stage may prejudice the continuing credibility of the team and the later acceptance of its findings and recommendations. For instance, on one occasion an auditor foolishly made a grossly inaccurate guess at the liquid capacity of a tank: he later confessed that he thought he never regained his credibility with line management, who thought he did not understand their problems and were, from the outset, predisposed to reject his recommendations which they suspected would not be worth taking seriously and might create more problems than they might solve.

## B4.2.22   The fact-finding interview

More audit interviews of this nature occur than of any other type. Yet the opportunity for holding such interviews should be used discriminatingly. If the information being sought is available in the form of records, procedures manuals or by observation, then that is usually the preferred method of obtaining it.

Similar interviews may be used to gain access to dependable data or to obtain an authority to conduct an observation. These interviews may all be necessary to determine facts that vary (census data). There will usually be no alternative to an interview of this type to determine opinions, attitudes or trends of belief. Certainly the use of these interviews should be limited to worthwhile issues of significance to the interviewee if the auditor is to avoid being seen as an impractical, non-productive time-waster.

The auditor must realise that the choice of interviewee will determine the answers obtained. For instance, it is likely the interviewee will tell how a job *should* be done if he or she is the manager in charge; it is more likely that the answers will relate to how the job *is* done if the interviewee is the person who does the job.

The auditor must interview enough people to provide a representative basis for the information he or she receives. A skilful interviewer will be able tactfully to impress upon the interviewee that the interviewee is being depended upon, and is responsible for, the accuracy of the information being given.

## B4.2.23   Interviews to discuss audit findings

The audit team should keep in close touch with line management throughout the audit. Significant findings should be brought to management's attention when they are made, in oral or written progress reports. The initial meeting at the commencement of the audit should establish that this will occur and provide a mechanism for it. Towards the end of an audit, the audit team leader, and perhaps the most senior audit staff in the team, should meet with the head of the audited unit, who may be accompanied by the most senior staff of that unit, for a final 'wrap-up' meeting. Ideally a draft audit report should have been issued beforehand and should be the basis for the discussion at this meeting. It is not easy to achieve the drafting and first typing of the audit report in time for the wrap-up meeting just prior to the end of the audit field work: consequently many auditing departments compromise in one of two ways:

1.   Discuss their findings with line management in a 'wrap-up' meeting towards the end of the audit visit, without the benefit of a drafted audit report, in which case the draft audit report should be sent to line management of the unit audited before it is finally issued.

2. Return to the site at a later date to discuss the draft report.

Discussion of audit findings prior to issuance of the final audit report is essential for several reasons. First, it primes line management as to what they can expect and makes them less disposed to react hostilely when the final audit report arrives. Secondly, it provides an opportunity to incorporate the auditee's responses into the audit report – which, inter alia, may help the auditee to save face. Thirdly, it provides a final opportunity for the auditor to check audit findings and thereby reduces the likelihood of errors appearing in the final audit report. While there may be disagreements over the auditor's recommendations as these are matters of judgement, there should be no disagreement over the auditor's findings as these should be matters of fact: such disagreements should be resolved. Any remaining disagreements should be referred to in the final audit report. Fourthly, this interview provides an opportunity to establish clearly the action expected of line management on receipt of the audit report. Many companies require the manager to whom the report is addressed to respond formally to the internal auditing department within two or three weeks of receipt of the audit report.

## B4.2.24  *Interviewing Approach*

### Preparing for the interview

The following sections are written in the style of instructions to an auditor on his or her audit approach.

First, don't barge in unprepared. *Know your field* – swat up the background by reviewing any factual matter in the area you will be discussing.

Secondly, *know what you want to accomplish.* You may even go to the extent of planning the interview by writing out its objectives, possible problems which you may encounter during the interview, and possible modifications of approach you may then adopt. Certainly you may prepare a list of questions even though you are likely not to follow them too obtrusively or stubbornly.

Thirdly, if possible, *know the interviewee.* Just as you should tailor a written report to its reader, so you should prepare for, and conduct, an interview in a way which is personalised to the interviewee. Try to anticipate the interviewee's point of view; even during the interview you should try to imagine the impact that your approach is having upon the interviewee.

You should also endeavour to *know yourself* as well as possible: this includes and appreciation of your mannerisms and the impact they have on people. It also includes an appreciation of your own personal bias towards particular forms of question.

Administrative preparation includes obtaining a proper introduction to the interviewee where appropriate, making the appointment in good time, and providing for adequate privacy in order to establish a relaxed working relationship.

Finally, make sure that enough time is allowed; if the interviewer has inadequate time he or she will tend to force the interview, losing the opportunity to obtain valuable information and risking the interviewee misinterpreting the auditor as being uncommitted, uncertain and unprofessional; if the interviewee has inadequate time he or she is likely to adopt a false stance in order to expedite the termination of the interview.

## B4.2.25 At the start of the interview

Endeavour to establish a relationship of mutual confidence. While this is more a matter of the interviewer's attitude as perceived by the interviewee (and vice versa), there are some techniques which are useful. Remember that an interview is an exercise in communication, and communication is a two-way process. For instance, the interviewee will expect to receive signals from the interviewer which indicate that the interviewer has understood what the interviewee has said.

The interviewee should be put at ease, and a prerequisite for this is that the *interviewer* is at ease. Don't rush the start of the interview. On the other hand, don't delay so long that impatience sets in and the interviewee suspects you are hesitant because you are unsure of yourself. Try to put the interviewee at ease by establishing, if possible, some pleasant associations which you both can share. Your early questions should be on topics which are easy to talk about. If possible, commence with questions which enable the interviewee to take pride in his or her knowledge of achievements: the early questions should certainly be ones which the interviewee will be able to answer and is unlikely to refuse to answer.

## B4.2.26 During the interview

Tact, patience and firmness on the part of the interviewer are the qualities which are called for. The tactful interviewer avoids resentment which would lead to friction. He or she will never rebuke, ridicule or show annoyance. Certainly he or she must never seem bored. It is usually fatal to appear to be patronising and this is likely to be the case if the interviewer projects an image of being an expert. While the interviewer's questions should be as simple and straightforward as possible, he or she must be astute enough not to have the tables turned on him or her.

The interviewer is principally at risk in three ways:

- the interviewee may fluster the interviewer by a display of rudeness or impatience, or by deliberately unintelligible explanations;
- the interviewee may try to draw the interviewer into expressing ill-considered 'off-the-cuff' responses to questions posed by the interviewee;
- the interviewee may wander from the subject or give ambiguous answers.

The interviewer must be tactfully persistent in cutting short irrelevancies or repetition and in coming back to points inadequately explained. Otherwise the interviewee will form the view that the questioner does not know what he or she is after or is afraid of making the main point.

Most important, the auditor must be a good listener. After all, it is the interviewer who is interviewing the other party. The interviewee should be helped to tell the story and then, if necessary, to supplement it. Interruptions should only be in order to return the conversation to the subject or to cut short repetition.

Attentive pauses are often productive but should not be over-used: this is a technique frequently followed by television interviewers who find their interviewees then tend to feel obliged to carry on talking. It may be their supplementary remarks which are the most interesting.

A good listener is generally also one who asks questions in such a way that the interviewee feels the questioner is genuinely interested in the answers. Many auditors fail to do this when they are asking questions relating to accounting practices or administrative procedures!

Finally, a good listener learns to see behind the spoken words to the hidden feelings of the interviewee and to half-expressed or unexpressed ideas.

### B4.2.27    At the end of the interview

There is an art in knowing how to stop when you are through – but that is what must be done. At the end of an interview there may be a case for briefly summarising what has been covered. The summary at the end of the meeting should focus upon what has been agreed during the meeting as action which will be taken after the meeting: it is rarely appropriate to extend the summary so that it becomes a précis of the entire contents of the meeting. The interviewer should certainly check if the interviewee has anything to add, and should also be alert for any new information which might be dropped as a casual remark by the interviewee during the informality of the end of the interview.

Finally, a word of appreciation may be appropriate together with an outline of the next steps which will be taken (such as a later meeting, or a series of meetings with the interviewee's staff).

### B4.2.28    After the end of the interview

The auditor should record all data collected during the interview as soon as possible. Clear distinction should be made in the audit notes between fact, inference and opinion. Written confirmation should be secured where appropriate. The results of the interview should be checked to other sources for confirmation.

It is wise for the auditor to review his or her own performance in the interview, in order to learn lessons for the future.

### B4.2.29    *Interviewing style*

There are many different types of question, some of which auditors should be wary of using. In general terms we can say that the interviewer should use the interviewee's language, be unambiguous and easily understood, be quiet in manner yet indicative of interest in the answer. It is as well to be methodical in the questioning but only to ask one question at a time. Even when the question has been fully answered some interviewers find it difficult to drop the question and move on to the next.

Frequently it is appropriate to check answers by repeating them back to the interviewee in a different form – for instance, percentages can be converted into numbers. Be alert for common errors – people tend to be inaccurate about dates, times, percentages and such like.

## B4.2.30 *Suitable types of question in appropriate contexts*

The Elephant's Child
I keep six honest serving-men
(They taught me all I knew);

Their names are What and Why and When
And How and Where and Who.

I send them over land and sea,
I send them east and west;
But after they have worked for me,
I give them all the rest.

I let them rest from nine to five,
For I am busy then,
As well as breakfast, lunch, and tea,
For they are hungry men.
But different folk have different views,
I know a person small -
She keeps ten million serving-men,
Who get no rest at all!

She sends 'em abroad on her own affairs,
From the second she opens her eyes -
One million Hows, two million Wheres,
And seven million Whys!

| **TYPE** | | **EXAMPLES** |
|---|---|---|
| **Closed** | | |
| | A) | Were you present on that occasion? |
| | B) | Did you sign the document? |
| **Forced choice** | | |
| | A) | Is your job full-time or part-time? |
| | B) | Did you check it yourself or did you get someone else to check it? |
| **Direct** | | |
| | A) | *What* are your responsibilities? |
| | B) | *Why* did you authorise it? |

440

| **TYPE** | | **EXAMPLES** |
|---|---|---|
| | C) | *When* were you asked to do this? |
| | D) | *How* often do you review these procedures? |
| | E) | *Where* can I find the documentation? |
| | F) | *Who* is responsible for authorising this? |
| **Open** | | |
| | A) | Could you give me a picture of your daily (or weekly) routine of work? |
| | B) | Tell me about customer relations – what you see the problems to be and how these are being tackled. |
| | C) | Some people I find are broadly satisfied with the ways things are going in their department, while others feel there is room for change. I wonder how you feel? |
| | D) | What happened? |
| | E) | What did you do then? |
| | F) | How do you feel about that? |
| | G) | What would you like to do next? |
| | H) | Why do you think she said that? |
| | I) | What's the worst that could happen? |
| | J) | Tell me about ..............? |
| **Probe** | | |
| | A) | What exactly did that entail? |
| | B) | How did you go about doing that? |
| | C) | You didn't mention any colleagues – was anyone working with you on the project? |
| | D) | And how did you feel about that? |
| | E) | In what way? |
| **Encouraging** | | |
| | A) | When dealing with the public you must have come across many interesting people – and perhaps some awkward ones? |
| **Link** (for making smooth transitions from one topic to another) | | |
| | A) | Among other things you mentioned figure work – so perhaps we could discuss that now. Can you tell me more about the work you did in Accounts? |
| **Reflecting back** | | |
| | A) | You felt you had been by-passed? |

441

| TYPE | | EXAMPLES |
|------|------|----------|
| | B) | It seemed to you rather unfair? |

### B4.2.31   *Types of question to be wary of*

| TYPE | | EXAMPLES |
|------|------|----------|
| **Leading** | | |
| | A) | You get on well with colleagues, I take it? |
| | B) | And you would be willing to do humdrum jobs such as filing? |
| | C) | What I really want to know is – are you going to take the job then be off within three months? (The question suggests a desired answer) |
| **Fatuous/redundant** | | |
| | A) | So you've been a stamp collector all your life. You must be pretty interested in stamps then? |
| | B) | And then [looking at application form] you went to college I see? |
| **Loaded** (Emotionally slanted, putting the interviewee in an awkward position) | | |
| | A) | Then you went to university and took a degree. Did you get a first? |
| | B) | What do you mean by an interest in travel – that could be anything from an annual holiday to a real interest? |
| | C) | Do you merely eliminate those who appear unsuitable or do you have a positive selection policy? |
| | D) | Did they warn you about us? |
| | E) | Are you prepared to work in this madhouse? |
| **Multiple** | | |
| | A) | When did you move to London? Was it by choice or necessity? And did this cause any problems for your wife – and, of course, for your children's schooling? |

### B4.2.32   *Audit interviewing – practical tips*

**General points**

1.   Try to develop the habit of considering the impact of your words before you speak them.

2.   Be firm with an obstructive interviewee, but do not waste time if he or she is being unhelpful.
3.   Mannerisms may distract and/or irritate, but not all mannerisms are dysfunctional. They are likely to be harmful if they are either annoying or excessively repetitive – eg:
   –   wriggling in your seat;
   –   waving a hand with or without a pencil in it;
   –   waving papers;
   –   scratching your head;
   –   hand over your mouth;
   –   expressions such as 'ugh', 'you know', 'um', 'right', 'yes', 'OK', 'you see', 'I see'.
4.   Prepare your interview well.
5    Don't say anything which raises the suggestion that you may think the interviewee's cooperation is in doubt, as this amounts to a negative assessment of the interviewee and will tend to alienate him or her and get the very response you are intending to avoid. The only exception might be well on into the middle of an interview when an auditee has demonstrated beyond any doubt that he is being openly obstructive and unhelpful.

**At the commencement**
1.   Don't omit pleasantries, and don't cut them too short – respond to the interviewee's remarks by adding something in context.
2.   Make sure you introduce yourself (though preferably this should have been done beforehand by a mutual acquaintance).
3.   Quickly go through the purpose of the meeting.
4.   Be cheerful.
5.   Be confident.

**Asking questions**
1.   Common errors:
   –   not actually asking a question;
   –   asking a question which is so broad as to be meaningless;
   –   asking forced choice questions;
   –   asking more than one question at a time;
   –   firing questions too fast so that it seems like an interrogation;
   –   appearing to work through a shopping list of fixed questions.

**Listening to answers**
1.   Look attentive.
2.   *Do* actually listen to the answer: avoid allowing yourself to be distracted into thinking what your next question will be.
3.   Don't study your papers too much.

**Reactions to answers**
1.   Don't rebuke. For instance, don't say 'You should know the answer to that question!'

2. Respond in a way that indicates both interest and the fact that you have absorbed the answer, eg:
   - repeat part of the answer in an animated way;
   - link the answer to the next question by asking a supplementary question, or by connecting to the next question with a 'logical phrase';
   - supplementary questions can also be used to test initial answers;
   - don't over-use the same type of response so that it becomes an irritating mannerism.
3. Make sure you don't overlook unclear, inadequate answers – ask the question again in a different way.
4. If an answer indicates that the question was misunderstood, make sure that no blame is attributed to the interviewee for misunderstanding the question. Don't say: 'No, my question was ...'; instead say: 'I'm sorry, I didn't make my question clear; I meant to ask ...'.
5. Don't imply that it doesn't matter that the interviewee can't answer a question, as this implies that the question was a waste of his or her time. It may also suggest that the quality of answers to later questions does not really matter very much.
6. Some questions should follow leads given by the interviewee's answers to earlier questions.
7. Take quick, brief notes whenever it is obvious that you will not be very likely to remember the answer to the question without an aide-memoire.

**Conclusions**
1. Don't be patronising. For instance, don't say: 'You gave me good answers to my questions'.
2. Don't presume. For instance, don't say: 'I'll come to see you first thing tomorrow to conclude this discussion'.
3. Give the interviewee the chance to say anything he may particularly want to say.
4. Make sure you give the interviewee an idea of what happens next. For instance, what you will do next, what you will do with the information he or she has given you, or when (if at all) you would appreciate the opportunity to talk with him or her again.

## B4.2.33  Audit engagement checklists

Audit management checklist

Report:-

Audit Year:-

[To be used by the person planning, organising and controlling the audit]

This checklist is an example in use. It is not perfect and is offered to suggest ideas.

|  |  | Target date for comple-tion | Actual date com-pleted |
|---|---|---|---|
| 1 | Arrange start dates with local and head office management |  |  |
| 2 | Book hotels and make any necessary travel arrangements |  |  |
| 3 | Review audit files and other background information on the audit area |  |  |
| 4 | Pre-audit visit to operation to be audited |  |  |
| 5 | Advise plans to external auditor |  |  |
| 6 | Plan audit programme (within overall audit budget) |  |  |
| 7 | Brief audit team on allocation of responsibilities |  |  |
| 8 | Review progress of audit work with individual team members |  |  |
| 9 | Control the work of the audit team within the context of the audit programme |  |  |
| 10 | Discuss audit comments with local management |  |  |
| 11 | Communicate details of audit work to external auditors |  |  |
| 12 | Write the audit report and obtain clearance from the Director of Internal Auditing |  |  |
| 13 | Issue draft audit report to local management |  |  |
| 14 | Discuss draft audit report with local management |  |  |
| 15 | Clear audit report with local management |  |  |
| 16 | Final approval of the audit report by the Director of Internal Auditing |  |  |
| 17 | Issue audit report and send copies to all parties responsible for implementing audit recommendations |  |  |
| 18 | Complete an appraisal of the unit audited |  |  |
| 19 | Review the adequacy of the audit files and ensure that all papers are properly filed away |  |  |
| 20 | Review budget and actual times and suggest any amendments for subsequent years |  |  |
| 21 | Follow-up action taken on audit recommendations |  |  |

AUDIT WORK CHECK LIST

System:-

Target start date:-

Target finish date:-

[To assist each auditor in the audit team]

This checklist is an example in use. It is not perfect and is offered to suggest ideas.

Auditor ....................................................

| 1 | Read details of the control area in the Audit Manual | | |
|---|---|---|---|
| 2 | Review: | Permanent file | |
| | | Last set of audit working papers | |
| | | Previous audit report | |
| | | Other relevant papers | |
| 3 | Discuss the work with the audit manager and agree audit objectives and programme | | |
| 4 | Review: | Budgets and operating statements | |
| | | Other relevant management information | |
| 5 | Obtain background information relevant to the system being examined | | |
| 6 | Ensure that senior line management are aware of the work which the auditor intends to make | | |
| 7 | Contact person in charge | | |
| 8 | Conduct fact finding and appraise soundness of the system | | |
| 9 | Test-check operation of the system | | |
| 10 | Update/write system notes (including flowcharts) | | |
| 11 | Complete/update computer flowcharts | | |
| 12 | Annotate previous year's reports to show action taken on matters previously raised | | |
| 13 | Formulate any audit comments and discuss these with the Audit Manager and line management | | |
| 14 | Complete audit work check list | | |
| 15 | Complete final draft of audit comments | | |
| 16 | Complete or update internal control questionnaires [ICQs] | | |
| 17 | Complete an appraisal of the system | | |
| 18 | Discuss work with the audit manager | | |
| 19 | File papers in audit files | | |

[1]   Mints, F E, 'Behavioural Patterns in Internal Audit Relationships', The Institute of Internal Auditors, Research Report No 17, 1972.

# Performing the engagement – case studies

## B4.3.1   **Audit testing**

CASE STUDY FOR DISCUSSION

Compliance testing during an internal audit of the mortgages department in a home loans business discloses to the audit team that management is not complying with a control procedure. This procedure authorises the home loans company to send its staff to audit the books of brokers who are arranging home loans for members of the public with this home loans company. Brokers are independent people who act as 'middle people' between the home loans company and members of the public who need finance to purchase homes. The lawyer who is needed for each transaction is often recommended to the member of the public concerned by the broker and while the home loans company could appoint its own lawyer to act for it in addition to the other lawyer acting for the borrower, this is invariably not done.

This particular incident of non-compliance related to one broker. The home loans company's management had been reluctant to upset the broker by insisting upon a visit as the broker was arranging a large amount of business for the home loans company. The broker had resisted a request from management to audit his books as he was extremely busy.

After discussion between the internal audit team and line management, management concedes the point and agreed to insist on visiting the broker.

So, audit compliance tests detected a failure to comply and management agreed to remedy the position.

**Question**

Had the audit team fully discharged its audit responsibilities in this case – except for following up to confirm that management had taken the action they had agreed to take?

How should the auditors have followed up on this point? Should they have made a follow-up audit visit to the mortgages department to confirm that line management had taken the agreed action – and, if so, how long after the end of the original audit fieldwork?

**Suggested answer**
1.     Although you would not have known the outcome of this case, neither would the auditors have known the outcome at the time of the audit.

2.    In the event, line management finally endeavoured to arrange to visit the premises of the broker six months after the conclusion of the internal audit which had drawn their attention to this matter and had obtained their agreement to comply with this important control. Line management had not been approached by internal audit following the conclusion of the audit fieldwork (other than to receive a copy of the final audit report – to which they had replied confirming their agreement to the actions to be taken by line management).

3.    The broker still resisted the visit to inspect his books – even though this was a standard, routine procedure with respect to brokers. This time, line management became a little suspicious and decided to take alternative action, as follows:

  (i)    They inspected the land registry entries against the properties upon which mortgages had been arranged by this broker. These entries should provide details of charges, including mortgages, secured against the properties.

  (ii)   They physically inspected the properties themselves.

4.    To cut a long story short, it quickly emerged that there was a major fraud running to many millions of pounds. It had been achieved by the broker working in collusion with a 'bent' lawyer and a 'bent' property valuer. The values of the properties had been grossly exaggerated and consequently unjustified mortgages had been granted against the properties which were inadequate security for the mortgages. Multiple mortgages had been arranged simultaneously against the same properties with different home loans companies – which was clear from the land registry entries. However, it had not been clear at the time the mortgages were arranged as (a) processing of charges takes three weeks, and (b) the home loans companies involved relied on the 'bent' lawyer to make the necessary searches of the register. The mortgage loans had been granted and paid to the lawyer who had kept mortgage repayments up-to-date on these accounts.

5.    When the fraud was discovered the 'gut reaction' in the company was 'Where were the internal auditors?'. The auditors thought they were in the clear as they had discovered this particular case of non-compliance and management had agreed to remedy the matter. But the auditors, having discovered this weakness of control, had not conducted a 'weakness' or 'substantive' test to determine whether the weakness had led to actual losses. Should they have conducted such 'weakness tests'? They clearly could not probe in depth every case of every sort of non-compliance, and line management has the primary responsibility to administer controls. Nevertheless, what management had told the auditors about this case of non-compliance might have alerted the auditors to the advisability of pursuing the matter further as part of their audit.

6.    It is arguable, too, that the auditors should have followed-up on the implementation of their agreed recommendation so that six months would not have passed before management took the necessary action – during which time the fraud grew much larger.

7.    Whatever the faults of the auditor, if any, line management were certainly not blameless!

## B4.3.2 Using random numbers in audit testing

CASE STUDY

**The case**
1.  You are given three tables of random numbers.
2.  Consider the audit uses of the data contained in Tables 1, 2 and 3
3.  How would you use each of these tables?

**Table 1: 300 random numbers in the range 00001 to 99999, in random sequence.**

| | | | | | |
|---|---|---|---|---|---|
| 50049 | 98219 | 95747 | 41478 | 32500 | 33275 |
| 63769 | 88447 | 56183 | 92569 | 25857 | 97632 |
| 18492 | 99565 | 20152 | 13986 | 77497 | 19573 |
| 78266 | 30716 | 51675 | 17288 | 73548 | 50205 |
| 17732 | 40667 | 11875 | 91064 | 39045 | 47895 |
| 81446 | 85059 | 9211 | 16085 | 46875 | 44238 |
| 26192 | 23091 | 5005 | 33188 | 332 | 87364 |
| 52636 | 75836 | 92391 | 35403 | 35090 | 76001 |
| 75888 | 65290 | 52682 | 39051 | 47030 | 57455 |
| 62115 | 84566 | 25404 | 80992 | 53687 | 37674 |
| 2734 | 66448 | 15653 | 95574 | 42307 | 74103 |
| 69021 | 51770 | 17536 | 47245 | 63708 | 59826 |
| 18381 | 33952 | 47288 | 93065 | 68840 | 16248 |
| 94641 | 51507 | 3246 | 64828 | 80601 | 89082 |
| 32274 | 43902 | 71198 | 52426 | 43579 | 45005 |
| 23229 | 25945 | 64105 | 29929 | 26857 | 1407 |
| 54586 | 52099 | 46876 | 65567 | 6126 | 74275 |
| 64209 | 83739 | 29802 | 98057 | 62649 | 62331 |
| 10941 | 93614 | 529 | 5860 | 95260 | 64284 |
| 44619 | 22468 | 26898 | 80128 | 27265 | 59093 |
| 87077 | 19037 | 72266 | 96300 | 41732 | 98365 |
| 41001 | 18622 | 97034 | 71462 | 87338 | 14914 |
| 72575 | 91205 | 445 | 89715 | 63877 | 8139 |
| 4768 | 48140 | 13136 | 82638 | 15299 | 35079 |
| 94082 | 58925 | 72939 | 5556 | 84277 | 72120 |
| 33578 | 59090 | 47191 | 49854 | 5303 | 31768 |
| 46783 | 94768 | 82818 | 52479 | 30832 | 2588 |
| 7351 | 61315 | 40786 | 97901 | 38568 | 25650 |
| 18157 | 75102 | 65245 | 93361 | 37615 | 14187 |
| 54736 | 58527 | 89141 | 19103 | 83070 | 72956 |

| | | | | | |
|---|---|---|---|---|---|
| 85155 | 24374 | 74497 | 93000 | 81753 | 51706 |
| 37586 | 18859 | 67585 | 24368 | 59887 | 40478 |
| 21855 | 33309 | 40884 | 58638 | 41521 | 61567 |
| 75390 | 4240 | 79082 | 48015 | 1260 | 81194 |
| 43991 | 78966 | 96695 | 71231 | 1951 | 3605 |
| 94900 | 12917 | 11136 | 73893 | 44134 | 73519 |
| 58894 | 48929 | 58719 | 7733 | 81862 | 69580 |
| 56249 | 98434 | 2168 | 54098 | 36267 | 56935 |
| 31285 | 13553 | 94104 | 33788 | 90993 | 35915 |
| 33107 | 37597 | 9309 | 73891 | 2081 | 81522 |
| 64816 | 84174 | 40522 | 74337 | 97025 | 25798 |
| 92871 | 13097 | 30455 | 74105 | 10173 | 90614 |
| 65881 | 75503 | 7120 | 69124 | 83676 | 72519 |
| 55720 | 1782 | 61114 | 59474 | 93527 | 35122 |
| 9869 | 81414 | 51178 | 66916 | 70107 | 7071 |
| 54201 | 72025 | 41665 | 73138 | 53356 | 70150 |
| 24697 | 1225 | 93075 | 31671 | 12546 | 65611 |
| 50962 | 38727 | 98283 | 62660 | 41063 | 65716 |
| 3479 | 85321 | 17814 | 9991 | 31594 | 13931 |
| 50347 | 95500 | 93772 | 42837 | 80895 | 17280 |

**Table 2: 300 random numbers in the range 00001 to 99999, in ascending sequence**

| | | | | | |
|---|---|---|---|---|---|
| 562 | 663 | 1926 | 2687 | 4334 | 4666 |
| 4711 | 4781 | 5189 | 5301 | 5370 | 5424 |
| 5804 | 5867 | 6113 | 6373 | 6466 | 6487 |
| 6580 | 6825 | 6933 | 8063 | 8243 | 8757 |
| 9188 | 10823 | 11171 | 11325 | 12038 | 12259 |
| 13118 | 13217 | 13335 | 13387 | 13675 | 13744 |
| 13789 | 13803 | 14886 | 14914 | 15766 | 15955 |
| 17235 | 18030 | 18179 | 18347 | 18534 | 19518 |
| 19687 | 20008 | 20035 | 20253 | 20856 | 21223 |
| 21683 | 21737 | 21857 | 22224 | 22282 | 22996 |
| 23066 | 23090 | 23174 | 23230 | 23410 | 24105 |
| 24299 | 24902 | 25747 | 26584 | 27370 | 27410 |
| 27439 | 27816 | 28066 | 28311 | 28647 | 28880 |
| 29101 | 29230 | 29513 | 29721 | 29831 | 29917 |
| 29935 | 30849 | 31121 | 31314 | 31543 | 32136 |
| 32437 | 33234 | 33333 | 33444 | 33657 | 33770 |
| 33846 | 33962 | 34818 | 34854 | 34857 | 34884 |

| | | | | | |
|---|---|---|---|---|---|
| 36039 | 36191 | 36502 | 37162 | 38077 | 38360 |
| 38826 | 39013 | 39014 | 39638 | 40391 | 40504 |
| 40506 | 40630 | 41426 | 41451 | 41742 | 42094 |
| 42196 | 42357 | 42971 | 43729 | 44268 | 44401 |
| 44470 | 44952 | 45193 | 45422 | 45572 | 45661 |
| 46355 | 47374 | 48166 | 48227 | 48420 | 48484 |
| 48852 | 48871 | 48963 | 49052 | 49096 | 49137 |
| 49296 | 49878 | 50157 | 50207 | 50465 | 51167 |
| 51542 | 51824 | 52095 | 52980 | 53058 | 53063 |
| 53122 | 53233 | 54038 | 54499 | 54818 | 54907 |
| 55596 | 56882 | 57346 | 57500 | 57827 | 58057 |
| 58120 | 58140 | 58336 | 58508 | 58670 | 58793 |
| 59019 | 59262 | 59884 | 60465 | 60717 | 61391 |
| 61465 | 62730 | 63027 | 63419 | 63484 | 63585 |
| 63603 | 63952 | 64013 | 64672 | 65046 | 65104 |
| 65171 | 65315 | 65766 | 65915 | 65932 | 66353 |
| 66410 | 67202 | 67223 | 68135 | 68260 | 68813 |
| 68950 | 69010 | 69200 | 69284 | 69498 | 70547 |
| 71786 | 71856 | 72194 | 72285 | 72618 | 72657 |
| 73051 | 73162 | 74181 | 74528 | 74544 | 74596 |
| 74681 | 74833 | 75046 | 75285 | 75414 | 76396 |
| 76673 | 76722 | 76850 | 77042 | 77220 | 77430 |
| 77562 | 78511 | 78566 | 79017 | 79068 | 79760 |
| 79781 | 79800 | 80682 | 80848 | 81565 | 82075 |
| 82740 | 83627 | 83678 | 83691 | 83839 | 83987 |
| 84138 | 84557 | 84567 | 84592 | 85497 | 86646 |
| 86783 | 86978 | 87394 | 88339 | 88750 | 88846 |
| 89139 | 89146 | 89212 | 89345 | 89809 | 89945 |
| 90301 | 90353 | 90505 | 91600 | 91705 | 91803 |
| 91938 | 92698 | 92733 | 92925 | 93112 | 93842 |
| 94074 | 94445 | 94735 | 94984 | 95029 | 95427 |
| 95521 | 96431 | 96617 | 96672 | 97160 | 97341 |
| 97412 | 97753 | 98223 | 99148 | 99322 | 99868 |

**Table 3: 100 random numbers in the range 0001 to 9,999, in ascending sequence**

| | | | |
|---|---|---|---|
| 1090 | 1190 | 1248 | 1308 |
| 1356 | 1386 | 1410 | 1464 |
| 1467 | 1490 | 1528 | 1548 |
| 1569 | 1570 | 1587 | 1609 |

| 1687 | 1733 | 1813 | 2220 |
|------|------|------|------|
| 2246 | 2254 | 2255 | 2276 |
| 2341 | 2503 | 2631 | 2672 |
| 2693 | 3034 | 3121 | 3162 |
| 3242 | 3247 | 3252 | 3349 |
| 3369 | 3436 | 3576 | 3596 |
| 3632 | 3751 | 3813 | 4252 |
| 4372 | 4482 | 4635 | 4747 |
| 5227 | 5264 | 5395 | 5653 |
| 5671 | 5910 | 6170 | 6195 |
| 6196 | 6268 | 6405 | 6534 |
| 6612 | 6717 | 6787 | 6873 |
| 7026 | 7200 | 7236 | 7261 |
| 7330 | 7393 | 7416 | 7506 |
| 7548 | 7553 | 7743 | 7882 |
| 7910 | 7968 | 8090 | 8406 |
| 8482 | 8535 | 8642 | 8730 |
| 8746 | 8769 | 8804 | 9069 |
| 9194 | 9242 | 9324 | 9416 |
| 9430 | 9434 | 9464 | 9522 |
| 9546 | 9731 | 9855 | 9991 |

**Suggested answer**

Random sampling is appropriate for the selection of samples for scientific (ie statistical) sampling work. Random samples are representative of the population as a whole – if the sample is of sufficient size. Prerequisites of random selection are:

- Know the population
- Ensure each item has an equal chance of selection.

A sample may be selected at random in a variety of ways:

- Random number tables can be used to determine the items to be selected. The table should be entered at random and proceeded through in a predetermined order. If a selected number does not exist in the population, the table should be proceeded with in the usual way rather than picking out the next item in the population after the missing item (which could create significant bias in sample selection). **Table 1** would be used in this way.
- In **Table 2** the 5 digit number groups are given in ascending sequence. It is difficult to see that a table like this would have any use other than as a basis for selecting a sample of 300 from a population numbered 00001 to 99,999 where the data to be selected is stored sequentially.
- **Table 3** would have a similar use to Table 2, except that the sample would be 100 and the population would be numbered between 0001 and 9,999.

## B4.3.3  Attribute sampling

*Introduction to attributes sampling*

1.  We use the expression 'audit sampling plan' to refer to a statistical sampling technique designed to achieve a particular type of audit objectives.

2.  Attribute sampling is an example of an audit sampling plan. Attribute sampling allows the auditor to obtain reliable estimates on 'how many?' within a universe have a certain attribute, for instance:
    (a)  How many credit limits have been exceeded?
    (b)  How many errors have occurred?
    (c)  How many accounts are overdue?
    (d)  How many customers' accounts are dormant?
    (e)  How many purchases have been for items which have cost more than $1,000?

3.  Stop-or-go sampling and discovery sampling are two variants of attribute sampling. Stop-or-go sampling gives a rapid way of concluding on the maximum probable number of instances within a population which have a certain attribute. Discovery sampling tells the auditor how large the sample should be in order to be able to conclude (assuming no instance is discovered within the sample) that there are probably fewer than a certain number of instances in the entire population. Neither of these two variants of attribute sampling allow reliable conclusions to be drawn on the likely number of instances of the attribute: they only allow the user to conclude that there are unlikely to be more than a certain number. Because of this relative lack of precision they are quicker to use, requiring the auditor to examine smaller samples.

4.  Attribute sampling and its variants are not designed to give an estimate of 'how much?' (ie 'what value?') – for that we must use a sampling for variables sampling plan. The emphasis of attribute sampling is upon 'how many?'

5.  Here we look at the principal method of attribute sampling. We do not deal here with stop-or-go and discovery sampling.

6.  We have several choices about how to use this sampling plan:
    (a)  We can rely on statistical sampling tables and avoid using a formula.
    (b)  We can use a single formula (Formula A1 below) *plus* make reference to a simple Table of Standard Deviation Factors (Table 1 [below]).

7.  One of the attractions of attribute sampling is that the auditor does not need to calculate the standard deviation from a pilot sample of the population. The measure of variability (which corresponds to the standard deviation) in this method is [*p*] and the auditor estimates this usually judgementally without reference to the population, as we explain below. To use this attribute sampling plan the auditor must:
    (a)  **Know** the Population Size [*N*].
    (b)  **Decide** the Desired Precision [*A*].
    (c)  **Suggest** an Expected Error Rate (or incidence of another condition if the attribute being examined is not an error attribute – eg number of customers in the US) [*p*].
        (i)  The auditor can determine [*p*] in a variety of ways:

<ul>
<li>– consult management.</li>
<li>– use his or her experience.</li>
<li>– test a pilot sample.</li>
<li>– select a value for [p] which is not greater than a rate which the auditor would find acceptable. This is likely to be the principal determinant the auditor will use.</li>
</ul>

(ii) If the results of the statistical test indicate that the auditor understated [p], then the auditor will need to rework the test using the *actual rate* as [p] – and so on until the result of the test indicates that the auditor's final suggestion for [p] was not an understatement – which means that the sample was large enough for the auditor to draw conclusions about the population as a whole with the degree of confidence (eg 95.5%) and precision (eg ±4%) which were used.

(iii) We can use two formulae in two steps. The first step requires us to use Formula B1 [below], and the second step uses Formula B2 [below] which makes use of the result of Formula B1. As with Formula A1, Formula B1 also requires reference to be made to the Table of Standard Deviation Factors (see Table 1 below).

This is a slightly improved method. It adjusts the sample size to fit the population by adding a finite correction factor.

(iv) We can replace tables by building formulae into spreadsheets. Keying in the variables allows the spreadsheet to specify required sample size.

## Formula A1 – Attribute Sampling

The auditor can determine sample size in attribute sampling by using tables, or alternatively by using a combination of a table and the following formula:

$$\text{Sample size} = \frac{Z^2 \times N \times p(1-p)}{(A^2 \times N) + (Z^2 \times p(1-p))}$$

where:

| | | |
|---|---|---|
| N | = population size | (eg: 500) |
| p | = expected error rate or incidence of any other condition | (eg: 1 in 20 = .05) |
| A | = desired precision | (eg: + 4 per cent = .04) |
| Z | = standard deviation factor at the desired confidence level | (eg: $\overline{9}5.5$ per cent = 2.0000) |

## Formula B1

Step one:

$$n(e) = \frac{Z^2(p)\,(1-p)}{A^2}$$

where:

n(e) = first estimate of sample size
N p A and Z as shown for Formula A1

## *Formula B2*

Step two:

$$n(f) = \frac{n(e)}{1 + (n(e)/N)}$$

where:

*n(f)* = final sample size
*N p A* and Z as shown for Formula A1

## *Table 1 – Table of Standard Deviation Factors*

('Z' in attribute sampling)

(Confidence levels in percentages converted to standard deviation units, based on the normal distribution curve).

| Confidence level | Factor |
|---|---|
| 99.9 | 3.2905 |
| 99.7 | 3.0000 |
| 99.5 | 2.8070 |
| 99.0 | 2.5758 |
| 98.0 | 2.3263 |
| 95.5 | 2.0000 |
| 95.0 | 1.9600 |
| 90.0 | 1.6449 |
| 85.0 | 1.4395 |
| 80.0 | 1.2816 |
| 75.0 | 1.1503 |
| 70.0 | 1.0364 |
| 68.3 | 1.0000 |
| 60.0 | 0.8416 |
| 50.0 | 0.6745 |
| 40.0 | 0.5244 |

| Confidence level | Factor |
|---|---|
| 30.0 | 0.3853 |
| 20.0 | 0.2534 |
| 10.0 | 0.1257 |

eg 95.5% of the population is within 2 standard deviations of the mean (in a normal distribution).

## *Attribute sampling – case studies*

| **Assume:** | Population size | 1000 |
|---|---|---|
| | Expected error rate | 1 in 50 |
| | Desired precision | ±2% |
| | Desired confidence | 95% |

| **Re-quired:** | (Round your answers to the next 10 above) | |
|---|---|---|
| | **Case 1** | Using Formula A1 and the Table of Standard Deviation Factors (Table 1), calculate the required samplesize. |
| | **Case 2** | Reduce your confidence level from 95% to 70% with a precision of ±5%. What is the required sample size? |
| | **Case 3** | Why is the required sample size which you have calculated in **Case 2** too small to be usable? |
| | **Case 4** | Recalculate **Case 2** except with a population size of 1,000,000, and consider the implications of the result you get. |
| | **Case 5** | Explore the impact upon required sample size if all the assumptions in **Case 1** are held steady, except that the Population Size is altered from 1000 to 500. |
| | **Case 6** | As **Case 1** but with a population size of 1,000,000. What is the required sample size? |
| | **Case 7** | If the auditor tests a sample of the size suggested in **Case 1** and finds that the actual error rate in this sample is 1 in 20 (rather than 1 in 50 which had been expected), how many *additional* items in the population should the auditor examine so as to test whether he or she can be confident that this new error rate is not exceeded in the population as a whole? |
| | **Case 8** | The auditor decides to work at 95% confidence ±2% but intends to achieve a maximum of 15% of this 95% through his or her assessment of the quality of management and of internal control. In the event, the auditor rates this at 10% leaving 85% to be obtained from the statistical test. Therefore, compute sample size on the following assumptions: |
| | | Population size       1,000,000 |
| | | Expected error rate     1 in 50 |

| Desired precision | ±2% |
| Desired confidence (from the statistical test) | 85% |

## Suggested answers

### Case 1

**Required sample size if population = 1,000:**

$$\text{Sample size} = \frac{1.96^2 \times 1000 \times .02 \,(1-.02)}{(.02^2 \times 1000) + (1.96^2 \times .02 \,(1-.02))}$$

$$= \frac{75.29536}{0.4 + 0.07529536} = \text{sample size of } 158.42 \text{ to 3 significant places } (\text{say } 160)$$

### Case 2

Population size is 1,000 but the required audit confidence is 70% ± 5%:

$$\frac{1.0364^2 \times 1000 \times .02 \,(1-.02)}{(.05^2 \times 1000 + (1.0364^2 \times .02 \,(1-.02)))}$$

$$= \frac{21.053}{2.52} = \text{sample size of } 8.35$$

### Case 3

Because a sample size of 8 or 9 does not allow a reliable assessment to be made of whether the Expected Error Rate assumption (1 in 50) has been met.

### Case 4

$$\frac{1.0364^2 \times 1,000,000 \times 0.2 \,(1-.02)}{(.05^2 \times 1,000,000 + (1.0364^2 \times .02 \,(1-.02)))}$$

$$= \frac{21053}{2500 + 0.021} = \text{sample size of } 8.42$$

The same observation applies as per the answer to **Case 3**.

### Case 5

If 1000 is altered to 500 in the above calculation, the required sample size becomes 137:

$$\frac{1.96^2 \times 500 \times .02 \, (1-.02)}{(.02^2 \times 500 + (1.96^2 \times .02 \, (1-.02))}$$

$$= \frac{37.64768}{0.27529536} = \text{sample size of 136.75 to 3 significant places (say 140)}$$

**Case 6**

**Required sample size if population = 1,000,000:**

$$\text{Sample size} = \frac{75295.36}{400 + 0.07529536} = 188.2$$

**Case 7**

If the *Actual Error Rate* in **Case 1** above turns out to be 1 in 20 rather than the 1 in 50 which had been expected then 154 *additional* items in the population must be examined, making 313 in all, viz:

$$\frac{1.96^2 \times 1000 \times 0.5 \, (1-.05)}{(.02^2 \times 1000) + (1.96^2 \times .05 \, (1-.05))}$$

$$= \frac{182.476}{0.4 + 0.182476}$$

$$= \frac{182.476}{0.582476}$$

313.28

= 313–159 = 154 additional items to be tested

**Case 8**

$$\frac{1.4395^2 \times 1,000,000 \times .02 \, (1-.02)}{(.02^2 \times 1,000,000) + (1.4395^2 \times .02 \, (1-.02))}$$

$$= \frac{40,614.3409}{400.0406112}$$

= 102 sample size

## B4.3.4 Sampling for variables

### Introduction to variables sampling

1. Attribute sampling is a method of estimation sampling to obtain reliable estimates of the number of times a particular feature is present in a population. Sampling for variables is another method of estimation sampling – this

time to determine the value of something which is present within a population.

2. Monetary unit sampling combines attributes sampling and sampling for variables in one sampling plan and is not covered here. It may tell the auditor, for instance, both how many items in a population are likely to be in error and also the value of those erroneous items.

3. Sampling for variables is most frequently used to estimate money values but can be used to estimate other values such as volumes, hours worked and so on.

4. The steps involved in sampling for variables are as follows:
   - Determine the population size.
   - Find out what management says is the value of the population (this is what the sampling plan will set out to test for reliability).
   - Take a pilot sample of not less than 100 and calculate the standard deviation.
   - Use formulas or tables to determine whether an additional sample needs to be tested, and if so how large this supplementary sample should be. In this session we call the formulae to be used **A1** and **A2** (**A1** should be used first). Note that formula **A1** makes use of the standard deviation factor (Z) which we also use in attribute sampling. **Table 1** allows you to determine the standard deviation factor.

## *Table 1 – Table of Standard Deviation Factors*

('Z' in attribute sampling)

(Confidence levels in percentages converted to standard deviation units, based on the normal distribution curve).

| Confidence level | Factor |
|---|---|
| 99.9 | 3.2905 |
| 99.7 | 3.0000 |
| 99.5 | 2.8070 |
| 99.0 | 2.5758 |
| 98.0 | 2.3263 |
| 95.5 | 2.0000 |
| 95.0 | 1.9600 |
| 90.0 | 1.6449 |
| 85.0 | 1.4395 |
| 80.0 | 1.2816 |
| 75.0 | 1.1503 |
| 70.0 | 1.0364 |
| 68.3 | 1.0000 |
| 60.0 | 0.8416 |
| 50.0 | 0.6745 |
| 40.0 | 0.5244 |

| Confidence level | Factor |
|---|---|
| 30.0 | 0.3853 |
| 20.0 | 0.2534 |
| 10.0 | 0.1257 |

e.g. 95% of the population is within 2 standard deviations of the mean (in a normal distribution).

## Formula A1

$$n(e) = \frac{(Zs)^2}{A}$$

where:

| | |
|---|---|
| $n_{(e)}$ | = first estimate of sample size |
| Z | = standard deviation factor (per Table 1) |
| s | = standard deviation of the sample |
| A | = precision (sampling error) |

## Formula A2

This uses the first estimate of sample size and adjusts it to fit the population:

$$n(f) = \frac{n(e)}{1 + (n(e)/N)}$$

5.  Test the supplementary sample and this time from the pilot and supplementary samples taken together:
    (i)  Determine the average value of an item in the population and therefore estimate the likely total value of the population (average value x number of items in the population).
    (ii) The revised standard deviation.
6.  Use another formula (**B1**) to determine the reliability of the estimate of the total value.

## Formula B1

$$A = z\frac{s}{\sqrt{n}}\left(\sqrt{1 - \frac{n}{N}}\right)$$

where:

| | |
|---|---|
| A | = precision |
| Z | = standard deviation factor (per Table 1) |

| | |
|---|---|
| s | = standard deviation of sample |
| n | = sample size |
| N | = population size |

## VARIABLES SAMPLING – CASE STUDIES

| | |
|---|---|
| **Case 1** | We want to estimate the likely value of inventories and we consider our confidence level should be 90% (with a precision of ± 5%). Management has a book value for inventory of £1,000,000, but we want to perform our own valuation. There are 10,000 line items in the inventory. We have taken at random a pilot sample of 100 of these line items and from this have ascertained a pilot sample standard deviation of £50. |
| | **Required:** Using Formula A1 and then Formula A2 determine the size of the *additional* sample (ie beyond the original 100 sample) which must be examined and evaluated in order for the auditor to be able to conclude on the likely value of inventories at the level of confidence which the auditor requires (ie 90% ± 5%) |
| **Case 2** | Assume that the examination of the additional sample shows that the standard deviation remains £50. Assume also that our valuation of the 264 line items is £30,000 against a book value of £26,400. Our average valuation of a line item in our sample is therefore £30,000/264 = £113.64 and our estimated total value of the inventory would therefore be £113.64 x 10,000 = £1,136,400. |
| | **Required:** Use Formula B1 to determine (a) how reliable is our estimate (ie what is the precision (sampling error) at our 90% confidence level?), and (b) whether management's book value of the inventory (£1,000,000) can be relied upon. |

## Suggested answers

### Case 1

**Formula A1**

$$n(e) = \frac{(1.6449 \times 50)^2}{5} = 271$$

**Formula A2**

$$n(f) = \frac{271}{1 + (271/10,000)} = 264$$

**Additional sample needed**

$$264 - 100 = 164$$

**Case 2**

**Formula B1**

$$\text{Precision} = 1.6449 \left( \frac{50}{\sqrt{264}} \right) \times \left( \sqrt{1 - \frac{264}{10,000}} \right) = \pm £5$$

A precision of ±£5 for each line item calculates out at ±£50,000 for the entire population of 10,000 units, so the value of the entire inventory is:

$$£1,136,400 \pm £50,000$$

or, in other words, the value of the inventory is between £1,086,400 and £1,186,400 at our 90% confidence level – which we may consider is close enough to management's book value of the inventory to be acceptable (in view of our low (90%) confidence level).

## B4.3.5   Working papers: Case for consideration based on Practice Advisory 2330–1

1. Do your audit working papers document the engagement and are they reviewed by management of the internal audit activity?
2. Do they record the information obtained and the analyses made and do they adequately support the bases for the observations and recommendations reported?
3. Are they usually complete and include support for engagement conclusions reached? Do they document:
   - planning;
   - examination and evaluation of the adequacy and effectiveness of the system of internal control;
   - the engagement procedures performed, the information obtained, and the conclusions reached;
   - review;
   - communicating;
   - follow-up
4. Would you say that your working papers achieve the following:
   - Provide the principal support for the engagement communications.
   - Aid in the planning, performance, and review of engagements.
   - Document whether the engagement objectives were achieved.
   - Facilitate third party reviews.
   - Provide a basis for evaluating the internal audit activity's quality program.
   - Provide support in circumstances such as insurance claims, fraud cases, and lawsuits.

- Aid in the professional development of the internal auditing staff.
- Demonstrate compliance with the *Standards*.

5.   PA 2330–1 says that working paper *may* include:

- Planning documents and engagement programs.
- Control questionnaires, flowcharts, checklists and narratives.
- Notes and memoranda resulting from interviews.
- Organisational data, such as organization charts and job descriptions.
- Copies of important contracts and agreements.
- Information about operating and financial policies.
- Results of control evaluations.
- Letters of confirmation and representation.
- Analysis and tests of transactions, processes, and account balances.
- Results of analytical auditing procedures.
- The engagement's final communications and management's responses.
- Engagement correspondence if it documents engagement conclusions.

Which of the above might yours include?

# Communicating results – best practice guidance

**B5.1.1**   While we also refer to other important pronouncements, our main source of guidance for the parts of this Handbook which describe internal auditing best practice has been the *Professional Practices Framework* of The Institute of Internal Auditors. This *Framework* includes their *Definition* of internal auditing, *Code of Ethics*, *Standards*, and *Practice Advisories*. Of these, only the *Practice Advisories* are non-mandatory: they do explain and elaborate upon best practice in most circumstances, and are important for practitioners and students. Readers can see the current complete list of *Practice Advisories* at www.theiia.org. Those current on 1 January 2005 are shown at APPENDIX 3 of this Handbook, including a useful topical classification at APPENDIX 3.2.

In addressing this subject we have drawn more widely than those *Practice Advisories* classified by The Institute as applicable to this part of our Handbook, which are:

| Practice Advisories, by Standard Number | Release date |
|---|---|
| Practice Advisory 2400–1: Legal Considerations in Communicating Results | 28 March 2001 |
| Practice Advisory 2410–1: Communication Criteria | 5 January 2001 |
| Practice Advisory 2420–1: Quality of Communications | 4 October 2001 |
| Practice Advisory 2440–1: Recipients of Engagement Results | 5 January 2001 |
| Practice Advisory 2440–2: Communications Outside the Organization | 15 May 2001 |
| Practice Advisory 2440–3: Communicating Sensitive Information Within and Outside of the Chain of Command | 12 June 2003 |

We address Practice Advisory 2440–3 in CHAPTER B7.1 rather than in this part of the Handbook.

*Practice Advisories* carry the *Standard* number to which they principally refer. Readers are advised to consult the applicable *Standards* as we do not in every case reproduce them here. They are to be found at APPENDIX 2.

## B5.1.2   Using the planning stage of the audit to consider approach to communicating results

The appropriate form of communication of engagement results should be considered as early as the planning phase of the audit engagement:

'The final engagement communication format should be considered, since proper planning at this stage facilitates preparing the final engagement communication.'[1]

and:

'The chief audit executive is responsible for determining how, when, and to whom engagement results will be communicated. This determination should be documented and communicated to management, to the extent deemed practical, during the planning phase of the engagement.'[2]

## B5.1.3 Communication style and approach

Usually engagement results will be communicated in the form of an audit report, but internal audit activities should weigh up carefully whether the written audit report is the most effective means of communication in a particular case. It is unlikely to be effective on its own, needing to be supplemented by carefully prepared face-to-face meetings, presentations and so on. The way in which the different selected means of communication are coordinated with each other and their timing are important determinants of their effectiveness, as is the quality of each.

We should not assume that the only *formal* engagement communication is the written audit report. Practice Advisory 1210.A2–1 allows that other forms of communication may be formal.[3]

The audit report should be produced to a standard associated with very important internal management reports. If it were more or less, it would create an inappropriate impression. It is advisable that audit reports have a distinctive and attractive 'house-style' so that they are not overlooked as an audit report when they reach someone's desk.

It is mistaken to believe that an unnecessarily elaborate report with complex phraseology will communicate better or make a stronger impression. Management and the audit committee members are over-taxed with too much material to be read and digest: they will appreciate it is the auditor puts things simply. Conciseness is a key quality of effective communication in whatever format:

'Concise communications are to the point and avoid unnecessary elaboration, superfluous detail, redundancy, and wordiness. They are created by a persistent practice of revising and editing a presentation. The goal is that each thought will be meaningful but succinct.'[4]

Timing is particularly important. An engagement report loses its impact and value if it is delayed.

'Timely communications are well-timed, opportune, and expedient for careful consideration by those who may act on the recommendations. The timing of the presentation of engagement results should be set without undue delay and with a degree of urgency and so as to enable prompt, effective action.'[5]

Internal auditors should be alert to the possibility that management may seek to delay the communication of audit results to higher levels of management or to the audit committee of the board. One way that this may be done is for management to delay responding to a draft audit engagement report so that the internal audit activity is delayed in finalising the report and issuing it to more senior levels. If an audit committee meets just once every three months, this can have a very signifi-cant impact on the timing of chief audit executive reports through to the audit committee. To avoid this risk, standard audit procedures should include an override so that audit results are reported upwards without undue delay in such cases.

Auditors should not consider the written audit report to be the end product of the audit engagement. Rather it is a means to an end – and can be a very effective means. The end result should be reassurance to management and to the board that their risk management, internal control and governance processes are sound, and persuasive advice to improve these where improvement is needed. The quality of audit communications, including the quality of the written audit report, impacts significantly on whether the internal audit activity is able to persuade management and the board on action that is needed. In CHAPTER B7.1 we address the situation where management has been unwilling to take the action which the internal audit activity is commending.

The written audit report has a secondary purpose. It is a permanent record of the results of the audit.

While the content of the audit engagement report is a matter for the chief audit executive (or his or her delegate), it is helpful to view the audit report is a dynamic, collaborative venture. It is usually discussed in draft with management and management's responses are incorporated into the final version of the audit report. In this way a higher degree of commitment by management to 'agreed action' can be achieved; and mortifying or belittling of management can be avoided.

Internal auditors should not subordinate their judgement on professional matters to that of others. This is particularly important with respect to (a) the determination of the scope of audit work, and (b) the content and tone of engagement and other audit reports. Examples of the scope of audit work would be the content of the annual plan of audit engagements, or the content of the plan of an individual audit engagement. An example of 'other audit reports' – apart from the audit engagement report – would be an annual report from the chief audit executive to the audit committee of the board, perhaps containing the CAE's overall opinion of the effectiveness of risk management, internal control and governance processes. If the internal audit activity has been required to bend their judgement on these matters, then it is important that the most senior point within the entity to whom internal audit reports (usually the audit committee of the board) is cognisant of this compromise: this means that the chief audit executive has a professional obligation to make sure that they are made so aware.

With respect to an audit engagement report, by way of example, senior manage-ment asked internal audit to 'tone down' their report to the audit committee in order to avoid worrying the audit committee, and also because the regional executive about whom internal audit was concerned was responsible for half the earnings of the bank that year and top management wished that nothing should be done to upset him. Later, after the bank had collapsed, internal audit was able to point out that they *had* informed the audit committee; but the anodyne language they had used in their report to the audit committee, following management pressure, had not been sufficient to alert the audit committee to the gravity of the matter.

## B5.1.4  Quality of communications

At B5.2.1 to B5.2.7 we discuss quality issues with respect to style of written audit reports. To the extent possible, auditors should adopt a positive style of reporting, concentrating on opportunities for improvement rather than dwelling on failure. A positive style will also be facilitated if internal audit can show within their report how their audit results and recommended/agreed action will assist management *to achieve their objectives better*. Management see themselves as in business more to achieve objectives and less to prevent things going wrong; auditors and audit reports will be more acceptable if they also have this slant.

> 'Constructive communications are helpful to the engagement client and the organization and lead to improvements where needed. The contents and tone of the presentation should be useful, positive, and well-meaning and contribute to the objectives of the organization.'[6]

> 'Management reporting and communication should convey risk management conclusions and recommendations to reduce exposures. For management to fully understand the degree of exposure, it is critical that audit reporting identify the criticality and consequence of the risk exposure to achieving objectives.'[7]

Hallmarks of quality in audit communications are that they are:[8]

- accurate;
- free from errors and distortion;
- faithful to underlying facts;
- fair, impartial, unbiased, balanced;
- clear;
- concise;
- constructive;
- complete – lacking nothing essential;
- timely.

## B5.1.5  Errors and omissions

An error is an unintentional misstatement or omission of significant information in a final engagement communication. If it is determined that a final engagement communication contained an error, the chief audit executive should consider the need to issue an amended report which identifies the information being corrected. The amended engagement communications should be distributed to all individuals who received the engagement communications being corrected.

'**Standard 2421 – Errors and Omissions**
If a final communication contains a significant error or omission, the chief audit executive should communicate corrected information to all parties who received the original communication.'

## B5.1.6 Engagement disclosure on non-compliance with the *Standards*

At A4.1.10 we discussed that practice varies between internal audit activities as to whether reports of every audit engagement include a routine reference to compliance by the internal audit activity with the *Standards*; and compliance by both the internal audit activity and also by individual internal auditors with the *Code of Ethics*. Note that the *Code of Ethics* states that:

'This Code of Ethics applies to both individuals and entities that provide internal auditing services.'

An alternative approach is to include, within the internal audit activity's annual or more frequent overall reports to the audit committee of the board, reference to whether or not internal audit has been in compliance with the *Code of Ethics* and *Standards*. However, it is mandatory to disclose within an audit engagement report when non-compliance has impacted upon the specific engagement:

'**Standard 2430 – Engagement Disclosure of Noncompliance with the Standards**
When noncompliance with the Standards impacts a specific engagement, communication of the results should disclose the:
- Standard(s) with which full compliance was not achieved,
- Reason(s) for noncompliance, and
- Impact of noncompliance on the engagement.'

## B5.1.7 Disseminating results

In essence, what we describe below is common sense, it is designed to achieve openness and maximum participation. That way, there will be greater 'buy-in' to audit results and to agreed action.

One of the matters which should be determined according to the professional judgement of the chief audit executive, along with the scope of work and the content of audit reports, is to whom engagement results should be communicated:

'The chief audit executive is responsible for determining how, when, and to whom engagement results will be communicated. This determination should be documented and communicated to management, to the extent deemed practical, during the planning phase of the engagement. Subsequent changes which affect the timing or reporting of engagement results should also be communicated to management, if appropriate.'[9]

The principle is that there should be openness as to whom, when and how audit results will be communicated, and the decision on circulation should be made by the chief audit executive. It is desirable that the protocols for determining circulation of audit reports should be set out in the charter of the internal audit activity, which should however state that the determination is to be made by the chief audit executive in each instance.

While the chief audit executive should determine the content and circulation of audit reports, the position may be more complex if the audit report relates to an engagement which was outsourced:

> 'When the chief audit executive issues engagement communications, and an outside service provider was used, the chief audit executive may, as appropriate, refer to such services provided. The outside service provider should be informed and, if appropriate, concurrence should be obtained prior to such reference being made in engagement communications.'[10]

The *Standards* and *Practice Advisories* fail to make the useful distinction between to whom an audit report is *addressed*, and to whom it may be *copied*. The addressee is the person from whom a response to internal audit is expected.

We consider that it is desirable that a report on an audit engagement is addressed, where practical, to just one person. That should be the executive who needs to know and is capable of ensuring that appropriate action is taken on the results of the audit. It will usually to be the executive to whom the manager of the audited unit reports. Addressing the report to that executive engages the right person in actioning the audit report. Primarily, the audit has been undertaken for that executive: he or she is responsible for reviewing risk management, internal control and governance processes in the operations headed by managers who report directly to him or her. But, not having the time to undertake this review for himself or herself – and perhaps not knowing how to undertake it – the review has been entrusted to an internal audit activity that both has the time and knows how to do it.

> 'Final engagement communications should be distributed to those members of the organization who are able to ensure that engagement results are given due consideration. This means that the report should go to those who are in a position to take corrective action or ensure that corrective action is taken.'[11]

The audit findings and the draft audit report will have been discussed with the manager of the audited unit whose responses will have been built into the final audit report:

> 'Internal auditors should discuss conclusions and recommendations with appropriate levels of management before issuing final engagement communications.'[12]

This may happen 'during the course of the engagement and/or at post-engagement meetings (exit interviews)'[13] or later using the draft audit report as the basis for discussion, or in a combination of these ways. The draft audit report would also be discussed with the responsible executive to whom the manager of the audited unit reports. It is not enough for the final report to land on his or her desk without prior warning as to its contents, or without the opportunity to influence its contents and to have his or her responses incorporated into the final report:

'Although the level of participants in the discussions and reviews may vary by organization and by the nature of the report, they will generally include those individuals who are knowledgeable of detailed operations and those who can authorize the implementation of corrective action.'[14]

The final audit report will be copied to the manager of the audited unit:

'The final engagement communications should be distributed to management of the activity under review.'[15]

It will probably also be copied to a small number of additional parties – such as the finance director, the chief executive, group internal audit (in the case of a subsidiary internal audit function) and perhaps the external auditor. The latter has a right to see all company documentation including internal audit reports; but it may be inefficient and uneconomic to copy all internal audit engagement reports to the external auditor as a matter of routine – when the external auditor has a right to ask to see those which are relevant. A satisfactory compromise is for the chief audit executive to keep the external auditor informed of the audit engagements which have been reported, and to give the external auditor copies of the audit engagement reports as requested.

Many of those to whom audit reports are copied may welcome receiving just a summary audit report. Some internal audit activities follow the practice of commencing the full audit report with a summary covering just one or two pages, which is then followed by the supporting detail. This allows the busy, senior reader to read just the front page or two and only to dip into the detail if necessary. Rather than sending the whole to everyone, most of those to whom audit reports are copied may be sent just the front one or two page summary: they can then ask to receive the full report if they need it. The summary report will cross-reference to the supporting detail.

'Higher-level members in the organization may receive only a summary communication. Communications may also be distributed to other interested or affected parties such as external auditors and the board.'[16]

Audit committees of the board will generally find even the one or two page summary report to be too much detail: they will usually be prepared to settle for a one or two paragraph summary of each audit engagement completed – with carefully chosen wording to place the right emphasis on the main audit results. If they wish to do so, audit committees may on occasion ask to see the full engagement report. Sometimes one member of the audit committee will be nominated by the audit committee to routinely receive the full version of each internal audit report. That person may or may not be the chair of the audit committee.

In general there should be no secret distribution list. There may be very occasional exceptions. For instance, occasionally the audit committee of the board may directly commission an audit engagement to be undertaken on their behalf by the internal audit activity, with the report to go directly to the audit committee. The audit engagement itself may not be known about by management who would not see the report before it went to the audit committee. An example of this was an occasion when the chief audit executive used his direct reporting line to the audit committee to express his concerns to the chair of the audit committee about the conduct of the entity's chief executive. The audit committee asked him to investigate further and report the results directly and confidentially to the audit committee.

Circulation of audit results should not be wider than is needed to achieve their purpose. This respects confidentiality, it assists in preserving the dignity of managers upon whom some of the content may not reflect well, and it sets an appropriate example of economy and efficiency.

Some internal audit activities, especially smaller ones, follow the practice of every audit report being issued in the name of the chief audit executive. Where this does not occur, it needs to be understood that delegation does not mean abdication: the chief audit executive remains responsible for the content of all internal audit reports and will need to actively supervise their preparation accordingly, directly or indirectly through audit managers who report to him or her. Audit reports may be signed by the chief audit executive or his or her designee, but there is no mandatory requirement for this:

> 'The chief audit executive or designee should review and approve the final engagement communications before issuance and should decide to whom the report will be distributed. The chief audit executive or a designee should approve and may sign all final reports. If specific circumstances warrant, consideration should be given to having the auditor-in-charge, supervisor, or lead auditor sign the report as a representative of the chief audit executive.'[17]

## B5.1.8   Reporting on audits of business processes

Some audit engagements are of business activities which cut across sectional boundaries within the entity and follow a natural business process from start to finish. Examples might be where the subject of the audit is 'launching a new product', or 'handling customer complaints', or 'the revenue cycle'.

There is usually considerable merit in determining the plan of audit engagements so that it includes some business activities or processes of this sort. Internal audit is one of the few agencies with the authority to follow a process across departmental frontiers. It may be that the process has not been reviewed in this holistic way in the past. There is considerable opportunity to generate audit results which will be valuable. Risks are often greatest (and controls weakest) where they exist at the interfaces between departments: these may go unnoticed in an audit whose scope corresponds to a section, department, function or division of the entity.

Audits which cut across departmental frontiers, while potentially very valuable are usually more difficult to do in a traditional way. Control self-assessment (see B2.2.39 and B2.2.61) lends itself well to this. One of the challenges in an audit of a business process which cuts across departmental frontiers, is to determine to whom to address the audit report. The audit report should be addressed to the executive who can take ownership of the issues raised. There may be more than one such executive – each taking ownership of some of the issues raised within the audit report. They will often need to take joint ownership since action will need to be jointly undertaken. In such a case, therefore, the audit report is likely to need to be addressed to more than one senior, responsible executive.

One alternative may sometimes be to address the engagement report of an audit of a business process to the chief executive, or another very senior executive to whom the other executives all report. Another alternative might be to sectionalise the audit engagement report, addressing each section to a particular responsible executive.

If appropriate action is not taken on the audit report by the executive to whom it is addressed, then the chief audit executive needs to consider whether there is now a more senior level of management who needs to know and would be capable of ensuring that appropriate action was taken. Again, this has to be a matter of professional judgement by the chief audit executive, based on the circumstances in each case. Not every matter should be escalated upwards without limit. We discuss this in B7.1.1.

## B5.1.9  Communicating about fraud

Additional guidance is applicable for engagement communications issued as a result of fraud investigations. Once the incidence of significant fraud has been established with reasonable certainty, senior management and the board should be notified immediately. If the fraud impacts the reliability of financial statements already issued, senior management and the board should be notified of that. A written report or other formal communication should be issued at the conclusion of the investigation phase, and it should include all observations, conclusions, recommendations, and corrective action taken. The Institute, reflecting the intense and distinctive legal character of US society and business, recommends that a draft of proposed final communications on fraud should be submitted to legal counsel for review, and that in those cases in which the internal auditor wants to invoke client privilege, consideration should be given to addressing the report to legal counsel rather than to senior management or the board.[18]

## B5.1.10  Whistleblowing by internal auditors

Although the Practice Advisory 'Communicating Sensitive Information Within and Outside of the Chain of Command'[19] is classified by The Institute within the section of the *Standards* covered in this chapter, we have chosen to discuss it at B7.1.2 within the chapter on 'Resolution of management's acceptance of risks'. That Practice Advisory deals with whistleblowing by internal auditors as well as with other matters.

## B5.1.11  Audit report writing

'Internal auditors should be skilled in oral and written communications so that they can clearly and effectively convey such matters as engagement objectives, evaluations, conclusions, and recommendations.'[20]

We offer suggestions on report writing at B5.2.1 to B5.2.7.

Every engagement final communication should contain, at a minimum, the purpose, scope, and results of the engagement.[21] The results should include observations, conclusions (opinions), recommendations and action plans. Practice Advisory 2410–1: 'Communication Criteria' should be consulted on the meaning of these. This Practice Advisory has a useful explanation of the attributes upon which observations and recommendations should be based:

- 'Criteria: The standards, measures, or expectations used in making an evaluation and/or verification (what should exist).
- Condition: The factual evidence that the internal auditor found in the course of the examination (what does exist).
- Cause: The reason for the difference between the expected and actual conditions (why the difference exists).
- Effect: The risk or exposure the organization and/or others encounter because the condition is not consistent with the criteria (the impact of the difference). In determining the degree of risk or exposure, internal auditors should consider the effect their engagement observations and recommendations may have on the organization's operations and financial statements.'[22]

1   Practice Advisory 2200–1: 'Engagement Planning', para 3.
2   Practice Advisory 2200–1: 'Engagement Planning', para 2.
3   Practice Advisory 1210.A2–1: 'Identification of Fraud', para 11.
4   Practice Advisory 2420–1: 'Quality of Communications', para 4.
5   Practice Advisory 2420–1: 'Quality of Communications', para 7.
6   Practice Advisory 2420–1: 'Quality of Communications', para 5.
7   Practice Advisory 2010–2: 'Linking the Audit Plan to Risk and Exposures', para 6.
8   Practice Advisory 2420–1: 'Quality of Communications'.
9   Practice Advisory 2200–1: 'Engagement Planning', para 2.
10  Practice Advisory 1210.A1–1: 'Obtaining Services to Support or Complement the Internal Audit Activity', para 11.
11  Practice Advisory 2440–1: 'Disseminating Results', para 5.
12  Practice Advisory 2440–1: 'Disseminating Results', para 1.
13  Practice Advisory 2440–1: 'Disseminating Results', para 2.
14  Practice Advisory 2440–1: 'Disseminating Results', para 3.
15  Practice Advisory 2440–1: 'Disseminating Results', para 5.
16  Practice Advisory 2440–1: 'Disseminating Results', para 5.
17  Practice Advisory 2440–1: 'Disseminating Results', para 4.
18  Practice Advisory 1210.A2–1: 'Identification of Fraud', paras 11 and 12.
19  Practice Advisory 2440–3.
20  Practice Advisory 1210–1: 'Proficiency', paras 2 and 3.
21  Practice Advisory 2410–1: 'Communication Criteria', para 1.
22  Practice Advisory 2410–1: 'Communication Criteria', para 7.

# Communicating results – supplementary guidance

## B5.2.1  Audit reports and audit follow-up

'I'm sorry I've written you such a long letter: I didn't have the time to write a short one.'

George Bernard Shaw

'I know you believe that you understand what you think I said, but I am not sure you realise that what you heard is not what I meant ... so I'm sending you this report.'

'Say what you mean.
Mean what you say.
Know what you mean.'

'The only person who says what he actually means gets fired'

Jonathan Baird (1999)

## B5.2.2  *Communicating audit findings and recommendations*

Audit reports are not the end-product of internal auditing although they fulfil the incidental purpose of being an excellent formal record of the audit and its conclusions. Principally, audit reports are a means to the end – which is reassurance to management that their systems of control are sound or persuasive advice to management to improve them. They are an invaluable means of communication. Yet audit findings and recommendations should be discussed orally with management and staff prior to incorporation into a written audit report. And frequently the written audit report should be presented in a formal presentation supported by good visual aids.

In some contexts it may be difficult to induce auditors to write audit reports on their work. It has been noted that this is more frequently the case with specialist auditors such as computer auditors. Audit reports should be written even when the auditors find things are satisfactory.

Audit reporting is inextricably bound up with audit productivity. Audit findings and recommendations may be valuable and yet they may be ignored by management. The internal auditing unit should aim to achieve a 'sale' on each audit recommendation. Audit recommendations may be ignored because they are not communicated to management effectively. They should be communicated to the level of management who need to know and who are capable of ensuring that appropriate action is taken

## B5.2.3   *Circulation of audit reports*

A distinction can usefully be made between those to whom an audit report is *addressed,* and those to whom it is *copied.* The report should be addressed to managers for whom the audit is being conducted. It has been said that internal audit does what management would do if management had the time and knew how. A senior manager may have several operations for whom he or she is responsible – each headed up by a senior executive. The responsible manager needs to know that each operation is under control. He or she could conduct their own investigation to determine this – if they knew how, and if they had the time. It is generally more efficient to rely on internal audit to review the operation on behalf of the responsible manager, and therefore the audit report will be addressed to the responsible manager who is the primary 'client' for the audit. It will of course be discussed in draft with the executive who heads up the operation which is the subject of the audit and that executive's response to the audit findings and recommendations will be built into the audit report.

In general the audit report will be addressed to only one person – the responsible executive – but it may be copied as a matter of routine to several people.

The determination of to whom the report should be addressed and copied should be at the discretion of the head of the internal auditing unit.

Circulation of audit reports should be kept to the practical minimum as they usually contain confidential material, and nobody likes their 'dirty linen to be washed unduly in public'. Rather than addressing the full audit report to more than one responsible manager when the scope of the audit embraces operations which fall within the remit of more than one responsible manager, it is usually preferable to sectionalise the report, addressing one report to one responsible manager and another report to another. The audit report will invariably be copied to the executive who manages the operation which has been audited, and may as a matter of routine also be copied to:

- the external auditors;
- group internal audit in case of an audit performed by a more 'junior' internal auditing unit;
- the chief executive (usually a summary report only);
- the audit committee of the Board (usually a summary report only).

## B5.2.4   *Follow-up and the status of audit recommendations*

As a measure to maximise audit productivity, internal auditing units should maintain a schedule of the status of their audit recommendations, showing for each:

- date first communicated to management;
- date of audit report which contained the recommendation;
- date management accepted the recommendation;
- date by which management undertook to implement the recommendation;
- date that recommendation was implemented;
- date that the internal auditing unit confirmed satisfactory implementation.

It is all too easy for auditors to walk away from an audit after the audit report has been issued, leaving management to accept and implement audit recommendations (or to fail to do so as the case may be). If line management become used to a lack of attention from the internal auditing unit after their issuance of an audit report, it becomes more likely that line management will lack the incentive to action responsibly the audit report. It is good practice for management's indication of acceptance of audit findings and recommendations, together with their undertakings will respect to implementation, to be incorporated into the audit report.

It is also good practice for there to be a formal, known requirement for there to be a written response to the internal auditing unit from management to whom the report is addressed. This requirement might be for a response within 28 days of issuance of the audit report. An indication that this is a requirement should be incorporated into the Introduction section of the audit report.

Follow-up on audit findings and recommendations is a shared responsibility between the internal auditing department and line management.

- The internal auditing unit is responsible for ensuring that line management understands its (line management's) responsibilities for action on receipt of an audit report.
- The internal auditing unit is also responsible for ensuring so far as is practical that it knows the status of each audit recommendation. Usually it will suffice for audit to rely on the written response to the audit report from line management, or for internal audit to make enquiries of line management to ascertain the status of audit recommendations. On occasion, if the importance of the issues raised by audit warrant it, or if internal audit has reservations about the reliability of management, *follow-up audit visits* may be conducted to confirm the status of audit recommendations. Since follow-up audit visits are time consuming and often unpopular they should be used sparingly.
- The internal auditing department is responsible for ensuring that audit findings and recommendations are communicated to the appropriate level of management. When there has been a lack of satisfactory action by line management to whom audit findings and recommendations have been addressed, the internal auditing unit is responsible for considering whether more senior management (and ultimately the audit committee of the Board) now need to be informed and, if so, to inform them appropriately.
- Line management is responsible for the management and control of their operations and therefore have the responsibility for following-up upon the receipt of audit reports. It is their responsibility to determine what action should be taken, to make arrangements for that action to be taken, to monitor

the successful implementation of that action and to keep the internal auditing unit informed of progress.

## B5.2.5   *Audit report structure*

Many internal auditing units follow a general structure for their audit reports which corresponds to a fairly standardised format with the following sections within the report. Sections 1 to 4 can be bound separately to make a summary report for senior management who do not need to be given the detail.

**Audit report sections:**

- Introduction

  To set the scene for the report. For instance it may include:
  - The dates when the fieldwork took place
  - Reference to the date of the previous audit
  - Why the audit was conducted.
- Objectives and Scope

  It is particularly important to indicate limitations of scope so that the reader of the report does not obtain a false sense of reassurance as to, for instance, the breadth of the audit's coverage.
- Conclusion

  The internal auditing units overall conclusion which should relate directly to the objectives and scope of the audit.
- Summary of Main Findings and Recommendations

  The purpose of this is to highlight the main points which are explored later in the Supporting Detail section, preferably taking only approximately a page to do so. The points in this section usefully can be cross-referenced to the Supporting Detail section.
- Supporting Detail

  This should be divided into sections, *each section* containing the following – preferably laid out clearly in this sequence, using these as subsection titles:
  - Subject
  - Work Done
  - Findings
  - Recommendations
  - Management Response
  - Appendices
- Relegate to appendices material which is necessary but which would distract the reader from grasping the argument in the Supporting Detail section, because it would represent a significant digression into excessive detail at that stage.

## B5.2.6　*Writing style*

The so-called 'limited cognitive capacities' of people are particularly germane to writing reports which communicate effectively. The rules are:

- Begin at the end
  - Start all long documents with the main arguments and conclusions.
  - Cut long words and long sentences.

  The aim should be a 'fog factor' of three or less (where the fog factor is computed as the number of words with three or more syllables divided by the number of sentences).
- Be direct

Active verbs are better than passive verbs or nouns.
- Be brief

Cut unnecessary words and sentences.
- Revise

Nobody gets it right first time.

## B5.2.7　*'Fog' or 'clarity' indices*

Turnbull suggests that 'information and communication' is one of the aspects that the board may wish to consider and discuss with management when regularly reviewing reports on internal control and carrying out its annual assessment of internal control and risk management. Before Turnbull, Rutteman had, similarly, regarded the five COSO essential components of an effective system of internal control – one of which is 'information and communication' – as the criteria which might be used to assess internal control effectiveness.

Of course, 'information and communication' has many aspects to it, and the Turnbull report draws attention to a few of these. 'Communication' itself is a multifaceted challenge. Just one part of this is the place played by written communication in a business as well as between the business and its stakeholders. In this, the clarity of written text is crucially important.

Clarity is a function of a variety of techniques. Here we look exclusively at the use of 'fog indices' to measure the likely readability of written text. The same technique is at least equally applicable to assess the likely comprehension that will be achieved by listeners to, for instance, the chairman's speech to the shareholders at the Annual General Meeting.

A fog index lets you check how clear is a piece of text. There is more than one way to work out a fog index. Clarity is improved by the use of short sentences and short words and it is entirely misguided to think that use of these makes a poor impression. If communication is the purpose, it is a mistake to try to dress things up with an impressive show of verbosity. Readers and listeners are likely to be more impressed if they have been able to clearly and easily understand the message. If they cannot understand, they will be inclined to conclude that the messenger does not clearly understand what he or she is trying to communicate – what is not understood clearly cannot be communicated clearly.

The opposite of clarity is 'fog'. There are ways of calculating the degree of fog of a report. Two alternative methods of doing so manually are suggested below.

Microsoft Word allows this to be automated to provide readability scores computed using two methods different from those suggested in this article. There are a number of ways of obtaining statistics about text in Word. The most straightforward is to click on File > Properties > Statistics: this will give you data on the number of words and the number of sentences:

Word can also supply full 'readability' data using two methods. One is the Flesch Reading Ease Score – the higher the score, the easier it is to understand the text, and we should aim for a score of 60–70. The other method is the Flesch–Kincaid Grade Level Score which computes readability according to the school grade of someone who would be able to understand the text, and for general reports we should aim for a score of between 7.0–8.0.

To obtain this data from Word, when the Word file is open, click on 'Tools > Options > Spelling & Grammar > Check grammar with spelling > Show readability statistics > Click OK'. Then, the readability information will be available whenever you invoke 'Tools > Spelling and Grammar'. Guidance is available under 'Readability statistics' in Microsoft Word 'Help'. It is also possible for Word to generate the key words used in a file.

To achieve broadly similar results manually, one way is to work out the average number of words of three or more syllables in a sentence, ie:

$$\frac{\text{Number of words with three or more syllables}}{\text{Number of sentences}}$$

Table 1 below sets out this way of calculating the fog index of text.

Usually, if this calculation is done for half a page of text within a report, the score is likely to be quite close to that for the report as a whole. Aim for a fog factor of 3.0 or lower.

Most famous speeches, written as much to be read as to be listened to, have very low fog factors. Churchill's speech in the House of Commons, 18 June 1940, is an example. It has a fog factor of 1.4. It is reproduced here with words of three or more syllables in **bold**:

'I expect the battle of Britain is about to begin. Upon this battle depends the **survival** of Christian **civilisation**. Upon it depends our own British life and the long **continuity** of our **institutions** and our Empire.

The whole fury and might of the **enemy** must very soon be turned on us. Hitler knows that he will have to break us in this island or lose the war.

If we can stand up to him all Europe will be free, and the life of the world may move forward into broad, sunlit uplands, but if we fail then the whole world, **including** the **United** States, and all that we have known and cared for, will sink into the abyss of a new dark age made more **sinister**, and perhaps more prolonged, by the lights of a **perverted** science.

Let us therefore brace ourselves to our duty that if the British **Commonwealth** and Empire lasts for a thousand years men will say, "This was their finest hour".'

Below is an abridged version of what Lieutenant Colonel Tim Collins told his troops on 19 March 2003. There are 24 sentences and 28 words of three or more syllables giving a fog factor of 28/24 or only 1.17. Again, we have highlighted the longer words below: most of them could not have been avoided. Further notable features of this speech which contribute to its clarity and therefore to its effectiveness are (a) the very small number of words with four or more syllables, and (b) the short length of paragraphs.

'We go to **liberate**, not to conquer. We will not fly our flags in their country. We are **entering** Iraq to free a people and the only flag which will be flown in that ancient land is their own. Show respect for them.

There are some who are alive at this moment who will not be alive shortly.

Those who do not wish to go on that journey, we will not send. As for the others, I expect you to rock their world. Wipe them out if that is what they choose. But if you are **ferocious** in battle, **remember** to be **magnanimous** in victory.

Iraq is steeped in history. It is the site of the Garden of Eden, of the Great Flood and the birthplace of **Abraham**. Tread lightly there.

You will see things that no man could pay to see and you will have to go a long way to find a more decent, **generous** and upright people than the **Iraqis**.

If there are **casualties** of war then **remember** that, when they woke up and got dressed in the morning, they did not plan to die this day.

Allow them **dignity** in death.

Bury them **properly** and mark their graves.

The **enemy** should be in no doubt that we are his **nemesis** and that we are bringing about his rightful **destruction**.

There are many **regional commanders** who have stains on their souls and they are stoking the fires of hell for Saddam. He and his forces will be destroyed by this **coalition** for what they have done.

If someone **surrenders** to you then **remember** they have that right in **international** law and ensure that one day they go home to their **family**.

The ones who wish to fight, well, we aim to please.

If you harm the **regiment** or its **history** by **over-enthusiasm** in killing or in **cowardice**, know it is your **family** who will suffer.

> You will be shunned unless your conduct is of the highest – for your deeds will follow you down through history.
>
> We will bring shame on neither our **uniform** nor our nation.'

Lowering the fog factor of text can be achieved readily by dividing sentences into two or more sentences, and by using short rather than long words. Some long words may be unavoidable.

Table 2 provides an alternative way of calculating reading fog, and Table 3 goes on to suggest a way of getting an indication of the required reading age to comprehend the written text. We should not forget that people start reading at (say) 7½ years of age and stop learning to read at age 16, even if they carry on being educated thereafter.

Using 'method 2' (Table 2), Example 1 shows the fog index of an original section of text, and Example 2 shows the same sentiments written more clearly with a more acceptable fog index.

**Table 1**

**CALCULATING FOG – METHOD 1**

**This method calculates the average number of words with three or more syllables in a sentence – which reflects sentence length and frequency of long words**

The average number of words with three or more syllables in the text:

1. Choose about half a page of text which looks typical.
2. Count the number of words with three or more syllables in the text (exclude names):

**(A)** [                    ] **Total number of long words**

3. Count the number of sentences in this same text:

**(B)** [                    ] **Total number of sentences**

4. Divide (A) by (B) to give your fog index (which is the average number of words with three or more syllables in a sentence):

**(C)** [                    ] **Long words per sentence (average)**

- Aim for a score of 3 or less.
  - Score of 3 or less: easy to follow
  - Score of 4 or less: getting hard to follow
  - Score above 5: Gobbledegook!

**Table 2**

## CALCULATING FOG – METHOD 2
**This method reflects sentence length and frequency of long words**

1. Choose about half a page of text which looks typical.
2. Count the number of words in this text:

**(A)** [ ] **Number of words in this text**

3. Count the number of sentences in this same text:

**(B)** [ ] **Number of sentences in this text**

4. Divide (A) by (B) to give the average number of words in a sentence:

**(C)** [ ] **Average words per sentence**

5. Count the number of words with three or more syllables in the text (exclude names):

**(D)** [ ] **Total long words**

6. Divide (D) by (A) and multiply by 100 to give the average percentage of words with three or more syllables in a sentence:

**(E)** [ ] **Long words per sentence (% average)**

7. Add (C) and (E) to give your fog index (which reflects sentence length and frequency of long words):

**(F)** [ ] **Fog ('clarity') index**

- Aim for a score of 36 or less.
  - Score of 36 or less: easy to follow
  - Score of 36 to 45: getting hard to follow
  - Score of over 45: Gobbledegook!

**Table 3 (read in conjunction with Table 2)**

## CALCULATING REQUIRED READING AGE
**Reading age to follow the text (Method 2):**

8. Multiply the result in the box of step 7 by 0.4 to find the number of reading years (ie the number of years of education) needed to understand this writing on a 'single read' of it:

(G) [ ] **Reading years to follow the text**

9. Since people start reading at (say) 5 years of age, add (G) + 5 to find the age of a person who can follow this text:

(H) [ ] **Actual age to follow the text**

*Note:*

People stop learning to *read* at age 16, even if they carry on being educated thereafter.

EXAMPLE 1

**Recruiting**

'It is generally recognised that a shortage of engineers and physical scientists exists. Although the actual magnitude of the shortage depends on the informational source, even the most conservative say this shortage is at least 10,000. A review of studies dealing with the future supply of engineers indicates that the earliest that the supply will approximately the demand will be approximately ten years hence. Since this agency requires for replacement purposes alone approximately 75 scientists each year, it is imperative that immediate steps be taken to improve our recruiting position with reference to new engineers and scientists.

It is generally recognised that the in-hiring rate of recent engineering college graduates has steadily increased due to competition for these people.'

**Method 2:**

| | | |
|---|---|---|
| Total number of words: | | 121 |
| Words of 3 or more syllables | | 32 (27%) |
| Average sentence length: | | 24 |
| Fog ('clarity') index | 27+24 = | 51 |

EXAMPLE 2

**Recruiting**

'There is a shortage of engineers and physical scientists. It is thought to be at least as high as 10,000. Also, the shortage may not be overcome for another ten years.

This Agency needs 75 scientists a year for replacement alone.

Therefore we must start a recruiting campaign straight away. Starting salaries will have to increase to encourage recruits.'

**Method 2:**

| | | |
|---|---|---|
| Total number of words: | | 58 |
| Words of 3 or more syllables | | 10 (18%) |
| Average sentence length: | | 9 |
| Fog ('clarity') index | 18+9 = | 27 |

# Communicating results – case studies

## B5.3.1 Published reports on internal control by internal audit

In B2.1.7 we consider the growing interest of internal audit in the external aspects of corporate governance.

Not least because of the reluctance of boards and of external auditors to become deeply involved in, respectively, reporting publicly on internal control effectiveness and providing assurance on directors' corporate governance statements, perhaps in the medium term there could be a role here for internal audit. Notwithstanding any on-going external audit involvement here, internal auditors should nevertheless now be considering the case for their active involvement. Too little attention has been given to the merits of internal audit reporting publicly on internal control in the annual report.

It is not new for internal auditors to report publicly in the annual reports of entities. Here we reprint and analyse a set of such reports which appeared as early as the 1970s.[1] We do so as the approach taken by Anglian, although a long time ago, offers practical suggestions for internal auditors to approach this in the future.

These internal audit reports, which appeared in the annual reports of Anglian Water during the 1970s, have many points of interest. Clearly internal audit was primarily an audit of accounting and financial matters, under the direction and control of the director of finance (1974–75). But, as we shall see, its financial and accounting 'home base' was not allowed to be a significant restriction upon internal audit scope.

## B5.3.2 *Internal audit coverage*

Three years after being set up, internal audit was able to report that it had reviewed all financial systems in operation (1977–78), not a bad achievement although, admittedly, by the start of 1975 the department had its full complement of as many as 17 audit staff (1974–75), even though they regarded internal audit resources as being 'scarce' (1974–75). It is interesting to speculate how many internal auditors would be in post today in an equivalent but downsized function.

It is unlikely that the contemporary downsizing of internal audit can be attributed reasonably to either a more optimal allocation of internal audit resources to the areas of greatest relative need, nor to a better use of IT to assist in internal audit work by automating aspects of it.

### B5.3.3    Risk assessment

With regard to the former, it looks as if internal audit in Anglian Water in the 1970s applied rather similar risk assessment methods in audit planning as we would today. Take, for instance, their statements that:

> 'A formal system of audit planning and control has been instituted to ensure that the scarce audit resources are allocated to the best advantage of the Authority.'
>
> (1974–75)

### B5.3.4    IT auditing

With regard to the latter it is striking that the internal audit function recruited a computer professional into it from its inception (1974–75). By 1977–78 the internal audit function had a computer audit terminal connected to Anglian Water's new mainframe and by then there is a clear suggestion that audit software was being built into the new IT systems being developed. The policy was:

> 'Wherever possible, use is made of the computer to aid audit work.'
>
> (1977–78)

A year later they were able to report in similar terms, this time that:

> 'Considerable use is made of the computer installation to aid audit work'

and one notable example was the audit software built into their new direct billing applications.

### B5.3.5    A multi-disciplinary function

Despite its financial and accounting orientation, it was clearly considered that internal audit should be a multi-disciplinary function, capable, for instance, of making a positive contribution in the areas of contracting and IT. Internal audit staff 'were recruited from a wide variety of sources'. Apart from an IT specialist, another internal auditor was an engineer (1974–75).

### B5.3.6    *Internal audit's mission*

The first of this set of reports had outlined the role and responsibilities of internal audit (1974–75). As we have pointed out, its accounting and financial vantage point did not appear to have narrowed its scope significantly. Its mission, *inter alia*, was:

> 'to detect fraud, misappropriation, irregular expenditure and losses due to waste or extravagance'

and

> 'to review the monitoring procedures in use … which ensure the physical security of assets and the privacy and confidentiality of information.'
>
> (1974–75)

## B5.3.7 Scope of internal audit work

This must have allowed it a broad role. In 1977–78 they were starting to audit information relating to demand forecasting and to the formulation of the authority's capital development programme.

In 1978–79 we note an internal audit focus on (a) 'information systems that lead to decision making' and to (b) internal audit involvement at the development stage of an improved project appraisal system and in (c) the development of new controls over capital expenditure.

In 1976–77 internal audit had reported they conducted comprehensive examinations of capital spending and had also completed internal audits on 'energy' and 'research'. In 1976–77 internal audit was involved in the planning for the introduction of Anglian Water's new mainframe computer.

In 1978–79 we find them appraising every new IT application 'to ascertain whether all basic control requirements have been met'. As early as 1976–77 they make it clear that internal audit is concerned that Anglian Water's procedures and policies lead to 'best possible value for money'.

## B5.3.8 *'External' internal control*

An organisation's internal control often extends to the systems in place within outside businesses, and that management and auditors should therefore consider the extent to which these should be reviewed before coming to an opinion on internal control. A foretaste of this appears in the 1976–77 internal audit report which describes a number of audits conducted by Anglian Water of District Councils who had an agency relationship with Anglian Water.

## B5.3.9 *Proactive role*

Although internal audit is described as having a protective role (1976–77), it is also seen as being proactive in assisting in promoting improvements; whether financial, administrative or operational.

## B5.3.10 *The 'total audit'*

Commencing 1974–75, reference is made to the close liaison and co-operation between internal and external audit particularly with regard to the elimination of duplication (1977–78) and in 1978–79 the very modern concept of the 'total audit coverage' is introduced within internal audit's public report.

## B5.3.11 *The opinion on internal control*

Perhaps it is particularly interesting to see how internal audit expresses overall opinion on internal control in these published reports. Understandably, for a newly established function, it takes a few years before internal audit expresses such an opinion which first features in the 1977–78 report using the words:

'The standard of financial administration achieved throughout the Authority is now considered by the Chief Internal Auditor to be generally satisfactory.'

Internal audit points out that it had not expressed this opinion until they had been able to report that they had by then reviewed all financial systems in operation.

The following year (1978–79) the opinion was fleshed out:

'The standard of financial administration achieved is considered to be generally satisfactory. This opinion has been formed following reviews of all major financial systems, carried out in each division and at headquarters designed to ensure that systems, controls and procedures were effective, remained relevant in the light of changing circumstances and were adhered to in practice.'

It was in 1978–79 that the very modern phrase 'reasonable assurance' was used in connection with the objectives of internal control, as it is currently in both the COSO and Rutteman reports and thus in directors' internal control reports following the COSO[2] or Rutteman[3] guidance.

By 1979–80 there had been a refinement of emphasis in that the wording of the opinion joined internal audit and management together as endorsing the sentiment expressed:

'During the year all major financial systems have been audited sufficiently to satisfy management on the soundness, adequacy and application of controls, and that the assets and interests of the organisation have been accounted for and protected from serious losses due to any reason, including fraud and poor value for money.'

As with the 1990s reports on internal control, these opinions from Anglian Water were not 'point of time' opinions as of the year end date but rather related to the whole of the year being reported though perhaps without expressly stating so. They also, as with 1990s reports, tended to imply a current and even future assurance rather than merely assurance relating to the old year which was being reported. While they overtly focused upon internal financial control, arguably they were broader than that.

Unlike so many 1990s published reports on internal control, undoubtedly these statements included expressions of opinion on internal control in various terms – 'generally satisfactory', 'effective', 'relevant', 'adhered to', 'sound', 'adequate', 'applied', 'protected from serious losses', and 'value for money'.

## B5.3.12   *Conclusion*

So we have observed a thoroughly modern internal audit function in place a generation ago. Indeed in certain respects it was not only ahead of its time, but in advance of contemporary practice at the turn of the millennium.

## B5.3.13   **Internal audit**

Under the *Accounts and Audit Regulations 1974* [superseded by *Accounts and Audit Regulations 1996 (SI 1996/590)*] the Authority was required to carry out, under the direction and control of the Director of Finance, an internal audit of the accounts of the Authority and of its officers.

At its meeting in November 1974 the Authority agreed that the role and responsibilities of internal audit should be:

(a)  to secure the installation of soundly based systems of control within each area of directorate or divisional responsibility;

(b)  to review and where necessary make recommendations for the improvements of systems, controls and procedures in order to ensure that they are both efficient and effective, that they remain adequate in the light of changing circumstances and that they are adhered to in practice;

(c)  to assist in protecting the assets and interests of the Authority by carrying out a continuous examination of activities in order to detect fraud, misappropriation, irregular expenditure and losses due to waste or extravagance;

(d)  to review the monitoring procedures in use within the Authority which ensure the physical security of assets and the privacy and confidentiality of information.

Internal audit is an integral part of the Finance Directorate, but to ensure its objectivity and independence in reviewing, appraising and reporting on systems and procedures it does not have any responsibility for developing and installing procedures, preparing records or engaging in any activity which will subsequently be subject to audit review and appraisal. The Chief Internal Auditor is directly responsible and reports to the Director of Finance personally, while all internal audit staff based either at Headquarters or at four area offices located in various parts of the region are responsible to the Chief Internal Auditor and not to the Headquarters' directorates or divisions whose work they review and appraise.

A very close liaison has been maintained by internal audit with the Authority's external auditors, Price Waterhouse & Co, since the start.

Although recruitment of internal audit staff did not begin until a late stage, by January 1975 all 17 audit staff were in post, and by the end of the financial year each division had been the subject of an audit visit, although inevitably the initial coverage could not be as extensive as would have been desired following the considerable changes which occurred at and after the April 1974. Considerable emphasis has been placed on the internal training of audit staff, who were recruited from a wide variety of sources, and it is believed that this will provide to be a very sound investment for the future.

A formal system of audit planning and control has been instituted to ensure that the scarce audit resources are allocated to the best advantage of the Authority.

An unusual feature has been the recruitment of two non-accountants – an engineer and a computer professional – to ensure that the necessary expertise is available to enable internal audit to make a positive contribution in the vital areas of contract procedures and administration and of data processing.

**Anglian Water Annual Report 1974–75**

The Authority's internal audit staff carry out a continuous independent appraisal of accounting, financial and related processes to ensure that in all aspects of the Authority's work adequate internal controls are operating, and that where such controls are considered not to be operating effectively management are informed and appropriate action is taken. Internal auditors are expected to adopt a positive attitude and assist in promoting improvements to financial, administrative and operational procedures and policies so that the Authority may obtain the best possible value for the money it spends. This requirement to promote improvements arises out of internal audit's prime protective role and is not in substitution for it.

In addition to audits of divisional and headquarters activities, teams of internal audit and divisional staff carried out audits of expenditure incurred by district councils as agents of the Authority under Sections 7 and 15 of the Water Act 1973. In many cases these audits have resulted in the negotiation of substantial reductions in the amounts claimed from the Authority by the agent councils.

Other internal audit work during the financial year included planning for the introduction of the Authority's new computer, a comprehensive examination of capital spending and audits of spending on energy and research.

**Anglian Water Annual Report 1976–77. Part 6 – Finance**

The Authority's internal audit staff carry out a comprehensive and independent appraisal of accounting, financial and related processes as a service to management. Internal audit is a managerial control which functions by measuring and evaluating the effectiveness of other controls. By the end of the financial year all financial systems in operation throughout the Authority had been reviewed and, in many cases, recommendations had been made and accepted for improvements to systems, controls and procedures to ensure that they remained both efficient and effective. The standard of financial administration achieved throughout the Authority is now considered by the Chief Internal Auditor to be generally satisfactory. Without losing sight of internal audit's prime protective role, increasing effort was devoted to appraising and evaluating information systems that lead to decision making in the Authority. A start was made in auditing the information relating to demand forecasting and the formulation of the Authority's capital development programme.

During the year, the internal audit headquarters team moved from Diploma House to Brook House, Huntingdon, and took delivery of the computer audit terminal connected to the new mainframe. This move was aimed at ensuring that the development of audit techniques in relation to the new systems, particularly direct billing, went in hand with the development of those systems themselves. Wherever possible, use is made of the computer to aid audit work.

Close co-operation between the Authority's internal auditors and the external auditors, Price Waterhouse and Co., has continued throughout the year, particularly in respect of the elimination, as far as has been possible, of duplication of work by the various teams.

**Anglian Water Annual Report 1977–78. Part 6 – Finance**

The Authority has a system of internal control to provide reasonable assurance that its transactions are appropriately recorded and reported, its assets are protected, established policies are followed and costs are properly controlled and managed. This system is prescribed by the Financial Regulations, written delegation of duties to responsible officers and other clearly defined procedures. These are supplemented by a comprehensive internal audit appraisal of all accounting, financial and related processes.

The standard of financial administration achieved is considered to be generally satisfactory. This opinion has been formed following reviews of all major financial systems, carried out in each division and at headquarters designed to ensure that systems, controls and procedures were effective, remained relevant in the light of changing circumstances and were adhered to in practice.

Internal audit effort continued to be devoted to appraising and evaluating the information systems that lead to decision making. During the year a contribution was made to the introduction of an improved project appraisal system and to the development of controls over capital expenditure. With the publication of divisional revenue output measures a start was made on inter-divisional comparisons of performance.

Considerable use is made of the computer installation to aid audit work, and during the year an important innovation in the form of a special reports feature was developed jointly by the computer audit staff and Honeywell. This system is now operating on all direct billing applications. In addition, each new computer application is independently appraised by internal audit to ascertain whether all basic control requirements have been met.

The internal auditors liase with the external auditors, Price Waterhouse and Co., to ensure that total audit coverage is adequate and to eliminate any unnecessary duplication of work.

**Anglian Water Annual Report 1978–79. Part 6 – Finance**

The scale and complexity of the Authority's organisation is recognised by the framework of control which is set down in Financial Regulations, Rules of Contract and the Schemes of Delegations. Within that structure management is responsible for ensuring that detailed systems of control exist to safeguard the Authority's assets, ensure reliability of records, promote operational efficiency and monitor adherence to policies and directives.

Management in turn relies on an effective internal audit to review, appraise and report on these systems of control.

During the year all major financial systems have been audited sufficiently to satisfy management on the soundness, adequacy and application of controls, and that the assets and interests of the organisation have been accounted for and protected from serious losses due to any reason, including fraud and poor value for money.

**Anglian Water Annual Report 1979–80. Part 6**

[1]    We have not been able to obtain a copy of the 1975–76 report.
[2]    'Internal control – integrated framework' (September 1992) Committee of Sponsoring Organizations of the Treadway Commission (COSO), American Institute of Certified Public Accountants.
[3]    'Internal control and financial reporting: guidance for directors of listed companies registered in the UK' (December 1994), 'The Rutteman Report', ICAEW.

## B5.3.14  Audit reports – case study

Select a sample of three audit reports and assess each with respect to the issues addressed in the table below.

**B5.3.14** *Communicating results – case studies*

## FORM FOR GROUP USE IN EVALUATING INTERNAL AUDIT REPORTS

|  |  | **Report 1** | **Report 2** | **Report 3** |
|---|---|---|---|---|
| 1. | Is it clear that this is an audit report? | | | |
| 2. | Is necessary 'housekeeping' information provided (dates of audit, members of team, etc)? | | | |
| 3. | Is appropriate contextual information given, probably in the introduction to the report? | | | |
| 4. | Is the report attractive and to the standard usually associated with an important internal company communication? | | | |
| 5. | What do you think of the general flow of the report (sections used in the report, sequencing of contents, use of English, etc)? | | | |
| 6. | Is the report concise and easy to understand? | | | |
| 7. | Is it clear from whom the report comes? | | | |
| 8. | Is the circulation disclosed and appropriate? | | | |
| 9. | Is management's response appropriately incorporated into this report? | | | |
| 10. | Is it clear to whom the report is addressed and the action expected from the addressee? | | | |
| 11. | Any evidence of appropriate use of a transmittal memorandum? | | | |
| 12. | Is it easy to find and understand the main conclusion and the main issues arising from the audit? | | | |
| 13. | Does the report show that the issues addressed in this report and the overall conclusion arise naturally from the reported audit work done? | | | |

|     |                                                                                             | Report 1 | Report 2 | Report 3 |
|-----|---------------------------------------------------------------------------------------------|----------|----------|----------|
| 14. | Are there any other issues of note on audit report writing practice apparent from this report? |          |          |          |

## B5.3.15   Effective use of English

Each of these sentences/words has been extracted from an audit report. Rewrite these sentences and expressions to communicate more clearly and acceptably.

|     |                                                                                                                              |  |
|-----|------------------------------------------------------------------------------------------------------------------------------|--|
| 1.  | The functional area attributed its operational deficiencies to a lack of personnel resulting from budget limitations        |  |
| 2.  | The concept of a trade discount has ceased to exist.                                                                         |  |
| 3.  | The value has been determined for disposal purposes of these assets.                                                        |  |
| 4.  | The policy provides as a maximum provision for replacement 25 per cent of the initial cost and is adjusted in accordance with the inflation rate. |  |
| 5.  | These figures, which were net of allowances for depreciation, expenses, prepayments and the costs of other estimated services, were omitted. |  |
| 6.  | However, it is not envisaged that a detailed study of the costings of every tender will be made.                            |  |
| 7.  | We project that the results of this classification of project results …                                                     |  |

| 8. | We do not believe the management accounts can be trusted. | |
|---|---|---|
| 9. | No response has been made by management. | |
| 10. | The elimination of the waste could be accomplished. | |
| 11. | It is thought by management ... | |
| 12. | During the course of our audit we noted that invoices are ... | |
| 13. | This surplus is after giving effect to deductions therefrom by reason of ... | |
| 14. | Numerous other products are produced or processed, in addition to the above items. | |
| 15. | We discussed this with the auditee. | |
| 16. | We engaged in an audit commensurate with staff availability. | |
| 17. | modification | |
| 18. | initial | |
| 19. | optimum | |
| 20. | encounter | |
| 21. | demonstrate | |
| 22. | aggregated | |
| 23. | audit findings | |
| 24. | audit recommendations | |
| 25. | inflexible | |
| 26. | obdurate | |
| 27. | stubborn | |
| 28. | pigheaded | |
| 29. | A supplier should be required to sign in when he arrives. | |

# Monitoring progress – best practice guidance

'Internal auditors should determine that corrective action was taken and is achieving the desired results, or that senior management or the board has assumed the risk of not taking corrective action on reported observations.'[1]

'Follow-up by internal auditors is defined as a process by which they determine the adequacy, effectiveness, and timeliness of actions taken by management on reported engagement observations and recommendations, including those made by external auditors and others.'[2]

While we also refer to other important pronouncements, our main source of guidance for the parts of this Handbook which describe internal auditing best practice has been the *Professional Practices Framework* of The Institute of Internal Auditors. This *Framework* includes their *Definition* of internal auditing, *Code of Ethics*, *Standards*, and *Practice Advisories*. Of these, only the *Practice Advisories* are non-mandatory: they explain and elaborate upon best practice in most circumstances, and are important for practitioners and students. Readers can see the current complete list of *Practice Advisories* at www.theiia.org. Those current on 1 January 2005 are shown at APPENDIX 3 of this Handbook, including a useful topical classification at APPENDIX 3.2.

In addressing this subject we have drawn more widely than those *Practice Advisories* classified by The Institute as applicable to this part of our Handbook, which are:

| Practice Advisories, by Standard Number | Release date |
|---|---|
| Practice Advisory 2500–1: Monitoring Progress | 5 January 2001 |
| Practice Advisory 2500.A1–1: Follow-up Process | 5 January 2001 |

*Practice Advisories* carry the *Standard* number to which they principally refer. Readers are advised to consult the applicable *Standards* as we do not in every case reproduce them here. They are to be found at APPENDIX 2.

### 'Standard 2500 – Monitoring Progress

The chief audit executive should establish and maintain a system to monitor the disposition of results communicated to management.'

Monitoring the disposition of audit engagement results overlaps with disseminating engagement results which we discussed in B5.1. This is because audit decisions need to be taken, as a consequence of this monitoring, on whether there is a need to communicate audit results to higher levels within the chief audit executive's 'chain of command' when, in the judgement of internal audit, action by management has been unsatisfactory. Ultimately the board, or its audit committee, may need to be informed – and so there is also overlap with CHAPTER B7.1 'Resolution of management's acceptance of risks'.

> '... If the communications result in a conclusion that management, by its inadequate or lack of actions, is exposing the organization to an unacceptable level of risk, the chief audit executive (CAE) should consider other options to achieve a satisfactory resolution. Among those possible actions, the CAE could discuss his or her concerns about the risk exposure with senior management within his or her normal chain of command. Since the audit or other committee of the governing board would also be expected to be in the CAE's chain of command, the members of the board committee would normally be apprised of the CAE's concerns.'[3]

Practice Advisory 2440–3: 'Communicating Sensitive Information Within and Outside of the Chain of Command' goes on to discuss extreme circumstances where it might be acceptable for the chief audit executive to communicate *outside* the normal chain of command (see B7.1.2).

## B6.1.2   Audit engagement follow-up

In CHAPTER B3.1 we stressed that thorough planning of an audit engagement is a necessary prerequisite of a successful engagement. Similarly, careful follow-up may be equally important. It would be futile to perform an audit well and then to lose track of whether or not audit recommendations are accepted and agreed action is implemented successfully. An absence of audit follow-up may encourage management to ignore audit recommendations and forget about, or defer, agreed action. Audit follow-up can be the essential catalyst to turn a good audit into improved business processes.

Follow-up takes time – even when follow-up audit visits are not conducted. But it is well worthwhile. It will be preferable to schedule fewer audits in order to allow adequate time for follow-up. The primary objective is for internal audit to 'make a sale' on every audit recommendation and each agreed action. A secondary objective is for internal audit to know the status of each of these – so as to be able to advise senior management and the audit committee more reliably on the quality of risk management, control and governance processes.

## B6.1.3   *Internal audit's responsibilities for audit engagement follow-up*

The Institute assigns responsibility for follow-up to the chief audit executive:

> 'The nature, timing, and extent of follow-up should be determined by the chief audit executive.'[4]

This is consistent with giving to the chief audit executive the responsibility to determine the programme of audit engagements, the content of audit reports, to whom audit results are disseminated – and so on. Internal audit should not subordinate it judgement on professional matters to that of others. In a broad sense, engagement follow-up is a shared responsibility between internal audit and management. Internal audit is responsible to follow-up so that internal audit knows the status of all audit recommendations and all agreed actions, and is therefore in a position to take further appropriate action where necessary. As we have said, internal audit also has the responsibility to report to the audit committee the status of past audit recommendations and agreed actions:

> 'Techniques used to effectively monitor progress include:
>
> ...
>
> • Reporting to senior management or the board on the status of responses to engagement observations and recommendations.'[5]

Further, internal audit has a responsibility to ensure that appropriate policies and procedures are agreed within the organization covering both internal audit's and management's responsibilities for follow-up:

> 'The chief audit executive should establish procedures to include the following:
> • A time frame within which management's response to the engagement observations and recommendations is required.
> • An evaluation of management's response.
> • A verification of the response (if appropriate).
> • A follow-up engagement (if appropriate).
> • A communications procedure that escalates unsatisfactory responses/actions, including the assumption of risk, to the appropriate levels of management.'[6]

and:

> 'Techniques used to effectively monitor progress include:
> • Addressing engagement observations and recommendations to the appropriate levels of management responsible for taking corrective action.'[7]

The audit duty to follow-up varies between assurance and consulting engagements, reflecting that consulting engagements are 'agreed upon'[8] with the audit client.

> **'Standard 2500.A1 –**
> The chief audit executive should establish a follow-up process to monitor and ensure that management actions have been effectively implemented or that senior management has accepted the risk of not taking action.'

> **'Standard 2500.C1 –**
> The internal audit activity should monitor the disposition of results of consulting engagements to the extent agreed upon with the client.'

## B6.1.4  *Audit engagement follow-up by a separate function*

Some organizations set up a separate function for this follow-up, and it is often assigned to a separate section within the internal auditing activity:

> 'Techniques used to effectively monitor progress include:
>
> ...

- Receiving and evaluating information from other organizational units assigned responsibility for procedures of a follow-up or corrective nature.'[9]

## B6.1.5  *Management's responsibilities for follow-up*

Management is responsible for follow-up in the sense that those to whom engagement reports are addressed have a responsibility to consider them carefully and to act upon them in accordance with the policies and procedures of the organization.

'Techniques used to effectively monitor progress include:

...

- Receiving and evaluating management responses to engagement observations and recommendations during the engagement or within a reasonable time period after the engagement results are communicated. Responses are more useful if they include sufficient information for the chief audit executive to evaluate the adequacy and timeliness of corrective action.
- Receiving periodic updates from management in order to evaluate the status of management's efforts to correct previously communicated conditions.'[10]

## B6.1.6  *Approaches to audit engagement follow-up*

'Monitoring progress' is one part of audit engagement follow-up. The other part of follow-up is for the internal auditing activity to take further action when they judge it to be necessary.

It is a matter of professional judgement to determine the nature, extent and timing of audit follow-up:

'Certain reported observations and recommendations may be so significant as to require immediate action by management. These conditions should be monitored by the internal audit activity until corrected because of the effect they may have on the organization.'[11]

Whether or not immediate and continuous follow-up is justified, and the urgency and means with which it is undertaken, will require the auditor to weigh up:

- the relative importance of the matter;
- the past record of management to deal promptly and effectively with audit recommendations:

'There may also be instances where the chief audit executive judges that management's oral or written response shows that action already taken is sufficient when weighed against the relative importance of the engagement observation or recommendation. On such occasions, follow-up may be performed as part of the next engagement.'[12]

- whether the matter has been communicated to the level of management who legitimately can decide whether to tolerate the risk of inaction:

'Factors that should be considered in determining appropriate follow-up procedures are:

- The significance of the reported observation or recommendation.

- The degree of effort and cost needed to correct the reported condition.

- The impacts that may result should the corrective action fail.

- The complexity of the corrective action.

- The time period involved.'[13]

## B6.1.7  Follow-up audit visits

Follow-up audit engagements should be undertaken only when appropriate in view of the urgency and importance of the matter. They can be disruptive of audit schedules as well as being unpopular with management and staff. They provide the opportunity to confirm whether agreed action, which management may have reported to internal audit that they have untaken, has indeed been implemented and the results are working satisfactorily:

> 'Internal auditors should ascertain that actions taken on engagement observations and recommendations remedy the underlying conditions.'[14]

When follow-up engagements are to be conducted, they should appear within the audit plan:

> 'The chief audit executive is responsible for scheduling follow-up activities as part of developing engagement work schedules. Scheduling of follow-up should be based on the risk and exposure involved, as well as the degree of difficulty and the significance of timing in implementing corrective action.'[15]

[1]    Practice Advisory 2500.A1–1: 'Follow-up Process', para 1.
[2]    Practice Advisory 2500.A1–1: 'Follow-up Process', para 2.
[3]    Practice Advisory 2440–3: 'Communicating Sensitive Information Within and Outside of the Chain of Command', paras 2 and 3.
[4]    Practice Advisory 2500.A1–1: 'Follow-up Process', para 3.
[5]    Practice Advisory 2500–1: 'Monitoring Progress', para 3.
[6]    Practice Advisory 2500–1: 'Monitoring Progress', para 1.
[7]    Practice Advisory 2500–1: 'Monitoring Progress', para 3.
[8]    See definition of 'Consulting Services' within the *Glossary* to the *Standards*, which defines terms as they are used within the *Standards.*
[9]    Practice Advisory 2500–1: 'Monitoring Progress', para 3.
[10]   Practice Advisory 2500–1: 'Monitoring Progress', para 3.
[11]   Practice Advisory 2500–1: 'Monitoring Progress', para 2.
[12]   Practice Advisory 2500.A1–1: 'Follow-up Process', para 4.
[13]   Practice Advisory 2500.A1–1: 'Follow-up Process', para 3.
[14]   Practice Advisory 2500.A1–1: 'Follow-up Process', para 5.
[15]   Practice Advisory 2500.A1–1: 'Follow-up Process', para 6.

# Resolution of management's acceptance of risks – best practice guidance

**B7.1.1**   While we also refer to other important pronouncements, our main source of guidance for the parts of this Handbook which describe internal auditing best practice has been the *Professional Practices Framework* of The Institute of Internal Auditors. This *Framework* includes their *Definition* of internal auditing, *Code of Ethics*, *Standards*, and *Practice Advisories*. Of these, only the *Practice Advisories* are non-mandatory: they explain and elaborate upon best practice in most circumstances, and are important for practitioners and students. Readers can see the current complete list of *Practice Advisories* at www.theiia.org. Those current on 1 January 2005 are shown at APPENDIX 3 of this Handbook, including a useful topical classification at APPENDIX 3.2.

In addressing this subject we have drawn more widely than those *Practice Advisories* classified by The Institute as applicable to this part of our Handbook, which are:

| **Practice Advisory, by Standard Number** | **Release date** |
|---|---|
| Practice Advisory 2600–1: Management's Acceptance of Risks | 5 January 2001 |

In addition, we address here Practice Advisory 2440–3: 'Communicating Sensitive Information Within and Outside of the Chain of Command' rather than in Chapter B5.1 which would reflect the classification of that Advisory given by the Institute.

*Practice Advisories* carry the *Standard* number to which they principally refer. Readers are advised to consult the applicable *Standards* as we do not in every case reproduce them here. They are to be found at APPENDIX 2.

**'Standard 2600 – Resolution of Management's Acceptance of Risks**
When the chief audit executive believes that senior management has accepted a level of residual risk that may be unacceptable to the organization, the chief audit executive should discuss the matter with senior management. If the decision regarding residual risk is not resolved, the chief audit executive and senior management should report the matter to the board for resolution.'

As worded, this Standard is ambiguous as to whether or not consensus should be obtained before an unresolved matter is taken to the board, or to the audit committee of the board, for resolution. Whether this ambiguity is intentional, we are not sure. If intentional, it has the effect of avoiding within the *Standards* themselves any overt suggestion that internal audit might legitimately undermine the authority of management. Undoubtedly there are many business contexts where it would be an explosive matter for the chief audit executive to take a matter to the board or to the audit committee against the wishes of senior management. It appears, for instance, that recently a multi-national oil company's internal auditors did not notify the audit committee of the 20%+ overestimate of proven and provable oil reserves, of which senior management were aware for over two years.

While the wording of this Standard may be ambiguous, we have no doubt that the chief audit executive should not subordinate his or her judgement on this professional matter to that of even senior management. It is a matter of internal audit independence and objectivity. The tenor of Practice Advisories in general, and those that we discuss in this section in particular, endorses this view.

In B5.1 we said that if appropriate action on the audit report is not taken by the executive to whom it is addressed, then the chief audit executive needs to consider whether there is now a more senior level of management who needs to know and would be capable of ensuring that appropriate action was taken. Again, this has to be a matter of professional judgement by the chief audit executive, based on the circumstances in each case. Not every matter should be escalated upwards without limit.

Management has the discretion to determine whether to act.

> 'Management is responsible for deciding the appropriate action to be taken in response to reported engagement observations and recommendations.'[1]

Senior management may decide to assume the risk of not correcting the reported condition because of cost or other considerations.[2]

Internal audit is an advisory function without executive authority except over internal audit matters. However, it is the chief audit executive's responsibility to ensure that audit concerns are communicated to the appropriate levels within the entity and, to be able to do so, it is important that the chief audit executive has a direct reporting line through to the audit committee of the board (B1.2.3).

> 'The chief audit executive is responsible for assessing such management action for the timely resolution of the matters reported as engagement observations and recommendations. In deciding the extent of follow-up, internal auditors should consider procedures of a follow-up nature performed by others in the organization.'[3]

and:

> 'The chief audit executive should establish ... a communications procedure that escalates unsatisfactory responses/actions, including the assumption of risk, to the appropriate levels of management.'[4]

## B7.1.2   Communicating sensitive information within and outside of the chain of command

> 'Ultimately, the internal auditor must make a personal decision. The decision to communicate outside the normal chain of command should be based on a well-

informed opinion that the wrongdoing is supported by substantial, credible evidence and that a legal or regulatory imperative or a professional or ethical obligation requires further action. The auditor's motive for acting should be the desire to stop the wrongful, harmful, or improper activity.'[5]

Practice Advisories 2440–3: 'Communicating Sensitive Information Within and Outside of the Chain of Command' (12 June 2003) is an important addition which grapples with the vexed issue of whistleblowing (reporting outside one's chain of command) and other related matters. Practice Advisory 2600–2: 'Communicating Sensitive Information and Whistleblowing' (December 2002) was withdrawn almost as soon as it was issued, to be replaced by PA 2440–3. We recommend strongly that internal auditors faced with the prospect that whistleblowing might be the right action for the auditor to take should study this Practice Advisory carefully.

Practice Advisory 2440–3 is about matters which constitute an unacceptable level of risk if not appropriately dealt with by management and thus subject to Standard 2600 (above). It is about:

'information that is critically sensitive and substantial to the organization and has significant potential consequences. That information may relate to exposures, threats, uncertainties, fraud, waste and mismanagement, illegal activities, abuse of power, misconduct that endangers public health or safety, or other wrongdoings. Those types of matters may adversely impact the organization's reputation, image, competitiveness, success, viability, market values, investments and intangible assets, or earnings. They are likely to increase an organization's risk exposures.'[6]

Much of the focus of Practice Advisory 2440–3 is on a particular category of unacceptable risk, that is wrongdoing of which the internal auditor is aware and which is substantial. While there may be additional, appropriate actions by the internal auditor (which we discuss later), the fundamental internal audit response should be guided by the Standard:

'If the communications result in a conclusion that management, by its inadequate or lack of actions, is exposing the organization to an unacceptable level of risk, the chief audit executive (CAE) should consider other options to achieve a satisfactory resolution. Among those possible actions, the CAE could discuss his or her concerns about the risk exposure with senior management within his or her normal chain of command. Since the audit or other committee of the governing board would also be expected to be in the CAE's chain of command, the members of the board committee would normally be apprised of the CAE's concerns. If the CAE, after those discussions with senior management, is still unsatisfied and concludes that senior management is exposing the organization to an unacceptable risk and is not taking appropriate action to halt or correct the situation, senior management and the CAE would present the essential information and their differences of opinion to the members or a committee of the governing board. That simple chain-of-command communication scenario may be accelerated for certain types of sensitive occurrences … .'[7]

Practice Advisory 2440–3 discusses the need to weigh the professional internal auditor's:

'broad responsibilities to the public and its protection of the general welfare'[8] against:

'the duty of confidentiality, imposed by the IIA Code of Ethics, to respect the value and ownership of information and avoid disclosing it without appropriate authority, unless there is a legal or professional obligation to do so.'[9]

1    Practice Advisory 2600–1: 'Management's Acceptance of Risks', para 1.
2    Practice Advisory 2060–1: 'Reporting to the Board and Senior Management', para 3; and Practice Advisory 2600–1: 'Management's Acceptance of Risks', para 2.
3    Practice Advisory 2600–1: 'Management's Acceptance of Risks', para 1.
4    Practice Advisory 2500–1: 'Monitoring Progress', para 1.
5    Practice Advisory 2440–3: 'Communicating Sensitive Information Within and Outside of the Chain of Command', para 11.
6    Practice Advisory 2440–3: 'Communicating Sensitive Information Within and Outside of the Chain of Command', para 1.
7    Practice Advisory 2440–3: 'Communicating Sensitive Information Within and Outside of the Chain of Command', paras 2, 3 and 4.
8    Practice Advisory 2440–3: 'Communicating Sensitive Information Within and Outside of the Chain of Command', para 9.
9    Practice Advisory 2440–3: 'Communicating Sensitive Information Within and Outside of the Chain of Command', para 10.

# Resolution of management's acceptance of risks – case studies

## B7.2.1   Case studies on whistleblowing

CASE 1

A director of internal auditing uncovers an apparent long-running taxation fraud within the privately owned company whose internal audit service she heads. She discloses the matter as fully and as clearly as possible within the company, exhausting all her formally laid down reporting opportunities. The company has no audit committee and the 'terms of reference' of its internal audit function does not provide its head of internal auditing with direct access to the board (which is 50% non-executive).

Management's response to this disclosure by the head of internal audit includes casting some doubt upon whether internal audit has interpreted the facts and the tax implications correctly; and consequently whether there really is a fraud and, if so, whether the internal auditor's assessment of its size is reliable. In summary, management thanks the internal auditor for her work in this area, but asks her to take no further action.

It is apparent to the head of internal audit that the company itself has no intention of taking any action either to prevent the continuance of the alleged fraud or to make disclosure to the taxation authorities.

What is the position of the head of internal audit, and what should she do?

**Guidance on Case 1**

It appears that the head of internal audit has fully discharged her professional internal auditing responsibilities by (a) discovering the fraud and (b) communicating it as clearly and effectively as her reporting authority allows. Internal auditors, as advisors, do not have the executive authority to compel the actions they recommend.

It should go without saying that internal auditors owe a duty of professional care to ensure that audit findings are soundly based and that audit recommendations are appropriate and arise from the audit findings. We are assuming that such is so in this case.

We note that the head of internal audit has accepted a role within this company which is inconsistent with The IIA's *Standards for the Professional Practice of Internal Auditing* in that internal audit has no access to an audit committee of the board or to the board itself. In determining whether this amounts to professional misconduct, we would be influenced by any evidence that the head of internal audit (a) in the past had used her best endeavours to achieve full implementation of the *Standards* – which requires wholehearted support from the board and management as well as from internal audit; and (b) in this case had reported the matter to the board of directors notwithstanding that she was not authorised so to do. So, with respect to (a) we consider a head of internal audit should not 'acquiesce without protest' in a state of affairs which does not measure up to the *Standards* and the best time to influence these affairs is when there is not a current issue at stake; with respect to (b) we therefore consider whistleblowing when necessary *within* the business (including to the board of directors) to be consistent with best internal audit practice. Internal auditors should not subordinate their judgement to that of others, and so the decision whether to refer the matter to the board should be that of the internal auditor alone.

Before the head of internal audit opts to 'blow the whistle' externally, we are clear that she should have exhausted all internal communication of the matter – including (a) communication to the board which exceeds her laid down authority in this case, and (b) communication to the external auditor whether or not authorised.

If the law *requires* the internal auditor to make any external disclosure, or if such is necessary to avoid personal culpability, then we believe it to be consistent with best practice for professional internal auditing that the auditor should make such a disclosure. However, in this case we do not believe that there is such a legal obligation.

Depending upon the full circumstances of this case, it is likely that the UK's Public Interest Disclosure Act (1998) could afford a measure of protection for the internal auditor exercising her rights to 'go public' about this case. No advice we give should be construed as seeking to restrict any internal auditor from exercising rights granted to him or her under this or any other law. For instance, we do not advise that the internal auditor should necessarily resign her position before 'going public' with the disclosure, though this is certainly a matter which the internal auditor should decide upon.

In this case we take the position that it would be unprofessional for the internal auditor *not* to consider whether to 'go public' and, if so, in what way(s). In coming to her judgement on this, the internal auditor should in particular be influenced by the balance of the relevant provisions in The Institute's *Code of Ethics*.

We recommend that the head of internal audit takes legal advice as necessary. She should also make and retain a full and contemporary record (a) of the evidence, and (b) to account for the decision she came to about whether or not to 'go public' and, if so, how.


CASE 2

An inexperienced internal auditor within an internal auditing function detects an incident of apparent wrongdoing. He has checked and rechecked this and is confident of the facts and his interpretation of these facts. No action is taken when he reports it to the head of internal audit, but no satisfactory explanation of the incident or the lack of action is given. With insufficient explanation, the head of internal audit insists that any reference to this incident be omitted from (a) the internal audit report on this assignment, and (b) the summary which goes before the audit committee of the board.

The company has a procedure set out within its *Code of Business Conduct* whereby any staff (including internal auditors) may communicate their concerns about alleged wrongdoing. The mechanism for doing this is to communicate first with one's immediate boss or, if that is not appropriate or has been ineffective, to the Group Head of Internal Audit. There is an established procedure for the Group Head of internal Audit to follow upon receipt of such communications.

### Guidance on Case 2

The procedure set out above is of limited use in this case. Nevertheless, the concerned internal auditor should formally invoke this procedure, notwithstanding that his functional head (the group head of internal auditing) already appears to have failed to have taken appropriate action.

Senior internal auditors have an important duty to support and protect their staff in situations like this, and this includes giving full explanation for causes of action which are determined in response to expressions of concern.

It is best practice that all staff should be empowered to take their concerns to any other senior point within the business, at their discretion – including to the chief executive and to the board or its audit committee. Certainly all internal auditors should have direct access to the chair of the audit committee and, at that chairman's discretion, be empowered to arrange for items of concern to be placed on the agendas of audit committee meetings.

The indications are that none of the powers exist in this case which are set out in the previous paragraph. Even so, we consider that the concerned internal auditor has a personal professional responsibility (which he should not subordinate to the judgement of the head of internal audit) to use his best endeavours to ensure that his audit finding is communicated to the level of management (and the board) who needs to know and who is capable of ensuring that appropriate action is taken. It has to be the internal auditor's personal judgement in this case to what level that communication ultimately should be made, and the timing of any escalation in reporting. We consider that the internal auditor should do this even if, as in this case, he has been ceded no formal powers to 'blow the whistle' internally in this way. Once again, we advise that a careful record is kept of the evidence and of the formulation and execution of the strategy to disclose.

In coming to his personal professional judgement as outlined in the above paragraph, the internal auditor will of course weigh the advice accorded to him by others, not least by the head of internal audit.

As in our guidance on **Case 1** above, we take the position that it would be unprofessional for the internal auditor *not* to consider whether to 'go public' and, if so, in what way(s). Once again, in coming to his judgement on this, the internal auditor should in particular be influenced by the balance of the relevant provisions in The Institute's *Code of Ethics*.

If the motivation for external disclosure involves malicious intent, disclosure is unlikely to be the appropriate professional act for an internal auditor.


## CASE 3

The head of internal audit of a leading bank is effectively removed from his position. He had highlighted a problem of £600 million worth of 53,000 bogus non-resident accounts and other serious losses internally among senior colleagues. It was the bank's customers who were evading tax, but arguably the bank had colluded with them to such an extent that it quickly repaid £14 million out of its own resources, and had a further, much larger, potential liability.

The head of internal audit had pressed the bank to clarify its position with the tax authorities and with the country's central bank. He complained that his position, and that of the internal auditing function he headed, were effectively undermined after he had highlighted these problems. He had made sure that executive management and the audit committee of the board had been informed about these problems. The chief executive of the bank had told the audit committee that he considered raising the matter externally would cause the bank great damage, and that the problem of this sort of 'bogus accounts' was in any case an 'old industry-wide problem' of which the tax authorities and the central bank were well aware and about which they were said to be very understanding.

The bank claimed that the removal of the head of internal audit was unrelated to this matter but merely a matter of career development since he had been head of internal audit for several years.

At about that time, a *Code of Best Practice* for the bank's internal audit function enjoined internal auditors *inter alia* to 'exercise objectivity, independence and professionalism in the performance of their duties and responsibilities', to 'display loyalty in all matters pertaining to the Group' and to 'be guided by the principles of Integrity, Confidentiality, Professionalism, Loyalty and Legality'. Furthermore, the internal audit function's *Charter* stipulated that the function advised 'all levels of management and the audit committee' who required it 'to function professionally and ethically' and to whom it had 'full and complete access'. The internal audit function was charged with communicating its findings and recommendations 'as appropriate, to (a) the levels of management who need to know and those who are capable of ensuring that action is taken as necessary and (b) the Audit Committee.'

While this case relates to happenings that date back to the beginning of the 1990s and earlier, it finally came into the public domain in the late 1990s. We are unaware of how this came about – other than that a large number of internal auditing documents reached the national press. It has had the effect of giving the issue a new lease of life as politicians have now started to ask questions. This may be a classic case of ultimately bringing the matter into the public domain because of a perceived public interest dimension. Was this justified in order to blow a hole in the informal accommodation which appears to have been made between the bank and the authorities?


### Guidance on Case 3

The right mechanisms were in place to enable the internal audit findings and recommendations to be communicated all the way through to the non-executive audit committee of the board who, it would appear, initiated a measured, appropriate response by the bank. The head of internal audit thus needed to act in no *unauthorised* way to make the audit committee aware of this matter. He appears to have communicated the audit findings and recommendations clearly but there is some suggestion here of a 'scatter-gun' audit approach (an apparently well informed press report suggests the head of internal audit 'sent a flurry of letters to other executives, to the audit committee and to senior board members of the bank, warning them of the consequences of not dealing quickly with the situation'). Possibly internal audit alienated management and the board by a rather tactless, too wide dissemination of these damaging audit findings?

We could see no indication that either the *Code of Best Practice* for internal audit nor the internal audit function's *Charter* protected the head of internal audit from removal without the prior consent of the audit committee. This would have been a valuable safeguard – in the interests of the business as well as of the head of internal audit. While there is no indication that his removal was without the prior knowledge of the audit committee, it is possible that management may have been less inclined to initiate and/or support such a move if this safeguard had been built into the constitutional documents of the business. What we need to achieve is that management does not react to these situations by contemplating the removal of the head of internal audit – which is a matter of 'shooting the messenger'. There was clearly a loss of confidence between top management and the head of internal audit, but we would suggest that this was a collective failure which a mature business, and the individuals involved, should endeavour to avoid especially in cases such as this.

Regardless of the compensation terms for the head of internal audit, it does appear that top management, the board and the board's audit committee reacted unduly defensively to an internal audit which they had set up to be able to work in a professional way, and which had been conducting itself well. There is some indication that this undermined the general effectiveness of internal audit to this business. It must also have dented the morale of internal audit.

## CASE 4

On 28 June 2001, *The Wall Street Journal Europe* carried an excellently researched article by James Bandler and Mark Maremont titled 'Gunning for Xerox takes a heavy toll on James Bingham – the hard life of a corporate whistleblower' (pp 1 & 11).

Xerox shares, which had traded as high as the low 60s in the first half of 1999, had fallen to less than $4 in late 2000[1] against a backcloth of a downturn in the copier market as printers replaced copiers for many business uses. For any company, it would have been an anxious time, focussing management's attention on what could be done to turn in results up to market expectations in order to maintain or grow the share price. In this hostile climate, if there were any ways in which Xerox had been significantly understating profits, these would naturally be candidates for rectification.

James F Bingham, aged 46, had been with Xerox Corp for 15 years ending up as assistant treasurer on $350,000 pa before he was fired for alleged insubordination after he had claimed to top Xerox executives that the company was using undisclosed bookkeeping methods to hide worsening results. He was later to call this 'accounting fraud' when he blew the whistle publicly and filed a lawsuit against Xerox. Not uniquely amongst whistleblowers, Bingham is said to have had a record for being 'brash', 'brisk', an 'arrogant free spirit' and to have been a rebel even in his schooldays.

Bingham had disclosed his views in a memo, addressed to Xerox's president as well as to their chief financial officer. He did so shortly after the scandal had become public. Bingham is reported as considering that Xerox was driving itself into bankruptcy through bad decisions based on faulty accounting. He says he thought his arguments and the correctness of his data were so strong that Xerox executives would change course.

A year after his dismissal, *The Wall Street Journal Europe* reported that his family was suffering as income from his work had plummeted to $50,000 per year, work had been unsteady and he had been unable to concentrate upon work because of the demands of his dispute with Xerox – all consequences regrettably familiar to many whistleblowers. It was said that his focus on the case had distracted him from his family and led to Bingham starting to drink heavily – this had stopped recently with medical assistance. Xerox colleagues were said to be avoiding him as are other friends in a community dominated by Xerox, a large employer.

For months Xerox have called Bingham's claims 'baseless'. But the fact is that they have now restated their past three years results and have accepted that they misapplied accounting rules including improperly using a $100m reserve to offset unrelated expenses – which, amongst other things, Bingham had claimed.

One of Bingham's assertions was of aggressive or creative accounting and this gained some credibility when Xerox (as a footnote to an SEC filing, 'to give shareholders more information in the light of the intense scrutiny of Xerox's accounting practices') revealed that profits for 1998, 1999 and 2000 had been overstated by $845million (or 40% of the total pre-tax profits of $2.1billion for those three years) by a series of one-off transactions and changes in accounting estimates. Xerox still maintain these were appropriate and they have not been restated. Indeed Xerox have stated that reviews by outside auditors and directors found only small problems – a salutary example of how the performance of auditors and audit committees may later be used to defend accounting practices.

Bingham is a witness in an on-going SEC investigation into Xerox which commenced in May 2000 following Xerox's first suggestion of trouble with its accounting, linked to 'serious accounting irregularities in its Mexico and Latin America operations'. In December 2000 Bingham told the SEC that Xerox's accountants were expected to find income through accounting actions. One aspect of this investigation is said to be whether Xerox deliberately misled investors by not initially disclosing these large gains achieved through 'aggressive accounting practices'. Bingham concedes that he himself was a party to rebundling overseas short-term rental agreements so as to make them appear long-term, and then taking notional future rental revenue as immediate profit. He says that he became depressed by some of the things he was involved in.

Allegedly Bingham refused an offer of one year's severance and sued Xerox for wrongful dismissal for endeavouring to rectify Xerox's 'fraudulent accounting and financial accounting practices', which Xerox denied. In June 2001 Xerox asked the court to silence Bingham as being in breach of his confidentiality obligation to Xerox.

*The Wall Street Journal Europe* reported Bingham's claim that Xerox's director of world-wide audit had a meeting in his office when over $500 million of special accounting actions in 1998 and 1999 were discussed as well as the need to do everything possible to keep the investigation in Mexico. So far as we know, this claim has not been confirmed by Xerox, but if it were to be, it would raise some interesting questions about the independence of the internal auditor.

## Outcome

Early in April 2002 Xerox and the SEC agreed that Xerox should pay a $10 million civil penalty and to restate its books back to 1997 to settle SEC charges, including fraud. Xerox neither admitted nor denied the allegations. The SEC believes Xerox booked about $2billion of revenues from long-term office equipment leasing deals upfront – instead of over the period of the contract – as part of its effort to disguise its flagging operations. They claim that '... at least from 1997 to 2000' Xerox '... disguised its true operating performance by using undisclosed accounting manoeuvres, most of which were improper.' – in all amounting to a $3 billion overstatement of revenue and a $1.5 billion increase in earnings between 1997 and 2000.[2] The SEC says 'for Xerox, the accounting function was just another revenue source and profit opportunity'. The accounting manoeuvres have variously been called 'accounting tricks', 'accounting actions' and 'accounting opportunities'.[3]

On 18 April 2002, in a filing to the SEC, Xerox, with debts around $(US)16 billion and cash of $5 billion, admitted that it may not be able to repay a $(US)7 billion loan due in October which 'would raise substantial doubt about our ability to continue as a going concern', according to the filing. Standard & Poors promptly placed the company on credit watch, making it more expensive for Xerox to raise money.[4]

In April 2002 it was also reported that KPMG and more than a dozen others, including Xerox's chairman and their chief financial officer, has received warnings from the SEC that they could face civil charges over the affair. In KPMG's case they had refused to sign Xerox's 2000 accounts until the company had conducted an independent investigation into its accounting methods – an investigation which led to the first restatement of the company's results. Xerox replaced KPMG with PricewaterhouseCoopers.

## Wider issues suggested by Case 4
1.    What circumstances may lead to creative/aggressive accounting?
    a.    Analysts earning expectations.
    b.    Declining profitability.
    c.    Pressure to meet financial targets.
    d.    Other?
2.    In these circumstances what will discourage/detect/rectify creative aggressive accounting?
    a.    Disclosure.
    b.    Strong, independent audit.
    c.    Informed, independent, competent board.
    d.    Other?

3. When is it wrong to look for accounting actions that will 'generate' extra income?
   a. When they would not be there – were accounting principles and standards applied in a 'high quality' way.
4. Much creative accounting results in taking future income in the current year, or deferring the charge for current expenditure to future years. Examples which may or may not be justifiable and should probably be disclosed as an accounting policy or a change in accounting policy:
   a. Amortising affinity group marketing costs.
   b. Inappropriately changing the computational basis of material items in the accounts which entail the exercise of significant management judgement (eg provisions).
   c. Rearranging contracts from short term to long term and taking all the profits 'up front'.
   d. Other?
5. Is there anything we can learn from 'reputational management' about how a company should react to this sort of whistleblowing by a member of staff?
   a. Have a crisis management plan.
   b. Respond in ways which are convincing.
   c. Resist 'shooting the messenger'.
   d. But, avoid the risk in the first place.
6. Is the personality (and work situation) of whistleblowers ever an impediment to the resolution of the issue(s) at stake? What motivates whistleblowers to blow the whistle?
   a. Note that Bingham had at first been involved in Xerox's alleged intricate accounting manoeuvres.
   b. We are told he blew the whistle to top people in Xerox shortly after the Mexico problem had reached the public domain.
7. What is the lot of a whistleblower and therefore how should a prospective whistleblower conduct him/herself before, during and after blowing the whistle?
   a. Fighting the case requires single-mindedness and makes it difficult to focus on anything else.
   b. Re-entry into employment is difficult.
   c. Family and marriage are put under strain.
8. Does resignation alter a whistleblower's duty to his/her ex employer?
   a. Note that Xerox is suing Bingham not to disclose confidential information gained during his employment with Xerox.
9. What are the general principles to be applied by a head of internal audit in determining the extent of internal audit's involvement in the type of issues raised by this type of case?
   a. Should internal audit be involved in determining accounting treatment?
   b. Should internal audit be involved in trying to contain an external investigation to just one part of the world?
   c. What should determine who, if anyone, internal audit sides with in a disputed case of whistleblowing?

(Note that an internal auditor may have a successful defence in court when he/she knew of a malpractice if (a) he/she had done his/her job well as an internal auditor, and (b) he/she had not assumed any executive role in the affair.)

---

[1] Up to $9 by late June 2001.

2   Simon English 'Xerox slated for "trick accounting" ' (2002) *Daily Telegraph*, 12 April, p33; and
    Chris Ayres 'SEC warning on Xerox audit surprises KPMG' (2002) *The Times*, 11 April, p27.
3   'SEC approves $10m Xerox settlement' (2002) *US Today*, 12 April, p7A.
4   Simon English 'Xerox admits debt may force it to collapse' (2002) *Daily Telegraph*, 19 April,
    p36.

*Part C*

# Selected advanced audit engagements

# The internal audit role in mergers and acquisitions

**C1.1**   The IIA is now defining internal audit as comprising both 'assurance' and 'consulting' services. The definition of internal auditing near the start of the Standards makes this clear, and both these services are defined in the Glossary which appears at the end of the Standards, with a revised version of 'consulting services' commencing 1 January 2004, as shown below.

## C1.2   Definition of 'internal auditing'

'Internal auditing is an independent, objective assurance and consulting activity designed to add value and improve an organization's operations. It helps an organization accomplish its objectives by bringing a systematic, disciplined approach to evaluate and improve the effectiveness of risk management, control, and governance processes.'

## C1.3   Definition of 'assurance services'

'An objective examination of evidence for the purpose of providing an independent assessment on risk management, control, or governance processes for the organization. Examples may include financial, performance, compliance, system security, and due diligence engagements.'

## C1.4   Definition of 'consulting services'

'Advisory and related client service activities, the nature and scope of which are agreed with the client and which are intended to add value and improve an organization's governance, risk management, and control processes without the internal auditor assuming management responsibility. Examples include counsel, advice, facilitation and training.'

The above definition of assurance services classifies 'due diligence' investigations by internal auditors as belonging to the internal audit 'assurance' role. But Practice Advisory 1000.C1–2 on 'Additional Considerations for Formal Consulting Engagements'[1] states in the section on 'Definition of consulting services' that the consulting role of internal auditors may include:

'special consulting engagements – participation on a merger and acquisition team or system conversion team.'

(Compliance with Practice Advisories is discretionary, but adherence to the Standards is mandatory.)

A question is whether internal audit involvement in mergers and acquisitions fits into their 'assurance' or into the 'consulting' role, or both. The Institute of Internal Auditors is not being inconsistent here, as it is possible to reconcile the above apparently conflicting statements, as follows.

- When internal audit is involved in conducting a due diligence investigation, it could be said to fit into the 'assurance services' role since it contributes to providing assurance on the statements that are being relied upon by a party to the merger or acquisition. This might be what is being referred to as 'due diligence' in The IIA's Glossary definition on 'assurance services'.
- Internal audit may also conduct audit engagements to provide assurance on the reliability of the due diligence process itself – in particular cases when due diligence is taking place, or of the due diligence process in general. This is different from internal audit being involved in performing the due diligence investigation. Undoubtedly such an audit engagement would be an example of internal audit discharging its 'assurance role', and this certainly must be included in what is meant by the reference to 'due diligence' in The IIA's glossary definition on 'assurance services'. Arguably this sort of involvement by internal audit is important for any company involved in mergers and acquisitions since such activities represent high risks for companies.
- Internal audit 'participation on a merger and acquisition team', which is referred to in Practice Advisory 1000.C1–2 as an example of a possible internal auditing 'consulting service', is presumably referring to *neither* internal audit involvement in a due diligence investigation, *nor* to an internal audit of the due diligence process itself. Instead it is referring to such activities as assisting in integrating the acquired business into the business of the acquirer.

[1]   Practice Advisory 1000.C1–2 on 'Additional Considerations for Formal Consulting Engagements' is an interpretation of Standard 1000.C1 (and other related Consulting Implementation Standards).

*Chapter C2*


# Auditing subsidiaries and remote operating units


**C2.1**   Here we examine the specific practical considerations that apply in the auditing of subsidiaries or remote operating units (for instance those located in other countries).

The modern corporation is increasingly organised into decentralised profit centres, some of which may be located overseas. It is normally the role of the centre to provide leadership, inspiration and direction in order to achieve the necessary performance potential. This presupposes that the required objectives and performance standards have been established, agreed and accurately communicated to those affected.

The degrees to which functions are devolved to the subsidiary and remote units will, of course, vary. Senior management will have to decide what business aspects remain the prerogative of the centre, for example these could include:

- approving budgets;
- setting production schedules;
- reviewing divisional strategies;
- allocating capital resources;
- responsibility for research and development;
- defining standards;
- appointing divisional managers; and so on.

The roles and responsibilities of group and subsidiary management will need to be defined and clear policies generated; for example on such matters as trading within the group, where *inter alia* the stances on sourcing from within the group and selling on to other subsidiaries will need to be defined.

For the most part, the fundamental audit approach to the bulk of the audit fieldwork will be the same in this type of operational review as it would be for those conducted within either the parent company or head office. In other words, the systematic review and assessment of the controls and measures in place to both counteract the inherent risks within the operation(s) being examined and to ensure that the established objectives are achieved. On the ground there may be some potential additional practical matters to address, such as the local language and legislative considerations. However, of prime concern to the audit manager will be how can he/she ensure that the time spent during the audit visit is productive and focussed upon the appropriate things. This will be especially true if this is to be the first audit of the operation.

The audit manager may be under pressure to deploy his precious resources in a cost effective manner and in proportion to the perceived level of risks. This may be especially true when the additional costs of travel, accommodation and subsistence have to be added to the fixed payroll costs of the audit function. In the eyes of senior management there can be no justification for wasting audit time on low risk operations with little overall significance to the organisation.

When contemplating the total audit universe of possible review projects, the audit manager may apply some form of relative risk assessment in order to identify auditing priorities as the basis for forming the audit plan for the coming year. We do not examine such formal risk assessment methods here, but rather suggest two possible techniques for gathering key data about any subsidiary or remote operation as the basis for assessing the audit priorities within an review project.

This chapter mainly concentrates upon on how auditors can acquire the information necessary to ensure that the field visit is effectively directed towards the key areas of the operations, especially those which represent greater degrees of risk to the organisation as a whole.

First, we consider effective fact finding prior to the main field audit visit as a means to set the scene for the forthcoming operational review. Secondly, we look at the process of conducting a high level review as a means of identifying key operational areas where audit review attention should be concentrated at either a system or activity level. Within these two approaches, we provide comprehensive examples of the types of questions to be posed.

## C2.2  Fact finding

In the course of preparing for an audit visit, one method of gathering the key background and performance data and environmental facts about a potential audit review target would be to use a fact finding programme. The data collected during this process may be obtained from a number of sources including existing management information and accounting records, senior management representatives and local operating reports.

In sections A to D below, we provide some examples of the sort of questions and subjects that should be considered for inclusion into such a fact finding programme. Our example assumes that the target is located overseas; however, where this is not the case, some of the supplied questions will not apply. The data is divided into a number of logical categories, ie:

(a)   Nature and Scale of Business
(b)   Organisation and Key Contacts
(c)   Economic and Political Background
(d)   Policies and Procedures

It may be possible to gather the required facts and data without visiting the target operation and thus avoid the costs associated with field visits. Alternatively, a form of brief reconnaissance trip may be justified where the required information is only available on-site. In either case, the intelligence obtained should aim to provide a reliable basis for subsequently scoping and focussing the planned audit visit activities upon the key areas of the target operations.

The information gathered during this sort of fact finding exercise can be used to ensure that appropriate arrangements are put in place for the detailed audit review visit and that key circumstances are taken into account during the creation of the detailed audit review programmes. By following this sort of process, the possibility of wasting valuable time during the site visit is potentially reduced (although there is no guarantee that it can be completely eradicated).

Where the data is related to either financial or performance matters, care should be taken to ensure that the sources are reliable and the data is both accurate and up-to-date. Where there is the likelihood of a prolonged delay between the date the data was gathered and the intended date of the audit field visit, the contents may have to be reviewed in the interim so that more current and credible information is made available to support the determination of audit coverage.

Particular attention should be paid to the appropriate interpretation of data trends or performance variances, as these may be influenced by legitimate events, such as either seasonal sales patterns or the effects of local fiscal regulations. Where necessary, unusual data or underlying implications should be subject to further validation enquiries.

When the auditor is compiling the fact finding document care should be taken to ensure that commercially sensitive and confidential data is adequately protected from unauthorised access and leakage.

One other practical consequence of using the fact finding approach is that it should ensure that the auditors engaged in the project and the subsequent review visit are suitably aware of the key environmental considerations. This will hopefully demonstrate to local management that the audit function has taken the time and effort to set the operation in context and obtained an accurate impression of the business under review. This sort of informed preparation can enhance the perceived credibility of the auditing function.

Noted below is an example Fact Finding programme. Please bear in mind that it is only an illustrative example. In practice, there may be further elements that could be legitimately included in such a programme. Conversely, items currently included may be irrelevant for use within your organisation.

## C2.3  Example fact finding programme

NATURE AND SCALE OF BUSINESS

| A.1  What categories of business operation are conducted within this unit? (ie sales, production, or R & D). |
| --- |

A.2 List all the relevant types of products and services marketed through this operation.

A.3 Provide an indication of the scale of each operation in terms of either turnover, size of expenditure budget, or level of capital invested. Clearly indicate the currency used.

A.4 Is this operation solely funded by the parent company? (If no, see A.5 below.)

A.5 If external or joint funding applies to this operation, note the names of the other interested parties, their defined role in the relationship, and the level of their investment. Consider the implications for conducting the audit and the possible requirement to access records held by third parties.

A.6 What is the unit's trading and business relationship with the parent company? (ie marketing outlet for centrally produced products, marketing of locally produced and licensed products, agent, or distributor, etc).

A.7 Have the taxation implications of the relationship with the parent company been considered, planned for and authorised? Obtain overview details and consider whether any specific aspect of the operation will need to be reviewed in order to ensure that the taxation objectives are being achieved.

A.8 When was the operation first established?

A.9 Note the nature of the significant events in the development and growth of this operation (with approximate dates).

A.10 Has the parent company defined the performance expectations for the business? If so, obtain the details and note any specific sales, turnover or other financial targets for the current accounting year.

A.11 Determine the accounting year dates. (Is this consistent with the parent company? If not, why?) Additionally, have accounting reporting lines been established with the parent company with a defined timetable for submission?

A.12 Obtain a copy of the official trading and management accounts and summarise the key performance figures for a twelve month period. Key data should include (when applicable) sales turnover, profit on sales, total expenditure, inventory values, net profitability, etc.

A.13 Using the data summarised per point A.12 above, highlight any unusual trends or anomalies for investigation and clarification.

A.14 Record details of the banking arrangements including the number and type of accounts, their purpose, and the established authorisations.

A.15 Where applicable, determine the arrangement for reconciling the 'payables' to the parent company .

A.16 Determine and note the details of any significant local trading relationships with agents, distributors or major customers. Provide an indication of the relative levels of such key relationships.

A.17 Further to point A.16, determine whether there are legally binding agreements in place for key relationships, and if possible note the main operational elements.

A.18 Is there a local direct sales force? If so, obtain details of the authorised expense rates and the actual travel expenses for marketing and sales staff for the past six months.

A.19 If budget versus actual data is available for key performance factors, obtain a copy and note any major variances. Are local management obliged to report upon major variances to the parent company? If so, are explanations of unusual items available centrally?

A.20 Obtain and review any available management information or progress reports, and record summary details of specific and relevant events (noting any action that is either planned or being taken).

A.21 Have any specific large-scale investments been made in this operation? Obtain and summarise the key details (ie value, commercial objectives, investment period, funding basis, progress against targets, etc).

A.22 If medium and long-term (strategic) plans are available, note the key objectives and their current status.

A.23 Are there warranty implications for the operation? If so, determine what facilities are provided for servicing and maintaining products (including the availability of adequate stocks of spare parts).

A.24 Record when the operation was last audited and note the significant findings and concerns.

A.25 Determine whether there were any major recommendations arising from the last audit visit and their status (ie accepted, rejected, actioned, or outstanding).

## ORGANISATION AND KEY CONTACTS

B.1 Obtain current organisation charts and note likely key contacts with their locations and telephone numbers

B.2 Establish those responsible for key functions and confirm their availability during the planned audit visit.

B.3 Determine whether there have been any recent changes in senior management, and assess whether this is likely to influence the effectiveness of the audit visit.

B.4 Are up-to-date job descriptions available for the key positions (if so, obtain a copy and assess whether the key responsibilities are adequately defined)?

B.5 Record overview statistics on the number of staff employed in key operational areas (ie sales, administration and accounting, production, development, etc) and the level of staff turnover.

B.6 Determine whether there have been any recent major changes in staffing establishment levels (ie contraction due to poor economic conditions or expansions due to increased opportunities and demand).

B.7 Determine whether parent company executives have been given responsibilities for the local operations (ie note the nature and scope of such involvement). NB: Dependent upon the nature of the responsibility, it may be desirable to arrange a meeting with the relevant executive in order to enhance the understanding of the local trading and fiscal situations.

B.8  Has initial contact been made with key local managers and if so have any potential logistic, operational or practical difficulties been identified?

B.9  Note the location(s) of the operations to be subject to audit review (and consider the implications for travel, accommodation, required audit resources, etc).

B.10 Note the relevant national language(s) and whether key personnel are fluent in any others. Consider the implications for the audit visit.

B.11 Where external agents, distributors, etc are involved in the operations, are there agreements in place permitting the parent company auditors to inspect the third party records and documentation? Consider whether any likely restrictions or problems of access will influence the quality and scope of the proposed audit visit.

## ECONOMIC AND POLITICAL BACKGROUND

C.1  What is the local trading currency?

C.2  What are the current key business exchange rates? (See also C.4.)

C.3  What are the principal characteristics of the local/national economies? (ie the basis of national trade, growth, recession, etc.)

C.4  What has been the nature of currency exchange rates over the previous 12 months and are there any implications for the performance and profitability of the operation? Note any dramatic fluctuations and the nature of any action taken (internally or externally) to stabilise the currency.

C.5  Ascertain the local rate of inflation over the past 12 months and note any apparent trends. When applicable, what is local government apparently doing in relation to inflation, and are their measures showing any signs of success?

C.6  Have any specific plans been established by the company to counteract or reduce the effects of local currency or inflation instability?

C.7  Where relevant, determine the level of local commercial interest rates and their relationship to those applicable to the parent company/country.

C.8  Describe the political nature of the host country, paying particular regard to its fundamental principles (ie capitalistic), stability, whether or not a change is imminent/likely, etc. Discuss relevant points with management and note any implications for the business operations and the planned audit visit.

C.9  To what extent are local conditions (economic and political) likely to affect the business operations? (NB: such influences are likely to vary and be dependent upon the nature of the business being conducted.)

C.10 Have documented and authorised pricing and discount policies been established? (If so, obtain an overview of their main elements, and determine if they are reviewed and adjusted against the background of any local economic and political events).

C.11 Note any specific local accounting requirements and their effect on records and accounting conventions.

> C.12 Note the principal elements of those local taxation conditions with implications for the business (ie sales taxes, corporation taxes, income or other employment taxes, etc).
>
> C.13 What steps have been taken to optimise the taxation implications for the parent company?
>
> C.14 What are the characteristics of the local employment market and what are the implications for the business operations? (ie levels of unemployment, available skills in relation to operational skill requirements, effects of local employment legislation, levels of employment related taxation, etc).

## POLICIES AND PROCEDURES

> D.1 Are local operations generally governed by the policies and procedures developed by the parent company? If not, are local variants in place? (See also D.8)
>
> D.2 Determine the operational systems in use and whether documented and authorised procedures are provided.
>
> D.3 Obtain details of the computing arrangements in place and whether the installation conforms to any defined standards established by the parent company.
>
> D.4 Establish the degree of reliance upon computer systems as a basis for considering the necessity of computer audit reviews.
>
> D.5 Record details of the main computer application systems in use (ie accounting, stock control, customer billing, etc).
>
> D.6 Determine whether the key computer applications are those used or recommended by the parent company. If not, consider whether they are likely to be adequate, stable and obtained from reliable sources.
>
> D.7 Establish if a 'control environment' ethic is applied to the operation and if this is supported by the stance of the parent company. Obtain details of any documented requirements.
>
> D.8 Have local policies, procedures or objectives been developed, authorised and implemented for the following areas? (NB not all of those listed below will necessarily apply in every situation):
>
> - general operational and administration procedures;
> - control environment;
> - management information;
> - planning (strategic, tactical, manpower, etc);
> - accounting (including pricing and discount policies);
> - financial information and reporting;
> - staffing and employment;
> - risk management;
> - quality management;
> - capital projects;
> - legal and industry regulation and compliance;

- treasury and investments ;
- authority procedures;
- budgeting and monitoring;
- taxation;
- stock inventories;
- purchasing and procurement;
- production and manufacturing operations;
- marketing and sales;
- after sales support;
- research and development;
- information technology;
- contracting.

D.9 Where necessary and practical (taking into account any language implications) obtain and review key policy and procedure documents in relation to their apparent scope, quality, relevance, etc.

## C2.4 High level review programme

Having concluded that a particular subsidiary or operation should be subject to operational audit review, it will be necessary to obtain an accurate impression of the relative risk priorities within the organisation, so that audit review resources can be suitably targeted. In the real world, this may present practical difficulties, especially where the chosen operation is located overseas. In such circumstances, the auditor may have to resort to a range of information sources so that a comprehensive picture of the operations can be formed. These sources may include:

- reviewing and analysing accounting, performance and other data sent to the parent company;
- conducting interviews with senior (parent company) executives with line responsibility for the relevant operation;
- getting local senior management to complete and return questionnaires covering the key areas of audit interest;
- where available, reviewing previous audit working papers and reports.

One possible solution to gathering the relevant data about the prevailing condition of internal controls and management attitudes is to conduct a high level review of the operation. This can either be undertaken by the audit department as a reconnaissance exercise prior to the main audit visit, or by soliciting the cooperation of local managers to provide the necessary data. This latter option may be more pragmatic in the case of an overseas operation where the associated travelling and accommodation costs may prevent two audit visits, especially where audit management are keen to ensure that any review time spent on site is productive and not used to gather background facts. If the responses were to be completed by local management, they would obviously require some guidance as to the purpose of the process and the type and level of information required.

The following section of this chapter contains a series of example high level risk and control issues relevant to either a subsidiary or remotely located company. The fictitious company depicted is known to be primarily involved in sales and marketing activities, but also has the usual management, accounting, and personnel functions. Accordingly the risk and control issues focus upon these areas at a high level. The responses to the noted questions can be used in variety of ways by the audit department. It primarily provides the basis for a high-level examination of an operating unit from the point of view of the prevailing management and control structure.

Audit management also has the option to use the previously described 'fact finding programme' to bring together a wide range of relevant facts about the nature and type of business operation being considered for an audit review. The data contained in that programme could, in itself, indicate selected activities which could benefit from a full-scale audit review (for example, by virtue of the level and significance of a particular business activity or trading relationship). However, the additional use of the high level programme approach can provide yet further insight into the underlying quality and effectiveness of management within the business.

## C2.5   Example high level review programme

The issues are presented (in this example version) in categories relevant to the key system/activity areas and are structured around the main organisation elements, such as management, finance and accounting, personnel, etc. Given that every organisation has a specific and often unique business or operational environment, it is highly probable that either additional or alternative key questions could apply. Additionally, the functions and activities addressed in this example programme are likely to be subject to differing scales of relevance within a range of organisations, and this will have a notable bearing on the appropriateness of the questions. When reading through the listed points, consider your own organisation and whether changes are required to adequately reflect its activities and corporate direction.

The questions should be answered by providing details of the controls and measures in place. Following entry of the current controls and measures, audit management can take a view of their relative or potential effectiveness. In instances where there are concerns about the quality of control, etc, a comprehensive review can then be applied using a more detailed SAPG during the field work visit.

---

**1. Management and administration**

   **1.1   The control environment**

   Are there in place satisfactory Codes of Conduct and other policies which define acceptable business practice, conflicts of interest and expected standards of integrity and ethical behaviour?

   Do senior managers frequently visit outlying locations for which they are responsible?

   Is disciplinary action sufficiently taken and communicated in the case of control or ethical violations?

---

### 1.2 Organisation

How does management ensure that the organisational structure is optimised and appropriate to the achievement of strategic objectives?

Have documented terms of reference, responsibilities and authorities been agreed, authorised and implemented for all functions and departments, and are they maintained up-to-date?

### 1.3 Management information

Is applicable *external* information (eg about the market) available– as well as internally generated information about business performance?

Has the business considered the scope to develop strategic information systems (targeted at suppliers and/or staff and customers) which achieve a competitive advantage by reducing costs and/or improving service and reliability?

Is information sufficiently *timely, complete, and accurate* to be used reliably by management?

Are all exception reports followed up?

Is an inventory maintained of confidential and sensitive corporate information, and is the handling and issuance of this information subject to proper authorisation controls?

### 1.4 Planning

What processes ensure that the organisation will continue to develop in an effective manner?

What mechanisms ensure that the achievement of authorised objectives is adequately planned for?

Are all plans fully assessed, costed and authorised prior to implementation?

Are there mechanisms in place to enable management to measure the success of business operations against defined objectives?

### 1.5 Risk management

What steps has management taken to accurately identify potential risks?

Have adequate plans been developed to counteract, reduce or avoid risks to assets, persons and the organisation's reputation?

Where the organisation is heavily dependent upon the use of information technology, has specific consideration been given to the effects on the business of a loss (or disruption) of computing facilities?

### 1.6 Quality management

Have the objectives of the quality programme been clearly defined (ie in terms of potential competitive advantage, improved customer satisfaction, etc)?

What steps have management taken to ensure that the appropriate national or international quality standard accreditation will be achieved and maintained?

Are all the quality initiatives subject to ongoing monitoring in order to ensure that targets and objectives are realised?

### 1.7 Estates management and facilities

How does management accurately identify requirements for buildings and premises in order to address the operational objectives of the organisation?

What measures ensure that all the relevant prevailing building laws and regulations are identified and complied with?

What processes ensure that all property costs are correctly accounted for, authorised and monitored?

How does management ensure that adequate and effective security, fire prevention and protection facilities are provided, maintained, and tested?

### 1.8 Environmental issues

Has an approved and documented environmental policy been established which defines the required approach for business operations?

How does management ensure that all the relevant environmental legislation and regulations are fully complied with?

Are measures in place which ensure that all environmental impacts are identified, monitored, and effectively managed (and what is the evidence for this)?

### 1.9 Insurance

How does management ensure that all insurable risks are identified, assessed and adequately covered?

How does management ensure that insurance costs are competitive and represent value for money?

How can management be sure that all insurance claims are accurately assessed, costed, and eventually settled?

### 1.10 Security

What measures are in place to prevent the following?:

- unauthorised access to company premises;
- theft of company property from premises;
- damage and disruption caused by vandalism, burglary, and other security threats.

Have potential risks and security threats been adequately defined and assessed, and how can management be assured that security measures are effective?

Have documented procedures and instructions been implemented for emergency drills, building evacuations, and contingency arrangements (and how is their effectiveness assessed)?

### 1.11 Media, public and external relations

Has an agreed and authorised public and media relations policy been implemented, and if so how is management to be assured that the policy is always complied with?

What steps does management take in order to remain aware of local community issues and to foster good relations with the local community?

What action does management take to ensure that the organisation is actively represented within the relevant trade and industry bodies?

## 2. Financial & Accounting

### 2.1 Treasury

Has senior management established and issued a written policy governing treasury operations, objectives, authorised transaction types, financial limits, etc?

Are working capital requirements defined, communicated, monitored, and reacted to?

Are all treasury transactions and fund movements accurately accounted for, correctly recorded in the accounting system, and reported to management?

### 2.2 Payroll

What mechanisms prevent payroll payments being made to invalid or unauthorised persons?

How can management be certain that the amounts paid via the payroll are correctly calculated and that income taxation and other deductions are accurately calculated and disbursed?

How can management be sure that all payroll transactions are correctly reflected in the accounting system in the proper accounting period?

### 2.3 Accounts payable

How can management be certain that only valid invoices are paid where the goods and services have been correctly and fully received?

Are all invoices authorised prior to payment and confirmed as being within the agreed budget?

What processes ensure that the values of paid accounts and outstanding invoice liabilities are accurately and completely reflected in the accounting system?

### 2.4 Accounts receivable

How can management be assured that all goods delivered and services performed are identified and accurately invoiced to customers using the appropriate prices and discounts?

What procedures ensure that all invoices are recorded, despatched, and accounted for within the accounting system?

How can management be certain that all customer remittances are correctly identified, recorded, and accounted for?

Are overdue accounts promptly identified and effectively progressed?

### 2.5 General ledger and management accounts

How can management be certain that the general ledger accounting data is accurate, complete and up-to-date?

How does management ensure that the accounting records and systems comply with the prevailing laws, regulations and recognised accountancy good practice?

How is accuracy of published and statutory accounting statements confirmed?

What prevents the processing of unauthorised or invalid accounting entries?

### 2.6 Fixed assets and capital charges

Have management implemented an authorised policy governing capital acquisitions and expenditure, depreciation, etc which conforms with recognised accounting practice?

How can management be assured that all asset acquisitions are authorised, and correctly reflected in the accounts?

Are assets subject to adequate protection and regular verification, with the follow up of anomalies?

### 2.7 Budgeting and monitoring

Have management developed and implemented a documented budgeting process for use throughout the organisation, and does this clearly allocate responsibilities for action and follow up of variances?

How is the budget and actual data reflected by the budget system confirmed as authorised, accurate and complete?

How can management be certain that all subsequent amendments to the budget data are justified, authorised and accurately applied?

### 2.8 Bank accounts and banking arrangements

Are corporate bank accounts only established at the request of senior management for a defined and authorised purpose (and how is this process evidenced)?

Are the prevailing banking terms and conditions optimised in terms of account type, transaction levels, interest payable on balances, levels of charges, etc?

How are management assured that all banking transactions are accurate, complete, and authorised?

### 2.9 Sales tax accounting (where applicable)

How does management ensure that all input and output VAT on applicable transactions is accurately identified, accounted for and included on the appropriate returns?

What processes ensure that all the required VAT returns are accurately completed in accordance with the current legislation, and that the correct amount is either paid over or recovered?

Is the current company registration for VAT confirmed as correct and up-to-date?

### 2.10 Taxation

How can management be assured that all taxation liabilities are correctly calculated and discharged in accordance with the prevailing regulations?

What measures ensure that taxation liabilities are minimised within the prevailing legislation?

How does management ensure that all the regulations are complied with and the underlying accounting data accurately supports the official returns?

### 2.11  Inventories

How can management be certain that the accounting systems and year-end financial statements accurately reflect the values of inventory stocks?

What processes ensure that all processed stock movements are valid, correctly priced, and accurately posted to the relevant stock accounts?

Are stock values adequately and regularly verified, and how is this evidenced?

Are all stock adjustments, write-offs, disposals suitably authorised?

### 2.12  Petty cash and expenses

How can management be assured that only valid, accurate and authorised expenses are processed and correctly reflected in the accounts?

Has management established clear policies and procedures for recording, authorising and processing petty cash and expense claims?

### 2.13  Financial information and reporting

How are management assured that all the required external and statutory financial reports/returns are accurately generated and released on time?

Have management identified, documented, and addressed all their financial information requirements?

What processes prevent the creation and circulation of inaccurate, invalid or out-of-date financial data?

How can management be certain that all accounting records are maintained in accordance with the current accounting regulations, standards, and professional good practice?

## 3. Personnel

### 3.1  Human resources function

Have documented policies been established for staff recruitment, training, remuneration, performance appraisal, and disciplinary matters?

How is ongoing compliance with all the prevailing employment regulation and laws confirmed, and would failure to comply be promptly detected?

How can management ensure that the personnel records are up-to-date, accurate and adequately protected from unauthorised use and access?

### 3.2  Recruitment

Have standard remuneration scales and employment conditions been implemented, and would management be made aware of staff engagements which fall outwith these standards?

How can management be certain that all staff recruitment and appointments are warranted and authorised?

How can management be sure that the most appropriate and cost effective method of recruitment is utilised?

What steps are taken to confirm the previous employment record and educational qualifications of candidates, and what prevents the engagement of staff with either an invalid or unsuitable record?

Are all staff engagements supported by an accurate contract of employment?

What measures ensure that new employees are correctly set up on the payroll?

### 3.3 'Manpower' and succession planning

Have management implemented a structured approach to manpower and succession planning?

Have the implications of the mid to long-term strategic business objectives been taken into consideration (with all the other internal and external influences) when determining the manpower requirements?

Have current and future skill requirements been accurately identified, and what action is being taken to ensure that staff are appropriately developed to meet the requirements?

### 3.4 Staff training and development

How are management assured that all training and staff development activities are justified, authorised and appropriately targeted?

Has management determined the required skill and knowledge base for the workforce and planned to ensure that employees remain competent and able to discharge their duties?

Are training activities monitored for their effectiveness, and how are the most suitable and cost effective training methods selected?

### 3.5 Pension scheme (and other benefits)

How can management be assured that the pension scheme is correctly established and operated, and that it complies with the current legislation and recognised good practice?

How can management and trustees be certain that all pension funds are kept strictly separate from company activities and remain fully accounted for?

How can members, management and trustees be assured that all pension contributions are valid, correctly calculated, deducted, paid over, and fully accounted for?

Is the pension fund subject to regular scrutiny by suitably qualified external auditors (or any regulatory bodies)?

Are there processes in place to ensure that all payments from the fund are valid, authorised, correctly calculated, paid over to bona fide person, and fully accounted for?

How can management be assured that the operations of any other schemes (ie Employee Share, Share Options, Profit Related Pay, etc) fully comply with the current legislation and are fully accounted for?

### 3.6   Staff appraisal and disciplinary matters

How does management confirm that staff are performing at the appropriate level and standard?

Are staff performances assessed against realistic and measurable factors and objectives, and how are these recorded and monitored?

Are performance shortcomings used as the basis for determining and agreeing the personal training and development needs of staff (and are these subject to justification)?

Do all staff appraisal and disciplinary procedures comply with the current legislation?

Are management confident that cases of persistent absenteeism or serious misconduct would be detected and appropriately dealt with?

### 3.7   Health and safety

How can management be assured that they have identified and adequately addressed all the Health & Safety risks and hazards within the organisation?

What processes ensure that staff are fully aware of workplace risks and how to correctly utilise safety equipment and protect themselves?

Has sufficient and appropriate safety equipment been provided and what measures ensure that it all remains in working order and effective?

Have sufficient fire prevention and protection systems been provided and are they regularly tested?

Have adequate first aid, medical, hygiene and cleanliness facilities been provided?

Are all incidents and accidents reported and appropriately dealt with?

How can management be assured that all hazardous materials are safely, correctly and securely stored?

### 3.8   Labour relations

Has the basis for communicating with the workforce and their representatives been clearly established, endorsed and communicated?

Have suitably experienced and qualified staff, familiar with negotiation and other relevant techniques, been employed and allocated the responsibility for dealing with labour relations?

## 4. Procurement

### 4.1   Purchasing

How can management be assured that all purchase orders are justified, authorised, within budget and accounted for within the correct accounting period?

How does management ensure that adequate and appropriate supplies (of a suitable quality) are obtained to sustain the required business objectives?

How does management ensure that goods and services are always obtained as the most economical and fair price?

## 5. Stock

### 5.1 Stock control

How does management determine the current and future stock requirements, and how can they be sure that actual stock levels can accurately meet the sales and production demands?

What measures ensure that all stock movements are valid, authorised, correctly processed, and accounted for?

Are management made aware of either overstocking or stock shortages, and how are their reactions evidenced?

### 5.2 Distribution, transport and logistics

Is there adequate and timely liaison and information flow between the sales, production, stock control, distribution and transport functions in order to ensure that customer demands are efficiently fulfilled?

How can management be assured that the most appropriate, efficient and cost effective distribution and transport options are utilised?

How can management be certain that all deliveries are undertaken in the required timescale, that they are received in good condition, agreed and signed for?

## 6. Marketing and sales

### 6.1 Product development

Has management defined and authorised strategic business objectives, and how can they be sure that all product developments comply with these targets?

Has management established, authorised and implemented documented procedures for the development and evolution of all product ranges?

### 6.2 Market research

What steps are taken to ensure that customer requirements are identified and effectively addressed?

Are all market research activities accurately costed, justified as being worthwhile and authorised?

How does management identify potential new markets or opportunities to differentiate their products?

### 6.3 Promotion and advertising

How can management be assured that advertising and promotional expenditure is adequately targeted, budgeted, effectively used, monitored for its effectiveness, and fully accounted for?

What measures ensure that all advertising and promotional activities are lawful, accurate and project a positive corporate image?

### 6.4 Pricing and discount policies

Have documented pricing and discount policies been authorised and implemented?

What steps are taken to ensure that prices remain competitive, profitable and sustainable?

How is management assured that the correct prices and discounts are always applied to invoices?

### 6.5 Sales management

What measures are in place to ensure that current and potential customers are identified and that customer data is accurately maintained up-to-date?

How can management be assured that adequate (and justifiable) sales staff are provided and that they are suitably trained and knowledgeable about the company products?

What measures are applied to ensure that customers are financially stable and reliable (and what prevents the acceptance of unsuitable customers)?

How are individual customer credit limits determined, and are they subject to a higher level of authority prior to orders being accepted?

### 6.6 Sales performance and monitoring

How does management ensure that projected sales targets are accurately and realistically determined?

How can management be assured that they are provided with accurate and timely sales performance statistics, and what action is taken to detect and react to shortfalls, etc?

How does management determine and justify the staffing establishment of the sales function so as to avoid either under or over-staffing?

### 6.7 Order processing

What measures ensure that all orders (from all possible sources) are correctly identified, logged, reviewed, authorised to proceed, and accounted for?

What measures are applied to ensure that orders are only accepted from established, authorised and bona fide customers?

How is management assured that credit limits are strictly observed and only amended when suitably authorised?

What measures ensure that all orders are acknowledged and efficiently fulfilled?

How is management assured that accurate invoices are subsequently raised and accounted for within the accounts receivables systems?

# Outsourced business activities, and implications for internal audit

## C3.1   Meaning

Sometimes termed 'contracting out', outsourcing occurs when services previously provided by in-house personnel are handed over to an outside contractor to provide. This often takes place after a due process of market testing which requires that a fully specified tender document is prepared and potential outside contractors are invited to tender for the work against the specification contained within the tender document. The in-house personnel who previously provided the services (sometimes known as the direct labour) may be invited to tender for the work in competition with the outside tenderers.

## C3.2   Impact upon in-house personnel

Very often, a condition of tendering which is imposed upon the outside tenderers is that they must agree to take on the direct labour personnel if they, the outside tenderers, are successful in winning the contract. Common complaints of those whose contract of employment transfers in this way from the business to the outside contractor is that their terms and conditions of service as well as their job security are often not so good with the outside contractor as they were previously when perhaps they had been insulated from the effect of market forces. Large organisations often end up paying premium employment costs (such as profit-sharing and pension schemes) to peripheral employees for whom they were not originally intended: outsourcing their work can eliminate that premium.

## C3.3   Broadening scope of outsourcing

In recent years there has been a general trend to outsourcing non-core activities such as catering, security, office cleaning and, in the case of local authorities, refuse collection. More recently, more fundamental activities such as accounting, computer operations and site maintenance have been seen as candidates for outsourcing. Outsourcing computer operations is termed 'facilities management'.

## C3.4   Cost-benefit issues

In the public sector, the push towards outsourcing has often happened in order to inject a competitive element into the tendering for these services and in the subsequent provision of them by the outsourced contractor. It is believed that this can lead to lower costs of public services as well as higher quality. Great care must be taken to ensure that it is not just costs which are reduced but that essential standards of service provision are maintained. In essence, the outside contractor is unlikely to provide any service unless it is part of the contract, nor a standard of service unless such is specified, with penalty clauses for shortfall, in the contract. It also has the effect of reducing the size of (or at least reducing the rate of growth of) the public sector in a national economy – which is perceived as having certain macroeconomic advantages.

## C3.5   Cost escalation

At first, outsourced services may be provided on favourable terms. Once the contractor is well established as the preferred provider of the service, and as soon as the contractual terms permit, the contractor may raise the price of providing the service. Then, with the in-house provision no longer being available, the business may be in a weak position to resist escalating costs of ensuring that the service continues to be provided. Of course, if there is an open market in the provision of these services, the services can be market tested again so that a competitive provider is found. Nevertheless when contracting out is fashionable, it is likely that contractors in general will price low ('low balling') in order to get the work, with an intention of contractors in general being to raise their prices when the opportunity permits.

Low price tenders initially are often feasible as they can often be costed on a marginal cost basis for a while. For instance, firms of public accountants may tender for outsourced internal audit work in anticipation that they will be able to resource that work using staff at a time of the year when they are not heavily engaged upon year-end external audit work.

A common practice is to bid for a market tested service at cost price and, once the contract has been won, to charge at expensive rates for services which the client needs but which the client omitted to include in the tender document and which are therefore not covered by the contract. Careful specification of the job and careful wording of the contract can reduce this risk.

## C3.6   Re-invigorating a business through outsourcing

The cultural implications of outsourcing are considerable. The net effect of a significant amount of outsourcing is to make the organisation smaller and simpler to run. There is a reduced requirement for staff functions such as a large personnel department. So there are these indirect cost savings as well. Many of the popular approaches to contemporary management are designed to achieve this. Outsourcing can help a business keep or regain its dynamism – its ability to adapt more rapidly. Management have more freedom to make changes without the inertia effect of large cohorts of staff who may be resistant to change or at least have to be managed effectively during times of change. Management are able to focus more singlemindedly on the main issues.

## C3.7   Impact on human resource inventory

On the other hand, outsourced activities provide outside contractors with a learning experience *on the job* so that the reservoir of in-house trained and experienced human resource talent is reduced and the business may consequently become less competent, more vulnerable and perhaps *less* able to competently handle a future need to change. Experience gained by outsiders may be a potential competitive threat – in effect the business is developing outsiders who may set up in competition or take their resultant know-how to a rival business for whom they also provide outsourced services. Outsiders working in and for the business may also represent a security risk. Most businesses take incredible risks with their contract cleaners who may have virtually unrestricted access to premises out of hours.

## C3.8   The decision to outsource

How does management decide what and whether to outsource? First, they apply cost-benefit principles to the decision. Secondly, they consider which are their non-core activities which might be done better by outsiders who specialise in those activities – in other words by outsiders for whom those activities *are* core.

## C3.9   Core activities

It is not always immediately apparent what *are* the core activities of a business, and they may change over time. For instance, a domestic home loans company may develop special expertise in collecting overdue debts to the extent that it becomes the market leader in collections. In such a case its core business might be regarded as having changed from having been a home loans company (expert at making a margin on the money it borrows in order to lend on to people to buy houses) to having become a collections company which may tender for the collections work of other home loans and consumer credit companies. An automobile manufacturer might not regard its core business as involving machining – it may buy in all its components and merely assemble and market its products. Much of the marketing is also likely to be contracted out.

## C3.10   Strategic implications

The decision to outsource may have strategic implications. Businesses must consider the security of their supplier and distribution lines. Outsourcing may make the business more dependent on outside suppliers and distributors. On the other hand, if these outsiders are in plentiful supply the strategic risks are less, and vertical integration may not be appropriate.

Vertical integration is the process whereby a business expands so that it absorbs other businesses in the supply and distribution chain. Since each of these businesses intends to make a profit, gathering them all together so that they are all 'in-house' ensures that all the profit margins are retained. However, the business may not be so successful at making a profit on non-core activities in which it has relatively low expertise.

One way of identifying what is the business' *core* activity is to determine what it is that it is consistently able to do at greatest profit in terms of return on capital employed.

There may be broader issues at stake which militate against outsourcing. For instance, customers and clients of the business might expect that certain elements of the service they receive are provided internally and not outsourced.

## C3.11   Implications for internal audit

Much of the above discussion points to control risks which may be associated with outsourcing and which are therefore of particular interest to the internal auditor. We summarise some of them here.

- Do the tender document and the subsequent contract specify an adequate minimum standard of service, and ensure that unanticipated contingencies will be serviced effectively?
- Are the contracting procedures for outsourcing adequate to ensure the contractor is selected objectively, and are these procedures followed?
- Is it evident that contracted out services are value-for-money?
- Has management considered and are management managing the security risk associated with utilization of outsiders for contracted out work?
- Is contracted out work periodically market tested so as to ensure the service is provided competitively?
- Are all services currently performed by in-house personnel considered on an impartial basis for market testing?
- Has the business a clear strategic grasp of what is its core activity which is not to be regarded as a candidate for outsourcing?
- Is partial outsourcing (whereby contract staff work alongside in-house staff) rationally considered as an option wherever it may be applicable?
- Is contracting out leading to excessive dependence on one supplier, and does management regularly consider this risk?
- Does management review the discharge of contracts for outsourced services with a view to learning lessons from cost overruns, etc?

# Reputational risk – control and audit

## Questionnaire

### C4.1   *General overview (1)*

**Overall control objective(s) for reputation management:**

(a) To manage reputation consistent with the goals and values of the enterprise and the specific goals for reputation management; (b) to strengthen the 'corporate brand' (ie 'corporate personality, identity and image') by building up a substantial bank of goodwill with each stakeholder group (customers, partners, investors, staff, suppliers); (c) to know the value of our corporate reputation; (d) to avoid our responsible approaches to our business being interpreted cynically by our stakeholders; (e) to manage effectively all areas of potential legal exposure, and to monitor the potential impacts of new laws upon our reputation; (f) to manage the disclosure of bad news to minimise its reputational damage and where possible to enhance our reputation by effective management of bad news; (g) to maximise the safety of our processes, products and services; (h) to ensure that there is no mismatch between reputation and reality; (i) to develop the reputation of our product and/or service brands; (j) to transfer reputational risks by means of insurance and in other ways where appropriate.

| 1.1 | Key issues | Illustrative scope or approach |
|---|---|---|
| 1.1.1 | **Do the goals and values of the business, as well as its principal policies on conduct, sufficiently address the main areas of reputational risk?** (See also 1.2.2 and 8.1.3 below) | These have been formally adopted by board resolutions, and communicated effectively in the name of the board throughout the business. |

| 1.1 | Key issues | Illustrative scope or approach |
|---|---|---|
| 1.1.2 | **Does the business manage each of the principal drivers of reputation?** | These are becoming accepted as generally being:<br>– Financial performance, profitability and long-term investment value;<br>– The chief executive and the senior management team;<br>– Quality of products and services – brand image;<br>– Treatment of staff;<br>– Social responsibility;<br>– Customer service;<br>– Ability to communicate. |
| 1.1.3 | **How does the business protect its financial position from reputational damage?** | – Availability of loan facilities, and their terms.<br>– Insurance against initial losses from a catastrophe (crisis management plan helps to protect against secondary losses).<br>– Insuring operational risks (property, employer's liability, etc).<br>– Insuring financial risks (hedging, trade indemnity insurance, etc).<br>– Insuring business risks (political risk insurance, patent infringement insurance, professional indemnity insurance, rehabilitation cover[1]).<br>– Insuring people risks (key person insurance, fidelity bonding insurance, etc). |
| 1.1.4 | **Does the business understand its reputation?** | – Conduct a straightforward SWOT analysis (reputational strengths, weaknesses, opportunities and threats).<br>– Conduct a vulnerability audit (see also 3.1.9 below).<br>– Enquire using analogies[2] as to how stakeholders regard the business.<br>– Is there premium value associated with our products/services indicative of a relatively strong reputation? |

| 1.2 | Detailed issues | Illustrative scope or approach |
|---|---|---|
| 1.2.1 | How is sufficient coverage of different business issues achieved within the policy statements and codes of practice of the business, and is reputational risk addressed appropriately in each case? | Policies and codes of conduct may need to be formulated in these areas, eg:<br><br>– business ethics and conduct;<br><br>– scientific ethics and conduct;<br><br>– product supply chain ethical principles;<br><br>– health and safety;<br><br>– fraud;<br><br>– whistleblowing;<br><br>– IT security;<br><br>– e-commerce;<br><br>– data protection. |
| 1.2.2 | Are policies governing reputation management clearly laid down? | Avoidance of dual standards re ethics, environment, human rights, equity, etc (difficult in global businesses). |

## C4.2  *Financial performance, profitability and long-term investment value (2)*

**Specific control objective(s) for this aspect of reputation management:**

(a) To maximise the enhancement of shareholder value which comes from a good reputation; (b) to ensure that investor expectations are well informed and realistic; (c) to ensure that the business understands its investing stakeholders' needs and intentions; (d) to maximise the potential of disclosure practices, accountability and audit to enhance reputation; (e) to ensure that the business has an excellent reputation for corporate governance in general; (f) to manage reputation so as to reduce vulnerability to economic downturn.

| 2.1 | Key issues | Illustrative scope or approach |
|---|---|---|
| 2.1.1 | How does the business ensure it has a reputation for observing the highest standards of corporate governance? | – Compliance with the principles and provisions of the Combined Code for Corporate Governance and any other relevant codes and regulations.<br><br>– Openness and clarity of disclosure of this compliance.<br><br>– A record for leading edge progressiveness in corporate governance and public reporting practices. |

| 2.1 | Key issues | Illustrative scope or approach |
|---|---|---|
| 2.1.2 | Is the business's record for accountability sufficient to enhance the reputation of the business? | – Completeness of disclosure?<br><br>– Promptness of disclosure?<br><br>– Compliance with accounting standards?<br><br>– Consistency of accounting basis?<br><br>– Conservativeness of financial statements? |
| 2.1.3 | Has the company built shareholder value well and is the perception that it will continue to do so? | – Inter-company comparisons over time.<br><br>– Analysis of market expectations.<br><br>– Development of business plans to deliver market expectations and communication of these to investors. |
| 2.1.4 | Are the expectations of investors accurately understood, and what are the risks that these will not be met? (See also 2.2.1 and 2.2.2 below.) | Analysis of who are the principal stakeholders and their expectations and intentions (see also 2.1.3 above). |
| 2.1.5 | How does the business ensure that the past track record of the directors and top management is reassuring to investors? | – Careful selection.<br><br><br>– Media promotion. |
| 2.1.6 | How does the organisation ensure that the annual statutory audit process enhances its reputation? (See also 2.2.3–2.2.5 below.) | – Regular appraisal by the audit committee of external audit performance.<br>– Observance of Combined Code's provision that the audit committee keep under review the scope and results of the audit and its cost effectiveness and the independence and the objectivity of the auditors, and that where the auditors also supply a substantial volume of non-audit services to the company, the committee should keep the nature and extent of such services under review, seeking to balance the maintenance of objectivity and value for money. |

| 2.1 | Key issues | Illustrative scope or approach |
|---|---|---|
| 2.1.7 | Are appropriate approaches taken to avoiding material losses, whether fraudulent or not sufficient to safeguard the reputation of the business? | – Responsibilities for preventing and detecting fraud are specifically assigned.<br><br>– Business methods are chosen to minimise the risks of avoidable losses.<br><br>– There is a fraud policy statement which is sound, understood and enforced. |
| 2.1.8 | How does the business ensure that it has a high reputation for successful acquisitions of other businesses? | – Thorough due diligence conducted on each prospective acquisition.<br>– Dilution of prospective acquisition on shareholders' investment is assessed and avoided.<br>– Rationalisation of acquired businesses takes place promptly (eg integration with existing businesses, disposal of unwanted operations, etc).<br>– Extravagant acquisitions are avoided. |
| 2.1.9 | How does the business ensure that economic downturns do not sabotage its reputation? | – A balanced portfolio of businesses resistant to sector specific downturns.<br><br>– Minimisation of fixed costs through outsourcing, etc. |

| 2.2 | Detailed issues | Illustrative scope or approach |
|---|---|---|
| 2.2.1 | How are (a) unfulfilled promises, and (b) misleading assertions avoided in the chairman's report and in other parts of the published interim and annual report and accounts, as well as in prospectuses and other published information? | – Prudence of content.<br><br><br><br>– Careful scrutiny by the board.<br><br><br><br>– Consistency and reliability. |

| 2.2 | Detailed issues | Illustrative scope or approach |
|---|---|---|
| 2.2.2 | Is the board, and in particular its chairman and chief executive, sensitive and responsive to the concerns of investors and representative bodies of investors (such as PIRC)? | – Regular meetings with main investors and investor groups.<br><br>– Feedback from company's stockbroker.<br><br>– Careful reaction to expressed concerns. |
| 2.2.3 | How does management avoid a delayed or qualified external audit opinion? | – Good financial accounting control.<br>– Careful scheduling.<br>– Tight deadlines.<br>– Close liaison with external auditors. |
| 2.2.4 | How is it ensured that the external audit is conducted by a firm whose reputation contributes positively to this enterprise? | (See 2.1.6 above)<br><br>– Sector experience of the firm.<br><br>– Size of the firm.<br><br>– Litigation record of the firm. |
| 2.2.5 | How is the independence of the external audit firm monitored and ensured? | (See 2.1.6 above)<br>– Extent of reliance of the firm upon this client.<br>– Length of time they have been this company's auditor. |
| 2.2.6 | How does the business ensure that it is fully aware of all clauses (covenants etc) in financing arrangements which could lead to default: and how is care taken to minimise these risks? | – Careful maintenance of records on contracts.<br><br><br><br>– Directors made aware of all key clauses of this type. |

**C4.3** *The board, the chief executive and the senior management team (3)*

**Specific control objective(s) for this aspect of reputation management:**

(a) To ensure that the board is in command of reputational risk; (b) to ensure that senior management are managing reputational risk effectively; (c) to ensure that effective measures are taken when a crisis threatens the corporate reputation; (d) to involve all levels of management and in the mitigation of reputational risk.

| 3.1 | Key issues | Illustrative scope or approach |
|---|---|---|
| 3.1.1 | Is reputation management approached systematically at the level of the board downwards? | Board agenda papers show that the board consciously and specifically considers and oversees the management of the organisation's reputation. |
| 3.1.2 | Is the business's approach to reputation management monitored objectively? | – By internal audit reporting to the board and to senior management? (See also 3.1.9 below.)<br>– Within the control risk self assessment programme? (See also 3.2.2 below.)<br>– - By external consultants? |
| 3.1.3 | How does the business ensure that the board contributes optimally to the 'corporate brand' reputation? | Directors (executive and non-executive) are chosen in part for their established reputations in areas which are important to the reputation of the business. |
| 3.1.4 | How is the reputational contribution of individual directors ensured? | – Individual director development programmes provide an up-to-date basis for the reputations of individual directors.<br>– The organisation gives directors opportunity and support to project their reputations with stakeholders, and directors avail themselves of this effectively.<br>– Annual assessment of director performance (executive and non-executive) includes a consideration of the individual's contribution to the reputation of the business.<br>– The process of board succession planning takes account of the reputational needs of the business. |

| 3.1 | Key issues | Illustrative scope or approach |
|---|---|---|
| 3.1.5 | **Is the board well set up to respond swiftly and capably in a crisis?** | – How long does it take for the board to convene?<br>– How accessible and available is the chairman of the company?<br>– How accessible and available are the non-executive directors of the company?<br>– Is there appropriate board representation on the crisis management team(s)?<br>– Is the board served well by its secretariat?<br>– Is authority to respond clearly defined? |
| 3.1.6 | **How does the company set about avoiding publicly aired squabbles?** | – A united board.<br>– An effective chairman.<br>– A strong PR function.<br>– Good media relations.<br>– Clearly defined responsibilities for individual directors and for board committees.<br>– Regular, adequate, timely board and board committee meetings so that the board is on top of its business. |
| 3.1.7 | **Does senior management manage reputation across *all* areas of the business?** | A systematic analysis of reputation risk exposure. |
| 3.1.8 | **How is business continuity assured?** | – Risks to business continuity are assessed.<br>– Measures are taken to avoid supply chain failures.<br>– Etc. |
| 3.1.9 | **How does the internal auditing function have regard to reputational management?** (See also 1.1.4 above.) | – Does the audit needs assessment of the internal auditing function give weight to reputational risk:<br>   – in determining priorities for assignments;<br>   – in determining audit focus within assignments.<br>– Is there evidence that internal audit reports are addressing reputational issues? |

| 3.2 | Detailed issues | Illustrative scope or approach |
|---|---|---|
| 3.2.1 | **Are the expectations of top management accurately understood, and what are the risks that these will not be met?** | Quality of communication 'downwards'. |
| 3.2.2 | **Is reputation management a consultative, inclusive process?** | – Involvement of as many staff as possible.<br>– Inclusion of reputation risk issues in the programme of control risk self assessment (see also 3.1.2 above).<br>– Existence of a corporate value which makes all employees share a responsibility for reputation management.<br>– Involvement of business partners (especially suppliers) in the conscious management of reputational risk. |
| 3.2.3 | **Is there an appropriate contingency plan(s) (crisis response plans) ready to be used to manage a reputational crisis (crisis management plan/crisis response plan)? Does it mean that there is a quick, clear, consistent, credible, efficient and responsive reaction to a crisis?** | – Develop approaches in advance to deal with the various types of risk which could occur.<br>– Determine what crisis management teams might be needed, and their responsibilities – then set them up.<br>– Carefully select the members of the teams.[3]<br>– Select understudies for all team positions where they may be needed.<br>– Train team members and their understudies.<br>– Write procedures tailored for each team.<br>– Update. |

| 3.2 | Detailed issues | Illustrative scope or approach |
|---|---|---|
| 3.2.4 | **Are the reputational risks associated with the compensation packages of the board and senior executive team managed effectively?** | A job evaluation process which takes account of the extent of responsibilities for managing reputational risks. |
| 3.2.5 | **How is the risk of loss of regulatory approval managed; how are regulatory investigations managed; how in general is the risk of unfavourable publicity from the regulator avoided?** | – A strong regulatory compliance function.<br><br>– Active involvement in trade associations and professional bodies.<br><br>– Constructive responses to regulatory investigations. |
| 3.2.6 | **How does the organisation's approach to reputational management compare to that of other organisations?** | Benchmarking. |
| 3.2.7 | **How does the company ensure that the earnings of board members cannot reasonably attract unfavourable comment?** | – Remuneration committee of non-executive directors determines the remuneration of the executive.<br>– Executive directors determine the remuneration of non-executive directors.<br>– Non-executive directors receive a fee commensurate with their time commitment and their contribution to the business.<br>– Non-executive directors have no financial interest in the business other than their directors' fees and any shareholdings they may own.<br>– Search consultants or similar are used to advise on levels of compensation which correspond to market rates. |

## C4.4  *Quality of products and services – brand image (4)*

**Specific control objective(s) for this aspect of reputation management:**

(a) To make sure that our corporate reputation has a halo effect upon our product and/or service brands; (b) to ensure that the reputation of our brands enhances our corporate reputation; (c) to develop and safeguard the reputations of our product and/or service brands.

| 4.1 | Key issues | Illustrative scope or approach |
|---|---|---|
| 4.1.1 | Do(es) our brand name(s) and visual imaging project an apt image? | – Product analysis. <br> – Market analysis. |
| 4.1.2 | Are opportunities taken to develop the ethical reputation of our products and services? | – Identification and communication of ethical qualities. <br> – Product recall strategy. |
| 4.1.3 | Is the strength of our corporate reputation exploited in product marketing and advertising? | – Co-ordination of PR, marketing. <br> – Measures to ensure consistency between the corporate brand and product/service brands. |
| 4.1.4 | Do we protect our brands by copyright/patent etc and do we actively pursue violations? | – Copyrights/patents – worldwide. <br> – Active pursuit of violations. |
| 4.1.5 | Do we value our brands and compare with competitors' brand values? | Perhaps using Interbrand's methodology. |

| 4.2 | Detailed issues | Illustrative scope or approach |
|---|---|---|
| 4.2.1 | Does the hype about product and service quality correspond to the reality? | – Record and analysis of customer complaints. <br> – Customer satisfaction surveys. <br> – Use of skilled marketing and advertising specialists. |

| 4.2.2 | **Do we know the level and nature of loyalty to our brands, is it stronger than that of our competitors, and do we endeavour to retain and increase it?** | - Customer analysis.<br><br>- Measures which indicate commitment to customers.<br><br>- After sales service (see also section 7). |
|---|---|---|
| 4.2.3 | **Have we considered whether it is better to segment our brands or to promote a monolithic brand image across the whole range of our products or services?** | Avoid monolithic brand image? |

## C4.5   *Treatment of staff (5)*

**Specific control objective(s) for this aspect of reputation management:**

(a) To ensure that our treatment of our staff not only avoids the risk of damaging our corporate reputation but enhances our reputation as a good employer in the eyes of our stakeholders, including with the community and with prospective employees; (b) to ensure that our staff are motivated to conduct themselves responsibly so as to enhance our corporate reputation; (c) to handle severance with employees with sensitivity; (d) to utilise to the full the opportunities which exist for furthering our corporate reputation through our direct and indirect contacts with relations and friends of our employees and with those who have in the past been in our employ (alumni relations).

| 5.1 | **Key issues** | **Illustrative scope or approach** |
|---|---|---|
| 5.1.1 | **How do we ensure that staff and the company subscribe to the same values?** | – Corporate values are defined and communicated.<br><br>– Staff participate in the development of our corporate values. |

| 5.1 | Key issues | Illustrative scope or approach |
|---|---|---|
| 5.1.2 | How do we ensure that staff understand what constitutes acceptable conduct? | – Code of business conduct.<br>– Other codes of conduct in more specialised areas.<br>– Example set by management.<br>– Consistency of treatment re violations, etc.<br>– Training. |
| 5.1.3 | How do we ensure we measure up to societal expectations with respect to the treatment of our staff at home and abroad? | – Quality of information.<br>– Comparative analysis.<br>– Full awareness of legal requirements.<br>– Focus on working conditions.<br>– Focus on terms of employment.<br>– Fair rewards.<br>– Diverse cultural staffing. |
| 5.1.4 | How do we ensure we react to employee concerns appropriately? | – Good channels for staff representation (staff associations, union representation, etc).<br>– Defined, high quality grievance procedures.<br>– Policies and procedures to avoid victimisation.<br>– A whistleblowing policy for staff. |
| 5.1.5 | How specifically do we ensure we maximise the commitment of staff to promote the company positively? | – Communication to staff of corporate goals, objectives and targets.<br>– Openness and honesty with staff about corporate performance and management intentions. |
| 5.1.6 | In recruitment, how do we ensure that we have a reputation as the employer of choice? | – Careful selection to ensure we take on staff who will fulfil themselves in our employment.<br>– Straight dealing in terms of job offers, terms of employment etc.<br>– Known for significant investment in the development of staff. |

| 5.2 | Detailed issues | Illustrative scope or approach |
|---|---|---|
| 5.2.1 | How do we ensure that staff have and display the right attitudes? | – Clarity re what is required.<br>– Training.<br>– Analysis of perceptions. |

## C4.6   *Social responsibility* (6)

**Specific control objective(s) for this aspect of reputation management:**

To ensure the enterprise conducts itself in a manner which is acceptable to the community/ies within which we operate and upon whom we impact.

| 6.1 | Key issues | Illustrative scope or approach |
|---|---|---|
| 6.1.1 | **Are the expectations of the wider body of stakeholders (community, etc) accurately understood, and what are the risks that these will not be met?** | – Identification of community values and trends in these.<br><br>– Formulation of corporate policies which are leading edge in terms of social responsibility, and effective communication of these internally and externally. |
| 6.1.2 | **Is care taken to acquire materials, products and other inputs from socially and environmentally responsible sources?** | – Supply chain analysis.<br><br>– Social and environmental audits of suppliers.<br><br>– Supplier warranties on social and environmental responsibility. |
| 6.1.3 | **Do we care properly for our suppliers?** | – Prompt payments.<br>– Fair trading.<br>– Good relationships.<br>– Research co-operation. |
| 6.1.4 | **Are we appropriately active in the community?** | – Charitable work and contributions.<br><br>– Sensitivity to cultural diversity. |

| 6.2 | Detailed issues | Illustrative scope or approach |
|---|---|---|
| 6.2.1 | **Have we assessed our reputation for social responsibility and its impact on our business prosperity?** | – External consultants' review. |
| | | – A rough correlation analysis between P/E ratios and reputations for social responsibility of ourselves and our competitors. |

## C4.7  *Customer service (7)*

**Specific control objective(s) for this aspect of reputation management:**

(a) To maximise the opportunity to ensure that our relationship with our customers enhances our corporate reputation; (b) to learn from our customers about our reputation.

| 7.1 | Key issues | Illustrative scope or approach |
|---|---|---|
| 7.1.1 | Are the expectations of customers accurately understood? | – Customer research.<br><br>– Trends analysis.<br><br>– Feedback from customers. |
| 7.1.2 | How is the company guarding against the risk that customer concerns will not be properly addressed? | – Effective procedure for responding to customer complaints.<br><br>– Customer complaints analysis and feedback to sales and production. |

| 7.2 | Detailed issues | Illustrative scope or approach |
|---|---|---|
| 7.2.1 | How well does our reputation for customer service serve us? | – Is it a barrier to entry for the prospective competition?<br><br>– Does it lead significantly to repeat business? |

## C4.8  *Information and communication (8)*

**Specific control objective(s) for this aspect of reputation management:**

To ensure we utilise the art of communication (a) to spread the good news about our business with maximum impact, (b) to hear clearly what our stakeholders have to say, and (c) to minimise damage to reputation at times of crisis.

| 8.1 | Key issues | Illustrative scope or approach |
|---|---|---|
| 8.1.1 | Are policies governing reputation management clearly communicated internally? | – A reputation management policy statement.<br><br>– Communication of this policy in managers' guides and through training. |

| 8.1 | Key issues | Illustrative scope or approach |
|---|---|---|
| 8.1.2 | Is there a 'Crisis communications management strategy'? | – Appointment of a core group of people as 'the communications management team' (senior staff, PR personnel, external advisors (even expert witnesses).<br><br>– Measures to ensure the team are up and running promptly in a crisis.<br><br>– Measures to ensure that all communications are channeled through the team.<br><br>– Preparation by the team of contingency statements/information material.<br><br>– Measures to ensure that communications with staff will be maintained.<br><br>– A proactive approach to public communication (eg call a press conference).<br><br>– Measures to maintain momentum after the crisis so as to turn the situation around. |
| 8.1.3 | Are our corporate values within the public arena? (See also 1.1.1 above.) | – Be proactive at making our statements of vision, mission, values, promises etc available to our stakeholders, including the public.<br><br>– Similarly with our codes of conduct, unless for security reasons their issuance needs to be restricted (as, for instance, with our information security policy). |
| 8.1.4 | Does public disclosure of reputational issues convey the right impression successfully? | – Early disclosure can limit damage.<br><br>– Inaccurate disclosure will accentuate damage. |
| 8.1.5 | Is communication with main stakeholders taken seriously? | Regular stakeholder meetings with:<br>– investors;<br>– community;<br>– employees;<br>– suppliers and creditors;<br>– customers. |

| 8.1 | Key issues | Illustrative scope or approach |
|---|---|---|
| 8.1.6 | Is the enterprise's use of IT likely to damage reputation – eg Y2K, Web extortion, e-commerce, etc? | – Policies covering these areas. <br><br> – Effective project management. <br><br> – Good quality management. |

| 8.2 | Detailed issues | Illustrative scope or approach |
|---|---|---|
| 8.2.1 | How are communication links between crisis management teams ensured? | Updated and communicated team lists with their specific responsibilities (including for internal and external communication). |
| 8.2.2 | Are there secure avenues for staff and others to communicate their concerns, and are these known and used? | – Whistleblowing policy statement. <br><br> – Provision for staff to communicate their concerns confidentially to (eg) the director of internal auditing. |
| 8.2.3 | Is equipment up to scratch for handing a crisis? | Mobile phones, pagers, laptop computer, televisions, etc. |

1   A type of insurance which provides a fighting fund to combat reputation damage and re-promote an affected brand: introduced in the 1980s in response to malicious tampering with brands.

2   For instance, ask which motor car the business most reminds them of – and why?

3   You will need a team leader and depending upon the purpose of the team, a team co-coordinator, an administrative representative., a legal expert, a communications advisor, a finance representative, an insurance representative and an IT expert.

# Information technology

## C5.1   Standard Audit Programme Guide

| SAPG Ref: IPF2 | Function: Information Technology | Activity/System: Information Processing Facility |
|---|---|---|

*Management checklist version with example controls and measures*

| Company: | Division: | Country: | Site: |
|---|---|---|---|
| Audit Ref: | Date: | Completed by: | Reviewed by: |

**Control Objective(s):** (a) To ensure that IT facilities and services support both the strategic objectives of the business and the maintenance of competitive advantage; (b) To ensure that adequate and appropriate IT resources and skills are provided to support the business; (c) To provide a secure and reliable environment for all IT activities, and to ensure that all facilities are protected from damage, loss or disruption; (d) To ensure that all data processing is valid, authorised and accurate; (e) To ensure that data is protected from unauthorised access and use; (f) To ensure that the required service levels are achieved in support of business objectives; (g) To ensure that only authorised and tested programs are utilised; (h) To ensure that only accurate, complete and timely data is provided; (i) To ensure that IT processing facilities are operated at optimum performance/efficiency without jeopardising system integrity and reliability; (j) To ensure that critical systems and data are adequately backed-up so that prompt recovery can be achieved; (k) To ensure that only authorised and reliable systems and operating software is utilised; (l) To ensure that adequate and effective system access controls are in place to prevent unauthorised activities; (m) To ensure that personal computers are securely and consistently used throughout the organisation; (n) To ensure that appropriate hardware is obtained from stable suppliers; (o) To ensure that all IT hardware is adequately protected from loss, theft or damage; (p) To ensure that only suitably approved and thoroughly tested system amendments are correctly applied when necessary; (q) To ensure that all key systems are adequately documented and trailed in order to support their ongoing use and maintenance; (r) To ensure that local area network facilities are secure and protected from unauthorised access and tampering; (s) To ensure that all database systems are accurately maintained, suitably protected and continue to serve the information needs of the business; (t) To ensure that the principles of the prevailing Data Protection legislation are fully complied with; (u) To ensure that, when necessary, adequate control is exercised over external Facilities Management arrangements; (v) To ensure that system development activities are adequately managed and that all deliverable systems are secure and subject to effective prior testing; (w) To ensure that only reliable, secure and supportable software products are acquired and utilised; (x) To ensure that adequate and effective contingency plans are in place to support the prompt recovery of IT facilities; (y) To provide adequate and effective user support services so as to ensure that IT facilities are consistently, correctly, and securely utilised; (z) To ensure that IT resources and facilities are accurately and appropriately accounted for and monitored.

| Seq. | Risk/Control Issue | Current Control/Measure |
|------|--------------------|-------------------------|
| 1 | Key Issues | |
| | IT strategic planning | |
| 1.1 | How does management ensure that the provision of all IT hardware, software, methods and resources remains in step with the strategic direction of the business and the achievement of competitive advantage, etc? | – IT strategic planning exercise conducted in accordance with a proven methodology.<br><br>– IT requirements and action plans documented and authorised by the Board.<br><br>– All acquisitions of hardware and software are verified against the agreed plan. |
| 1.2 | What measures ensure that only authorised and appropriate IT systems and facilities are provided? | – All IT projects have to be formally assessed, justified and authorised against the Strategic Plan.<br><br>– IT steering committee signifies approval to proceed in their minutes. |
| 1.3 | How does management ensure that the information needs of the business are adequately served? | – A data model has been established for the organisation and all new and amended systems have to comply with the model structure.<br><br>– Requests to amend the data structure are assessed and authorised where necessary.<br><br>– Corporate information flow has been mapped and reporting requirements established. |
| 1.4 | What measures ensure that the existing IT facilities remain appropriate to the underlying business needs? | – Business objectives are re-assessed periodically and mapped against the current and planned IT facilities. Any perceived change requirements for IT have to be justified and authorised.<br><br>– Performance and operational criteria are monitored for the key IT systems and facilities. Shortcomings are highlighted and addressed in relation to the underlying business requirements. |

| Seq. | Risk/Control Issue | Current Control/Measure |
|------|--------------------|--------------------------|
|      | **IT organisation** | |
| 1.5 | **Has management adequately defined the organisational structure and responsibilities of the IT function (and how is this maintained up-to-date and relevant)?** | – Formal terms of reference have been defined for the IT division.<br><br>– IT action plans generated by the strategic plan define the resource, skill and procedural requirements.<br><br>– Manpower planning exercise undertaken for the IT division.<br><br>– Organisational structure reflects the logical association of activities and lines of communication. Conflicts of interest and the potential for malpractice are minimised by the defined segregation of duties.<br><br>– Organisational structure is formally reviewed every year against the updated business objectives. |
| 1.6 | **How can management be assured that sufficient levels of IT resource (including suitably skilled staff) are provided to support the current and future needs of the business?** | – Manpower and skill planning exercise undertaken for the IT division.<br><br>– Specific or specialist recruitment requirements are identified and addressed in tandem with the human resources department |
| 1.7 | **What steps does management take to ensure that the skills of the IT staff remain relevant (and what specific measures are in place to ensure the maintenance of a minimum skill level)?** | – Existing staff are continuously monitored for their skills against the requirements for the current and planned environments. Training and development needs are identified and addressed.<br><br>– Each member of staff has a job specification which incorporates their specific minimum skill requirements. |
| 1.8 | **Have management provided an adequate framework of operating standards and policies as a means of ensuring secure and reliable IT related activities?** | Authorised and documented standards and policies have been implemented for the following areas:<br><br>– operations dept;<br><br>– system development methodology;<br><br>– data control procedures;<br><br>– programming standards including testing requirements;<br><br>– safety standards;<br><br>– access control and logical security policy;<br><br>– data back-up and media handling procedures;<br><br>– disaster and contingency plan;<br><br>– data protection policy. |
| 1.9 | **How does management prevent potential staff fraud or malpractice in the operation of key systems?** | – Key duties are strictly segregated as a means of reducing the opportunity for malpractice without a high degree of collusion.<br>(ie operations and programming functions are separated in order to prevent unauthorised program amendments being applied to the live environment). |

| Seq. | Risk/Control Issue | Current Control/Measure |
|---|---|---|
| | IT sites | |
| 1.10 | How does management ensure that all IT sites are secure and adequately protected from unauthorised access? | – Main building entrance manned by security personnel who check staff and visitors.<br>– Access beyond reception is controlled by key-card system. The key-cards are programmed in relation to activity zones and allocated on a 'needs' basis.<br>– Intruder alarms are installed and regularly tested and serviced.<br>– Access to the central computer room is restricted to key personnel only via programmed key-card. |
| 1.11 | What specific measures control the access of visitors, delivery staff, etc (and what prevents unauthorised access to the main computer room)? | See responses to 1.10 above<br><br>– All visitors are registered upon arrival and escorted whilst in the building. |
| 1.12 | Have adequate physical security and fire prevention systems been installed, and how does management ensure that they remain operational and effective? | – Intruder alarms are installed and regularly tested and serviced.<br>– Main computer room covered by CCTV system monitored by security staff.<br>– Premises are patrolled after normal working hours.<br>– Fire detection and alarm system installed and linked to fire station – regularly tested and serviced.<br>– Main computer room is protected by an ozone friendly gas smothering system. |
| 1.13 | Are regular emergency and fire drills conducted as a means of evaluating the effectiveness of the prevailing measures? | Building evacuation drills are regularly conducted and assessed for their effectiveness. |
| 1.14 | What measures are in place to both prevent and detect the unauthorised removal of IT equipment? | – Goods moving in or out of the premises are inspected for the relevant written authorities.<br>– All corporate hardware is identified with a non-removable label.<br>– Personal computers are securely fixed to desks with flexible metal cords. |
| 1.15 | How does management ensure that staff are sufficiently aware of their responsibilities in respect of fire prevention and emergency evacuation drills? | – All health and safety requirements are contained in the relevant procedures manual given to all employees.<br>– Building evacuation drills are regularly conducted and assessed for their effectiveness. |
| 1.16 | How is management assured that adequate and appropriate levels of insurance cover are in place for the IT facilities? | Legal department undertake an annual review of insurance cover based upon a formal risk assessment and the events in the past year. |

| Seq. | Risk/Control Issue | Current Control/Measure |
|------|-------------------|------------------------|
| | **Processing operations** | |
| **1.17** | **What general measures ensure that processing activity is valid, accurate and authorised?** | – Only valid, tested and authorised program versions are available in the production environment. |
| | | – All runs are authorised prior to operation. |
| | | – JCL ensures that correct files, data and programs are called during processing. |
| | | – System access controls prevent unauthorised access to data and mainframe facilities. |
| | | – Data preparation is reconciled to source documents. |
| | | – Data is validated for errors. |
| **1.18** | **What specific measures prevent unauthorised transactions and/or system amendments being applied?** | – System access controls prevent unauthorised access to data and mainframe facilities. |
| | | – Production program files are read only and cannot be directly amended. |
| | | – Production and development program libraries are separated and subject to strict program movement authorities and processes. |
| **1.19** | **How can management be assured that data is accurate, complete, authorised and reliable?** | See responses in sections 1.17 and 1.18 above. |
| **1.20** | **How is commercially sensitive or confidential data protected from unauthorised access or leakage?** | – System and data 'owners' define the access rights to their data and these definitions are reflected in the access control system. |
| | | – Access controls in place which give each user a defined range of access to systems and data, and prevent access to all other systems. |
| | | – Especially sensitive data is further protected in that it is only accessible from a restricted number of securely located terminals. |
| | | – All confidential output is routed to the laser printer and shrink wrapped. |
| **1.21** | **What measures ensure that only authorised and tested versions of programs are utilised?** | – Production and development program libraries are separated and subject to strict program movement authorities and processes. |
| | | – Following development and comprehensive testing, development programs are moved to the production library on the authority of the operations manager and end-users. |
| | | – The production program library only contains current and approved versions. The contents are regularly independently checked against an approved schedule of programs. |
| | | – Access to the production library is restricted and in live use is controlled by the JCL or SCL. |

| Seq. | Risk/Control Issue | Current Control/Measure |
|------|-------------------|------------------------|
| 1.22 | **What specific steps would prevent the loading and use of either unauthorised or untested programs or system amendments?** | – Production and development program libraries are separated and subject to strict program movement authorities and processes.<br><br>– Access to the production library is restricted and in live use is controlled by the JCL or SCL.<br><br>– Unauthorised programs located in the production library would be detected during the regular verification of the contents. |
| 1.23 | **Would management be promptly made aware of any abnormal processing activities?** | – Job runs are controlled by authorised JCL or SCL. The ability to introduce unauthorised JCL is prevented by access control measures.<br><br>– All activity is logged and exception reports highlighting defined categories of activity are produced and sent to management for review, investigation and sign-off. |
| 1.24 | **What steps are in place to prevent development staff directly accessing the live production environment?** | Access to the production facilities is restricted to privilege users only and augmented by password control. |
| 1.25 | **How is management assured that the skills of the operating and technical support staff are maintained up-to-date and relevant?** | – Existing staff are continuously monitored for their skills against the requirements for the current and planned environments. Training and development needs are identified and addressed.<br><br>– Each member of staff has a job specification which incorporates their specific minimum skill requirements. |
| 1.26 | **How can management be assured that the mainframe and distributed systems are operated at optimum efficiency (and that facility overloads are prevented)?** | – Job scheduling is planned in advance for mainstream production tasks.<br><br>– Loading requirements are based on historical evidence of resource requirements and run times.<br><br>– On-line resource usage monitoring is applied on all key systems and warning signals activated if defined parameters are exceeded.<br><br>– Operations and technical support staff are on call to affect schedule amendments and activate reserve capacity if necessary.<br><br>– Performance statistics are generated and reviewed by management. |
| 1.27 | **What measures prevent unauthorised usage of mainframe facilities?** | – Access to mainframe facilities is restricted by user ID and password.<br><br>– Runs are controlled by authorised JCL and generating JCL requires specific skills.<br><br>– All non-standard jobs are reported on the system logs and reported to management for sign-off or investigation |

| Seq. | Risk/Control Issue | Current Control/Measure |
|---|---|---|
| 1.28 | How can management be assured that the operating system is efficiently configured and that adequately skilled staff are available to maintain and/or rebuild the system in the event of a major failure? | – Performance statistics are generated and reviewed by management.<br><br>– Manufacturers recommended configurations are taken into account when the system is set up.<br><br>– Experienced technical support staff are employed and supported by ongoing training and development.<br><br>– Regular exercises are conducted to simulate system failure and environment rebuilds. These are evaluated for their effectiveness. |
| 1.29 | Have adequate steps been taken to ensure that all key hardware is regularly and appropriately maintained in order to avoid unnecessary disruption of services etc? | – All mainframe equipment is subject to regular preventative maintenance by the supplier.<br><br>– Fault diagnostic software is used to highlight potential problems.<br><br>– Contingency plans are in place to counter the effects of any disruption to services. |
| 1.30 | Is access to the Job Control Language (JCL) or System Control Language (SCL) facilities adequately restricted? | Access to JCL and SCL facilities is restricted to experienced personnel outwith the operations department. |
| 1.31 | What measures ensure that the use of JCL and SCL is optimised and that inefficient or inappropriate tasks are not loaded? | All JCL and SCL is tested prior to use and authorised prior to transfer into the production environment. |
| 1.32 | How does management ensure that access to and use of utility programs is valid, appropriate and trailed? | – Utilities are not held on-line and their use (and loading) is subject to written authorisation.<br><br>– Utility program usage features on the management review log of system activity and has to be checked against the written authorities. |
| 1.33 | What steps ensure that only authorised, accurate and appropriate data is loaded for access by users? | – System controls (including JCL parameters) confirm that the correct data and system files are accessed during processing.<br><br>– System access and validation controls contribute to the accuracy and reliability of data. |
| 1.34 | Have management defined the required service provision levels and what measures ensure that such performance is adequately monitored and reacted to? | – Job Scheduling and prioritisation contributes to meeting the defined service levels.<br><br>– On-line performance and job progress monitoring is in place and subject to review.<br><br>– Delays or problems are detected and promptly reacted to. |

| Seq. | Risk/Control Issue | Current Control/Measure |
|------|-------------------|------------------------|
| 1.35 | What measures prevent unauthorised access to confidential data output, and how is such data securely distributed to authorised users? | – All confidential and sensitive output is routed to the laser printer and shrink-wrapped prior to distribution.<br>– Alternatively, confidential data can only be accessed and displayed on nominated securely located terminals. |
| | **Back-up** | |
| 1.36 | How does management ensure that all key systems and data are protected in the event of a failure or breakdown? | – Back-up policy and procedures are in place as the basis for effective data protection.<br>– Each system has an agreed back-up schedule and timetable. Mainframe systems automatically back-up as part of the control procedures.<br>– Separate PC procedures are in place.<br>– Regular confirmatory checks are conducted to ensure that the requirements are being complied with. |
| 1.37 | How can management be certain that the prescribed data back-up routines are being applied in practice? | – Contents of back-up store are checked regularly to ensure that the required files are available.<br>– Regular confirmatory checks are conducted to ensure that the requirements are being complied with. |
| 1.38 | What measures ensure that all data and system back-ups are securely stored and adequately protected from damage, deterioration or loss? | – Secure and remote back-up store is provided and all back-up media are moved out to the store on a daily basis.<br>– Store is adequately protected by alarms and out-of-hours patrol.<br>– Store is air-conditioned and the environmental conditions are monitored and controlled to ensure the optimum conditions for the media. |
| 1.39 | How can management be assured that end-users are applying adequate data back-up routines in order to protect their PC-based activities? | – Guideline and procedures are circulated to all end-users.<br>– Regular visits are conducted by the user support staff to verify if users are applying sufficient back-up to their systems and data. |
| 1.40 | What measures ensure that all key data and system back-ups can be accurately and promptly identified and traced? | – Physical and magnetic labelling standards are in place as a means of identifying specific media.<br>– Mainframe media is tracked using a library control system which identifies each item of media. The storage location is recorded for each item. |
| 1.41 | Does management ensure that all key back-ups are regularly accounted for? | Mainframe media store contents are reconciled on a monthly basis. |

| Seq. | Risk/Control Issue | Current Control/Measure |
|------|-------------------|------------------------|
| 1.42 | How can management be certain that organisation is correctly complying with all the relevant data retention legislation? | – The retention periods for key corporate data (ie accounting records) are defined in accordance with any prevailing legislation.<br><br>– Destruction dates for media are established which comply with the regulations. |
| 1.43 | What measures ensure that long-term back-up media remains readable and useable? | Key system back-up media are checked periodically to ensure that the contents remain readable. Secondary copies are provided for crucial systems in the event that the prime copy fails to read. |
| 1.44 | What specific measures prevent the premature erasure or reuse of back-up media? | – Write protect devices activated.<br><br>– Usage of media items is controlled by the library system and the incorrect loading of media would be detected by the JCL or SCL parameters. |
| 1.45 | How is the disposal of outdated or unwanted media controlled so that valid items are not destroyed or overwritten? | Usage of media items is controlled by the library system. |
| 1.46 | What measures are in place to prevent and detect virus infection of media? | – All external media is checked for virus infection before use.<br><br>– PC users are required to run all external media through virus software located on a free-standing machine before loading onto their systems. |
| 1.47 | How can management be assured that virus infections would be promptly detected, contained and effectively dealt with? | – All external media is checked for virus infection before use.<br><br>– All PCs have virus detection software loaded which runs on boot up. Any virus infections have to be reported immediately to technical support department for corrective action. |
|      | Systems/operating software | |
| 1.48 | What measures ensure that only recognised, reliable and correctly configured operating systems are utilised? | – Only tested and approved operating software is utilised.<br><br>– Operating software is configured (in accordance with the suppliers recommendations) to ensure maximum efficiency and appropriate functionality. |
| 1.49 | Does management ensure that adequate and appropriately skilled staff are available to maintain operating and systems software? | Experienced technical support staff are employed. Relevant training is provided so that their skills are maintained at the required level. |
| 1.50 | What measures prevent the inappropriate or disruptive configuration of operating/systems software? | – Configuration amendments are only applied by the technical support staff.<br><br>– All amendments are subject to prior management authority.<br><br>– All potential amendments are subject to rigorous prior testing outwith the production environment. |

| Seq. | Risk/Control Issue | Current Control/Measure |
|------|--------------------|-----------------------|
| 1.51 | What measures prevent unauthorised access to and amendment of operating systems? | Access is restricted via the access control system which only permits access by authorised Technical Support staff. Specialist knowledge requirements also have the effect of reducing the opportunity for unauthorised access. |
| 1.52 | Are all system software upgrades and fixes adequately assessed, tested and authorised prior to application to the live environment? | – All potential amendments are subject to rigorous prior testing outwith the production environment.<br>– Test results are reviewed by management prior to the granting of update authority. |
| 1.53 | Are systems and operating software facilities effectively configured so that unauthorised access to data and systems is prevented? | – The access control system operates in tandem with the operating system to ensure that access is controlled on a 'needs' basis.<br>– The mainframe system is further protected by runs being controlled via the JCL or SCL which defines those systems and files to be accessed during the job. |
| 1.54 | How can management be assured that the efficiency and performance of the operating system is optimised? | Operating software is configured (in accordance with the suppliers recommendations) to ensure maximum efficiency and appropriate functionality. |
| 1.55 | How can management be assured that full recovery from a major systems failure can be promptly achieved? | – All the necessary recovery journals are maintained. Recovery is regularly tested.<br>– Rebuilding of the operating environment is tested as part of the Disaster Recovery Plan tests. |
| 1.56 | Are abnormal or unauthorised events promptly and independently brought to the attention of management? | – Attempted access violations are logged and circulated for review.<br>– All errors and non-standard runs are reported to management for review and sign-off. |
| 1.57 | Is access to 'privilege user' facilities adequately restricted and trailed? | – Access control system permits access to the high level facilities for named users with double password access control.<br>– Amendments applied to configuration files are logged and reported to management. |
| 1.58 | Is access to utility and diagnostic facilities suitably restricted and trailed? | Identical to methods described in 1.57 above. |
| 1.59 | Have management established adequate and appropriate levels of operating system journals in order to maintain an awareness of system usage and operating efficiency? | – All standard journals are generated.<br>– In addition, specific journals and logs have been established to highlight the application of either sensitive or wide-ranging amendments. Such reports are circulated to management for action. |
| 1.60 | How does management ensure that all personal computers throughout the organisation are appropriately and consistently configured? | – Operating systems are initially loaded and configured by technical support staff in accord with the suppliers recommendations and operational requirements of the company.<br>– Regular checks are conducted by technical support to ensure that the machines retain their original and authorised configurations. |

| Seq. | Risk/Control Issue | Current Control/Measure |
|------|--------------------|-------------------------|
| 1.61 | **What specific measures prevent the use of unauthorised or unreliable PC operating systems?** | Regular checks are conducted by technical support to ensure that only authorised operating systems are present on company PCs. |
| 1.62 | **What measures prevent users from applying unauthorised or inappropriate amendments to PC configurations?** | Regular checks are conducted by technical support to ensure that the machines retain their original and authorised configurations. |
| | **System access control** | |
| 1.63 | **Has management established a policy of system and data ownership whereby users take responsibility for their systems and data?** | – All data and systems are allocated to users.<br>– Users grant access rights and these are reflected in the database administration system. |
| 1.64 | **What measures are in place to ensure that data and systems are effectively protected from unauthorised access and/or amendments?** | – Access control system is in place which supports the access rights granted by the users/owners (as defined in the DBMS).<br>– Access control system operates on a user-ID and password basis. Each user-ID has a range of access permissions defined.<br>– Access is not permitted to systems or data where rights have not been granted and set-up on the system. |
| 1.65 | **What measures ensure that the access control arrangements are maintained up-to-date and relevant to the underlying business needs?** | – Managers are periodically provided with departmental summaries of users and required to confirm that the details are correct.<br>– Access usage is monitored and redundant user-IDs highlighted for removal.<br>– System level access rights are granted on a 'needs' basis in accord with defined standard patterns of access. |
| 1.66 | **Who controls the granting of access rights and how can management be assured that this operation is correctly conducted?** | – The granting of rights is related to the current policy.<br>– The data administrator is held responsible for maintaining the access control system in accord with the policy and the wishes of system owners.<br>– Managers are periodically provided with departmental summaries of users and required to confirm that the details are correct. |
| 1.67 | **Are attempted security breaches or violations capable of prompt detection and effective reporting to management?** | The system only allows three unsuccessful log-on attempts before reporting the events to the data administrator for follow-up investigation. |
| 1.68 | **What additional measures are in place to ensure that high-level or privilege access rights are effectively controlled and that relevant actions are trailed?** | – Use of high level facilities is protected by two levels of access control and two passwords.<br>– All usage of utilities and privilege facilities are logged and reported to management for sign-off. |

| Seq. | Risk/Control Issue | Current Control/Measure |
|------|--------------------|--------------------------|
| 1.69 | How can management be certain that staff are fully aware of their responsibilities with regard to data and system security? | – The system security and access policy is given to all employees and is augmented by documented procedures which specify responsibilities for data and system security measures.<br><br>– Spot checks are conducted by the technical support team to verify that the prescribed procedures are being complied with. |
| 1.70 | How can management be assured that user access passwords are effective, and are protected from leakage and misuse? | – The system enforces password changes every six weeks and prevents the re-use of previous passwords.<br><br>– The system enforces a minimum password length and rejects blank passwords and selected words.<br><br>– Procedures define action to be taken if user suspects a breach of password confidentiality. |
| 1.71 | What measures prevent the casual use of terminals left switched on and unattended? | – Unattended and inactive terminals are automatically logged off after a fixed time period. Re-entry of the user id and password are required to re-activate the system.<br><br>– Personal computers require the entry of a password to reactivate after a period of inactivity. |
|      | **Personal computers** | |
| 1.72 | How does management ensure that PC facilities are justified and contribute to business efficiency? | – PC acquisitions have to be justified against the business requirements and also conform with the IT strategic plan.<br><br>– All purchase requests have to be authorised. |
| 1.73 | How does management ensure that suitable personal computers are obtained from reliable suppliers and that they meet the relevant performance and facility requirements? | – Only industry standard PC hardware is permitted and specification guidelines have been established.<br><br>– All authorised purchase requests are checked against the defined standard criteria and preferred supplier lists.<br><br>– Preferred suppliers are assessed as to their reliability and stability before any trading relationship is established.<br><br>– Underlying user requirements and performance criteria are established as the basis for acquisition. |
| 1.74 | Does management take steps to ensure that PC hardware is of an appropriate type and quality, and is capable of suitable future expansion? | – Only industry standard PC hardware is permitted and specification guidelines have been established.<br><br>– Expansion capabilities are assessed as part of the review of preferred suppliers. |

| Seq. | Risk/Control Issue | Current Control/Measure |
|------|--------------------|--------------------------|
| 1.75 | **What steps does management take to protect PC hardware from theft, damage or misuse?** | – Personal computers are fixed to desks with lockable flexible steel cables.<br><br>– All PC hardware is identified with a non-removable label bearing a unique fixed assets register number.<br><br>– Hardware can only be removed from the premises if accompanied by a written authority. Security staff challenge all persons removing equipment and check for the required authority documentation. |
| 1.76 | **How can management ensure that only authorised and appropriate software is loaded onto personal computers (and what specifically prevents users from loading their own software files)?** | – Only established and proven software packages are obtained.<br><br>– A register of licensed copies and their locations is maintained as the basis for regular spot checks on PC hard disk contents.<br><br>– Staff are not permitted to load their own or unlicensed software. All official software is loaded and configured by members of the technical support team, who undertake regular software audits.<br><br>– In selected instances, users PCs have the floppy drive disabled with a lock to prevent the loading of unauthorised software and data. |
| 1.77 | **What measures prevent users from applying unauthorised or inappropriate configuration amendments which could affect performance and reliability?** | – All official software is loaded and configured by members of the technical support team, who undertake regular software and configuration audits.<br><br>– Access to specific configuration facilities is restricted by the use of a password only issued to technical support staff. |
| 1.78 | **How is the unauthorised use of personal computers and the relevant data prevented?** | – The system boot-up process is augmented by the use of an access control system requiring the correct entry of a user-ID and password.<br><br>– On-line systems have additional access controls in place which aim to support the access rights granted by the system owners. |
| 1.79 | **How can management be sure that staff are adequately trained in the correct and efficient use of PC facilities?** | – General training materials are available to support the efficient and controlled use of PC facilities.<br><br>– Specific application and software package training courses and materials are made available as part of the introduction of new or amended systems.<br><br>– Users have access to the technical and user support team to assist them with day-to-day problems. |
| 1.80 | **Are all hardware and software upgrades only applied by suitably trained and authorised staff (and how is this confirmed)?** | All hardware and software upgrades are applied by the technical support team. |

| Seq. | Risk/Control Issue | Current Control/Measure |
|------|-------------------|------------------------|
| 1.81 | **What steps does management take to ensure that the requirements of the prevailing Data Protection legislation are fully complied with?** | – A Data Protection Policy is in place and reinforced by specific procedures and practices. Training is provided for relevant staff.<br><br>– System access controls and validation measures contribute to the accuracy and relevance of data.<br><br>– Data security and circulation procedures contribute to the protection of data and the prevention of unauthorised disclosure. |
| 1.82 | **What steps are in place to prevent undue disruption in the event of hardware failure?** | – Preventative maintenance contracts are in place with suppliers for PC and related hardware.<br><br>– Faults are reported and dealt with on a 'same day' basis.<br><br>– Limited numbers of reserve and standby hardware are available in the event of prolonged fault and resolution. |
| 1.83 | **What measures protect personal computers from virus infection?** | – All incoming media have to be scanned on a free-standing machine designated for that purpose, before being loaded onto company machines.<br><br>– All PCs have virus detection software installed, which is automatically run upon boot-up.<br><br>– Staff are obliged to report all potential virus infections to the Technical Support team for investigation, isolation and corrective action. |
| 1.84 | **What measures prevent users from making unauthorised copies of licensed software and sensitive data files?** | – Unless justified by management, floppy disk drives are locked and therefore unavailable to staff.<br><br>– Original source system diskettes are held by the technical support team. |
| 1.85 | **What measures prevent users from circumventing access and operating system controls?** | Disk drive locks prevent users from booting their PCs via a system disk in the floppy drive. |
| | **Software maintenance** | |
| 1.86 | **Are all key systems adequately documented so as to ensure that they can be effectively maintained?** | – All corporate application systems are documented to a defined standard.<br><br>– The details of all authorised program amendments are updated on the system documentation as a trail for subsequent use. |

| Seq. | Risk/Control Issue | Current Control/Measure |
|------|--------------------|--------------------------|
| 1.87 | What steps ensure that all software amendments are justified, authorised and fully tested before being applied to live use? | – All system amendments are subject to specification by users and assessment and justification processes. Formal authorisation is required from the IT steering committee.<br><br>– Development and programming standards are in place which define the minimum testing standards.<br><br>– Management and users have to signify their acceptance of the amendment and the test results before transfer to the production environment is permitted. |
| 1.88 | How can management be assured that all software amendments are appropriately coded and are valid for the purpose? | – Development and programming standards are in place which define the minimum testing standards.<br><br>– Users are required to sign off the testing results and signify their confirmation that the amendment fulfils the specified purpose. |
| 1.89 | What specific measures prevent the unauthorised application of invalid software amendments? | – Strict version control is exercised over program amendments. The introduction of an unauthorised amendment would require simultaneous amendments to the relevant JCL/SCL and written authority to permit the transfer from the development environment to the production library.<br><br>– Direct update access to the production library is not permitted. All amendments have to be generated in the development environment and then authorised prior to update in the production area. |
| 1.90 | How can management be assured that only authorised and current versions of programs are utilised in the live production environment? | The program contents of the production library are periodically verified against the register of authorised program versions. This check is independently carried out in order to circumvent any possible collusion between operations and development staff. |
| 1.91 | Are all software amendments adequately specified and documented? | – The details of all authorised program amendments are updated on the system documentation as a trail for subsequent use.<br><br>– Program amendments have to conform to the prescribed documentation standards. |
| 1.92 | What specific arrangements are in place to ensure that only authorised and valid software amendments are applied to personal computers? | – All application software updates are handled by the technical support team in a consistent manner.<br><br>– Staff are not permitted to introduce their own or unofficial software amendments. Any such unauthorised software would be detected by the technical support team during their regular software audits. |

| Seq. | Risk/Control Issue | Current Control/Measure |
|------|-------------------|------------------------|
| | **Local Area Networks (LANs)** | |
| 1.93 | **How does management ensure that LAN requirements are fully assessed, justified, and fit in with future expansion requirements?** | – Assessment of current and future LAN requirements was undertaken as part of the strategic planning exercise. <br> – Future expansion flexibility taken into account when designing and installing LANs. |
| 1.94 | **Are performance and service availability requirements identified as the basis for determining the optimum networking solution?** | – Critical performance and response criteria were identified and incorporated into the LAN requirements specification. <br> – Various LAN solutions were fully assessed and costed as the basis for selection. |
| 1.95 | **What steps prevent unauthorised access to the networked facilities and protect user systems and data from invalid access?** | User-ID and password system in place to control access to systems and data on a 'needs' basis. |
| 1.96 | **How can management be assured of the integrity of the network system software and its contribution to general data and system security?** | – Only industry standard hardware and network software are utilised. <br> – All the appropriate access and facility control mechanisms are enabled. |
| 1.97 | **How are file and system servers adequately protected from unauthorised access?** | – File servers, gateway PCs and PCs used for overnight back-up are located in a separate lockable area. <br> – File server keyboards are disabled by locks. |
| 1.98 | **How is the usage of Supervisor and high-level facilities protected from unauthorised usage?** | – Such facilities only accessible via the file server keyboard, which is disabled by a lock. <br> – Supervisor facilities are subject to enhanced access controls using double passwords. |
| 1.99 | **Have management made adequate arrangements to provide suitable skills for the maintenance and amendment of the network facilities?** | – Suitably experienced staff have been engaged. <br> – Additional training is provided when necessary. |
| | **Database** | |
| 1.100 | **How does management ensure that the data needs of the organisation are accurately identified and reflected in current systems and databases?** | – A data modelling exercise was conducted as part of the IT strategic planning review. <br> – A corporate data model has been developed and accepted by senior management as the basis for future business requirements. <br> – All new and amended systems are required to comply with the agreed data structure. |
| 1.101 | **How does management ensure that appropriate, secure, reliable, and flexible Database Management Systems (DBMS) are in place and maintained?** | – Selection of DBMS was subject to formal software evaluation and selection methodology. <br> – Stability and reliability of DBMS supplier fully assessed prior to purchase being approved. |

| Seq. | Risk/Control Issue | Current Control/Measure |
|------|-------------------|------------------------|
| 1.102 | How can management be assured that appropriate control is exercised over data ownership and the determination of access rights? | – All systems and associated data are allocated to key users as 'owners'. The owners determine and agree the access rights of all others.<br><br>– The Database Administrator is responsible for ensuring that the agreed access rights are reflected in the database system.<br><br>– The access arrangements established to the database are subject to periodic review and agreement by 'owners'. |
| 1.103 | How is data protected from unauthorised access and amendments, and how is management assured of the accuracy of corporate data? | – Partly through the application of the access system described in section 1.102 above.<br><br>– Data is subject to various validation and range checks during input. Additionally, data exception reports are generated by the relevant applications for management review and action. |
| 1.104 | How is management assured of the accuracy and relevance of database set-up in support of the business? | All new database systems are subject to a planned implementation including the loading of new or set-up data. Such data is reconciled to source and tested for integrity prior to live operation. |
| 1.105 | How is the initial and ongoing integrity of the database structure and records assured? | – See 1.104 above<br><br>– DBMS has integral integrity checking facilities, ie valid pointers, block sums, etc. |
| 1.106 | Has management made adequate arrangements for the ongoing maintenance and operation of the database? | – The data administrator is responsible for ensuring that adequate day-to-day procedures are in place covering the updating and maintenance of the system.<br><br>– Performance is monitored against agreed service levels and problems are promptly reported and followed-up. |
| 1.107 | Are all subsequent amendments to the database structure and contents subject to authorisation, and what measures prevent unauthorised structural amendments? | – All subsequent database structure amendments are authorised in writing and only applied and thoroughly tested by the data administrator, who then provides confirmation that the appropriate action has been taken.<br><br>– High level access control is exercised over database amendments and all are reported on activity reports. |
| 1.108 | What specific measures ensure that the database can be promptly and accurately rebuilt in the event of major failure? | – DBMS incorporates effective tracking of all transactions with before and after images to enable recovery to a defined point in time.<br><br>– DBMS rebuilds are regularly tested in the development environment as part of the contingency plan tests. |
| 1.109 | How are management assured that adequate and effective database back-up precautions are taken? | – DBMS incorporates effective tracking of all transactions with before and after images to enable recovery to a defined point in time.<br><br>– Back-up is daily. Data is retained in secure back-up store. |

| Seq. | Risk/Control Issue | Current Control/Measure |
|---|---|---|
| 1.110 | How would management be made aware of any attempts to violate access arrangements or other unusual database activities? | – All accesses are logged.<br><br>– Unsuccessful or invalid log-on attempts are restricted to three. All attempted violations are logged and reported to the data administrator and access system manager for follow up. |
| 1.111 | How can management be sure that query languages are efficiently and appropriately used (and that enquiries are neither excessive nor over-demanding on system resources)? | – User training has been provided for the DBMS query language.<br><br>– Overnight batch processing of extensive query language runs to minimise disruption.<br><br>– Query language runs greater than x minutes are switched into background mode to avoid degradation of services. |
|  | **Data Protection Laws** |  |
| 1.112 | What steps has management taken to ensure that all affected staff are made aware of their responsibilities under the prevailing Data Protection legislation? | – All new staff receive training in Data Protection.<br><br>– Data Protection principles are incorporated into corporate procedures and instructions. |
| 1.113 | How does management ensure that all the Data Protection requirements are cost effectively complied with? | – Data Protection principles are incorporated into corporate procedures and instructions.<br><br>– Data Protection Co-ordinator is responsible for monitoring compliance and following-up procedural shortcomings, etc. |
| 1.114 | What measures ensure that the organisation's registration details remain accurate and up-to-date (eg for new systems and business activities)? | – Registration is periodically reviewed in order to ensure that it remains up-to-date and accurate.<br><br>– All new activities and systems are reviewed for potential Data Protection implications. |
| 1.115 | What steps ensure that Data Protection implications are considered for all systems under development (or where significant amendments are being applied)? | – The system development methodology incorporates a module for assessing the Data Protection implications of new systems.<br><br>– All new activities and systems are reviewed for potential Data Protection implications. |
| 1.116 | What systems are in place to effectively deal with enquiries from data subjects? | – Each data subject enquiry is logged by the Data Protection co-ordinator and referred to the responsible system manager for action.<br><br>– Each enquiry is investigated and assessed – a decision is reached and the enquirer informed of the proposed action. |
| 1.117 | What processes ensure that data errors are promptly corrected? | Any detected data errors (or those arising from a data subject enquiry) are corrected or erased as appropriate, and the action is confirmed by the Data Protection co-ordinator. |

| Seq. | Risk/Control Issue | Current Control/Measure |
|------|--------------------|-------------------------|
| | **Facilities management** | |
| 1.118 | **Where necessary, how does management justify the use of external facilities management services?** | – Current and proposed IT facilities were subject to full cost/benefit assessment. <br><br> – The requirements of the IT strategic plan were taken into account and the approval of the Board sought. |
| 1.119 | **How does management ensure that the required levels of service provision and cost saving are being achieved?** | – The contractual relationship with the facilities management supplier incorporates minimum service level requirements. These are monitored and reacted to. <br><br> – Anticipated cost savings were calculated and actual costs are monitored to ensure that predicted benefits are being achieved. |
| 1.120 | **How does management ensure that the optimum facilities management solution is selected, taking into account service quality, reliability, and cost?** | – Quality, service and operational criteria were established for the full assessment of all the possible options. <br><br> – The determination of the type of facilities management service was subject to justification as part of the strategic planning exercise. |
| 1.121 | **What processes ensure that all the required responsibilities, rights and liabilities are identified and appropriately allocated between the parties?** | – A comprehensive contract has been established which defines rights, responsibilities, performance requirements and liabilities. <br><br> – Ongoing performance and achievement monitoring is applied to ensure that targets are attained. |
| 1.122 | **How can management be assured that adequate and effective security will be exercised over company data?** | Third party facilities and security arrangements were subject to a full review by the company auditors. |
| 1.123 | **Has management clearly established the ownership of hardware, general software and specific company systems?** | Ownership of all elements has been clearly defined in the contract. |
| 1.124 | **Are actual costs and performance measures monitored against defined targets, and what action is taken in the event of either service disruption, poor performance or general failure?** | – Ongoing performance and achievement monitoring is applied to ensure that targets are attained. <br><br> – Actual costs are monitored to ensure that predicted benefits are being achieved. <br><br> – Shortfalls and problems are highlighted for management follow-up and action. |
| 1.125 | **Has management confirmed that adequate and regularly tested contingency plans are in place to protect ongoing processing and service provision?** | – The third party supplier has confirmed that documented contingency plans are in place and are regularly tested. <br><br> – Company auditors have attended contingency testing exercises and confirmed that they are satisfied with the arrangements. |
| 1.126 | **Are steps in place to ensure that all new systems or process amendments are agreed and fully tested prior to live usage?** | All amendments to existing programs are justified, agreed, documented, tested and signed-off by the users before live usage. |

| Seq. | Risk/Control Issue | Current Control/Measure |
|------|--------------------|-------------------------|
| | **System development** | |
| 1.127 | How is management assured that all system developments are conducted to a required standard and are appropriately secure? | – A recognised systems development methodology has been established which incorporates best practice.<br>– All aspects of the development are addressed in the methodology including documenting systems, testing, etc. |
| 1.128 | Does management ensure that all new systems are fully tested to the satisfaction of users prior to live usage (and how is this evidenced)? | – All system developments are subject to formal testing to a prescribed standard.<br>– Users are involved in the testing process and are required to sign-off the system as meeting their requirements. |
| | **Software selection** | |
| 1.129 | How does management ensure that only reliable proven and secure software products are acquired? | – Software package evaluation procedures are in place.<br>– Products are fully assessed against requirements. Existing users are contacted and their opinions obtained on quality, performance and user support facilities. |
| 1.130 | What steps does management take to confirm the reliability and stability of software suppliers? | – Existing users are contacted and their opinions obtained on supplier performance and reliability.<br>– Only established software suppliers are utilised. |
| 1.131 | Are all the impacts, costs and implications of software acquisition assessed and is the purchase subject to formal testing and authorisation procedures? | – All costs are identified (ie customising, maintenance, training, implementation, etc).<br>– All purchases have to conform with the documented standards and requirements. Authorisation to purchase is obtained from the IT steering committee. |
| 1.132 | How does management ensure that the software supplier is capable of providing initial and ongoing support? | – Support services are assessed. The frequency and costs of upgrades are assessed for reasonableness.<br>– The opinion of existing users is sought. |
| 1.133 | How does management ensure that the optimum software solution is selected (and are all possible solutions examined)? | The formal evaluation of possible solutions should take in the market leaders. All are subject to full assessment as the basis for an informed selection. |
| 1.134 | Does management ensure that software products have a demonstrable upgrade path and are capable of meeting user requirements? | The potential for future flexibility and expansion is taken into account during the assessment process. All facilities are reviewed against the requirements specification agreed with users. |

| Seq. | Risk/Control Issue | Current Control/Measure |
|------|--------------------|--------------------------|
| 1.135 | Does management ensure that adequate user support facilities (including documentation and training) are provided in order to maximise the benefits of the system? | – Support services are assessed.<br><br>– Adequate user and technical documentation has to be supplied – the quality of this will be reviewed prior to purchase. The supplier will be expected to address any shortcomings.<br><br>– Training needs will be identified during the assessment process. Training proposals and associated costs will, whenever necessary, be incorporated in the proposed solution. |
| 1.136 | What measures ensure that the implementation of new software is planned for and that adequate resources are made available? | All implementation impacts are identified and addressed. An implementation plan is produced and resource requirements determined. |
| | **Contingency planning** | |
| 1.137 | What procedures have management provided to ensure that any emergency or major failure can be promptly and effectively rectified? | – A full risk assessment was conducted and a documented Contingency and Recovery Plan has been developed, agreed and introduced.<br><br>– All possible recovery options were examined and the optimum solution selected. |
| 1.138 | How can management be assured that the prevailing contingency arrangements remain up-to-date, appropriate and effective? | All systems and IT facility changes are assessed for their impact on the Contingency and Recovery Plan, which is accordingly updated. |
| 1.139 | How can management be certain that the current contingency arrangements are the most appropriate and cost effective in the circumstances? | – All possible recovery options were examined and costed.<br><br>– The arrangements are reviewed every year in order to ensure that they remain appropriate. |
| | **User support** | |
| 1.140 | Has management taken steps to ensure that adequate and appropriate user support facilities are provided, as a means to ensure the consistent and secure use of corporate IT facilities? | – Helpdesk and user support team established. Appropriate skills and facilities provided to address support needs of users throughout the company.<br><br>– Use of IT is supported by documented procedures, policies and guidelines. |
| 1.141 | Have reporting lines been established for both hardware and software faults, and how can management be assured that such problems are promptly and effectively addressed? | – All faults are initially reported to the helpdesk, where the details are logged and action is initiated.<br><br>– Call and rectification progress is monitored by the helpdesk supervisor. Problems are escalated in accord with an agreed timetable.<br><br>– The service provided by external engineers and suppliers is subject to monitoring against the contractual service levels. Problems and delays are escalated. |
| 1.142 | What measures prevent end-users taking unauthorised action to investigate and rectify faults? | Standing instructions prohibit users tampering with computer equipment. They could be held liable for any damage. |

| Seq. | Risk/Control Issue | Current Control/Measure |
|---|---|---|
| 1.143 | Have service level requirements been established for the user support function, and how is management assured that such levels are being achieved in order to minimise disruption? | – All calls are logged and subsequent corrective progress is timed against established service level requirements.<br><br>– Failures to meet the established deadlines are reported and escalated for further action. Overall performance statistics are maintained and reviewed by management. |
| | IT accounting | |
| 1.144 | Has management agreed, circulated and established an accounting policy for the IT function? | – User management participated in the development of an agreed IT accounting policy incorporating charge out rates for IT services.<br><br>– Procedures are in place governing the flow of IT accounting information and the process for challenging charges. |
| 1.145 | Have budgets been established and are they subject to effective monitoring and follow-up? | Monthly budget and actual reports circulated to all key user managers. |
| 1.146 | Have end-users been allocated responsibility for their IT related costs? | – Users are made aware of the basis for incurring IT charges based upon service provision and transaction levels.<br><br>– Usage of query systems and report generators is in hands of users. Estimated costs are displayed at the end of the appropriate processing session.<br><br>– Costs can be broken down to individual user-IDs if required. |
| 1.147 | What measures have management taken to ensure that IT usage costs are fairly, accurately and completely accounted for and charged out to users where necessary? | – Users have been involved in the determination of the charge-out basis.<br><br>– System statistics can be supplied in support of queried charges if required. |

# C5.2 Standard Audit Programme Guide – systems

## *System interfaces for information processing facility*

It is unlikely that any activity or system will operate in complete isolation, but will need to interact with other data and systems in order to be fully effective. At a simple level, such interaction could relate to the input of data from a source system and the generation of amended or enhanced data which can be output to the next process. For example, taking coded transactions from an accounts payable system into the general ledger as the basis for subsequently producing management accounts information.

It is often at the point of interaction between systems where controls are critical. Auditors should be satisfied that the data moving between systems is consistent, complete and accurate, in order that the subsequent processes are undertaken upon a reliable basis.

# Contracting

## C6.1 Standard Audit Programme Guide

| SAPG Ref:<br>CON2 | Function: Contracting | Activity/System: Contract<br>Management |
|---|---|---|

*Management checklist version with example controls and measures*

| Company: | Division: | Country: | Site: |
|---|---|---|---|
| Audit Ref.: | Date: | Completed by: | Reviewed by: |

**Control Objective(s):** (a) To ensure that contracting activities support the cost-effective achievement of agreed business objectives; (b) To provide and maintain suitable documented procedures in order that contracting activities are effectively administered and so that staff malpractice and fraud are prevented; (c) To ensure that contract requirements are correctly identified, appraised, justified, and documented; (d) To ensure that the optimum contracting solution is selected; (e) To ensure that contracts awarded represent value for money and meet the required quality and performance standards; (f) To ensure that only stable, financially secure, and appropriately qualified contractors are engaged; (g) To ensure that there is a fair and equitable basis for selecting contractors; (h) To ensure that all requirements and objectives are identified, documented and met; (i) To ensure that all payments against the contract are valid, authorised, and correctly accounted for; (j) To ensure that contracts are completed on time, within budget and to the required standard; (k) To ensure that responsibilities are identified and allocated; (l) To ensure that management information is accurate, appropriate, complete and timely; (m) To ensure that progress is adequately monitored and that problems are promptly reacted to; (n) To ensure that all statutory and regulatory issues are identified and correctly addressed; (o) To ensure that the most appropriate form of contract is utilised and that the organisation is adequately protected in the event of contractor default; (p) To ensure that any design requirements are fully explored and accurately communicated; (q) To ensure that subsequent design changes are authorised and/or minimised; (r) To ensure that delays and extensions of time are reported, minimised and authorised where necessary; (s) To ensure that price fluctuations throughout the course of the contract are justified, authorised and correctly applied; (t) To ensure that contractual claims are minimised, controlled and satisfactorily resolved; (u) To ensure that all project assets, plant and materials are adequately protected and correctly accounted for; (v) To ensure that valid claims for damages are correctly raised, pursued and settled.

| Seq. | Risk/Control Issue | Current Control/Measure |
|------|-------------------|-------------------------|
| 1 | **Key Issues** | |
| 1.1 | **How does management ensure that significant contract activity is in accord with, and supports the achievement of, the business objectives of the organisation?** | – All contracts with a value >$5Million are approved by the relevant executive committee in accordance with the prevailing delegations of authority.<br><br>– Decisions are taken in light of the agreed strategic/business plan(s). Any contract or project outwith the agreed plan are subject to separate Board ratification. |
| 1.2 | **How can management be assured that contracting activities are appropriately, cost effectively, and consistently conducted?** | – An agreed and documented contract administration procedure is in place. Key stages (ie project appraisal, budget authorisation, etc) are subject to formalised management review and authorisation prior to any commitment.<br><br>– The legal department has a defined role in independently assessing potential contractual relationships. |
| 1.3 | **What specific steps are in place to prevent and/or reveal staff malpractice and/or fraud in the placing of contracts?** | – All key duties in the contract administration process are subject to strict segregation and documented authority limits.<br><br>– Employees with the power to commit the organisation to expenditure are prevented from authorising payments to contractors. |
| 1.4 | **What steps ensure that all potential contracts or projects are fully appraised for viability, cost-effectiveness and justification (and how is this evidenced)?** | – Formal project/contract appraisal procedures are in place. All contracts valued in excess of $X million are subject to a full feasibility study addressed to the commissioning committee/business board.<br><br>– Full risk and financial assessments are conducted as part of the feasibility process.<br><br>– Delegation of authority procedures define agreed limits for ultimate authorisation to proceed. |
| 1.5 | **How can senior management be assured that they are made aware of all potential and actual contracts (and their financial and operational implications)?** | – The feasibility research involves representatives from all the affected functions as a means of identifying the full range of possible options. Additionally, representatives from the operational and finance areas are responsible for ensuring that full impact studies are undertaken.<br><br>– All identified options are subject to the feasibility process and comparative study. |
| 1.6 | **What measures ensure that only suitably justified and authorised contracts are progressed (and what specifically prevents the establishment of unauthorised contract relationships)?** | – All contracts are subject to documented authority being given (ie within the relevant Board or committee minutes).<br><br>– Legal department will only enact a contractual relationship where evidence of the relevant authorisation is sighted and confirmed. |

| Seq. | Risk/Control Issue | Current Control/Measure |
|------|-------------------|------------------------|
| 1.7 | How are management assured that realistic and accurate contract cost estimates are generated and subject to adequate ongoing monitoring throughout the contract? | – The financial assessment conducted as part of the feasibility study is used as the foundation for building an accurate cost model for the contract/project.<br><br>– Any modifications to the original requirements are subject to review and management authorisation, with the amended figures being applied to the cost model.<br><br>– Budgets are established, and responsibilities allocated for ongoing monitoring and reaction to variances, etc as part of the documented contract administration procedures. |
| 1.8 | What processes ensure that the most appropriate form of contract/project funding is selected and authorised (and how is this evidenced)? | – The financial assessment process within the feasibility study will incorporate a review of the financing options. Consultation with the Treasury function is required during this process and the financial implications of the various options are assessed.<br><br>– Due regard is taken of any prevailing strategic financing considerations established as part of the long-term financial planning for the organisation.<br><br>– Where justified, the financing options are summarised and presented to the appropriate board or committee for authorisation (ie in accord with the current delegation of authority procedures). The relevant minutes record the authorisation. |
| 1.9 | How can management be assured that the most suitable form of contract is used, and that the clauses represent a fair balance of the risks between the parties? | – The legal department (and where necessary external legal advisors) are consulted as part of the contract administration procedures, and their advice is sought on the choice of contract form and the specific clause contents.<br><br>– Whenever practical, established standard forms of contract are utilised (but still subject to review by the company legal experts).<br><br>– If necessary, legal department. staff will negotiate any specific clauses with potential contractors. |
| 1.10 | What steps are taken to ensure that contracts are legally enforceable and correctly enacted? | See 1.9 above<br><br>– The legal department are charged with the responsibility for correctly enacting contracts and confirming that all the relevant processes (ie signing and sealing, etc) have been correctly conducted.<br><br>– A register of all external contracts is maintained and updated with action taken, claims raised, etc. |

| Seq. | Risk/Control Issue | Current Control/Measure |
|------|--------------------|-------------------------|
| 1.11 | How can management be certain that contracts represent the best value for money? | – All contracts valued in excess of $Xmillion are subject to formal tendering processes as a means of testing the market. |
| | | – Where appropriate, recognised national, trade or professional terms are utilised in contract relationships. |
| 1.12 | What steps ensure that all the relevant quality and performance issues are accurately identified, documented and ultimately delivered? | – The design and requirements specification stages of the prevailing procedures ensure that all the relevant quality and performance parameters are identified and incorporated into the tender and contract documentation. |
| | | – Potential contractors are assessed for their technical reputation and practical ability to address the defined requirements (ie membership of a recognised trade or professional body, etc). |
| | | – Throughout the duration of the contract, the project manager appointed by the organisation is held responsible for ensuring that technical, performance and workmanship standards are achieved. Shortfalls are reported and monitored for suitable remedy. The relevant payments are withheld until the standards are attained. |
| 1.13 | How does the organisation avoid the engagement of unstable, financially insecure or inadequately skilled contractors? | – All potential contractors are subject to a full financial assessment including examination of their accounts. |
| | | – References are obtained and reviewed. Membership of trade associations and professional institutions are verified. |
| | | – Contractors must provide evidence of the proficiency of their staff and an undertaking that adequate resources will be made available throughout the life of the contract. |
| | | – Contractor's previous performances are investigated and assessed (ie partly through contact with previous clients). |
| | | – Liquidated damage clauses are built into the contract where relevant. |
| | | – Performance bonds and parent company guarantees are obtained where applicable. |
| 1.14 | What measures ensure that contractors are selected on a fair and equitable basis (and how is staff malpractice and fraud prevented)? | – Tendering procedures in place and applied. |
| | | – Strictly enforced procedure governing the blind submission of tenders, and the opening and logging of same by staff who are not involved in either the instigation of contracts or the final award of the contract. |
| | | – Key duties throughout the contract administration processes are strictly segregated. |

| Seq. | Risk/Control Issue | Current Control/Measure |
|------|--------------------|-----------------------|
| 1.15 | How can management be assured that all the relevant requirements, design, performance and quality criteria are accurately identified and reflected in the contracting documentation? | – Formal requirements specification processes in place involving all the affected functions.<br><br>– Once agreed, all the requirements are incorporated into the contract documentation as the basis for subsequent contractual obligations. This process is overseen by the legal department and subject to quality control by the relevant operational department. |
| 1.16 | What measures ensure that contracts are completed on time, within budget, and to the required standards? | – Formal project management methods are applied.<br><br>– Milestones and key targets are identified and responsibilities allocated for ongoing monitoring and reporting of progress.<br><br>– Accounting budgets agreed and established and updated with actual accounting data. Variances are reported and allocated to individuals for follow-up action.<br><br>– Quality control and technical monitoring responsibilities are allocated. Work/goods are signed off by company project manager as being of the required standard prior to payment of the contractor's account. |
| 1.17 | How are specific responsibilities and contractual obligations identified and allocated? | Allocated within the project management process. The project manager is responsible for ensuring that all key stages and tasks are duly allocated. |
| 1.18 | What measures ensure that contract/project progress and the achievement of contractual obligations are accurately and effectively monitored (and how can management be assured that problems, delays and shortcomings would be promptly identified and dealt with)? | – Regular progress and financial status reports are produced by the project team and circulated to key management (per the project management procedures).<br><br>– Procedure in place to highlight, report and escalate significant problems and delays.<br><br>– Escalation procedure requires the definition of a solution and the allocation of remedial action to a named individual. |
| 1.19 | How can management be assured that all contract and related management information is accurate, complete, up to date and appropriately routed to all affected parties? | – Prior to the commencement of a contract, the likely management information needs are identified and planned for.<br><br>– Data sources, reporting frequencies, etc are defined and resources allocated to provide the required data.<br><br>– Key data (ie cost versus budget) is verified by reconciliation of summaries back to the data source.<br><br>– Processing controls in place to ensure that only authorised and valid data is processed correctly. |

| Seq. | Risk/Control Issue | Current Control/Measure |
|------|--------------------|--------------------------|
| 1.20 | What steps ensure that all contract payments are for work actually completed? | – All contractor accounts are subject to verification to either work done or goods supplied and formal authorisation, prior to payment.<br>– Unproven charges are rejected. |
| 1.21 | How can management be certain that contract payments are accurately calculated in accordance with the contract provisions (ie including interim and staged payments)? | – Responsibility for verifying the calculation of contractor's invoices in allocated. All charges are checked against the records of completed work and delivered goods.<br>– Charges are agreed to the costing basis or specific prices featured in the contract documentation. |
| 1.22 | What specific measures prevent the processing of unauthorised, invalid, duplicated or incorrect contract payments (ie either for work not completed or for goods not supplied)? | See 1.21 above<br>– Evidence of account checking and authorising signature is confirmed before transaction entry and payment processing.<br>– Invoice numbers verified upon entry to prevent processing of duplicates. |
| 1.23 | What measures ensure that all contract payments are accurately reflected in the project and main accounting systems? | – Transaction batch totals and accounts codings verified.<br>– Invalid data rejected.<br>– Regular reconciliation of control accounts.<br>– Circulation of system output (ie budget versus actual) and regular review and sign-off by responsible managers. |
| 1.24 | When applicable, what measures are in place to effectively deal with price fluctuations during the course of a contract (and how is the organisation protected from unreasonable amendments to contract costings)? | – Accepted and proven price fluctuation methods incorporated into contracts.<br>– Price fluctuation charges verified against the contract conditions and relevant activity documentation, prior to formal authorisation to pay being sought. |
| 1.25 | Whenever necessary, what measures ensure that all statutory and regulatory issues are correctly addressed (and would non-compliance be promptly identified)? | – All contracts reviewed by the legal department, regulatory and statutory implications highlighted, discussed and action plan agreed to ensure that they are satisfactorily addressed.<br>– Compliance monitored as part of project management process. |
| 1.26 | Does management take steps to either prevent or minimise the effects of potential contractor default? | – Performance bonds are taken out for contracts valued >$Xmillion.<br>– Parent company guarantees obtained where appropriate. |

| Seq. | Risk/Control Issue | Current Control/Measure |
|---|---|---|
| 1.27 | Are all extensions of time subject to management authorisation, and what prevents unauthorised extensions? | – Requests for extensions are routed through the project manager and formally reported to management for sanction. |
| | | – Agreement to extend completion dates is confirmed in writing. Copies of documentation held on contract file in legal department. |
| | | – In the absence of the above noted documentation, unauthorised delays would be pursued with the contractor and remedy sought. |
| 1.28 | What steps are taken to minimise contractual claims and potentially costly disputes? | – Contractors' previous claim activity is reviewed and contractors with adverse levels of claims are discounted. |
| | | – The project management framework and established communication channels aim to promptly identify potential claim problems. Prescribed processes are available to deal with claims. |
| | | – Each claim is formally reviewed, assessed, and if necessary justified and authorised for settlement under the terms of the contract. |
| | | – Costly litigation is only used as a last resort, and only after a full professional assessment of the circumstances. |
| 1.29 | What measures ensure that all contractual claims for damages against the contractor are fully assessed, accurately costed, and authorised to proceed (and how is this evidenced)? | – The project manager is responsible for monitoring the progress of the contractor's work and detecting circumstances where a damage claim is relevant. |
| | | – Potential damage claims are reported to responsible management for formal assessment against the contract conditions, confirmation of the accuracy of the costing applied, and written authorisation to proceed. A copy of the written authorisation to proceed is filed in the legal department with the other relevant contract documents. |
| | | – Claims are lodged by the legal department in accord with the contract and/or discussed with contractors in order to reach agreement. |
| 1.30 | What processes ensure that all valid/authorised damage claims are pursued, settled and correctly paid? | – The details and status of all damage claims are recorded by the legal department and periodically reviewed for their progress. Overdue settlements are pursued and confirmed with the finance department. |
| | | – Claim settlements are verified for accuracy by the legal department and then processed through the accounts system. Periodic reports are circulated detailing (for each contract) the value of settled claims. |

| Seq. | Risk/Control Issue | Current Control/Measure |
|------|--------------------|--------------------------|
| 1.31 | How can management be certain that all contractor claims are identified, assessed, and authorised (and what prevents the settlement of unauthorised or invalid claims)? | – Each claim is logged when received, formally reviewed, assessed, and if necessary justified and authorised for settlement under the terms of the contract.<br><br>– The legal department maintain detailed records of all claims received for each contract. Copies of the documented authorisation to proceed are retained and used as a point of reference when settlement payments are made. The legal executive signs the payment authority documentation to certify that the claim has been previously authorised to proceed. Rejection of the payment request or the absence of a suitable authority signature will prevent the payment being processed. |
| 1.32 | How does management ensure that all project/contract assets, plant and materials are accounted for and adequately protected from loss or damage? | – Contract-specific asset registers are maintained and key project assets are identified upon receipt.<br><br>– Periodic checks are undertaken by the finance department to confirm the existence of project assets and items of capital plant, and to reconcile the asset registers.<br><br>– Usage of materials is controlled through the use of authorised requisitions. Stock records are maintained and subject to regular confirmatory checks by the finance department. Variances and anomalies are followed-up and project management held responsible for any losses, etc.<br><br>– Appropriate (and cost effective) security measures and storage facilities are provided to protect items from theft, damage and deterioration. |
| 1.33 | How does management confirm that the anticipated benefits arising from contract activities are actually subsequently achieved, and what action is taken to address weaknesses in both the specific and general contract administration processes? | – All aspects of the project and contract administration are subject to a formal post completion review. This process reviews the outcome of the project against the previously established performance criteria.<br><br>– Concurrent with the assessment of the project outturn, a review is undertaken of the relevant contract administration procedures. Any weaknesses or shortcomings are reported and when necessary amendments to the administration framework are authorised and implemented. |

| Seq. | Risk/Control Issue | Current Control/Measure |
|---|---|---|
| 2 | **Detailed Issues** | |
| 2.1 | **What specific measures would prevent any contractual activities which do not comply with the strategic direction of the organisation?** | – All contracts have to be authorised to proceed by the relevant Board or committee (in accordance with the prevailing delegation of authority procedure).<br><br>– Authorisation to proceed is evidenced in writing (ie board minutes, etc).<br><br>– Contract activities outwith the agreed strategic direction of the company must be specifically authorised by the main board.<br><br>– Periodic reports of all contractual activity are provided to the executive committee. The Secretary to the committee is charged with ensuring that prior written authorities are available for all the contracts listed. |
| 2.2 | **How are management and staff made aware of their responsibilities with regard to contracting activities, and has a suitable and workable procedural framework been provided for their guidance?** | – Documented contract administration procedures have been authorised and circulated. These define the relevant responsibilities and required actions.<br><br>– Staff involved in contract administration are provided with suitable training in the required administration procedures.<br><br>– The procedures define the relevant duties and lines of communication. Segregation of key duties ensures that the potential for fraudulent activities is minimised. |
| 2.3 | **Are all the potential options and solutions explored as part of the appraisal process (and what prevents options being overlooked)?** | – Documented project assessment and feasibility procedures/guidelines are in place which reinforce the necessity to examine all the possible solutions and options (including doing nothing).<br><br>– Wide ranging representation in the assessment process ensures that the review will be correspondingly broad in nature.<br><br>– Prior to commencement of detailed assessment work, a scope brief is issued by the commissioning management group as the basis for the work that follows. This brief is discussed and evolved until all affected parties are satisfied with the contents and implied range of the exercise. |

| Seq. | Risk/Control Issue | Current Control/Measure |
|------|-------------------|------------------------|
| 2.4 | How does management prevent either personal bias or undue subjectivity from affecting the appraisal process? | – Segregation of key duties and adequate representation reduces the opportunity for unbalanced influences being brought to bear on decisions, etc.<br><br>– The assessment and feasibility processes will identify a range of key criteria for the project/contract which will have to be satisfied by the eventual solution.<br><br>– Tendering procedures are applied to contracts valued >$Xmillion. The identity of the tenderers is protected and staff removed from the awarding of the contract are responsible for the receipt and custody of tenders.<br><br>– Tender submissions are evaluated by a balanced review committee against predetermined criteria. The recommended tender is present to the relevant board or committee for sanctioning. |
| 2.5 | What measures ensure that all the implications and costs are identified and reviewed (ie including ongoing running or maintenance costs)? | – A full financial assessment of the project/contract is undertaken as part of the formal assessment and feasibility procedures.<br><br>– Procedures are in place to guide participants as to the required level of financial analysis, which includes determining the ongoing maintenance and running costs.<br><br>– A standard form of financial report is prepared as part of the feasibility and justification submission to management for their review and authorisation to proceed.<br><br>– Authorised costs are incorporated into the contract conditions and confirmed for accuracy and completeness prior to the enactment of the contract. |
| 2.6 | How can management be assured that all relevant insurance arrangements are optimised and current throughout the life of the contract? | – Insurance and bonding factors should be highlighted during the assessment and tendering processes. The relevant requirements (both internal and external to the organisation) are determined and communicated to the affected parties.<br><br>– The legal and secretarial departments will liase and ensure that the relevant level and type of cover is arranged and maintained throughout the life of the contract. Any lapses in cover should be reported and acted upon as part of the administration procedures. |

| Seq. | Risk/Control Issue | Current Control/Measure |
|------|--------------------|--------------------------|
| 2.7 | How does management ensure that contractors under consideration have adequate and suitably skilled resources to meet the demands of the contract? | – Written undertakings are sought from contractors as part of the tendering and contract letting processes in order to confirm that the relevant levels of appropriate staff will be available throughout the life of the contract.<br><br>– Positive evidence is sought as to the proficiency and skills of the contractor's workforce. Additionally membership of any relevant trade or professional bodies is confirmed prior to the letting of the contract. |
| 2.8 | Whenever appropriate (or when required by legislation) are fair and properly controlled tendering procedures applied, and if so, what measures ensure that all the bids are impartially reviewed? | – The tendering procedures have been examined by an external legal advisor and confirmed as being in accord with both best practice and the prevailing EEC regulations (when applicable).<br>Also see notes under point 2.4 above. |
| 2.9 | How can management be assured that the design and specification processes are adequate in order to avoid subsequent (and potentially costly) design changes? | – A design team is assigned to the project and given a brief to explore all the possible technical options. The brief also defines the essential performance criteria.<br><br>– Established quality and technical standards are applied.<br><br>– Possible design options are fully costed and submitted for management authorisation.<br><br>– Users and affected parties are involved in the requirements specification and design criteria processes to ensure that all the relevant issues are identified and included in the design brief.<br><br>– Where necessary, external specialist design/specification consultants are engaged to advise on the design criteria and feasible options. |
| 2.10 | Are measures in place to review and specify the required design and technical standards? | – Users and affected parties are involved in the requirements specification and design criteria processes to ensure that all the relevant issues are identified and included in the design brief.<br><br>– Where necessary, external specialist design/specification consultants are engaged to advise on the design criteria and feasible options. |

| Seq. | Risk/Control Issue | Current Control/Measure |
|------|--------------------|--------------------------|
| 2.11 | What steps are taken to ensure that realistic and workable targets and milestones are established and communicated as the basis for subsequent progress monitoring? | – Project management and critical path analysis techniques are applied in order to generate an overall project/contract administration plan with key milestones and progress points.<br><br>– A computer-based project management system is used to record and report actual progress against the agreed plan. Shortfalls and potential conflicts are reported for management action and follow up.<br><br>– The project manager is held responsible for monitoring progress and the achievement of the plan. Regular summary reports are presented to the sponsoring management committee and the board in order to keep them informed of progress and any problems, etc. |
| 2.12 | How can management be sure that adequate and appropriate resources are provided (at the correct time) by the organisation in order to fulfill their obligations? | – The feasibility and project assessment process incorporate the identification of resource and skill requirements. Plans are then drawn up which define how the organisation will meet the recognised demands. Where necessary, additional and suitably experienced staff are engaged, and existing staff are assessed and/or trained to meet the requirements.<br><br>– The human resources department will be consulted as to the implications for the manpower plan.<br><br>– All affected staff are contacted (via their managers) and their commitment to the project is confirmed in writing. Alternative arrangements are made to provide adequate coverage for their original or mainstream tasks. |
| 2.13 | What steps are taken to ensure that the organisations' staff resources are adequately skilled and trained to discharge their contractual and administrative obligations? | – Specific skill and knowledge requirements are identified. Existing staff skills are assessed against these requirements and a training plan is formulated and implemented.<br><br>– Training and skill acquisition costs are determined and approved as part of the project/contract costing and authorisation processes. |
| 2.14 | What measures ensure that key contract/project activities are adequately documented and trailed? | – Documentation requirements are defined in the contract administration procedures.<br><br>– The flow of key contract documentation (ie sign-off reports, project progress reports, transaction summaries, etc) is defined.<br><br>– Key documents are filed in relationship to each contract or project as the basis for trailing activities, decisions, etc. |

| Seq. | Risk/Control Issue | Current Control/Measure |
|------|-------------------|------------------------|
| 2.15 | What action is taken to provide for adequate and accurate channels of communication and representation (both between the employer and contractor, and between affected areas within the employing organisation)? | – The need for regular project team and contractor meetings is defined in the administration procedures. The frequency and form of such meetings are defined, and minutes are required and circulated.<br><br>– Key individuals are identified for each affected party and charged with responsibility for the flow of relevant information, etc.<br><br>– Matters for higher management consideration and authorisation are documented and circulated in accord with defined requirements.<br><br>– Regular progress reports and project management data are produced and circulated. |
| 2.16 | Are actual costs adequately monitored against authorised budgets, and would variances be promptly identified for follow-up? | – A suitably detailed project/contract accounting system is established. Actual costs are compared with the agreed budgets and monitored as part of the progress reporting responsibilities allocated to named individuals.<br><br>– Variances and unusual entries are required to be investigated, resolved and/or reported to senior management. All key financial transactions are subject to prior agreement and authority which reduces the possibility of unexpected charges, etc. |
| 2.17 | If subsequent design changes prove necessary, are they subject to accurate costing and authorisation (and how is this evidenced)? | When necessary for the success of the contract/project, design changes are assessed, fully costed and then submitted to the commissioning committee or board for authorisation to proceed. |
| 2.18 | What measures are in place to avoid the excessive cost and disruption of litigation for disputed contract claims? | – It is intended that all contractual and damage claims should be settled within the contract conditions.<br><br>– Arbitration clauses are included where relevant and independent arbitration is sought if the claims cannot be settled by mutual agreement.<br><br>– Court litigation is only pursued as a last resort where the case has been appropriately assessed for its likely success and where previous negotiations and arbitration have failed.<br><br>– Litigation is subject to senior management approval on the advice of the legal advisors. |

# Appendices

# The Institute of Internal Auditors *Code of Ethics*

To obtain permission to translate, adapt, or reproduce any part of this document, contact:

Administrator, Practices Center
The Institute of Internal Auditors
249 Maitland Avenue
Altamonte Springs,
Florida 32701–4201, USA
Phone: +1 (407) 830–7600, Ext. 256
Fax: +1 (407) 831–5171

## Introduction

The purpose of The Institute's *Code of Ethics* is to promote an ethical culture in the profession of internal auditing.

*Internal auditing is an independent, objective assurance and consulting activity designed to add value and improve an organization's operations. It helps an organization accomplish its objectives by bringing a systematic, disciplined approach to evaluate and improve the effectiveness of risk management, control, and governance processes.*

A code of ethics is necessary and appropriate for the profession of internal auditing, founded as it is on the trust placed in its objective assurance about risk management, control, and governance. The Institute's *Code of Ethics* extends beyond the definition of internal auditing to include two essential components:

1  Principles that are relevant to the profession and practice of internal auditing;
2  Rules of Conduct that describe behavior norms expected of internal auditors. These rules are an aid to interpreting the Principles into practical applications and are intended to guide the ethical conduct of internal auditors.

The *Code of Ethics* together with The Institute's *Professional Practices Framework* and other relevant Institute pronouncements provide guidance to internal auditors serving others. 'Internal auditors' refers to Institute members, recipients of or candidates for IIA professional certifications, and those who provide internal auditing services within the definition of internal auditing.

## Applicability and Enforcement

This *Code of Ethics* applies to both individuals and entities that provide internal auditing services.

For Institute members and recipients of or candidates for IIA professional certifications, breaches of the *Code of Ethics* will be evaluated and administered according to The Institute's Bylaws and Administrative Guidelines. The fact that a particular conduct is not mentioned in the Rules of Conduct does not prevent it from being unacceptable or discreditable, and therefore, the member, certification holder, or candidate can be liable for disciplinary action.

## Principles

Internal auditors are expected to apply and uphold the following principles:

### Integrity

The integrity of internal auditors establishes trust and thus provides the basis for reliance on their judgment.

### Objectivity

Internal auditors exhibit the highest level of professional objectivity in gathering, evaluating, and communicating information about the activity or process being examined. Internal auditors make a balanced assessment of all the relevant circumstances and are not unduly influenced by their own interests or by others in forming judgments.

### Confidentiality

Internal auditors respect the value and ownership of information they receive and do not disclose information without appropriate authority unless there is a legal or professional obligation to do so.

### Competency

Internal auditors apply the knowledge, skills, and experience needed in the performance of internal auditing services.

# Rules of Conduct

## 1. Integrity
Internal auditors:
1.1.    Shall perform their work with honesty, diligence, and responsibility.
1.2.    Shall observe the law and make disclosures expected by the law and the profession.
1.3.    Shall not knowingly be a party to any illegal activity, or engage in acts that are discreditable to the profession of internal auditing or to the organization.
1.4.    Shall respect and contribute to the legitimate and ethical objectives of the organization.

## 2. Objectivity
Internal auditors:
2.1.    Shall not participate in any activity or relationship that may impair or be presumed to impair their unbiased assessment. This participation includes those activities or relationships that may be in conflict with the interests of the organization.
2.2    Shall not accept anything that may impair or be presumed to impair their professional judgment.
2.3    Shall disclose all material facts known to them that, if not disclosed, may distort the reporting of activities under review.

## 3. Confidentiality
Internal auditors:
3.1    Shall be prudent in the use and protection of information acquired in the course of their duties.
3.2    Shall not use information for any personal gain or in any manner that would be contrary to the law or detrimental to the legitimate and ethical objectives of the organization.

## 4. Competency
Internal auditors:
4.1.    Shall engage only in those services for which they have the necessary knowledge, skills, and experience.
4.2    Shall perform internal auditing services in accordance with the Standards for the Professional Practice of Internal Auditing.
4.3    Shall continually improve their proficiency and the effectiveness and quality of their services.

Adopted by The IIA Board of Directors, June 17, 2000

*Appendix 2*

# International Standards for the Professional Practice of Internal Auditing

To obtain permission to translate, adapt, or reproduce any part of this document, contact:

Administrator, Practices Center
The Institute of Internal Auditors
249 Maitland Avenue
Altamonte Springs,
Florida 32701–4201, USA
Phone: +1 (407) 830–7600, Ext. 256
Fax: +1 (407) 831–5171

## Introduction

Internal auditing is an independent, objective assurance and consulting activity designed to add value and improve an organization's operations. It helps an organization accomplish its objectives by bringing a systematic, disciplined approach to evaluate and improve the effectiveness of risk management, control, and governance processes.

Internal audit activities are performed in diverse legal and cultural environments; within organizations that vary in purpose, size, complexity, and structure; and by persons within or outside the organization. While differences may affect the practice of internal auditing in each environment, compliance with the *International Standards for the Professional Practice of Internal Auditing* is essential if the responsibilities of internal auditors are to be met. If internal auditors are prohibited by laws or regulations from complying with certain parts of the *Standards*, they should comply with all other parts of the *Standards* and make appropriate disclosures.

Assurance services involve the internal auditor's objective assessment of evidence to provide an independent opinion or conclusions regarding a process, system or other subject matter. The nature and scope of the assurance engagement are determined by the internal auditor. There are generally three parties involved in assurance services: (1) the person or group directly involved with the process, system or other subject matter – the process owner, (2) the person or group making the assessment – the internal auditor, and (3) the person or group using the assessment – the user.

Consulting services are advisory in nature, and are generally performed at the specific request of an engagement client. The nature and scope of the consulting engagement are subject to agreement with the engagement client. Consulting services generally involve two parties: (1) the person or group offering the advice – the internal auditor, and (2) the person or group seeking and receiving the advice – the engagement client. When performing consulting services the internal auditor should maintain objectivity and not assume management responsibility.

The purpose of the *Standards* is to:

1. Delineate basic principles that represent the practice of internal auditing as it should be.
2. Provide a framework for performing and promoting a broad range of value-added internal audit activities.
3. Establish the basis for the evaluation of internal audit performance.
4. Foster improved organizational processes and operations.

The *Standards* consist of Attribute Standards, Performance Standards, and Implementation Standards. The Attribute Standards address the characteristics of organizations and parties performing internal audit activities. The Performance Standards describe the nature of internal audit activities and provide quality criteria against which the performance of these services can be evaluated. While the Attribute and Performance Standards apply to all internal audit services, the Implementation Standards apply to specific types of engagements.

There is one set of Attribute and Performance Standards, however, there are multiple sets of Implementation Standards: a set for each of the major types of internal audit activity. The Implementation Standards have been established for assurance (A) and consulting (C) activities.

*The Standards* are part of the Professional Practices Framework. The Professional Practices Framework includes the Definition of Internal Auditing, the Code of Ethics, the Standards, and other guidance. Guidance regarding how the Standards might be applied is included in Practice Advisories that are issued by the Professional Issues Committee.

The *Standards* employ terms that have been given specific meanings that are included in the Glossary.

The development and issuance of the *Standards* is an ongoing process. The Internal Auditing Standards Board engages in extensive consultation and discussion prior to the issuance of the Standards. This includes worldwide solicitation for public comment through the exposure draft process.

All exposure drafts are posted on The IIA's website as well as being distributed to all IIA Affiliates. Suggestions and comments regarding the *Standards* can be sent to:

The Institute of Internal Auditors
Global Practices Center, Professional Practices Group
247 Maitland Avenue
Altamonte Springs, FL 32701–4201, USA
E-mail: standards@theiia.org
Web: www.theiia.org

The latest additions and amendments to the *Standards* were issued in December 2003, and became effective January 1, 2004.

## Attribute Standards

### *1000 – Purpose, Authority, and Responsibility*

The purpose, authority, and responsibility of the internal audit activity should be formally defined in a charter, consistent with the *Standards*, and approved by the board.

**1000.A1** – The nature of assurance services provided to the organization should be defined in the audit charter. If assurances are to be provided to parties outside the organization, the nature of these assurances should also be defined in the charter.

**1000.C1** – The nature of consulting services should be defined in the audit charter.

### *1100 – Independence and Objectivity*

The internal audit activity should be independent, and internal auditors should be objective in performing their work.

### *1110 – Organizational Independence*

The chief audit executive should report to a level within the organization that allows the internal audit activity to fulfill its responsibilities.

**1110.A1** – The internal audit activity should be free from interference in determining the scope of internal auditing, performing work, and communicating results.

### *1120 – Individual Objectivity*

Internal auditors should have an impartial, unbiased attitude and avoid conflicts of interest.

## 1130 – Impairments to Independence or Objectivity

If independence or objectivity is impaired in fact or appearance, the details of the impairment should be disclosed to appropriate parties. The nature of the disclosure will depend upon the impairment.

**1130.A1** – Internal auditors should refrain from assessing specific operations for which they were previously responsible. Objectivity is presumed to be impaired if an internal auditor provides assurance services for an activity for which the internal auditor had responsibility within the previous year.

**1130.A2** – Assurance engagements for functions over which the chief audit executive has responsibility should be overseen by a party outside the internal audit activity.

**1130.C1** – Internal auditors may provide consulting services relating to operations for which they had previous responsibilities.

**1130.C2** – If internal auditors have potential impairments to independence or objectivity relating to proposed consulting services, disclosure should be made to the engagement client prior to accepting the engagement.

## 1200 – Proficiency and Due Professional Care

Engagements should be performed with proficiency and due professional care.

## 1210 – Proficiency

Internal auditors should possess the knowledge, skills, and other competencies needed to perform their individual responsibilities. The internal audit activity collectively should possess or obtain the knowledge, skills, and other competencies needed to perform its responsibilities.

**1210.A1** – The chief audit executive should obtain competent advice and assistance if the internal audit staff lacks the knowledge, skills, or other competencies needed to perform all or part of the engagement.

**1210.A2** – The internal auditor should have sufficient knowledge to identify the indicators of fraud but is not expected to have the expertise of a person whose primary responsibility is detecting and investigating fraud.

**1210.A3** – Internal auditors should have knowledge of key information technology risks and controls and available technology-based audit techniques to perform their assigned work. However, not all internal auditors are expected to have the expertise of an internal auditor whose primary responsibility is information technology auditing.

**1210.C1** – The chief audit executive should decline the consulting engagement or obtain competent advice and assistance if the internal audit staff lacks the knowledge, skills, or other competencies needed to perform all or part of the engagement.

## 1220 – Due Professional Care

Internal auditors should apply the care and skill expected of a reasonably prudent and competent internal auditor. Due professional care does not imply infallibility.

**1220.A1** – The internal auditor should exercise due professional care by considering the:

- Extent of work needed to achieve the engagement's objectives.
- Relative complexity, materiality, or significance of matters to which assurance procedures are applied.
- Adequacy and effectiveness of risk management, control, and governance processes.
- Probability of significant errors, irregularities, or noncompliance.
- Cost of assurance in relation to potential benefits.

**1220.A2** – In exercising due professional care the internal auditor should consider the use of computer-assisted audit tools and other data analysis techniques.

**1220.A3** – The internal auditor should be alert to the significant risks that might affect objectives, operations, or resources. However, assurance procedures alone, even when performed with due professional care, do not guarantee that all significant risks will be identified.

**1220.C1** – The internal auditor should exercise due professional care during a consulting engagement by considering the:

- Needs and expectations of clients, including the nature, timing, and communication of engagement results.
- Relative complexity and extent of work needed to achieve the engagement's objectives.
- Cost of the consulting engagement in relation to potential benefits.

## 1230 – Continuing Professional Development

Internal auditors should enhance their knowledge, skills, and other competencies through continuing professional development.

## 1300 – Quality Assurance and Improvement Program

The chief audit executive should develop and maintain a quality assurance and improvement program that covers all aspects of the internal audit activity and continuously monitors its effectiveness. This program includes periodic internal and external quality assessments and ongoing internal monitoring. Each part of the program should be designed to help the internal auditing activity add value and improve the organization's operations and to provide assurance that the internal audit activity is in conformity with the *Standards* and the *Code of Ethics*.

## 1310 – Quality Program Assessments

The internal audit activity should adopt a process to monitor and assess the overall effectiveness of the quality program. The process should include both internal and external assessments.

## 1311 – Internal Assessments

Internal assessments should include:

- Ongoing reviews of the performance of the internal audit activity; and
- Periodic reviews performed through self-assessment or by other persons within the organization, with knowledge of internal audit practices and the *Standards*.

## 1312 – External Assessments

External assessments, such as quality assurance reviews, should be conducted at least once every five years by a qualified, independent reviewer or review team from outside the organization.

## 1320 – Reporting on the Quality Program

The chief audit executive should communicate the results of external assessments to the board.

## 1330 – Use of 'Conducted in Accordance with the Standards'

Internal auditors are encouraged to report that their activities are 'conducted in accordance with the *International* Standards for the Professional Practice of Internal Auditing.' However, internal auditors may use the statement only if assessments of the quality improvement program demonstrate that the internal audit activity is in compliance with the *Standards*.

## 1340 – Disclosure of Noncompliance

Although the internal audit activity should achieve full compliance with the *Standards* and internal auditors with the *Code of Ethics*, there may be instances in which full compliance is not achieved. When noncompliance impacts the overall scope or operation of the internal audit activity, disclosure should be made to senior management and the board.

# Performance Standards

## *2000 – Managing the Internal Audit Activity*

The chief audit executive should effectively manage the internal audit activity to ensure it adds value to the organization.

## *2010 – Planning*

The chief audit executive should establish risk-based plans to determine the priorities of the internal audit activity, consistent with the organization's goals.

**2010.A1** – The internal audit activity's plan of engagements should be based on a risk assessment, undertaken at least annually. The input of senior management and the board should be considered in this process.

**2010.C1** – The chief audit executive should consider accepting proposed consulting engagements based on the engagement's potential to improve management of risks, add value, and improve the organization's operations. Those engagements that have been accepted should be included in the plan.

## *2020 – Communication and Approval*

The chief audit executive should communicate the internal audit activity's plans and resource requirements, including significant interim changes, to senior management and to the board for review and approval. The chief audit executive should also communicate the impact of resource limitations.

## *2030 – Resource Management*

The chief audit executive should ensure that internal audit resources are appropriate, sufficient, and effectively deployed to achieve the approved plan.

## *2040 – Policies and Procedures*

The chief audit executive should establish policies and procedures to guide the internal audit activity.

## *2050 – Coordination*

The chief audit executive should share information and coordinate activities with other internal and external providers of relevant assurance and consulting services to ensure proper coverage and minimize duplication of efforts.

## 2060 – Reporting to the Board and Senior Management

The chief audit executive should report periodically to the board and senior management on the internal audit activity's purpose, authority, responsibility, and performance relative to its plan. Reporting should also include significant risk exposures and control issues, corporate governance issues, and other matters needed or requested by the board and senior management.

## 2100 – Nature of Work

The internal audit activity should evaluate and contribute to the improvement of risk management, control, and governance processes using a systematic and disciplined approach.

## 2110 – Risk Management

The internal audit activity should assist the organization by identifying and evaluating significant exposures to risk and contributing to the improvement of risk management and control systems.

**2110.A1** – The internal audit activity should monitor and evaluate the effectiveness of the organization's risk management system.

**2110.A2** – The internal audit activity should evaluate risk exposures relating to the organization's governance, operations, and information systems regarding the

- Reliability and integrity of financial and operational information.
- Effectiveness and efficiency of operations.
- Safeguarding of assets.
- Compliance with laws, regulations, and contracts.

**2110.C1** – During consulting engagements, internal auditors should address risk consistent with the engagement's objectives and be alert to the existence of other significant risks.

**2110.C2** – Internal auditors should incorporate knowledge of risks gained from consulting engagements into the process of identifying and evaluating significant risk exposures of the organization.

## 2120 – Control

The internal audit activity should assist the organization in maintaining effective controls by evaluating their effectiveness and efficiency and by promoting continuous improvement.

**2120.A1** – Based on the results of the risk assessment, the internal audit activity should evaluate the adequacy and effectiveness of controls encompassing the organization's governance, operations, and information systems. This should include:

- Reliability and integrity of financial and operational information.
- Effectiveness and efficiency of operations.
- Safeguarding of assets.
- Compliance with laws, regulations, and contracts.

**2120.A2** – Internal auditors should ascertain the extent to which operating and program goals and objectives have been established and conform to those of the organization.

**2120.A3** – Internal auditors should review operations and programs to ascertain the extent to which results are consistent with established goals and objectives to determine whether operations and programs are being implemented or performed as intended.

**2120.A4** – Adequate criteria are needed to evaluate controls. Internal auditors should ascertain the extent to which management has established adequate criteria to determine whether objectives and goals have been accomplished. If adequate, internal auditors should use such criteria in their evaluation. If inadequate, internal auditors should work with management to develop appropriate evaluation criteria.

**2120.C1** – During consulting engagements, internal auditors should address controls consistent with the engagement's objectives and be alert to the existence of any significant control weaknesses.

**2120.C2** – Internal auditors should incorporate knowledge of controls gained from consulting engagements into the process of identifying and evaluating significant risk exposures of the organization.

## 2130 – Governance

The internal audit activity should assess and make appropriate recommendations for improving the governance process in its accomplishment of the following objectives:

- Promoting appropriate ethics and values within the organization.
- Ensuring effective organizational performance management and accountability.
- Effectively communicating risk and control information to appropriate areas of the organization.
- Effectively coordinating the activities of and communicating information among the board, external and internal auditors and management.

**2130.A1** – The internal audit activity should evaluate the design, implementation, and effectiveness of the organization's ethics-related objectives, programs and activities.

**2130.C1** – Consulting engagement objectives should be consistent with the overall values and goals of the organization.

## 2200 – Engagement Planning

Internal auditors should develop and record a plan for each engagement, including the scope, objectives, timing and resource allocations.

## 2201 – Planning Considerations

In planning the engagement, internal auditors should consider:

- The objectives of the activity being reviewed and the means by which the activity controls its performance.
- The significant risks to the activity, its objectives, resources, and operations and the means by which the potential impact of risk is kept to an acceptable level.
- The adequacy and effectiveness of the activity's risk management and control systems compared to a relevant control framework or model.
- The opportunities for making significant improvements to the activity's risk management and control systems.

**2201.A1** – When planning an engagement for parties outside the organization, internal auditors should establish a written understanding with them about objectives, scope, respective responsibilities and other expectations, including restrictions on distribution of the results of the engagement and access to engagement records.

**2201.C1** – Internal auditors should establish an understanding with consulting engagement clients about objectives, scope, respective responsibilities, and other client expectations. For significant engagements, this understanding should be documented.

## 2210 – Engagement Objectives

Objectives should be established for each engagement.

**2210.A1** – Internal auditors should conduct a preliminary assessment of the risks relevant to the activity under review. Engagement objectives should reflect the results of this assessment.

**2210.A2** – The internal auditor should consider the probability of significant errors, irregularities, noncompliance, and other exposures when developing the engagement objectives.

**2210.C1** – Consulting engagement objectives should address risks, controls, and governance processes to the extent agreed upon with the client.

## 2220 – Engagement Scope

The established scope should be sufficient to satisfy the objectives of the engagement.

**2220.A1** – The scope of the engagement should include consideration of relevant systems, records, personnel, and physical properties, including those under the control of third parties.

**2220.A2** – If significant consulting opportunities arise during an assurance engagement, a specific written understanding as to the objectives, scope, respective responsibilities and other expectations should be reached and the results of the consulting engagement communicated in accordance with consulting standards.

**2220.C1** – In performing consulting engagements, internal auditors should ensure that the scope of the engagement is sufficient to address the agreed-upon objectives. If internal auditors develop reservations about the scope during the engagement, these reservations should be discussed with the client to determine whether to continue with the engagement.

## 2230 – Engagement Resource Allocation

Internal auditors should determine appropriate resources to achieve engagement objectives. Staffing should be based on an evaluation of the nature and complexity of each engagement, time constraints, and available resources.

## 2240 – Engagement Work Program

Internal auditors should develop work programs that achieve the engagement objectives. These work programs should be recorded.

**2240.A1** – Work programs should establish the procedures for identifying, analyzing, evaluating, and recording information during the engagement. The work program should be approved prior to its implementation, and any adjustments approved promptly.

**2240.C1** – Work programs for consulting engagements may vary in form and content depending upon the nature of the engagement.

## 2300 – Performing the Engagement

Internal auditors should identify, analyze, evaluate, and record sufficient information to achieve the engagement's objectives.

## 2310 – Identifying Information

Internal auditors should identify sufficient, reliable, relevant, and useful information to achieve the engagement's objectives.

## 2320 – Analysis and Evaluation

Internal auditors should base conclusions and engagement results on appropriate analyses and evaluations.

## 2330 – Recording Information

Internal auditors should record relevant information to support the conclusions and engagement results.

**2330.A1** – The chief audit executive should control access to engagement records. The chief audit executive should obtain the approval of senior management and/or legal counsel prior to releasing such records to external parties, as appropriate.

**2330.A2** – The chief audit executive should develop retention requirements for engagement records. These retention requirements should be consistent with the organization's guidelines and any pertinent regulatory or other requirements.

**2330.C1** – The chief audit executive should develop policies governing the custody and retention of engagement records, as well as their release to internal and external parties. These policies should be consistent with the organization's guidelines and any pertinent regulatory or other requirements.

## 2340 – Engagement Supervision

Engagements should be properly supervised to ensure objectives are achieved, quality is assured, and staff is developed.

## 2400 – Communicating Results

Internal auditors should communicate the engagement results.

## 2410 – Criteria for Communicating

Communications should include the engagement's objectives and scope as well as applicable conclusions, recommendations, and action plans.

**2410.A1** – Final communication of engagement results should, where appropriate, contain the internal auditor's overall opinion and or conclusions.

**2410.A2** – Internal auditors are encouraged to acknowledge satisfactory performance in engagement communications.

**2410.A3** – When releasing engagement results to parties outside the organization, the communication should include limitations on distribution and use of the results.

**2410.C1** – Communication of the progress and results of consulting engagements will vary in form and content depending upon the nature of the engagement and the needs of the client.

## 2420 – Quality of Communications

Communications should be accurate, objective, clear, concise, constructive, complete, and timely.

## 2421 – Errors and Omissions

If a final communication contains a significant error or omission, the chief audit executive should communicate corrected information to all parties who received the original communication.

## 2430 – Engagement Disclosure of Noncompliance with the Standards

When noncompliance with the *Standards* impacts a specific engagement, communication of the results should disclose the:

- *Standard(s)* with which full compliance was not achieved,
- Reason(s) for noncompliance, and
- Impact of noncompliance on the engagement.

## 2440 – Disseminating Results

The chief audit executive should communicate results to the appropriate parties.

**2440.A1** – The chief audit executive is responsible for communicating the final results to parties who can ensure that the results are given due consideration.

**2440.A2** – If not otherwise mandated by legal, statutory or regulatory requirements, prior to releasing results to parties outside the organization, the chief audit executive should:

- Assess the potential risk to the organization.
- Consult with senior management and/or legal counsel as appropriate
- Control dissemination by restricting the use of the results.

**2440.C1** – The chief audit executive is responsible for communicating the final results of consulting engagements to clients.

**2440.C2** – During consulting engagements, risk management, control, and governance issues may be identified. Whenever these issues are significant to the organization, they should be communicated to senior management and the board.

## 2500 – Monitoring Progress

The chief audit executive should establish and maintain a system to monitor the disposition of results communicated to management.

**2500.A1** – The chief audit executive should establish a follow-up process to monitor and ensure that management actions have been effectively implemented or that senior management has accepted the risk of not taking action.

**2500.C1** – The internal audit activity should monitor the disposition of results of consulting engagements to the extent agreed upon with the client.

## 2600 – Resolution of Management's Acceptance of Risks

When the chief audit executive believes that senior management has accepted a level of residual risk that may be unacceptable to the organization, the chief audit executive should discuss the matter with senior management. If the decision regarding residual risk is not resolved, the chief audit executive and senior management should report the matter to the board for resolution.

# Glossary

**Add Value** – Value is provided by improving opportunities to achieve organizational objectives, identifying operational improvement, and/or reducing risk exposure through both assurance and consulting services.

**Adequate Control** – Present if management has planned and organized (designed) in a manner that provides reasonable assurance that the organization's risks have been managed effectively and that the organization's goals and objectives will be achieved efficiently and economically.

**Assurance Services** – An objective examination of evidence for the purpose of providing an independent assessment on risk management, control, or governance processes for the organization. Examples may include financial, performance, compliance, system security, and due diligence engagements.

**Board** – A board is an organization's governing body, such as a board of directors, supervisory board, head of an agency or legislative body, board of governors or trustees of a non profit organization, or any other designated body of the organization, including the audit committee, to whom the chief audit executive may functionally report.

**Charter** – The charter of the internal audit activity is a formal written document that defines the activity's purpose, authority, and responsibility. The charter should (a) establish the internal audit activity's position within the organization; (b) authorize access to records, personnel, and physical properties relevant to the performance of engagements; and (c) define the scope of internal audit activities.

**Chief Audit Executive** – Top position within the organization responsible for internal audit activities. Normally, this would be the internal audit director. In the case where internal audit activities are obtained from outside service providers, the chief audit executive is the person responsible for overseeing the service contract and the overall quality assurance of these activities, reporting to senior management and the board regarding internal audit activities, and follow-up of engagement results. The term also includes such titles as general auditor, chief internal auditor, and inspector general.

**Code of Ethics** – The Code of Ethics of The Institute of Internal Auditors (IIA) are Principles relevant to the profession and practice of internal auditing, and Rules of Conduct that describe behavior expected of internal auditors. The Code of Ethics applies to both parties and entities that provide internal audit services. The purpose of the Code of Ethics is to promote an ethical culture in the global profession of internal auditing.

**Compliance** – Conformity and adherence to policies, plans, procedures, laws, regulations, contracts, or other requirements.

**Conflict of Interest** – Any relationship that is or appears to be not in the best interest of the organization. A conflict of interest would prejudice an individual's ability to perform his or her duties and responsibilities objectively.

**Consulting Services** – Advisory and related client service activities, the nature and scope of which are agreed with the client and which are intended to add value and improve an organization's governance, risk management, and control processes without the internal auditor assuming management responsibility. Examples include counsel, advice, facilitation and training.

**Control** – Any action taken by management, the board, and other parties to manage risk and increase the likelihood that established objectives and goals will be achieved. Management plans, organizes, and directs the performance of sufficient actions to provide reasonable assurance that objectives and goals will be achieved.

**Control Environment** – The attitude and actions of the board and management regarding the significance of control within the organization. The control environment provides the discipline and structure for the achievement of the primary objectives of the system of internal control. The control environment includes the following elements:

- Integrity and ethical values.
- Management's philosophy and operating style.
- Organizational structure.
- Assignment of authority and responsibility.
- Human resource policies and practices.
- Competence of personnel.

**Control Processes** – The policies, procedures, and activities that are part of a control framework, designed to ensure that risks are contained within the risk tolerances established by the risk management process.

**Engagement** – A specific internal audit assignment, task, or review activity, such as an internal audit, Control Self-Assessment review, fraud examination, or consultancy. An engagement may include multiple tasks or activities designed to accomplish a specific set of related objectives.

**Engagement Objectives** – Broad statements developed by internal auditors that define intended engagement accomplishments.

**Engagement Work Program** – A document that lists the procedures to be followed during an engagement, designed to achieve the engagement plan.

**External Service Provider** – A person or firm, outside of the organization, who has special knowledge, skill, and experience in a particular discipline.

**Fraud** – Any illegal acts characterized by deceit, concealment or violation of trust. These acts are not dependent upon the application of threat of violence or of physical force. Frauds are perpetrated by parties and organizations to obtain money, property or services; to avoid payment or loss of services; or to secure personal or business advantage.

**Governance** – The combination of processes and structures implemented by the board in order to inform, direct, manage and monitor the activities of the organization toward the achievement of its objectives.

**Impairments** – Impairments to individual objectivity and organizational independence may include personal conflicts of interest, scope limitations, restrictions on access to records, personnel, and properties, and resource limitations (funding).

**Independence** – The freedom from conditions that threaten objectivity or the appearance of objectivity. Such threats to objectivity must be managed at the individual auditor, engagement, functional and organizational levels.

**Internal Audit Activity** – A department, division, team of consultants, or other practitioner(s) that provides independent, objective assurance and consulting services designed to add value and improve an organization's operations. The internal audit activity helps an organization accomplish its objectives by bringing a systematic, disciplined approach to evaluate and improve the effectiveness of risk management, control, and governance processes.

**Objectivity** – An unbiased mental attitude that *allows* internal auditors to perform engagements in such a manner that they have an honest belief in their work product and that no significant quality compromises are made. Objectivity requires internal auditors not to subordinate their judgment on audit matters to that of others.

**Residual Risks** – The risk remaining after management takes action to reduce the impact and likelihood of an adverse event, including control activities in responding to a risk.

**Risk** – The possibility of an event occurring that will have an impact on the achievement of objectives. Risk is measured in terms of impact and likelihood.

**Risk Management** – A process to identify, assess, manage, and control potential events or situations, to provide reasonable assurance regarding the achievement of the organization's objectives.

**Should** – The use of the word 'should' in the Standards represents a mandatory obligation.

**Standard** – A professional pronouncement promulgated by the Internal Auditing Standards Board that delineates the requirements for performing a broad range of internal audit activities, and for evaluating internal audit performance.

# *Practice Advisories* by Standard number

Per www.theiia.org on 1 January 2005.

| Practice Advisories, by Standard Number | Release date |
|---|---|
| Practice Advisory 1000–1: Internal Audit Charter | 5 January 2001 |
| Practice Advisory 1000.C1–1: Principles Guiding the Performance of Consulting Activities of Internal Auditors | 15 May 2001 |
| Practice Advisory 1000.C1–2: Additional Consideration for Formal Consulting Engagements | 7 January 2002 |
| Practice Advisory 1100–1: Independence and Objectivity | 5 January 2001 |
| Practice Advisory 1110–1: Organizational Independence | 5 January 2001 |
| Practice Advsiory 1110.A1–1: Disclosing Reasons for Information Requests | 5 January 2001 |
| Practice Advisory 110–2: Chief Audit Executive (CAE) Reporting Lines | 3 December 2002 |
| Practice Advisory 1120–1: Individual Objectivity | 5 January 2001 |
| Practice Advisory 1130–1: Impairments to Indepence or Objectivity | 5 January 2001 |
| Practice Advisory 1130.A1–1: Assessing Operations for Which Internal Auditors were Previously Responsible | 5 January 2001 |
| Practice Advisory 1130.A1–2: Internal Audit Responsibility for Other (Non-Audit) Functions | 1 February 2003 |
| Practice Advisory 1200–1: Proficiency and Due Professional Care | 5 January 2001 |
| Practice Advisory 1210–1: Proficiency | 5 January 2001 |
| Practice Advisory 1210.A1–1: Obtaining Services to Support or Complement the Internal Audit Activity | 5 January 2001 |
| Practice Advisory 1210.A2–1: Identification of Fraud | 5 January 2001 |
| Practice Advisory 1210.A2–2: Responsibility for Fraud Detection | 5 January 2001 |
| Practice Advisory 1220–1: Due Professional Care | 5 January 2001 |
| Practice Advisory 1230–1: Continuing Professional Development | 5 January 2001 |

Practice Advisory 1300–1: Quality Assurance and Improvement Program — 25 May 2004

Practice Advisory 1310–1: Quality Program Assessments — 19 December 2001 Rev 25 May 2004

Practice Advisory 1311–1: Internal Assessments — 19 December 2001 Rev 25 May 2004

Practice Advisory 1312–1: External Assessments — 19 December 2001 Rev 25 May 2004

Practice Advisory 1312–2: External Assessment – Self Assessment with Independent — 25 May 2004

Practice Advisory 1320–1: Reporting on the Quality Program — 5 January 2001 Rev 25 May 2004

Practice Advisory 1330–1: Use of 'Conducted in Accordance with the Standards' — 21 February 2003 Rev 12 February 2004

Practice Advisory 2000–1: Managing the Internal Audit Activity — 5 January 2001

Practice Advisory 2010–1: Planning — 5 January 2001

Practice Advisory 2010–2: Linking the Audit Plan to Risk and Exposures — 7 March 2001

Practice Advisory 2020–1: Communication and Approval — 5 January 2001

Practice Advisory 2030–1: Resource Management — 5 January 2001

Practice Advisory 2040–1: Policies and Procedures — 5 January 2001

Practice Advisory 2050–1: Coordination — 5 January 2001

Practice Advisory 2050–2: Acquisition of External Audit Services — 7 February 2002

Practice Advisory 2060–1: Reporting to Board and Senior Management — 5 January 2001

Practice Advisory 2060–2: Relationship with the Audit Committee — 3 December 2002

Practice Advisory 2100–1: Nature of Work — 5 January 2001

Practice Advisory 2100–2: Information Security — 1 February 2001

Practice Advisory 2100–3: Internal Audit's Role in the Risk Management Process — 7 March 2001

Practice Advisory 2100–4: Internal Audit's Role in Organizations Without a Risk Management Process — 7 March 2001

Practice Advisory 2100–4: Legal Considerations in Evaluating Regulatory Compliance Programs — 28 March 2001

Practice Advisory 2100–6: Control and Audit Implications of e-Commerce Activities — 12 June 2003

Practice Advisory 2100–7: The Internal Auditor's Role in Identifying and Reporting Environmental Risks — 12 June 2003

# Index to IIA Practice Advisories – by topic

Per www.theiia.org on 1 January 2005.

## Audit charter

## Assumption of non-audit duties

## CAE responsibilities

## Compliance with the Standards

## Consulting

# Disclosures

# Engagement communications

# Engagement performance

## Engagement planning and scope

## Engagement workpapers

## Governance

## Independence and objectivity

## Internal control

## Outsourcing or co-sourcing

## Risk-based planning

# Government Internal Audit Standards

The Standards for the Professional Practice of Internal Auditing of The Institute of Internal Auditors Inc are reproduced at APPENDIX 2.

The following are the standards published by the Audit Policy and Advice Unit in HM Treasury, July 2001. To check for updates, visit www.hm-treasury.gov.uk/ Documents/Public_Spending_and_Services/ Guidance_for_Government_Departments/, and for this guidance in particular see www.hm-treasury.gov.uk/Documents/Public_Spending_and_Services/ Guidance_for_Government_Departments/pss_ggd_gias.cfm?

## Contents

## *Introduction*

Government accounting requires Accounting Officers, in accordance with their terms of appointment, to make provision for internal audit in accordance with the standards set out in the Government Internal Audit Manual.

The definition of internal audit, code of ethics and accompanying Standards for the professional practice of internal audit in central government organisations which are subject to the provisions of government accounting are addressed to both accounting officers and to heads of internal audit. The definition and Standards have been updated to reflect the Institute of Internal Auditor's new Standards, so aiming to minimise any possible conflict for internal auditors in government who are members of the Institute. They nevertheless continue to reflect both the unique accountability structures of central government, and the developing nature of internal audit as it continues, in a context of rapid change and development, to add value[1] to the organisations it serves (see below for a definition of internal audit).

We hope they will also prove beneficial (as have previous Standards and versions of the Government Internal Audit Manual) to the wider public sector.

The Standards define the way in which the internal audit service should be established and undertake its functions. They cover both assurance-related and consultancy work. They apply equally to internal audit services which are provided by in-house audit units, by in-house audit units under service level agreements following market tests, and by external contractors who provide either partial services in support of an in-house team or the whole internal audit service.

The Standards form two groupings. The first encompasses the organisational and structural aspects of internal audit; the second encompasses the activity and operation of internal audit:

| Organisational Standards | Operational Standards |
|---|---|
| 1. Scope of internal audit | 6. Audit strategy |
| 2. Independence | 7. Management of audit assignments |
| 3. Audit committees | 8. Due professional care |
| 4 Relationships with management, other auditors and other review bodies | 9. Reporting |
| 5. Staffing, training and development | 10. Quality assurance |

If any organisation subject to these Standards knowingly (unavoidably or deliberately) does not comply with them on a long-term basis, the reasons for the non compliance should be documented and discussed with HM Treasury.

## Definition of internal audit

Internal audit is an independent and objective appraisal service within an organisation.

- Internal audit primarily provides an independent and objective opinion to the accounting officer[2] on risk management, control and governance, by measuring and evaluating their effectiveness in achieving the organisation's agreed objectives.[3] In addition, internal audit's findings and recommendations are beneficial to line management in the audited areas. Risk management, control and governance comprise the policies, procedures and operations established to ensure the achievement of objectives, the appropriate assessment of risk, the reliability of internal and external reporting and accountability processes, compliance with applicable laws and regulations, and compliance with the behavioural and ethical Standards set for the organisation.

- Internal audit also provides an independent and objective consultancy service specifically to help line management improve the organisation's risk management, control and governance. The service applies the professional skills of internal audit through a systematic and disciplined evaluation of the policies, procedures and operations that management put in place to ensure the achievement of the organisation's objectives, and through recommendations for improvement. Such consultancy work contributes to the opinion which internal audit provides on risk management, control and governance.

## Code of ethics for internal auditors in central government

The purpose of this code of ethics is to set the central and local Standards for the performance and conduct of the staff and units to which it applies. This code is intended to clarify the standard of conduct expected from all members of the internal audit unit when carrying out their duties. The code applies to all staff and units who are required to comply with the Government Internal Audit Standards, but does not supersede or replace the Civil Service Code.

There are four main principles that should be observed:

- integrity;
- objectivity;
- competency; and
- confidentiality.

### *Integrity*

All members of the internal audit team should demonstrate integrity in all aspects of their work. The relationship with fellow colleagues and external contacts should be one of honesty and fairness. This establishes an environment of trust which provides the basis for reliance on all activities carried out by the internal audit team.

### *Objectivity*

Objectivity is a state of mind that has regard to all considerations relevant to the activity or process being examined without being unduly influenced by personal interest or the views of others. Members of the internal audit team should display appropriate professional objectivity when providing their opinions, assessments and recommendations.

## Competency

Members of the internal audit team should apply the knowledge, skills and experience needed in the performance of their duties. They should carry out their work to the Standards set out in the Government Internal Audit Standard. They should not accept or perform work that they are not competent to undertake unless they receive adequate advice and support to competently carry out the work.

## Confidentiality

Members of the internal audit team should safeguard the information they receive in carrying out their duties. There should not be any unauthorised disclosure of information unless there is a legal or professional requirement to do so.

Confidential information gained in the course of audit duties should not be used to effect personal gain.

# Organisational Standards

## *1. Scope of internal audit*

### 1.1 Provision of terms of reference

1.1.1 The purpose, authority and responsibility of internal audit should be formally defined by the accounting officer in terms of reference set out below.
   (a)   Are consistent with the definition of internal auditing and with these Standards.
   (b)   Specify the requirements for the appointment of the head of internal audit and their staff, including professional skills and experience.
   (c)   Establish the responsibilities and objectives of internal audit.
   (d)   Establish the relationship of the head of internal audit with the accounting officer and audit committee.
   (e)   Establish the relationship between the head of internal audit and accounting officers or third parties to be reported to.[4] The terms of reference should specify that heads of internal audit should review any such report with their accounting officer and audit committee prior to publication.
   (f)   Establish the organisational independence of internal audit, including the direct accountability of internal audit to the accounting officer and make appropriate provision for the objective assessment of the resource requirements of internal audit.
   (g)   Embrace the risk management, control and governance processes of the organisation including all its operations, resources, services, and responsibilities for other bodies.
   (h)   Enable the head of internal audit to deliver an audit opinion of the nature specified by the accounting officer.
   (I)   Define the consultancy role of internal audit.

(j)     Establish internal audit's right of access to all records, assets, personnel and premises, and its authority to obtain such information as it considers necessary to fulfil its responsibilities.

1.1.2  The head of internal audit should advise the accounting officer on the content of the terms of reference and should regularly consider whether any amendment is required.

## 1.2    Scope of work

1.2.1  Internal audit should fulfil its terms of reference by systematic review and evaluation of risk management, control and governance which comprises the policies, procedures and operations in place to:

(a)     Establish, and monitor the achievement of, the organisation's objectives.

(b)     Identify, assess and manage the risks to achieving the organisation's objectives.

(c)     Advise on, formulate, and evaluate policy, within the responsibilities of the accounting officer.

(d)     Ensure the economical, effective and efficient use of resources.

(e)     Ensure compliance with established policies (including behavioural and ethical expectations), procedures, laws and regulations.

(f)     Safeguard the organisation's assets and interests from losses of all kinds, including those arising from fraud, irregularity or corruption.

(g)     Ensure the integrity and reliability of information, accounts and data, including internal and external reporting and accountability processes.

1.2.2  Internal audit should devote particular attention to any aspects of the risk management, control and governance affected by material changes to the organisation's risk environment.

1.2.3  If the head of internal audit or the audit committee consider that the level of audit resources or the terms of reference in any way limit the scope of internal audit, or prejudice the ability of internal audit to deliver a service consistent with the definition of internal auditing, they should advise the accounting officer in a formal minute, emphasising the consequent limitations to the scope and value of the head of internal audit's opinion and the risks which may arise as a result. If the accounting officer decides to accept any such limitation, this decision should be recorded formally. (Standard 6.1.10.)

## 1.3    Responsibilities in respect of other bodies

1.3.1  The head of internal audit should make provision for the derivation of appropriate opinion about:

(a)     control over any subsidiary bodies;

(b)     the adequacy of the arrangements for internal audit in any subsidiary bodies (Standard 10.1);

(c)     control in inter-departmental or cross-cutting systems; and

(d)     control in contractors or service providers where that control is material to the achievement of organisational objectives.

1.3.2 Internal audit should decide whether to conduct the work to derive the required opinions themselves or rely on the opinions provided by other auditors.

1.3.3 The head of internal audit should advise on the provision of relevant access rights in the drafting of contracts let by the organisation.

## 1.4   Fraud

1.4.1 Audit procedures alone, even when performed with due professional care, cannot guarantee that fraud will be detected. Internal audit should not have responsibility for the prevention or detection of fraud. However internal auditors should be alert in all their work to risks and exposures that could allow fraud.

1.4.2 Managing the risk of fraud is the responsibility of line management. Line management may establish a functionally independent fraud detection and prevention organisation. Where they establish a separate fraud unit, the relationship between this organisation's head and the head of internal audit should be formally defined.

1.4.3 The head of internal audit should arrange to be informed of all suspected or detected fraud so that they can consider the adequacy of the relevant controls, evaluate the implication of the fraud for their opinion of the risk management, control and governance, and consider making recommendations to line managers regarding any need for more detailed investigation and improvement in control.

## 2.   Independence

### 2.1   The principles of independence

2.1.1 Internal audit should be sufficiently independent of the activities which it audits to enable auditors to perform their duties in a manner which facilitates impartial and effective professional judgements and recommendations. They should have no executive responsibilities.

2.1.2 Accountability for the response to the advice and recommendations of internal audit lies with the line managers who either accept and implement the advice or formally reject it. Audit advice and recommendations are without prejudice to the right of internal audit to review the relevant policies, procedures and operations at a later date.

### 2.2   Organisational independence

2.2.1 Internal audit is primarily a service to, and should report directly to the accounting officer. Internal audit may also have additional or secondary reporting lines to other accounting officers for the audit of cross cutting projects or to external bodies in cases where internal audit is appointed for the delivery of compliance and other assurances required by regulators or other authorities.

2.2.2 The accounting officer should be advised on the discharge of their responsibilities in respect of internal audit by their audit committee. In particular (amongst its other responsibilities), the audit committee should advise on internal audit in accordance with Standard 3.2. The audit committee should not obstruct the head of internal audit's direct access to the accounting officer (Standard 9.1.6).

2.2.3 The accounting officer should make appropriate arrangements for the routine provision and management of the budget and resources of internal audit (including staff appraisal arrangements) without prejudice to the direct accountability of internal audit to the accounting officer. These arrangements will normally involve delegation of these particular responsibilities to the principal finance officer.

## 2.3 Status of the head of internal audit

The head of internal audit should be graded with sufficient status to facilitate the effective discussion and negotiation of the results of internal audit work with senior management in the organisation. Evaluation tools used to grade the post should give due weight to the influence of the head of internal audit on the risk management, control and governance of the organisation.

## 2.4 Independence of individual auditors

2.4.1 Individual auditors should have an impartial, unbiased attitude, characterised by integrity and an objective approach to work, and should avoid conflicts of interest. They should not allow external factors to compromise their professional judgement.

2.4.2 Objectivity is presumed to be impaired when individual auditors review any activity in which they have previously had executive responsibility, or in which they have provided consultancy advice. Auditors should not be assigned to assurance work in business areas where they have had an executive or other involvement, and where the head of internal audit deems that this may impair their objectivity, until a suitable period has elapsed. The head of internal audit should develop appropriate guidelines for determining the duration of such periods.

2.4.3 Long-term responsibility for the audit of a particular aspect of an organisation can also affect independence; assignment of ongoing audit responsibilities should be rotated from time to time.

## 2.5 Independence of audit contractors

Objectivity could be impaired if an audit contractor also provides other services to the organisation. Steps should be taken to avoid or manage such conflicts of interest.

## 2.6 Declaration of conflict of interest

2.6.1 Individual auditors should declare any conflicts of interest arising from audit work assigned to them by the head of internal audit. Such potential conflicts of interest include previous executive or consultancy responsibilities and personal relationships with staff with current executive responsibilities.

2.6.2 Internal audit should plan the allocation of audit work to minimise the risk of conflicts of interest whenever possible.

# 3. Audit committees

*This Standard only encompasses internal audit issues and does not define the full role or constitution of an audit committee.*

## 3.1 Principles of the audit committee

The 'Policy Principles for Audit Committees in Central Government'[5] provide that the accounting officer should establish an audit committee unless there are clearly identified reasons for the decision not to.

## 3.2 Internal audit issues on which the accounting officer should seek the audit committee's advice

The accounting officer should ask the audit committee to advise them on:
(a)   the skill, experience and competency requirements for the post of head of internal audit;
(b)   the terms of reference for internal audit;
(c)   the effectiveness of the internal audit strategy and periodic plan in addressing the organisation's risks;
(d)   the resourcing of internal audit;
(e)   the periodic work plans of internal audit, and material changes to these plans the head of internal audit's annual and interim audit report(s) and any implications arising from their findings and opinion;
(f)   the arrangements for and the results of quality assurance processes;
(g)   the adequacy of management response to internal audit advice and recommendations; and
(h)   the arrangements made for co-operation between internal audit, external audit and other review bodies.

## 3.3 The head of internal audit's relationship with the audit committee

3.3.1 The head of internal audit should attend audit committee meetings unless, exceptionally, the audit committee decides they should be excluded from either the whole meeting or particular agenda item(s). The reasons for any such exclusion should be made known to the accounting officer.

3.3.2 The head of internal audit should have a right of access to the chair of the audit committee to discuss any issues they wish to raise.

## 4. Relationships with management, other auditors and other review bodies

### 4.1 Principles of good relationships

Heads of internal audit should co-ordinate internal audit plans and activities with line managers, other internal auditors, external audit and other review agencies to ensure the most effective audit coverage is achieved and duplication of effort is minimised.

### 4.2 Relationships with management

4.2.1 Internal audit provides a service to management. Its strategy, planning and delivery should aim to maximise the value added for management without jeopardising internal audit's responsibilities to the accounting officer.

4.2.2 Management and staff at all levels of the organisation should have complete confidence in the integrity, independence and capability of internal audit. The relationship between internal auditors and line managers is a privileged one, and information gained in the course of audit work should remain confidential to those with a legitimate interest within the organisation.

4.2.3 Co-operative relationships with line management enhance the ability of internal audit to achieve its objectives effectively. Audit work should be planned in conjunction with management as far as possible, particularly in respect of the timing of audit work (except where unannounced visits are essential to the achievement of the audit objectives).

4.2.4 When fraud is suspected or detected, decisions to involve external agencies such as the police should be taken by line management. If internal audit does not consider that line management have made appropriate decisions in this respect, this should be reported internally to the accounting officer.

### 4.3 Relationships with other internal auditors

Where internal auditors need to work with internal auditors of another organisation (for example, in interdepartmental systems or cross cutting projects), the roles and responsibilities of each party should be agreed and endorsed by each accounting officer. Whenever possible agreement to joint working or to placing professional reliance on work carried out by one party should be sought.

### 4.4 Relationships with external auditors[6]

4.4.1 Internal audit should seek to meet regularly with the external auditor to consult on audit plans, discuss matters of mutual interest, discuss common understanding of audit techniques, methods and terminology, and to seek opportunities for co-operation in the conduct of audit work. In particular, internal audit should offer the external auditor the opportunity to rely on their work where appropriate, provided this does not prejudice internal audit's independence.

4.4.2 In any case of conflict with the external auditor, the head of internal audit will consult with, or refer the matter to, the accounting officer.

### 4.5 Relationships with other review bodies

4.5.1 Where other assurance and review bodies such as management inspection or compliance teams are in place, internal audit should look for opportunities to gain assurance from, and place reliance on, their work. If it is intended to place formal reliance on work by such bodies, an appropriate audit or quality assurance exercise should be carried out to ensure that each body's work is carried out to a suitable standard to enable reliance.

4.5.2 The head of internal audit should establish a means to gain an overview of other assurance providers' work to enable them to identify and consider individual or common material issues or themes emerging. If appropriate, they should be reported to the accounting officer.

## 5. Staffing, training and development

### 5.1 Principles of staffing, training and development

Internal audit should be appropriately staffed in terms of numbers, grades, qualification levels, and experience, having regard to its objectives and to these Standards. Internal auditors should be properly trained to fulfil their responsibilities and should maintain their professional competence through an appropriate ongoing development programme.[7]

### 5.2 The Government Internal Audit Certificate

5.2.1 The Government Internal Audit Certificate (GIAC) defines the minimum level of skill, knowledge and experience required of an internal auditor.

5.2.2 The head of internal audit should be both GIAC-qualified and have a wide experience of management.

5.2.3 All internal audits should be led or supervised by internal auditors who hold the GIAC.

### 5.3 Staffing the internal audit unit

5.3.1 The head of internal audit is responsible for ensuring that they have access to the full range of knowledge, skills, qualifications and experience to meet the unit's audit objectives and these Standards. In addition to internal audit skills, the head of internal audit should specify any other professional skills which may be needed by the internal audit unit. They should also make provision for appropriate administrative support.

5.3.2 The head of internal audit is responsible for recruiting staff with the appropriate intellectual qualities, personal attributes, and qualifications (or perceived ability to undertake professional training).

5.3.3 The head of internal audit may appoint non GIAC-holders to the internal audit unit where they deem such appointees' specialist knowledge, training and experience enhances the organisation's overall audit capability, and does not jeopardise its compliance with these Standards.

5.3.4 The head of internal audit should set criteria for the appointment of the more senior staff in the internal audit unit based on demonstration of training and experience in accordance with the competencies framework in the 'Internal Audit Training and Development Handbook'.

### 5.4 Continuing professional development

5.4.1 All internal auditors should undertake a programme of continuing professional development to maintain and develop their skills. They should maintain a record of such training activities.

5.4.2 Heads of internal audit should ensure that appropriate provision is made for maintaining and developing the competence of audit staff. They should monitor the ongoing training activity of all staff in their internal audit unit.

## Operational Standards

### *6.  Audit strategy*

#### 6.1   Developing the internal audit strategy

6.1.1 The head of internal audit should develop and maintain a strategy for providing the accounting officer, economically and efficiently, with objective evaluation of, and opinions on, the effectiveness of the organisation's risk management, control and governance arrangements.[8] The head of internal audit's opinions are a key element of the framework of assurance and the accounting officer needs to inform their completion of the annual Statement of Internal Control (SIC).[9]

6.1.2 The strategy should also aim to add value for the organisation's line managers by providing them with audit analyses, findings and recommendations. In addition, where internal audit judge it appropriate, they can offer consultancy to support management in implementing the recommendations.

6.1.3 The strategy should be developed to meet the audit needs of the organisation, as assessed by the head of internal audit, using the organisation's objectives and risk assessment as a primary resource.

6.1.4 The strategy should include provision for the head of internal audit to consider, at least annually, the adequacy of the organisation's risk assessment and, if necessary, make recommendations for its review.

6.1.5 The strategy should include a systematic and prioritised review of how effectively the organisation's risks are managed by its policies, procedures and operations.

6.1.6 The head of internal audit should consider any risk which they think may be material to the organisation's risk management, control and governance, even if it is not included in management's risk priorities.

6.1.7 The strategy should establish the resources and skills required for its delivery.

6.1.8 The strategy should describe the audit techniques selected as the most effective for delivering the audit objectives.

6.1.9  The strategy should set out the relative allocation of audit resources between assurance work and consultancy work. The exact allocation will be determined in the periodic plans.

6.1.10 The strategy should be approved by the accounting officer. This approval should include acceptance of risks or other areas of potential audit coverage which cannot be resourced, and identification of consequent residual risk exposure. The accounting officer should be advised by the head of internal audit that they are responsible for that residual exposure. (Standard 1.2.3).

#### 6.2   Developing the periodic audit plans

6.2.1 Internal audit should prepare periodic work plans, designed to implement the audit strategy, for approval by the accounting officer.

6.2.2 The periodic plans should set out details of the assignments to be carried out in the period covered by the plan, providing sufficient detail for the accounting officer and management to understand the assignments' purpose and scope. They should establish the broad resources and skills required for each assignment, and should set relative priorities for each assignment. These periodic plans should be approved by the accounting officer.

6.2.3 The periodic audit plans should be kept under review to identify any amendment needed to reflect changing priorities and emerging audit needs. They should make provision for an element of contingency to accommodate audit assignments which could not have been reasonably foreseen. Material changes to the periodic audit plans should be approved by the accounting officer.

# 7.   Management of audit assignments

## 7.1   Planning

7.1.1 For each audit assignment a detailed plan should be prepared and discussed with relevant line managers. These plans should establish detailed objectives for the assignment, the level of assurance that management wishes to derive from the opinion to be delivered, resource requirements, audit outputs and target dates. They should set out:
   (a)   the scope and objectives and timing of the work to be done, allocating internal audit resources and establishing their targets;
   (b)   any requirements for participation by line management including supplying IT system or other data to the auditors;
   (c)   the schedule and timing of the assignment; and
   (d)   to whom the assignment findings will be disclosed (without prejudice to the right of disclosure of all audit findings to the accounting officer). For audits of cross cutting projects, the assignment plan should clearly identify the reporting lines to each accounting officer involved.

7.1.2 Internal audit should seek a 'sponsor' for each assignment. This will normally be the manager with overall responsibility for the business risk area to be audited.

7.1.3 Assignment plans should be agreed with the sponsor before work is done, and the agreement recorded. They should take account of any concerns of the sponsor about aspects of the policies, procedures and operations within the area to be audited. Any material objection to the assignment plans which cannot be resolved by negotiation should be referred to the accounting officer.

## 7.2   Approach

7.2.1 Assignments intended to provide an audit opinion should be approached using a risk based systematic approach which should clearly:
   (a)   identify and record the objectives, risks and controls;
   (b)   establish the congruence of the objectives with higher level corporate objectives;

(c)    evaluate management's risk analysis, taking account of their acceptance of specific risks;

(d)    evaluate the controls in principle to decide whether or not they are appropriate and can be reasonably relied upon to achieve their purpose;

(e)    identify any instances of over-control;

(f)    evaluate the impact of any decision by management to accept risk(s) rather than transfer or control them;

(g)    determine an appropriate strategy to test the effectiveness of risk management and controls; and

(h)    arrive at conclusions and report, making recommendations as necessary and providing an opinion on the effectiveness of risk management and control in the audited area.

7.2.2 The scope and objectives, timing, and reporting arrangements should be defined and agreed for consultancy assignments in the same way as for assurance assignments. The objectives should make it clear that the internal auditors' involvement is in a consultancy role. The head of internal audit will reserve the right to audit any risk management, control and governance processes developed with internal audit acting in its consultancy role.

7.2.3 Internal auditors should apply the risk-based systematic audit approach by independent acquisition and examination of relevant evidence or by using risk and control evaluation methods.[10] At each stage of the assignment, auditors should consider what specific audit work needs to be conducted or to what extent review of evidenced management activity is sufficient to support an independent and objective audit opinion.

7.2.4 Audit opinion can also be derived by the use of supplementary audit techniques and approaches.[11]

7.2.5 The head of internal audit should develop local policies for the way in which assignment level opinion will be expressed, including definition of any terms of quantification.

7.2.6 Auditors should obtain and record sufficient relevant evidence to support their conclusions and to demonstrate the adequacy of evidence obtained to support professional judgements.

7.2.7 Internal audit should review their findings with the sponsor, making recommendations for dealing with any weaknesses and offering consultancy support if appropriate.

7.2.8 The head of internal audit should inform the accounting officer of any remaining material weaknesses. The head of internal audit should develop standards and retention requirements for all audit records and documentation, whether they are held on paper or electronically. They should control access to audit records and should obtain the approval of relevant management before releasing records to external parties (except where the National Audit Office has a right of access).

## 7.3 Follow-up

7.3.1 Internal audit should follow-up assignments. Follow-up will be a review of the effectiveness of management's response to assignments' findings and recommendations. The follow-up findings should be reviewed with the sponsor before being reported.

7.3.2 The head of internal audit should develop escalation procedures for any management responses which they judge to be inadequate in relation to the identified risk. These procedures should ensure that the risks of not taking action have been understood and accepted at a sufficiently senior management level.

7.3.3 Where follow-up reveals a change in the audit opinion, this change should be reported to the sponsor.

## 8. Due professional care

### 8.1 Principles of due professional care

8.1.1 Due professional care is the care and skill that a reasonably prudent and competent internal auditor will apply in performing their duties.
- Due care is working with competence and diligence. It does not imply infallibility or extraordinary performance.
- Due professional care is the use of audit skills and judgement based on appropriate experience, training (including continuing professional development), ability, integrity and objectivity.

8.1.2 Due professional care should be appropriate to the objectives, complexity, nature and materiality of the audit being performed.

8.1.3 Due professional care is achieved by adherence to these Standards.

### 8.2 Conduct of the individual auditor

Individual auditors are responsible for ensuring that they conduct their own work with due professional care. They should:
(a) be fair and not allow prejudice or bias to override objectivity;
(b) declare any conflicts of interest;
(c) not accept any gifts, inducements, or other benefits from employees, clients, suppliers or other third parties;
(d) consider and document the work needed to achieve audit objectives and the work which they perform in the course of an audit;
(e) consider and document the management or other criteria which they use in evaluation of audit findings;
(f) use all reasonable care in obtaining sufficient, relevant and reliable evidence on which to base their conclusions;
(g) be alert to the possibility of intentional wrongdoing, errors and omissions, inefficiency, waste, lack of economy, ineffectiveness, failure to comply with management policy, and conflicts of interest;
(h) have sufficient knowledge to identify indicators that fraud may have been committed;
(i) disclose any indicators identified that fraud may have been committed and recommend any further investigation which may be appropriate;
(j) disclose all material facts known to them which if not disclosed could distort their reports or conceal unlawful practice;
(k) disclose in reports any non-compliance with these Standards; and
(l) not use information which they obtain in the course of their duties for personal benefit or gain.

## 8.3 Organisational arrangements for due professional care

8.3.1 The head of internal audit should develop a programme of review to ensure that due professional care is achieved. This will principally be achieved through quality assurance methodologies (Standard 10).

8.3.2 The head of internal audit should ensure that appropriate processes are available for individual auditors to disclose any suspicions of fraud or improper conduct.

8.3.3 The head of internal audit should make provision in their plans for the basic training and continuing professional development of all internal audit staff, including themselves (Standard 5).

# 9. *Reporting*

## 9.1 Principles of reporting

9.1.1 The head of internal audit should determine the way in which audit findings will be reported, subject to the provisions of these Standards and the requirements of the accounting officer and any third parties.

9.1.2 The head of internal audit should set local Standards for all reports.

9.1.3 Internal audit should agree with report recipients the form and medium of those report(s), without prejudice to Standards 9.1.1 and 9.1.2.

9.1.4 All audit findings should be promptly reported to the sponsor.

9.1.5 A written audit report should be issued to the sponsor, at the close of each individual audit assignment undertaken in accordance with Standard 9.2.

9.1.6 The head of internal audit should provide a written report to the accounting officer timed to support their Statement of Internal Control.

9.1.7 The head of internal audit should be entitled to report any risk management, control or governance issue directly to the accounting officer.

## 9.2 Assignment recording and reporting

9.2.1 Internal audit's records of each assignment should include:
  (a)   the objectives and scope of the assignment;
  (b)   how these objectives have been achieved;
  (c)   a description of the objectives of the business area covered by the assignment;
  (d)   the risks, controls and all other material factors examined by the assignment; together with the evaluation criteria employed by the auditors (including an explanation of criteria formulated by the auditors rather than by management);
  (e)   an evaluation of the effectiveness of the risk management, disclosing weaknesses and non-effectiveness, over-control and poor value-for-money;
  (f)   the opinion given;
  (g)   any recommendations for improvement;
  (h)   any areas of disagreement between the auditor and management which cannot be resolved by discussion;

(i) disclosure of any relevant non-compliance with any of these Standards in the conduct of the audit and the reasons for the non-compliance;

(j) any indicators of fraud which may have been detected; and

(k) a record of how all these have been reported to the sponsor.

9.2.2 The head of internal audit should set Standards for reporting and should make arrangements for the review and approval of reports by audit management before issue.

9.2.3 A written report or reports should be issued to the sponsor at the conclusion of the assignment, encompassing at least (c), (d), (e), (f) and (g) from 9.2.1 above. Any audit findings presenting material concerns should be reported to the sponsor as soon as possible.

9.2.4 Reports should be clear, concise, and constructive. They should be issued promptly and within laid down timescales.

9.2.5 Reports should be security classified in accordance with organisational policies and with the material covered by the report to avoid unauthorised disclosure of material which would otherwise be subject to a security classification.

9.2.6 Reports should not be issued to third parties without the knowledge of relevant management.

9.2.7 In the event of a material error being discovered in a report this should be corrected and communicated to all who received copies of the report.

## 9.3 Annual reporting and presentation of audit opinion

9.3.1 The head of internal audit's formal annual report to the accounting officer should present their opinion of the overall adequacy and effectiveness of the organisation's risk management, control and governance processes. It should also:

(a) disclose any qualifications to that opinion, together with the reasons for the qualification;

(b) present a summary of the audit work undertaken to formulate the opinion, including reliance placed on work by other assurance bodies and accredited by internal audit;

(c) draw the accounting officer's attention to any issues the head of internal audit judges particularly relevant to their preparation of the Statement on Internal Control;

(d) compare work actually undertaken with the work which was planned and summarise performance of the internal audit function against its performance measures and criteria; and

(e) comment on compliance with these Standards and communicate the results of the internal audit quality assurance programme.

9.3.2 In addition to the formal annual report, the head of internal audit should make arrangements for interim reporting to the accounting officer in the course of the year. Such interim reports should address emerging issues in respect of the whole range of areas to be covered in the formal annual report. The head of internal audit should also provide information required by the accounting officer or audit committee on an *ad hoc* basis.

# 10. Quality assurance

## 10.1 Principles of quality assurance

10.1.1 The work of internal audit should be controlled at each level of operation to ensure that a continuously effective level of performance, compliant with these Standards, is being maintained.

10.1.2 The head of internal audit should develop a quality assurance programme designed to gain assurance by both internal and external review that the work of internal audit, including internal audit within their organisation's subsidiary bodies, is compliant with these Standards and achieves its objectives, and to sustain a commentary on compliance with these Standards in the annual audit report.

## 10.2 Management of internal audit

10.2.1 The head of internal audit should establish policies and procedures in a local audit manual to guide staff. The form and content of this manual should be appropriate to the size of the audit unit. At a minimum the manual should include audit's role and responsibilities, documentation Standards, local reporting Standards and targets, training requirements and expectations, and audit performance measures and indicators.

10.2.2 The head of internal audit should ensure that internal audit staff at all levels are appropriately supervised throughout all audit assignments to monitor progress, assess quality and coach staff. Supervision should include:
  (a) ensuring compliance with these Standards and local manuals;
  (b) providing suitable instructions at the outset of an audit;
  (c) approving audit objectives and work plans;
  (d) ensuring audits are conducted as planned or that variations are approved;
  (e) ensuring that appropriate audit techniques are used;
  (f) ensuring that audit findings, conclusions and recommendations are adequately supported by relevant and sufficient evidence;
  (g) ensuring that reports are accurate, objective, clear, concise and timely; and
  (h) ensuring that work is achieved within resource budgets, or variations are approved.

10.2.3 The extent of supervision will depend on the experience and training of the individual auditor. Particular care should be taken to ensure that all work by trainee auditors is subject to comprehensive supervision and that trainee auditors never work without the supervision of a professionally qualified auditor.

10.2.4 The head of internal audit should establish a set of performance measures and criteria for the internal audit function. Where there is a service level agreement or a contract, the performance measures and criteria should be contained within it. These measures and criteria should be approved by the accounting officer.

10.2.5 Supervisors should regularly discuss auditors' performance with them and identify any areas in which improvement or training is required.

## 10.3 Internal quality review

10.3.1 The head of internal audit should make provision for internal quality reviews to be undertaken periodically by experienced members of the internal audit function. These reviews should be undertaken at least every other year.

10.3.2 Internal reviews should appraise:
  (a) the quality of audit work;
  (b) the quality of supervision;
  (c) compliance with these Standards;
  (d) compliance with the local audit manual;
  (e) the ways in which the internal audit function adds value to the organisation; and
  (f) achievement of performance standards/indicators.

10.3.3 The sponsor for internal reviews should be the head of internal audit who should include comment on the results of such reviews in the annual audit report. Following an internal quality review the internal auditors involved should develop an action plan for addressing any weaknesses identified.

10.3.4 Internal reviews should be conducted by reviewing a range of completed and current audit assignments.

10.3.5 Internal reviews should be conducted according to a review programme approved by the head of internal audit, and should themselves be subject to the principles of objectivity and the acquisition of evidence contained in these Standards.

## 10.4 External quality review

10.4.1 The head of internal audit should make provision for external quality reviews to be commissioned periodically from appropriately qualified and independent reviewers. These reviews should be undertaken at least once every five years. External quality reviews should appraise:
  (a) the terms of reference for the internal audit function;
  (b) the independence and objectivity of internal audit;
  (c) the efficiency and effectiveness of the approach to formulating the audit strategy and plans;
  (d) the quality of supervision;
  (e) compliance with these Standards;
  (f) compliance with the local audit manual; and
  (g) achievement of performance Standards/indicators.

10.4.2 The sponsor for external quality reviews should be the accounting officer, who should discuss the results with the head of internal audit. Following an external quality review the head of internal audit should develop a programme for addressing any weaknesses identified and agree an action plan with the accounting officer. Progress against any such action plans should be reported upon in the annual audit report.

---

[1]    The way in which internal audit adds value is set-out in the 'Definition of Internal Audit'.

[2]    In the case of NDPBs the opinion may also be given to the statutory board where it has an executive function.

3      Audit work designed to deliver opinion on the risk management, control and governance of the organisation is referred to in these Standards as 'assurance work' because management use the audit opinion to derive assurance about the effectiveness of their controls.

4      Heads of Internal Audit in Executive Agencies or NDPBs may also be required to provide reports to the Accounting Officer of the sponsoring department. Again, some departmental Heads of Internal Audit may be required to report to the EC on aspects of their departments' control of expenditure of European funds.

5      Published by HM Treasury, December 2000

6      Detailed guidance on co-operation between internal and external auditors is contained in a good practice guide published jointly by the National Audit Office and HM Treasury

7      Detailed guidance on training requirements for Internal Auditors in central government is contained in the 'Internal Audit Training and Development Handbook' published by HM Treasury.

8      Where the Head of Internal Audit must also report to another Accounting Officer or to a third party the strategy should also set out how this requirement is to be met, including the timing of any such reports.

9      The Statement of Internal Control requires Accounting Officers to acknowledge their personal responsibility for the effective governance of their organisation; to confirm that they have, within the period covered by the Statement of Internal Control, reviewed the adequacy and effectiveness of the controls, and that any material weaknesses identified by the review have been addressed.

10     Such methods include Control and Risk Self-Assessment.

11     The full range of such techniques available to the internal auditor are described in the GIAM Best Practice guides which support these Standards.

*Appendix 5*

# Content Specification Outlines for the Certified Internal Auditor professional qualification of The Institute of Internal Auditors

Commencing 2003 The Institute of Internal Auditors, within their Certified Internal Auditor (CIA) content specification outlines (CSOs – which we would call 'syllabuses') have dropped the 'understanding' level and now distinguish only between 'proficiency' and 'awareness' levels:

> '**Proficiency** – Candidate is able to exhibit the competency in understanding and applying the subject matter in the workplace on a regular basis with skill and expertise.'

> '**Awareness** – Candidate exhibits awareness and knowledge. Candidate is able to define terms, recognise issues, and recall facts about the issues.'

Until 2003 the CSOs had defined 'understanding' as follows:

> '**Understanding** – Candidate exhibits sound understanding and ability to apply the competency. Candidates should understand relationships and problems involving the competency and apply the competency to new and different settings and the solution of problems.'

## CIA Syllabus 2004

*Part I: The internal audit activity's role in governance, risk, and control*

**Format: 125 multiple-choice questions**
**A.     Comply with The IIA's Attribute Standards**

**(Proficiency Level)**                                      **(15–25%)**

    1.    Define purpose, authority, and responsibility of the internal audit activity

        a.    Determine if the purpose, authority, and responsibility of the internal audit activity are clearly documented and approved.

        b.    Determine if the purpose, authority, and responsibility of the internal audit activity are communicated to the engagement clients

        c.    Demonstrate an understanding of the purpose, authority, and responsibility of the internal audit activity

    2.    Maintain independence and objectivity

        a.    Foster independence

**Format: 125 multiple-choice questions**

      (1)    Understand organizational independence

      (2)    Recognize the importance of organizational independence

      (3)    Determine if the internal audit activity is properly aligned to achieve organizational independence

   b.    Foster objectivity

      (1)    Establish policies to promote objectivity

      (2)    Assess individual objectivity

      (3)    Maintain individual objectivity

      (4)    Recognize and mitigate impairments to independence and objectivity

3.    Determine if the required knowledge, skills, and competencies are available

   a.    Understand the knowledge, skills, and competencies that an internal auditor needs to possess

   b.    Identify the knowledge, skills, and competencies required to fulfill the responsibilities of the internal audit activity

4.    Develop and/or procure the necessary knowledge, skills, and competencies collectively required by the internal audit activity

5.    Exercise due professional care

6.    Promote continuing professional development

   a.    Develop and implement a plan for continuing professional development for internal audit staff

   b.    Enhance individual competency through continuing professional development

7.    Promote quality assurance and improvement of the internal audit activity

   a.    Establish and maintain a quality assurance and improvement program

   b.    Monitor the effectiveness of the quality assurance and improvement program

   c.    Report the results of the quality assurance and improvement program to the board or other governing body

   d.    Conduct quality assurance procedures and recommend improvements to the performance of the internal audit activity

8.    Abide by and promote compliance with The IIA Code of Ethics.

**B.    Establish a Risk-based Plan to Determine the Priorities of the Internal Audit Activity (Proficiency level)**       **(15–25%)**

1.    Establish a framework for assessing risk

2.    Use the framework to:

   a.    Identify sources of potential engagements (eg, audit universe, management request, regulatory mandate)

   b.    Assess organization-wide risk

   c.    Solicit potential engagement topics from various sources

   d.    Collect and analyze data on proposed engagements

   e.    Rank and validate risk priorities

3.    Identify internal audit resource requirements

4.    Coordinate the internal audit activity's efforts with:

   a.    External auditor

   b.    Regulatory oversight bodies

   c.    Other internal assurance functions (eg, health and safety department)

5.    Select engagements

**Format: 125 multiple-choice questions**

    a.     Participate in the engagement selection process

    b.     Select engagements

    c.     Communicate and obtain approval of the engagement plan from board

  6.     Identify scope of engagements

**C.**     **Understand the Internal Audit Activity's Role in Organizational Governance (Proficiency level)**     **(10–20%)**

  1.     Obtain board's approval of audit charter

  2.     Communicate plan of engagements

  3.     Report significant audit issues

  4.     Communicate key performance indicators to board on a regular basis

  5.     Discuss areas of significant risk

  6.     Support board in enterprise-wide risk assessment

  7.     Review the positioning of the internal audit function within the risk management framework within the organization.

  8.     Monitor compliance with the corporate code of conduct/business practices

  9.     Report on the effectiveness of the control framework

  10.    Assist board in assessing the independence of the external auditor

  11.    Assess ethical climate of the board

  12.    Assess ethical climate of the organization

  13.    Assess compliance with policies in specific areas (eg, derivatives)

  14.    Assess organization's reporting mechanism to the board.

  15.    Conduct follow-up and report on management response to regulatory body reviews

  16.    Conduct follow-up and report on management response to external audit

  17.    Assess the adequacy of the performance measurement system, achievement of corporate objective

  18.    Support a culture of fraud awareness and encourage the reporting of improprieties

**D.**     **Perform Other Internal Audit Roles and Responsibilities (Proficiency level)**     **(0–10%)**

  1.     Ethics/Compliance

     a.     Investigate and recommend resolution for ethics/compliance complaints

     b.     Determine disposition of ethics violations

     c.     Foster healthy ethical climate

     d.     Maintain and administer business conduct policy (eg, conflict of interest)

     e.     Report on compliance

  2.     Risk Management

     a.     Develop and implement an organization-wide risk and control framework

     b.     Coordinate enterprise-wide risk assessment

     c.     Report corporate risk assessment to board

     d.     Review business continuity planning process

  3.     Privacy

     a.     Determine privacy vulnerabilities

     b.     Report on compliance

  4.     Information or physical security

**Format: 125 multiple-choice questions**

    a.    Determine security vulnerabilities

    b.    Determine disposition of security violations

    c.    Report on compliance

**E.**    **Governance, Risk, and Control Knowledge Elements**

                                                     **(15–25%)**

| | | |
|---|---|---|
| 1. | Corporate governance principles | **(Awareness level)** |
| 2. | Alternative control frameworks | **(Awareness level)** |
| 3. | Risk vocabulary and concepts | **(Proficiency level)** |
| 4. | Risk management techniques | **(Proficiency level)** |
| 5. | Risk/control implications of different organizational Structures | **(Proficiency level)** |
| 6. | Risk/control implications of different leadership Styles | **(Awareness level)** |
| 7. | Change management | **(Awareness level)** |
| 8. | Conflict management | **(Awareness level)** |
| 9. | Management control techniques | **(Proficiency level)** |
| 10. | Types of control (eg, preventive, detective, input, output) | **(Proficiency level)** |

**F.**    **Plan Engagements**

**(Proficiency level)**                                                      **(15–25%)**

1.    Initiate preliminary communication with engagement client

2.    Conduct a preliminary survey of the area of engagement

    a.    Obtain input from engagement client

    b.    Perform analytical reviews

    c.    Perform benchmarking

    d.    Conduct interviews

    e.    Review prior audit reports and other relevant documentation

    f.    Map processes

    g.    Develop checklists

3.    Complete a detailed risk assessment of area (prioritize or evaluate risk/control factors)

4.    Coordinate audit engagement efforts with

    a.    External auditor

    b.    Regulatory oversight bodies

5.    Establish/refine engagement objectives and identify/finalize the scope of engagement

6.    Identify or develop criteria for assurance engagements (criteria against which to audit)

7.    Consider the potential for fraud when planning an engagement

    a.    Be knowledgeable of the risk factors and red flags of fraud

    b.    Identify common types of fraud associated with the engagement area.

    c.    Determine if risk of fraud requires special consideration when conducting an engagement

8.    Determine engagement procedures

9.    Determine the level of staff and resources needed for the engagement.

10.    Establish adequate planning and supervision of the engagement.

11.    Prepare engagement work program

# Part II: Conducting the internal audit engagement

**Format: 125 multiple-choice questions**

**A.    Conduct Engagements**

**(Proficiency level)**                                                    **(25–35%)**

1.    Research and apply appropriate standards:

a.    IIA Professional Practices Framework (eg, Code of Ethics, Standards, Practice Advisories)

b.    Other professional, legal, and regulatory standards

2.    Maintain an awareness of the potential for fraud when conducting an engagement

a.    Notice indicators or symptoms of fraud

b.    Design appropriate engagement steps to address significant risk of fraud

c.    Employ audit tests to detect fraud

d.    Determine if any suspected fraud merits investigation

3.    Collect data

4.    Evaluate the relevance, sufficiency and competence of evidence

5.    Analyze and interpret data

6.    Develop workpapers

7.    Review workpapers

8.    Communicate interim progress

9.    Draw conclusions

10.    Develop recommendations when appropriate

11.    Report engagement results

a.    Conduct exit conference

b.    Prepare report or other communication

c.    Approve engagement report

d.    Determine distribution of report

e.    Obtain management response to report

12.    Conduct client satisfaction survey

13.    Complete performance appraisals of engagement staff

**B.    Conduct Specific Engagements**

**(Proficiency level)**                                                    **(25–35%)**

1.    Conduct assurance engagements

a.    Fraud investigation

(1)    Determine appropriate parties to be involved with investigation

(2)    Establish facts and extent of fraud (eg, interviews, interrogations, and data analysis)

(3)    Report outcomes to appropriate parties

(4)    Complete a process review to improve controls to prevent fraud and recommend changes

b.    Risk and control self-assessment

(1)    Facilitated approach

**Format: 125 multiple-choice questions**

        (a)     Client-facilitated

        (b)     Audit-facilitated

    (2)    Questionnaire approach

    (3)    Self-certification approach

  c.    Audits of third parties and contract auditing

  d.    Quality audit engagements

  e.    Due diligence audit engagements

  f.    Security audit engagements

  g.    Privacy audit engagements

  h.    Performance (key performance indicators) audit engagements

  i.    Operational (efficiency and effectiveness) audit engagements

  j.    Financial audit engagements

  k.    Information technology (IT) audit engagements

    (1)    Operating systems

        (a)     Mainframe

        (b)     Workstations

        (c)     Server

    (2)    Application development

        (a)     Application authentication

        (b)     Systems development methodology

        (c)     Change control

        (d)     End user computing

    (3)    Data and network communications/connections (eg, LAN, VAN, and WAN)

    (4)    Voice communications

    (5)    System security (eg, firewalls, access control)

    (6)    Contingency planning

    (7)    Databases

    (8)    Functional areas of IT operations (eg, data center operations)

    (9)    Web infrastructure

    (10)   Software licensing

    (11)   Electronic funds transfer (EFT)/Electronic data interchange (EDI)

    (12)   e-Commerce

    (13)   Information protection (eg, viruses, privacy)

    (14)   Encryption

    (15)   Enterprise-wide resource planning (ERP) software (eg, SAP R/3)

  l.    Compliance audit engagements

2.    Conduct consulting engagements

  a.    Internal control training

  b.    Business process review

  c.    Benchmarking

  d.    Information technology (IT) and systems development.

  e.    Design of performance measurement systems

**C.   Monitor Engagement Outcomes**

**(Proficiency level)**                                 **(5–15%)**

**Format: 125 multiple-choice questions**

1. Determine appropriate follow-up activity by the internal audit activity
2. Identify appropriate method to monitor engagement outcomes
3. Conduct follow-up activity
4. Communicate monitoring plan and results

**D.   Fraud Knowledge Elements**                              **(5–15%)**

1. Discovery sampling                              **(Awareness level)**
2. Interrogation techniques                        **(Awareness level)**
3. Forensic auditing                               **(Awareness level)**
4. Legal hazards                                   **(Awareness level)**
5. Use of computers in analyzing data              **(Proficiency level)**
6. Red flags                                       **(Proficiency level)**
7. Types of fraud                                  **(Proficiency level)**

**E.   Engagement Tools**                                      **(15–25%)**

1. Sampling                                        **(Awareness level)**
   a.   Nonstatistical (judgmental)
   b.   Statistical
2. Statistical analyses (process control techniques)  **(Awareness level)**
3. Data gathering tools                            **(Proficiency level)**
   a.   Interviewing
   b.   Questionnaires
   c.   Checklists
4. Analytical review techniques                    **(Proficiency level)**
   a.   Ratio estimation
   b.   Variance analysis (eg, budget vs actual)
   c.   Other reasonableness tests
5. Observation                                     **(Proficiency level)**
6. Problem solving                                 **(Proficiency level)**
7. Risk and control self-assessment (CSA)          **(Awareness level)**
8. Computerized audit tools and techniques         **(Proficiency level)**
   a.   Embedded audit modules
   b.   Data extraction techniques
   c.   Generalized audit software (eg, ACL, IDEA)
   d.   Spreadsheet analysis
   e.   Automated workpapers (eg, Lotus Notes, Auditor Assistant)
9. Process mapping including flowcharting          **(Proficiency level)**

## *Part III: Business analysis and information technology*

**Format: 125 multiple-choice questions**

**A.   Business Processes**                                    **(15–25%)**

1. Quality management (eg, TQM)                    **(Awareness level)**
2. The International Organization for Standardization (ISO) Framework   **(Awareness level)**
3. Forecasting                                     **(Awareness level)**

**Format: 125 multiple-choice questions**

| | | |
|---|---|---|
| 4. | Project management techniques | **(Proficiency level)** |
| 5. | Business process analysis (eg, workflow analysis and bottleneck management, theory of constraints) | **(Proficiency level)** |
| 6. | Inventory management techniques and concepts | **(Proficiency level)** |
| 7. | Marketing-pricing objectives and policies | **(Awareness level)** |
| 8. | Marketing-supply chain management | **(Awareness level)** |
| 9. | Human Resources | |
| | (Individual performance management and measurement; supervision; environmental factors that affect performance; facilitation techniques; personnel sourcing/staffing; training and development; safety) | **(Proficiency level)** |
| 10. | Balanced scorecard | **(Awareness level)** |

**B.**   **Financial Accounting and Finance**     **(15–25%)**

| | | |
|---|---|---|
| 1. | Basic concepts and underlying principles of financial accounting | |
| | (eg, statements, terminology, relationships) | **(Proficiency level)** |
| 2. | Intermediate concepts of financial accounting | |
| | (eg, bonds, leases, pensions, intangible assets, R&D) | **(Awareness level)** |
| 3. | Advanced concepts of financial accounting | |
| | (eg, consolidation, partnerships, foreign currency transactions) | **(Awareness level)** |
| 4. | Financial statement analysis | **(Proficiency level)** |
| 5. | Cost of capital evaluation | **(Awareness level)** |
| 6. | Types of debt and equity | **(Awareness level)** |
| 7. | Financial instruments (eg, derivatives) | **(Awareness level)** |
| 8. | Cash management (treasury functions) | **(Awareness level)** |
| 9. | Valuation models | **(Awareness level)** |
| | a.   Inventory valuation | |
| | b.   Business valuation | |
| 10. | Business development life cycles | **(Awareness level)** |

**C.**   **Managerial Accounting**     **(10–20%)**

| | | |
|---|---|---|
| 1. | Cost concepts (eg, absorption, variable, fixed) | **(Proficiency level)** |
| 2. | Capital budgeting | **(Awareness level)** |
| 3. | Operating budget | **(Proficiency level)** |
| 4. | Transfer pricing | **(Awareness level)** |
| 5. | Cost-volume-profit analysis | **(Awareness level)** |
| 6. | Relevant cost | **(Awareness level)** |
| 7. | Costing systems (eg, activity-based, standard) | **(Awareness level)** |
| 8. | Responsibility accounting | **(Awareness level)** |

**D.**   **Regulatory, Legal, and Economics**

**(Awareness level)**     **(5–15%)**

| | |
|---|---|
| 1. | Impact of government legislation and regulation on business |
| 2. | Trade legislation and regulations |
| 3. | Taxation schemes |
| 4. | Contracts |
| 5. | Nature and rules of legal evidence |

**Format: 125 multiple-choice questions**
    6.    Key economic indicators

**E.**    **Information Technology (IT)**

    **(Awareness level)**               **(30–40%)**

    1.    Control frameworks (eg, eSAC, COBIT)
    2.    Data and network communications/connections (eg, LAN, VAN, and WAN)
    3.    Electronic funds transfer (EFT)
    4.    e-Commerce
    5.    Electronic data interchange (EDI)
    6.    Functional areas of IT operations (eg, data center operations)
    7.    Encryption
    8.    Viruses
    9.    Information protection
    10.    Evaluate investment in IT (cost of ownership)
    11.    Enterprise-wide resource planning (ERP) software (eg, SAP R/3, Peoplesoft)
    12.    Operating systems
    13.    Application development
    14.    Voice communications
    15.    Contingency planning
    16.    Systems security (eg, firewalls, access control)
    17.    Databases
    18.    Software licensing
    19.    Web infrastructure

# *Part IV: Business management skills*

**Format: 125 multiple-choice questions**
    **A.**    **Strategic Management**

    **(Awareness level)**               **(20–30%)**

    1.    Global analytical techniques
        a.    Structural analysis of industries
        b.    Competitive strategies (eg, Porter's model)
        c.    Competitive analysis
        d.    Market signals
        e.    Industry evolution
    2.    Industry environments
        a.    Competitive strategies related to:
            (1)    Fragmented industries
            (2)    Emerging industries
            (3)    Declining industries
        b.    Competition in global industries
            (1)    Sources/impediments
            (2)    Evolution of global markets
            (3)    Strategic alternatives
            (4)    Trends affecting competition
    3.    Strategic decisions

**Format: 125 multiple-choice questions**

      a.     Analysis of integration strategies

      b.     Capacity expansion

      c.     Entry into new businesses

   4.     Portfolio techniques of competitive analysis

   5.     Product life cycles

**B.**    **Global Business Environments**

    **(Awareness level)**              **(15–25%)**

   1.     Cultural/legal/political environments

      a.     Balancing global requirements and local imperatives

      b.     Global mindsets (personal characteristics/competencies)

      c.     Sources and methods for managing complexities and contradictions

      d.     Managing multicultural teams

   2.     Economic/financial environments

      a.     Global, multinational, international, and multilocal compared and contrasted

      b.     Requirements for entering the global market place

      c.     Creating organizational adaptability

      d.     Managing training and development.

**C.**    **Organizational Behavior**

    **(Awareness level)**              **(15–25%)**

   1.     Motivation

      a.     Relevance and implication of various theories

      b.     Impact of job design, rewards, work schedules, etc

   2.     Communication

      a.     The process

      b.     Organizational dynamics

      c.     Impact of computerization

   3.     Performance

      a.     Productivity

      b.     Effectiveness

   4.     Structure

      a.     Centralized/decentralized

      b.     Departmentalization

      c.     New configurations (eg, hourglass, cluster, network)

**D.**    **Management Skills**

    **(Awareness level)**              **(20–30%)**

   1.     Group dynamics

      a.     Traits (eg, cohesiveness, roles, norms, groupthink)

      b.     Stages of group development

      c.     Organizational politics

      d.     Criteria and determinants of effectiveness

   2.     Team building

      a.     Methods used in team building

      b.     Assessing team performance

   3.     Leadership skills

**Format: 125 multiple-choice questions**

      a.      Theories compared and contrasted

      b.      Leadership grid (topology of leadership styles)

      c.      Mentoring

   4.     Personal time management

**E.**    **Negotiating**

    **(Awareness level)**                          **(5–15%)**

   1.     Conflict resolution

      a.      Competitive/cooperative

      b.      Compromise, forcing, smoothing, etc

   2.     Added-value negotiating

      a.      Description

      b.      Specific steps

# Certification in Control Self Assessment of The Institute of Internal Auditors

## CCSA Exam Content and Format

The topics tested on the CCSA exam are framed in the context of a variety of industry situations. Candidates are not expected to be familiar with industry-specific controls, but should be able to relate to risks and controls that generally apply to business processes in various industries. Exam topics are subject to change.

The CCSA exam covers the following domains.

| | |
|---|---|
| *Domain 1* | CSA Fundamentals (5–10 percent) |
| *Domain 2* | CSA Program Integration (15–25 percent) |
| *Domain 3* | Elements of the CSA Process (15–25 percent) |
| *Domain 4* | Business Objectives/Organizational Performance (10–15 percent) |
| *Domain 5* | Risk Identification and Assessment (15–20 percent) |
| *Domain 6* | Control Theory and Application (20–25 percent) |

**P** = Candidates must exhibit proficiency (thorough understanding; ability to apply concepts) in these topic areas.

**A** = Candidates must exhibit awareness (knowledge of terminology and fundamentals) in these topic areas.

## *Domain 1 – CSA Fundamentals (5–10%)*
A.  Code of Ethics (P)
B.  Ownership and accountability for control (P)
C.  Reliance on operational expertise (P)
D.  Comparison to traditional techniques of risk and control evaluation (P)
E.  Control awareness and education (P)
F.  Cooperation, participation, and partnership (P)

## *Domain 2 – CSA Program Integration (15–25%)*
A.  Alternative approaches to CSA (A)
B.  Supporting technology alternatives (A)
  1.  Database
  2.  Electronic voting
  3.  Presentation software and hardware
  4.  Project management software

C.  Cost/benefit analysis for implementation of the CSA process (A)
D.  Organizational theory and behavior (A)
    1.  Structure
    2.  Philosophy
    3.  Culture
    4.  Management style
    5.  Governance
E.  Strategic and operational planning processes (A)
F.  Change management and business process reengineering (A)
G.  Presentation techniques for successful integration (A)
H.  Organizational risk and control processes (A)
    1. Quality management
    2. Risk management
    3. Safety audits
    4. Environmental audits
    5. Internal and external audit
I.  Client feedback mechanisms (eg, interviews, surveys) (A)
J.  Strategic CSA program planning methodologies or techniques, including resource allocation (A)


## Domain 3 – Elements of the CSA Process (15–25%)

A.  Management's priorities and concerns (P)
B.  Project and logistics management (P)
C.  Business objectives, processes, challenges, and threats for the area under review (P)
D.  Resource identification and allocation (A)
    1.  Participants
    2.  CSA team
E.  Culture of area under review (P)
F.  Question development techniques (P)
G.  Technology supporting the CSA process (P)
H.  Facilitation techniques and tools (P)
I.  Group dynamics (P)
J.  Fraud awareness (A)
    1.  Red flags/symptoms of fraud
    2.  Communication and investigation channels
    3.  Responding to evidence
K.  Evaluation/analytical tools and techniques (trend analysis, data synthesis, scenarios) (A)
L.  Formulating recommendations or actions plans (practical, feasible, cost-effective) (P)
M.  Nature of evidence (sufficiency, relevance, adequacy) (A)
N.  Reporting techniques and considerations (types, audience, sensitive issues, access to information) (P)
O.  Motivational techniques (creating support and commitment for recommendations) (A)
P.  Monitoring, tracking, and follow-up techniques (A)
Q.  Awareness of legal, regulatory, and ethical considerations (A)

R.    Measuring CSA program effectiveness (A)


## Domain 4 – Business Objectives and Organizational Performance (10–15%)

A.    Strategic and operational planning processes (A)
B.    Objective setting, including alignment to the organization's mission and values (P)
C.    Performance measures (P)
  1.    Financial
  2.    Operational
  3.    Qualitative
D.    Performance management (P)
  1.    Aligning individual, group, and organizational objectives/goals
  2.    Designing congruent incentives
E.    Data collection and validation techniques (eg, benchmarking, auditing, consensus testing, etc) (A)


## Domain 5 – Risk Identification and Assessment (15–20%)

A.    Risk Theory (P)
  1.    Defining risk
  2.    Relationship of risk to strategic, operational, or process objectives
  3.    Risk tolerance, residual risk, and exposure
  4.    Impact assessment
B.    Risk models/frameworks (P)
C.    Understanding the risks inherent in common business processes (P)
D.    Application of risk identification and assessment techniques (P)
E.    Risk management techniques/cost-benefit analysis(P)
  1.    Transfer, manage, or accept
  2.    Impact/cost-benefit analysis


## Domain 6 – Control Theory and Application (20–25%)

A.    Corporate governance, control theory, and models (P)
  1.    Accountability and responsibility for control
  2.    Defining control
  3.    Relationship between risk, control, and objectives
B.    Techniques for determining control track record for the organization (eg, reviews, audits, other assessments) (A)
C.    Relationship between informal and formal controls (P)
D.    Techniques for evaluating formal controls (manual or automated) (P)
E.    Techniques for evaluating informal controls/control environment (P)
F.    Control documentation techniques (A)
  1.    Flowcharting
  2.    Business process mapping
  3.    Control charts
  4.    Control questionnaires

G.   Control design and application (P)
     1. Defining control objectives
     2. Control design (eg, preventive, detective, corrective; informal, formal)
     3. Cost/benefits
H.   Methods for judging and communicating about the overall effectiveness of
     the system of internal control (A)

# The Institute of Internal Auditors (UK) Practitioner of The Institute of Internal Auditors Programme – outline and contents

The Institute of Internal Audits (UK) offers three qualifications, in addition to a Certificate programme which is not regarded as a qualification. Practitioner of The Institute of Internal Auditors (PIIA) entails passing examination papers 1 to 5 as set out in this appendix. Member of The Institute of Internal Auditors (MIIA) is the full professional qualification and entails passing examination papers 7 to 10 as set out in APPENDIX 8. At present there is no longer a paper 6.

Paper 11 relates to The IIA(UK)'s third qualification – Qualification in Computer Auditing (QiCA).

The PIIA details given in this appendix are the result of a recent radical revision. The MIIA details given in APPENDIX 8 were current as of 1 January 2005 but are in the process of being revised.

## Module 1: Organisation and management – concepts and practices

| | |
|---|---|
| **Aims and Objectives** | This module is designed to enable the internal auditor to create and maintain an internal audit function that has a good fit with the structural, cultural, and political norms of the organisation in which he/she operates and to deliver effective assurance and consultancy services. |
| | It also ensures that the internal auditor has a command of the language that organisations use and enables the internal auditor to ask challenging questions. |
| **Competencies to be demonstrated** | The module develops knowledge, abilities and skills that are essential for identifying, understanding and implementing organisational and management concepts and practices. Those who have successfully completed the module will be able to demonstrate the following competencies: |

- The identification of the context within which organisations function and the various external and internal influences upon them
- An understanding of organisational and management objectives, structures and processes, including organisational culture and dynamics
- The identification of how management can contribute to organisational effectiveness and the impact of people and management styles on effective performance
- An understanding of performance measures and their part in monitoring organisational effectiveness
- An understanding of the key components of effective communication

● An understanding of the relationship between management and organisational theory and the internal audit function and the impact that this has on its organisational role and responsibility.

**Syllabus**  The syllabus comprises seven subject areas; environmental context and dynamics, organisational purposes and objectives, organisational structure, people in organisations communication in organisations, applied management change and measuring performance. The details of the content of each subject area are given below.

1.  **Environmental Context and Dynamics**

    1.1  Describes and explains the organisation in the context of its environment, including:

    ● the environmental influences on organisations in private, public and not-for-profit sectors and the importance of political, legal, ethical, economic, sociocultural factors and technological change and development

    ● the effects of competition on organisations such as threat, rivalry, power and supply and demand

    ● the range of stakeholder groups and the influences they may have on organisations, such as shareholders, suppliers, customers/clients, employees, lenders, elected representatives, government and regulators

    1.2  Explains any environmental, competitive and stakeholder influences on internal audit in an organisation.

2.  **Organisational Purposes and Objectives**

    2.1  Outlines the main purposes of organisations in private, public and not-for-profit sectors in terms of:

    ● their objectives, such as economic, protective, associative, local/central governmental

    ● organisation values, mission, goals and objectives

    2.2  Explains how an organisation sets its strategy and, in outline, how strategic analysis and planning techniques (including competitive advantage, best value, five forces and SWOT) are used

    2.3  Explains decision-making processes that organisations use with reference to relevant techniques and theories

    2.4  Explains the purposes of internal audit functions within an organisation.

3.  **Organisational Structure**

    3.1  Describes and explains different types of organisational structures in private, public and not-for-profit sectors, including functional, divisional, matrix, network, centralised/decentralised arrangements

    3.2  Explains the differences between formal and informal organisations

    3.3  Explains alliances, partnerships and joint ventures

    3.4  Explains the different ways in which internal audit fits into different types of organisation.

4. **People in Organisations**

4.1 Explains the characteristics of organisations in private, public and not-for-profit sectors and the impact on management styles. It also examines the following organisational and management theories:

- the organisation as a machine and scientific management
- the organisation as organic system and contingency theory
- the organisation as a political system and power relations
- the organisation as a social system and cultural and human behaviour

4.2 Identifies different styles of leadership, including authoritarian, participative, delegating and consensual

4.3 Identifies different management styles and techniques and their impact on teams

4.4 Explains what motivates individuals and teams drawing on relevant theory

4.5 Explains the contribution of development to individuals and teams, including the role of training, coaching and mentoring

4.6 Describes the role of internal audit in developing individuals throughout the organisation to manage risks and adapt processes to deal with them.

5. **Communication in Organisations**

5.1 Explains different approaches to communication in organisations, including formal and informal, downwards, upwards and across communications in private, public and not-for-profit sectors

5.2 Explains different communications media, when they are best used and their advantages and disadvantages and their impact on individuals and teams, including:

- written
- telephone
- email
- face-to-face
- broadcast
- non-verbal communication
- communication by default

5.3 Explains the importance of communication for internal audit.

6. **Applied Management and Change**

6.1 Describes the key processes of organisations in private, public and not-for-profit sectors and explains what 'Porter's value chain' says about organisational processes

6.2 Explains different levels of management and their contributions, including strategic, corporate, general and operational management

6.3 Explains key concepts in the manufacturing of products and the provision of services, including just-in-time and business-to-business services contrasted with business-to-consumer

6.4      Describes and explains the contribution of the following to business:

- quality marks and models, including the business excellence model
- total quality management
- customer relationship management

6.5      Explains the importance of excellence, quality and customer relationships for internal audit

6.6      Explains the management of change, including the tools and techniques used and the impact of change on individuals, teams and organisations

6.7      Describes and explains the contribution of change management techniques to internal audit

6.8      Explains the principles of project management and its value to organisations.

**7.     Measuring Performance**

7.1      Explains the ways in which management can measure the performance of organisations in private, public and not-for-profit sectors, including the use of externally accredited performance measures such as ISO 9000, Investors in People (IiP), Chartermark and benchmarking

7.2      Describes and explains the contribution of management control and assurance models to organisational performance.

# Module 2 Accounting and financial systems

**Aims and Objectives**

This module is designed to enable the internal auditor to understand financial systems and interpret accounting information. It is also designed to enhance the internal auditor's analytical, numerical and general business skills. In particular, the module focuses on:

- Providing internal auditors with a knowledge and understanding of financial systems and the main risks and controls associated with them
- Enabling internal auditors to understand and interpret key financial and management accounting information thus enhancing financial literacy
- Developing the analytical and numerical skills of internal auditors in undertaking calculations, analysing numerical and accounting information and making accounting adjustments
- Enabling internal auditors to use the results of interpretation and analysis of accounting information for further audit work.

**Competencies to be demonstrated**

The module develops knowledge, abilities and skills that are essential for understanding and analysing accounting and financial systems. Those who have successfully completed the qualification will be able to demonstrate the following competencies:

- Identifying the main risks and associated controls within financial systems based on a given scenario
- Understanding the conditions and activities associated with financial systems that could lead to fraud or improper activities
- Undertaking accurate calculations and analysis and presenting numerical information in the most effective manner for management decision making

- Understanding the purpose of published financial statements and critically evaluating their usefulness and limitations
- Interpreting the external financial reporting of organisations in the private, public and not-for-profit sectors
- Understanding the methods of preparing management accounting information and the assumptions that have been made
- Applying accounting information during audit work
- Communicating at an acceptable level of financial literacy with financial managers within the organisation and with external auditors
- Appreciating the importance of accounting controls within financial systems and understanding their role in preventing and detecting errors and fraud
- Understanding and the ability to comment upon the differences between published financial statements and internal management information
- Awareness of subjectivity in decision making by those preparing accounting information.

**Syllabus**     The syllabus comprises seven subject areas; nature and financing of organisations, financial systems and the accounts functions, accounting controls, external financial reporting, concepts underlying the preparation of financial statements, management accounting and interpreting and analysing accounting information. The details of the content of each subject area are given below.

1. **Nature and Financing of Organisations**

   1.1     Identifies the main types of organisation and the sectors in which they operate

   1.2     Distinguishes between the business objectives of different types of organisation

   1.3     Describes the main internal and external sources of finance for an organisation

   1.4     Identifies appropriate sources of finance for given organisational needs

   1.5     Explains risks associated with types of organisation and types of finance.

2. **Financial Systems and the Accounts Function**

   2.1     Explains the role of the main functions within a finance/accounts department

   2.2     Identifies the main risks and describes key controls in the following financial systems:

   - cash and banking
   - income and debtors
   - expenditure and creditors
   - payroll
   - fixed assets
   - stock

   2.3     Describes how fraud or improper activities can occur within financial systems

   2.4     Explains the basis of double entry and the presentation of ledger accounts (questions will *not* be set requiring preparation of ledger accounts using double entry)

2.5    Explains the main components and operation of an integrated computerised accounting system

2.6    Explains the operation of a coding system in a computerised accounting system

2.7    Explains the role and risks of using the journal for correcting errors and making adjustments (questions will *not* be set on preparation of journal entries)

2.8    Explains the purpose of a trial balance.

## 3.    Accounting Controls

3.1    Explains the role of accounting controls in preventing and detecting errors and fraud

3.2    Explains the role of the sales and purchase ledger control accounts

3.3    Explains the use of reconciliations as a control mechanism

3.4    Requires the preparation of a bank reconciliation from given data from the cash book and bank statement and comment on the significance of items identified

3.5    Explains the impact on audit work of errors and discrepancies shown up by accounting controls.

## 4.    External Financial Reporting

4.1    Explains the use of the income statement to measure profit or surplus

4.2    Explains the layout of income statements for different types of organisation and how to interpret the information given about income and expenses

4.3    Explains the concept of a balance sheet in showing the capital employed/funds and net assets of an organisation

4.4    Explains the layout of a balance sheet and the classification of assets and liabilities

4.5    Distinguishes between capital and revenue income and expenditure and explains the relationship between the income statement and balance sheet

4.6    Explains the purpose and main contents of a published annual report

4.7    Explains how to understand and interpret a cash flow statement from the published accounts of an organisation

4.8    Explains the distinction between cash resources and profits earned

4.9    Describes the role of the external auditor in giving an opinion on the financial statements.

## 5.    Concepts Underlying the Preparation of Financial Statements

5.1    Explains the role of accounting standards in regulating the preparation of financial statements

5.2    Describes the impact of adopting different accounting methods allowed by accounting standards on the financial statements, including:

- choice of estimation techniques for provision for depreciation
- methods of calculating the cost of stock

5.3    Explains and gives examples of the application of accounting concepts:

- going concern
- accruals (matching)

5.4    Explains the accounting objectives of:
- relevance
- reliability
- understandability
- comparability

5.5    Explains the need for accounting adjustments when preparing financial statements:
- accruals and prepayments
- provision for depreciation
- provision for doubtful debts

5.6    Requires the calculation of depreciation using the straight line and reducing balance methods and explanations of the benefits of each method (estimation technique)

5.7    Explains the basis for valuation of stock as the lower of cost and net realisable value.

## 6.    Management Accounting

6.1    Explains the main purposes of management accounting

6.2    Distinguishes between direct and indirect costs

6.3    Explains fixed, variable and semi-variable costs

6.4    Explains the role of cost centres in cost accounting

6.5    Explains the use of absorption costing and the assumptions made in the allocation of overheads

6.6    Explains the use of marginal costing for decision making, including the concept of contribution

6.7    Distinguishes between marginal and absorption costing and explains when each is most appropriate to use

6.8    Identifies the steps and assumptions in the budget setting process

6.9    Describes the function of budgetary control and identifies the action to be taken when variances are identified (a knowledge of standard costing is *not* required)

6.10    Requires the preparation of a cash budget (cash flow forecast) from given information and the identification of future funding needs based on the forecast

6.11    Explains the use of financial and non-financial performance indicators to monitor performance

6.12    Describes the key features of capital investment appraisal techniques and how to undertake calculations using:
- net present value
- payback period
- accounting rate of return.

## 7.    Interpreting and Analysing Accounting Information

7.1    Describes the benefits of good presentation of numerical information and the need for analysis of this information by internal auditors

7.2    Explains the usefulness of computerised data interrogation techniques for analysis of financial data

| | |
|---|---|
| 7.3 | Requires the preparation of numerical tables from given data to convey appropriate management information, including the use of ratios, fractions and percentages and calculations of the mean, median and mode from given data |
| 7.4 | Requires the presentation of numerical information in graphical form |
| 7.5 | Requires the calculation of accounting ratios relating to profitability, efficiency and liquidity and explains how to use them to draw conclusions about organisational performance |
| 7.6 | Explains the limitations of financial statements in providing information about organisational performance |
| 7.7 | Requires the interpretation of a given cash flow statement and comment on the liquidity of the organisation |
| 7.8 | Requires the use of results of accounting information analysis to suggest areas for further audit work |
| 7.9 | Requires analysis of the results of capital investment appraisal techniques for a project and comment on management decision making |
| 7.10 | Requires the preparation of reports for management on the analysis of financial and management accounting information. |

# Module 3: Internal auditing

**Aims and Objectives**

This module is designed to enable the internal auditor to understand the focus, responsibilities and methodologies associated with the effective delivery of internal audit services. In particular the module focuses on:

- Developing an understanding of the Professional Practices Framework that underpins the professional requirements of internal auditing
- Describing and explaining the range of services that can be provided to audit clients, and specifically those concerned with the assessment of risk, control and governance processes and the provision of assurance
- Explaining how to apply the tools and techniques associated with audit services and activities to realistic situations
- Describing how to develop an effective communications strategy to enable the internal auditor to work in partnership with audit clients.

**Competencies to be demonstrated**

This module develops knowledge, abilities and skills that are essential for effective internal auditing. Those who have successfully completed the module will be able to demonstrate the following competencies:

- An understanding of the development of the profession of internal auditing and an ability to contribute to the range of services internal audit can provide to clients
- An understanding of how to work within the Professional Practices Framework and apply the *Standards for the Professional Practice of Internal Auditing* and *Code of Ethics*
- The ability to carry out assignments/projects using the full range of audit tools and techniques
- The provision of assurance to the organisation on the adequacy and effectiveness of its governance and risk management processes
- An understanding of good communication skills and the means to develop client auditor relationships that contribute to the delivery of an added value service to audit clients

- The ability to analyse situations for organisations across the full range of their activities and systems, and develop solutions to resolve issues.

**Syllabus** The syllabus comprises three topic areas; Professional Practices Framework and the development of internal auditing, delivering audit services, and communication and client-auditor relationships. The details of the content of each topic and subject area are given below.

## Part A: Professional Practices Framework and the Development of Internal Auditing

**1. Definition of Internal Audit and Code of Ethics**

1.1 Describes the focus and purposes of internal audit as outlined in the definition of internal audit

1.2 Explains the key terms and requirements of the *Code of Ethics* and explains its purpose and role.

**2. Professional Auditing Standards**

2.1 Describes and explains the main components of the IIA's Professional Practice Framework, including attribute and performance standards and how these relate to the work of internal audit.

**3. The Development and Focus of Internal Audit**

3.1 Explains the purpose and historical role of internal audit

3.2 Describes and explains the changing focus of internal auditing, for example, the shift from an internal control focus to a risk-based auditing

3.3 Describes the nature, objectives and types of control

3.4 Explains the range of risk-based services that internal audit can provide, including control risk self-assessment, control education seminars/workshops, system development, business process reviews and compliance reviews

3.5 Explains the need for internal audit to promote improvement opportunities for audit clients

3.6 Explains the need for internal audit to provide assurance on the adequacy of internal control and the methodology by which such assurance can be provided

3.7 Develops an awareness of the circumstances in which the internal auditor can act as a consultant and how the results of such work can be used to provide assurance

3.8 Explains and describes the role and responsibilities of key stakeholders in internal audit, including the audit committee, senior and operational management, and the ways in which internal audit can develop and sustain relationships with such stakeholders to an organisation's benefit

3.9 Explains the importance of developing positive relationships with other audit and compliance functions, including external audit, regulatory bodies, quality, environmental and compliance functions

3.10 Describes how internal audit can add value to the organisation.

## Part B: Delivering Audit Services

**1. Macro Audit Planning**

1.1 Explains the importance and purpose of audit planning

1.2    Describes the different types of plan and the strengths and limitations of each, including strategic, annual, periodic and operational plans

1.3    Describes the factors which contribute to a strong control environment and explains the importance of assessing the control environment as part of the planning process

1.4    Explains risk-based audit planning and describes the techniques used for gathering information to evaluate and assess risk

1.5    Considers the degree of reliance internal audit can place on the results of an organisation's risk management processes when planning the audit schedule

1.6    Explains why business activities that are subject to audit should be prioritised according to risk

1.7    Describes the different ways in which audits can be selected for the audit plan, including cyclical and risk-based audits, and in what circumstance each is appropriate

1.8    Demonstrates an awareness during the planning process of the types of circumstances and activities that can give rise to inefficiency, fraud and irregularity

1.9    Describes the importance of determining audit resource and specialist needs as an outcome of the planning process

1.10    Describes the process of and need for agreeing audit plans with the audit committee and senior management.

**2.    Micro Audit Planning**

2.1    Describes the sources of material for audit assignment planning, including risk register, previous audit reports, organisational documentation and how to use them

2.2    Explains the use of statistical data and analytical review in assessing and evaluating risk

2.3    Describes how the likelihood and consequence of risks arising can be assessed

2.4    Explains audit scope and how the risk assessment exercise sets the boundaries or scope of the audit

2.5    Defines audit objectives and the mitigating actions (risk strategies, including controls) that should be in place to ensure identified risks are managed

2.6    Explains the link between audit scope, audit objectives, mitigating actions (including controls) and test strategy within the planning process

2.7    Explains how audit resources are determined as a result of the assignment planning process

2.8    Explains how and with whom the audit brief should be agreed.

**3.    Documenting Information, Testing and Evidence**

3.1    Describes the methods used to document information, including process diagrams, system notes, and control matrices, and explains how and in what circumstances internal auditors would use the different methods

3.2    Describes the nature and purpose of different types of test, including walk-through, compliance and substantive testing and the circumstances when it would be appropriate to use them

3.3    Describes the purpose and use of non-statistical and statistical sampling methods and the use of CAATs as a sampling tool

3.4    Explains how test results are evaluated and the need to consider the significance of audit findings in terms of risk

3.5    Explains the types of audit evidence and where each is appropriate in terms of underpinning audit findings.

## 4.   Reporting

4.1    Explains why internal audit reports on audit assignments

4.2    Describes the different methods of reporting an audit assignment, including the formal written report with executive summary and detailed audit findings, the one page summary report, red/green/amber risk assessment reports and oral presentations and the circumstances when each is appropriate

4.3    Describes how the audit report can add value through pragmatic, business-focused solutions that involve the client in their development

4.4    Describes the attributes of effective reporting, including format, style, timeliness, achieving buy-in and agreement on the part of the client and implementation of report items

4.5    Explains the need for the logging and monitoring of the results of audit assignments to enable the follow-up of significant issues within an appropriate timescale

4.6    Explains the influence of senior management and the audit committee in ensuring that appropriate attention is given to implementing the results of audit work

4.7    Explains the use of key summary reporting procedures, including activity reports to the audit committee, performance management statistics and annual assurance reports.

## 5.   Quality Assurance

5.1    Explains the purpose and benefits of an independent or supervisory review and the monitoring of audit assignments

5.2    Explains the purpose and benefits of quality assurance procedures

5.3    Describes the role and purpose of benchmarking and the use of performance measures to compare performance between organisations and within the same organisation over time.

## 6.   Audit Documentation

6.1    Describes the content and purpose of current and permanent audit files and the impact of data protection legislation on records

6.2    Describes the content and purpose of the audit manual

6.3    Develops an understanding of the importance and range of audit working papers in both manual and electronic formats.

## Part C: Communication and Client-Auditor Relationships

## 1.   Communication

1.1    Explains why the communication of the internal audit role and responsibilities to audit clients is needed

1.2    Describes how to use communication techniques to develop good organisational understanding and to contribute to the effectiveness and marketing of internal audit activity

1.3   Explains different interview techniques and how they can achieve the best outcomes, including types of interview, structuring of interviews, types of questions and the impact of body language

1.4   Describes the importance of negotiation, including the framework for negotiation, how negotiation works in practice and how to use negotiation within the audit approach.

**2.   Client-Auditor Relationships**

2.1   Explains the characteristics of a good auditor

2.2   Describes and explains what contributes to good client-auditor relationships

2.3   Explains the barriers to developing good client-auditor relationships

2.4   Describes how internal audit can work in partnership with audit clients and the circumstances when this approach is not appropriate

2.5   Describe how to effectively work in partnership with other review agencies, including external audit, regulatory bodies and third party reviewers of internal audit activities.

Note: The Skills Module: Communication and Client-Auditor Relations supplements Part C of this module.

# Module 4: Business information systems auditing

**Aims and Objectives**

This module is designed to enable the internal auditor to understand business information systems and the purposes and techniques of information systems auditing. In particular, the module focuses on:

- Developing an understanding of the value of information systems and their contribution to meeting corporate objectives and managing risk
- Explaining how to critically evaluate the effectiveness of an organisation's controls relating to its information and processes
- Developing an understanding of the main infrastructure components within the information systems environment
- Identifying risks to the confidentially, integrity and availability of information and processes, and the control measures to effectively manage those risks
- Explaining how to critically evaluate the effectiveness of an organisation's information system developments and project management
- Explaining how information systems and technology can be used to deliver audit objectives.

**Competencies to be demonstrated**

The module develops competencies that are essential for the delivery of business information systems auditing. Those who have successfully completed the module will be able to demonstrate the following competencies:

- The provision of assurance on the effectiveness of an organisation's information and processes, and the effective use of resources
- The ability to carry out reviews covering areas where technical terminology is common and to effectively communicate any findings to senior management
- The provision of assurance on the effectiveness of information security and the ability to recommend actions to manage risks to acceptable levels

- An understanding of standards for information security and the ability to measure the degree of compliance with best practice
- The provision of advice to management on how to deliver successful information system projects
- The timely completion of audit reports at each stage of a systems development project to assist project stakeholders in making effective decisions
- The ability to formulate an effective audit plan, covering information systems topics and produce audit programmes for each topic
- An understanding of the use information systems and technology to help the audit department successfully deliver its objectives.

**Syllabus**

The syllabus comprises five subject areas; business information processes, information systems infrastructure, security and control of information systems, information systems development and project management, and information systems auditing role and techniques. The details of the content of each subject area are given below.

**1. Business Information and Processes**

1.1 Explains the value of information systems to organisations in providing requisite information and effective business processes, and in the delivery of customer service requirements and competitive advantage

1.2 Explains how to assess the risks to the organisation of not having effective information systems and business processes

1.3 Explains the need for requisite information for decision making, such as the importance of providing the right information, pertinent to agreed policies and objectives, to the right person at the right time in the right medium in a clear and unambiguous form

1.4 Explains how to assesses the risks to business of not using requisite information

1.5 Describes the range of information from manual, basic accounting to advanced operational information for decision making

1.6 Explains how information can help to exploit opportunities and manage business risk

1.7 Describes and evaluates the use of the internet and intranets as information sources

1.8 Explains what is understood by knowledge management and differentiates between knowledge, information and data

1.9 Defines data quality and explains how it underpins effective information

1.10 Outlines an effective information strategy and explains how it links with corporate objectives.

**2. Information Systems Infrastructure**

2.1 Identifies and appraises information delivery methods and types of user interfaces

2.2 Summarises the main software components, including operating software, network software and databases, and the risks associated with each

2.3 Summarises internet and e-commerce software and the associated risks

2.4     Summarises the main types of corporate application software, including business applications, enterprise resource planning systems and customer relationship management systems, and the risks associated with each

2.5     Summarises the enabling software components, including email, workflow, document management and data warehousing

2.6     Summarises office and end-user applications and the associated risks

2.7     Summarises the main hardware components, including mainframes, servers, PCs, networks and network equipment, and the risks associated with each

2.8     Explains the different roles and responsibilities within an information systems department and the risks associated with each.

### 3.    Security and Control of Information Systems

3.1     Explains the requirement for information security and data protection, including the protection of key corporate data, personal data and intellectual property

3.2     Outlines the main statutory and regulatory powers giving access to and governing the disclosure of information

3.3     Identifies the internal and external threats to information systems, including computer fraud and abuse, malicious software and viruses

3.4     Summarises standards for information security and how to measure the degree of compliance with best practice

3.5     Describes how to appraise an information security policy and summarise its coverage, including the categorisation of data, levels of access, passwords, data retention, internet and email use

3.6     Describes the main information security controls and explains how each mitigates risk, including:

- physical and environmental controls
- business continuity planning and disaster recovery
- network controls
- system software controls
- database controls
- application controls
- internet and e-commerce controls
- installation and operational controls
- change controls
- access controls
- encryption, authentication and non-repudiation
- personnel controls
- end-user controls
- software licensing controls.

### 4.    Information Systems Development and Project Management

4.1     Explains why an organisation benefits from effective project management and how it realises the benefits of business process change

4.2      Summarises the risks associated with information systems projects and identifies mitigating controls

4.3      Explains what is meant by project methodologies, milestones and decision points

4.4      Identifies the requisite information required by project stakeholders at each decision point

4.5      Summarises the process for procuring and developing systems, the development controls and explains how the latter mitigate risk

4.6      Compares different types of development, including incremental, prototyping and rapid application development

4.7      Identifies the main types of systems documentation and explains what they evidence

4.8      Describes how to assess the effectiveness of system design and explains the role of quality assurance

4.9      Explains why an organisation would outsource facilities and identifies the risks and mitigating controls

4.10      Identifies the main types of outsourcing, including bureau, application service provision, facilities management, maintenance

4.11      Identifies the use of service level agreements and methods of service measurement

4.12      Identifies the main stages of systems implementation, including system configuration, data migration and interfaces to legacy systems, and the risks and mitigating controls

4.13      Compares different types of post project and development process reviews, including post-implementation reviews and learning from experience.

## 5.    Information Systems Auditing Role and Techniques

5.1      Describes the information systems audit role and objectives

5.2      Summarises the audit process, based on a general risk assessment of the organisation's information and computing use, the formulation of an effective audit plan covering information systems topics and the production of audit programmes for each topic

5.3      Explains the role of internal audit in relation to systems development, including the review of the development process and participation in systems under development

5.4      Describes and evaluates the main audit uses of information systems and technology, explaining how each contributes to successfully delivering objectives:

- risk and control assessment

- data interrogation and extraction

- systems testing

- audit automation

5.5      Summarises data forensics and how to secure and preserve evidence.

# Module 5: Corporate governance and risk management

**Aims and Objectives**

This module is designed to enable the internal auditor to provide independent and objective assurance to the board on the existence and effectiveness of internal control and risk management systems in the context of good corporate governance. It is also designed to provide the internal auditor with the knowledge and skills to provide advice and assistance to management in the establishment and maintenance of corporate governance and risk management structures and processes. In particular, the module focuses on:

● Understanding corporate governance and the management of risk, including the role of internal audit

● Identifying and critically evaluating the elements of governance and risk management in an organisation

● Co-ordinating and facilitating risk assessment exercises.

**Competencies to be demonstrated**

The module develops knowledge, abilities and skills that are essential for identifying, understanding and implementing good corporate governance and risk management reporting and practices. Those who have successfully completed the module will be able to demonstrate the following competencies:

● Understanding of the concept and development of corporate governance and critically evaluating structures and processes in organisations

● Understanding of the theory of risk management in the context of corporate governance and the critical evaluation of structures and processes in organisations

● Identifying and explaining the role(s) of internal audit in this context

● Communication of advice and assistance to management in the establishment and maintenance of corporate governance structures and processes

● Communication of advice and assistance to management in the establishment and maintenance of a risk management framework.

**Syllabus**

The syllabus comprises two subject areas; corporate governance and risk management. The details of the content of each subject area are given below.

1. **Corporate Governance**

    1.1    Explains the principles and development of corporate governance in the UK and Ireland in public, private and not-for-profit sectors, including

        ● definitions

        ● historical developments and future trends, including European Community and global influences and trends

        ● key themes in governance failures and reputational crisis, including unsound structure, suppression of information, poor risk management, insensitivity to stakeholders; with illustrated examples such as Maxwell, Barings, Railtrack, Enron, Nestlé, Nike and MacDonalds.

        ● organisational stewardship, shareholders and stakeholders

        ● business ethics

    1.2    Explains the characteristics of good governance in public, private and not-for-profit organisations including:

        ● the role of the board and its sub-committees, including the audit committee; also executive and non-executive directors as individuals

- the role of management at all levels
- the role of internal auditors, internal and outsourced
- the role of external auditors
- reporting responsibilities and processes, including whistleblowing

1.3     Describes the influence of external bodies on private sector organisations and their shareholders and stakeholders, including PIRC, Hermes, the Association of British Insurers, the Bank of England, the Financial Services Authority and the Department of Trade and Industry

1.4     Describes the influence of external bodies and agencies on public and not-for-profit organisations and shows awareness of stakeholders' interests, sensitivities and organisational accountability; including public sector accountability, political sensitivity, ministerial responsibilities, elected members, Public Accounts Committee, Accounting Officers, sponsoring departments of central government, Treasury, European Court of Auditors, National Audit Office, Charity Commission

1.5     Explains the main concerns of stakeholders as regards corporate social responsibility and sustainability, including:

- equal opportunities
- health and safety
- environment
- community investment.

## 2.    Risk Management

2.1     Explains the principles of risk management, including

- definitions of risk, including (enterprise wide) risk management and risk assurance, risk appetite and risk management strategies
- the relationship of risk management to corporate governance
- the differences between risk management standards, for example the ANZ Standard, and the common use of similar terms in financial services, insurance and project management

2.2     Explains the structures and processes of (enterprise wide) risk management, including:

- structures and roles of the board and of executive and non-executive directors, chief risk officer, risk committee, general management, internal audit and functional experts such as health and safety officers, security, insurance, finance, human resources, information technology
- risk types, including operational, reputational and financial
- risk frameworks
- risk identification at all levels
- risk analysis
- risk evaluation
- routine assurance and embedded monitoring
- organisational learning from risk experience
- risk management assurance

- embedding risk management in the organisation

2.3     Explains how organisations manage risks, including:

- risk management strategies, including tolerate, terminate, transfer or treat
- controls as a means for managing risks
- control frameworks including CoCo and COSO
- control models and types of control including preventive, detective, corrective, automated, manual, environmental, managerial and clerical

2.4     Explains the relationship between internal audit and risk management, including the choice of roles available to internal audit and the consequences for corporate governance

2.5     Explains the theoretical approaches to risk identification, analysis and evaluation, including top-down and control risk self-assessment

2.6     Describes the practical techniques for the implementation of risk identification, analysis and evaluation in an organisation

2.7     Describes the building of a risk-based audit work plan.

# The Institute of Internal Auditors (UK) Member of The Institute of Internal Auditors Programme – outline and contents

The Institute of Internal Auditors (UK) offers three qualifications, in addition to a Certificate programme which is not regarded as a qualification. Practitioner of The Institute of Internal Auditors (PIIA) entails passing examination papers 1 to 5 as set out in APPENDIX 7. Member of The Institute of Internal Auditors (MIIA) is the full professional qualification and entails passing examination papers 7 to 10 as set out in this appendix. At present there is no longer a paper 6.

Paper 11 relates to The IIA(UK)'s third qualification – Qualification in Computer Auditing (QiCA).

The MIIA details given below were current as of 1 January 2005 but are in the process of being revised. At the end of this Appendix we reproduce The Institute of Internal Auditors' statement defining the learning aims of the new qualification.

## Module 7: Advanced management

**Aim**    To develop the internal auditor's understanding of current management techniques, methods and issues including the management of internal auditing activities.

**Syllabus 1.    Business Policy and Strategy**

   1.1    Overview of business policy; case histories, definitions of business policy and strategy, link between strategy and operational management, business policy an internal audit

   1.2    Strategic analysis; the strategist's toolkit – strategic fit, SWOT analysis, competitive strength rating, industry analysis, generic strategy, value chain, PESTEL analysis, understanding the customer, financial analysis

   1.3    Creating strategy; inventing strategy alternatives – SWOT approach, generic strategies approach, competitive strategy approach, resources approach, multiplicity of strategic options

   1.4    Selecting the best strategy; discounted cash flow, multi-criteriate analysis

1.5     Strategy implementation; monitoring actual performance, applications and the need for management information decision taking.

## 2.    Corporate Governance

2.1     Business environment; companies and their stakeholders – shareholders, employees, customers, lenders, government and the community

2.2     Requirements of boards and individual directors; types of director

2.3     Corporate fraud and control failures; examples – Guinness, Blue Arrow, BCCI, Maxwell, Barings

2.4     External pressures on boards; North American experience – FCPA, SEC, the Treadway Commission; COCO; UK experience – regulation of financial services, the Combined Code

2.5     Motivation for change; future actions

2.6     Management of risk
- risk appetite and acceptance
- risk identification and measurement
- managing business risks.

## 3.    Management of operations and services

3.1     Introduction – types of operation function, the service encounter, the transformation process, resources and their use, operations performance.

3.2     Management of demand, resources and productivity – process flow, demand and supply, resource capacity planning, productivity of resources, loading and sequencing, effects of queuing, linked processes

3.3     Quality management – what is it?, characteristics, inspection and quality control, quality assurance, quality management systems, performance improvement, statistical process control

3.4     Capacity acquisition and work management – master scheduling, internal and external resources, resource procurement, work sequencing.

## 4.    Management of Marketing

4.1     Marketing strategy – design and implementation

4.2     Marketing information systems

4.3     Marketing of services.

## 5.    Human Resource Management

5.1     HR planning and link to business strategy

5.2     Role of personnel – salary policy administration and structure, profit sharing, bonus schemes

5.3     Recruitment and selection – examination of current practice

5.4     Performance management – work planning and review, performance appraisal, managing work behaviours, competencies

5.5     Training and development – developing self-reliant executives.

**6.   Management of the Working Environment – Internal Auditing**

6.1     Planning – risk needs assessment, effects on staff, approval and co-ordination

6.2     Control – time management, allocating assignments, agreeing objectives, procedures and guidelines, protocols

6.3     Use of computers – hardware and software, laptops, security, back-up

6.4     Use of technology, storage, networks

6.5     Changing workforce – outsourcing, quality of performance, communications, team building

6.6     Training and development – need for, evaluation of outcomes, developing people, health and safety, external accreditation

6.7     Data protection principles, audit use of data, matching data, breaches of the Act, corporate procedures

6.8     Managing relationships – the board/ governing body, audit committee, regulatory bodies.

**7.   Management of Organisational Change**

7.1     Importance for organisations today, different types of change, business and the environment

7.2     Models of organisations and beliefs about how organisations can be changed

7.3     Strategies of change

7.4     Tools for change – team building, TQM, business process re-engineering performance measurement, business excellence

7.5     Making change happen – implementation process, consulting skills for internal auditors, resistance to change, adaptation to change, cultural factors.

**8.   Project Management**

8.1     Role of project manager – appointment – definition of project, planning, decision making, monitoring, controlling

8.2     Project planning – method statement, work breakdown structure, cost plan, network and bar charts, resource charts and curves

8.3     Critical path methods and networks analysis – network diagrams networks for large projects, programme evaluation review technique

8.4     Monitoring and control – measuring performance, controlling change minimising delay, controlling extra costs

8.5     Suppliers and contractors – distribution of work, subcontracting, payment

8.6     Suppliers and contractors selection.

# Module 8: Financial management and business analysis

**Aim**     To develop the internal auditor's ability to analyse, interpret, and assess the validity of accounting, financial and other information including published reports and that prepared for use within the organisation.

**Syllabus**  **1.**   **Legal and Financial Reporting Requirements**

1.1     Accounting practice, company formation, listing

1.2     Share capital and reserves, loan capital, bank loans, creditors

1.3     Assets, investments, stocks, debtors

1.4     Turnover, investments, stocks, debtors

1.5     Group accounts, subsidiaries

1.6     Cash flow statements

1.7     Annual reports

1.8     Acquisitions and mergers

1.9     Foreign exchange.

**2.**   **Analysis of Published Statements**

2.1     Historical summaries

2.2     Other sources of information

2.3     Trends and ratios, guide to analysis.

**3.**   **Financial Management**

3.1     The framework of financial management:
- financial management and financial objectives
- money and capital markets

3.2     Economic influences:
- overview of macro economic policy
- fiscal policy and monetary policy
- inflation

- government intervention
3.3 Long-term finance and capital structures
3.4 Working capital management
3.5 Budgeting:
- budgetary control and behavioural implications,
- quantitative aids,
- alternative budget systems.

**4. Decision Making**

4.1 Information and techniques
4.2 Project appraisal:
- investment decisions
- discounted cash flow
- project appraisal and risk
- capital rationing
- leasing decisions.

**5. Monitoring**

5.1 Performance measurement:
- principles
- manufacturing and service industries
- non-profit making organisations.
5.2 Divisional control:
- transfer pricing
- transfer pricing and profit maximisation
- divisional performance evaluation.

# Module 9: Advanced information systems auditing

**Aim**    To develop the internal auditor's understanding of risks and controls in information systems, and audit approaches available. Understanding the benefits of using information technology in the internal auditing department.

**Syllabus**  **1. IT Management**

1.1 Organisation and management of information systems
1.2 IT strategies including mainframe, mid-range and microcomputer approaches
1.3 IT project management
1.4 Systems development approaches, including computer aided software engineering (CASE), principles of object orientated development and end user computing developments
1.5 Performance management and planning

1.6　Outsourcing IT – the control and audit implications.

## 2.　Security and Control of IT Systems

2.1　Security and control of IT facilities in mainframe/mid range/PC environments

- developing and enforcing an IT security policy
- physical security, locations, buildings, services, fire, flood, electronic radiation and access control to computing facilities
- personnel security
- file security
- terminal security
- communications security
- systems development and application chance control security
- computer operations security
- internet security.

2.2　Audit objectives of the above.

## 3.　Disaster Recovery and Contingency Planning

- business resumption planning
- disaster recovery methods
- developing and testing the disaster recovery plan
- managing the disaster (total or partial)
- contingency planning in the PC environment.

## 4.　Networks and On-Line Systems

4.1　Hardware and software characteristics, basic components of on-line and real time systems

4.2　Networks and telecommunications – technical descriptions, control and security issues, audit objectives of networks and telecommunications

4.3　Local Area Networks (LANS) and Wider Area Networks (WANS) – technical descriptions, control and security implications, audit objectives of WANS and LANS

4.4　Client server architecture and PCs – technical descriptions, control and security implications and audit objectives in the client/server environment.

## 5.　Operating Systems

5.1　Operating systems software and the role of systems programmers

- concepts, components, functions and operating systems software

- role of systems programmers and other technical staff in configuration of systems software and change control
- installation/modifications/maintenance of system software
- auditing objectives relating to operating systems software.

## 6.  Database Management Systems

6.1  Database management system software and the role of the database administration function in large database systems

- database concepts, types, file organisation structures
- principal functions of database management software
- data dictionary and its use by database specialists, users and auditors
- control functions of database administration software
- database design, testing and implementation
- functions and controls over the database administration function
- audit objectives relating to database systems.

## 7.  Auditing Application Systems

7.1  Components of application systems

7.2  Types and classifications of controls, general approach to systems audits, IT environments

7.3  System reviews

7.4  Key risks and controls

7.5  Audit considerations

7.6  Examples:

- integrated financial information systems
- integrated human resource information systems
- public utilities customer service systems.

## 8.  Internal Audit Management and Audit Automation

8.1  Strategy for auditing systems

8.2  The benefits of using information technology in the internal auditing department

8.3  Using information technology to assist in managing the department

8.4  Planning and administration of the individual audit

8.5  Using information technology during the audit (CAATS)

8.6    Audit reporting

8.7    Implementing and managing the use of information technology in audit.

**9.   Knowledge Management**

9.1    Knowledge, information and data

9.2    Requisite information

9.3    Intranets and internets.

# Module 10: Advanced internal auditing

**Aim**     To apply the knowledge, understanding and skills acquired from MIIA studies and personal experience to real life and assumed situations.

There is no prescribed syllabus for this module. The module is examined by means of a case study, which is provided four weeks before the examination date. Questions are not disclosed prior to the examination.

# Revised MIIA Syllabus Summary

The following statement has been agreed by the Chief Examiner as defining the learning aims of the new qualification:

> 'Successful candidates should be able to interact with directors and senior management at a strategic level on complex issues of risk, ethics and governance in the context of a global business environment.'

The following pages set out how the 'old' and 'new' MIIA modules relate to one another and a brief description of the three core modules from the new syllabus.

| Old Syllabus | New Syllabus Equivalent |
| --- | --- |
| Advanced Management | Strategic Management (see summary below) |
| Financial Management and Business Analysis | Financial Management (see summary below) |
| Advanced Information Systems Auditing | No equivalent module. The Information Systems topic area is now embedded across all aspects of the syllabus. |
| No equivalent module | Risk and Assurance Module (see summary below) |
| Advanced Internal Auditing | Case Study Module (to be taken last) |
| No Skills Module Requirement | Skills Module – Advanced Communications |

## Core Module Summaries

There follows a summary of the three new core syllabus modules so that you may see what is included.

## Financial Management Module Aims and Objectives

The aim of this module is to enable the internal auditor to provide effective assurance and advice to all levels of management, including board level, on strategic and operational financial issues. Successful candidates should be able to operate effectively in a rapidly changing technological and global environment.

Successful candidates will be able to:

1.  Demonstrate financial literacy in order to contribute and operate effectively at strategic level
2.  Analyse and synthesise internal and external accounting, financial and economic and other information
3.  Evaluate the significance of the outcome of analyses against the strategic objectives of the organisation
4.  Evaluate risks in financial systems and financial information and recommend mitigating strategies
5.  Apply accounting, financial and economic knowledge and skills to decision-making and performance monitoring

## Risk and Assurance Module Aim and Objectives

This module is designed to develop and enhance the internal auditor's knowledge and understanding of risk management, internal audit and corporate governance. The application of this knowledge provides the basis for enhancing the quality of the assurance opinion provided to internal audit stakeholders. The module also raises the awareness and sensitivity of internal auditors to broader strategic issues and how they may impact both upon the organisation and the internal audit function. In particular, the module focuses on:

1.  Being able to critically evaluate current control models and assurance frameworks that support corporate governance requirements.
2.  Honing analytical skills and being able to appreciate and exploit the cultural and political environment, particularly where organisational management and/or the board require an informed judgement and opinion about corporate governance arrangements.
3.  Understanding the different stakeholder perspectives that underpin effective risk management within an organisation.
4.  Understanding, and being able to assess, the balance between managing risk and taking risks as it affects the overall strategy of the organisation.
5.  Evaluating the effectiveness of reporting in relation to risk management and corporate governance.

6.   Developing a thorough grasp of the hard (processes and procedures) and soft (skills and competencies) factors required to manage an internal audit function.
7.   Being able to apply the Professional Practices Framework and ethical standards in an organisational environment.
8.   Developing a detailed understanding of the more advanced theoretical concepts and best practice requirements which underpin the assurance and consulting roles, responsibilities, and management of internal audit.
9.   Developing a more detailed understanding of IT risks and their impact on the organisation and how information systems may be used to help manage risk and providing assurance across the whole of the organisation.

## Strategic Management Module Aim and Objectives

The aim of this module is to enable students to appreciate the dynamics of the organisational environment and how governance, corporate and business strategies can be used to enable competitive advantage, value and sustainability

Successful candidates will be able to understand how organisations ensure that:

1.   Legal, ethical and economic responsibilities of corporate leaders are managed effectively
2.   Corporate and business strategy is properly formulated, implemented and monitored including performance management
3.   The strategy successfully exploits opportunities to create current and future value for all stakeholders

The resources and capabilities of the organisation are used and developed effectively to enable the achievement of the strategy.

## Advanced Communication Skills module

The aim of the skill module is to prepare auditors for some of the critical communications and interpersonal relationships with the board and senior management. As with the PIIA skills modules, this module will be workshop based and will not be formally assessed.

## Case Study Module

As at present, this module will be an integrated case study that requires students to draw from their knowledge, skills and experiences to analyse and evaluate the case. No syllabus is specified. This module will be taken last by all students.

# Websites for internal auditors

## Introduction

In this section we list sites of interest to internal auditors. While some sites are shown in more than one category of this listing, users are advised to refer across sections as some entries are applicable to other categories within which they may not appear. The categories in this listing are:

- Internal auditing (APP 9.1)
- IT governance (APP 9.2)
- Audit products/services (APP 9.3)
- Internal control (APP 9.4)
- Fraud, whistleblowing etc (APP 9.5)

Users of this listing will realise that websites change rapidly, so success will not always be achieved. We would like to learn of any changes or additions we should make for the next edition of this handbook. Please e-mail us at achambers@management-audit.com.

## APP 9.1  Internal auditing

| Organisation/ Title | URL/Country of Location | Comments/Further Links |
|---|---|---|
| **Audit Force** Audit Force is a consulting organisation that provides internal audit and compliance expertise. | http:// www.auditforce.com/ USA | This site provides an on-line magazine with articles of interest to auditors. |
| **Auditing the Human Resource Function** | http:// www.auxillium.com/ audit.htm USA | This is an example of an audit programme provided by Auxillium West, a human resources consulting firm, which outlines the basic approach as well as information that should be included to cover a regulatory compliance review (for the USA). |

| Organisation/ Title | URL/Country of Location | Comments/Further Links |
|---|---|---|
| **AuditNet** | http:// www.auditnet.org USA | AuditNet is an information and resources site developed for the benefit of the audit profession by Jim Kaplan. It now incorporates The IIA Inc. AuditBahn, the information superhighway for auditors, accountants and financial professionals.<br>There are a number of discrete areas on AuditNet, and some of these are listed below in alphabetical sequence.<br>A useful glossary of Internet terms can be found at: http://www.auditnet.org/tag.htm The IIA Inc is now the host of this site which has links to and from www.theiia.org and www.itaudit.org |
| **AuditNet – Audit Best** | http:// www.auditnet.org/ best.htm USA | The Audit Best Practices section of AuditNet is designed to encourage internal auditors to share with others their best practices.<br>An Index of available documents is provided and items can be downloaded. |
| **AuditNet – Audit Surveys** | http:// www.auditnet.org/ audsurvy.htm USA | A listing of audit customer surveys submitted by the world-wide network of auditors that form AuditNet. |

| Organisation/ Title | URL/Country of Location | Comments/Further Links |
|---|---|---|
| AuditNet – Auditors Sharing Audit Programs | http:// www.auditnet.org/ asapind.htm USA | This site features a collection of audit programmes used by auditors from around the world. The audit programmes listed cover Management, Financial and IT subjects. The listed programmes can be downloaded. In addition, there are further links to sources of audit programme and audit tool materials, such as the two following examples: Standardised Audit Workplans can be accessed on: http://www.aetna.com/audit/ ST-WPLNS.htm Gallaudet University (Washington DC), Audit Programs and Review Kits on: http://www.gallaudet.edu/ ~auditweb/index.html |
| AuditNet – Clearing house for Audit Research on Internet Topics | http:// www.auditnet.org/ carit.htm USA | Listing of student research papers on the joint topics of auditing and the Internet. |
| AuditNet – FraudNet | http:// www.auditnet.org/ fruadnet.htm USA | This section of AuditNet is devoted to the sharing of fraud policies, procedures, code of ethics and resources. |
| AuditNet – Audit Books | http:// www.auditnet.org/ booklist.htm USA | Listing of books relating to auditing and technology issues. |
| AuditNet – AuditZine | http:// www.auditnet.org/ aud_zine.htm USA | A compendium of articles about the Internet for auditors and accountants. |

| Organisation/ Title | URL/Country of Location | Comments/Further Links |
|---|---|---|
| **AuditNet – KARL (Kaplan's AuditNet Resources List).** Maintained by James Kaplan. | http:// www.auditnet.org/ karl.htm Previously http://users.aol.com/ auditnet/karl.htm USA | Launched by Kaplan in the early 1990s, a very comprehensive listing (now over 105 pages) of sites of interest to the auditing community. Most of the listed items have active links to the relevant WWW sites. Updates to the KARL site can be automatically notified by email using the subscription form at: http://www.itaudit.org/ auditnet_area/subscribe.htm Jim Kaplan is the author of The Auditor's Guide to Internet Resources (published by IIA Inc). |
| **AuditNet – PolicyNet** | http:// www.auditnet.org/ iupaudit.htm USA | Provides links to various Internet Use Policies (IUPs) that can be used as models for internal auditors in their own situations. |
| **AuditNet Audit Training** | http:// www.auditnet.org/ train.htm USA | Listing of conferences, seminars and training courses relevant to internal auditors. |
| **Australian & New Zealand University Internal Audit Group** | http:// www.curtin.edu.au/ curtin/audit/ anzuiag1.htm Australia | ANZUIAG is a discussion group of internal audit staff from Australian and New Zealand universities. Full contact details for the group and the minutes of previous meetings are accessible on the site. |
| **Canadian Environmental Auditing Association. (Association Canadienne de Verification Environnemen-tale)** | http:// www.mgmt14k.com. ceaa/ Canada | The CEAA/ACVE is a non-profit organisation dedicated to furthering the development and professional practice of environmental auditing. A useful Guidelines area is available together with details of environmental auditing qualifications. |
| **Compliance Desk** | http:// www.complian-cedesk .com/ USA | This site provides news and resources for the compliance professional. There are links to Y2K resources and articles. |

| Organisation/ Title | URL/Country of Location | Comments/Further Links |
|---|---|---|
| **Data Protection Registrar** | http:// www.open.gov.uk/ dpr/dprhome.htm UK | General information on the *Data Protection Act 1998* and the work of the DPR. Online search of the public register. Ability to download texts of the Data Protection Guidelines in Adobe Acrobat PDF format. Included in this listing are items related to the work of the European Commission Working Party on the Protection of Individuals with Regard to the Processing of Personal Data. |
| **Institute of Internal Auditors Inc** The website of the Institute of Internal Auditors Inc. | http://www.theiia.org USA | Full range of on-line documents, auditor's discussion groups, publication details and qualifications. |
| **Institute of Internal Auditors Singapore** | http://www.iia.org.sg Singapore | A site representing the 622 members of the IIA Singapore. Membership details, standards, examinations, and links to other sites. |
| **Institute of Internal Auditors Spain Instituto de Auditores Internos de España** | http:// www.arrakis.es/~iai Spain | In Spanish only Membership details, etc. |
| **Institute of Internal Auditors UK** The website of the Institute of Internal Auditors (UK) | http://www.iia.org.uk UK | Sections covering membership, publications, training and links to sites of interest. |
| **Institute of Internal Auditors Uruguay** | http:// www.uruguaytrade. com/congresso Uruguay | In Spanish only |

| Organisation/ Title | URL/Country of Location | Comments/Further Links |
|---|---|---|
| **Internal Auditing World Wide Web** | http://www.bitwise.net/iawww USA | Conceived by John K Peterson, this site is a warehouse of information and knowledge pertaining to the internal auditing profession and functions across all associations, industries and countries. Comprehensive international contacts section. |
| **Quality Auditor** | http://www.earthlink.net/~rj143/qa-home.htm USA | Reference point for those engaged in quality auditing. Links listing. |
| **Risk Assessment and Risk Management** | http://www.mc2consulting.com/riskpage.htm | Details of tools and articles on the subject of risk. Useful internal audit risk bibliography. Some articles available in French |
| **The Information Systems Audit and Control Association** | http://www.isaca.org USA | A worldwide not-for-profit association of more than 19,000 members. Administrators of the Certified Information Systems Auditor (CISA®) certification. The ISACA's Information Systems Audit & Control Foundation also features on the site with the Control Objectives for Information Technology (COBIT). Year 2000 resources list can be found at http://www.isaca.org/yr2000.htm |

## APP 9.2   IT governance

| Organisation/ Title | URL/Country of Location | Comments/Further Links |
|---|---|---|
| **Canaudit Inc** Canaudit Inc performs technical audits of a range of IT platforms. | http://www.canaudit.com/ Canada | This site contains information on training courses addressing IT audit and security review methods. |

| Organisation/ Title | URL/Country of Location | Comments/Further Links |
|---|---|---|
| **Center for Education and Research on Information assurance and Security** CERIAS has subsumed a former project at Purdue University called COAST (Computer Operations, Audit, and Security Technology). | http:// www.cerias.purdue. edu/about.html USA | The mission of CERIAS is to provide innovation and leadership in technology for the protection of information and information resources, and in the development and enhancement of expertise in formation assurance and security. |
| **Centre for Internet Security** | http:// www.cisecurity.org | |
| **CERT Co-ordination Center** | http://www.cert.org/ security- improvement/ | |
| **Computer Audit BCS Specialist Group** Membership enquiries can be directed to Jean Brown. Telephone: +44 (0)1803 872775 or email: 100125.66@ compuserve.com | http:// www.bcs.org.uk/ siggroup/sg07.htm | This British Computer Society group exists to support practitioners in the areas of computer audit and security and to promote the awareness and use of computer auditing and control techniques. The following membership fees apply: BCS: £15 Non-BCS: £25 Student: £10 Corporate: £75 |
| **Computer Security Institute** | http:// www.gocsi.com/ USA | Established in 1974, the CSI is an international membership organisation offering training specifically targeted to information security professionals. Useful features and an article archive are available, as well as listings of links to relevant sties. |

| Organisation/ Title | URL/Country of Location | Comments/Further Links |
|---|---|---|
| **Computer Security Resource Clearinghouse** This site is part of the NIST (National Institute of Standards and Technology), which is part of the US Department of Commerce's Technology Administration. | http:// www.csrc.ncsl.nist. gov/ USA | The CSRC is designed to collect and disseminate computer security information and resources to help users, systems administrators, managers and security professionals better protect their data and systems. |
| **Information Systems – Best Practice Guidelines** Developed by the Queensland Audit Office in Australia. | http:// www.qao.qld.gov.au/ bestprac.html Australia | This document, provides a comprehensive guide to the key areas of control over IS security. |
| **IT Governance Institute** | http:// www.itgovernan- ce.org | Linking Business objectives and information technology. Resource Section: http://www.itgovernance.org/itgi/ resources.htm IT Governance Institute, 3701 Algonquin Road, Suite 1010, Rolling Meadows, IL 60008 USA Tel: +1.847.590.7491. Fax: +1.847.253.1443. E-mail: info@itgi.org |
| **IT Security Cookbook** | http:// www.boran.com/ security | |

| Organisation/ Title | URL/Country of Location | Comments/Further Links |
|---|---|---|
| **IT Audit Forum** Supported by sponsorship and advertising. ACL is an active sponsor. Built and managed by Online Networks Inc, Portland, Oregon, USA. Contact John Yu via email on editor@itaudit.org or telephone 1–503-644–1001 | http:// www.itaudit.org | Launched in September 1998, a website geared specifically to the information technology needs of audit professionals. The site's most visible feature is 'The Forum' – which contains a number of articles on timely topics that address the special interests, needs and concerns of auditors. Readers can initiate or participate in threaded discussions in response to the issues raised in the articles. 'The Forum' is published twice a month. The 'Conference Center' is a threaded discussion area which allows visitors to post questions on topics of interest, respond to the entries of other professionals and obtain views and opinions on modern technology issues. In addition there is an online chat area for the exchange of information and ideas in real time, and 'Yellow Pages' on available products, services and resources. |
| **Software Engineering Institute** | http:// www.sei.cmu.edu/ arm/ | Software acquisition management improvement |
| **Software Engineering Institute** | http:// www.sei.cmu.edu | Software Risk Evaluation Method – Version 1.0 |
| **System Administration, Networking and Security Institute** | http://www.sans.org | |
| **United States General Accounting Office – Accounting and Information Management Division** | http://www.gao.gov/ special.pubs/ pdf_sing.pdf | Information security management |

| Organisation/ Title | URL/Country of Location | Comments/Further Links |
|---|---|---|
| **United States General Accounting Office – Information Security Risk Assessment** | http://www.gao.gov./ special.pubs/ ai00033.pdf | Information Security Risk Assessment – Practices of Leading Organizations |

## APP 9.3   Audit products/services

| Organisation/ Title | URL/Country of Location | Comments/Further Links |
|---|---|---|
| **Audit Command Language** | http://www.acl.com USA | ACL is software, which provides data analysis, presentation and management facilities. The site offers product information, training schedules, and details of consultancy services. Site contents available in English, German, Spanish, French and Portuguese. |
| **Audit Department Manager Plus (ADM Plus)** Pleier & Associates | http:// www.admplus.com USA | ADM Plus is a software package to automate the management of the internal auditing function. The site gives an overview of system facilities together with price and ordering details. Site visitors can also view, print or download copies of the quarterly newsletter Audit Productivity Trends. |
| **auditMASTER-PLAN** J.E. Boritz Consultants Ltd | http:// www.jebcl.com Canada | auditMASTERPLAN is a computer-based risk assessment, planning and work tracking system for internal auditors. Full product overview, licensing and ordering details are provided. |
| **Auditor Assistant** Auditor Assistant is a registered trade mark of First Chicago NBD | http:// audit.wordlink.com/ aahome/ USA | A risk-based audit management system created in Lotus Notes. A demonstration presentation is available for download in PowerPoint format. |

| Organisation/ Title | URL/Country of Location | Comments/Further Links |
|---|---|---|
| **IDEA** | http:// www.caseware-idea.com | IDEA for Windows is a productivity tool that allows the display, analysis, manipulation, sampling and extraction of data from a wide variety of file formats. |
| **Management Audit Limited** | http:// www.management-audit.com UK | Provider of software, training and consultancy specifically for the internal audit and corporate governance communities. |
| **MIS Training Institute** | http:// www.misti.com USA | Founded in 1978, MIS Training Institute offers audit and information security education courses, details of which can be interrogated on the site. The security and consulting division of MIS training Institute, Information Security Institute (ISI) focuses exclusively on providing high-quality infosecurity training and consulting services. Details can be found on: http://www.misti.com/ISI.asp |
| **Risk Alert** J.E. Boritz Consultants Ltd | http:// www.jebcl.com/risk/ risk2.htm Canada | Risk Alert, the business condition analyst, is a tool designed to support the evaluation of the business condition of an enterprise, including the validity of going concern assumption that underlies the preparation of most general purpose financial statements. |

## APP 9.4  **Internal control**

| Organisation/ Title | URL/Country of Location | Comments/Further Links |
|---|---|---|
| **Control Self Assessment Tool** | http://www.vpf-web.harvard .edu/audit/home/ CSA_frame. bot.html USA | This site features an example CSA Questionnaire designed by the internal audit department (in co-operation with the financial deans) at Harvard University, to assist in the performance of reviews of controls over financial systems and activities. In addition to the questionnaire, guidance on its' completion is also provided. |
| **Control Self Assessment Resource Center** Site maintained by John Wyckoff, Internal Audit Manager for Portland Teachers Credit Union. | http:// www.teleport.com/ ~jhw/csa USA | Website provides links to CSA resources, consultants, facilitators and trainers available via the Internet. Links to CSA software and tools are listed at: http://www.jhw.com/csa/tools.htm |
| **Fraud and Investigation Links** Originally developed for a presentation to the Alabama Chapter of the Association of Certified Fraud Examiners. | http:// www.bham.net/ users/jwrhymes/ fraud/fraud.html USA | A page of links to federal agencies, information sources on security, auditing, investigations, etc. |
| **Fraud Report** | http://www.hm-treasury.gov .uk/pub/html/ docs/fraud/9596fr/ main.html UK | The text of a report that analyses reported fraud in UK government departments. Includes a section of guidance on the management of the risk of fraud. |

| Organisation/ Title | URL/Country of Location | Comments/Further Links |
|---|---|---|
| Internal Control Resources | http:// pw1.netcom.com/ ~jstorres/ internalaudit/ content.html USA | Listing of links to organisations, resources, books and articles. |
| Management Control Association | http:// www.ms.rhbnc.ac.uk/ mca2001 UK | The Association holds doctoral colloquia and also research conferences. The secretary of the Association is Dr Derek Purdy of the Department of Economics, University of Reading |
| MIS Training Institute | http:// www.misti.com USA | Offers a wide range of training courses, many related closely to internal control issues. |

## APP 9.5   Fraud, whistleblowing etc

| Organisation/ Title | URL/Country of Location | Comments/Further Links |
|---|---|---|
| A collaborative site of fraud information | http:// www.fraud.org.uk UK | The site is supported by The Association of British Insurers, The Arson Prevention Bureau, The Institute of Chartered Accountants in England & Wales, The British Bankers' Association, The Confederation of British Industry, Crimestoppers, The Department of Trade and Industry, The Department of Social Security, The Financial Services Association, The Credit Industry Avoidance System and The Home Office. |
| Centre for Fraud Management Studies | http:// www.fraudstudies- .com UK | Liverpool Business School, Liverpool John Moores University, Liverpool, L3 5UZ (tel: +44 (0)151 231 3440; fax: +44 (0)151 709 3156) |
| Fraudwatch (US) | http:// www.fraudnewslet- ter.com USA | |

| Organisation/ Title | URL/Country of Location | Comments/Further Links |
|---|---|---|
| Internet Scambusters | http:// www.scambuster-s.org | |
| National Fraud Information Center (US) | http://www.fraud.org USA | |
| Whistleblowers' website | http:// www.fraudhot-line.net http:// www.forensicac-counting.co.uk UK | In July 2001 Forensic Accounting, a breakaway from PwC, launched this website to allow employees to send in anonymous tip-offs which are then relayed to top management if the company in question has signed up. Contact Raj Bairoliya at Forensic Accounting. |

# Index

**Introduction.** Alphabetical arrangement is word-by-word, where a group of letters followed by a space is filed before the same group of letters followed by a letter, for example 'Product quality' appears before 'Productivity'.

The use of 'Internal audit' and related terms as main headings is minimal, and references should be sought elsewhere.